CONTEMPORARY ISSUES AND CHALLENGES IN BUSINESS MANAGEMENT:
POST-COVID 19

CONTEMPORARY ISSUES AND CHALLENGES IN BUSINESS MANAGEMENT:
POST-COVID 19

Patron

Prof. (Dr.) Atmanand, Director, MDI Murshidabad

Editors

Dr. Biranchi Narayan Swar
Dr. Chetan G K
Dr. Neeraj Singhal

First published 2022
by Routledge
605 Third Avenue, New York, NY 10158

and by Routledge
2 Park Square, Milton Park, Abingdon, Oxon, OX14 4RN

Routledge is an imprint of the Taylor & Francis Group, an informa business

Library of Congress Cataloging-in-Publication Data
A catalog record for this title has been requested

ISBN: 978-1-032-21444-3(pbk)

Contents

Foreword   *x*

Preface   *xi*

Acknowledgements   *xii*

Section I:
CONTEMPORARY ISSUES AND CHALLENGES IN MARKETING

1. Reimagining the New Norms: Customer Shopping Behaviours in India during COVID Times – *Dr. Badal Bihari Rath*   2

2. Assessing Indian Consumers' Perception Towards Attributes of Active and Intelligent Packaging Using Kano Model – *Kumar Akash, Prabha Krishna, Arora Sapna*   14

3. Rationales of Factors Affecting Consumer Purchase Behavior for E-Pharmacy in the Presidency Region of West Bengal – *Aman Jha, Sudip Kundu*   28

4. Cars are now online too: Dawn of 'Click to buy' model in India due to Covid19 – *Samantak Chakraborty, Dr. Mohammad Khalid Azam*   46

5. The Experience of Salons with Deals and Coupons – *Krunal Joshi, Janvi Joshi*   54

6. Nudge Theory and its Application in Organic Consumer Products: A Review Study – *Dr. Deepti Kakar, Mr. Deepak Sharma*   65

7. What We "sense" is What We Believe-Impact of Multisensory Environmental Cues on Purchase Intention – *Dr. Rupa Rathee, Dr. Pallavi Rajain*   80

8. Effect of CRM on Customer Satisfaction in the Insurance Sector – *Dr. Bhavneet Kaur, Ms. Anuradha Jain, Mr. Mohit Chadha*   93

9. Post COVID-19: The Change in Consumer Behavior and Implications to Retailers – *Dr. Biranchi Narayan Swar*   105

Section II:
CONTEMPORARY ISSUES AND CHALLENGES IN FINANCE AND ACCOUNTING

10. Energy Finance Challenges in Covid Lockdown Days: Lessons from Pandemic – *Dr. Mahantesh Kuri, Dr. Prasad Kulkarni, Dr. Jyoti Jamnani, Dr. Joel Gnanapragash*   114

11. Determinants of Book Built IPO Underpricing - Differential Issue
Size and Market Momentum Approach Revisited. – *Suresha B, Ravikumar T* 131

12. Whether the Impact of the Acquisition is Reflected on the Share Price
of Acquiring Companies! - A Study Based on A Few Acquisitions by
Indian Corporates. – *Mr. Sudipta De, Dr. Ashoke Mondal* 147

13. An Analysis of Efficiency of Foreign Exchange Reserves among Nine
Countries: An Application of DEA. – *Dr. Rachna Agrawal, Ashima Verma* 158

14. Product Complexity of Indian Exports: Restructuring
due to COVID-19 – *Dr. Purvi Pujari,* 170

15. Nexus Between Financial Liberalization, Financial Stability
Index and Crises – *Dr. Anjala Kalsie, Dr. Jappanjoyt Kaur Kalra* 181

16. Relationship Between Portfolio Flows and Currency Crisis: An Empirical
Analysis – *Dr. Anjala Kalsie, Ms. Jyoti Dhamija* 195

17. Impact of Corporate Governance on the Dividend Policy: Empirical Evidence from the
Indian Corporate Sector. – *Dr. Ruchita Verma, Dr. Dhanraj Sharma, Ms. Priyanka* 206

Section III:
CONTEMPORARY ISSUES AND CHALLENGES IN OB AND HRM

18. Job Performance and Its Correlates: An Empirical Study of Public
Sector Employees – *Iqra Zaffar, Abdul Gani* 220

19. Understanding Employer Branding Through Sentiment Analysis of
Employee Reviews of India's Best Companies to Work for – *Dr. Tavleen Kaur,
Dr. Chirag Malik, Dr. Neeraj Singhal* 235

20. Work from Home During and After COVID: Need for Competence
Satisfaction and Its Implications for Employee Wellbeing – *Navya Kumar,
Dr. Swati Alok, Dr. Sudatta Banerjee* 249

21. Integration of Artificial Intelligence in to Human Resources: Challenges
and Scope – *Shreya Srivastava, Oamkaar Sadarangani* 262

22. Developmental Idiosyncratic Deals and Career Commitment: Mediation Effect
of Organization Commitment – *Biswa Prakash Jena, Dr. Archana Choudhary,
Dr. Manas Kumar Pal* 273

23. Grittier and Embedded: An Analysis of Hotel Employees
During Covid 19 Pandemic – *Kerwin Savio Nigli, Shruti Agrawal* 283

Section IV:
CONTEMPORARY ISSUES AND CHALLENGES IN OPERATIONS AND SCM/ ITM/
BUSINESS POLICY, STRATEGY AND ENTREPRENEURSHIP

24. A Study of Supply Chain Practices and its Challenges in Indian
Pharmaceutical Companies. – *Dr. Mritunjay Kumar* 300

25. Total Quality Management (TQM): A Managerial Technology to
Fight COVID-19 – *Ashutosh Samadhiya, Rajat Agrawal* 308

26. Moderating Role of Project Flexibility Between Top Management Commitment
and Project Success in Financial Services – *Pankaj Tiwari, Suresha B*   319

27. The Role of College Level Intervention in Improving the Entrepreneurial
Aptitude of Young Entrepreneurs in Oman: An Empirical Study – *Thangarasa
Tiburtrious Andrew Rohanaraj*   332

28. Progress of Digital Payment Ecosystem in Unorganised Indian
Markets: A Systematic Literature Review – *Aditi Mehtani, Dr. Saima Rizvi*   347

29. Management Lessons from Unorganized Restaurants
in South India – *Sandeep H, Georgy Kurien*   360

30. Women Entrepreneurship in India and China: An Institutional
Perspective – *Dr. Meghna Chhabra, Dr. Rajat Gera, Ms. Anita Sharma*   371

31. CSR-An Empirical Study to Understand the Dynamics Affecting Strategic
Initiatives from Industries for Crafting A Sustainable Ecosystem in
Future – *Dr. Vaishali Rahate, Dr. Parvin Shaikh*   385

32. Framework for Integrating Sustainability Across Value Chain:
An Industry 4.0 Perspective – *Dr. Neeraj Singhal*   399

About the Editors

Dr. Biranchi Narayan Swar

Dean – Continuing Education and Professor, Marketing

Dr. Biranchi Narayan Swar has over 17 years of work experience both in the industry and academia. He is currently Professor of Marketing and Dean-Continuing Education at Management Development Institute, Murshidabad, India. Prior to his stint in MDI, he taught in Symbiosis International (Deemed University). His teaching, research and training interests include Shoppers' buying behavior, Online retailing, Service quality, Marketing analytics, Customer Relationship Management and Branding. Dr. Biranchi has got his Ph.D in Marketing from Utkal University. He has published more than 30 research papers in various Scopus and ABDC listed Journals. He has presented research papers in more than 50 scholarly and professional conferences organized within and outside India. He has got the best paper awards for his contribution to the research in various conferences. He is the reviewer and in the editorial board of the various peer reviewed national/international journals. He is an alumnus of IIM Indore.

Dr. Chetan G. K.

Chairperson-MDP and Consulting and Associate Professor, Finance

Dr. Chetan is presently working as Associate Professor – Finance at Management Development Institute, Murshidabad. He pursued MBA degree in Finance from Karnatak University, Dharwad and holds Doctorate degree in Finance from Jain University, Bengaluru. He served as Associate Professor of Finance at Kirloskar Institute of Advanced Management Studies (KIAMS), Harihar for six years. He also taught courses of Finance at KIAMS - Pune as part of faculty exchange programme. He worked as lecturer of Finance at Bapuji B-Schools, Davangere for about five years prior to joining KIAMS.

Dr. Chetan also worked as Dealer for Equities and F&O at Kotak Securities Ltd. before joining academia. He is passionate in teaching finance courses such as: Corporate Finance, Investment Analysis and Portfolio Management, Corporate Valuation, Financial Modeling, Equity Research, and Financial Services. His broad research interests include Event Studies and Lead - Lag Relationship. He completed various certification courses of National Stock Exchange and Bombay Stock Exchange, Mumbai.

Dr. Neeraj Singhal

Assistant Professor, Strategic Management

Dr Neeraj Singhal is Assistant Professor in Strategic Management area at Management Development Institute (MDI), Murshidabad, West Bengal, India. He has more than 2 decades of teaching, research, and institution building experience. Dr Singhal contributed research papers in international and national journals of repute published from Sage, Springer, Elsevier indexed in ABDC/Scopus etc. He is also the reviewer for Cambridge, Sage and other reputed publishers. He has published in the area of strategy, sustainable development, climate change, green business, carbon market etc. He is a member of Academy of International Business, USA, Strategic Management Society, USA. He is also an alumnus of IIM Ahmedabad and IIM Indore.

Foreword

It gives me immense pleasure to introduce you to the edited volume brought out by MDI Murshidabad, titled "Contemporary Issues and Challenges in Business Management: Post Covid-19".

This book fosters the multidisciplinary discussion about issues and challenges during post Covid-19 with respect to management practices. The four sections of the book cover the contemporary issues and challenges in the post Covid-19 scenario faced by various business domains such as Marketing, Finance, Human Resources, Operations and Supply Chain Management, ITM, Business Policy, Strategy and Entrepreneurship.

MDI is a leading business school of India, launched its Murshidabad campus in the year 2014. MDI Murshidabad is fostering the culture of research among faculty members, researchers, corporate and students. This book is an effort in that direction.

Prof. (Dr.) Biranchi Narayan Swar and his colleagues, Dr. Chetan G K and Dr. Neeraj Singhal has done a great job in editing this book. They all have a rich experience in teaching, research, and writing books. And I am sure that this book will create interest among the readers, and will have a great impact on the society at large.

I wish them great success.

Prof. (Dr.) Atmanand
Director, MDI Murshidabad

.

Preface

MDI Murshidabad organized the International conference on Changing Business Paradigm (ICCBP-2021). ICCBP 2021, the international conference is organized with an aim at capturing the role of innovations in management practices. The basic theme of the conference was the changing business paradigm during post COVID. One of the primary objectives of the conference is to identify the challenges faced by marketers or corporates during and post COVID.

Apart from this, one of the added advantages of ICCBP 2021 is to promote research and related activities in the area of Marketing, Finance and Accounting, OB and HRM, Operations and SCM, IT, Strategy, Entrepreneurship and case studies with respect to various functional activities. The conference provided a platform to practitioners, researchers and consultants and students to exchange their thoughts and contribute or share their views and expertise in formulation and implementation of various strategies during these uncertain times. We hope this book will find some space in the minds of the stakeholders and provide some important strategies for the future.

Dr. Biranchi Narayan Swar

Dr. Chetan G. K

Dr. Neeraj Singhal

Acknowledgements

We would like to thank Prof. (Dr.) Atmanand, Director, MDI Murshidabad, West Bengal, India for his continuous support and encouragement in organizing this International Conference on Changing Business Paradigm-2021 (ICCBP-2021). As an outcome of this conference, we are publishing this book from Taylor & Francis. MDI Murshidabad has wholeheartedly supported and funded the publication of this book. We would also like to thank all the faculty members, non-teaching staff and students of MDI Murshidabad for extending their unwavering support at all times.

We would also like to thank the international conference advisory committee for their continuous support and encouragement in organizing this event. We take this opportunity to thank all keynote speakers, session chairs for sharing their valuable insights during the conference. A sizable number of acclaimed authors from academia and seasoned managers from the industry have set out intense interest in contributing their research papers and cases for this conference. As a result of their contribution we were able to come with this book. We would like to thank our editorial team for their continued guidance, inputs, and review comments which helped immensely in enhancing the quality of the papers. We also thank Taylor & Francis publication, their editors, production experts and their entire team for their cooperation in bringing this book in time.

We value the feedback and suggestions given by you to improve the quality of this book. We look forward to your comments on emails: iccbp@mdim.ac.in in order to bring out a better innovative book in future.

Dr. Biranchi Narayan Swar

Dr. Chetan G. K

Dr. Neeraj Singhal

SECTION I

Contemporary Issues and Challenges in Marketing

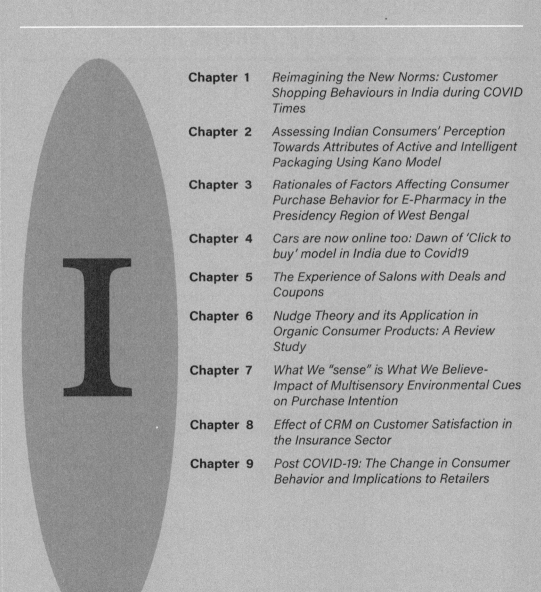

Chapter 1   *Reimagining the New Norms: Customer Shopping Behaviours in India during COVID Times*

Chapter 2   *Assessing Indian Consumers' Perception Towards Attributes of Active and Intelligent Packaging Using Kano Model*

Chapter 3   *Rationales of Factors Affecting Consumer Purchase Behavior for E-Pharmacy in the Presidency Region of West Bengal*

Chapter 4   *Cars are now online too: Dawn of 'Click to buy' model in India due to Covid19*

Chapter 5   *The Experience of Salons with Deals and Coupons*

Chapter 6   *Nudge Theory and its Application in Organic Consumer Products: A Review Study*

Chapter 7   *What We "sense" is What We Believe-Impact of Multisensory Environmental Cues on Purchase Intention*

Chapter 8   *Effect of CRM on Customer Satisfaction in the Insurance Sector*

Chapter 9   *Post COVID-19: The Change in Consumer Behavior and Implications to Retailers*

CHAPTER 1

Reimagining the New Norms: Customer Shopping Behaviours in India during COVID Times

Dr. Badal Bihari Rath
Product Manager
Webinar Planet
Faridabad, India
badalrath@gmail.com

Abstract

The current CORONA pandemic has disrupted the way business is done across the world. Every day new ways of doing business are being explored and implemented to achieve better margins and profits. Customer experience is also changing during COVID times across the globe including India. Indian customers are usually choosy and always prefers specific product and services while evaluating various options and alternatives. Various players have adopted different marketing strategies to sell during COVID and minimize the infections. Since product and services touch points are the likely source of infections spread, the overall objective is to limit these customer touchpoints. This is leading to a change in customer experience and impacting the way product and services are displayed and sold both in online and offline marketplaces. Indian consumers were adapted to first try and then buy behaviour. In current COVID scenario the situation is reversed to first buy and then try. During Corona pandemic sellers are asking customers to first buy and then to go for a trial resulting in customer behaviour changes due to changed market dynamics.

This research paper explores Customer Shopping Behaviour trends and sentiments in India during pandemic lockdown. The study also aims to focus on how marketing companies are redesigning marketing strategies to engage consumers during and post COVID 19 pandemics.

Keywords: Consumer Behaviour, COVID 19, Customer experience, Shopping Behaviour, Corona Pandemic, Customer behaviour

1. INTRODUCTION

The current Corona virus (COVID 19) pandemic which was first detected in Wuhan, China has infected people and spread across the globe. The spread has led to socio and economic down fall and left businesses around the world counting the costs. Due to Government enforced lockdowns, businesses have temporarily shut down and many more are on verge of permanent closure and job loss. Fearing spread of virus people are staying at home or working remotely to prevent being infected or transmitting infections. Every day new ways of doing business are being explored and implemented to achieve better margins and profits. Customer experience is also changing during COVID 19 times across the globe including India. Indian customers are usually choosy and always prefers specific product and services while evaluating various options and alternatives. While purchasing clothes, consumers will prefer to try the new garment for best fit and design. Consumers would try various options available and then make a purchase or look for other alternatives. Since COVID 19 spreads through various modes including touching infected surfaces, sellers and manufacturers are displaying restraint to prevent transmission of infections. Various players have adopted different marketing strategies to sell during COVID 19 and minimize the infections. Since product and services touch points are the likely source of infections spread, the overall objective is to limit these customer touchpoints. This is leading to a change in customer experience and impacting the way product and services are displayed and sold both in online and offline marketplaces.

2. LITERATURE REVIEW

Consumer Behavior Approaches during Crises

Consumer is a person who has a specific need or desire for a product or service. Then makes a purchase and consumes or disposes during the consumption process. Consumer utility as a function is dependent on consumption of services, housing, wealth, industrial goods, and agriculture (Grundey, 2009). While no two of them are same since every consumer is influenced by different external and internal factors which forms the basis of consumer behaviour. Consumer behaviour involves a constant decision-making process involving series of steps like searching, evaluating, purchasing, consuming, and disposing of products and services (Valášková, Kramárová and Bartosova, 2015). As per a research by Valaskova et.al the approaches towards explaining consumer behaviour can be divided into three groups. First group is based on psychical, which is the relation between psyche and behaviour of the consumer, second group is sociological approach which is the reaction of consumers under various situations. These behaviours are influenced due to various social occasions, social leadership, and economics. Economics approach is based on the basic knowledge and understanding of micro economy under which the consumers define their needs and requirement. (Valášková, Kramárová and Bartosova, 2015). Post liberalisation in India, consumer behaviour types has been explained by such approaches in the borderless world, although defeating individual identity and in the process giving rise to a collective identity through brand culture. Amalia et.al (Amalia, Mihaela and Ionuţ, 2012) in their research explained not all people are same nor all people have same perception and expectation about a situation which can be good or negative effects like a crisis or pandemic. New trends in consumer behaviour emerges during crisis. Two key factors which models the consumer behaviour during crisis are risk perception and attitude. Risk perception reflects the consumer intention to be exposed to the risk content. Risk attitude interprets consumers exposure to the risk content and the level of like or dislike to that content. Although much research has been undertaken to understand the consumer behaviour during various economic crisis, Hoon Ang et al. found that these changes in consumption behaviour during an economic crisis may be moderated by personality characteristics too. The personality characteristics include the level of orientation which consumers are value conscious, risk avoidance and materialistic (Hoon, Sim, Lim and Kuan, 2001). Earlier studies have indicated behavioural changes within consumers during crisis with significant changes in utility pattern. A significant study conducted by Flatters and Willmott during crisis showed new trends like demand simplification due to limited offers which even continued post crisis where people were buying simple offerings but offering greater value. This research also reported that rich people post crisis expressed behaviour involving dissatisfaction associated with excess consumption and focused on recycle. This study proved the impact of recession on consumer attitude and trends are critical. During recession, some behavioural trends are advanced, some are slowed while others are diminished. The most important trend during crisis is the demand for simplicity. Consumers looks for products and services which are uncomplicated, have value for money (Flatters and Willmott, 2009). Some of the above trends were shown by consumers during current Corona -19 pandemic and subsequent lockdown.

3. SHOPPING BEHAVIOR DURING PANDEMIC LOCKDOWN

India is a mosaic market which offers huge potentials in terms of population size, socio economic and cultural factors, revenue, and growth too. Indian consumer market is also both complex and diverse and it is important to customize the marketing strategies as per local needs and preferences. There is also intense competition from both large and small local as well as international players. Consumer market is also mosaic in nature with people from various cultural backgrounds and a country with has differing levels of wealth and a huge land mass (Business, 2021). At retail level the Indian retail industry has is emerging as one of the most dynamic and fast paced industry due to several players in the market. India also ranks as the world's fifth largest global destination in the retail space (Equity Foundation, 2020). Indian retail segment constitutes of more than 15 million modern and traditional retailers. Indian retail sector currently accounts for more than 10 percent of the India's gross domestic product (GDP) and contributes around 40 percent to India's consumption. Also, this sector is a leading employment generator and contributes to eight percent employment employing around 40-50 million people directly. This includes more than 6 million people in modern trade and equals to approx. 12 percent of total retail consumption in India. (RAI, 2020). Within the market, consumers drive the market competition, economic integration, and growth. With dynamics economic changes, consumers are also experiencing a change or transformation in behaviour. The needs and wants of Indian consumer are many so always there is an inherent tendency of consumer to ask for products with more features and attributes.

Tough times require touch measures and taking clue from other nations, India went into a complete lockdown for 21 days from March 24th to control the infection. Stepping out of house was strictly prohibited and government allowed to do so only for medical treatments, buying grocery and other essentials as per lock down guidelines issued by Ministry of Home Affairs. PM later had to issue an appeal to the public to resist from panic buying was essential services was available during the lockdown. (Times, 2020). During this phase below are some of the major consumer behaviour changes and key trends which was exhibited:

1. **Panic Buying:** Hoarding is a common practice across the globe among consumers to stock essential products to manage the uncertain future supply of basic products. Similar panic buying scenes were observed when consumers in huge numbers landed at stores to buy essentials items on March 24th, the day when the lockdown started in India. Products just vanished from the stores in few minutes. Due to mass buying, there was a period of short supply of products and services due to supply challenges since transport services were also hampered.

2. **Healthy Living:** Since the lockdown was due to Corona infections, medical fraternity had a strong evidence that the infections although not completely stopped can be prevented by developing body immune systems through various methods including physical exercises, immune boosting medicines like Vitamin C and D and other healthy diets and drinks which builds the immune systems. Due to the association of physical well-being and warding off infection there was a surge in companies services offering healthy living themes. Companies like Cure.fit, Portea and online pharmacies selling medicines were booming during lock down. There was shift in consumer behaviour towards buying healthy foods and medicines to remain fit.

3. **Lockdown living:** Due to inability to access physical stores during lockdown, consumers went online to buy essentials items. During Demonetization phase, customers were forced to move from cash to cashless/digital payments system, in similar way during COVID 19 lockdown consumers moved from physical shopping to online shopping. Across India there was an increase in digital penetration. As per Nielsen, the time spent on mobile has increased to more than five hours per day. There was increase in number of new connections for broadband users as internet use has increased four times since April 2020. On a similar trend there were new users who ordered online grocery stores like grofers, big basket and supr daily. Going by these trends some of the E commerce service providers even diverted from their existing line of business to delivering groceries like Zomato. Due to closure of schools, colleges, and work from home for office users, electronics devices like smart phones, laptops were in considerable demands. (Community, 2020)

4. **Pent Up Demand:** As per a recent research on consumer behavior during COVID 19 pandemic, consumer behavior expert guru Jagdish N. Sheth found that it is an inherent tendency to postpone purchases or consumption of discretionary products or services during crisis. Such kind of behavior are noticed for durable goods and services like automobiles, homes and consumer appliances which are high priced. Although they might see a value for such items, however consumers will try to defer the purchase for few days or months and focus on products and services which are essentials. Due to this the demand shifts to the future. Pent Up Demand is familiar event when access to market is denied for a short period of time.

5. **Stores, work, and education come Home:** Due to lockdown, people were restricted to the home boundary. People were unable to go to the grocery stores or shopping stores. Instead, these stores came to customers doorsteps. Consumers had an option to place orders online and get delivered at home. Local kirana stores also took orders from online website and those who did not have one took orders through What's App platform. Online shopping behaviors kicked in and people who were not buying online also have shown interest due to safety and convenience considerations. As a result, first time online buyers increased in India during lockdown. Same trend continued for office work and education. Instead of going physically to office, school, and colleges, these came home. Students had to continue education through online mode and office workers worked remotely from home. This reversed the flow from physical presence to online presence. (Sheth, 2020)

4. SHOPPING BEHAVIOR DURING POST PANDEMIC LOCKDOWN

After a series of lock down extension, India slowly started to unlock with series of unlock phases to gradually boost the economy with the first Unlock 1.0 started on June 8th (Singh, 2020). To understand the overall consumer sentiments and behavior, McKinsey, conducted a research in India from November 9-20, 2020. Below are some of the key trends from the survey data.

-   **Consumers are shifting to value and essentials**: Up to 30 percent customers say that they will decrease the spending on discretionary categories

-   **Adoption of digital channel and Omnichannel**: There is up to 25% net increase in intent to shop and spend online even Post COVID-19

-   **Loyalty shock**: Around 94 percent of Indian consumers have changed brands, stores, and the way they shop. 60 percent consumers mentioned "value" and "convenience" as drivers for new shopping places. Value and quality are two most important factors to consider when looking for a new brand

-   **Out of Home normal**: 76 percent of the Indian consumers have not yet resuming normal out of home activities

-   Around 64 percent consumers still feel that impact on routine and finances will continue for another four months

-   About 50 percent of consumer continue to see reduction in their spending, savings, and income

-   Net intent of spending has increased since has increased across all categories except leisure, travel, and dining in restaurants (Chan, Das, Inoue and Malhotra, 2020)

Another research survey conducted by Deloitte indicated that maximum offline transaction happened before pandemic while during and after pandemic, consumers adopted digital technology and preferred to shop online (Refer to figure1 below).

Figure 1: *Changes in consumer shopping journey before, during, and after the pandemic*

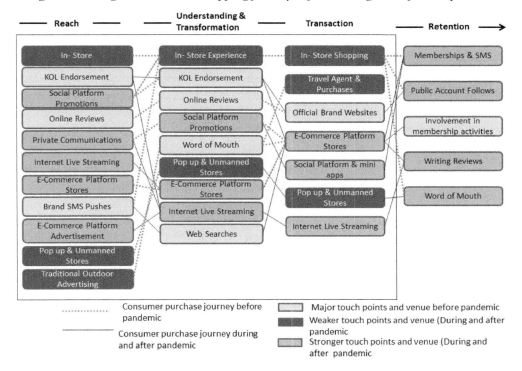

Source: https://www2.deloitte.com/content/dam/Deloitte/in/Documents/consumer-business/in-consumer-impact-of-covid-19-on-consumer-business-in-india-noexp.pdf

Consumers interest level was low towards in store shopping, travel, and agent purchases, pop up and unmanned stores and traditional outdoor advertisements. Consumers preferred social media promotions, private communications, live media streaming and e commerce stores (Wahi and Ramanathan, 2020)

Key Shopping and Marketing Trends post COVID-19 pandemic:

Post pandemic after shops were open to welcome customers, the whole consumer experience has changed. There were various factors leading to this change. While some were government mandate to follow, shop and mall managers had their own including government norms for shopping and marketing in public places. As per government mandate, wearing mask in public places and maintaining six feet distance was mandatory rule along with other safety measures like frequent sanitizations, thermal screening to track fever and sick patients. Even many shops and malls have switched off the air conditioning systems and replaced with regular ceiling fans. This made shopping even more uncomfortable since India weather is usually hot. Shoppers and retailers have displayed notice that without mask customers will not be allowed. Also, there was few interesting, enforced shopping behavior changes made by shoppers and retailers which totally changed the consumer buying habits. Some of these are below:

- **Consumers First buy Then Try:** While the days of window shopping is still intact during post lockdown, however the days are gone for trying without buying. Whether it is shoes or clothing customers are restrained to try at the stores. Some shop owners are bit flexible where they ask to first pay and then try out the clothes or shoes or any other products. The need of the hour is to prevent contamination of goods, consumers were not allowed to touch cloths, bags, shoes, and other items. While this strategy was good for consumers and staffers to keep safe from Corona infections, this made consumers finding the right size, cut, color, and fit has become a test of consumer own imagination and judgment. (Sharma, 2020)

- **No Touch Shopping:** Another interesting shopper strategy seen during post lockdown which for sure will warrant consumer behavior change was few shops adopting a "No Touch" policy. This behavior was observed in famous marketing place Janpath in New Delhi which is near to famous posh marketing venue Connaught Place. In this market there was both no try and no touch policy. Customers were asked to choose an item then pay. Once the payment was done then customer was offered a packed new item from stock and not from the one which was on display. Incase customer touched an item then it was sanitized again. Even some shops made consumers to wear gloves in case they insisted to touch an item before they buy. While no touch and no try policy are safe for customers and shop keepers from infection per se, but this makes consumer behavior change altogether. Indian customer mind set is to first touch the item to see its texture if it is a cloth. To feel the material for smoothness and color. Maximum customers will also try new clothes and shoes for a better fit. For a better and safe customer and shop owner experience, touch and try is ruled out making it difficult to consumers in making the right choice to buy the products and services (Sharma and Kumar, 2020)

- **Moving towards buy online and try at Home:** Product and marketing companies have been trying various methods to sale their products and services during pandemic. This list also includes E commerce and online companies. Various research and consulting companies in their research survey during and post lockdown surveys have found that safety of staff and customers is of paramount importance. Sellers were trying all possible ways to prevent and reduce infections while still offering best possible consumer interaction with products. Since during post lockdown sellers restricted customers to touch or try new products in the store itself, this overall had negative consumer experience. To offer customer good product experience, tryitfirst.com an online e shopping company based out of India has come out with an innovative model to sell as well as offer customers the options to try the product at the secure and convenience at home. Tryitfirst company offers mobile phone accessories including headsets and computer accessories. They offer genuine branded products online. The process involves customers first selecting products online for buying. Then they can choose up to 3 products for trying at home. A tryitfirst executive will go to the customers place and offer the three products for trial. First 20 minutes trial is free. If the customer wishes to try for few more minutes beyond the 20 minutes, then it is charged as trial duration increases as per table 1 below.

Table1: Tryitfirst trial charges

Duration	Cost
Upto 20 min	Free
20 minutes to 30 minutes	Rs 50 + GST
30 minutes to 40 minutes	Rs 100 + GST
40 minutes to 60 minutes	Rs 150 + GST

Source: https://tryitfirst.in/try-and-buy-policy

Customers have the option to buy or reject the trial product if customers feel that the order product is not up to the satisfaction level. If the customers want to purchase, then they have the option to pay online or by cash by paying to the company trial executive on the spot. However, customers must choose from the ordered product only. To prevent fake and misuse of this model customer can place only one order per day for trial. If they have placed more than one order for trial in a day, then first order is placed, and rest orders are automatically cancelled. This model offers customers to try product at convenience and safety by trying at home. This does not require to stand in long line in front of the store to buy products. Also, customer need not pay to buy the product first, they can try at home and then buy offering additional convenience of money. (Buy, 2020)

- **No return/exchange policy**: To avoid infection and frequent sanitization, few sellers during selling have announced that there will be no return or exchange. While customers were not allowed to try at stores, preventing them with options as no exchange and return was for sure a serious setback to customer shopping experience.

5. ANALYSIS:

Current Corona 19 pandemic have permanently altered the consumer behaviour pattern of Indian consumers. It is expected that some of the behaviour changes will be permanent and will continue even after pandemic is over. Maximum number of people have opted for online shopping during lockdown since stepping out of house was not a choice. Even online companies struggled to fulfil the demand since the volume of transaction was extremely high at the start of lockdown, although it stablished later. Customer have shown interest to shop online even after pandemic is over. Digital technology adoption increased due to Corona pandemic. People were working from home through remote means, watching movies online and attending online classes. All these possible through digital technology. During lockdown, customers preferred those products and services which offered high value. Due to low or nil income during the lockdown, consumers bought only those items which was essentials and stopped spending on discretionary categories. Post lockdown Indian customers even preferred to visit shops once they are opened. Even customers viewed that will carefully spend after lockdown. Discretionary expenditures are likely to remain low and spending on travel and leisure was not in plan of spending line. After, pandemic sellers adopted marketing and selling strategies in line to keep staffers and customers safe from infections. As a result, some sellers resorted to strategies like no touch shopping, no trying at stores, no exchange or refund policies. These strategies totally altered the pattern of Indian consumer behaviour. In future it is expected that companies should focus on offering products and services which have value, satisfaction in line with spiritual approach and develop products and services to enhance trust and credibility.

6. CONCLUSION

Reimaging Spiritual Consumerism as next normal in Consumer Behaviour

The pre pandemic lockdown consumer behaviour has been ruling the marketing dynamics since last three decades. With the onset of COVID 19 pandemic this behaviour has changed. As per Kotler and Keller (Kotler and Keller, 2012), it is important to understand the customers lives to offer most appropriate products and services and market it to the right person in most effective manner. During the lockdown customers were restricted to their houses with only digital media options open to the outside world. This has led to change in behaviour dynamics and redefined the social and individual orientation. Due to uncertainty, demand and supply challenges and financial distress has forced consumers to roll back to Maslow's need hierarchy of fulfilling basic level needs only. This includes, food, clothing, shelter, safe indoors and social love. People were managing the daily routine with the limited available products and services. Due to gap in demand and supply, people were forced to stock essentials beyond their needs and requirements. This included even common products like biscuits, where for the first time, Parle G biscuit brand was the largest selling biscuits due to low price. Also, online ready to eat food delivery companies moved to delivering essentials like fruits, groceries, and vegetables. The behaviour of social love, seeking out for products and services which are basic in nature during pandemic can be linked to consumer spirituality. Such behaviours are called as consumer spiritual behaviour. Several research studies have been done in past and these dimension of behaviour during crisis has been reported in literatures. One such study on such behaviours was reported by Thich (Thich, 2019), in his report titled 'A Buddhist Approach to Consumption'. He described the spiritual dimension in behaviour when a consumer decides to break away from the daily routine ways in which they consume and start exploring to find ways so that they can reduce the consumption even to an extent that they do not need even one more thing. This new consumer behaviour lies in impressions and experiences via our consciousness and senses. Kelemen and Peltonen (Kelemen and Peltonen, 2005) have also done similar research and named as consumer spirituality and defined it as an interrelated process and practices by which people buy and consume products and services which offers them 'spiritual utility'. Another similar research by Sheth et al have also reported the concept of spiritual consumption and its relationship with consumer behaviour during crisis (Sheth, Sethia and Srinivas, 2010). Marketing guru Philip Kotler in his research titled 'The Market for Transformation', described modern consumers as those who are increasingly looking for remedies, hopes and anchors that can change consumer persona to include mind and body and they see value in getting transformed (Kotler, 2019).

The next normal in consumer behaviour is most likely to be explored based on the below trends which will most likely reshape the future market:

- Rethinking on spiritual approach in understanding consumer behaviour inline with key drivers such as savings, economies of consumptions and health

- As per survey, maximum people prefer to buy products and services online and pay through digital means once the pandemic is over. This shift will be permanent which will force sellers to come up with innovative marketing and sales strategy to focus on online shoppers.

- Customers will prefer those products and services which offer high value and satisfaction in line with spiritual approach.

- Customers will shift towards purpose driven brands. Purpose driven brands are those brands that have proved trust and credibility during the Coronavirus crisis.

- Companies need to develop and offer product and service to conscious and spiritual generation.

7. RESEARCH IMPLICATIONS

Current corona pandemic scenario is very dynamic and due to which both companies and customers are getting impacted. Product and Services marketing company are leaving no stones unturned to not only fulfil the basic purchases need but also to delight the customers through better consumer behaviour experiences. Product and services companies need to continuously scan the market throughout the year for consumer behaviour pattern and changes. Also, the behaviour of shoppers changes quickly amid broader trends. Understanding these consumer behaviour trends during purchases will help marketing organisations to develop better marketing strategies, products, and services. The data provided in this research is focussed on India as a country and similar consumer behaviour mayor may not be seen across other countries. This research paper aims to highlight the various customer shopping behaviour during and after pandemic lockdown. Understanding these changing trends of consumer behaviour can give organizations a better understanding of how, where and when customers/consumers shop and then companies can customize their products and services as per needs of the customers.

8. LIMITATION AND SCOPE FOR FURTHER STUDY

Current corona pandemic scenario is very dynamic and there are multiple changes and forces which are sweeping across markets due to various policy changes implemented by government and nongovernment organizations impacting marketplace. It is expected that the new data which get generated may make current data provided in this research obsolete. The data provided in this research is current till the time of submission. Also, this research focusses on Indian consumer markets and same consumer behaviour and sentiments might not be displayed for other countries across the globe. Secondary research was used to develop this research paper. However, data limitation does exist which are commonly found while conducting secondary research.

9. REFERENCES:

- Amalia, P., Mihaela, D., Ionuţ, P. (2012). From market orientation to the community orientation for an open public administration: A conceptual framework. *Procedia: Social & Behavioral Sciences*, 62, 871–875. https://doi.org/10.1016/j. sbspro.2012.09.146
- Business, A., 2021. Marketing Your Business In India. [online] Asialink Business. Available at: <https://asialinkbusiness.com.au/india/sales-and-marketing-in-india/ marketing-your-business-in-india?doNothing=1> [Accessed 12 December 2020].
- Buy, T., 2020. Try & Buy And 365 Days Replacement : Tryitfirst.In : Try And Buy Guiding Policy. [online] Tryitfirst.in. Available at: <https://tryitfirst.in/try-and-buy-policy> [Accessed 12 December 2020].
- Chan, K., Das, R., Inoue, M. and Malhotra, A., 2020. Survey: Indian Consumer Sentiment During The Coronavirus Crisis. [online] Mckinsey. Available at: <https:// www.mckinsey.com/business-functions/marketing-and-sales/our-insights/survey-indian-consumer-sentiment-during-the-coronavirus-crisis#> [Accessed 27 December 2020].
- Community, N., 2020. COVID 19 And Indian Consumer Behavior. [online] NASSCOM Community |The Official Community of Indian IT Industry. Available at: <https://community.nasscom.in/communities/covid-19/covid-19-and-indian-consumer-behavior.html> [Accessed 12 December 2020].
- Equity Foundation, I., 2020. Retail Industry In India: Overview Of Retail Sector, Market Size, Growth...IBEF. [online] Ibef.org. Available at: <https://www.ibef.org/ industry/retail-india.aspx> [Accessed 12 December 2020].
- Flatters, P., Willmott, M. (2009). Understanding the post-recession consumer. *Harvard Business Review*, 87(7/8), 64–72. https://hbr.org/2009/07/understanding-the-postrecession-consumer
- Grundey, D., 2009. CONSUMER BEHAVIOUR AND ECOLOGICAL AGRI-BUSINESS: SOME EVIDENCE FROM EUROPE. *Journal of Scientific Papers ECONOMICS & SOCIOLOGY*, 2(1a), pp.157–170.
- Hoon Ang, S., Sim Cheng, P., Lim, E.A.C. and Kuan Tambyah, S. (2001), "Spot the difference: consumer responses towards counterfeits", Journal of Consumer Marketing, Vol. 18 No. 3, pp. 219-235. https://doi.org/10.1108/07363760110392967
- Kelemen, M. and Peltonen, T., 2005. Spirituality: A Way to an Alternative Subjectivity?. Organization Management Journal, [online] 2(1), pp.52-63. Available at: <https://www.tandfonline.com/doi/abs/10.1057/omj.2005.11>   [Accessed   12 December 2020].
- Kotler, P. and Keller, K., 2012. Marketing Management. France: Pearson.

- Kotler, P., 2019. The market for transformation. Journal of Marketing Management, [online] 35(5-6), pp.407-409. Available at: <https://www.tandfonline.com/doi/full/10.1080/0267257X.2019.1585713> [Accessed 12 December 2020].
- RAI, R., 2020. RAI Survey – Impact Of Covid-19 On Indian Retail. [online] Rai.net.in. Available at: <https://rai.net.in/COVID-19/RAI%20Survey_Impact%20of%20COVID-19%20on%20Indian%20Retail.pdf> [Accessed 12 December 2020].
- Sharma, R. and Kumar, R., 2020. #Coronaeffect: No Touching Of Items And Trying Out Clothes At Most Shops In Janpath Market | Delhi News - Times Of India. [online] The Times of India. Available at: <https://timesofindia.indiatimes.com/city/delhi/coronaeffect-no-touching-of-items-and-trying-out-clothes-at-most-shops-in-janpath-market/articleshow/76117838.cms> [Accessed 12 December 2020].
- Sharma, V., 2020. First Buy, Then Try: Covid Concern Takes All The Fun Out Of Shopping In Delhi | Delhi News - Times Of India. [online] The Times of India. Available at: <https://timesofindia.indiatimes.com/city/delhi/first-buy-then-try-covid-concern-takes-all-the-fun-out-of-shopping-in-delhi/articleshow/75931374.cms> [Accessed 12 December 2020].
- Sheth, J., 2020. Impact of Covid-19 on consumer behavior: Will the old habits return or die?. Journal of Business Research, [online] 117, pp.280-283. Available at: <https://www.sciencedirect.com/science/article/abs/pii/S0148296320303647?via%3Dihub> [Accessed 12 December 2020].
- Sheth, J., Sethia, N. and Srinivas, S., 2010. Mindful consumption: a customer-centric approach to sustainability. Journal of the Academy of Marketing Science, 39(1), pp.21-39.
- Singh, S., 2020. Covid-19: Here's A Timeline Of Events Since Lockdown Was Imposed In India. [online] Business-standard.com. Available at: <https://www.business-standard.com/article/current-affairs/here-s-a-timeline-of-events-since-lockdown-was-imposed-in-india-120070201413_1.html> [Accessed 12 December 2020].
- Thich, P., 2019. A Buddhist approach to consumption. Journal of Marketing Management, [online] 35(5-6), pp.427-450. Available at: <https://www.tandfonline.com/doi/full/10.1080/0267257X.2019.1588557> [Accessed 12 December 2020].
- Times, E., 2020. India To Be Under Complete Lockdown For 21 Days Starting Midnight: Narendra Modi. [online] The Economic Times. Available at: <https://economictimes.indiatimes.com/news/politics-and-nation/india-will-be-under-complete-lockdown-starting-midnight-narendra-modi/articleshow/74796908.cms?from=mdr> [Accessed 12 December 2020].
- Valášková, K., Kramárová, K. and Bartosova, V., 2015. Multi Criteria Models Used in Slovak Consumer Market for Business Decision Making. *Procedia Economics and Finance*, 26, pp.174–182. https://doi.org/10.1016/S2212-5671(15)00913-2
- Wahi, R. and Ramanathan, A., 2020. Impact Of COVID-19 On Consumer Business In India. [online] Www2.deloitte.com. Available at: <https://www2.deloitte.com/content/dam/Deloitte/in/Documents/consumer-business/in-consumer-impact-of-covid-19-on-consumer-business-in-india-noexp.pdf> [Accessed 12 December 2020]

CHAPTER 2

Assessing Indian Consumer's Perception Towards Attributes of Active and Intelligent Packaging Using Kano Model

Kumar Akash
Deptt of Food Business Management &
Entrepreneurship Development
National Instt of Food Technology
Entrepreneurship & Management
Kundli, Sonipat, India
visitak7@gmail.com

Prabha Krishna
Deptt of Chemical Engineering
Vignan's Foundation for
Science, Technology & Research
Guntur, Andhra Pradesh, India
prabha31094@gmail.com

Arora Sapna
Food Business Management
& Entrepreneurship
Development
National Institute of Food
Technology Entrepreneurship
& Management
Kundli, Sonipat-Hrayana
India
drsapna.niftem@gmail.com

Abstract

Food packaging plays a vital role from farm to fork throughout the distribution and supply chain facilitating storage, transportation, promotion and marketing processes by keeping quality, consumer safety and product integrity. The need for customer friendly features and attributes of packaging are growing due to changing lifestyles and it resulted in more innovative and creative packaging solutions with innovative features known as active and intelligent packaging. This study aims to assess the perception of customers towards the attributes of active and intelligent packaging for food products and measures the level of customer's satisfaction using the KANO model. The survey was conducted with 400 respondents and quantitative analysis was performed based on the Kano model to establish a relation between packaging attributes and consumer's satisfaction level. The respondents were selected through convenience sampling. A total of 12 attributes of innovative packaging are taken to collect costumers' opinion towards them through the online platform. The study finally concluded that "health & safety" is matter of utmost importance for customers. Most of the attributes fall under the "performance" category in discrete analysis while in the continuous analysis majority of attributes shifted to the "attractive" category. This study helps to understand consumer's behavioural intentions towards the innovative packaging attributes as well as their categorization into five categories. This also acts as a roadmap for future product development and a compass for investment decisions

Keywords: Active and Intelligent, Packaging, KANO Model, Innovative Packaging, Consumer Perception

I. Introduction

In today's market scenario packaging is not only limited to the containment of foods rather it works as a carrier to gauge the customer's attention. Customers are now very much conscious about purchasing packed food items. They need all the relevant information in the form of printed texts, company logos, graphic designs, symbols etc. Today's packaging techniques and methods must accommodate the lifestyles of customers for example ready to eat items, heat and eat meals which is convenient and also saves time. Packaging should be embedded with modern features along with conventional features of being handy and convenient to use. These modern features offer extra benefits and functionality like longer shelf life or indicating temperature of food stuff. The important elements in food packaging include traceability, leakage detection, & sustainability (Kotler & Armstrong, 2010). Such novel packaging techniques are termed as intelligent packaging. Intelligent packaging helps to increase the shelf life of the product, even improving the safety, quality and providing information regarding the product's past and present.

According to Fuertes et al. (2016), Active and intelligent packaging market is expected to reach 24,650 million USD by 2021 with a growth rate of 7 per cent. The major countries demanding active and intelligent packaging are the USA with 3600 million USD, followed by Japan with 2360 million, 1,690 million USD; UK, 1,270 million USD; and Germany, 1,400 million USD. In Indian context, the regional growth rate of active and intelligent packaging is similar to China and other Asian countries. Among global packaging leaders, Companies like Amcor and Tetrapak, are the lead market players of the packaging industry of India. India's active and intelligent market is not limited to the food and beverages sector, it expanded to other sectors like pharmaceutical, cosmetics and personal care. The research on consumer perception for smart packaging is not conducted in abundance and those which are conducted are scattered (Young et al, 2020). Yet it is found in surveys, around half of populations are unaware about the use of active and intelligent packaging (Kocetkovs et al., 2019)

In India, commercialization of active and intelligent packaging techniques at retail level is found to be minimal. Normally, customers are untouched with such packaging technology. This creates a void of opportunity for packaging companies to invest in novel packaging technology. The innovative packaging must have attributes which are preferred by customers. Selection of correct attributes for any product is important for its firm positioning in the market as the ultimate aim of any product is customer satisfaction. Kano et al. (1984) proposed that the various attributes of a product are not equal in regards to their relationship to the customer satisfaction level. KANO stated that some attributes may result in greater satisfaction and that consumer's requirements may differ from the functional attributes of products. KANO reformed the conventional customer satisfaction models by suggesting that the important core sources of customer satisfaction could be measured by recognizing the functional criteria and customer's satisfaction score.

Active and intelligent packaging industry is blooming day by day in the Asia Pacific region especially in India and China because of greater economic developments. Yet such packaging technologies are not common in Indian market. The aim of this study is to categorize the various attributes of active and intelligent packaging on the basis of their relationship to customer satisfaction levels. The main objective of the study is to assess the perception of consumers towards the attributes of active and intelligent packaging for food products using the KANO model.

II. REVIEW OF LITERATURE

This section is divided into three sections. The first section is based on food packaging, followed by the KANO model studies and the third dealing with reviews on consumer acceptance and awareness about smart food packaging around the world.

Food Packaging

It was during the industrial revolution, the concept of food packaging came into existence when metal cans were used for the first time to store food products which later was used for canning operations on commercial scale to extend shelf life of the food products (Risch, 2009). The primary purpose of food packaging is to act as a protective outer covering on food substance, generally made of metal, aluminum, cardboard, plastics or any other materials intended to protect food from hazardous external influences. The basic role of packaging is to provide a shield to the product from pollutants, loss in transportation, safety while another role starts when it gets placed on shelf which is to attract customers from its competitive products. It has become an essential component (Gillard et al, 2018) in order to gain attention from customers and sustain them (Silayoi & Speece, 2005). The packaging design has become a channel of communication with its customers (Silayoi & Speece, 2005) for consumer goods. The companies are more concerned about packaging as it can play a vital role for attracting customers as well as for competitiveness. Nowadays, packaging in food prodcuts plays a fundamental role from farm to fork throughout the distribution and supply chain facilitating storage, transportation, promotion and marketing processes by keeping quality, consumer safety and product integrity (Gokoglu, 2020; Kuswandi, 2020). The deterioration of food product quality can be due to endogenous (respiration, transpiration, ethylene sensitivity, enzymatic activity) and exogenous factors (temperature, relative humidity, ethylene, microorganisms, oxygen, Co_2, light), as food product remains an active biological system even after harvesting (Almenar,2020). Food packaging should prevent food items from any microbial contamination by acting as a barrier to water vapour, carbon dioxide, oxygen and other volatile compounds like flavours, taints etc. along with mechanical, thermal and optical properties (Rhim et al. 2013).

In today's market scenario, packaging is not only limited to the containment of foods rather customers are now very much aware about their selection of food items. They need all the relevant information in the form of written texts, brand logo, and graphics etc. Today's packaging techniques and methods must accommodate the lifestyles of customers with provision to features which are handy and convenient to use for example, easy opening, resealability and microwave ability. The packaging technique must be flexible enough to contain different shaped and sized products which aim for enhancing logistic efficiency. With advent in packaging technology, food industries and researchers are developing innovative food packaging methods to meet the market advantage, and to address consumer demands on food products with extended shelf life and controlled quality through mild preservation

(Dobrucka & Cierpiszewski, 2014). Schaefer and Cheung (2018) studied the prospects and challenges in the area of smart packaging and reported that by 2024, smart packaging market will be expecting to reach $26.7 billion. Researchers emphasized on development of sensor technology , nanotechnology, smart materials, thin film technology and printing technology for commercialization of smart packaging. India, the second most populous country of the world, is increasing its production capacity day by day but food preservation is still a concern. In the present scenario, though Indian food packaging industry stands as the fifth largest sector with a current worth of 40 billion, with a per capita consumption of 24 kg per year, the food packaging industry of India still remains in early stage (F & B News). In order to cope with food wastage and treatment of recyclable packaging, integrated packaging sensors should be developed which stores and shares various information to food suppliers, distributors, recyclers etc via the internet of things. With 80% of Indian food packaging industry still rely on rigid packaging, the Indian food industry requires an integration of passive packaging functions like protection and marketing with advanced packaging technologies to extend shelf life while maintaining and monitoring food safety and quality of the commodity (Dobrucka & Cierpiszewski, 2014).

Active and intelligent packaging techniques are one among such innovative and smart packaging techniques which not only extend shelf life of product, but help to maintain quality throughout the supply chain to the end consumer (Kuswandi, 2020). Kerry et al. (2006) defined active packaging as "incorporation of certain additives into packaging systems with the aim of maintaining or extending product quality and shelf-life" of commodity. Active packaging involves retaining the quality by incorporating some active materials like absorbers or emitters including oxygen scavengers, temperature controller, desiccants, etc. These active materials lengthen the shelf-life of food products and sustain the quality and safety of food. Active packaging helps to prevent various chemical, microbiological and physiological processes inside food packages for example lipid oxidation, spoilage from microbes, ripening, respiration of fruits and vegetables etc. (Kruijf et al., 2002).

Intelligent packaging is a recent technology used to monitor food inside packages by detecting, sensing, tracing, recording, communicating etc. the critical factors that result in spoilage of food using indicators, data carriers and sensors, barcodes etc. This includes TTI, freshness indicators, gas indicators, RFID (Radio Frequency identification) for quality management of stored products. Thus intelligent packaging provides dynamic feedback of the product estimating spoilage of packed food thus warning consumers from consumption (Wu et al., 2020; Kanatt, 2020).

KANO Model

Chen et al (2010) examined the relationship between service convenience and customer satisfaction for home delivery by using the Kano model. Borgianni (2018) used the KANO model in order to identify the trajectories of attributes of product development projects. Chen and Ko (2016) applied the KANO model to discuss the attractive factors of regional characteristics of the public and private realm for the Art Street in Taichung, Taiwan. Madzik et al (2019) also applied KANO Model in higher education to measure the common requirements i.e. practice, ethical and research orientation, quality resources, innovation orientation, skills orientation, and quality staff. The results showed that "practice orientation" and "quality resources" are the most stable requirements, while "quality staff" is the least stable. Salahuddin and A Lee (2020) have also applied the KANO model in order to identify the major quality features of wearable technology. The parameters i.e. Battery life, economical prices, comfortability, safety & durability are more important factors as the study results. Mikulic and Prebezac (2011) critically reviewed the KANO model for quality attributes and its theoretical and practical implications. Chul Oh et al (2011) also used the KANO model for measuring the quality attributes of e-shopping malls. The researcher used two dimensional studies for analysis. Gangurde and Patil (2017) applied the KANO model for product development as per customer requirements and increased customer satisfaction. Although the KANO model is quite popular for measuring the quality attributes, product development, and customer satisfaction, researchers did not find any study using the KANO model into the Food sector in context of active and intelligent packaging.

Consumer Acceptance Study

However, the application of these technologies into a commercial scale will occur only when consumers acknowledge and accept them (Yener, 2015). For that, it is necessary to understand the consumer awareness and attitude towards the new trends in packaging which acts as a valuable source of information for food manufacturers during development of new design and marketing strategies. The development and adoption involves multidimensional challenge and various researchers investigated the consumer awareness and acceptance of novel packaging technology including active and intelligent packaging. Van Wezemael et al. (2011) studied the acceptability of packaging technologies used for improved beef safety among European citizens. The revealed that, consumers preferred familiar packaging technologies like modified and vacuum packaging compared to novel packaging releasing preservative additives like antimicrobials. An online survey was conducted by O'Callaghan & Kerry (2016) using a questionnaire containing 16 questions among a network of University College Cork (Ireland) to analyse the acceptability of different packaging techniques (smart, active, intelligent, nanotechnology) on cheese products. It was found that unfamiliarity of advanced packaging techniques resulted in lower levels of recognition and acceptability as only 6 % responded positively towards commercial active packaging of cheese products. A similar result was found by Barska & Wyrwa. (2016), during a study conducted on knowledge and attitude among the inhabitants of the Lubuskie Region on active and intelligent packaging, in which only 4% of responders knew the term active packaging.

The consumer's ability to identify and recognize colour changes in time temperature indicators is considered an essential function in such high performance indicators (Dobrucka & Przekop, 2019). According to (Ortega et al., 2017; Qin et al., 2020), surface colour and light transmission are found to be important parameters on consumer choice on packaged food. Silayoi and Speece (2018) studied the role of packaging design and impact of involvement level and time pressure during purchase decisions for packaged food products. Researchers utilized the focus group methodology (two focus groups, 6 of housewives and 6 of working women) to understand the behaviour of consumers and how packaging elements affect purchasing decisions. It is found that visual elements like graphics, shape, size, colour etc. play an important role in purchase decisions under time pressure hence it reduces the level of involvement. While the informational elements like product information and technology used, play an important role during high involvement decision making. Involvement is basically output of individual interest in a particular brand and its association with individual's feeling, values and self-concept.Wilson et al. (2018) conducted a study on impact of visual sachets inside fresh cut cantaloupe package on consumer acceptance and perception. The respondents preferred packages without drip-absorbent pads (sachets) though the participants are willing to pay more for the packages that extends shelf life of food commodities. Similarly, a study conducted among 365 Turkish consumers by Adey and Yener. (2015) found that 74.79% responded to the fact that visual ability to track the history and freshness of food plays an important role in purchase decisions. They also mentioned the unwillingness to purchase food with active sachets in food packages due to the possibility of being mistaken. Researchers also stated that customers only spend a few seconds finalizing their purchasing material as its influence on the customer's mind is high. Any product with attractive packaging and sufficient information on labels will have more chances of attracting customers. From these studies, it is clear that consumers pay attention to the visuals aspects of packaging materials.

In contrast to the aforementioned studies, Azad & Hamdavipour (2011) studied the effects of packaging characteristics on consumer's purchasing confidence. This survey was done in chain store covering 270 participants through a questionnaire based on likert scale and the information of packaging are divided into two groups of visibility and informative and results shown that informative factor like trade name and product information are main factor for buying a product while graphic and size had virtually no influence over it. The study conducted by Kuswandi, et al. (2011) stressed about the importance of labelling and information to be embedded in packaging materials. According to Lim. (2019), more information is required in the decision making process from a customer standpoint, beyond relying on "best before date" that often fail to reflect actual quality of the food product. Imiru (2017) studied the effect of packaging attributes on consumer buying decision behaviour in major commercial cities in Ethiopia. The survey consists of 384 participants from standard supermarkets in Addis Ababa and other major cities in Ethiopia. Questions were asked regarding cereal packed food and Packaging attributes studied under this survey includes packaging material, packaging colour, background image, font style, printed information and innovation. It was found that innovation has the strongest effect on the purchase decision of cereal packed food followed by printed information, background image and font size. Rundh (2009) studied the packaging designs of products and how they help to gain competitive advantage in the market. This study has been done by analysing five "corporate stories" of their new packaging development. The study presented the influence of external (consumers, environment, technology, logistics & distribution, market and international influences) and internal factors (choice of packaging material, packaging laboratory, designer, supplier etc.) in process design of new packaging. The study suggests interaction with customers for planning and development of packaging design as per their requirement.

Price of the packaging material is also considered as a very important factor in purchase decisions among customers of various food products in different packaging materials. Shepherd (2005) states appearance, freshness and price as key factors influencing purchase decisions of consumers of Asia. The study conducted by Adey and Yener (2015) found that consumers who considered price as a prime factor in purchasing decision were willing to accept the food product with innovative packaging facility even with an increased price lesser than 10%. Similarly, the online survey conducted by Koutsimanis et al. (2012) among 292 participants residing in the US, found that price of the fresh produce significantly affected the purchase decisions and ranked first (25%) among secondary attributes studied including container size and shelf life of produce. The willingness to purchase and pay more for food products (cheese) using novel packaging technologies was deemed unacceptable especially by elder population, though willingness increased after receiving appropriate knowledge on these technologies. Also Wongprawmas & Canavari (2017) studied the willingness to pay for products with Government and private food safety brands and labels on fresh produce among 350 Thai consumers from Bangkok. The study revealed a positive attitude and increased willingness to purchase fresh produce with both government led food safety labels and private brands. With growing population, it is important to create awareness of people in India about advanced and innovative technologies like active and intelligent packaging so that these technologies can be adapted easily on a commercial scale. Though many studies regarding consumer perception towards smart packaging were conducted based on clusters in Europe and few clusters in America, consumer perception is not studied as much as other areas of smart packaging (Young et al, 2020). However, researchers couldn't find much literature supporting awareness, attitude and perception of Indian consumers towards smart packaging with respect to the food sector.

III. RESEARCH METHODOLOGY

Objectives of the Study

Understanding the perceptions of consumers towards attributes of active and intelligent packaging and their influence over the customer satisfaction level helps to develop a new packaging model which carries the attributes preferred by the customer. Therefore, the study was aimed to assess the perception of consumers towards the attributes of active and intelligent packaging for food products using the KANO model.

Data Collection

The study is primarily based on primary data. A self administered questionnaire based on the KANO model was prepared by taking into account 12 attributes or features of smart packaging and circulated among consumers through Google forms. The data was collected from 400 respondents selected through non -probabilistic convenience sampling. The Kano Model is being implemented in this study to quantify customer satisfaction levels for attributes of innovative packaging. A total of 12 attributes of innovative packaging has been selected to make a comparative study regarding the preference and satisfaction level it produces among customers.

Scope of Study

Understanding the perceptions of consumers towards attributes of active and intelligent packaging and their influence over the customer satisfaction level helps to develop a new packaging model which carries the attributes preferred by the customer. The scope of study further extends as different attributes of innovative packaging can be segregated on the basis of customer satisfaction level. This would help organizations to adopt more effective investment and marketing plans to boost up their profit. The findings of this research might assist the Indian firms for better operational and financial decisions pertaining to product development, marketing in the context of innovative packaging. For example companies could use it to enhance customer satisfaction experience, achieve competitive advantage over competitors, or to distinguish oneself in the market.

Analysis Tools

The present study applied KANO model for prioritizing the attributes of active and intelligent packaging. Further, standard deviation, mean score and graphs have been used to exhibits the results.

KANO model

The satisfaction of the consumers depends on the functionality being provided regarding the product features, how many and in which way these are implemented. As the present study is based on attributes preferences of active and intelligent packaging by the consumers, the Kano model has been applied to measure the attributes. The Kano Model is an approach to priorities featured on a product roadmap based on the degree to which they are likely to produce satisfaction in customers. The KANO model is named after its researcher's name i.e. Dr. Noriaki Kano, professor at Tokyo University. Dr Noriaki Kano developed a framework based on factors which contributed to customer satisfaction and loyalty (Kano et al., 1984). This framework consists of a two way quality model that helps to determine the degree of customer satisfaction with product features.

Functional		Dysfunctional	Category
Like it	+	Dislike it	Performance
Expect it	+	Dislike it	Must-Be
Like it	+	Don't care	Attractive
Don't care	+	Don't care	Indifferent
I dislike it	+	I expect it	Reverse
Like it	+	Like it	Questionable

The questionnaire is designed into two forms named as functional Vs dysfunctional. The functional form is based on asking consumers feelings which requires fulfillment and dysfunctional form is asking consumer feelings in case of non-fulfillment of the attribute. The KANO model maps the features or attributes of a product into five categories, depending on customers respond to the intensity of functionality: Performance, Must – be, Attractive, Indifferent, Reverse and Questionable.

Example of Mapping

Response Analysis
Once responses are obtained, continuous and discrete analysis is being done for prioritizing of attributes. The mathematical models help to map the responses and deduce suitable categories for attributes of active and intelligent packaging.

Discrete Analysis

Discrete analysis is following steps:

1) Categorization of feature or attribute by matching each respondent's functional and dysfunctional answer using the Evaluation table discussed earlier.
2) Count the total responses in each category for each feature or attribute. The table below shows the number of responses (frequency) for the feature "Shelf Life" fall under the particular category.
3) The category of each feature is decided by the mode i.e the category having highest frequency. In this case, "shelf life" attribute of innovative packaging falls under the "Performance" category as it has the highest frequency.
4) Whenever, there is a tie between categories, research must consider the rule below mentioned:
5) Must-be > Performance > Attractive > Indifferent.

Continuous Analysis

Though discrete analysis helps to understand the requirement of the customers yet has several issues like a lot of information lost during analysis.

Each respondent's twenty five answer combinations are being condensed to one of the six categories, further shorten it to one category for each attribute. DuMouchel (1993) suggested a continuous analysis method for categorization of attributes or features. First, each answer of a functional and dysfunctional question is converted to a mathematical scale ranging from -2 to 4. To understand this, larger the number, more preference for that attribute by the respondent. The Kano Model is being implemented in this study to quantify customer satisfaction levels for attributes of innovative packaging. A total of 12 attributes of innovative packaging has been selected to make a comparative study regarding the preference and satisfaction level it produces among customers.

IV. ANALYSIS AND INTERPRETATION

A total of 400 responses were collected after rejecting incomplete responses and table-1 exhibits the social demographic profile of the respondents. Out of which 222 were male respondents and 178 were the female respondents. A total of 326 respondents were in the age group of 18-25 years who usually purchase food items for self consumption. As far as educational qualification is concerned, 57.5 percent of the sample is graduated followed by postgraduate with a percentage of 28 percent. The majority of the respondents (78.25 percent) are students and these are trend setters for any product. Nowadays, companies are targeting youth as India has the largest population of youth and they could be carriers

Table 1: Socio-demographic Profile of the Respondents

Characteristics	Frequency (n)	Frequency (%)
Gender		
Male	178	44.5
Female	222	55.5
Age		
Below 18 years	4	1
18-25 Years	326	81.5
25-35 Years	56	14
35-50 Years	10	2.5
Above 50 Years	4	1
Education		
Primary	3	0.75
High School	2	0.5
Senior Secondary	21	5.25
Graduation	230	57.5
Post Graduation	211	28
Others	32	8
Profession		
Student	313	78.25
Government sector	22	5.5
Private	51	12.75
Farmer	2	0.5
Business	2	0.5
Others	10	2.5
Annual Income		
No Income	282	70.5
Below 1 Lakh	23	5.75
1-3 lakh	34	8.5
3-5 Lakh	28	7
Above 5 Lakh	33	8.25
Food Science/ Technology Background		
Yes	236	59
No	164	41

Source: Compiled from data obtained through survey

Table 2: Categorization of Attributes using Discrete Analysis

Feature	M	P	A	I	R	Q	Total	Category
Shelf Life	17	113	114	33	21	102	400	A
Sachets	23	21	57	72	98	129	400	Q
Price	53	34	51	90	33	139	400	Q
Eco-Friendly	36	172	66	27	20	79	400	P
Time Temp	37	79	109	71	24	80	400	P
Visual Inspection	29	93	122	52	29	75	400	P
Informative Labeling	74	113	66	49	26	72	400	P
Health & Safety	72	165	31	37	22	73	400	P
Anti-Microbial & Anti-Oxidant	54	147	63	34	20	82	400	P
Freshness Indicator	28	105	105	50	24	88	400	P
Leakage Indicator	46	106	86	51	18	93	400	P
Offers & promotion	29	104	99	60	16	92	400	P

Source: Compiled from data obtained through survey

of their market leader or success. Further, these respondents were also asked about background knowledge of Food technology or science. A total of 236 respondents were having knowledge of food technology or Science.

The reason for sachet under questionable may be that consumers are not comfortable with the presence of sachet in food item due to image barrier or habit (Young et al, 2020, Wilson et al, 2018, Aday & yener, 2015). In order to draw a more accurate picture of categorization of attributes, a continuous analysis method is taken into account. The results of continuous analysis are exhibited in Table-3 and Figure -1 is prepared to provide a cumulative figure to decide the category for attributes.

Unlike discrete analysis there is no loss of information and the influence of variance in responses taken into account. Price as well as Sachets attributes are of the "Indifferent" category. It is also found that the "Health & Safety" attribute is the most important feature for customers having importance score 7.93 followed by eco-friendly with a score of 7.83 while the TTI is least important feature to customers with score of 6.85.

It clearly indicates that customers don't want to compromise with their health and safety so whatsoever features or functionality being implemented in innovative packaging, it must ensure that they don't cause any health hazard. As today's consumers are more health and environment conscious, they prefer to have products in the similar way focusing upon these two aspects. Consumers are having more concerns for adopting technology in case of food products and willing to adopt innovative packaging to prevent from microbial spoilage (Aday & Yener, 2015)

Table 3: Continuous Analysis using KANO Model (Standard Deviation)

Feature	S.D of Functional	S.D of Dysfunctional	S.D of Importance Score
Health & Safety	1.37	2.55	1.83
Eco-Friendly	1.25	2.54	1.74
Anti-Microbial & Anti-Oxidant	1.49	2.51	1.8
Informative Labeling	1.49	2.51	1.64
Leakage Indicator	1.64	2.41	1.98
Visual Inspection	1.46	2.34	1.9
Offers& promotion	1.58	2.39	1.8
Freshness Indicator	1.36	2.42	1.68
Shelf-Life	1.29	2.47	1.65
Price	2.21	2.23	1.97
Sachets	2.11	2.07	1.92

Source: Compiled from data obtained through survey

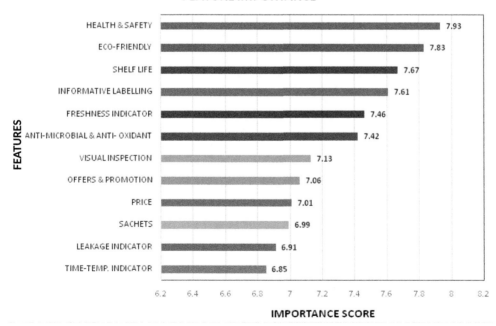

FEATURE IMPORTANCE

Fig. 1: *Ranking of Attributes based on Importance Score*

V.   LIMITATIONS AND FUTURE SCOPE OF THE STUDY

The present study is conducted to prioritize the attributes for active and intelligent packaging using the KANO model but discrete analysis of the KANO model has itself few limitations which also affect the study's results. Under discrete analysis, there is no record of the variance in data as well as softer answers get the same weight as harder ones. For example "Attractive" with a dysfunctional answer "expect it" got the same weight age as the answer "live with". Further, the present study is limited to responses obtained from consumers only. The study can be extended by considering manufacturer or service provider point of view. Secondly, the study exhibits the results obtained from the KANO model, further advanced statistical tools can be applied to get more in- depth results into smart packaging for food sector specific. The study is being conducted for the basic attributes of active and intelligent packaging which is also a limitation. The study can be extended by focusing on each attribute and for that attribute which variable is most of the important for the consumers. Moreover, the study can be extended sub sector wise of Indian food sector as each sub sector of the food sector is different in nature. The study can be further extended on the type of smart packaging that consumers prefer in order to increase consumer acceptability.

VI.   Acknowledgment:

The authors are thankful for the support provided by National Institute of Food Technology Entrepreneurship & Management (NIFTEM), Kundli, Sonipat (Haryana), India- 131028.

VII.   REFERENCES

1.   Aday, M. S., & Yener, U. 2015. Assessing consumers' adoption of active and intelligent packaging. *British Food Journal*, 117:1, 157–177.
2.   Azad, N & Iran, L. 2012. A study on effects of packaging characteristic on consumer's purchasing confidence. *Management Science Letters*, 2:1, 397- 402.
3.   Biji, K. B., Ravishankar, C. N., Mohan, C. O., & Srinivasa Gopal, T. K. 2015. Smart packaging systems for food applications: a review. *Journal of Food Science and Technology*, 52:10, 6125–6135.
4.   Borgianni, Y. 2018. Verifying dynamic Kano's model to support new product/service development. *Journal of Industrial Engineering and Management,* 11:3,569-587. https://doi.org/10.3926/jiem.2591
5.   Dobrucka, R., Cierpiszewski, R. 2014. Active and Intelligent Packaging Food - Research and Development – A Review. *Polish Journal of Food and Nutrition Sciences*, 64:1, 7–15.
6.   DuMouchel, W. 1993. Thoughts on Graphical and Continuous Analysis on Kano's Methods for Understanding Customer-defined Quality. *Center for Quality of Management Journal*, 2:4, 20–23.
7.   Fang, Z., Zhao, Y., Warner, R. D., & Johnson, S. K. 2017. Active and intelligent packaging in meat industry. *Trends in Food Science & Technology*, 61, 60–71.

8. Fuertes, G., Soto, I., Carrasco, R., Vargas, M., Sabattin, J., & Lagos, C. 2016. Intelligent Packaging Systems: Sensors and Nanosensors to Monitor Food Quality and Safety. *Journal of Sensors*, 1–8.

9. Imiru, G. A. 2017. The Effect of Packaging Attributes on Consumer Buying Decision Behavior in Major Commercial Cities in Ethiopia. *International Journal of Marketing Studies*, 9:6, 43

10. Janjarasskul, T., &Suppakul, P. 2017. Active and intelligent packaging: The indication of quality and safety. *Critical Reviews in Food Science and Nutrition*, 58:5, 808–831.

11. Kano, N., Seraku, N., Takahashi, F., & Tsuji, S. 1984. Attractive quality and must–be quality. *Journal of Japanese Society for Quality Control,* 14, 39–48.

12. Kocetkovs, V., Muizniece-Brasava, S., & Veipa, J. 2019. Consumer awareness and attitudes towards active and intelligent packaging systems in the Latvian market. In Baltic Conference on Food Science and Technology: conference proceedings, LLU (pp. 222–226).

13. Kotler, P & Armstrong, G .2010. *Principles of Marketing*, 13th edition, New Jersey: Pearson Prentice Hall

14. Lee, S. Y., Lee, S. J., Choi, D. S., & Hur, S. J. 2015. Current topics in active and intelligent food packaging for preservation of fresh foods. *Journal of the Science of Food and Agriculture*, 95:14, 2799–2810.

15. Ming-Shih Chen & Yao-Tsung Ko. 2016. Using the Kano Model to Analyze the Formation of Regional Attractive Factors of Art Street in Taichung, Taiwan, *Journal of Asian Architecture and Building Engineering,* 15:2, 271–278, DOI: 10.3130/jaabe.15.271.

16. N. De Kruijf , M. Van Beest , R. Rijk , T. Sipiläinen-Malm , P. Paseiro Losada & B. De Meulenaer. 2002. Active and intelligent packaging: applications and regulatory aspects, *Food Additives & Contaminants*, 19:S1, 144–162, DOI: 10.1080/02652030110072722

17. Rhim, J.-W., Park, H.-M., & Ha, C.-S. 2013. Bio-nanocomposites for food packing applications. *Progress in Polymer Science,* 38:10–11, 1629–1652.

18. Rundh, B. 2009. Packaging design: creating competitive advantage with product packaging. *British Food Journal*, 111:9, 988–1002.

19. Schaefer, D., & Cheung, W. M. 2018. Smart Packaging: Opportunities and Challenges. *Procedia CIRP*, 72, 1022–1027.

20. Siegrist, M., Cousin, M.-E., Kastenholz, H., & Wiek, A. 2007. Public acceptance of nanotechnology foods and food packaging: The influence of affect and trust. *Appetite*, 49:2, 459–466.

21. Silayoi, P., &Speece, M. 2004. Packaging and purchase decisions. British Food Journal, 106:8, 607–628.

22. Yam, K. L., Takhistov, P. T., &Miltz, J. 2005. Intelligent Packaging: Concepts and Applications. *Journal of Food Science*, 70:1, R1–R10.

23. Young, Erin; Mirosa, Miranda and Bremer, P .2020. A Systematic Review of Consumer Perceptions of Smart Packaging Technologies for Food; *Frontiers in Sustainable Food Systems,* May, 4:63, 1–20.

CHAPTER 3

Rationales of Factors Affecting Consumer Purchase Behavior for E-Pharmacy in The Presidency Region of West Bengal

Aman Jha
Research Scholar
Department of Management Studies
NSHM Knowledge Campus, Kolkata
Kolkata, India
amanjhabose@gmail.com

Sudip Kundu
Assistant Professor
Department of Management Studies
NSHM Knowledge Campus, Kolkata
Kolkata, India
sudipkundu1905@gmail.com

Abstract

This study aims to examine the factors influencing the adoption and usage of online pharmacies in the West Bengal Presidency Division. The key goal is to figure out what are the drivers and obstacles to the buying of drugs online and which considerations could make it easier to address perceived barriers for the consumer. A mixture of online quantitative surveys and qualitative literature was conducted; with target group being 18–75-year-olds, residing in Presidency division of West Bengal who have made an online medicine purchase. Quantitative analysis of the sample was carried out using version 22.0 of the IBM SPSS and other qualitative data was analysed using traditional methods.

The paper identified and defined a specific scaled model for measuring behavioural traits of respondents relating to buying medicine from e-pharmacy portal and specific demographic factors like income and education level, individual living status, place of residence, played a significant role. As consumers have started preferring to make purchases at the ease and safety of home, the conclusions of this paper can provide marketers with evidences and parameters to strategically design their marketing mix.

Keyword: Consumer behaviour, E-pharmacy, Confirmatory Factor Analysis, Purchase Intention, Online Marketing

Introduction

The Internet has transformed and altered our lifestyles, the way we interact, and our purchasing methodologies (*Von Rosen et al., 2017*). As access to the internet expands, the use for the quest for medical information is also widening. Worldwide data suggests that about 4.5% of all online searches are connected to health-related problems or information (*Das al., 2014*). Initially, selling focused on e-commerce was on reliable, non-food products such as books, but nowadays almost any commodity can be sold, and so major retailers have capitalised on this delivery format (*Bourlakis et al. 2008*).

E-pharmacies are new entrants to the Indian e-commerce scene, attracting increased attention from government and investors in the last three to five years. Today, the market potential of e-pharmacy is worth more than $1 trillion, *(Sinha et al., 2019)* with more than 30 start-ups supporting this segment's growth in various regions of India. The increasing trend internet pharmacy industry is driven by a gradual growth of the Internet, an ever-increasing focus on physical well-being, a transition from direct doctor-patient interactions to self-diagnosis, customer experience of online sales, ease of mail order, and distance selling (*Nayyar et al., 2016); (Gabay et al., 2015*). The online pharmacy market is slowly gaining momentum in the space of the e-commerce industry with an impressive rate of market penetration in both India's rural and urban regions (*Wood et al., 2018)*, with the help of big market players like, 1mg, Netmeds.com, PharmEasy and Easy Medico Several entrepreneurs and investors are keen to take the initiative of becoming part of the fast-growing E-pharmacy industry.

As the year 2020 was greeted by the global pandemic COVID-19, which emerged in China and had its first recorded case in India on 30 January, most e-pharmacies saw a surge in demand, with consumers starting to accept them as cleaner, quicker, and cheaper than traditional stores. The threat of catching the virus has driven people to go to internet channels, either to pay bills or to meet with doctors. E-pharmacies are no deviation from this. Key point, the development that these channels have undergone during the last few months, is something experts say is here to live. For example, after the lockdown was declared in March, 1mg, a digital customer health network, saw a 100% rise in demand in the first three to four weeks. Cut to June, orders were only 30-40% higher than pre-COVID days (*Annapurani et al., 2020*).

REVIEW OF LITERATURE

Consumer Behaviour

Customer purchasing activity is aligned with consumer behaviour and also how they work as they want to purchase a commodity that fits their needs. It is the study of consumer perceptions that pushes them to buy and use those goods. The study of consumer buying behaviour becomes more essential for advertisers, since they may recognize consumer desires. It aims to understand what causes a consumer buy a product. In order to be placed on the marketplace, it is important to decide the type of goods that consumers want. Performance based, advertisers can identify the desires and despises of consumers and plan their marketing strategies.

(*Kotler et al., 2011*) state that due to many reasons, the significance of examining customer purchasing behaviour as a field of marketing is growing. In order to resource consumers with any product or service, companies must consider the community, social category and many other aspects of their clients. Understanding these variables allows companies to draw up an efficient marketing plan in order to more effectively satisfy their customers' needs. The intense pace of globalisation is another explanation for increasing the value of the study of consumer purchasing behaviour. Globalization, according to *(Nargunkar et al., 2008)*, has changed the way corporations work and target their customers. It is important to consider the purchasing actions of *(Lancaster et al., 2002)* customers to make these possible. Quick developments in technology are another aspect adding to the value of understanding consumer buying behaviours. It is also reported that major and global corporations are making substantial investments in improving their IT processes in order to better understand their buyers' expectations and preferences. In turn, this helps them to determine what and how often their customers are purchasing *(Brink and Berndt et al., 2009)*.

Importance of Studying Consumer Behaviour

Knowledge of thorough consumer behaviour is important for a company to be competitive both in terms of its existing products and in terms of new product releases. A consumer has a complicated process of thinking and an approach towards the buying of a different product. If a company fails to understand the buyer's response to a service, there is a high probability of product loss. Consumer behaviour too is changing respond to altering behaviours, technologies, demographics, lifestyle, spending power and related factors. The marketer must consider the factors that differ so that the marketing effort can be adjusted accordingly.

When it comes to marketing, the division of consumers is a way of distinguishing consumers from a range of other buyers. *(Katalin Eibel et al., 2013)*. It helps to create a target demographic with the same or similar actions *(Barmola et al., 2010)*. Consumer behaviour is not only important for gaining new customers, but it is also very important for existing customers to be maintained *(Turki et al., 2010)*. The study of customer behaviour would be the first to demonstrate a transition in the industry environment *(Adebola et al. 2019)*. Analysing consumer behaviour makes it easy to grasp and compete. Depending on customer preferences, the brand must broaden its strategic advantages. *(Elena et al. 2017)*.

In short, concepts and ideals of consumer conduct are of the highest concern to sales staff or marketers. When goods are manufactured in order to satisfy the needs and wishes of the consumer, the products can also be well marketed in order to fulfil the goals of the business. The analysis of customer behaviour helps one to analyse a variety of factors that have an effect on consumer buying decisions. If the advertisers did not know these factors, they would not have accomplished their targets.

Consumer Behaviour in accordance to E-Pharmacy

Medicines have always been a very important part of people's lives to protect and cure people from different diseases and injuries *(Shekhar et al. 2019)*; *(Ricks et al., 2012)* ;*(Singh et al. 2005)*. If not medicines, most of the diseases in this world would still have been incurable *(Mathialagan et al., 2012)*. People have been using medications in various ways since centuries, in order to keep them stable and safe from harmful diseases. E-Commerce is a revolution in how business can be conducted in the future, and everyone will have to adapt to evolving patterns. Because e-Pharmacy is just technical innovation, it is recommended that it be permitted and that its benefits be made available to consumers in India, but with adequate protections and under strict regulatory regulation to protect the interests of consumers (*Frost and Sullivan 2019*).

The growth in online pharmacy business is steady, but there is a positive trend in India. According to CLSA's foreign exchange report, Singapore's Indian pharmacy market is growing at around 12% per year and at this rate the Indian Pharmacy market would be $35 billion from the current $20 billion dollar market (*Frost and Sullivan 2018*). There are many e-pharmacy operators in the Indian market; however, the top players are Net meds, Pharmeasy, Medlife and 1mg with a pan-India approach *(Sharma et al., 2019)*. In the current situation, Indians are witnessing a significant change in health problems with a relatively high level of chronic diseases, where medications are needed for a prolonged period. Owing to busy schedule and day-to-day responsibilities, the need for health care shifts to the secondary focus, and that results in a pause in taking the prescription drug on schedule or in a prompt visit to the physicians. But the most difficult aspect is the buying of drugs, which involves lengthy prescription searches, price differences and long trips to a single chemist *(Jimmy et al., 2011)*. It saves a lot of consumers' available time.

Currently, e-Pharmacy is at inception stage in India, much like other sectors, but also has the promise to be a really big industry field in the near future. Demand-driven factors involve larger numbers of people with unmet medical needs due to broad populations and increased digital penetration across both developed and emerging areas. The e-Pharmacy model is projected to compensate for 5-15% of total pharmacy sales in India, largely through improved adherence and access to medicines for several underserved communities *(Alamelu R. et al. 2016)*. E-pharmacy is very well associated with national growth goals and provides direct and concrete results for both customers and business. Meanwhile, it has also been recognised that e-commerce and retail growth are compatible and mutually reinforcing. By using technology in a smart way and under tight regulatory supervision, e-Pharmacy has the ability to bring tremendous value to the current retail industry in India. E-Commerce provides many benefits for customers and the most important is the comfort or ease with which medications can be purchased. The advantages of the e-Pharmacy model should be the first concern of the Government for customers, who are the majority. It is important that the regulatory system in the world be conceptualised, bearing in mind the broader needs of customers in the country. If technology is available to minimise the intermediary prices of medications, it must be allowed to be used to its maximum extent as it lowers the selling price of certain drugs and supports the middle class, which is most affected by the price hikes (*Ahmed Shaikh et al. 2019*).

Buying Behaviour Factors for E-Pharmacy

Table1: Validated Questions Used in Relevant Prior Studies Utilized In the Questionnaire

Construct	Label	Sources
Purchase Intention	Positive Recommendation (PI1)	Venkatesh et al., 2003; Yin et al., 2016
	Positive about buying online (PI2)	Moe et al., 2003; Roblek et al., 2018
	Intend to re-purchase online (PI3)	Holtgäfe et al., 2012
	Likely to buy medicines online (PI4)	Venkatesh et al., 2003; Yin et al., 2016
Experience	Satisfied with online pharmacy (E1)	Gurău C et al., 2005
	More involved online portal (E2)	Szekely et al., 2010
	Satisfied with online services (E3)	Misra et al., 2000
	I have decent knowledge (E4)	Wiedmann et al., 2010
Perceived Ease of Use	I consider ordering online is easy (PE1)	Ray et al., 2012
	Online site is easy to use (PE2)	Vida et al., 2018
Search of information	Site is goodinformation source (SI1)	Kim et al., 2012; Roblek et al. 2018
	E-portal provides useful info (SI2)	Wiedmann et al., 2010
	Non-prescribed drug info on web (SI3)	Holtgäfe et al., 2012
	Sort out relevant reliable info (SI4)	Lostakova et al., 2012; Gurau et al., 2005
	Interact with doctors in the web (SI5)	Haynes et al., 2001
	Familiar with the search info (SI6)	Holtgäfe et al., 2012

Perceived Risk	Concerned of personal info (PR1)	Büttner et al., 2006
	Authenticity of medicine (PR2)	Koufaris et al., 2004; Yin et al., 2016
	Concerned on payment gateway (PR3)	Yin et al., 2016
	Concerned of delayed delivery (PR4)	Wiedmann et al., 2010
	Concerned about return policy (PR5)	Dalton et al., 2017
Perceived Usefulness	Saves time spent on shopping (PU1)	Venkatesh et al., 2003
	Don't have to discusson face (PU2)	Wiedmann et al., 2010
	Convenient and effortless 24/7 (PU3)	Roblek et al., 2018
	Easier to gather information (PU4)	Holtgäfe et al., 2012
	Buy medicine unfound in OTC (PU5)	Surratt et al. 2010
Perception on value added services	Transparency of information (VAS1)	Pelton et al., 2009
	Clear information with picture (VAS2)	Lombardo et al. 2016
	Multiple payment options (VAS3)	Desai et al., 2016
	Multiple delivery time options (VAS4)	Arya et al., 2019
	Wide range of product (VAS5)	Liang et al., 2012
	Better price compared to OTC (VAS6)	Levaggi et al., 2009

Source: Own Source (Primary Data)

RESEARCH OBJECTIVE

This paper aims to highlight the factors amidst demographic profile which plays a role in influencing shopper's perception towards buying products from e-pharmacy. The basic aim of the paper was to identify the factors that affect the e-purchase of pharmaceutical products. This research is conducted to get a superior comprehension of inspirations driving consumer choices on acquiring professionally prescribed medicines on the web. The paper gives new insights into consumer behaviour and their viewpoints for online pharmacies and draws a theoretical framework that explicit the relationship between influencing factors of online medicine buying, during the post pandemic conditions.

RESEARCH METHODOLOGY

The research was conducted across four districts of Presidency Division of West Bengal, which by 2001 census has a population of 32,741,224. The study was conducted across districts, falling under the Presidency area of West Bengal, namely Howrah (n=77), Kolkata (n=105), North 24 Parganas (n=130), and South 24 Parganas (n=98). The sampling method used was Stratified Random Sampling. The sample units were people who have made an online purchase of pharmacy and all possible subsets of a population (from across demographic variables) were given an equal probability of being selected. The sample size, taken for the study was 410, distributed among four districts. The target population of the study is identified as people aged 18 to 75 years who have made an online purchase of medicines earlier. The total valid sample for the study was 410 respondents.

Demographic Summary

Table1: Description of the Sample's Demographic Characteristics (n = 410)

Variable	Percentage (%)	Frequency	Variable	Percentage (%)	Frequency
Gender			**Distance From Medical Stores**		
Male	51.7	212	Less Than 1km	59.8	245
Female	48.3	198	1Km - 3 Km	40.2	165
Age			**District Of Residence**		
Below 30 Years	39.5	162	North 24 Parganas	31.7	130
30-45 Years	23.2	95	Howrah	18.8	77
45-65 Years	20.7	85	Kolkata	25.6	105
> 65 Years	16.6	68	South 24 Parganas	23.9	98
Income Level			**Level Of Education**		
< 4 Lakhs	18.8	77	Under Graduate	17.1	70

4-8 Lakhs	18.3	75	Graduate	39.8	163
8-12 Lakhs	38.5	158	Post Graduate	30.2	124
>12 Lakhs	24.4	100	Professional	12.9	53
Living Status			**Family Size**		
Living Alone	15.1	62	Less Than 3	31.0	127
Living with Spouse	43.0	176	3 to 4	53.9	221
Living with Parent	22.2	91	5 & Above	15.1	62
Living with S & P	19.7	81			

Source: Own Source (Primary Data)

HYPOTHESIS STATEMENT

H$_{1:}$ The identified factors of buying behaviour of e-pharmacy are not significant predictor of the model.

H$_{2:}$ Demographic profile has no role to influence shopper's perception towards buying products from e-pharmacy.

DATA ANALYSIS

Measurement fit and Validity of the factor constructs

Relative Chi-square (x^2) = 1472.145, df = 44, p = .000; model fit: minimum discrepancy (CMIN/df) = 3.33, GFI = .781, NFI = .797, RFI = .772, IFI = .849, TLI = .829, CFI = .848 and RMSEA = .075. (Hu et al., 1999) ;(Yu et al., 2002): [Cut-off Criteria for Several Fit Indexes: Absolute/predictive fit – Chi-Square (x^2) - Ratio of x^2 to df ≤ 2 or 3; NFI ≥ .95; TLI ≥ 0.95; CFI ≥ .80; GFI ≥ .95; and RMSEA < .05 to .08 are acceptable level.] The model of measurement was calculated, after a confirmatory factor analysis was carried out which yielded above mentioned results. Results show that the data match the estimation model well and all measurement fit is as per recommendation. *(Hair et al. 2010)*

All items loaded on their respective latent factors with substantial [p=.000] factor loadings ≥.80 indicated a clear converging validity of the models used in this analysis. – *(Hair et al. 2010)*

Figure 1: *Unstandardized Estimate of Buying Behaviour Constructs*

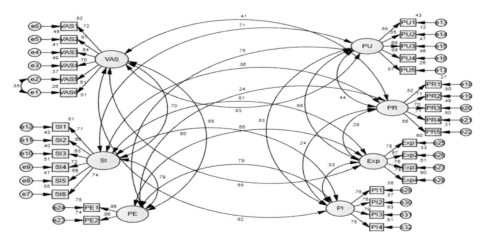

Source: Own Source (Primary Data)

Figure 2: *Standardized Estimate of Buying Behaviour Constructs*

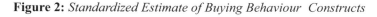

Source: Own Source (Primary Data)

H1: The identified factors of buying behaviour of e-pharmacy are not significant predictor of the model.

The test result indicates that all the underlying labels that create a factor are important predictors where p = .000 [p<0.05] is present. We thus dismiss the null hypothesis.

Table 3: Regression Weights (Default Model) - Consumer Purchase Behaviour

Factor	Regression Weights (Default Model)	Estimate	S.E.	C.R.	P
Perception on value added services	Better price compared to OTC (VAS1) < ----- Perception	1.000			
	Availability of a range of product (VAS2) < --- Perception	1.169	.092	12.727	***
	Multiple delivery options (VAS3) < --- Perception	1.035	.111	9.356	***
	Multiple payment options (VAS4) < --- Perception	.972	.109	8.931	***
	Clear provided information (VAS5) < --- Perception	.910	.099	9.157	***
	Transparency of information (VAS6) < --- Perception	.864	.091	9.485	***
Search of information	Familiarity with the search (SI1) < --- Information	1.000			
	Interact with doctors/ groups (SI2) < --- Information	.963	.072	13.405	***
	Sort relevant reliable information (SI3) < --- Information	.899	.064	14.095	***
	Easy to find non-prescription drug (SI4) < --- Information	1.051	.085	12.329	***
	Provides useful information (SI5) < --- Information	.850	.066	12.893	***
	Preferred source of information (SI6) < --- Information	.826	.059	13.991	***
Perceived Usefulness	Decreases time spent on shopping (PU1) < --- Usefulness	1.000			
	Don't have to face with OTC (PU2) < --- Usefulness	.731	.113	6.488	***
	Can do shopping 24*7 (PU3) < --- Usefulness	1.142	.097	11.754	***
	Gather information/compare price (PU4) < --- Usefulness	1.304	.112	11.667	***
	Buy medicines, not available OTC (PU5) < --- Usefulness	1.127	.123	9.162	***

Perceived Risk	Sharing my personal information (PR1) < --- Risk	1.000			
	Authenticity of medicine delivered (PR2) < --- Risk	1.454	.162	8.984	***
	Sharing payment gateway information (PR3) < --- Risk	1.501	.168	8.915	***
	Delayed or incorrect delivery (PR4) < --- Risk	1.371	.153	8.968	***
	Return or reimbursement of money (PR5) < --- Risk	1.132	.143	7.897	***
Perceived Ease of Use	Online pharmacy site easy to use (PE1) < --- Ease of Use	1.000			
	Ordering in online portal is easy (PE2) < --- Ease of Use	1.033	.050	20.829	***
Experience	Satisfied with the functionality (E1) < --- Experience	1.000			
	More involved in online portal (E2) < --- Experience	1.336	.115	11.647	***
	Pleased with customer service (E3) < --- Experience	1.486	.089	16.624	***
	Knowledge in searching medicine (E4) < --- Experience	1.422	.086	16.572	***
Purchase Intention	Positively recommend (PI1) < --- Intention	1.000			
	Feel good about my decision to buy (PI2) < --- Intention	1.458	.093	15.648	***
	Intend to re-purchase (PI3) < --- Intention	1.322	.080	16.452	***
	Likely to buy medicines online (PI4) < --- Intention	1.304	.080	16.271	***

Source: Own Source (Primary Data)

Design validity and psychometric properties were tested with confirmatory factor loading, composite reliability and mean variance values extracted. The calculation model of research demonstrated high psychometric convergent validity with built-in reliability and average variance explained (AVE). The construct reliability (C.R.) values are as following: 0.797 for perception on value added services, 0.716 for perceived usefulness, 0.778 for perceived risk, 0.845 for search of information, 0.850 for perceived ease of use, 0.821 for experience, 0.856 for purchase intention. All the C.R. values maintained the recommended minimum level of 0.70 – (Hair et al. 2010) ;(Lowry et al., 2014). The A.V.E values are: 0.398 for perception on value added services, 0.346 for perceived usefulness, 0.416 for perceived risk, 0.478 for search of information, 0.740 for perceived ease of use, 0.538 for experience, 0.597 for purchase intention, all maintained the recommended minimum level of 0.50 –

(Hair et al. 2010). The values of AVE extracted has been further validated and compared with Maximum Shared Variance (M.S.V.) and Average Shared Variance (A.S.V.) as a part of discriminant validity.

Table 4: Construct Validity - Consumer Purchase Behaviour

Constructs	Convergent Validity			Discriminant Validity		
	Construct Reliability (C.R.)	Average Variance Explained (A.V.E.)	Recommended Level	Maximum Shared Variable (M.S.V.)	Average Shared Variable (A.S.V.)	Recommended Level
Purchase Intention	0.856	0.597	C.R. > 0.70 A.V.E. > 0.50 C.R.> A.V.E.	0.865	0.447	A.V.E. > M.S.V. A.V.E. > A.S.V.
Experience	0.821	0.538		0.865	0.495	
Perceived Ease of Use	0.850	0.740		0.740	0.467	
Search of information	0.845	0.478		0.656	0.481	
Perceived Risk	0.778	0.416		0.194	0.109	
Perceived Usefulness	0.716	0.346		0.865	0.476	
Perception on VAS	0.797	0.398		0.865	0.442	

Source: Own Source (Primary Data)

H2 – Demographic profile has no role to influence shopper's perception towards buying products from e-pharmacy.

Anova analysis

Variables relating to demographic profile of the respondents were tested against purchasing intention, experience, perceived ease of use, perceived risk, perceived usefulness, information search and value-added services to examine, if demographic profile of respondents plays any significant influence on the factors For the identification of discrepancies in demographic characteristics, the measurement of variance for each factor was conducted on scores using the groups of each demographic characteristic as a factor of heterogeneity. Where the results were large, authentic variations were measured using the Tukey test. Differences were found to be important when $p \leq 0.05$ [Table 5].

Table 5: The table showing all factor ANOVA analysis

Demographic Profile		Gender	Age	Distance	District	Education	Family Size	Income Level	Living Status
Purchase Intention	F	76.612	4.01	0.062	39.001	28.108	2.836	20.923	15.12
	P value	0	0.01	0.804	0	0	0.06	0	0
	Sig	S	S	NS	S	S	NS	S	S
Experience	F	80.438	3.95	0.571	40.194	24.207	3.414	16.676	15.485
	P value	0	0.01	0.45	0	0	0.034	0	0
	Sig	S	S	NS	S	S	S	S	S
Perceived Ease of Use	F	78.962	3.78	0.778	25.199	20.6	2.396	14.169	12.941
	P value	0	0.01	0.378	0	0	0.092	0	0
	Sig	S	S	NS	S	S	NS	S	S
Perceived Risk	F	75.468	9.54	1.097	3.065	1.371	6.148	0.965	6.055
	P value	0	0	0.295	0.028	0.251	0.002	0.409	0
	Sig	S	S	NS	S	NS	S	NS	S
Perceived Usefulness	F	89.07	1.6	0.057	14.07	11.534	5.181	7.621	13.546
	P value	0	0.19	0.811	0	0	0.006	0	0
	Sig	S	NS	NS	S	S	S	S	S
Search of Information	F	86.684	1.58	2.148	27.482	17.446	2.192	13.798	14.986
	P value	0	0.19	0.144	0	0	0.113	0	0
	Sig	S	NS	NS	S	S	NS	S	S
Value Added Services	F	86.537	1.58	0.158	13.329	9.428	5.09	6.615	12.932
	P value	0	0.19	0.691	0	0	0.007	0	0
	Sig	S	NS	NS	S	S	S	S	S

**S= Significant, NS= Not Significant
Source: Own Source (Primary Data)

Experience: The demographic profile of the respondents was studied with respect to experience of shopper's making purchases through e-pharmacy. The identified demographic factors like age [F (3, 406) =3.953, p=0.008 (p<0.05)], district [F (3, 406) =40.194, p=0.000 (p<0.05)], education level [F (3, 406) =24.207, p=0.000 (p<0.05)], family size [F (2, 407) =3.414, p=0.034 (p<0.05)], income level [F (3, 406) =16.676, p=0.000 (p<0.05)], and living status [F (3, 406) =15.485, p=0.000 (p<0.05)] were found significant. Thus, it signifies a difference in the mean score among the group. However distance from OTC (F=0.571, p=0.450) was not significant. A detailed post hoc test using Tukey's method was conducted to find which particular profiles are statistically significant between the groups.In the study of age of the respondents a significant mean score was found amid the mean score of 45 to 65 years and above 65 years (p=0.005), while in the study of domicile, Kolkata had much higher propensity to make a purchase, compared toHowrah (p=0.000), North 24 pgs (p=0.000), and South 24 pgs (p=0.000). Education levels had a positive impact on the purchase from e-pharmacies as Higher the education higher is the propensity to use pharmacy.

Perceived Ease of Use: The demographic profile of the respondents was analysed with regard to the perceived ease of use of online platforms for transactions made by shoppers via e-pharmacy. Significant demographic variables have been established, such as age [$F(3,406)=3,776$, $p=0,011$ ($p<0,05$)], district [$F(3,406)=25,199$, $p=0,000$ ($p<0,05$)], educational level [$F(3,406)=20,600$, $p=0,000$ ($p<0,05$)], income level [$F(3,406)=14,169$, $p=0,000$ ($p<0,05$)], and living status [$F(3,406)=12,941$, $p=0,000$ ($p<0,05$)]. This indicates a disparity in the mean score of the group. That being said, distance from OTC ($F=0.778$, $p=0.378$) and the family size ($F=2.396$, $p=0.092$) was not significant. A detailed post hoc test using Tukey's method was conducted to find to find which particular profiles are statistically significant between the groups. A significant mean score was found amid the mean score of45 to 65 years and above 65 years ($p=0.017$) in the study of respondents' age. Respondents living in the urban regions of Kolkata found the e-pharmacy platforms much easier to use compared to the regions of Howrah ($p=0.000$), North 24 pgs ($p=0.000$), and South 24 pgs ($p=0.000$). Educational backgrounds or profiles had a beneficial influence on the buying through e-pharmacies, as higher the level of education higher is perceived ease of usage of the platform. A significant mean score was also found between people living alone and Living with Parent ($p=0.000$), Living with Spouse ($p=0.001$), and Living with S & P ($p=0.000$),

Perceived Risk: The identified demographic factors like age [$F (3, 406) =9.541$, $p=0.008$ ($p<0.05$)], district [$F (3, 406) =3.065$, $p=0.028$ ($p<0.05$)], family size [$F (2, 407) =6.148$, $p=0.002$ ($p<0.05$)], and living status [$F (3, 406) =6.055$, $p=0.000$ ($p<0.05$)] were found significant, as the demographic profile of the respondents was studied with respect to perceived risk of shopper's making purchases through e-pharmacy. Thus, it signifies a difference in the mean score among the group. However, distance from OTC ($F=1.097$, $p=0.295$), education level ($F=1.371$, $p=0.251$), and income level ($F=0.965$, $p=0.409$) was not significant. A comprehensive post hoc test using Tukey's test was performed to figure out the specific profiles are statistically significant amongst the categories. People above 65 years of age and families with less than 3 people were found to be more prone to perceiving risks in making online e-pharmacy purchases.

Perceived Usefulness: The demographic profile of the respondents was studied with respect to perceived usefulness of shopper's making purchases through e-pharmacy. The identified demographic factors like district [$F (3, 406) =14.070$, $p=0.000$ ($p<0.05$)], education level [$F (3, 406) =11.543$, $p=0.000$ ($p<0.05$)], family size [$F (2, 407) =5.181$, $p=0.006$ ($p<0.05$)], income level [$F (3, 406) =7.621$, $p=0.000$ ($p<0.05$)], and living status [$F (3, 406) =13.546$, $p=0.000$ ($p<0.05$)] were found significant. Thus, it signifies a difference in the mean score among the group. However, distance from OTC ($F=0.057$, $p=0.811$) and age ($F=1.602$, $p=0.188$), was not significant. A comprehensive post hoc test using Tukey's test was performed to figure out the specific profiles are statistically significant amongst the categories. Respondents domiciling in the urban city of Kolkata and having graduated, perceived the online pharmacy portals as a useful source of products and product related information.

Search of Information: The identified demographic factors like district [$F (3, 406) =27.482$, $p=0.000$ ($p<0.05$)], education level [$F (3, 406) =17.446$, $p=0.000$ ($p<0.05$)], income level [$F (3, 406) =13.798$, $p=0.000$ ($p<0.05$)], and living status [$F (3, 406) =14.986$, $p=0.000$ ($p<0.05$)] were found significant, when the demographic profile of the respondents was studied with respect to requirements around search of information of shopper's making purchases through e-pharmacy.. Thus, it signifies a difference in the mean score among the group. However, distance from OTC (F=2.148, p=0.144), age (F=1.578, p=0.194), and family size (F=2.192, p=0.113) was not significant. A detailed post hoc test using Tukey's method was conducted to find to find which particular profiles are statistically significant between the groups. Respondent living in North 24 pgs, South 24 pgs and Howrah had a much less propensity to search for information online compared to the ones from Kolkata. A person with education level higher that graduation was more prone to search for all related information's before making a purchase and families with less than 4 lakhs of income also were more into researching about products online before making a purchase.

Value Added Services: The demographic profile of the respondents was studied with respect to value added services on portals for shopper's making purchases through e-pharmacy. The identified demographic factors like district [F (3, 406) =13.329, p=0.000 (p<0.05)], education level [F (3, 406) =9.428, p=0.000 (p<0.05)], family size [F (2, 407) =5.090, p=0.007 (p<0.05)], income level [F (3, 406) =6.615, p=0.000 (p<0.05)], and living status [F (3, 406) =12.932, p=0.000 (p<0.05)] were found significant. Thus, it signifies a difference in the mean score among the group. However, distance from OTC (F=0.158, p=0.691), and age (F=1.584, p=0.193) was not significant. A comprehensive post hoc test using Tukey's test was performed to figure out the specific profiles are statistically significant amongst the categories. Respondents from Kolkata and having a higher educational level were found to seek much more value-added services from the service providers People with a higher family size and the ones living with both their spouse and parents also looked upon to have value added services with their products.

Purchase Intention: The demographic profile of the respondents was studied with respect to purchase intention of shopper's making purchases through e-pharmacy. The identified demographic factors like age [F (3, 406) =4.014, p=0.008 (p<0.05)], district [F (3, 406) =39.001, p=0.000 (p<0.05)], education level [F (3, 406) =28.108, p=0.000 (p<0.05)], income level [F (3, 406) =20.923, p=0.000 (p<0.05)], and living status [F (3, 406) =15.120, p=0.000 (p<0.05)] were found significant. Thus, it signifies a difference in the mean score among the group. However, distance from OTC (F=0.062, p=0.804) and family size (F=2.836, p=0.060) was not significant. A detailed post hoc test using Tukey's method was conducted to find to find which particular profiles are statistically significant between the groups. People living in Kolkata and below the age of 30 showed more intentions of making an online pharmacy purchase compared to people of 45 to 65 years (0.005) and above 65 years (p=0.005). Responds with higher educational degrees and having higher family income levels were also inclined towards e-pharmacy portals.

CONCLUSION

A clear demographic variation in regard to the behavioural experience of consumers in e-pharmacy is discovered in the study. Age and education levels are found to play a major role in behavioural approach of consumers. The younger population finds the technologically abled platform easy to use, and are more focussed on obtaining the value-added services like cheaper product and various delivery options. While the older population perceive online pharmacy as a risk prone platform and the required technical knowledge to operate applications and websites have been a major barrier in getting them to make purchases. As the concept of e-pharmacy has not penetrated much into the rural demographics, people living in the urban city of Kolkata are far more expected to make online purchases compared to people living in other allied districts.

It can be inferred that an intense public awareness campaign is required by the state or firms, to let a larger pool of consumers get aware of uses and methods of operation of e-pharmacy, as the barriers are currently dominating the consumer decision making process. Analysis of the online consumer experience to purchase OTC medicines offered valuable insights into what kind of knowledge is needed and from which platforms to purchase OTC medicines. The Internet has proven to be the main source of information and, in addition to basic information on pharmaceutical products, there has also been a clear need for price reviews and quality comparisons. According to this study, online pharmacies should invest in well-functioning, real-time chat facilities and proper product details on their websites, as well as in simple, easy-to-use websites. In addition, consumers seemed to enjoy a fairly priced and fast (home) delivery. Publicity of their services cannot be overemphasised, particularly because the use of their services is not yet so widespread.

Due to the pandemic around, the study could only be done around the Presidency Division of West Bengal, and the views differed depending upon the region in the studied sample. Future study on the topic can be exercised on a larger demographic. Additionally, two new groups of retailers and physicians might be added in the study, in order to have a complete and distinct visualization of the e-pharmacy market, and also of the factors impacting e-pharmacy purchase behavior.

RESEARCH LIMITATIONS AND SCOPE FOR FURTHER STUDIES

As e- pharmacy use was self-reported and vulnerable to participants' bias recall and false reporting, further difference in rural and urban marketplace and consumer behavior scenarios were not accounted for. Further pre-pandemic behavior and post-pandemic behavior of consumers both need to be studied in order to obtain insight into shifts in customer behavior in e-pharmacy.

Further research must be conducted with the need to identify the behavioral and demographic sub market formation and customer tailoring communication statement to cater to each such cluster of identified demographics and even behavioral significance of each such clusters with identified variables needs to be studied further.

REFERENCES

A Mathialagan, S Kaur, Community Perception on the Use of Over the Counter (OTC) Medications in Malaysia, International Journal of Scientific & Engineering Research, 3: 1–10, 2012.

Adebola Orogun and Bukola Onyekwelu; Predicting Consumer Behaviour in Digital Market: A Machine Learning Approach. International Journal of Innovative Research in Science, Engineering and Technology; August 2019; Vol. 8, Issue 8 pg. 8391–8402.

Alshurideh, Muhammad, Turki (2010) Customer Service Retention A Behavioural Perspective of the UK Mobile Market. Doctoral thesis Durham University.

Anand A, Sethil N, and Sharon G et al. Internet Pharmacy: Need to be implemented in India. Chronicles of Young Scientists. 2010; 1: 1– 10.

Beena Jimmy and Jimmy Jose 2011 May; Patient Medication Adherence: Measures in Daily Practice 26(3): 155–159, Oman Medical Journal

Bellman S, Lohse GL, Johnson EJ. Predictors of online buying behaviour. Communications of the ACM. 1999; 42: 32–8

Bessell TL, Anderson JN, Silagy CA et al. Surfing, self-medicating and safety: buying non-prescription and complementary medicines via the internet. Quality and Safety in Health Care. 2003; 12: 88–92.

Brink, A. & Berndt, A. (2009) "Relationship Marketing and Customer Relationship Management" Juta Publications.

Charnock D. The DISCERN handbook: Quality criteria for consumer health information on treatment choices. Oxford: Radcliffe Medical Press, 1998.

Das A, Faxvaag; What influences patient participation in an online forum for weight loss surgery? A qualitative case study; An Interact J Med Res. 2014 Feb 6; 3(1):e4.

Frost & Sullivan 2015, E-Pharmacy in India: Last Mile Access to Medicines FICCI &.

Gabay M.; Regulation of Internet Pharmacies: A Continuing Challenge. Hosp Pharm. 2015 Sep; 50(8):681–2.

Gray NJ, Klein JD, Cantrill JA et al. Buying medicines on the Internet: young consumers' perceptions. Journal of the American Pharmaceutical Association. 2002; 42: 313.

Gurău C. Pharmaceutical marketing on the Internet: Marketing techniques and customer profile. Journal of Consumer Marketing. 2005; 22: 421–8.

J Ricks, I Mardanov, Journal of Medical Marketing: The effect of pharmacists on drug purchasing behaviour of price-sensitive consumers Device, Diagnostic and Pharmaceutical Marketing, 12: 177-187, 2012.

K.C. Barmola and S.K. Srivastava, 2010. "The Role of Consumer Behaviour in Present Marketing Management Scenario". Productivity, 51(3), 268–27

Katalin Eibel-Spanyi & Agnes Hofmeister-Toth, 2013. "The impact of values on consumer behaviour," International Journal of Economics and Business Research, Inderscience Enterprises Ltd, vol. 5(4), pages 400–419.

Kotler, P. and Keller, K. (2011) "Marketing Management" (14th edition), London: Pearson Education.

Kung M, Monroe KB, Cox JL. Pricing on the Internet. Journal of Product and Brand Management. 2002; 11: 274–87.

Lancaster, G., Massingham, L. and Ashford, R. (2002) "Essentials of Marketing" (4th edition), London: McGraw-Hill.

Laura Wood, India E Pharmacy Market Opportunity Outlook 2024: E-Healthcare & Digital India Initiatives by the Government, Dublin, May 22, 2018, PR Newswire.

Lynch JG, Ariely D. Wine online: search costs affect competition on price, quality and distribution. Marketing Science. 2000; 19: 83–103.

M. Bourlakis, S. Papagiannidis and Helen Fox; E-consumer behaviour: past, present and Future trajectories of an evolving retail revolution International Journal of E-Business Research, 4(3), 64–76, July-September 2008.

Mackey TK, Nayyar G Br Med Bull. Digital danger: a review of the global public health, patient safety and cyber security threats posed by illicit online pharmacies. 2016 Jun; 118(1):110–26.

Nargundkar, R. (2008) "Marketing Research: Text and Cases" Tata McGraw-Hill Educational.

R, A., A. R, L. C. S. Motha, and N. R. "Online Pharma Retail Is a Promising/Unpromising Avenue: An Indian Context". Asian Journal of Pharmaceutical and Clinical Research, Vol. 9, no. 2, Mar. 2016, pp. 26–29.

Simoens S, Lobeau M, Verbeke K et al. Patient experiences of over-the-counter medicine purchases in Flemish community pharmacies. Pharmacy World and Science. 2009; 31: 450–7.

Sunny Sinha, Anand Kotiyal Current status of E-Pharmacy in India: 2019 Review by 1Mg Technologies Private Limited PharmaTutor.

Suraj Kushe Shekhar, Tony P. Jose and Rehin K R 2019." Consumer buying behaviour and attitude towards pharmaceuticals", Int. J. Res. Pharm. Sci., 10(4), 3392–3397.

T Singh, D Smith, Journal of Consumer Marketing, Direct-to-consumer prescription drug advertising: a study of consumer attitudes and behavioural intentions 22: 369–378, 2005.

This Fledgling Online Market Too Is Facing Brick-And-Mortar Backlash in India by Nishant Sharma, December 2019, Bloomberg Quint

Vătămănescu, E.M., Nistoreanu, B.G. and Mitan, A., 2017. Competition and Consumer Behaviour in the Context of the Digital Economy. Amfiteatru Economic, 19(45), pp. 354–366.

Von Rosen AJ, von Rosen FT, Tinnemann P, Müller-Riemenschneider F.; Sexual Health and the Internet: Cross-Sectional Study of Online Preferences among Adolescents; J Med Internet Res. 2017 Nov 8; 19(11): e379.

Wagner ML, Alonso J, Mehlhorn AJ. Comparison of Internet and community pharmacies. The Annals of Pharmacotherapy. 2001; 35: 116–9.

CHAPTER 4

Cars are Now Online Too: Dawn of 'Click to Buy' Model in India Due to Covid19

Samantak Chakraborty
Research Scholar
Business Administration
Aligarh Muslim University, Aligarh, U.P.
samantakchakraborty@gmail.com/
schakraborty@myamu.ac.in

Dr. Mohammad Khalid Azam
Professor
Business Administration
Aligarh Muslim University,
Aligarh, U.P.
mkhalidazam@rediffmail.com

Abstract

Purpose

The purpose of this case study is to highlight the changes that have taken place in the market and what has been the initial sales performance of these platforms. How the different companies ranging from the luxury brands like Mercedes and BMW to the old trusted stalwarts of the Indian market likes of Maruti-Suzuki, Hyundai, Honda have reciprocated these changes.

Design/methodology/approach

The present case study follows a qualitative research approach. The case collates secondary data pertaining to the online platforms launched by the top companies and their innovativeness that they put forward through these websites. Also, the published materials in newspapers and magazines were used to provide the background information of these top companies. It presents the facts persisting the information regarding the online market of car selling in India.

Findings

Extending the knowledge body from existing research, this study found that ten companies launched their online digital platform which has their specific offerings to their buyers and allows different services to them and Maruti-Suzuki has the lead in sales in the market. The companies have started grooming the online channels as they believe that it is the future for the industry but they have tried to build it on the traditional foundation of the retail-dealership/showrooms across the country.

Practical/Research implications

Managers of the dealerships/showrooms need to learn and implement the strategies that are apt for the online sales, as the sales pitch to the buyers have transitioned to the online space from the physical space and that possesses its own set of challenges. The managers need to develop sales strategies that don't compromise on their quality of services to their buyers. While the market researchers have a new branch of the market at their hands that promises to evolve its patterns of consumer behaviour.

Originality/value
The online market is a must for every small or big company today. While e-commerce companies have made their stance strong in midst of the pandemic and this made other companies also follow in their footsteps. And cars selling online is the new normal heading in the future which will play an important role in extending the pervasiveness of the online market.

Social Implications
The post-pandemic world is going to be uncertain as it is believed to have changed our way of living. And the online space has become more crucial than ever. And the introduction of the augmented reality is going to be a game-changer that will provide the consumer a sense of tangibility up to a certain extent while buying the product on offer.

Keywords: Pandemic, Digital Platforms, Cars, Covid-19, Online Car Sales.

INTRODUCTION

The online market in the past decade has seen a tremendous surge in the business world. As dependence on the internet has surged that has enabled us to search for information at our fingertips. Also, the growth of different models has been evident in diversified product portfolios. The online market started as the extension of the offline market's channels but in the past few years, it has established itself as a separate entity. This has given birth to many unconventional business models that only have an online presence and not a brick and mortar outlet. Today, in this new decade there is hardly any product or services that don't have an online platform. And, it all changed with the unprecedented circumstances, a global pandemic hitting the world have galvanised all kinds of markets, especially the offline market. A disease that spreads through contact was the last thing that was needed for the offline market that was already facing online market competition. The e-commerce market has been instrumental in this regard as the major product portfolios of the market have already made the transition to these platforms some of which include FMCG, Electronics, etc. are being sold at better prices online than the offline market. And the happenings of the year 2020 have also pushed the other traditional business models to take note of the online space in these new normal times. One of the major sectors that have also put the foot on peddling due to this pandemic is the Automobile sector of many countries especially the Indian automobile industry. However, cars selling online aren't a new thing in the first world countries where they exist with the help of traditional dealership outlet sales. But in India, majorly the online sales of cars have been limited to the sales of the used cars. The selling and buying platforms like CarDekho, Cars24, and Droom, etc. have been the major players in this trade. But the forced online selling due to Covid19 has accelerated the transition of the premium automobile manufacturers to have their platform each with unique offerings.

DESIGN/METHODOLOGY/APPROACH

The present case study follows a qualitative research approach. The case collates secondary data pertaining to the online platforms launched by the top companies and their innovativeness that they put forward through these websites. Also, the published materials in newspapers and magazines were used to provide the background information of these top companies. It presents the facts persisting the information regarding the online market of car selling in India.

PURPOSE

Pandemic hitting the market has taken many marketers by surprise but few of them have started to adapt to it, while certainly it had an adverse effect which some of the market experts predicted but there is also a silver lining in all of this. Pandemic has made marketers around the globe adopt new strategies to keep afloat with the persisting 'new normal' scenarios. The market has been forced to transform itself and adapt the online channels for retailing their product following the 'Click to buy' model. And the present case study is about the automobile manufactures of India adopting these channels as they are traditionally retailing their products using dealerships. This case study discusses the different companies taking up online selling to the next level and the first impressions of the sales made by these companies during the lockdown. It also sheds light on the challenges it possesses for the current business model in the Indian market.

FINDINGS

E-commerce coming to the cars wasn't intended but it got accelerated due to the present circumstances. Buying cars online was present in other parts of the world like the U.S. where Tesla has been making its name in the market by adapting to this channel better than its competitors. But traditionally, this market is hugely dependent on the dealership-showroom model. In the pre-pandemic world, the buyers were adopting the online channels as compared to the dealerships because of their way of making profits i.e., by selling add-ons during the lengthy car-buying process. The three automakers of Detroit namely General Motors, Fiat Chrysler, and Ford have emphasised the online platforms because of the recent developments (Page, 2018; Wilmot, 2020).

In India, the story of car selling has been more or less the same as the American market where the buyers depend on the dealerships of the companies to take their new ride home. But the lockdown badly hit the Indian Automobile industry due to the pandemic where April 2020 recorded zero sales, the worst in its history. And as time passed and the government relaxing the norms the companies had to come up with online platforms to keep themselves afloat with the traditionally run dealerships spread across the country where previously the buyer had to visit the showroom physically, test drive the car, book a car and then complete the proper documentation before they delivered the car. But today all of this is available at a press of a button. The companies have launched their official websites or platforms where all these tasks can be completed with the comfort of sitting at home (Gupta, 2020). The major companies that have launched online services are:

1. *Audi:* The digital platform incorporated by the German carmakers includes both the online sales and provides service of its cars. The process allows the buyers to book for purchasing cars online. For this, an account needs to be created by the user (under **Audi Shop**). Where the models of car and its options are displayed can be selected, nearest dealership can be located with making a selection of payment options. After all of this is done, the selected dealership contacts the buyer and guides them for the rest of the process of purchase providing them a total 'touch-less' doorstep delivery buying experience. Additionally, the company has also introduced some interesting features, like an in-depth configuration with a 360° visualizer, that is accompanied with an augmented feature which allows the buyer to visualize their configured car (via smartphone camera) at their home vicinity without going anywhere (Bahadur, 2020a).

2. *Mahindra & Mahindra:* Company launched its digital platform under the name 'Own-Online. The sales platform enables the buyer to purchase any model of its vehicles without any physical contact. Through the Own-Online platform, buyers can finance, insure, exchange, accessorize, and then own a Mahindra vehicle having completed the entire process online. It also provides the access to Mahindra's Pan-India network of 270+ dealers and 900+ touchpoints. The process starts with selecting the model of the vehicle, personalise it as per their taste, followed by choosing their dealer, then getting the online approval for the finance and insurance options, and finally making an online payment then choose a preferred location for 'contactless' delivery. Mahindra has also provided expert help regarding the Own-Online process, Mahindra's product, and the process experts are available online via video chat and text messages. The company claims that the Own-Online is the only mass-market digital sales platform that gives buyers on-road prices of the cars, and also breakdowns its components such as registration, road taxes, and insurances, as well as benefits likes offers and discounts (Thakur, 2020).

3. *Volvo:* Volvo's digital platform has been given simpler outlook as compared to other companies. A buyer has to visit the official website and leave all the contact details with the preferable time and date. Hence, after this the dealership gets into touch with the buyer. The representative from the nearest of all the 25 dealerships present in the country provides with the further buying process that may require documentation, and payment transfer (Shah, 2020).

4. *Honda:* The Japanese brand introduced its digital platform under the name 'Honda from Home'. The platform provides buyers to manage to "manage their car purchase from the comfort of their homes without having to visit the dealership." And the company is trying to integrate the platform with the countrywide network made up of 375 touchpoints spread over 263 cities. The forthcoming buyers can start the process of buying by accessing the official website and opt the 'Book Now' button which will then directs to the portal where, they need to provide their details. The buyer is able to go through a range of cars and their fitting models, transmission option, fuel type,

and colour. After this, they are contacted by the pertinent dealership for the proper guidance of the sales process, the documentation, and finance or payment options they can choose from. After the formalities are finalized, the bought car is home delivered to the buyer (Gandhi, 2020).

5. ***Volkswagen:*** Company introduced a digitised sales platform that allows buyers to select and book their desired Volkswagen car or services, directly from the company's website. The platform joins the 137 dealerships and 117 service centres spread over the country. While booking the buyers can handpick their desired dealership and are provided the prospect to digitally interact with the sales consultant as required. They similarly have an option to visit the dealership or the service centre physically if they choose to do so, instead of availing the pick-up and drop service option. The website also has a secure transaction process where verifications are authenticated via an OTP-based system as per the company claims (Mehra, 2020b).

6. ***Jeep:*** Jeep named its online selling initiative as 'Book My Jeep' on Jeep India's website. The module helps the buyers through the primary process of selecting the model, variant, engine, and gearbox option, colour, and other details such as the locality of the buyer and documentation. Once done with these, the payment for booking can be made using internet banking or credit card, or other available online payment options. Then buyer is then contacted by the sales representative (via video or phone call) to aid set up a test drive. Hence, completing the purchase by making the payment on the Book My Jeep online platform. Jeep is also offering special benefits on online bookings (Rivan, 2020).

7. ***Hyundai:*** Hyundai launched a pilot in the NCR first then rolled out the service across India. They named it **'Click to Buy'** that integrated over 500 dealerships on to the platform where all the models are available. The buyer requires to create an account with Hyundai on the 'Click to Buy' website. After the registration, the process is straightforward, where they can select the dealership, model, variant, colour, and any other configurable options. After that, they are provided with the quotation and all the financing options, as well as the delivery method for the purchase car. After all of this, they can place the order (Bahadur, 2020c).

8. ***Tata Motors:*** Following the footsteps of Hyundai, Tata Motors released its 'Click To Drive' digital platform connecting the buyers to its 750 dealerships from all over the country. To avail of their service, the buyer has to make a registration on the Click To Drive website of the company, handpick their desired car, surf through video brochures enlightening its many features and book the model in their desired variant and colour from the dealership that they choose. After the booking, the buyer is contacted by the Tata Motors call centre and a sales representative from the selected dealer guides them through the entire buying process which includes information like on-road prices, the choice for financial assist, and estimate of their current car. Buyers can select to finish the process over email, WhatsApp, or video call. Lastly, the buyer can choose whether they want to pick up the car from the dealership or get it delivered at home on a later date (Mehra, 2020a).

9. ***BMW:*** Company launched its digital retail and service platform in India and called it BMW Contactless Experience. The buyer has to make an account on the website.

Once the account is created the buyer can go through the model, version, and the various options for the vehicle they would like to buy using the configurator. The nearest dealership needs to be selected if the buyer's location is serviceable and then only the car can be bought online. The same account that was created for buying the new BMW can also be used for buying the pre-owned BMWs. This account can also be used to schedule services for their vehicles (Bahadur, 2020b).

10. *Mercedes-Benz:* Mercedes-Benz launches its online platform named 'Shop' powered by *Roadster.com* where a buyer can find the entire product line along with the comprehensive specifications to the on-road price of the car. Before going full-blown online Mercedes-Benz used to sell used cars using 'Shop' but now they have started to retail new cars as well under the portfolio 'Merc from Home' campaign (Ahed, 2020). The above-listed companies were the companies that launched their digital platform in 2020, while the biggest stalwart of the Indian market Maruti-Suzuki had launched its digital platform in the year 2017 under the name of 'Maruti-Suzuki Arena'. And this gave them the first mover advantage which made them the biggest platform for online space as well as gave them a head start as compared to other companies as Maruti-Suzuki has 1000+ dealerships nationwide are integrated with its online platform. The sales figures have also spoken of this advantage as they sold 2 lac cars in the past year using their online platform (AutomotiveWorld, 2020) while others are struggling to find a strong foothold in these deep unknown waters.

As these online platforms are not the business-to-consumer model and involve dealers and the dealerships currently working all across the country, the buyers have to go through the process of choosing their suitable dealership for carrying out the paperwork and documentation of the purchase, this model of business is distinguishable from the e-commerce channels. So, this intermediary channel born because of the pandemic could be a potential market in the e-commerce space for the country. In conclusion, it can be stated that the rise of such websites will open new vicinities for different players in the market not only from the automobile sector but the players of like the tech developers for making the websites closer to the real world experience in near future.

Practical/research implications:

As this market is in its nascent stage, but these developments are going to affect the consumer behaviour of the buyers. Martin Schwenk, MD and CEO at Mercedes-Benz India, in an interview with Autocar India, had stated that "We believe that ordering a car should be as easy as ordering food online – 25 percent of sales by 2025 will be online." This technology adoption of the consumers to make a purchase remains to be seen, as this is fairly early days where the early adopters have started making the purchase but there is still time to analyse the performance of this sector and it will be done in the coming years. And this poise a great opportunity for the market researchers to study these changes in the behavioural patterns. The established models like the Technology Adoption Model (TAM) (Taylor & Todd, 1995), Unified Theory of Acceptance and Use of Technology (UTAUT) model (Venkatesh et al., 2003, 2011) can be utilised to study these consumer behaviour or a new model can be developed as well.

Social implications:

In conclusion, it can be stated that the post-pandemic world is going to be uncertain as it is believed to have changed our way of living. And the online space has become more crucial than ever. And the introduction of the augmented reality will prove to be beneficial for selling such products in which the sense of tangibility of the product is ranked high by the buyer.

REFERENCES

Ahed, A. (2020). *Mercedes-Benz India's Merc from Home online sales platform for new cars goes live - Autocar India.* https://www.autocarindia.com/car-news/mercedes-benz-india-to-sell-new-cars-online-via-its-digital-shop-417007

AutomotiveWorld. (2020). *Maruti Suzuki's 1000+ online dealerships help to sell 2 lakh cars | Automotive World.* https://www.automotiveworld.com/news-releases/maruti-suzukis-1000-online-dealerships-help-to-sell-2-lakh-cars/

Bahadur, N. (2020a). *Audi India introduces new online sales, service initiatives - Autocar India.* AutoCar India. https://www.autocarindia.com/car-news/audi-india-introduces-online-sales-service-initiatives-417220

Bahadur, N. (2020b). *BMW launches online retail platform called Contactless Experience - Autocar India.* https://www.autocarindia.com/car-news/bmw-contactless-experience-online-retail-platform-launched-417048

Bahadur, N. (2020c). *Hyundai 'Click to Buy' service now available pan-India - Autocar India.* https://www.autocarindia.com/car-news/hyundai-click-to-buy-service-available-across-india-416842

Gandhi, S. (2020). *Honda Cars India introduces 'Honda from Home' online vehicle booking platform - Autocar India.* https://www.autocarindia.com/car-news/honda-launches-online-new-car-booking-platform-417050

Gupta, R. (2020). *Online Car Sales in India | Will it Kill the Dealership Business?* https://gomechanic.in/blog/online-car-sales-in-india/

Mehra, J. (2020a). *Tata Motors introduces 'Click to Drive' digital retail platform - Autocar India.* https://www.autocarindia.com/car-news/tata-launches-click-to-drive-digital-sales-platform-416894

Mehra, J. (2020b). *Volkswagen launches online car and SUV buying service in India - Autocar India.* https://www.autocarindia.com/car-news/volkswagen-launches-online-car-buying-service-in-india-417049

Page, F. (2018). *Online car buying services: which brands have one? | Autocar.* AutoCar India. https://www.autocar.co.uk/car-news/new-cars/online-car-buying-services-which-brands-have-one-0

Rivan, R. (2020). *FCA India launches online retail platform for Jeep - Autocar India.* https://www.autocarindia.com/car-news/fca-india-launches-online-retail-platform-for-jeep-417112

Shah, S. (2020). *Volvo introduces a contactless car-buying programme - Autocar India.* AutoCar India. https://www.autocarindia.com/car-news/volvo-introduces-a-contactless-car-buying-programme-417128

Taylor, S., & Todd, P. A. (1995). Understanding information technology usage: A test of competing models. *Information Systems Research*, *6*(2), 144–176. https://doi.org/10.1287/isre.6.2.144

Thakur, S. (2020). *Mahindra introduces 'Own-Online' digital sales platform - Autocar India*. AutoCar India. https://www.autocarindia.com/car-news/mahindra-introduces-own-online-digital-sales-platform-417203

Venkatesh, V., Morris, M. G., Davis, G. B., & Davis, F. D. (2003). User acceptance of information technology: Toward a unified view. *MIS Quarterly: Management Information Systems*, *27*(3), 425–478. https://doi.org/10.2307/30036540

Venkatesh, V., Thong, J. Y. L., Chan, F. K. Y., Hu, P. J. H., & Brown, S. A. (2011). Extending the two-stage information systems continuance model: Incorporating UTAUT predictors and the role of context. *Information Systems Journal*, *21*(6), 527–555. https://doi.org/10.1111/j.1365-2575.2011.00373.x

Wilmot, S. (2020). *E-commerce is finally coming to cars*. https://www.livemint.com/news/world/e-commerce-is-finally-coming-to-cars-11589719084380.html

CHAPTER 5

The Experience of Salons With Deals and Coupons

Krunal Joshi
Associate Professor
Shri Jairambhai Patel Institute of Business Management (NICM), Gandhinagar, Gujarat
krunaljo@yahoo.co.in

Janvi Joshi
Assistant Professor
Shri Jairambhai Patel Institute of Business Management (NICM), Gandhinagar, Gujarat
visit_janvi@yahoo.co.in

Abstract

Deals and coupons provided by salons on deal aggregators like LittleApp, Nearbuy, Dineout and Zomato have been in existence for some time now and have also gained popularity among the consumers. The reason for popularity of these deals and coupons among the consumers is their value for money. Due to consumer pull, more and more salons have started offering deals on the aggregator platforms. Through this study an attempt has been made to understand as to what is the experience of salons with such deals, and are they equally popular with them? Structured interviews of owners / managers[1] of 20 salons operators of Ahmedabad city were conducted. Only salons which were currently selling deals/coupons or had sold deals/coupons in the past on deal aggregator platforms were included in the sample. The interviewees were quizzed on their experience with deals and coupons in relation to sales growth, foot falls, type of customers and their loyalty, profitability and aggregator support to name a few. Some operators praise the merits of deals/coupons, while some others found them not very helpful considering the profitability issues and the type of customers the deals attract.

Keywords: Daily Deals, Deal Aggregators, Online Deals, Online Coupons, Coupon Promotions, Groupon, Social Couponing

---

[1]In the first place, an attempt was made to ensure that the interviewee was the owner of the salon as he/she was expected to have sufficient exposure in the subject matter of the study. Only under unavoidable circumstances the manager with sufficient exposure was interviewed.

INTRODUCTION

Sales promotions tools try to induce immediate purchase/sale by incentivizing either consumers, trade partners or the company's own sales force. According to Kotler and Keller (2016), "sales promotions consist of a diverse collection of incentive tools, mostly short term, designed to stimulate quicker and / or greater purchase of particular products / services by consumers or the trade". Doyle (2016) also explains sales promotions as usually a range of tactical marketing techniques that incentivize the sale of products and services in order to achieve specific sales and marketing objectives.

Consumer Sales Promotions

Consumer sales promotions are one of the many ways in which marketers communicate the value that they propose to deliver to the final consumers (Kanagal, 2013, p. 2; Kotler & Keller, 2016). According to Kotler, Keller, Koshy and Jha (as cited in Kanagal, 2013, p. 2) sales promotions as marketing communication tools have gained importance over the years. Consumer sales promotions take various forms like contests, cashbacks (rebates), free gifts, samples, loyalty (reward) programs, and coupons & deals to name a few (Biswal, 2011, para. 1-14; Kanagal, 2013, pp. 11-12).

Coupons and Deals

Coupons and deals are special type of time bound promotions that enable customers to get a pre-decided amount of discount on the full value of the purchase or an opportunity to purchase a bundle of items at a reduced rate as compared to what he/she would have paid for the items individually. Couponing is one of most widely used tools by the marketers to promote sales and is also one of the oldest and most effective (Belch & Belch, 2012). Coupons and deals in various forms have been popular in providing incentives to the customers. "Couponing is an important marketing tool, particularly for attracting the attention of new customers and less loyal ones (Santella & Associates, 1999a)" (Collard, Pustay, Roquilly, & Zardkoohi, 2001, p. 64). Coupons and deals have been in existence in physical forms (printed and distributed to prospective and existing customers by the marketer and/or newspaper cutouts) for quite some time. The history of coupons dates back to 1887, when Coca-cola created the world's first coupon which were mailed to homes throughout the country and strategically placed in magazine periodicals, offering potential customers a free glass of the year-old drink (Donnelly, 2012, p. 85).

Online Deals and Coupons

Donnelly (2012) also observed that due to the advent of internet, over the years coupons and deals have become popular in the online mode (downloadable and printable) due to their easy of availability (p. 85). According to Byers, Mitzenmarcher and Zervas (2012), last decade or so has seen a spur in the number of daily deal websites[2] providing localized discounted offers to customers for restaurants, ticketed events, services, and other items.

---

[2]Also known as daily deals applications / deals discovery platforms / deal aggregators / group -buying websites

Groupon and LivingSocial, though not the pioneers, are one of the most popular group-buying daily deals websites (Ming, Yulan, & Xianghua, 2016, p. 280; Yijing & Qiongshen, 2011, p. 1). Yijing and Qiongshen (2011) examined that the group-buying websites primarily originated in United States and in late 1990s two companies viz. Mobshop.com and Mercata.com were operating as market leaders with a lot of popularity. In Europe also websites Letsbuyit.com (Sweden) and Coshopper.com (Norway) had been heavily funded by enthusiastic entrepreneurs for expansion over 10 countries. These early players were not so successful. Regions like Latin America, Japan and China had also seen the existence of such group-buying websites for quite some time. However, Groupon is considered to be a representative of the recent generation group-buying websites (pp. 1-2).

Online Deals and Coupons – Scenario in India

In India also, many such deals discovery platforms (websites and applications) have come into existence in past one decade. Some of such websites and applications are : Nearbuy (formerly Groupon India), Stylofie, Zomato, EazyDiner, Dineout, Coupondunia.com, LivingSocial, MagicPin, Little Internet, MyDala.com, Sosasta.com, and Couponguru. com. A lot of turbulence has happened in this industry and some major developments include the taking over of LivingSocial (Indian operations) by Groupon India ("Star India hires", 2017, para. 6); Groupon exiting its Indian operations by selling-off a majority stake to a private equity firm Sequoia in 2015 and subsequent rebranding of Groupon India operations as Nearbuy ("Groupon Inc rebranded", 2015, para. 1); merger of Little Internet and Nearbuy and the subsequent majority stake-holding of Paytm in the merged entity in 2017 ("Nearbuy and Little", 2017, para. 1). The merged entity (Nearbuy and Little Internet) is the market leader with about 88 percent share and a total of 40,000 merchants listed on its platform (para. 4-5). Until recently, both the platforms, Little Internet and Nearbuy were operating independently, even after the merger. Towards the end of 2019, Little Internet gradually moved to Nearbuy platform after an official prolonged notice to the subscribers about the same.

Online Deals and Coupons - Basic Business Model

Group-buying websites like Groupon generally have one or more deals of the day for a specific geographical market which they prominently promote on their webpage / emails (Byers et al., 2012, p. 543). These deals provide a coupon for a particular product / service at a discount (often more than 40 to 50 percent) to the list price (p. 543). Each deal has a minimum threshold size that must be reached for the deal to become active and there can be a maximum threshold limit also set by the seller to restrict the number of coupons sold. Groupon retains approximately half the revenue generated from the discount coupons (p. 543). Other platforms offer deals and coupons to be bought at a discount to the list price without any lower or upper threshold limits to the number of coupons sold.

In India, Nearbuy and similar platforms have local deals listing for restaurants, salons & spas, health & fitness centers and events, thought the restaurants deals have a predominance followed by salons & spas deals and a few deals related to health & fitness centers and local. These platforms charge a certain commission (as a percentage of the total revenue generated from coupons) from the business operators against the listing of the deals. Most of them do not charge anything to the coupon buyers where as a few platforms are subscription/fee based[3].

PURPOSE OF THE STUDY

The industry seems divided on the positives and negatives of such daily deals promotions. Deals aggregators and some industry experts believe that these promotions provide great benefit for small and medium-sized local businesses, by promoting their products and services to a large buyer base and are a good platform for advertising. On the other side, there are views that daily deal promotions are quite expensive and harmful for many small and medium-sized businesses (Barr, 2012; Cooper, 2011). This raises a pertinent question about the overall experience of the operators with deals and coupons offered through deal aggregators. This is the focus area of the current study.

To the best of the knowledge of the researcher, there is a general lack of studies in India on daily deal promotions, their impact on the revenues and profitability of business operators which are offering them on various deal aggregators' platforms and also what has been the operators' overall experience with deal aggregators and dail deal promotions. This study is an attempt towards filling this gap.

Study Objectives

1. To explore about the reasons why salons list deals on daily deal platforms.
2. To get a comprehensive understanding on the overall experience of salons with deals and coupons as well as with deal aggregators.
3. To arrive at the future implications for the daily deals industry.

LITERATURE REVIEW

Studies on coupon promotions & their effects

In a study by Dholakia and Tsabar (2011), the effect of Groupon promotion, that was run by a startup restaurant, was analysed on its revenues, profitability (overall as well as per transaction) and repeat purchase rate after the promotion ended[4] (pp. 4-5). It was concluded that even though the Groupon promotion generated significant revenue growth for the startup but it did not have any impact on its overall profitability, neither negatively nor positively (p. 5). The significant growth in sales (revenue) had been conceptualized as the *'exposure value'* that the startup received due to Groupon (p. 6). The per transaction profits also dipped significantly during the promotion period because of the higher number of Groupon customers as compared to non-Groupon customers (who paid full price) (pp. 8-9). Also, only about 4 percent of the Groupon users returned for at least a second

---

[3]Based on scanning of details on various deal aggregators' websites/applications, September 10, 2020.

[4]Every single customer transaction data since the firm was launched as well as during the period it ran the Groupon promotion was analysed for the purpose of the study.

time within two weeks after the promotions ended (pp. 11-12). However, the startup considered Groupon to be a cost-effective advertising medium as well as a viable feedback mechanism (p. 13).

Dholakia (2011) found that Groupon promotions were profitable for some of the businesses (around 66%). Interestingly, these businesses had a higher percentage (31 percent) of coupons buyers coming back for a repeat purchase at full value than the same for businesses with unprofitble promotions (13 percent) and also about 50 percent of the coupon buyers at these businesses bought beyond the Groupon's coupon value as compared to only 25 percent for businesses with unprofitable promotions (p. 6). Thought these two variables (coupon buyers buying more and coupon buyer returning) were not significant predictors of profitability nor were variables like number of coupons sold, coupon value, discount off on the price. Effectiveness of Groupon promotions in reaching new customers (and not cannibalizing existing customers) and employee satisfaction with coupon buyers were found to be significant predictors of Groupon profitability (pp. 7-8).

Wu, Kimes, & Dholakia (2012) found that only 40 percent of the daily deals customers were new to the restaurants, resulting into a lot of cannibalization of existing sales for the restaurants (p. 17), which could be a serious concern for businesses using deals and coupons. Although many restaurant operators said their revenues increased, their number was about the same as those who reported losing money (p. 17).

Kumar and Rajan (2012) concluded, even though coupons are successful in capturing a significant number of new customers, huge losses during campaign periods result into significant financial burden on the businesses which can only be recovered if majority of those coupon customers return (p. 13). Non-returning coupon customers can result into extended recovery periods from losses and so businesses do not initiate new coupon launches. Poorly designed coupon campaigns can do serious damage to business's profit margins.

Based on a survey of 108 hotels (one-fourth of all Italian hotels that have run social coupon campaigns through Groupon) on the perceived benefits of social coupon campaigns, Cassia, Magno and Ugolini (2015) found them to have a higher effectiveness in increasing brand awareness and low effectiveness with regards to attracting new customers and retaining them (72 hotels reported that they were not able to retain any of the coupon users, whereas the remaining 36 hotels retained 8.65 per cent of them, on average). Also, the social coupon campaigns did not stimulate existing customers' demand significantly (p. 1606-1607). The probable reason for this could be a specific nature of the hotel industry of low or variable recurring demand. In this sense, cannibalization of existing customers due to social coupon campaigns may not be considered as a serious issue.

Edelman, Jaffe and Kominers (2016) have observed that deals and coupons (voucher discounts) are likely to be profitable if they predominantly attract new customers who come for a repeat purchase, paying full price, but if vouchers provide discounts to many existing customers, vouchers could drastically reduce the firms' profit (p. 40). They also observed that, discount vouchers offer opportunities for price discrimination opportunities to firms as well as advertising exposure to new customers. Successful price discrimination is achieved if the valuation of consumers with access to vouchers must generally be lower than the consumers who do not have access to vouchers (consumer heterogeneity) and for the advertising effects to be important, a firm must begin with sufficiently low recognition among prospective customers (p. 41) implying that discount vouchers will be more beneficial for newer, lesser know firms (p. 49).

METHODOLOGY ADOPTED

Structured interviews of owners / managers[5] of salons of Ahmedabad city were conducted and analysed. Only salons which were currently selling deals/coupons on Nearbuy[6] were included in the population. Upon a detailed analysis of the Nearbuy platform, it was found that there were around 70 such salons in Ahmedabad, offering one or more deals. These were a combination of independent salons and salons operated as a chain/franchisee. Interviews of owners / managers of 20 salons, which is around 29 percent of the total deal offering salons, were conducted. Thought the sampling method adopted for selecting the salons for the study was that of convenience sampling, while conducting interviews, analysing and preparing the results the researcher took a basic care that only such salons are included which were older than 1 year in operations and were running the deals / coupons promotions for minimum 6 months. Wherever possible a prior appointment was fixed with the interviewee before approaching for the interaction. In other cases, the researcher approached the interviewee at the place of business and conducted the interview if the interviewee agreed to it. In either case a small briefing on, the objectives of the study, its academic (non-commercial) nature as well as the assurance on confidentially of the data and responses was given prior to beginning the interview. The interviewees were quizzed on their experience with deals and coupons promotions and their impact on growth in awareness, sales, foot falls, profitability, the type of customers and their loyalty, and aggregator support to name a few. A qualitative analysis of the responses was done to bring out the finding and conclusions.

FINDINGS

- *Purpose for listing and offering deals on deal aggregators' platforms:* Three main objectives, why the salons list and offer deals on aggregators' platforms, in the order of their importance are: *increasing awareness* about their salons, ***increasing footfalls*** and they find ***deal aggregators' platforms as no cost (free) form of advertising.*** The salons consider the platforms to be no cost (free) form of advertising may be because they do not have to pay any money upfront for listing, but they fail to consider the commission that they need to pay on each deal that gets sold through the platform.

---

[5]In the first place, an attempt was made to ensure that the interviewee was the owner of the salon as he/she was expected to have sufficient exposure in the subject matter of the study. Only under unavoidable circumstances the manager with sufficient exposure was interviewed.

[6] Nearbuy is one of the oldest and the largest deal aggregators in India with a large number of salons on its platform. A basic analysis of various aggregators (other than Nearbuy) revealed that a salon listed on their platform is most likely to have a listing on Nearbuy as well. So, Nearbuy was used as a platform to selected salons under the study.

When quizzed about why don't they consider the commission paid on each deal that gets sold through the platform as a cost advertising associated with advertising, most of them said that it is still cheaper than other forms of advertising like newspapers, radio, billboards and other traditional methods.

- *Increase in awareness and footfalls after listing on deal aggregators' platform:* Most of the salons (80 percent) said there has been a low to medium increase in awareness & the resulting footfalls (due to deals after listing on deals aggregators' platforms (not as expected), and the rest (20 percent) said their awareness has increased on higher levels. To be specific, the salons were asked to mention on an average what percentage of their total customers (footfalls) in a month were deal customers? There was a mixed response from salons ranging from 5 percent to 50 percent. 8 salons experienced the lower percentage (5-10) of deal customers footfalls, 6 salons had about 25 to 30 percentage of their footfalls as deal customers and the rest had a higher percentage (about 35-50) of these customers. On analyzing the number of deals listing for all the salons and comparing with the footfalls data, it was seen that the salons with highest footfalls (due to deals) also had a far larger number of deals listed as compared to the salons that had lowest footfall. Though not tested statistically, this may be an important qualitative finding that there is a **probable positive relationship between the number of deals offered on the platforms and the increase in footfalls**.

- *New customers or repeat ones:* Also, the footfalls due to deals were a mix of new customers (with deals for the first time) and repeat customers (with the deals for the second, third or repeated time), repeat ones on a higher side. This hints at loyalty on the side of the customers, but the negative side to this is that these repeat customers come along with deals, which somehow reduces their profit potential, unless they buy beyond deals.

- *Additional purchases beyond coupon value (at full price) by coupon customers:* For most of the salons a small number (15%) of deal customers bought anything beyond coupon/deals they came with. Only in case of 2 salons a higher number (35-40%) of coupon customers bought beyond the deals / coupons they came with. Interestingly though, the customers would ask if others services are also on deal or not. In such cases, some of the salons, **as a relationship building measure**, offered discounts even if no deal existed. 2 salons also ran their **own store-based deals/promotions** over and above the deals listed on aggregators' platform.

- *Profitability per coupon customer:* Profitability from coupon customers for all the salons was a concern. They either made **very low profits or no profits** at all due to heavy discounts and commissions on the coupons that they pay to the aggregators. **Tough no salons ever made losses on deal customers**.

- *Cannibalization of existing customers' business:* About half of the salons experienced their older customers coming up with coupons, now that they have started offering it, but on a **lower side (less than 10%), something which was not a major reason of worry**. It would be a reason for worry if it increases further. Only 1 salon said they have experienced about 25% of their older customers now coming up with coupons.

- *Feeling bad in serving coupon client:* Neither of the salons ever felt bad about serving a coupon customer and though a couple of salons had a few instances of bad experience with coupon customers *(The customers were rude/ill-behaved).* The salon owners/ managers see coupon customers as an opportunity to build new relationship, especially because salons as a business is very much service driven and if the customer feels comfortable at our place he is definitely going to come back.

- *Negative impact of coupons on brand image:* None of the salons felt that their brand image will get hampered due to listing on a deal aggregators' platform.

- *Coupon customers' likely chances of returning at full price (after discontinuing coupons):* All the salons felt that there will be some impact on footfalls and the coupon customers may stop coming if they discontinued the coupons, but not much to worry about, because the salons are confident about their quality of service and believe that the customers would return for good service. Only **the price sensitive and deal prone ones would not return**.

- *Any specific characteristics of coupon customers:* Some of the characteristics that defined the majority of the coupon customers were: young aged (though no specific age range mentioned), technology savvy, price sensitive (due to limited income). A few instances of higher aged group customers were also experienced by some salons.

- *Overall experience with deal promotions:* All the salons were overall **reasonably satisfied (not highly satisfied)** with the deal promotions as it had helped them to improve their awareness and footfalls to some extent, though not as much as expected.

- *Continue coupon promotions in future:* All the salons said that they *would continue using coupons promotions in future* as well, though they might change the structure of the deals / coupons. Two most important reasons for the same were: Firstly, the salons feel that today a lot of consumers were becoming internet savvy and they used internet for a lot of things including searching for a salon and its various information like deals, packages and feedback before visiting. *So, it was important to be present on platforms like deal aggregators to be visible to the customers, at least from the awareness point of view.* Secondly, **they had a fear of missing out (FOMO[7])**, because if other salons (in their vicinity) were offering deals and coupons on the aggregators' platforms and if they did not, the chances of customers not preferring their salon and the resulting loss in business increased. So, in a way they have **no choice but to continue offering the coupons**.

- *Overall experience with deal aggregators:* The experience for all the salons with the deal aggregators in terms of technical support and payment processing was satisfactory. The salons would receive the coupon payments within 7-10 days of their redemption

---

[7]Fear of missing out (FOMO) is described as "a pervasive apprehension that others might be having rewarding experiences from which one is absent". The phenomenon was first identified in 1996 by Dr. Dan Herman, a marketing strategist, who researched it and published the first academic paper on the topic in 2000 in *The Journal of Brand Management.* Author Patrick J. McGinnis coined the term FOMO and made it popular in 2004.

by the customers, directly in their bank accounts. The commission charged by the deal aggregators ranges from 15 to 30 percent depending upon the type salons. Neither of the salons every experienced any instance of push / force from the deal aggregators with regards to offering minimum or a certain percentage of discounts while listing their deals. Only one common concern that most of the salons shared was that the POCs (their Point of Contact with the deal aggregators) would change quite often and they had to deal with newer people time and again.

- *Future of deal aggregators / online coupon promotions:* All the salons felt that the **concept of online coupon promotions (and so deal aggregators) would continue in near future**. Some reasons mentioned were: Customers want deals / coupons so somebody will offer it (either existing deal aggregators or a new entrant if existing aggregators go out of business); customers have become internet savvy and this phenomenon cannot be ignored. Though, all of them also agreed to the fact that *the whole business model cannot continue for a long time in its present form.* Salons cannot continue offering high discounts for a longer period of time, neither they can pay high commissions. Rationalization in both these aspects will have to come if this concept / business model / industry has to continue for long.

CONCLUSIONS AND IMPLICATIONS FOR THE INDUSTRY

Though online coupon promotions (and so deal aggregator platforms) are considered cheaper and effective alternatives of advertising and they help in promoting the business (though in varying proportions for the salons included in the study) without affecting the brand negatively, for it to continue for a longer time and generate long term benefits for the salons as well as the deal aggregators it is important that the current model of high discounts and commissions changes to something reasonable. This is more so important because profitability from coupon promotions (coupon customers) is an issue considering the fact that it attracts price sensitive (or deal prone) customers and their tendency to buy in addition to the coupon value (at full price) is low. Cannibalization of existing customers due to coupon promotions is also not a major concern for the salons currently. This could be probably because of the lower awareness about availability of online coupon promotions and their lower usage among the larger existing customer base of the salons. But as and when the popularity and awareness of deal aggregators increases among them and they start adopting it, the salons may start facing the issues of cannibalization and thereby reduced overall profitability. Salons would not mind even serving the existing customers coming in with deals and coupons in future (without worrying about cannibalization) provided it is overall profitable to serve them. Currently salons are using online coupon promotions probably out of compulsion because of the fear of missing out. Rather they would want to do it willingly, out of choice. For this also, some major structural changes would be required in the way online coupon promotions are designed and run. In addition to rationalizing discounts and commissions on coupons, limiting their usage in some way on the side of the consumers can be looked at.

LIMITATIONS AND FUTURE SCOPE FOR RESEARCH

This study was a qualitative one at a small level limited to just the salons in the city of Ahmedabad. In that sense the results may not be generalizable easily across other geographic regions as well as businesses beyond salons, though the study surely hints towards some important developments and challenges the online coupon promotions industry is experiencing. The daily deal promotions as an industry is still evolving, resulting into a lot of scope for research on the side of the various business operators (like restaurants, hotels, theme parks etc.) offering coupons on various platforms. Research on the side of consumers buying such deals (like their motivations for coupon buying, experiences with deals & coupons and their future orientation towards the coupon promotions) can also be a potential area in the future.

REFERENCES

Barr, A. (2012, January 3). Groupon shares drop on concern about merchants. Reuters. Retrieved November 16, 2020, from https://www.reuters.com/article/us-groupon-merchants/groupon-shares-drop-on-concern-about-merchants-idUSTRE80210020120103

Biswal, J. (2011, November 28). Sales promotion [Blog Post]. Retrieved December 29, 2020, from http://philipkotler2013.blogspot.com/2011/11/sales-promotion.html

Belch, G. E., & Belch, M. A. (2012). Introduction to Advertising and Promotion: An Integrated Marketing Communications Perspective (9th ed.). New York: McGraw-Hill/Irwin.

Byers, J. W., Mitzenmarcher, M., & Zervas, G. (2012). Daily deals: Prediction, social, diffusion, and reputational ramifications. WSDM'12: Proceedings of the fifth ACM international conference *on Web search and data mining* (pp. 543-552). New York, NY, United States: Association of Computing Machinery. Retrieved October 1, 2020, from https://doi.org/10.1145/2124295.2124361

Cassia, F., Magno, F., & Ugolini, M. (2015). The perceived effectiveness of social couponing campaigns for hotels in Italy. *International Journal of Contemporary Hospitality Management, 27*(7), 1598-1617.

Collard, C., Pustay, M., Roquilly, C., & Zardkoohi, A. (2001). Competitive cross-couponing: Comparison of French and U.S. perspectives. *Journal of Public Policy & Marketing, 20(1)*, 64-72. Retrieved January 1, 2020, from https://www.jstor.org/stable/30000645

Cooper, J. (2011, March 15). I consider Groupon the single worst decision I've ever made as a business owner. Business Insider, Australia. Retrieved November 16, 2020, from https://www.businessinsider.com.au/jesse-burke-groupon-nightmare-2013-03

Dholakia, U. M. (2011). How effective are Groupon promotions for businesses? Working Paper, Rice University. Retrieved from http://ssrn.com/abstract=1696327

Dholakia, U. M., & Tsabar, G. (2011, May 1). A Startup's experience with running a Groupon promotion. Retrieved from https://ssrn.com/abstract=1828003

Donnelly, K. (2012). Coupons of the 21st century: The golden age of the daily deal industry. The Elon Journal of Undergraduate Research in Communications, 3(2), 85–93. Retrieved October 19, 2020, from https://www.elon.edu/docs/e-web/academics/communications/research/vol3no2/07DonnellyEJFall12.pdf

Doyle, C. (2016). *A dictionary of marketing.* Oxford University Press. doi:10.1093/acref/9780198736424.001.0001

Edelman, B., Jaffe, S., & Kominers, S. D. (2016). To groupon or not to groupon : The profitability of deep discounts. *Marketing Letters, 27*, 39–53. doi:10.1007/s11002-014-9289-y

Groupon Inc rebranded as Nearbuy, to focus more on mobile apps. (2015, August 10). The Economic Times. Retrieved October 3, 2020, from https://economictimes. indiatimes. com/small-biz/startups/groupon-inc-rebranded-as-nearbuy-to-focus-more-on-mobile-apps/articleshow/48417876.cms

Kanagal, N. B. (2013, May). Promotions as market transactions. *Journal of Management and Marketing Research, 13*, 1–13. Retrieved September 14, 2020, from https://www. aabri.com/manuscripts/131510.pdf

Kotler, P., & Keller, K. L. (2016). *Marketing management* (15th ed.). Chennai, India: Pearson.

Kumar, V., & Rajan, B. (2012). The Perils of social coupon campaigns. *MIT Sloan Management Review, 53*(4), 13–14.

Ming, Z., Yulan, W., & Xianghua, G. (2016). Signalling effect of daily deal promotion for start-up service provider. *Journal of the Operational Research Society, 67*(2), 280–293. doi:10.1057/jors.2014.47

Nearbuy and Little Internet merge, Paytm gets majority stake. (2017, December 07). Retrieved January 3, 2020, from https://economictimes.indiatimes.com/small-biz/startups/ newsbuzz/nearbuy-and-little-internet-merge-paytm-gets-majority-stake/articleshow/ 61956544.cms

Star India hires LivingSocial CEO Gautam Thakar to head sports business. (2017, December 26). The Economic Times. Retrieved January 3, 2020, from https://economictimes. indiatimes.com/industry/media/entertainment/media/star-india-hires-livingsocial-ceo-gautam-thakar-to-head-sports-business/articleshow/62257545 .cms

Varuni, K. (2019, August 31). Why restaurants and aggregators are locking horns over discounts? The Economic Times. Retrieved November 1, 2020, from https:// economictimes.indiatimes.com/small-biz/startups/newsbuzz/why-restaurants-and-aggregators-are-locking-horns-over-discounts/articleshow/70916348.cms? from=mdr

Wu, J., Kimes, S. E., & Dholakia, U. (2012). Restaurant daily deals: The operator experience. *Cornell Hospitality Report*. Retrieved August 14, 2020, from https://scholarship.sha. cornell.edu/chrpubs/168/

Yijing, J., & Qiongshen, W. (2011). The differences between Groupon and other group-buying intermediaries: : from transactional and relational coordination perspectives (Dissertation). Retrieved August 10, 2020, from http://urn.kb.se/resolve? urn=urn:nbn:se:liu:diva-7079

CHAPTER 6

Nudge Theory and its Application in Organic Consumer Products: A Review Study

Dr. Deepti Kakar
Professor Management
Jagan Institute of Management Studies
Delhi, India
deeptikakar@jimsindia.org

Mr. Deepak Sharma
Research Scholar
Jagan Institute of Management Studies
Delhi, India
deepak.sharma@jimsindia.org

Abstract

Nudging can be described as the phenomenon that offers subtle and often indirect influence(s) to yield an expected choice from a decision maker. Unlike explicit mandates of law or product promotions, nudging does not drastically change the alternative options available for choice but attempts to impact the thought process of the decision maker. The concept of Nudge theory that won Nobel Prize for Economic Sciences in 2017 was propounded by Richard H. Thaler & Cass R. Sunstien in the book, Nudge – Improving decisions about Health, Wealth and Happiness in the year 2008.

From the past few years, this concept has been used by governments in several nations including the Government of India in its various welfare schemes. For instance, Selfie with daughter – Beti Bachao Beti Padhao, Swachhagrahis - Swachh Bharat Mission, Give it up - a campaign for LPG Subsidy. The theory has been applied in the competitive market place. Hybrid or electric vehicles, health and wellness products, organic products, green products, etc. are few examples that have involved the use of nudging by marketers/sellers.

Now people have become highly informed about their surroundings and internet penetration has played a key role in this transition. These information friendly 'homo economicus' can be nudged towards positive outcomes with greater ease. Since 2008 there are many pieces of research done in this field. This study aims to explore the finer details of the nudge theory and collate its application via various nudge based campaigns around the globe. Formulated as a review study of existing research, the emphasis is to arrive at the achievement level of such attempts. To do so, this study will be based on about 85 research papers and research articles published during 2008 - 2020 in various application areas of nudging including organic consumer goods (in India and rest of the world). The unbiased perspective emerging from the proposed study will prove to be useful for marketers in the industry of organic consumer products in their future plans regarding promotion and sales outcomes.

Keywords: Nudge theory, nudging, organic products, consumer goods, review paper.

I. INTRODUCTION

Decision making is essentially inescapable in human life. Decisions, tiny or big take most of our day and days of life. There are some decision making situations that are intuitive and hence do not consciously involve time and mental effort to analyse the options to arrive at the final choice, while the more involved decision making is thirsty on resources and takes an explicitly visible form in the course of things. Distinct from making decisions for one, decisions by others may significantly impact the desired outcomes and goal achievement. Illustrative in context are the behavioural decisions of citizens, impacting the welfare outcomes for the society at large that can make or mar the goal achievement of administrators and policy makers. Similarly, very critical is the decision of the potential buyer/consumer for a marketer/business organization.

What all goes into the decision making process and influences the consumer choice have been the focus of a mountain of research in consumer behaviour over the decades. Marketer's intention to stimulate a positive intention in the consumer, to buy her product is as active today as was decades ago. Thus, leaning on to behavioural studies such as psychology and behavioural economics to comprehend the cognitive forces that underlie all decision-making by customers is not a recent development. Foundation of behavioural theories developed on experimental analysis can be credited to Bernard (1927), Skinner (1938, 1953), Pavlov (1960), Bushell and Burgess (1969). Further unravelling of choice and consumption behaviour, similarly on the basis of experiments notably include studies by Catania (1963), Catania and Reynolds (1968), Hursh (1978), Hursh and Natelson (1981), Hursh (1984). Tracking the evolution of marketing perspective on consumer behaviour, Sheth (1985) highlights the coming together of behavioural sciences and marketing practices in better understanding consumers. As Pierce and Cheney (2004) clearly classify the causes of behaviour to be either internal or external to people, the possibility of controlling the external environment in context of potential consumers can fruitfully direct the consumer behaviour in desired direction of effecting a purchase. Decision making is not always rational and emotions/irrational behaviour too guide our choices has been ratified in the recent past (Kahneman, 2003, 2011; Thaler & Sunstein, 2008). And these are heavily influenced by the context or circumstances in which decisions are made. Interestingly, the coining of 'choice architecture,' (Thaler & Sunstein, 2008) demonstrates the significance of environmental setup in influencing patterns of consumption spending.

Choice architecture is an example of the broad phenomenon of nudging that entails subtle and covert measures that alter/influence consumer behaviour aiming to entice her to make the intended decision. Nudging does not create loud and visible incentives for decision makers. Nudging is unlike paternalism. Paternalism as a term dates back to the late 19th century with eloquent descriptions made by Immanuel Kant in 1785 and John Stuart Mill in 1859 (Thompson, n.d.). It encompasses all actions that restricts the set of available options for the decision maker without her consent and done with the intention of yielding benefit to the decision maker (Dworkin, 1972). On the other hand, nudging is in tune with libertarian paternalism (Thaler and Sunstein, 2003). It does not exclude any of the available options for the decision maker neither attempts to radically alter her behaviour by attaching incentives to the options. Thaler and Sunstein (2008) clear the distinction, "Nudges are not mandates." Nudges are gentler signals that target the understanding at subconscious level and thus influence decision making. Use of nudges in policy spheres and commercial arena has been done and researched to a commendable extent. Research involving in-depth studying and commenting on the usefulness of nudges, instances of their success and failure, reasons for their goal achievement or otherwise, all exist for their individual, isolated application. However collation of the studies to string the commonalities of success cases and failed attempts is significant to better understand the possibility of generalizing the case for/against the use of nudge theory by policy makers and marketers. Moreover, the usefulness of nudge(s) to stimulate behavioural changes to encourage the purchase of organic consumer products is conspicuously scarce especially in Indian context.

This paper is divided into three major sections in addition to the introduction; methodology, literature review and analytical discussion. Sequentially these appear as follows and are culminated with concluding remarks.

III. LITERATURE REVIEW

Nudging as a concept

Conception of 'nudge' or the 'nudge theory' and its formalization happened in 2008 by the Nobel Award Winner (2017) Richard H. Thaler, who co-authored the book, 'Nudge: Improving decisions about health, wealth, and happiness,' with Cass R. Sunstein. The understanding of irrationality about human behaviour that lies at the base of bad decisions was extended by Thaler and Sunstein (2008) as the idea of irrational thoughts and behaviour was already established and extensively researched by practitioners and learners of psychology. Without use of the term 'nudge' or 'nudging,' their previous work, Thaler and Sunstein (2003) brought to fore the idea of libertarian paternalism, a new term that provided an alternative to the coercive ideology of paternalism, yet possessing the ability to achieve same results. Highlighting the biases in-built in all humans, Thaler and Sunstein (2008) explained the logic behind erroneous or poor decision making which ultimately results in non-desired or poor outcomes in areas of health, education, and finances. Overcoming these, has been propounded by the authors via nudging; with the help of interesting illustrations they showcased and defended the strength of nudging in driving decision making on the right path and therefore outcomes. Thaler, Sunstein and Balz (2014) added to the earlier contribution on the concept and design of environment of the decision maker. Without undermining the traditional economic theory and relevance of market forces, Thaler, et.al lay down six principles of structuring the system of options that could lead to improved decisions for people in different life dimensions. In a recent study, Grayot (2019) furthered the clarity on the ambiguities relating to valid psychological factors that explain the internal dynamics of decision making process ingrained in the dual-process theory.

A critically acclaimed challenge to the theory was put forward by Hansen and Jespersen (2013) who went on to explain that the non-nudge environment of a decision maker is not necessarily a sure failure in yielding desired outcomes. However, Hansen and Jespersen (2013) support and explain Thaler and Sunstein (2008) view on nudges being non-manipulative in nature. They propose a framework of creating four types of nudges - transparent type 2, transparent type 1, non-transparent type 1 and transparent type 2; each either being manipulative or not (non-transparent and transparent) and conforming to System 2 thinking or System 1 (Kahnemann, 2011) thinking referring to the reflective and automatic thinking modes respectively (Thaler and Sunstein, 2008). In addition to revisiting the conceptual framework of nudging, Sunstein (2014) stressed on the characteristic transparency of nudges and their advantages over the traditional incentive system that would be manipulative and cost guzzling. A comparison of the efficiency of decisions from traditional price incentives with nudges has been the basis of 'a set of general principles for choosing whether to employ a nudge or a price instrument,' formulated by Galle (2014). In-spite of considerable literature on the conceptual build-up on nudging, borderline cases and misclassification of information and advice as nudges (Hausman and Welch, 2010) is a critical issue. Difference of opinion and debates though enrich and make the theory more robust, they may confound the perspective of choice architects. Also, more criticism of the theory and its application has involved raising issues related to ethics (Hausman & Welch, 2010; Selinger and Whyte, 2011) in modern day pluralistic societies and across societies (Selinger and Whyte, 2010; Bovens, 2010). Questioning the implicit assumption of people being naïve to think the best for themselves, Selinger and Whyte (2011) opine that social anxieties related to nudging are less serious as compared to ethical doubts. Wary of the non-manipulative nature of nudging, Rizzo and Whitman (2009) doubt the long run sustainability of the concept especially in the sphere of policy making as it may transcend and become more intrusive hurting personal freedom and choice. The choice architecture may end up being designed with impressionistic components thereby defying its definitional transparency. The intention of the choice architects is not doubtful although their perception of helping decision makers make better decisions is subject to their own interpretation of being better (Baldwin et al., 2011; Cartwright and Hight, 2020).

To what extent would nudges result in desired outcomes is largely dependent on unpredictable factors (Baldwin et al., 2011) and also raises suspicion on nudging implications) which may turn libertarian paternalism into its traditional spirit and appearance (Goodwin, 2012; Bradbury et. al, 2013). Responding to such disapprovals, Cass Sunstein wrote, 'Misconceptions about nudges' and gave counter-arguments to allegation of nudges being exploitative, covert, manipulative, ineffective and extend too much dependence on government. This was further supported by Sunstein, et. al. (2018) with the help of results from five nation survey covering 15 nudges in diverse areas proving presence of high approval for nudges as policy tools though not without variations across nations and cultures. An alternative to trounce the ingrained human biases (Kahneman and Tversky, 2000) and their impact in the form of bad decisions (Thaler and Sunstein, 2008) was put forward by Richard E. Nisbett; by training people to help them reason out and understand events and decision situations (Kelly, 2019) while Morewedge, et.al. (2015) via experimental training endorse Nisbett but suggest to supplement incentives and nudges with training interventions rather than replace them.

Nudging and policy making

Soon after the concept of nudging and its potential implications to modify decisions came to be known and understood, governments in various countries began to take very keen interest in using behavioural expertise to effect policy making.

Policy making in India is not bereft of influence by nudging theory. For instance, there is a chapter titled, 'Policy for Homo Sapiens, Not Homo Economicus: Leveraging the Behavioural Economics of Nudge' in The Economic Survey for 2019. Also, NITI Aayog (think-tank of the Government of India) Behavioural Insights Unit that would concentrate on improving the outcome of public programs in education, health and nutrition, financial inclusion and skill development, agriculture and water resources and basic infrastructure sector specifically in the identified underdeveloped districts (Behavioural Insights Unit, n.d.). UK was the first nation to make a conscious inclusion of behavioural understandings into policy making and action, where the then Prime Minister David Cameron set up the very first Behavioural Insights Team in 2010. The initial popular success was the formulation of a nudge based strategy to encourage donation of organs at Driver's Licence Centres in London that went on to add one million volunteers in one year (Walters, 2014; Ehrenhalt, 2019). The global spread of the influence of nudging can be gauged from the study report of Whitehead, et. al. (2014) who found "evidence of public initiatives that had been influenced by the new behavioural sciences (but were not centrally orchestrated) in a total of 135 states and Taiwan." Use of nudges by regulators/administrators to effect desired changes in areas of sanitation, health, energy conservation, etc. have been acknowledged, used (Ruggeri, 2018) and studied as a part of nudging for effective policy making. Some popular ones are mentioned in the following paragraph.

An experiment in Britain involving nudging to change people's behaviour so as to keep public places clean, was able to successfully lower littering by 46% in parks and by 42.4 % in commercial sites (Keep Britain Tidy, 2015). Similarly positive results were obtained by a field experiment by Altmann and Traxlerk (2012) involving reminder messages about the importance of dental health, dental check-up, flossing, avoidance of sugary items, etc. sent to several patients (Bonn, Germany); the number of check-up appointments got doubled. The study by Guerassimoff and Thomas (2013) aiming at making people energy efficient involved sending common notifications to the experiment group of households (Cannes, France in 2012). Texas Department of Transportation (US) in an anti-littering campaign with the leading slogan, "Don't Mess with Texas" put up on billboards and run across news channels that led to a decline in the visible roadside litter by 34% during 2009-2013 (Don't' mess with Texas leads, September 3, 2013). To ensure greater effectiveness of policy actions Bhargav and Looewenstein (2015) have made suggestions for policy makers including simplification of the potential benefits of choosing a particular alternative and protection of customers from the potential threat of behavioural exploitation by marketers. Clearly the use of simple nudges via awareness campaigns, notifications, reminders, and slogans as part of behaviourally informed policy making (Shafir, 2012) brought about significant and effective results. Resolution of complicated issues through behaviourally guided public policy is far from satisfactory (Selinger and Whyte, 2011; Ewert, 2019) and complexity of human behaviour is at the root of the insufficiency of nudging which is however cost effective and empirically driven (Mont, Lehner and Heiskanen, 2014). Mont, et. al (2014) advised against indiscriminate replication of nudging in contexts different from where it may have been successful and at best using it for supplementing existing policies rather than their replacement. Undoubtedly, use of nudges is meant to make policies more favourable and effective but the Carnegie Mellon study suggests they may jeopardize policy making and implementation as they may be seen as a cheap substitute (Yoder, 2019). The study involving several experiments over several years show up weakness of nudges in helping fix long term, larger and more complicated issues.

Nudging and marketing

Though marketers and salespersons have been using it for decades, research and studies using the term 'nudging' as a part of marketing strategy to drive consumer behaviour in a favourable direction emerged in the last decade. Majority of such studies have showed that nudging can be a powerful tool to study and influence consumer behaviour.

A recent study (Singh, 2019), made it more substantial by claiming that nudging not only enables marketers and companies in better understanding of consumer behaviour but also assists consumers in making more educated choices. Considering policy approaches to improve eating behaviour of people to help overcome dietary related disorders, Gutherie, et.al. (2015) stress on the role of information for producers/marketers as well as consumers for good choices. Nudging can also be used as an instrument to encourage sustainable consumer behaviour and it can bring positive changes in specific conduct. (Mont, et.al. 2014). Experiments to evaluate the decisions made by consumers when nudged by default options (VonBergen et.al. 2016; Kraak, et.al. 2017; Kaiser, 2018) reveal that consumer decisions are better. Since default options come with the convenience of 'no action required,' they are able to direct the decision maker's choice in the desired direction. VonBergen, et.al. (2016) throw light on the concept and consideration of defaults options as nudges only if the customer has an option to choose other alternative or to opt-out. However, Kaiser, (2018) questions the usage of digital nudges as they may end up producing more favourable results for the choice architect rather than the customers. Several studies to examine the linkage between nudging and consumer decision making (Nguyen 2019; Petit et.al. 2018) have shown nudging is a positive way to influence decision making to enhance sales. Experiments specifically to enhance healthy eating among consumers (Hollands, et.al. 2011; Hollands, et.al. 2017; Cheung, et.al. 2019; Huitink et.al. 2020; Fennis et.al. 2020; Matheus Mistura, 2012; Kraak et.al. 2012, Boehm et.al. 2019; Huitink et.al. 2020, Petit et.al. 2018) by the use of nudging has been reported to be effective. Interestingly, Huitink et.al. (2020) propose that the combination of price and nudging worked best in boosting sales for healthy products rather than their independent application. Experimenting to analyse the role of nudging versus marketing to modify human behaviour towards healthy eating options (Boehm et.al., 2019; Petit et.al. 2018) led to similar outcomes however, Huitink et.al. (2020) and Cheung et.al. (2019) obtained contradictory results in use of social norm nudges to induce healthy eating. Designing nudges, keeping in mind the personality traits of the decision makers (Kaiser, 2018) is instrumental in improving their effectiveness.

Linkage between nudging and pricing (Welch, 2010; Kraak et.al. 2017; Hoenink et.al. 2020) shoe different results as price strategy may at times be better while in some instances it works the same way as s nudge, however, price must be justified for the nudged product implying consumer decision making highly influenced by the idea of 'value for money,' when attempting a purchase deal. Studies by Hollands et.al. (2017) and Vandenbroele et.al. (2018) have mentioned the use of 'Traffic Light Labelling' in their experiment interventions. Both the studies were designed to encourage healthy eating habits among consumers via labelling nudges. Similarly experiments involving changes in packaging sizes (Petit et.al. 2018; Hollands et.al. 2017) throw up effective outcomes in shifting consumers from unhealthy products to healthy products with specific reference to food, alcohol and tobacco. In addition to experimental study by Vandenbroele et.al. (2018), a study in Indian settings by Soniya and Meena (2020) proves nudge to be an effective tool to encourage people to buy more organic products.

However, criticising the use of nudging by marketers, Dholakia et.al. (2016) emphasize on the right amount of nudging and its possibility of failing if the marketer attempts to show-off superiority. Findings of Nguyen (2019) establish nudges as ineffective, undermine democracy, evade main issues, and tantamount to shaming.

II. METHODOLOGY

Structured to review the existing literature, the present paper is in the nature of an integrated review paper that identifies relevant research articles/papers, combines and collates the similarities and dissimilarities and attempts to build additional perspective in context. The methodology thus draws from the works of Toracco (2016), Grant and Booth (2009) and Callahan (2010) generously. Though the mapping of this review paper with the category of critical or integrative research review as defined by Toracco (2016) and detailed by Grant and Booth (2009) is less than perfect, it does transcend mere identification and collation of existing research studies. In keeping with the analytical framework used by Grant and Booth (2009) - SALSA, acronym for Search, Appraisal, Synthesis and Analysis has been used to lay down the methodology. In consonance - the Search is largely focused on primary studies; the Appraisal is on the basis of contribution made by the existing research studies (in India and elsewhere); Synthesis is mostly narrative; Analysis is non-quantitative and characterises the spotting of similarities and distinctive aspects in the existing research studies. The proceeding methodology detailing is attempted on lines suggested by Callahan (2010). For accessing the existing literature, scope was defined to include primary studies on use of nudging in policy action and commercial use of nudging specifically in organic consumer goods; both in various countries. On line searching was done using Google and Google Scholar search engines and two databases, namely Emerald and ProQuest were relied for extracting relevant literature. The retrieved research studies are non-exhaustive and time bound by the origination of the term nudging formally by Thaler and Sunstein (2008) to publications in the most recent possible and completed year, 2020. The review research due to its very nature and reliance on secondary data via World Wide Web was completely desk based and was done over seventeen weeks beginning September 2020 and culminating in the third week of January 2021. This being a two author work, the research initiation, processing and outcomes had been chalked with division of focus areas. A balanced contribution in the areas of - one, searching and identification, two, collating and three, appraisal and formal writing was achieved with frequent communication and short term goal setting. The searching involved several combinations of keywords - nudge, nudging, use of nudging, nudging and policy making, nudging and consumer behaviour, nudging and consumer decisions, nudging and decision making. While the Google search results from 'nudging and policy making' threw up approximately 9.5 lakh results, 'nudging and consumer decision making' yielded about 7.5 lakh results. Given the unmistakably large number of search results and the time target for this review work, only the first 4 pages with 10 results each were studied in detail. With different combinations of the aforementioned keywords, a considerable number of search outcomes were same but after removal of such overlapping, the detailed search on Google returned searches was about 150. These were further reduced to about 90 by removing the search results linking to educational websites and blogs. In addition, Google Scholar provided about 27 thousand scholarly articles, referring to research publications for 'nudging and consumer decision making,' but the results narrowed to 17 thousand upon time scoping them over 2008-2020. Similarly for 'nudging and policy making,' the results were close to 25 thousand. As expected many scholarly results obtained from Google and Google Scholar were same but the latter yielded publication in Journals, non-objectively perceived to be superior in quality and adorned with citations. To ensure access to more such publications, Emerald and ProQuest were searched with similar combinations of keywords. The researchers had constrained access to these - bounded by their institution's (workplace) subscription to selected contents; nevertheless the database search led to accumulation of an additional 60 relevant research studies but full article access brought the number to less than 20 and this fell to half with specific reference to use of nudging in organic consumer products. However, there was only one study focusing exclusively on organic consumer products. Final number of research papers reviewed and included in the present study are: 17 for the background study; 23 uncovering nudge and nudging as a concept; 16 revealing the use of nudging in policy making and 29 involving nudging in commercial space/marketing; 1 for nudging and organic consumer products; there are three overlapping studies across the application of nudging in policymaking and marketing.

The soul of this study - the review of literature and the synthesis have been presented under the section on discussion are in the nature of a descriptive narration. These have been broadly split into three - nudging as a concept; nudging and policy making (and action); and nudging and marketing (including organic consumer products). The last section on discussion and conclusion attempts to subjectively tie together the broad insights drawn from the previous section. This description is a subjective amalgamation that attempts to balance the differing opinions put out by the reviewed studies.

IV. DISCUSSION AND CONCLUSION

Nudging as a concept has over the years generated massive opinions and counter-opinions that have gone to the extent of bestowing the concept originator a Nobel Prize to remarks of nudging being akin to shaming! Nevertheless, the literature reviewed as a part of the present study throws up some very significant insights.

Firstly, definitional clarity on nudging is weak and very thin as well as subjective lines demarcate regions that make preserve or impound on individual privacy and independence of decision making (Bovens, 2010; Hausman & Welch, 2010; Selinger and Whyte, 2010; Selinger and Whyte 2011). Thus, following the coining of the term nudge and nudge theory significant and significant number of studies have attempted to bring greater clarity in its conceptual and applicative understanding while others have added to the basket of problems and definitional fuzziness. This should not be surprising as the concept is in reference to human thoughts and behaviour which are highly involved and complicated enough (Mont, et. al., 2014) that despite having been the subject of in-depth studies over centuries and manage to startle researchers and others alike.

Secondly, nudging seems to be a new concept discovered (Thaler and Sunstein, 2008) and fine-tuned by several subsequent studies, its application has been in existence especially in the field of selling marketing. For instance, a popular component of psychological pricing strategy involves prices that end with 9, 99, etc. (charm pricing) like 5 in case of Rs. 5.99 and seems to be lower as compared to Rs. 6.00. The understanding of human cognition and its irrationality (e.g. cognitive biases) have been experimented and used by producers and sellers in the past (Thomas, et.al, 2007; Chandon and Ordabayeva, 2009; Biswas, et. al, 2013; Soster et. al., 2014). The success or otherwise has given a fillip to studies undertaking an understanding of consumer behaviour better to bring effectiveness to marketing strategies.

Thirdly, the enthusiasm of having stumbled on a gold mine in believing in the revolutionary nature of nudging as a panacea solving all problems is a misinterpretation. Nudging, per se is not a magic bullet. Its use in policy making as well as in commercial space has found to be less than guaranteed. There can be errors in understanding, interpreting or formulating the choice architecture are highly realistic.

Fourthly, nudging needs to be used in a wise manner. The concerns raised by critics of the nudge theory with respect to its application especially in the area of policy making and action (Rizzo and Whitman, 2009; Selinger and Whyte, 2011; Ewert, 2019; Baldwin et al., 2011; Cartwright and Hight, 2020) are not without merit. Undoubtedly, if better understanding of human behaviour is used for manipulating people's decisions it is a curtailment of individual freedom. Decisions arrived at via nudging undermine the ability of decision makers as well as ownership for their implications in near and distant future. Thus problems with nudging are not only at the level of its conception but also with the results. Nudging has the limitation to side-line the main issues (Dholakia, et al, 2016; Nguyen, 2019) and therefore confound the work of policy makers or marketers. Studies involving a comparison of traditional incentive system with nudging show that independent use of either is insufficient (Mont, et. al, 2014; Galle, 2014) and design of combinations may be more fruitful.

Fifthly, nudging applications cannot and should not be generalized in the hope that if they have worked in a sample, they will work in the entire population or if they have worked in a specific society/nation, they will bring similar results elsewhere (Selinger and Whyte, 2010; Bovens, 2010; Mont, et. al, 2014; Nisbett, 2015; Kaiser, 2018). Nudges and nudging is very sensitive to context and circumstances. And the possibility of nudges not working or in fact backfiring is possible due to this error. As errors in measurement of ingredients can result in a dish that the maker as well as the takers frown upon, errors in understanding human behaviour and specifically customer behaviour for a marketer can prove to yield results far from expected. Yet, designing the right choice architecture to nudge the potential customer into a loyal customer is not as simple as spelling 'nudge.' A failure to address the above listed observations, cautions a cry to be prepared for poor results.

Organic consumer products are grown/manufactured/processed without use of any chemicals or artificial agents and are therefore healthier for the human body. Since their creation does not involve the use of artificial inputs like chemical fertilizers, preservatives, synthetic colours, etc. they are environment friendlier relative to the widely available non organic products. Nudging consumers into purchase of organic products does not only serve to help the consumers arrive at decisions that are beneficial to them in the long run but are also devoid of environmental burden. Though information and awareness is growing in general and people are showing greater interest in choosing organic products, it may not be sufficient in making rapid and sustained changes. Specific nudging to impact purchase of organic consumer goods has not been widely researched and the researchers came across only one study in Indian context and a few in other countries although among the later none specifically aimed at 'organic consumer goods.' A wide gap in existing literature and the unsure success of nudging in context of other products, throws open an opportunity for researchers of behavioural sciences and marketing to contribute to enriching this vacant slot of applying nudging to stimulate consumption of organic products.

REFERENCES

[1] Books

Alemanno, Alberto & Sibony, Anne-Lise. 2017. *NUDGE AND THE LAW*. OXFORD: HART PUBLISHING.

Baldwin, Robert; Cave, Martin & Lodge, Martin. 2012. *Understanding regulation*. Oxford: Oxford University Press.

Kahneman, Daniel & Egan, Patrick. 2011. *Thinking, fast and slow*. New York: Random House Audio.

Kahneman, Daniel & Tversky, Amos. 2000. *Choices, values, and frames*. New York: Cambridge University Press and the Russell Sage Foundation.

Kaiser, Dennis. 2018. *Individualized choices and digital Nudging*. Karlsruhe Institute of Technology (KIT).

Mistura, Matheus. 2017. *Examining the use of food cues*. University of Victoria.

Nguyen, Cuong. 2019. *How Do Nudges Influence Consumer Decisions? - A Literature Review*. Espoo, Finland: Aalto University.

Ruggeri, Kai. 2019. *Behavioral insights for public policy*. Abingdon, Oxon: Routledge.

Thaler, Richard H & Sunstein, Cass R. 2009. *Nudge*. [Erscheinungsort nicht ermittelbar]: Penguin Books.

[2] Journals

Altmann, Steffen & Traxler, Christian. 2012. "Nudges at the Dentist". *SSRN Electronic Journal*. Elsevier BV. doi:10.2139/ssrn.2132500.

Bhargava, Saurabh & Loewenstein, George. 2015. "Behavioral Economics and Public Policy 102: Beyond Nudging". *American Economic Review* 105 (5): 396-401. American Economic Association. doi:10.1257/aer.p20151049.

Biswas, Abhijit et al. 2013. "Consumer Evaluations of Sale Prices: Role of the Subtraction Principle". *Journal of Marketing* 77 (4): 49-66. SAGE Publications. doi:10.1509/jm.12.0052.

Bovens, Luc. 2010. "Nudges and Cultural Variance: a Note on Selinger and Whyte". *Knowledge, Technology & Policy* 23 (3–4): 483–486. Springer Science and Business Media LLC. doi:10.1007/s12130-010-9128-2. https://link.springer.com/article/10.1007/s12130-010-9128-2#citeas.

Bradbury, Alice; McGimpsey, Ian & Santori, Diego. 2013. "Revising rationality: the use of 'Nudge' approaches in neoliberal education policy". *Journal of Education Policy* 28 (2): 247–267. Informa UK Limited. doi:10.1080/02680939.2012.719638.

Bushell, D., Jr., & Burgess, R. L. (1969). Characteristics of the experimental analysis. In R. L. Burgess & D. Cadario, R. & Chandon, P. 2018. "Which healthy eating nudges work best? A meta-analysis of field experiments". *Appetite* 130: 300-301. Elsevier BV. doi:10.1016/j.appet.2018.05.170.

Callahan, Jamie L. 2014. "Writing Literature Reviews". *Human Resource Development Review* 13 (3): 271-275. SAGE Publications. doi:10.1177/1534484314536705.

Cartwright, Alexander C & Hight, Marc A. 2019. "'Better off as judged by themselves': a critical analysis of the conceptual foundations of nudging". *Cambridge Journal of Economics*. Oxford University Press (OUP). doi:10.1093/cje/bez012.

Catania, A. Charles & Reynolds, G. S. 1968. "A QUANTITATIVE ANALYSIS OF THE RESPONDING MAINTAINED BY INTERVAL SCHEDULES OF REINFORCEMENT1". *Journal of the Experimental Analysis of Behavior* 11 (3S2): 327–383. Wiley. doi:10.1901/jeab.1968.11–s327.

Cheung, Tracy T. L. et al. 2019. "Cueing healthier alternatives for take-away: a field experiment on the effects of (disclosing) three nudges on food choices". *BMC Public Health* 19 (1). Springer Science and Business Media LLC. doi:10.1186/s12889-019-7323-y.

Dianoux, Christian et al. 2019. "Nudge: A relevant communication tool adapted for agile innovation". *Journal of Innovation Economics* 28 (1): 7. CAIRN. doi:10.3917/jie.028.0007.

Dworkin, Gerald. "PATERNALISM." *The Monist* 56, no. 1 (1972): 64-84. Accessed July 7, 2021. http://www.jstor.org/stable/27902250.

Ewert, Benjamin. 2019. "Moving beyond the obsession with nudging individual behaviour: Towards a broader understanding of Behavioural Public Policy". *Public Policy and Administration* 35 (3): 337–360. SAGE Publications. doi:10.1177/0952076719889090.

Fennis, Bob M. et al. 2020. "Nudging health: Scarcity cues boost healthy consumption among fast rather than slow strategists (and abundance cues do the opposite)". *Food Quality and Preference* 85: 103967. Elsevier BV. doi:10.1016/j.foodqual.2020.103967.

Goodwin, Tom. 2012. "Why We Should Reject 'Nudge'". *Politics* 32 (2): 85-92. SAGE Publications. doi:10.1111/j.1467-9256.2012.01430.x.

Grant, Maria J. & Booth, Andrew. 2009. "A typology of reviews: an analysis of 14 review types and associated methodologies". *Health Information & Libraries Journal* 26 (2): 91–108. Wiley. doi:10.1111/j.1471-1842.2009.00848.x.

Grayot, James D. 2019. "Dual Process Theories in Behavioral Economics and Neuroeconomics: a Critical Review". *Review of Philosophy and Psychology* 11 (1): 105–136. Springer Science and Business Media LLC. doi:10.1007/s13164-019-00446-9.

Guthrie, Joanne; Mancino, Lisa & Lin, Chung-Tung Jordan. 2015. "Nudging Consumers toward Better Food Choices: Policy Approaches to Changing Food Consumption Behaviors". *Psychology & Marketing* 32 (5): 501-511. Wiley. doi:10.1002/mar.20795.

Halpern, David & Sanders, Michael. 2016. "Nudging by government: Progress, impact, & lessons learned". *Behavioral Science & Policy* 2 (2): 52–65. Project Muse. doi:10.1353/bsp.2016.0015.

Hansen, Pelle Guldborg, and Andreas Maaløe Jespersen. "Nudge and the Manipulation of Choice: A Framework for the Responsible Use of the Nudge Approach to Behaviour Change in Public Policy." *European Journal of Risk Regulation* 4, no. 1 (2013): 3–28. doi:10.1017/S1867299X00002762.

Hausman, Daniel M. & Welch, Brynn. 2010. "Debate: To Nudge or Not to Nudge*". *Journal of Political Philosophy* 18 (1): 123–136. Wiley. doi:10.1111/j.1467-9760.2009.00351.x.

Hoenink, Jody C. et al. 2020. "The effects of nudging and pricing on healthy food purchasing behavior in a virtual supermarket setting: a randomized experiment". *International Journal of Behavioral Nutrition and Physical Activity* 17 (1). Springer Science and Business Media LLC. doi:10.1186/s12966-020-01005-7.

Hollands, Gareth J. et al. 2017. "The TIPPME intervention typology for changing environments to change behaviour". *Nature Human Behaviour* 1 (8). Springer Science and Business Media LLC. doi:10.1038/s41562-017-0140.

Houghtaling, Bailey et al. 2019. "A systematic review of factors that influence food store owner and manager decision making and ability or willingness to use choice architecture and marketing mix strategies to encourage healthy consumer purchases in the United States, 2005–2017". *International Journal of Behavioral Nutrition and Physical Activity* 16 (1). Springer Science and Business Media LLC. doi:10.1186/s12966-019-0767-8.

Huitink, Marlijn et al. 2020. "Social norm nudges in shopping trolleys to promote vegetable purchases: A quasi-experimental study in a supermarket in a deprived urban area in the Netherlands". *Appetite* 151: 104655. Elsevier BV. doi:10.1016/j.appet.2020.104655.

Hummel, Dennis & Maedche, Alexander. 2019. "How effective is nudging? A quantitative review on the effect sizes and limits of empirical nudging studies". *Journal of Behavioral and Experimental Economics* 80: 47–58. Elsevier BV. doi:10.1016/j.socec.2019.03.005.

Hursh, Steven R. & Natelson, Benjamin H. 1981. "Electrical brain stimulation and food reinforcement dissociated by demand elasticity". *Physiology & Behavior* 26 (3): 509–515. Elsevier BV. doi:10.1016/0031-9384(81)90180-3.

Hursh, Steven R. 1984. "BEHAVIORAL ECONOMICS". *Journal of the Experimental Analysis of Behavior* 42 (3): 435–452. Wiley. doi:10.1901/jeab.1984.42-435.

Kelly, Anne. 2019. "Decisions, Decisions: Review of Mindware: Tools for Smart Thinking by Richard E. Nisbett". *Numeracy* 11 (1). University of South Florida Libraries. doi:10.5038/1936-4660.12.2.16.

Kraak, V. I. et al. 2017. "A novel marketing mix and choice architecture framework to nudge restaurant customers toward healthy food environments to reduce obesity in the United States". *Obesity Reviews* 18 (8): 852–868. Wiley. doi:10.1111/obr.12553.

Leggett, Will. 2014. "The politics of behaviour change: nudge, neoliberalism and the state". *Policy & Politics* 42 (1): 3–19. Bristol University Press. doi:10.1332/030557312x655576.

Lu, Shouwang; Chen, Gong (Gordon) & Wang, Kanliang. 2020. "Overt or covert? Effect of different digital nudging on consumers' customization choices". *Nankai Business Review International* 12 (1): 56–74. Emerald. doi:10.1108/nbri-12-2019-0073.

Ly, Kim et al. 2013. "A Practitioner's Guide to Nudging". *SSRN Electronic Journal*. Elsevier BV. doi:10.2139/ssrn.2609347.

Morewedge, Carey K. et al. 2015. "Debiasing Decisions". *Policy Insights from the Behavioral and Brain Sciences* 2 (1): 129-140. SAGE Publications. doi:10.1177/2372732215600886.

Ordabayeva, Nailya & Chandon, Pierre. 2013. "Predicting and Managing Consumers' Package Size Impressions". *Journal of Marketing* 77 (5): 123–137. SAGE Publications. doi:10.1509/jm.12.0228.

Pavlov, Ivan P. 2010. "Conditioned reflexes: An investigation of the physiological activity of the cerebral cortex". *Annals of neurosciences* 17 (3). SAGE Publications. doi:10.5214/ans.0972-7531.1017309.

Rizzo, Mario J. & Whitman, Douglas Glen. 2008. "Little Brother is Watching You: New Paternalism on the Slippery Slopes". *SSRN Electronic Journal*. Elsevier BV. doi:10.2139/ssrn.1119325.

Selinger, Evan & Whyte, Kyle Powys. 2010. "Competence and Trust in Choice Architecture". *Knowledge, Technology & Policy* 23 (3-4): 461–482. Springer Science and Business Media LLC. doi:10.1007/s12130-010-9127-3.

Selinger, Evan & Whyte, Kyle. 2011. "Is There a Right Way to Nudge? The Practice and Ethics of Choice Architecture". *Sociology Compass* 5 (10): 923–935. Wiley. doi:10.1111/j.1751-9020.2011.00413.x.

Soster, Robin L.; Gershoff, Andrew D. & Bearden, William O. 2014. "The Bottom Dollar Effect: The Influence of Spending to Zero on Pain of Payment and Satisfaction". *Journal of Consumer Research* 41 (3): 656–677. Oxford University Press (OUP). doi:10.1086/677223.

Sunstein, Cass R. 2014. "Nudging: A Very Short Guide". *SSRN Electronic Journal*. Elsevier BV. doi:10.2139/ssrn.2499658.

Sunstein, Cass R. 2016. "Nudges That Fail". *SSRN Electronic Journal*. Elsevier BV. doi:10.2139/ssrn.2809658.

Thaler, Richard H & Sunstein, Cass R. 2003. "Libertarian Paternalism". *American Economic Review* 93 (2): 175-179. American Economic Association. doi:10.1257/000282803321947001.

Thaler, Richard H.; Sunstein, Cass R. & Balz, John P. 2010. "Choice Architecture". *SSRN Electronic Journal*. Elsevier BV. doi:10.2139/ssrn.1583509.

Thomas, Manoj; Simon, Daniel H. & Kadiyali, Vrinda. 2007. "Do Consumers Perceive Precise Prices to be Lower than Round Prices? Evidence from Laboratory and Market Data". *SSRN Electronic Journal*. Elsevier BV. doi:10.2139/ssrn.1011232.

Torraco, Richard J. 2016. "Writing Integrative Literature Reviews". *Human Resource Development Review* 15 (4): 404–428. SAGE Publications. doi:10.1177/1534484316671606.

Van Gestel, L. C.; Adriaanse, M. A. & De Ridder, D. T. D. 2020. "Do nudges make use of automatic processing? Unraveling the effects of a default nudge under type 1 and type 2 processing". *Comprehensive Results in Social Psychology*: 1–21. Informa UK Limited. doi:10.1080/23743603.2020.1808456.

Venema, Tina A. G. et al. 2020. "When in Doubt, Follow the Crowd? Responsiveness to Social Proof Nudges in the Absence of Clear Preferences". *Frontiers in Psychology* 11. Frontiers Media SA. doi:10.3389/fpsyg.2020.01385.

[3]   Online Sources

Ehrenhalt, Alan. 2021. "Why 'Nudge' Policies Should Be Used Gently". *Governing.* https://www.governing.com/assessments/gov-nudge-behavioral-economics.html.

Ezez. 2015. "A social experiment to nudge people towards responsible litter disposal". *www.keepbritaintidy.org.*   https://www.keepbritaintidy.org/sites/default/files/resources/KBT_CFSI_Green_Footprints_Report_2015.pdf.

Ezez. 2017. "The Importance of Misbehaving—A Conversation with Richard Thaler". https://deloitte.wsj.com/cfo/2017/10/16/the-importance-of-misbehaving-a-conversation-with-richard-thaler/.

Ezez. 2020. "Physical distancing: A behavioural science toolkit to aid physical distancing and people movement in a COVID-19 world | WARC". *Warc.com.* https://www.warc.com/content/paywall/article/physical-distancing-a-behavioural-science-toolkit-to-aid-physical-distancing-and-people-movement-in-a-covid-19-world/133654.

Ezez. 2021. "Behavioural science to tackle UK's litter epidemic". *Warwick Business School.* https://www.wbs.ac.uk/news/behavioural-science-to-tackle-uk-s-litter-epidemic/.

Ezez. 2021. "CSBC | Behavioural Insights Unit, NITI Aayog". *Csbc.org.in.* http://csbc.org.in/work/behavioural-insights-unit-niti-aayog/.

Ezez. 2021. "Don't mess with Texas Leads to Reduction in Roadside Trash". *Txdot.gov.* https://www.txdot.gov/inside-txdot/media-center/statewide-news/2013-archive/043-2013.html.

M. Dholakia, Utpal. 2021. "Why Nudging Your Customers Can Backfire". *Harvard Business Review.* https://hbr.org/2016/04/why-nudging-your-customers-can-backfire.

McAuley, Ian. 2010. "When does behavioural economics really matter?". *Home.netspeed.com.au.* http://www.home.netspeed.com.au/mcau/academic/confs/bepolicy.pdf.

Mirsch, Tobias; Lehrer, Christiane & Jung, Reinhard. 2017. "Digital Nudging: Altering User Behavior in Digital Environments". *CBS Research Portal.* https://research.cbs.dk/en/publications/digital-nudging-altering-user-behavior-in-digital-environments.

Nicholson, Zara. 2011. "Zille's HIV campaign gains momentum". *Iol.co.za.* https://www.iol.co.za/news/south-africa/western-cape/zilles-hiv-campaign-gains-momentum-1189372.

Nodjimbadem, Katie. 2017. "The Trashy Beginnings of "Don't Mess With Texas"". *Smithsonian Magazine.* https://www.smithsonianmag.com/history/trashy-beginnings-dont-mess-texas-180962490/.

Rowson, Jonathan. 2011. "'Nudge' is not enough, it's true. But we already knew that | Jonathan Rowson". *the Guardian.* https://www.theguardian.com/commentisfree/2011/jul/19/nudge-is-not-enough-behaviour-change

Soniya, V. & Meena, K. 2020. "A STUDY ON THE IMPACT OF NUDGE THEORY ON THE PURCHASE BEHAVIOUR OF CONSUMERS TOWARDS ORGANIC PRODUCTS IN NAGERCOIL TOWN, KANYAKUMARI DISTRICT". *Semanticscholar.org.*   https://www.semanticscholar.org/paper/A-STUDY-ON-THE-IMPACT-OF-NUDGE-THEORY-ON-THE-OF-IN-Soniya-K.Meena/6927a65b2a3b42a9786e5c789b315ecf18aa502a.

Subramanian, Krishnamurthy V. 2019. "Economic Survey 2019-20 Volume 1". *www. indiabudget.gov.in*. https://www.indiabudget.gov.in/budget2020-21/economicsurvey/ index.php.

VonBergen, Clarence W. et al. 2016. *Homepages.se.edu*. http://homepages.se.edu/ cvonbergen/files/2015/03/Cueing-the-Customer-Using-Nudges-and-Negative-Option-Marketing.pdf.

Walters, Jonathan. 2014. "How Britain's Getting Public Policy Down to a Science". *Governing*. https://www.governing.com/archive/gov-getting-public-policy-down-to-science.html.

CHAPTER 7

What We "Sense" is What We Believe-Impact of Multisensory Environmental Cues on Purchase Intention

Dr. Rupa Rathee
Department of Management Studies
Deenbandhu Chhotu Ram University of
Science and Technology
Murthal, India
ruparathee@gmail.com

Dr. Pallavi Rajain
Department of Management Studies
Deenbandhu Chhotu Ram University
of Science and Technology
Murthal, India
pallavirajain@gmail.com

Abstract

Sensory Marketing as defined by the American Marketing Association is "marketing technique that aims to seduce the consumer by using his senses to influence his feelings and behaviour". Each of the sense of sight, sound, touch, smell and taste has different influence on the consumer behaviour. The use or application of only a single sense is neither completely possible nor fruitful. Therefore, a combination of multiple sensory cues was found to be more effective. The present study was carried out to understand the influence of multisensory environmental cues (sight, sound, smell and touch) on the purchase intention of customers and also to find the sense which dominates their decisions. The data was collected from customers through mall-intercept survey. A standardized questionnaire adapted from previous authors was used to collect the data. The sample of the study included 450 respondents visiting the shopping malls in National Capital Region. The data was analysed using SPSS. The results revealed that there was a significant and positive impact of multisensory environmental cues on purchase intention of the customers. The highest impact was of the sense of sight as found through the beta values of regression analysis. The study has implications for marketers especially those related to organized retailing.

Keywords: Sensory Marketing, Multisensory Environmental Cues, Senses, Purchase Intention

I. INTRODUCTION

Sensory Marketing as defined by the American Marketing Association is "marketing technique that aims to seduce the consumer by using his senses to influence his feelings and behaviour". Each of the sense of sight, sound, touch, smell and taste has different influence on the consumer behaviour. In a way, "sensory marketing is an application of the understanding of sensation and perception to the field of marketing to consumer perception, cognition, emotion, learning, preference, choice, or evaluation" (Krishna, 2012). These sensory qualities serve as an attention-creating medium which may include lighting, colour, music, smell. The perception regarding these sensory qualities influences the customer's affective state. It can be said that the message-creating medium influences the affect-creating medium. A study of consumer behaviour is necessary because why consumers prefer one retail outlet over the other is important in deciding the future of that business. How the behaviour of consumers can be predicted or moulded forms a part of the subject of consumer behaviour or consumer psychology. Further these perceptions and emotions influence the consumer's purchase behaviour or buying decisions. This may have implications on the customer loyalty and repeat patronage. The role of each of the senses in influencing consumer behaviour is discussed in following paragraphs.

A. Sense of sight

This is the sense that seems to be most easily seduced as it is easier to convince someone with what he/she sees (Lindstrom, 2005). Visual stimuli include logos, colours, packaging, design etc. which are considered to be crucial for identifying any goods and services. Even in advertising, visual ads through television and internet along with print ads through newspapers and pamphlets are most commonly used. Usually, consumers who are brand loyal can easily identify the logos of their favourite brands and are easily attracted towards it. The colour associated with a product is another important visual stimulus as people generally associate certain colours with the previous associations developed due to different beliefs and cultures.

B. Sense of sound

It is also the most commonly used sense for marketing the products. Sound along with sight covers almost 99 per cent of all marketing communications. Sound can be in any form including jingles developed for advertising, sound made by the product, ambient music played by the retail stores where the product is sold. A jingle can contribute to the brand's sound communication as it is easily remembered. For example, most people remember the famous jingles like "Amul-the taste of India" by Amul or the older washing powder jingle by Nirma "Sabki Pasand Nirma" decades after they were first used.

C. Sense of smell

This sense can be said to be the one with the strongest emotional impact as 75 per cent of human emotions are induced with the sense of smell. Limbic system is the processing centre of scents in the human brain which is responsible for memory and emotional responses. Everyday thousands of smells are encountered and humans are capable of remembering as many as 10,000 distinct scents. In addition, studies have revealed that 90 per cent women and 80 per cent men associate scents with specific memories. What one smells influences mood in significantly greater proportion than any other sense.

D. Sense of touch

The sense of touch is the sense which provides a direct interaction between the customer and the product. There is difference between customers who like to touch products more and who do not. On the basis of this habit, touch has been categorised into two that is autotelic touch and instrumental touch. The autotelic Need for Touch (NFT) also called as fun touch is one where the customer touches product for amusement and not just for purchase driven goals. On the other hand, the instrumental Need for Touch arises out of requirement for purchase which is inevitable (Peck and Childers, 2003).

E. Sense of taste

Taste is mainly perceived through taste buds and women have more taste buds than men. These taste buds help is differentiating between the four kinds of tastes that is sweet, sour, salty and bitter. These taste buds wear out as a person grows old. Thus, older people may require stronger tastes to perceive the same level as the younger generation. Since what is eaten by humans is firmly connected to their endurance, taste gives the most explicit capacity of any of the five human sensations.

II. REVIEW OF LITERATURE

A. Impact of Senses on Behaviour

The influence on consumer behaviour due to sensory marketing is undeniable. Shabgou and Daryani (2014) proposed that the five senses can affect consumer behaviour. The aim of this study stated that advantage of human senses could be taken by using sensory marketing; it can surely have a good effect on the behaviour of customers. For attracting the customers and increasing their loyalty companies and retailers can apply vital incitement in marketing process using consumer senses. Seeing, smelling, hearing, touching and tasting a product plays a crucial role in perceiving a product. These roles have a valuable advantage in today's market perception. Based on information available from previous studies 5 hypotheses were developed regarding the influence of each of the mentioned senses on consumer behaviour and also their overall effect. In order to prove this the researcher conducted this study with the statistical population including customers in a shopping centre in Tabriz city. The researchers chose the statistical sample of 234 people using random sampling method. The software used to analyse the data was SPSS and inferential statistical methods like Freidman test and regression test etc were used. Based on the hypotheses of the study, they deduced that 5 senses usually impact 21.4 per cent of the consumer behaviour. Also, stimulation of the sense of sight has 6.1 per cent, stimulation of the sense of smell has 9.2 per cent, stimulation of hearing sense has 7.4 per cent, stimulation of the sense of touch has 11.7 per cent and stimulation of the taste sense has 14.4 per cent impact on consumer behaviour. Based on this study's observations, most customers basically shopped dependent on their internal want of enjoying what they bought, and product quality was also crucial but only secondarily. At the time of shopping, buyers wanted to take a look at the material and contact it by their hands, although any information about its production process was not available to them. Recently, Santos *et al.* (2019) explored the influence that wine tourism had on tourist's memorable impressions in terms of sensory elements. The researchers also found the effect of these impressions on their recommendation and loyalty behaviour. For this study 306 responses were collected from wine tourists in the

Tejo region which included both national and international tourists. SEM was applied to analyse the data and the results suggested that there was differential impact of the different sensory impressions on the behaviour of wine tourists. The results implied that wineries should attract customers by focusing more on the visual and taste elements of the wine tourism activities. Earlier, De Vries *et al.* (2018) investigated whether differences in touch interface (touch screen vs mouse) led to differences in psychological ownership as well as endowment effects. The authors also assessed the moderation effects of interactivity of objects (2D vs rotating 3D images), autotelic "Need for touch" and shopping enjoyment. The research was conducted on a sample of 50 students from a university in Netherlands with a 2*2*2 cross-over design with 8 treatment conditions. It was found that online shopping led to meaningful interactions between touch interactivity and interfaces leading to increased ownership and valuations of products. The outcomes did not suggest any directing job of autotelic NFT on mental proprietorship. Next, it was found that there was an impact of touch interface and interactivity on shopping enjoyment. It was also found that shoppers with high autotelic NFT experienced greater enjoyment with high interactivity touchscreens. Azeem and Hussain (2018) tried to find the impact of sensory elements on the image of the brand and customer loyalty. For this, the author conducted a quantitative study in three fast food restaurants namely KFC, Dominos's and Subway with a sample of 100 respondents from each. He found that all elements are effective together and the effectiveness increased on using the gustative, olfactory and haptic elements together. Further, it was found that olfactory elements were the most effective among all the sensory elements followed by gustative, haptic, visual and auditory elements.

Motoki *et al.* (2019) studied the effect of crossmodal correspondences between warmth and colour has an influence on visual attention as well as preference for products. For this, four experimental settings were used using within subjects' design with students as experimental subjects. The outcomes of the study showed the presence of crossmodal correspondences between feeling warm and light colours as shown in the first study. The second study showed how on increasing warmth the choice for light coloured goods increased as recorded by the visual attention received. The results of the third study were negative as there was no direct influence of these crossmodal correspondences on consumer preferences. However, the last study revealed that under conditions of comfortable warmth, consumer preference increased for light coloured goods. Biswas *et al.* (2019) examined strategies related to volume of ambient music as well as noise and its impact on the sale of healthy or unhealthy food items. This research comprised of a pilot study, five lab studies and two field experiments. The outcomes of the research revealed that in comparison to high volume, low volume music leads to healthy food choices as a result of relaxation that is induced by low volume music. On the other hand, high volume surrounding music improves energy among customers leading to unhealthy food options. Lin *et al.* (2018) studied the effectiveness of olfactory imagery in advertising on the basis of difference in olfactory sensitivity. Three studies were carried out to establish these hypotheses. The first two studies were conducted online using a combination of 8 ads in either food or non-food category. The third study was conducted using event related potential method where EEG machine was used to record the reactions of subjects to various ads. The outcome of the study showed that olfactory imagery can have a negative effect on ratings for ads and products as well as likelihood to buy especially in case of people who have sensitivity to smell. The study also found that sniffing along with olfactory imagery could reduce the negative effects for individuals with olfactory sensitivity.

Rodas-Areiza and Montoya-Restrepo (2018) analysed the importance of sensory stimulation in relation to consumer experiences. The study was conducted in two parts. The first part used observation and an online survey of 495 women regarding the choice of a face cream to evaluate the experience of consuming the product. The second part involved the use of Electroencephalogram or EEG, Eye Tracking and FaceReader for the same purpose. The results presented a model for the construction of a whole experience incorporating the specific emotions, impact and attention, and the rational argument of the consumer. Forster and Spence (2018) tried to test whether visual load modulated olfactory awareness. Visual inquiry task utilized via Cartwright-Finch and Lavie (2007) was utilized while presenting members to the surrounding smell of espresso. The experiment consisted of two conditions a high load and a low load. The impact of the two conditions was seen on critical-stimulus awareness, visual inquiry task execution, outside interruption, and brain meandering. In the three experiments that were conducted, the results were consistent with the hypothesis. It was found that task load had a modulating effect on olfactory awareness. Less than 42.5 per cent members in the high burden condition when contrasted with the low burden condition detailed the presence of coffee scent. The results also suggested that as a consequence of olfactory habituation, inattentional anosmia can persist even when attention becomes available. Vega-Gómez *et al.* (2020) studied the influence of scents on the perception, evaluation and behaviour of consumers inside a museum. The experiment was conducted at a museum over 30 days where the rooms of the museum were filled with congruent scents. MANCOVA analysis was performed to assess the influence. It was found that scent had significant effect on intention to revisit, perception and evaluation of consumers. Lowe *et al.* (2018) proposed that one aspect of sound that may cue alerting function of sound associations is pitch, with low-pitch (vs. moderate pitch) sound in the background non-consciously priming a threat response which results in higher anxiety among customers. The researchers conducted 7 studies in experimental settings for this purpose. They studied the impact of low pitch, moderate pitch or no pitch conditions on risk aversion. It was found through the 7 studies that in varied domains the low (vs. moderate) pitch foundation sound outcomes higher uneasiness, prompting hazard avoidant customer decisions, for example, choosing a food option with lower taste uncertainty or willingness to pay more for car insurance. In developing countries like India, Azeem and Hussain (2018) conducted a study in four Quick Service Restaurants (QSR). The researchers aimed to find the sensory factors that influenced the choice of customers regarding Quick Service Restaurants. The data was collected from 1600 customers of Subway, Domino's, KFC and McDonald's in four cities Mumbai, Bangalore, Chennai and Hyderabad. On applying factor analysis, three factors were found that influenced choice of QSR which included sensory influence, promotional influence and monetary influence. Further regression analysis revealed that sensory factors contributed the most to the choice of QSR.

B. Sensory Marketing in Retail Industry

McGrath *et al.* (2016) studied the influence of chocolate scent inside a bookstore to understand its effects on purchase behaviour. A trial was conducted at a bookstore in Canada for over 31 days. The authors could not find any influence of the presence of ambient chocolate scent on the sales. Even within the subset categories of sales there was no influence of the odour present on the within domain and out-of-domain products. The results suggested that the association between scents and sales was spurious but it could also be because the sales were already boosted due to the presence of smells from the café which left the chocolate scent to be ineffective. Flavián *et al.* (2017) studied how the use of vivid information through product presentation videos influences consumer's attitudes and intention to purchase with perceived ease of imagining acting as a mediator. The study also analysed the influence of vivid information on preference for channel of purchase. The data was collected from 217 business students in Spain using convenience sampling. The results of the study suggested that vivid information (promotional or demonstration videos) had a significant impact on consumer's attitudes and purchase intentions. The study also found that ease of imagining mediated the influence on purchase intentions. Lastly, the study found that showing vivid information to high NFT individuals lead them to purchase more from physical stores whereas in case of low NFT individuals, the vivid information was sufficient to make purchases online.

Krasonikolakis *et al.* (2018) studied the effect of store layouts on consumer behaviour in 3D online stores. The authors investigated the influence of in store atmospherics on consumer behaviour particularly store layouts. Firstly, a three round Delphi study was conducted with experts. Next, a laboratory experiment was conducted using 3D online stores as treatment. Five types of store layouts were used avant garde, warehouse, pragmatic, boutique and department. The consumer behaviour was evaluated on the following dimensions web-based shopping delight, amusement, simplicity of navigation, online client experience, online purchase intentions, word of mouth, telepresence. The results of the study indicated that the store layout types of 3D online environments had an influence on ease of navigation, entertainment and online shopping enjoyment. Lee *et al.*, (2018) performed a study on the hotel industry to find the influence of brand relationships, sensory information and review types (numeric rating or narratives) on customer's response. The authors performed two studies using a 2*2 experimental setup wherein the first study focused on sensory information and brand relationships. The second study consisted of 2*2 study between sensory information and review type. The data was collected from north-eastern university in USA. The first study suggested that there was an impact of brand relationship on sensory information particularly for story-format. This sensory information promoted customer's brand experience, transportation experience and emotional responses. The second study also identified influence of audit types on story-position tangible data which led to enhanced brand experience, transportation experience and trust.

III. OBJECTIVE OF THE STUDY

"To study the effect of multisensory environmental cues on consumer's purchase intention and find which sense dominates their decision-making process."

The past studies have shown that the sense of sight or visual cues dominate all other cues in information processing and throughout the twentieth century marketing efforts were based on visual orientation because of the prevalence of the visual medium (Lindstrom,

2005; Krishna, 2012). 62- 90 per cent of an item buying choice depends on the colour of the item and the choice is made close to observing it (Singh, 2006). As seen in package designing, in retail store design as well, colour is used to gain attention and attract, or to draw, the customer (Bellizzi and Hite, 1992). Also, in a recent article (Krishna *et al.*, 2016) it was suggested that sensory dominance is an area worth investigating. So, it can be hypothesized that:

H_1: There is a significant and positive impact of multisensory environmental cues on consumer's purchase intention.

H_2: The sense of sight significantly dominates the other senses in the consumer decision making process.

IV. METHODOLOGY

A. Sample and Procedure

The data was collected from customers visiting shopping malls in the National Capital Region during weekends from June 2019 to December 2019. There were 23 items in the scale. A five-point Likert scale (1= "strongly disagree" and 5= "strongly agree") was used for coding all responses. The sample taken for the study was 450 collected using non-probability sampling.

B. Measures

The data was collected using standardized scales which were checked for validity and reliability before proceeding with the analysis. The various senses were measured using the scale developed by Kang et al. (2011) and purchase intention which was measured using scales developed by Sahi *et al.*, 2016 and Hussain and Ali, 2015. The reliability of both the scales was tested using Cronbach's alpha. In case of sensory cues, the value was .893 and for purchase intention was .897. Since both values were above .7 (minimum required value), therefore the scale was considered good for further testing.

The first step of analysis included presentation of the descriptive statistics of the scale used for measurement (table 1). The values of minimum and maximum ranged from 1 to 5 as the items were measured on a 5-point scale. The mean values were in range from 3.48 to 4.31, standard deviation from .930 to 1.14. The absolute values of skewness and kurtosis ranged from .473 to 1.5 and .01 to 2.06 respectively. Thus, the data showed normal distribution.

Table 1: Descriptive Statistics

Items	Mean	Std. Deviation	Skewness	Kurtosis
Unstylish Interior / Stylish Interior	3.89	1.026	-.752	.018
Dirty mall /Clean mall	4.31	.956	-1.531	2.064
Uncomfortable Layout /Comfortable Layout	4.02	1.020	-.968	.400
Chaotic mall /Organized mall	4.21	.985	-1.273	1.175

Fast Music /Slow Music	3.75	1.108	-.540	-.454
Loud Sound /Light Sound	3.73	1.098	-.535	-.432
Harsh Sound /Sweet Sound	3.79	1.059	-.609	-.277
Unpleasant Music /Pleasant Music	3.81	1.060	-.664	-.132
Stale Smell /Fresh Smell	4.05	1.040	-1.053	.616
Unpleasant Scent /Pleasant Scent	3.95	1.003	-.823	.316
Strong Scent /Light Scent	3.83	1.028	-.650	-.034
Incongruent Scent (Unsuitable)/ Congruent Scent (Suitable)	3.82	.950	-.602	.170
Rough Fabric /Smooth Fabric	3.91	.975	-.680	.037
Hard Furniture (Chair, Table, etc) /Soft Furniture (Chair, Table, etc)	3.61	1.149	-.490	-.538
Uncomfortable Temperature / Comfortable Temperature	3.96	1.031	-.882	.245
In the future, I intend to use the same outlet for making purchases.	3.57	.930	-.617	.414
If I were in the market for buying products, I would be returning to this retail outlet.	3.49	.956	-.545	.064
I would like to shop longer in the retail outlet.	3.48	.934	-.385	.077
I would recommend this retail outlet to my family and friends.	3.69	.954	-.741	.493
I would often shop at this store in the next few months.	3.54	.959	-.440	-.072
I am likely to provide this store with the information it needs to better serve my needs.	3.61	.932	-.473	.118

Source: Data collected by researcher

V. RESULTS AND DISCUSSION

A. *Effect of Multisensory Environmental Cues on Consumer's Purchase Intention*

Regression analysis was applied in order to check the effect of multisensory environmental cues on consumer's shopping behaviour.

The value of R square in the table 2 suggests that 24.4 per cent of variance in purchase intention was caused by the multisensory cues.

Table 2: Model Summary[b]

R	R Square	Adjusted R Square	Std. Error of the Estimate	Durbin-Watson
.494[a]	.244	.243	.58443	1.855

a. Independent Variable: Senses

b. Dependent Variable: Purchase Intentions

Source: Data collected by researcher

The F value of 319.836 with p<.001 (value of significance) in the table 3 depicted the significance of impact of the multisensory cues (independent variable) on the purchase intention (dependent variable) of the customers.

Table 3: ANOVA[a]

Model	Sum of Squares	Df	Mean Square	F	Sig.
Regression	109.244	1	109.244	319.836	
Residual	338.487	991	.342		.000[b]
Total	447.731	992			

a. Dependent Variable: Purchase Intentions

b. Independent Variable: Senses

Source: Data collected by researcher

From the above table 4 it can be seen that there was significant impact of sensory cues (sight, smell and touch cues) (β=.617, p<.000) on the purchase intention of the customers. Thus, H_1 that there is a significant and positive impact of multisensory environmental cues on consumer's purchase intention was accepted. Further, to find the sense with the maximum impact an assessment of the impact of individual senses on the purchase intention as shown in table 4 was done.

Table 4: Coefficients[a]

Model	Unstandardized Coefficients		Standardized Coefficients	T	Sig.
	B	Std. Error	Beta		
(Constant)	1.326	.120		11.045	.000
Senses	.617	.034	.494	17.884	.000

a. Dependent Variable: Purchase Intentions

Source: Data collected by researcher

The highest impact was for sight cues (β=.213, p<.000) followed by touch cues (β=.166, p<.000) as shown in table 5. The outcomes of this research were in consistency with studies conducted previously which considered sight as the dominant sensory cue when studying the impact of multiple senses on consumer behaviour (Lindstrom, 2005; Singh, 2006; Oduguwa, 2015; Geci *et al.*, 2017). Therefore, hypothesis H_2 that the sense of sight significantly dominates the other senses in the consumer decision making process was also accepted.

Table 5: Coefficients[a]

Model	Unstandardized Coefficients		Standardized Coefficients	T	Sig.	Collinearity Statistics	
	B	Std. Error	Beta			Tolerance	VIF
(Constant)	2.191	.120		18.218	.000		
Sight	**.181**	.033	.213	5.529	.000	.588	1.700
Sound	-.048	.027	-.062	-1.744	.082	.696	1.438
Smell	.076	.034	.093	2.219	.027	.494	2.023
Touch	.129	.028	.166	4.535	.000	.649	1.542
a. Dependent Variable: Purchase Intention							

Source: Data collected by researcher

The regression equation for the model is:
Purchase Intention = 1.33 + .62 (Sensory cues)

Fig. 1: *Regression equation*

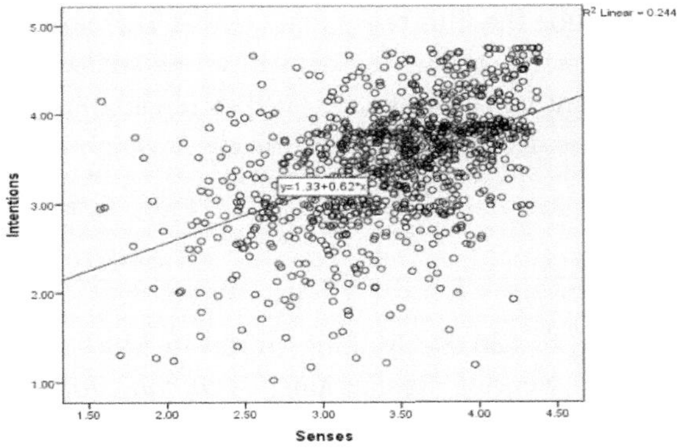

VI. CONCLUSION

The primary objective of the study was to find the impact of multisensory environmental cues on consumer behaviour. Particularly to assess the influence of multisensory cues (sight, sound, smell and touch) on consumer purchase intentions. The data collected through survey was analysed using regression analysis. The results of the study showed that there was significant impact of multisensory environmental cues on consumer behaviour. However, in case of sound cues the was non-significant in many cases. This may be due to the absence of music in some retail outlets or the music not being congruent to the type of store. Further, the most significant impact was that of sight cues. Thus, both the hypothesis of the study were accepted.

VII. IMPLICATIONS

In the times to come providing a wholesome experience to customers would be of utmost importance. Customers are attracted to a product or service if it is distinguishable from others and provides an emotionally connection. Multisensory marketing can be used by various manufacturing and service organizations to instil a sensitive appeal in their products which brings the product closer to the customer. Especially in case of organized retail outlets, the results of the study provided insight into how multisensory strategies appeal the customers. Satisfaction with products or services would lead to rebuy or repurchase and would ultimately provide loyal customers.

VIII. LIMITATIONS

1. The study was limited to organized retail outlets which usually focussed on the
2. The study focused on only four of the five senses and taste was not included as a sensory cue in this study.

IX. SCOPE FOR FUTURE RESEARCH

Since this study did not include the fifth sense that is taste. Therefore, future research can be conducted in which the impact of all the five senses can be studied. Secondly, as this study was conducted only for organized retail outlets. Further research can be conducted in other experiential or leisure industries using the same scale to check whether the results are consistent.

REFERENCES

Azeem, M. A., & Hussain, S. (2018). Making Sense in Marketing: Sensory Strategies for International Quick Service Restaurants. *Manthan: Journal of Commerce and Management, 5*(2), 37–52.

Bellizzi, J. A., & Hite, R. E. (1992). Environmental color, consumer feelings, and purchase likelihood. *Psychology & marketing, 9*(5), 347–363.

Biswas, D., Labrecque, L. I., Lehmann, D. R., & Markos, E. (2014). Making choices while smelling, tasting, and listening: The role of sensory (dis) similarity when sequentially sampling products. *Journal of Marketing, 78*(1), 112–126.

Cartwright-Finch, U., & Lavie, N. (2007). The role of perceptual load in inattentional blindness. *Cognition, 102*(3), 321–340.

de Vries, R., Jager, G., Tijssen, I., & Zandstra, E. H. (2018). Shopping for products in a virtual world: Why haptics and visuals are equally important in shaping consumer perceptions and attitudes. *Food quality and preference, 66*, 64–75.

Flavián, C., Gurrea, R., & Orús, C. (2017). The influence of online product presentation videos on persuasion and purchase channel preference: The role of imagery fluency and need for touch. *Telematics and Informatics, 34*(8), 1544–1556.

Forster, S., & Spence, C. (2018). "What smell?" Temporarily loading visual attention induces a prolonged loss of olfactory awareness. *Psychological Science.* 1–11

Géci, A., Nagyová, Ľ., & Rybanská, J. (2017). Impact of sensory marketing on consumer's buying behaviour. *Potravinarstvo Slovak Journal of Food Sciences, 11*(1), 709–117.

Hussain, R. and Ali, M. (2015). Effect of Store Atmosphere on Consumer Purchase Intention. *International Journal of Marketing Studies, 7*(2), 35–43.

Kang, E., Boger, C. A., Back, K. J., & Madera, J. (2011). The impact of sensory environments on Spagoer's emotion and behavioural intention. Retrieved 10-07-2011 from http:// scholarworks. umass. edu/cgi/viewcontent. cgi.

Krasonikolakis, I., Vrechopoulos, A., Pouloudi, A., & Dimitriadis, S. (2018). Store layout effects on consumer behavior in 3D online stores. *European Journal of Marketing, 52*(5/6), 1223–1256.

Krishna, A. (2012). An integrative review of sensory marketing: Engaging the senses to affect perception, judgment and behavior. *Journal of Consumer Psychology, 22*(3), 332–351.

Krishna, A., Cian, L., & Sokolova, T. (2016). The power of sensory marketing in advertising. *Current Opinion in Psychology, 10*, 142–147.

Lee, S., Jeong, M., & Oh, H. (2018). Enhancing customers' positive responses: Applying sensory marketing to the hotel website. *Journal of Global Scholars of Marketing Science, 28*(1), 68–85.

Lin, M. H., Cross, S. N., Laczniak, R. N., & Childers, T. L. (2018). The Sniffing Effect: Olfactory Sensitivity and Olfactory Imagery in Advertising. *Journal of Advertising, 47*(2), 97–111.

Lindstrom, M. (2005). Broad sensory branding. *Journal of Product & Brand Management, 14*(2), 84 – 87.

Lowe, M. L., Loveland, K. E., & Krishna, A. (2019). A quiet disquiet: Anxiety and risk avoidance due to nonconscious auditory priming. *Journal of Consumer Research, 46*(1), 159–179.

McGrath, M. C., Aronow, P. M., & Shotwell, V. (2016). Chocolate scents and product sales: a randomized controlled trial in a Canadian bookstore and café. *SpringerPlus, 5*(1), 670–675.

Motoki, K., Saito, T., Nouchi, R., Kawashima, R., & Sugiura, M. (2019). Light colours and comfortable warmth: Crossmodal correspondences between thermal sensations and colour lightness influence consumer behavior. *Food quality and preference, 72*, 45–55.

Oduguwa, E. (2015). *How Taste and Sight Impact Brand Loyalty in Sensory Marketing.* Undergraduate Student Research Awards.

Peck, J., and Childers, T.L. (2003). Individual Differences in Haptic Information Processing: The "Need for Touch" Scale. *Journal of Consumer Research, 30*, 430–442.

Rodas-Areiza, J. A., & Montoya-Restrepo, L. A. (2018). Methodological proposal for the analysis and measurement of sensory marketing integrated to the consumer experience. *Dyna, 85*(207), 54–59.

Sahi, G. K., Sekhon, H. S., & Quareshi, T. K. (2016). Role of trusting beliefs in predicting purchase intentions. *International Journal of Retail & Distribution Management, 44*(8), 860–880.

Santos, V., Caldeira, A., Santos, E., Oliveira, S., & Ramos, P. (2019). Wine Tourism Experience in the Tejo Region: The influence of sensory impressions on post-visit behaviour intentions. *International Journal of Marketing, Communication and New Media,* (5), 54–75.

Shabgou, M., & Daryani, S. M. (2014). Towards the sensory marketing: stimulating the five senses (sight, hearing, smell, touch and taste) and its impact on consumer behavior. *Indian Journal of Fundamental and Applied Life Sciences*, *4*(S1), 573–581.

Singh, S. (2006). Impact of color on marketing. *Management Decision, 44* (6), 783–789.

Vega-Gómez, F. I., Miranda-Gonzalez, F. J., Mayo, J. P., González López, O., & Pascual-Nebreda, L. (2020). The Scent of Art. Perception, Evaluation, and Behaviour in a Museum in Response to Olfactory Marketing. *Sustainability, 12*(4), 1384.

CHAPTER 8

Effect of CRM on Customer Satisfaction in The Insurance Sector

Dr. Bhavneet Kaur
Professor
JIMS Rohini
Delhi, India
bhavneet007@gmail.com

Ms. Anuradha Jain
Research scholar
JIMS Rohini
Delhi, India
anu_jain1993@yahoo.in

Mr. Mohit Chadha
Student
JIMS Rohini
Delhi, India
chadhamohit2@gmail.com

Abstract

Constant changes in the economic and financial landscape, the emergence of new technologies, and furling competition in the market have been a few compelling factors owing to which the insurance sector has progressed its approach towards attending customers. The sector has been investing in its technology infrastructure to engage the customers as well as to serve them in a superior manner. This paper aims to understand the dynamics between customer relationship management (CRM) and customer satisfaction with the insurance providing companies in the Delhi region. Paper proposes strategies for insurance companies to improve overall customer satisfaction. Both primary and secondary data sources were harnessed. The questionnaire was used for collection of data. First part of the questionnaire related to demographic variables of the respondents while the second part of the questionnaire explored the relationship between variables of CRM and customer satisfaction. A random sample of more than 180 insurance policyholders in Delhi was taken for survey through google forms. The data was analyzed for 150 fully completed questionnaires through various descriptive and inferential statistical tools such as ANOVA, correlation, and multiple regression analysis. According to this study, employee interface, service quality, and quality of infrastructure were found to be the significant contributors to overall customer satisfaction.

Keywords: CRM, Insurance industry, Customer Centricity, Marketing Strategies, etc.

INTRODUCTION

In today's time, customer retention is economical than working on acquiring new customers. Lindgreen *et al.* (2000) computed "it can be up to 10 times expensive to win a customer than to retain a customer." Many researchers also agree upon the fact that customer retention brings numerous economic benefits (Reichheld, 1996). One of the major tools which aims at retaining customers is customer relationship management (CRM). CRM refers to a bundle of techniques, methodologies & approaches that help businesses manage customer relationships in a planned way (Arman, 2009). Corporate sector has been relying on this business strategy to pick and manage customers to optimize their long-term value (Greenleaf and Winer, 2002). Insurance industry has also adopted and adapted to this approach for achieving customer centricity. Presently, the relationships of the insurance companies with their customers have undergone a paradigm shift. Private companies in the industry are challenging each other to provide superior services to their customers. CRM factors have been found to have a direct relation with the increase in demand for insurance products such as life insurance policies (Moradi, 2017). Hence, there is a need to develop CRM processes to attract and maintain customers.

The paper is organized as follows: The section- insurance industry in India, gives insights into the context of the paper. Literature review section gives an account of the previous studies made in the chosen arena. This section in followed by research gap, research objectives and methodology sections, which detail the rigour of the research. Next section is focused on the results from data analysis. The implications and conclusion sections establish the importance of the findings and give practical suggestions for the insurance industry.

Insurance industry in India

The Parliament of India passed the Life Insurance Corporation Act on 18th June 1956 and the Life Insurance Corporation of India was born on 1st September, 1956. The aim was to provide insurance at a reasonable cost especially in rural areas. Private investment was allowed in 1999. Since then, the competition in the market for insurance has been heating up with number of products, newer ways of distribution and plethora of players coming to the market. Some of them are- MAX, ICICI, Bajaj, Tata, Kodak, HDFC, Reliance, Aditya Birla, Aviva, Edelweiss Tokio etc.

Use of digital platforms has also helped in increasing the demand for insurance products. However, the huge portion of the market is untapped and represents a marketing opportunity for insurance services. According to a report by IBEF (2020), overall insurance penetration in India was 3.69 percent in 2017. The report also highlights that IRDAI is authorized to frame regulations as per the insurance bill. Buyers are attracted to invest in the insurance related products due to the fact that there are a number of tax incentives associated with them. 100 percent FDI is permitted for insurance intermediaries. The sector is expected to grow further due to changes in regulations, demographics, growing awareness for insurance products, further differentiation of services and surging investments in the sector. Thus, the knowledge and implementation of CRM practices, with an objective to acquire, sustain and retain customers, has become the need of the hour for insurance industry. However, due to the fact that the insurance products are highly differentiated with each category of products having unique characteristics, the implementation of CRM process has proved to be complex (Matis and Ilies, 2014). This paper explores the specifics of CRM in Indian insurance industry and its impact on customer satisfaction.

LITERATURE REVIEW

The literature review was carried out to identify the factors, which could broadly but conclusively be attributed to CRM. One of the important studies confirmed that satisfaction is positively related to customers repurchase intentions (Durvasula *et al.* 2004). They emphasized that the factors like word of mouth have significant impact on customer's purchase decisions. Khare (2008) explored how customer relations could be managed using CRM technology in India's financial sector by the usage of tools. Previous studies were analyzed to highlight the changes that emerged in their business processes for providing better value to the customer. The result depicted CRM as a facilitating technology rather a strategy that would enhance the productivity of the banks in India. The paper also pointed to the fact that in order to meet international standards, the industry has a long way to go. Chen and Mua (2009) emphasized that the customer trust in the company carries more weight and has more influence on customer loyalty as compared to their confidence in the salespersons. Hence, the Life insurance industry must invest in building a trustworthy brand. CRM in some selected insurance firms in Nigeria was studied by Oghojafor *et al.* (2011). Findings show that while most companies have a comprehensive database of their customers, not all make provisions for their customers to carry out major transactions online because they need not fully integrate their CRM with information technology. They further emphasized that the organization's profitability was enhanced by combining CRM with information technology through improved customer service.

The difference in the customers' expectations and perceptions from insurance services as a cause of dissatisfaction was pinpointed by Gulati *et al.* (2012). The study was focused on -CRM in Indian insurance industry. Gap analysis and t-test were used to draw conclusions. Isimoya *et al.* (2013) recommended that the management of an insurance company should empower the employees, focus on staff retention and imbibe values like loyalty and commitment. The paper also highlighted the importance of competency of staff and the ability of employees to communicate well with clients.

A study by Ramamoorthy *et al.* (2016) on Service quality and its impact on customer's behavioral intentions and satisfaction was carried out in context of Indian life insurance sector. A modified SERVQUAL instrument, exploratory factor analysis and Structural equation modeling were used. According to this study, reliable and responsive customer support were found to have a big impact on the satisfaction of the customer and his behavioral intentions. A comparative study on the CRM initiatives across retail, telecommunication, banking, and life insurance industry was carried out by Mujawar and Bodade (2016). The findings of the study revealed that the retail industry had the highest customer satisfaction. The lowest rate for satisfaction was observed for banking industry. It also isolated the fact that the life insurance industry has to deal with the high expectations of the customer. A study by Shanmugasundaram and Srilekha (2017) studied CRM in insurance sector using secondary sources like books, journals, reports, etc. They exposed that the importance of CRM should be known to company using it and suggested that the e-CRM implementation can save time and cost for the insurance players. The study on the factors affecting the successful implementation of CRM in the general insurance sector of Jammu city was conducted by Abrol (2017). Findings of this paper suggested that the effective implementation of CRM was significantly and positively influenced by customer satisfaction, trust, service quality, communication & knowledge. Harisha and Sulochna (2020) used regression test and descriptive statistics to analyze the responses collected through a questionnaire in a selected securities company. The results of the study indicated that in services industry, CRM practices help in retaining customers. Reddy (2020) studied customer retention with

CRM in the insurance sector in India. The survey of 35 insurance companies concluded that CRM and customer retention have a positive relationship. Study by Chang and Lee (2020) revealed that insurance service innovation is significant for generating word of mouth and behavioral intention in context of Taiwanese insurance sector.

RESEARCH GAP

There is abundant literature which enumerates the relationship between CRM and Customer satisfaction and explores their relationship in insurance sector also. Nevertheless, there are limited studies that have been carried out in the insurance sector examining the relationship between CRM and customer satisfaction in Delhi. Thus, there is a research gap which this paper proposes to address. Further, the present study attempts to recommend marketing strategies that improve CRM and customer satisfaction in the insurance sector in the chosen geographical area. Hence, this paper uses the data and information obtained through the study of various insurance companies in Delhi to build a complete prescriptive framework.

RESEARCH OBJECTIVE

This paper aims to analyze the satisfaction level of customers in insurance industry on several dimensions of CRM like- Quality of infrastructure provided by the insurance sector, Technology used, employee interface and service quality. The paper endeavored to identify the relationship between these dimensions and overall customer satisfaction with insurance services in Delhi.

RESEARCH METHODOLOGY

The present work is built on comparative and analytical data based on the perception of customers. Primary data was collected through a structured questionnaire. The research is exploratory as the secondary data along with brainstorming; advice of the experts and observation were used to draft a questionnaire. It consisted of 34 statements mapped on a 5-point likert scale. 150 questionnaires were obtained and used for data analysis. The reliability of the scale was checked by Cronbach's alpha and a very high overall reliability (0.903) was observed. KMO test results (.837) confirmed the sampling adequacy of data that was to be used for factor analysis. Factor analysis was carried out and factors were suitably grouped to compute/create new variables. The appropriate descriptive and inferential statistical tools like- t-test, ANOVA, Correlation, and Multiple Regression Analysis were used for examining data and achieving the objective mentioned above.

RESULTS - DESCRIPTIVE ANALYSIS

Statistics in Table 1 indicate that the employee interface dimension was more appealing and drives customer satisfaction more with a high construct mean score. Employee interface construct was a superset consisting of knowledge of employees, clarity of information provided by them, timeliness of the transactions done by them, confidentiality of those transactions, availability of employees and equal treatment provided by them to the customer categories. A higher mean score for this construct depicts that the customers are feeling satisfied with the employee behavior which is one of the critical factors for the success of an organization. Previous researches also support the fact that the expanding role of salespeople is necessary for successful implementation of CRM (Frederick Hong-kit, 2004)

TABLE 1: MEAN VALUE FOR VARIABLES

	N	Minimum	Maximum	Mean	Std. Deviation
Employee Interface	150	1.00	3.71	2.0648	.47872
CRM Technology	150	1.00	3.75	1.8517	.51740
Service Quality	150	1.00	3.33	1.8700	.44866
Quality of Infrastructure	150	1.00	4.20	1.8347	.55017
Valid N (listwise)	150				

Source : Author's data analysis

Demographic analysis- This section examines the relationship between the various demographics variables like gender, age and monthly income on the overall customer satisfaction.

Impact of Gender - The t-test results shown in Table 2 indicate that there are no significant differences between male and female respondents with regards to the various dimensions of CRM.

TABLE 2: T-TEST FOR TESTING THE IMPACT OF GENDER

		Levene's Test for Equality of Variances				
		F	Sig.	T	Df	Sig. (2-tailed)
Employee Interface	Equal variances assumed	1.093	.297	1.056	148	.293
	Equal variances not assumed			1.060	147.921	.291
CRM Technology	Equal variances assumed	.304	.582	.574	148	.567
	Equal variances not assumed			.570	141.358	.569
Service Quality	Equal variances assumed	1.805	.181	.111	148	.911
	Equal variances not assumed			.112	147.840	.911

Quality of Infrastructure	Equal variances assumed	.190	.664	.919	148	.359
	Equal variances not assumed			.920	147.451	.359
Overall Customer Satisfaction	Equal variances assumed	.022	.881	1.367	148	.174
	Equal variances not assumed			1.374	147.861	.172

Source : Author's data analysis

Impact of Age- The one-way ANOVA results shown in Table 3 indicate that there are significant differences between the customers of various age groups with regards to *CRM technology, quality of infrastructure, and service quality.* Thus, different age groups were found to have different expectations with regards to these CRM dimensions.

TABLE 3: ANOVA FOR TESTING THE IMPACT OF AGE

		Sum of Squares	df	Mean Square	F	Sig.
Employee Interface	Between Groups	.394	2	.197	.853	.428
	Within Groups	33.748	146	.231		
	Total	34.142	148			
CRM Technology	Between Groups	1.955	2	.977	3.763	.025
	Within Groups	37.922	146	.260		
	Total	39.877	148			
Service Quality	Between Groups	1.192	2	.596	3.022	.052
	Within Groups	28.799	146	.197		
	Total	29.991	148			
Quality of Infrastructure	Between Groups	2.627	2	1.313	4.520	.012
	Within Groups	42.418	146	.291		
	Total	45.044	148			
Overall Customer Satisfaction	Between Groups	.268	2	.134	.568	.568
	Within Groups	34.522	146	.236		
	Total	34.790	148			

Source : Author's data analysis

Impact of monthly income- According to the table 4, there is no significant difference between groups as demonstrated by one-way ANOVA (the value for F is more than 0.05).

However, the dependent variable of overall customer satisfaction is found to be statistically significant when the customers were grouped on basis of their monthly income.

TABLE 4: ANOVA FOR TESTING THE IMPACT OF MONTHLY INCOME

		Sum of Squares	df	Mean Square	F	Sig.
Employee Interface	Between Groups	1.368	4	.342	1.513	.201
	Within Groups	32.778	145	.226		
	Total	34.146	149			
CRM Technology	Between Groups	1.031	4	.258	.962	.431
	Within Groups	38.856	145	.268		
	Total	39.887	149			
Service Quality	Between Groups	.290	4	.073	.354	.841
	Within Groups	29.702	145	.205		
	Total	29.993	149			
Quality of Infrastructure	Between Groups	1.836	4	.459	1.538	.194
	Within Groups	43.264	145	.298		
	Total	45.100	149			
Overall Customer Satisfaction	Between Groups	2.615	4	.654	2.932	.023
	Within Groups	32.327	145	.223		
	Total	34.942	149			

Source : Author's data analysis

Correlation Analysis and Multiple Regression Analysis

Pearson's correlation was used to examine the relationship between the CRM factors and overall Customer Satisfaction. Correlation results as shown in Table-5 indicate that all the four CRM factors (independent variables) had significant positive association with overall customer satisfaction (dependent variable). This suggested that as the level of satisfaction on each of the CRM factors increases, the overall customer satisfaction increases. Thus, the correlations amongst the CRM factors and overall customer satisfaction are in congruence with the findings of previous research studies. Further, the correlation coefficients between all the independent variables (i.e., CRM factors) were less than 0.9. This reflects that the data was free of the co-linearity problem. But, due to the fact that the correlation analysis does not give information about the cause-and-effect relationship between the variables, Multiple regression was carried out.

TABLE 5: CORRELATION BETWEEN CRM FACTORS AND OVERALL CUSTOMER SATISFACTION

Variables	Employee Interface	CRM Technology	Service Quality	Quality Of Infrastructure	Overall Satisfaction
Employee Interface	1				
CRM Technology	.489**	1			
Service Quality	.401**	.578**	1		
Quality Of Infrastructure	.445**	.622**	.588**	1	
Overall customer Satisfaction	.422**	.442**	.519**	.527**	1

Source : Author's data analysis

To determine the overall model fit, Regression Analysis was carried out. Table 6, table 7 and table 8, depict the results of regression analysis. The regression results show that the model under study is significant. The ability of the independent variables to explain the dependent variable- overall customer satisfaction is 37.2%. All the variables considered in the paper collectively cause 37.2% variation in overall customer satisfaction. Nevertheless, the variables –employee interface, service quality, and quality of infrastructure are significant contributors to the regression model. This shows that improving upon these dimensions of CRM in insurance sector would significantly add up to the level of customer satisfaction. The association between the employee interface and customer satisfaction was found to be statistically significant with a p-value of 0.022 and a beta value of 0.181. This was interpreted to mean that customer satisfaction can be enhanced by 18% through focusing on employee interface. Previous studies suggested that customer satisfaction is often related to the employee attitudes and behavior (Alshurideh, 2017; Alshurideh, 2016a; Schmit & Allscheid, 1995). Customer satisfaction was found to have a causal relationship with employee interface.

The service quality dimension recorded a beta coefficient of 0.294 a p-value of 0.002. This means that consumer experience of the service quality (CRM dimension) explains customer satisfaction by 29%. The results were aligned with Ramamoorthy et al. (2016); Sadiartha & Apsari (2018), who found out that the dimensions of service quality, namely reliability and responsiveness, have a significant effect on customer satisfaction in the life insurance industry in India. Marcos and Coelho (2017) found significant positive relationship between service quality on customer loyalty in the insurance industry in Portugal.

The quality of infrastructure dimension of CRM had a beta value of 0.237, and a p-value of 0.004. The study thus notes that the quality of infrastructure explains customer satisfaction by 23%. Quality of infrastructure in this study refers to the physical aspects of the insurance facility including its size, cleanliness, availability of basic amenities like washrooms, drinking water facility and availability of parking spaces. Gogoi, 2020 enhances the study findings by signifying that quality of infrastructure plays an important role for customer satisfaction. The study was done in context of tourism industry. It pinpointed that a location which is attractive, has a clean image and is supported with reliable services, makes the traveler comfortable.

TABLE 6: REGRESSION ANALYSIS: MODEL SUMMARY

Model	R	R square	Adjusted R Square	Standard error of the estimate
1	.610[a]	.372	.354	.38911
a. Predictors:(Constant), Quality of Infrastructure, Employee Interface, Service Quality, CRM Technology				

Source : Author's data analysis

TABLE 7: REGRESSION TABLE

Model		Sum of Squares	df	Mean Square	F	Sig.
1	Regression	12.989	4	3.247	21.447	.000[b]
	Residual	21.953	145	.151		
	Total	34.942	149			
a. Dependent Variable: Overall Satisfaction, b. Predictors: (Constant), Quality of Infrastructure, Employee Interface, Service Quality, CRM Technology						

Source : Author's data analysis

TABLE 8 : REGRESSION RESULT-COEFFICIENTS

Model		Unstandardized Coefficients		Standardized Coefficients	t	Sig.
		B	Std. Error	Beta		
1	(Constant)	.453	.165		2.737	.007
	Employee Interface	.181	.078	.179	2.312	.022
	CRM Technology	.028	.086	.029	.319	.750
	Service Quality	.294	.094	.272	3.135	.002
	Quality of Infrastructure	.237	.080	.269	2.952	.004
a. Dependent Variable: Overall Satisfaction						

Source : Author's data analysis

IMPLICATIONS

The results of demographic analysis depicted that the satisfaction with some of the CRM dimensions varied across customers belonging to the different age groups. The relationship between the demographic variables and service quality expectation were well documented in earlier studies as well (Gagliano and Hathcote, 1994; Thompson and Kaminski, 1993). According to the study by Alinvi and Babri (2007), financial industry precisely focuses upon the young customer segment. Though targeting a specific age group is a strategic decision but understanding the perspective across various customer age groups is a significant approach to improve customer satisfaction. This guideline must be conscientiously and extensively followed in the case of insurance sector as well.

As the statistics in the study advocate, insurance industry is urged to work on the employee interface dimensions including their knowledge, communication and serviceability. The insurance provider must train the front-line employees so that they can conduct meaningful customer interaction across all the touch points and enhance customer satisfaction. In the present scenario of hyper-competition, quality of services provided by company has become a key success factor. The ultimate goal of all service-oriented organizations is to provide quality service, which in turn augments the organizational performance (Pulidindi and Aswini, 2015). Therefore, the aspects of service quality namely adequacy of the information provided, accessibility through various platforms, promptness in rectification of customer complaints etc must be paid due attention. Nevertheless, the importance of maintaining state of art physical infrastructure cannot be undermined with the insurance facility providing adequate parking and clean / hygienic utilities.

CONCLUSION

The study elucidates that the CRM dimensions considered in this paper (employee interface, service quality, CRM technology and quality of Infrastructure) explain customer satisfaction by 37.2%. Theoretically, the findings of the paper add to the existing strand of literature on CRM and customer satisfaction. On the practical front, the results of the study prescribe the guidelines for the insurance sector to improve customer satisfaction as the paper identifies the significant parameters of CRM.

REFERENCES

1. Abrol, D. (2017). Exploring the factors affecting the successful implementation of customer relationship management in insurance sector. *International Journal on Customer Relations, 5*(1), 37-44.
2. Alinvi, F. & Babr i, M. (2007). Customers' preferences of insurance services. Bachelor thesis, international business program.
3. Ammari,G., Al kurdi,B., Alshurideh,M., & Alrowwad, A.(2017).Investigating the impact of communication satisfaction on organizational commitment: a practical approach to increase employees' loyalty. *International Journal of Marketing Studies, 9*(2), 113–133.
4. Arman,S.M.(2014).Integrated model of social media and customer relationship management: a literature review. *International Journal of Information, Business and Management, 6*(3),118.
5. Alshurideh, M. T. (2016). Exploring the main factors affecting consumer choice of mobile phone service provider contracts. *International Journal of Communications, Network and System Sciences, 9*(12), 563–581.
6. Chang,J.-I. & Lee, C.-Y.(2020).The effect of service innovation on customer behavioral intention in the Taiwanese insurance sector: the role of word of mouth and corporate social responsibility. *Journal of Asia Business Studies, 14*(3), 341-360.
7. Chen, M. F.& Mau, L. H. (2007). The impacts of ethical sales behavior on customer loyalty in the life insurance industry. *The Services Industries Journal, 29*, 59-74.

8. Durvasula, S., Lysonski, S., Mehta, S. C., & Tang, B. P. (2004). Forging relationships with services: the antecedents that have an impact on behavioral outcomes in the life insurance industry. *Journal of Financial Services Marketing ,8* (4), 314-326.

9. India Brand Equity Foundation. (2021, June 9). Indian insurance industry overview & market development analysis. https://www.ibef.org/industry/insurance-sector-india. aspx

10. Isimoya, A. O., & Bakarey, B. E. (2013). Employees' empowerment and customers' satisfaction in insurance industry in Nigeria. *Australian Journal of Business and Management Research, 3*(5), 1-11.

1. Frederick, H. Y., Rolph, E. A. & Srinivasan, S. (2004). Customer relationship management: its dimensions and effect on customer outcomes. *Journal of Personal Selling & Sales Management, 24*(4), 263-278.

2. Greenleaf, E. & Winer, S. R. (2002). Special Session Summary Putting the Customer Back into Customer Relationship Management (CRM). *Advances in Consumer Research, 29*, 357-360.

3. Gulati,K.& Ravi,V.(2012).E-CRM and customer satisfaction in Indian insurance industry. *Asian Journal of Business and Economics, 2*, (2.3), 1-13.

4. Gagliano, K. G. & Hathcote, J. (1994). Customer expectations and perceptions of service quality in retail apparel specialty stores. *Journal of Services Marketing, 8*(1), 60-69.

5. Gogoi, B. J. (2020). Service quality measures: how it impacts customer satisfaction and loyalty. *International Journal of Management, 11*(3), 354–365.

6. Harisha, B.& Sulochana, N. M. (2020). A study on customer retention strategies through CRM at selected securities company. *Mukt Shabd, 9*(8), 1451-1453.

7. Khare, C. P. (2008). *Indian medicinal plants: an illustrated dictionary.* Springer Science & Business Media.

8. Lindgreen, A., Davis, R., Brodie, R.J. & Oliver, B. M. (2000). Pluralism in contemporary marketing practices. *International Journal of Bank Marketing, 18*(6), 294-308.

9. Marcos, A., & Coelho, A. (2017). Antecedents and consequences of perceived value in the insurance industry. *European Journal of applied Business and Management, 3*(2),29-51.

10. Matia C.& Ilies L. (2014). Customer relationship management in the insurance industry. *Procedia Economics and Finance,15*, 1138 – 1145.

11. Mujawar, S., & Bodade,P. (2016).Comparative study of crm initiatives in retail, telecommunication, banking and life insurance industry: a customer perspective. *International Journal of Research and Scientific Innovation, 3*(4), 52-59.

12. Oghojafor. B. E. A, Aduloju. S. A. & Olowokudeojo, F (2011). Information technology and customer relationship management (CRM) in some selected insurance firms in Nigeria. *Journal of Economics and International Finance, 3*(7), 452-461.

13. Ramamoorthy, R., Gunasekaran, R. M., Rai, K. B.& Kumar, S.A. (2016). Service quality and its impact on customers' behavioral intentions and satisfaction: an empirical study of the Indian life insurance sector. *Total Quality Management & Business Excellence, 29*(7-8), 834-847.

14. Reichheld, F. F. (1996). The loyalty effect: the hidden force behind growth, profits and lasting value. *Harvard Business School Press, 37*, 1-323.

15. Reddy (2020). Review on customer retention with customer relationship management in insurance sector in India. *Mukt Shabd, 9*(6), 6394-6401.

16. Shanmugasundaram, A. & Srilekha, K. S. (2017). Customer relationship management in insurance sector. *Journal of Business and Management, 19*, (6(II)), 31-35.

1. Sadiartha, A. A. N. G. & Apsari, G. A. M. (2018). Role of satisfaction in mediating the effect of services quality on the customers' loyalty in the village credit institutions of Pekraman, Indonesia. *Journal of Business and Social review in emerging Economies, 4*(2), 147-162.

2. Schmit, M. J. & Allscheid, S. P. (1995). Employee attitudes and customer satisfaction: Making theoretical and empirical connections. *Personnel Psychology, 48*(3), 521–536.

3. Thompson, A. M. & Kaminski, P. F. (1993). Psychographic and lifestyle antecedents of service quality expectations: a segmentation approach. *Journal of Services Marketing, 7*(4), 53-61.

4. Venugopal, P. & Aswini S.P. (2019). The perceptual differences of hospital employees on the use and adoption of electronic health records and telemedicine. *Journal of Testing and Evaluation, 47*(6), 4177-4191.

CHAPTER 9

Post COVID-19: The Change in Consumer Behavior and Implications to Retailers

Dr. Biranchi Narayan Swar
Professor-Marketing
Management Development Institute
(MDI), Murshidabad
West Bengal
drbiranchi.marketing@gmail.com

Abstract

The study of consumer behaviour plays a critical role for any marketers. Better understanding of consumer behaviour provides a competitive edge. The coronavirus pandemic has completely changed the consumer behaviour all over the world. So, the main objectives of this study are to understand about corona pandemic and its impact on consumer behaviour. The study explored the changes in consumer behaviour during the corona pandemic. The data was collected through telephonic interviews, online focus group discussions (FGDs) and secondary sources of data like internet and online data bases. The study have identified and summarized the changes in consumer behaviour during the pandemic. We have identified few changes in consumer behaviour due to this pandemic. The marketers can revisit their strategies to reach their customers during this pandemic. They can emphasize on the recommendations given in this study. The study has provided a unique contribution by understanding the shift in consumer behaviour during pandemic. This study provides valuable consumer insight during Covid 19 pandemic. The learning from this study can be used in other countries for marketing and reaching their customers and understand the shift in consumer behaviour.

Keywords: Covid 19, Consumer behavior, Retailers, Lockdown, Social distancing.

INTRODUCTION

Owing to the huge population of India, the country has a very huge demand of retail products and services. As such, the Indian Retail sector is among the largest sectors in the country and contributes to around 10% of the country's GDP (Gross Domestic Product) while providing employment to around 8% of the country's population. Price Waterhouse Coopers (pwc) India suggested that the cumulative annual growth rate of the retail sector is around 11-15%. This steady increase in the retail sector can be directly co-related with the growing middle-class population. Globally, it is seen that with an increase in disposable income, as a country's population goes through a positive economic change (i.e. lifting of lower class and lower middle class to middle class and upper middle class), the spending on retail products and services increases.

The nCovid'19 (SARS 2) virus pandemic came in unannounced at the later end of the year 2019 and slowly crept in to the lime light in the first half of 2020. The crisis gave very little time for businesses and industries to cope up with and due to which most sectors faced a negative financial position. The virus coupled with the government's measures to mitigate the crisis inadvertently led to a complete lockdown of the country. This saw the economy taking a downward slump and an already slow growing GDP of the country took a negative turn of around -20%. Like most industries, the retail industry also took a huge hit and is now trying to make a recovery at the end of this year. The combined factors of a growing retail sector and a post lockdown economy have led the consumers to have a different view point and behavior regarding expenditure and spending on the retail service sector. The new normal with face-masks, sanitizers and social distancing is proving to be a huge adaptation challenge for both the consumers as well as employees.

Some retail sectors are yet out of business as lockdown norms prevent opening of service providers like cinema halls. The health and fitness service sectors are open with limited capacities and restaurants are opened for dine out or less capacity to ensure meeting all the governmental procedures and regulations designed for the mitigation of the disease. Similar problems are faced by the travel and hospitability service sectors as well. Due to the reasons mentioned above it is imperative to know the shift or change in consumer behavior towards the retail sector. Having access to this knowledge will allow the service providers to better equip themselves to the new times. Knowing what is expected by the consumers will allow the businesses to better cater to their needs and demand. Thereby, focusing efforts towards the essentials and removing focus from things rendered obsolete or deemed unsafe. A simple example would be the knowledge of higher takeout sales post covid would lead a restaurant owner to increase kitchen space compared to dine in space. Therefore, the research tries to identify the various changes in consumer behavior and implications to retailers.

CONCEPTUAL FRAMEWORK

Retail: The word retail can be defined as the nuances and processes that constitute of selling consumer products or services to customers to earn revenues and skim profits. The choice of distribution used is up to the retail provider.

Retailers: A retailer is defined as a service provider who facilitates the customers by providing products and services in small quantities as per their requirements. Generally, the retailer provides the products to the customer nearby their door steps.

Retail Services: The host of services that are offered for an end user to pay for and consume can be termed as retail services. Examples can range from Restaurants, Delivery Services, Customer Care Services, Travel and Transportation Services, Hospitality services and Legal Services etc.

Consumer Behavior: Consumer Behavior, often abbreviated as CB, can be defined as the field of study comprising of researching individuals, groups or organizations in respect to the fundamental activities related with the purchase of, use of and finally the disposal of goods and services. It also tries to associate these with the consumer's emotions, attitudes and preferences that has a profound effect on buying behavior.

Consumers buying behavior is influenced by so many factors. Some of these factors are learning, reference groups, values, lifestyle, perception, quality, price and features etc. Generally when a consumer goes to a salesman to buy product or services, the salesman or service provider shows the products/services which are available with them or show the catalogue or brochures. If the customer likes any of the products/services then they take a decision to buy the product. But, today's scenario is quite different, as the consumer uses internet to search, evaluate (by comparing products), which enables them to make a purchase decision.

nCovid'19 (SARS 2): This is the newest strain of Corona Virus detected in the later part of the year 2019. "n" stands for novel referring to the uniqueness of the strain, "Covid" stands for Corona Virus Disease which has flu like symptoms paired with difficulty in breathing, "SARS" stand for Severe Acute Respiratory Syndrome and the number 2 represents the second time such a virus affected humanity. The first SARS outbreak was in 2002 believed to have been originated in Guangdong province of China. This is the virus causing the current global pandemic.

Pandemic: A pandemic is defined as a disease, symptom or complications affecting an organism (mainly humans) prevalent over a huge geographic area. Generally, the World Health Organization (WHO) declares a disease to be pandemic, if the outbreak of the disease is too fast for containment leading to the disease affecting the whole globe. Contrary to popular belief, humanity has faced 2 pandemics in recent times not counting the current one. The MERS and SARS outbreaks were both deemed to be pandemics. However, due to increased connectivity and globalization, the most recent pandemic has encompassed the globe more severely and affected a greater number of people than ever before.

Lockdown: It can be defined as a measure adopted in order to isolate a group of population. Generally, lockdowns are confinement measures and the term is closely related to prisoners and prisons. However, since the current Corona Virus Pandemic is highly communicable, the government has used this measure on a very large scale by preventing opening of all services, except essential services (like Medical, Police and Banking services) and enforcing strict regulations to penalize violators. This step is taken globally to reduce the growth and spread of the disease.

REVIEW OF LITERATURE

Corona pandemic has shaken up the economy and consumer behavior. As a result, both the public and private sectors are affected very badly. The product market will also be affected but consumable products are mostly categorized as essential leading to their sales despite the economic slow-down. Adding to this the lockdown restrictions meant no operation of services such as shopping malls, movie theaters, gyms and fitness centers and restaurants etc. In short, all non-essential services are stopped leading to huge losses in the sector and ultimately leading to pay cuts and job cuts.

To understand the impact of pandemic on the economy, consumer behavior and it's business implications, the research has conducted an in-depth literature review as follows:-

Chaudhary, M., Sodani, P. R., and Das, S. (2020) stated that despite the prevalent fears of job losses, loss in daily ration and absence of a proper structured social security net, the country should think on this unique development paradigm. nCoVid'19 has also provided some exciting opportunities to the nation. Since there is a growing distrust and negative sentiments towards China, there is a huge opportunity to participate in global supply chains. The '*Make in India*' campaign can spear head this effort. Since, there is no purely product-based industry; increasing production of any sector will inadvertently lead to an increase in employment for even the services sector. Another research conducted by Debdas Rakshit and Ananya Paul (2020), found that the pandemic revealed various pain points and weaknesses in Indian Business Survival Strategies. The paper pointed out the lack of reserved funds and capital in small and medium sized businesses leading to incurring heavy losses. Some businesses also went bankrupt and had to stop operation thus leading to a total job loss of all people involved with the operation.

Naeem, M. (2020) collected data from 40 UK consumers through telephonic interview to explore consumer psychology towards impulse buying behavior during COVID-19 pandemic. The study concluded that fear of illness, fear of empty shelves, fear of price rise and staying at home, increased the possibility of consumer' impulsive buying behavior. Mele, C., Russo-Spena, T. and Kaartemo, V. (2020) found that 'essential service provision' and 'responsible shopping practices' were the two major impacts on the business due to coronavirus pandemic. Bove, L.L. and Benoit, S. (2020) confirmed that safety measures provided by the service providers to their consumers will minimize the risk of infection while exchanging the services.

Anastasiadou, E., Chrissos Anestis, M., Karantza, I. and Vlachakis, S. (2020) compared Greece and Sweden to find out the changes in retail consumer behaviour due to the coronavirus. They concluded that in both the countries the retail consumer behaviour were different due to different in mentalities and motives. Chuang, Y., and Tai, Y. (2016) revealed that the benefits in switching costs and availability of attractive alternatives was the most commonly used predictors to explain shifting intentions in consumer behavior. The study was pre-pandemic but it already showed that customers are very fickle minded when choosing services. Consumers may have a favorite brand of toothpaste but are most likely to be neutral in terms of choosing a fast food restaurant. This can be because all fast food chains are cheap and satisfy the cravings. Leila Haghshenas, Afshin Abedi, Esmail Ghorbani, Abbas Kamali, and Mohammad naser Harooni (2013) stated that consumer behavior is a very challenging topic which includes how, what and why consumer buy or not buy something. Consumer behavior is a totality of psychology, anthropology, economics and sociology and tries to understand the buyers decision-making process related to both individual and group.

Consumer decision-making is one of the most critical areas in consumer behavior (Bettman, Luce, and Payne 1998; Simonson et al. 2001; Bargh 2002). Finally, the 3-stages model of service consumption (Tsiotsou, R. H., & Wirtz, J., 2012) such as the pre- purchase stage, the service encounter stage and the post-encounter stage. Thus, by identifying various factors the retailers can formulate the strategies to target the consumers at the various stages of their decision-making process.

Objective of the Research

1. To understand the changes in consumer behavior during post COVID 19 and its implications to Retailers.

METHODOLOGY

The study has used both primary and secondary sources of data. The method used for the data collection was telephonic interviews, online focus group discussions and other secondary sources of data like internet and online data bases. Apart from this, the research has also used newspapers, books and recently published company or research agencies reports related to COVID 19.

FINDINGS

Mckinsey & Co recently conducted a survey in 12 countries and found that 91 per cent Indians changed their shopping behavior due to this pandemic. After analyzing various sources of data, the paper has arrived at the following findings with respect to the shift in consumer behavior:-

1. Spending patterns: Particularly for emergency pantry items and health supplies.
2. More demand for packaged goods.
3. Changes in discretionary income and spare time, and reconsidered values and priorities of the consumer.
4. There has been a decrease in amount spent on services by consumers post-covid.
5. Social distancing is the need of the hour for businesses. Consumers try to avoid coming in contact with others, thus businesses should ensure social distancing norms are followed and other safety protocols are maintained.
6. There is huge surge in demand for health consultations services post covid as consumers are too varying of contacting corona.
7. Brand Loyalty of customers has seen mixed response during post covid as 51% consumers were not brand loyal but yet 49% were still brand loyal which shows brand loyalty totally relied consumer spending pattern post covid.
8. Online Entertainment services have seen a huge growth in consumption post covid 19 which could be due to consumers short of entertainment and time pass options during covid. This could heavily change the market scenario of this sector as consumer can soon become adapt to using these services.
9. Insurance sector has also seen a rise in its market post covid as consumers finally understood the importance of security of premium in these turbulent where lot of people had to suffer financial loss, damage, death.
10. Consumers' prefer to more of online shopping.
11. Buying workout equipment to use in their homes rather than attending a gym.
12. Increase in virtual consultation (tele-medicine).

13. Consumer prefers home delivery.
14. More usage of digital equipments, internet and social media platform.
15. Consumers are spending more time at home.
16. Adoption of cashless payment.
17. Less keen to invest their savings in the stock market.
18. More demand for essential goods and hoarding of essential goods.
19. Drop in branch visits.
20. Buy local.

Implications to the Retailers:

1. Challenges for the retailers to meet the high demand and changing purchase habits.

2. Retailers came with more of new products in the personal and home hygiene category.

3. Provided an opportunity to come with more Private Label Brands (PLBs) to meet the customer requirements.

4. Private labels came to the rescue of retailers as the supply lines of big FMCG firms were disrupted.

5. Insufficient delivery force.

6. Supply chain under pressure.

7. Logistics challenges (fast-shipping)

8. Retailers may seek out external funding sources.

CONCLUSIONS

After conducting the research, the study can conclude that the consumer behaviors have shown a slight change post covid in regards to services sector. The overall spending towards retail services has shown a reduction. Added to this, consumers are now focused on purchasing only services that they deem to be essential. The essentiality factor may vary from household to household. We can also see that consumers are now seeking extra facilities like sanitizers and social distancing norms etc. to avail services from any business. This adds an extra burden to business owners as consumers are asking extra amenities while demanding less accessibility and crowding. Post-Covid customers have put safety needs on top of the hierarchy index. Therefore, retail services business owners must take this into consideration while resuming operations post lockdown. Businesses may take heed of customer behavior patter change and act preemptively to gain competitive edge.

REFERENCES

Anastasiadou, E., Chrissos Anestis, M., Karantza, I. and Vlachakis, S. (2020), "The coronavirus' effects on consumer behavior and supermarket activities: insights from Greece and Sweden", *International Journal of Sociology and Social Policy*, Vol. 40 No. 9/10, pp. 893-907.

Bargh, J. A. 2002. Losing consciousness: Automatic influences on consumer judgment, behavior and motivation. Journal of Consumer Research 29 (2): 280–5.

Bettman, J. R, M. F. Luce, and J. W. Payne. 1998. Constructive consumer choice processes. Journal of Consumer Research 25 (3): 187–217.

Bove, L.L. and Benoit, S. (2020), "Restrict, clean and protect: signaling consumer safety during the pandemic and beyond", *Journal of Service Management*, Vol. 31 No. 6, pp. 1185-1202. https://doi.org/10.1108/JOSM-05-2020-0157.

Chaudhary, M., Sodani, P. R., & Das, S. (2020). Effect of COVID-19 on Economy in India: Some Reflections for Policy and Program. *Journal of Health Management, 22*(2), 169-180.

Chuang, Y., & Tai, Y. (2016). Research on customer switching behavior in the service industry. Retrieved November 22, 2020, from https://www.emerald.com/insight/content/doi/10.1108/MRR-01-2015-0022/full/html.

https://www.nielsen.com/in/en/insights/article/2020/covid-19-tracking-the-impact-on-fmcg-and-retail/ (accessed on January 05, 2020).

https://www.comscore.com/Insights/Blog/Coronavirus-pandemic-and-online-behavioural-shifts (accessed on January 05, 2020).

https://www.emarketer.com/content/the-biggest-business-impacts-of-the-coronavirus-pandemic-according-to-business-insider-intelligence (accessed on January 05, 2020).

Naeem, M. (2020), "Understanding the customer psychology of impulse buying during COVID-19 pandemic: implications for retailers", *International Journal of Retail & Distribution Management*, Vol. ahead-of-print No. ahead-of-print. https://doi.org/10.1108/IJRDM-08-2020-0317.

Mele, C., Russo-Spena, T. and Kaartemo, V. (2020), "The impact of coronavirus on business: developing service research agenda for a post-coronavirus world", *Journal of Service Theory and Practice*, Vol. ahead-of-print No. ahead-of-print. https://doi.org/10.1108/JSTP-07-2020-0180.

Rakshit, D., & Paul, A. (2020). Impact of COVID-19 on Sectors of Indian Economy and Business Survival Strategies. Retrieved December 02, 2020, from https://papers.ssrn.com/sol3/papers.cfm?abstract_id=3620727.

Simonson, I., Z. Carmon, R. Dhar, A. Drolet, and S. M. Nowlis. (2001). Consumer research: On search of identity. Annual Review of Psychology 52:249–75.

Tsiotsou, R. H., & Wirtz, J. (2012). Consumer Behavior in a Service Context. *Handbook of Developments in Consumer Behaviour*. doi:10.4337/9781781005125.00012.

W. O. (2020, December 25). Retail. Retrieved January 05, 2020, from https://en.wikipedia.org/wiki/Retail.

www.ETGovernment.com, M., Report. (2020). Opinion: Impact of covid-19 on the Indian Economy - ET Government. Retrieved December 25, 2020, from https://government.economictimes.indiatimes.com/news/economy/opinion-impact-of-covid-19-on-the-indian-economy/75021731.

Williams L. Wilke, consumer behaviors, John wiley & Sons inc, 2000, pp. 14

SECTION II

Contemporary Issues and Challenges in Finance and Accounting

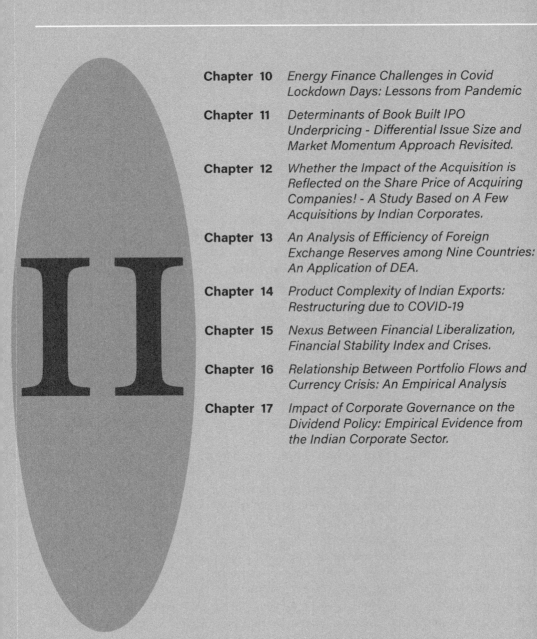

Chapter 10 *Energy Finance Challenges in Covid Lockdown Days: Lessons from Pandemic*

Chapter 11 *Determinants of Book Built IPO Underpricing - Differential Issue Size and Market Momentum Approach Revisited.*

Chapter 12 *Whether the Impact of the Acquisition is Reflected on the Share Price of Acquiring Companies! - A Study Based on A Few Acquisitions by Indian Corporates.*

Chapter 13 *An Analysis of Efficiency of Foreign Exchange Reserves among Nine Countries: An Application of DEA.*

Chapter 14 *Product Complexity of Indian Exports: Restructuring due to COVID-19*

Chapter 15 *Nexus Between Financial Liberalization, Financial Stability Index and Crises.*

Chapter 16 *Relationship Between Portfolio Flows and Currency Crisis: An Empirical Analysis*

Chapter 17 *Impact of Corporate Governance on the Dividend Policy: Empirical Evidence from the Indian Corporate Sector.*

CHAPTER 10

Energy Finance Challenges in Covid Lockdown Days: Lessons from Pandemic

Dr. Mahantesh Kuri
Assistant Professor, MBA
Rani Channamma
University
Belagavi, Karnataka
India
catchmahantesh@
yahoo.co.in

Dr. Prasad Kulkarni
Associate Professor, MBA
KLS Gogte
Institute of Technology
Belagavi, Karnataka
India
pvkulkarni@git.edu

Dr. Jyoti Jamnani
Assistant Professor, MBA
KLS Gogte Institute of
Technology
Belagavi, Karnataka
India
jntalreja@git.edu

Dr. Joel Gnanapragash
Associate Professor, MBA
Institute of Management
Christ University
Bengaluru, Karnataka
India
joel.gnanapragash@
christuniversity.in

Abstract

Purpose: Energy financing has become a thrust area for governments and corporations across the globe. Today, organizations are striving hard to minimize the climate risk. To achieve this objective, corporate are glancing towards investments through priority sector lending's, soft loans, crowd funding, green bonds and infrastructure debt funds. However, unclear policies, lack of synergy between energy and power departments of governments, cost of debt financing, energy actuaries and long term financing organizations have become major hurdles for energy financing. Added to these woes Covid-19 Corona virus outbreak has halted many investment decisions. Further, crude oil prices have reached the nadir level. This situation has bought ambiguity among governments either to invest in new energy sources or to continue with traditional energy sources. Hence, researchers wanted to explore the challenges faced by governments and corporations during a pandemic in the energy finance industry domain.

Methodology: Researchers divided energy and related companies into four divisions. They were oil and gas industries, Power companies, electrical equipment companies, and Auto manufacturing. This descriptive research used final account statements of 150 companies in India to assess cost of debt, investment, green bonds, green investment, government and private lending, technology investments, revenue and market data. Further, data visualization, correlations and ANOVA models used to conclude hypothesis acceptance or rejection.

Findings: Researchers found that the sector is enticing for big corporations due to its future potential. However, pandemic brought new challenges of sourcing raw materials from other than china. Further, governments concentrated on distribution of foods and medicine to people and diverted their attention from energy investment. Added to this, private funding agencies did not take risk of lending due to lower consumption of energy, volatile markets and falling large companies market capitalizations. In addition to this, higher energy costs with respect to green energy products during falling fossil fuel prices during lockdown had become unattractive. This has further put investment and return under huge risk. Data analysis had shown that energy companies in India worked towards supply security, employee safety and movement. On a reverse note, India's energy sector is a state subject and has differences with central policies. This resulted in lack of independence and flexibility. Contrary to above difficulties, lockdown also opened new avenues for energy companies for technology interventions though automation and digitalization.

Conclusions: Energy financing sector suffered limitations of funding and government support during the lockdown. However, it allowed companies to bring automation and digital technologies. Further, it forced companies to reassess their supply chain, investments, and employee safety.

Limitations: The paper focused mainly on Indian energy finance sector and omitted global corporations and their indirect impact on Indian energy sector.

Originality: This paper is written originally by authors and is not a part of any publications or chapters.

Keywords: Energy finance, carbon trading, covid-19 lockdown, crowd funding, green banking, priority sector lending, green bonds,

INTRODUCTION

The Kyoto agreement has opened new vistas in creating a clean environment by adopting Clean Development Mechanism (CDM) that intended to reduce pollution levels (Lewis, J., 2010). It has become imperative for all countries to follow the agreement. Countries across the world are striving hard to abide by the agreement by speeding up the energy financing activities. India is no exception to it.

Energy financing is spreading its tentacles into many areas. Today, corporations are putting their money to become more energy efficient. To do so they are allocating resources on assets. Another major area enticed by corporations is renewable energy. Here, companies are investing in new technology to generate energy from renewable sources. Apart from this, organizations are striving hard to minimize the waste in production and reduce water consumption. Similarly institutions are building green structures, transporting goods through green supply chains, and use personal cars fitted with electric devices.

The energy finance perspectives explained from different ways. Financial markets play a vital role in facilitating energy finance. These markets' positive activism encouraged the sector to act swiftly. Further, price discovery in the energy market has become a strategic tool. The price movements in energy markets strengthened the energy finance sector so far. However, the success of the energy finance sector depends upon decisions of top management. These executives influence investment decisions for a short term and a long term that kick start the campaign. Added to this, governments across the world are guaranteeing energy financing. Thus, green financing has become more greener with tax sops and rebate. Apart from this, a significant amount was raised through the derivatives market. However, risk involved in energy finance companies is very high. Mitigating this risk and to have proper actuarial science is a daunting task (Zhang. D, 2015)

According to Abolhosseini.S(2014) the energy finance raised through feed in tariffs, government guarantees, and bonds and certificates issued by a company. The interest in the energy finance domain highlighted as it provided a better image to corporate in the society. Similarly, energy finance companies had a better outlook in the global market and enabled them to fetch global contracts. On the other hand, in a few countries, energy efficiency has become a norm. Critically, many organizations focused on energy finance as a hedging instrument in the climate risk business (OECD, 2020). Having so many advantages in its kitty, energy financing domain allured investors and companies making it the fastest emerging financial sector.

To scale the renewable energy, the role of Indian government is crucial. It ensured investing firms have sufficient demand for a long term, conducive environment for equipment manufacturers, and space for OEM & AMC companies, and strong technical & advisory teams. Further, the government support in energy financing research by providing sufficient grants. More than this, the government established the regulatory body for smooth conduct of the projects and its grievances. On the support side, it is providing subsidies and tax incentives for green finance products. Above all, subsidies must cover cost of capital, risk and transaction costs. Apart from this, government subsidies play a crucial role in the success of renewable energy projects. It was observed that countries where subsidies were reduced interest in the energy projects also has gone down (Nie, P., 2016). The Government of India has set up a low cost infrastructure debt fund in 2011. This infrastructure debt fund can be raised either through mutual funds or thorough Non Banking Financial corporation's (NBFCs). The National Thermal Power Corporation has issued green bonds with 9.3% interest, which generated higher interest among investors. To boost the energy sector, Indian government set up the National Clean Energy and Environment Fund (NCEEF), changed lending structure and introduced priority lending. It also made soft loans available from Indian Renewable Energy Development Agency (IREDA). A major thrust was put by the government on crowd funding and green banks to facilitate the growth of the sector.

In a survey conducted by the consultancy Climate Policy initiatives (CPI) with project developers and infrastructure financiers had following outcomes:

Table 1: Financial instruments and their impact on debt.

Particulars	Potential reduction in cost(Points)	Potential increase in tenure(Years)
Government bonds	4.5 points.	10
Mutual funds	3	5
Credit assurance	1.8	5
Actuarial	1.8	8
Hedging	1.4	8

(**Source:** Climate Policy Initiatives (CPI))

The above table highlights that the government bond market reduces the cost and has a longer tenure. Similarly, organizations working in actuaries and hedging fetched longer tenure. However, mutual funds and credit assurance instruments were neither able to reduce cost nor increased the loan tenure.

The inefficiency in the government push for the accelerated growth in the energy sector overcomes the financial sector. The appetite for clean energy could not be met by the government, gradually fulfilled by private sector companies. However, they have hurdles of lack of clear government policies, consumer awareness, high project costs, transaction costs and behavioral inertia (Wu et.al, 2018). There are various ways of overcoming these hurdles. Some of them are : financing through advanced commercial project financing to achieve energy efficiency, enabling commercial financing, generating funds through bonds, credit lines with commercial and development banks, energy efficiency funds, utility financing, co financing and grants. Further, international donors are lending donations to financial institutions. These firms invest back in the energy projects. With all said and done, finance companies investment decisions depend on financial health, risk appetite, management support and commitment of institutions.

The cautious approach of private finance companies in the energy sector due to various risks involved. Construction risk is a major roadblock for energy finance. In this, companies are fixing the price for the project to avoid risks. Fuhrer, they awarded contracts to established players in the market. Apart from this, companies put contingency plans in place in case of project delays or failures. Lastly, companies are building flexible capacity options at the plant to meet the fluctuating demand. Lenders are putting stringent norms on project companies. Thereafter, project companies stipulate dates, guarantees and fine for construction companies (Bond, G. , 1995). Another notable risk involved in energy finance is market risk. This risk is observed between power purchase companies and individuals or enterprises. These power purchase companies have huge debt under its belt Thus, Debt is very crucial for the success of energy finance. The loan capital available to an entrepreneur makes him a success or failure(Nie, P. ,2016). To overcome this risk, a few financial institutions came out with innovative ways of lending namely mezzanine financing. In this type of financing financial institutions create a mix of debt and equity. Here, if the organization who availed the loan from venture capitalists is not able to pay, then the lender can convert their debt into equity. Another way of mitigating risk involved in energy finance is through the mode of project guaranteeing. Guarantees can be of two types. First, it may be private collaterals, or second, public sector backing. Certain countries are providing guarantees to energy finance companies that will allow the investors and companies to pay the tax or pay the lower tax. Furthermore, many bonds are certified to ensure the project guarantees. In India Indian infrastructure Finance Limited (IIFL) are providing guarantees for many green projects to increase their visibility in the marketplace. Public sector banks play a key role in generating interest in energy finance. It helps other banks to learn from the public sector banks experience and build trust in the project. Moreover, it provides first mover advantage to public sector banks (Geddes, A., 2018).

Generating funds for the energy sector is a herculean task. Banks and corporations in India adopted green bond mode to raise the capital. These bonds are floated by both private and public sector bodies across the world. In most of the countries, interest is paid by the governments such that it gets long term finance and reduces carbon in its nations (Mathews, J.A. ,2010).

It is evident that, since 2014, Indian financial institutions and companies have shown interest in the green bonds. State Bank of India, Axis bank, Yes Bank and Punjab National Bank are a few notable institutions in raising funds through green bonds and allocating funds to the renewable energy sector. The country also witnessed direct participation from corporations such as L&T, Hero future energy, Rewa Hero and Greenko. Further, NBFCs linked Tata Cleantech energy, and DCM facilitated the growth of the sector. The contributions from government bodies such as

IRFC, IREDA and IFC are worth mentioning.

Traditional financial instruments in the energy finance sector suffer from several limitations. The division of wealth, financial accessibility, and regulations are few notable features to mention here. Kenya is one such country wherein financial resources are limited to elite people. The government give solar equipment to customers in this unique approach called' pay as you go'. In this approach, customers pay the money to the equipment and usage in parts (Rolfis.P, 2015). Another model used to bring sustainability was micro financing. Companies like SKS micro financial in India revolutionized financial access to a large number of people. On the flip side, similar companies' faced closure due to lack of access to capital and non performing assets. The major reason for closure of such companies is lack of trust among stakeholders (Rolfis.P, 2015).

Energy finance is not away with hurdles. The sector faces the challenge of finance accessibility due to high interest rates in the ecosystem (Rolffs, P., 2015). Another major obstacle in the financial accessibility is most of the companies in the green energy areas are startups whose balance sheets are not attractive for financial institutions to sanction the loans. These startups' balance sheets are more in debt compared to other established players. Banks across the globe provide loans to startups who got funding from secured sources(Steffen, B. ,2018). These startups also have the challenges of securitization. Therefore non resource finance has emerged as the ebay mechanism to reduce the cost of capital compared to traditional corporate finance models. Added to this, banks in developing countries lack discipline in disbursing and collecting money (Brunnschweiler, C.,2010).

On the positive side of the development, renewable energy generation and installation cost has seen significant changes. The approximate cost in crore rupees per megawatt for solar has come down from 15.6 in 2010 to 4.2 in 2020. Similarly approximate cost rupees crore per mega watt in hydropower has increased from 7.8 to 14.

I. REVIEW OF LITERATURE

The Corona covid-19 outbreak has affected businesses across the nooks and corners of the world. However, the lockdown has not affected the renewable energy sector as they have to run continuously without interruption. Contrary to other streams of the energy sector that had shown ascending growth, the thermal sector has seen a steady decline in the demand during pandemic days(ET energy world, 8 December 2020).

Figure 2: *Electricity generation in 2019-20.*

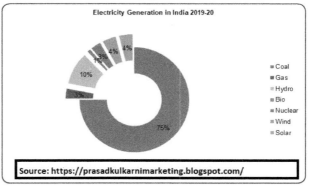

The decline in the thermal sector was noticed due to work from home and reduced office timings (Downtoearth, 2020). In India, 75% of the electricity generated comes from the thermal sector. In such situations, the government had asked its PSUs to step up and support power projects in India. Power Finance corporation (PFC) has disbursed Rs 11000 crore for power projects during the pandemic days. The company gave the due to its IT system and dedicated employee team(ET energy world, 2020)

Fund management 3nd energy financing

To succeed in the energy sector, funds should be available continuously for companies. The sector project management had a question due to several issues like demand, labor, and working capital availability. In India, financial institutions extend the loans based on balance sheet performance. However, dip in the demand and reduced usage of the energy impacted the nosedive of revenues and out coming in lack of working capital availability (hall.S, 2017). Moreover, energy projects of sector's companies earn revenue through government projects that have a stricter schedule. These unforeseen situations needed policy modification at both the state and central governments. The MNRE, a core organization in the energy sector had extended their project commissioning (downtoearth,2020). Further, Mr Yogi Adityanath , Chief Minister of Uttarpradesh, a state in India rescued solar electricity companies by infusing capital into the sector. On the same ground, Andhrapradesh and Punjab states of India, had ordered their divisional electricity supply companies (DISCOM's) to clear the renewable energy companies bill to infuse new capital into the sector. To understand the fund related issues affecting energy companies' researchers postulated the following hypothesis

H1: Fund management has a significant impact on the energy finance companies in India during the lockdown period.

Financial markets and energy financing

Private placements of corporate bonds in India have grown many folds. Rs 20548 crores in 2006-07 to Rs 67402 crores in 2019-20(Appendix 1) similarly climate bonds in emerging countries have shown remarkable progress. China is leading the ladder with $8800 billion and followed by India $800 billion (Appendix 2). Further, Green bonds share as a share of overall debt percentage is highest in France with 0.75% and India contributes 0.35 % (Appendix3). These interesting facts about market data enticed researchers to know the energy sector's performance during the lockdown. The lock down period had hit financial markets very badly. Except essential goods and services companies, others have seen their nadir during this time. The unattractive market and pandemic fear resulted in the exodus of foreign institutional investors who were prime investors in the energy sector. Further, foreign exchange markets had a volatile time. The currency dipped to all time low against dollars. This resulted in components required for the energy sector outsourcing unattractive and halted many projects' progress(downtoearth,2020). Hence researchers assumed financial markets have significant influence on the energy market and constructed the following hypothesis.

H2: Lack of capital support from the financial market reduced the growth of the energy sector during lockdown in India.

Cash Inflows and energy financing

The pandemic impacted the financial positions of the public. Job losses mounted across industry categories. In a few companies, compensations were reduced to half level to overcome the difficulties of lockdown period. Further, the corporate sector had seen their difficult days in terms of dip in demand, closure of facilities, and supply chain inefficiencies. These issues have aggravated their woes and were unable to pay energy bills. This onslaught from consumer and corporate front for bill realization kept energy companies in siege positions. Consequently, energy companies were not able to clear their supply chain member's bills. Renewable energy companies, one of the major supply chain members for project financing suffered adverse effects (downtoearth, 2020). Hence formulated the following hypothesis

H3: Inadequate cash flows derailed the progress of energy finance companies during the lockdown period.

Policy framework and energy financing.

Energy sector had tied their hands on several areas due to policy interventions by state and central governments. Inadequacies in fund management and lack of proper management control made financial regulators adapt to stricter norms in capital borrowing to energy companies. This has become a major obstacle to the energy sector. To overcome these situations, the central government has extended the borrowing limit of state governments so that DISCOMs bills would be cleared. This move acted as a helping hand to DISCOMs from state governments (IISD,2020). Added to this, energy companies in India whenever they buy electricity from the central grid have to pay a guaranteed amount. This obligation made electricity companies more responsible. However, during pandemic due to dip in their revenue performance energy companies were not able to meet the guarantee clause. At this time, central government intervened and had asked DISCOM's to meet 50% guarantee clause during lockdown period (IISD, 2020)

H4: Inadequate policy support from governments affected energy companies during the lockdown period.

Human Resource Management and energy financing

India had seen its worst labor shortage days during the lockdown. The spread of Coronavirus and job losses created the fear among the labor class. It has become difficult for them to lead a simple life. Thus, laborers started moving to their native places leaving projects in jeopardy. This resulted in delay in the project completion and increase in the cost of capital. (Downtoearth, 2020). Hence, researchers postulated the following hypothesis

H5: Human resource shortage had a direct impact on the project completion.

From the above review of literature and researchers prior experience in the domain, the following theoretical model constituted for the study:

II. THEORETICAL FRAMEWORK.

Fig. 3: *Theoretical framework.*

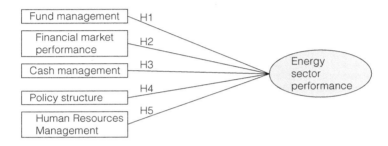

(**Source:** Model developed by researchers based on review of literature)

III. METHODOLOGY

Researchers divided energy and related companies into four divisions. They were oil and gas industries, Power companies, electrical equipment companies, and Auto manufacturing. This descriptive research used final account statements of 150 companies in India to assess cost of debt, investment, green bonds, green investment, government and private lending, technology investments, revenue and market data. The data was limited to April -June 2020 and July -September 2020 quarters. Further, data visualization, correlations, and ANOVA models used to conclude hypothesis acceptance or rejection.

IV. DISCUSSIONS

Fund Management: Covid 19 lockdown forced organizations to restructure their financial statements. Loans borrowed by companies in the power sector, Electrical sector, Automobile passenger cars, and automobile motorcycles went down significantly. Similarly, the interest to be paid on loans has touched new lows. Thus, the cost of debt after tax is 4.85% in the power sector, 4.95% in the electrical sector, 3.24% Automobile sector passenger cars, and 4.73% automobile motorcycle segment.

Table 2: Cost of debt of four industries' coming under direct impact of energy financing

Industry: Power

	Latest	2020	2019	2018	2017	2016
No.of Company	886	69	314	398	427	460
Secured Loans	971,217.3	309,934.91	790,521.6	786,116.0	631,480.7	700,288.1
Unsecured Loans	622,580.9	222,674.05	456,504.5	439,702.6	354,867.	371,429.3
Interest	127,490.4	36,881.99	102,731.8	110,295.7	79,079	87,515.38
cost of debt	0.0799915	0.0692477	0.0823814	0.0899772	0.0801	0.0816590
after tax (1-0.3)	0.0559941	0.0484734	0.057667	0.062984	0.0561	0.0571
before tax cost of debt	8.00	6.92	8.24	9.00	8.02	8.17
after tax	5.60	4.85	5.77	6.30	5.61	5.72

Industry : Electric Equipment - General - Medium / Small

Year	Latest	2020	2019	2018	2017	2016
No.of Company	267	30	71	93	112	129
Secured Loans	7,402.1	1,082.68	4,054.83	4,668.23	4,470.18	5,326.
Unsecured Loans	2,472.1	249.48	636.58	1,081.85	1,390.41	2,412.
Interest	997.79	94.16	332.97	448.2	592.99	768.14
cost of debt	0.10104	0.0706822	0.070974	0.07794674	0.10118264	0.09924969
after tax (1-0.3)	0.07073	0.0494775	0.049682	0.05456271	0.07082785	0.06947478
before tax	10.10	7.07	7.10	7.79	10.12	9.92
after tax	7.07	4.95	4.97	5.46	7.08	6.95

Automobiles - passenger cars

Year	Latest	2020	2019	2018	2017	2016
No.of Company	25	8	20	21	19	19
Secured Loans	5,388.7	369.73	1,993.03	2,255.99	3,179.00	3,309.92
Unsecured Loans	30,288	14,017.73	25,060.77	25,667.99	23,736.29	26,116.70
Interest	2,375.6	666.13	1,902.16	2,228.49	2,063.54	1,946.34
cost of debt	0.06658	0.0462993	0.070310	0.0798056	0.0766679	0.06614215
after tax (1-0.3)	0.04661	0.0324095	0.049217	0.05586392	0.05366756	0.04629950
before tax	6.66	4.63	7.03	7.98	7.67	6.61
after tax	4.66	3.24	4.92	5.59	5.37	4.63

Industry: Automobiles - Motorcycles / Mopeds

Year	Latest	2020	2019	2018	2017	2016
No.of Company	10	4	6	6	6	8
Secured Loans	1,121.66	902.1	552.33	335.62	444.38	929.37
Unsecured Loans	2,377.93	1,371.47	1,784.44	2,061.98	1,767.94	1,248.39
Interest	268.62	153.49	180.27	162.07	151.49	152.95
cost of debt	0.076757	0.0675105	0.0771449	0.067596	0.06847562	0.07023271
after tax (1-0.3)	0.053730	0.0472573	0.0540014	0.047317	0.04793293	0.04916290
before tax	7.68	6.75	7.71	6.76	6.85	7.02
after tax	5.37	4.73	5.40	4.73	4.79	4.92

Industry: Oil and Gas

Year	Latest	2020	2019	2018	2017	2016
No.of Company	31	7	14	17	19	20
Secured Loans	138,658.2	85,515.49	86,746.77	72,726.58	92,809.54	89,460.40
Unsecured Loans	427,590.61	412,979.33	288,236.72	210,736.23	192,760.69	190,933.18
Interest	29,707.37	25,134.31	21,938.56	15,466.95	14,192.16	13,780.19
cost of debt	0.05246345	0.0504204	0.0585054	0.054564	0.04969761	0.04914588
after tax (1-0.3)	0.03672441	0.0352942	0.0409537	0.038195	0.0347883	0.03440211
before tax	5.25	5.04	5.85	5.46	4.97	4.91
after tax	3.67	3.53	4.10	3.82	3.48	3.44

Note: Corporate Tax rate is assumed as 30%

(Source: Primary data)

These cost of debt data compared against previous five years of cost of debt and analysis of variance test is conducted to conclude the outcome of the Hypothesis 1.

Table 3: Analysis of variance test between cost of debt before lockdown and during the lockdown.

Groups	Count	Sum	Average	Variance
Power	6	33.84	5.64	0.21
Electrical	6	36.47	6.07	1.13
Cars	6	28.4	4.73	0.68
Motorcycle	6	29.94	4.99	0.09
Oil and Gas	6	22.04	3.67	0.06

ANOVA						
Sources of variables	SS	df	MS	F	p-value	F-crit
Between groups	20.41	4	5.1	11.64	0.0178	2.75
Within groups	10.95	25	0.43			
Total	31.32	29				

(**Source:** Primary data)

From the table 4 it is inferred that Hypothesis 1 is accepted (N=6, F=11.64,p<0.05). Thus, researchers have concluded that fund management had a significant impact on the working of energy finance companies in India during the lockdown period.

Financial Market Performance

A sectoral performance is depicted in the movement of shares. Investors do fundamental analysis and understand the market sentiments before investing money in the particular sector. Hence researchers identified market capitalization as a variable to measure the impact of lockdown on the energy sector. The detailed data of market capitalization of the energy sector is given below;

Table 4: Market capitalization (In Rs crores) of energy sector companies in India before and after the lockdown.

Year	2016	2017	2018	2019	2020
Automobiles	363631.	463685.	461777.	480310.1	352111.8
Oil and gas	691826.5	872187.6	977986.4	765695.5	455862.1
Power	984702.5	1309099	1414109	1624111	1143429
Electricals	162135.9	203070.8	190358.2	212027.7	142874

Table 5: Analysis of variance test of market capitalization of variance energy related companies across five **years.**

Groups	Count	Sum	Average	Variance
Automobiles	5	2121515.8	424303.16	3746186685
Oil and gas	5	3763558.08	752711.616	39254614941
Power	5	6475450.83	1295090.166	60489610668
Electricals	5	910466.6177	182093.3235	835220224

ANOVA						
Sources of variables	**SS**	**df**	**MS**	**F**	**p-value**	**F-crit**
Between groups	3.48E+12	3	1.16E+12	44.46	5.50E-08	3.2388
Within groups	4.17E+11	16	26081408130			
Total	3.90E+12	19				

The market capitalization of four industries of the energy financing domain had a drastic reduction in their market capitalization. Oil and Gas industries and Power industry experienced the decline due to lower expected revenues from the reduced demand. The restriction on movements of vehicles and delay in projects had curtailed revenue and profits of automobiles and electrical sector companies in the energy finance domain. The analysis of variance test is conducted to know the market capitalization significance before and during the lockdown on energy financing and found that ($N=5$, F-44.46, $p<0.05$) it significantly affects the sector.

Cash Management

Managing the cash is vital for the energy finance companies in project planning, execution and control. The corona covid-19 lock down days had mixed reactions for energy financing companies. The oil and gas companies were managing the cash better and similarly power has done better in cash management in the year 2020. However, researchers observed that Automobiles and electrical companies lacked demand and were shown reduced cash at the end of the lock down period.

Table 6: Cash and cash equivalent at the end of the years (in Rs crores)

	Cash and Cash Equivalents at End of the year(In Rs crores)				
Year	**Oil and Gas**	**Automobiles cars**	**Automobiles-Motorcycles**	**Electrical general-Medium and small**	**Power**
2016	8,223.14	7,127.74	1,240.58	772.24	30,955.94
2017	3,315.13	11,026.33	1,262.36	549.24	13,037.46
2018	3,247.30	19,801.96	3,695.52	331.2	8,698.32
2019	1,809.50	18,879.69	3,050.91	262.94	8,146.28
2020	8,573.13	4,699.04	581.21	64.01	9,825.48
2021	9,421.16	18,870.76	2,881.79	969.29	28,324.07

(**Source:** Primary data)

Table 7: Analysis of variance test between cash management before lockdown and during the lockdown.

Groups	Count	Sum	Average	Variance
Power	6	99987.52	16497.92	1.07+08
Electrical	6	2948.72	491.48	114223.12
Cars	6	80405.52	13400.92	44324712.79
Motorcycle	6	12712.37	2118.72	1561194.31
Oil and gas	6	34589.36	5764.89	11056

ANOVA						
Sources of variables	**SS**	**df**	**MS**	**F**	**p-value**	**F-crit**
Between groups	1.18E+09	4	2.95E+08	8.98	0.000122	2.75871
Within groups	8.21E+08	25	32850197			
Total	2E+09	29				

(Source: Primary data)

The analysis of variance test conducted to know the impact of lockdown in energy related companies by dividing the data as before and after lockdown. The result shows that (N=6, F=8.98, p<0.05) cash management had affected significantly in energy related companies during the lockdown.

Policy structure and energy financing sector

Indian energy sector had several limitations while borrowing capital, credit guarantees, storage issues, grid management, cash receivable management, and installation and set up cost. The lockdown raised the issues of coal imports, labor shortage on projects and equipment movement. The central government understood the long standing demands of clean energy sector and arrived at a few policy changes (table 5)

Table 8: Policy modifications in India during lockdown

Sl.No	Policy before the lockdown	Policy during the lockdown	Impact on energy sector
1	NPS withdrawal was subject to retirement	NPS withdrawal allowed partially(KPMG,2021)	Employees could manage their finance better during the lockdown
2	Policy repo rate 5.15%	Policy Repo rate 4.40%	Higher possibility of fund availability
3	Loan to SME without credit guarantee	Free loans with credit guarantees for SME	SMEs in the electrical sector benefited by this.

4	No receivables guarantees by state governments for liquidity infusion	Rs 90,000 crore liquidity infusion got state government guarantees for receivable with condition to utilize in power generating firms	Improved cash position of power firms.
5	No must run status for clean energy projects	Must run status for clean energy sector(Greentech media, 2021)	Uninterrupted power generation and financials
6	No peak power tender	Peak power tender solar and wind energy tenders together to meet grid storage needs	Reduced storage cost.

(**Source:** Primary data)

The hypothesis tested using concurrent deviation method of correlation

$r = \sqrt{+-(2c-m)/m} = +-\sqrt{\pm+-(12-6)/6} = 1$. (Where is c = 6 and m = 6)

The correlation shows that policy changes have a positive and significant impact on the improvement of the energy sector, particularly the renewable energy sector in the near future.

Human Resource Management and Energy companies

The Indian government had seen an exodus of laborers from urban areas to rural areas with fear of pandemic. This was a big blow to project management companies in the energy sector. A few of the energy projects were halted for a few months causing problems in meeting tender guidelines of the project. Apart from this, reduction in demand puts heavy weight on the heads of energy companies as it has to comply with regulatory compensation in India. At this juncture, the central government of India stood up and bought policy modifications. The table 6 explains the impact of human resource policies on the energy sector during the lockdown.

Table 9: Human resources and impact on energy sector during the lockdown

Sl.No	Human Resource before the lock down	Human Resource during the lockdown	Impact on Energy sector
1	PF contribution by both employer and employees	PF contribution of both employer and employee contribution(up to Rs 15000 salaried) paid by the government for three months(KPMG,2021)	+(companies saved their working capital)

2	Coal power companies ran with full capacity	Coal power companies ran with 55% capacity due to project delays(Greentech media, 2021)	Cost of production has gone up.
3	Renewable energy companies have to complete the Project on time.	Renewable energy sector companies can extend the project deadlines by 5 months due to labor shortages	Complete the project with limited human resources.

(Source: Primary data)

The hypothesis tested using concurrent deviation method of correlation

$$r = \sqrt{+-(2c-m)/m} = +-\sqrt{+-(4-3)/3} = 0.33 \text{ (where is c= 2 and m=3)}$$

The result showed that there is a positive relationship between human resource management in energy related companies during the lockdown on its performance but not highly significant.

CONCLUSIONS

The lockdown has made all renewable energy companies and finance companies look into their investments. Thus, there is a need for a change in the policy framework particularly in the solar energy policy framework. Further, the Government must enhance the confidence of lenders and request them to participate in the long term financing. Borrowings had seen drastic reduction during the lockdown due to reduction in the demand, closure of companies and delayed project execution. The interest to be paid on loans also came down dramatically due to government's interest deferment, financial assistance from governments and less requirement of capital for projects. The latest data on borrowings has shown a sharp rise depicting the influence of funds on working of energy related companies.

Lockdown days had mixed reactions to energy finance related domains. Oil and gas industry and power sectors had done better in cash management whereas the electrical and automobile sectors had a cash crunch situation due to lower demand, manufacturing and installation. Further, share markets reacted with negative sentiments across the energy finance domain. This is due to lack of demand, delay in projects and restriction on vehicular movements. Thus, the market capitalization of sectors across four industry verticals had seen sharp decline.

REFERENCES

1. Abolhosseini, S. (2014). The main support mechanisms to finance renewable energy development. Renewable and Sustainable Energy Reviews, 40, 876-885, ISSN 1364-0321, doi:10.1016/j.rser.2014.08.013

2. Bond, G. (1995). Financing energy projects. Experience of the International Finance Corporation. Energy Policy, 23(11), 967-975, ISSN 0301-4215, doi:10.1016/0301-4215(95)00099-2

3. Brunnschweiler, C. (2010). Finance for renewable energy: An empirical analysis of developing and transition economies. Environment and Development Economics, 15(3), 241-274, ISSN 1355-770X, doi:10.1017/S1355770X1000001X

4. Geddes, A. (2018). The multiple roles of state investment banks in low-carbon energy finance: An analysis of Australia, the UK and Germany. Energy Policy, 115, 158–170, ISSN 0301-4215, doi:10.1016/j.enpol.2018.01.009

5. Hall, S. (2017). Investing in low-carbon transitions: energy finance as an adaptive market. Climate Policy, 17(3), 280-298, ISSN1469-3062, doi:10.1080/14693062.2015.1094731

6. Lewis, J. (2010). The evolving role of carbon finance in promoting renewable energy development in China. Energy Policy, 38(6), 2875-2886, ISSN 0301-4215, doi:10.1016/j.enpol.2010.01.020

7. Mathews, J.A. (2010). Mobilizing private finance to drive an energy industrial revolution. Energy Policy, 38(7), 3263-3265, ISSN 0301-4215, doi:10.1016/j.enpol.2010.02.030

8. Nie, P. (2016). Subsidies in carbon finance for promoting renewable energy development. Journal of Cleaner Production, 139, 677-684, ISSN 0959-6526, doi:10.1016/j.jclepro.2016.08.083

9. Rolffs, P. (2015). Beyond technology and finance: pay-as-you-go sustainable energy access and theories of social change. Environment and Planning A, 47(12), 2609-2627, ISSN 0308-518X, doi:10.1177/0308518X15615368

10. Steffen, B. (2018). The importance of project finance for renewable energy projects. Energy Economics, 69, 280-294, ISSN 0140-9883, doi:10.1016/j.eneco.2017.11.006

11. "Wu, Yun; Singh, Jas; Tucker, Dylan Karl. 2018. Financing Energy Efficiency, Part 2 : Credit Lines. Live Wire;2018/91. World Bank, Washington, DC. © World Bank. https://openknowledge.worldbank.org/handle/10986/30386 License: CC BY 3.0 IGO."

12. (2020). Retrieved 8 December 2020, from https://www.oecd.org/env/outreach/2_6_DFIs-role-clean-energy-finance.pdf

13. Power Finance Corp disburses Rs 11K cr in first week of lockdown - ET EnergyWorld. (2020). Retrieved 8 December 2020, from https://energy.economictimes.indiatimes.com/news/power/power-finance-corp-disburses-rs-11k-cr-in-first-week-of-lockdown/74928962

14. COVID-19: Renewable power generation remains unaffected amid lockdown, says report - ET EnergyWorld. (2020). Retrieved 8 December 2020, from https://energy.economictimes.indiatimes.com/news/renewable/covid-19-renewable-power-generation-remains-unaffected-amid-lockdown-says-report/75566572

15. COVID-19: Prolonged lockdown can affect the renewable energy sector. (2020). Retrieved 8 December 2020, from https://www.downtoearth.org.in/news/energy/covid-19-prolonged-lockdown-can-affect-renewable-energy-sector-70341

16. (2020). Retrieved 9 December 2020, from https://www.nrdc.org/sites/default/files/catalytic-finance-underserved-clean-energy-markets-india-report-201810.pdf

17. Mukherjee, P. (2020). India's small renewables firms fighting consolidation wave. Retrieved 17 December 2020, from https://in.reuters.com/article/india-renewables/indias-small-renewables-firms-fighting-consolidation-wave-idINKCN1L60ND

18. How Can India's Energy Sector Recover Sustainably from COVID-19?. (2020). Retrieved 17 December 2020, from https://www.iisd.org/articles/how-can-indias-energy-sector-recover-sustainably-covid-19

19. (2021) India- Measures in response to COVID-19 - KPMG Global. Retrieved February 01, 2021, from https://home.kpmg/xx/en/home/insights/2020/04/india-government-and-institution-measures-in-response-to-covid.html

20. How India's Renewable Energy Sector Survived and Thrived in a Turbulent 2020. (2021). Retrieved 1 February 2021, from https://www.greentechmedia.com/articles/read/india-solar-

Determinants of Book Built IPO Underpricing- Differential Issue Size and Market Momentum Approach Revisited

Suresha B
Associate Professor in Finance
School of Business and Management
CHRIST (Deemed to be University)
Bangalore, India
suresh.b@christuniversity.in

Ravikumar T
Associate Professor in Finance
School of Business and Management
CHRIST (Deemed to be University),
Bangalore, India
ravikumar.t@christuniversity.in

Abstract

Initial Public offerings (IPOs) market dynamics concerning pricing, listing, and post-listing day performance are complex phenomena to understand. Price anomalies are commonly observed in IPO markets particularly in emerging markets due to information asymmetry. Participants' perceived underpricing creates undue market momentum during the offer period with asymmetric effect across different issue sizes.

Purpose and Design:
This study attempts to find the determinants of Book Built IPOs underpricing by taking a sample of 180 Book Built IPOs that went public in India between 2011 and 2020. The determinants were verified for different issue sizes. The listing day performance was measured using Listing Day-Absolute Return (LD-AR) and Listing Day-Market Adjusted Return (LD-MAR) model and tested for the explanatory capabilities of firm-specific and market momentum factors for underpricing using OLS models.

Results:
With differential issue size, we find a direct relationship between the issue size and underpricing, and dominant underpricing is observed in the case of moderate to large issue size with linear progressive return confirming that there is over-optimism on the part of investors. We also find that momentum specific factors have a significant influence along with the firm-specific factors such as the firm size, cash flows, subscription rate of QIBs and RIIs in the listing day return and the underpricing.

Keywords: Listing day return, Underpricing, differential Issue Size, Market Momentum, Firm Size

1. INTRODUCTION

Price anomalies are persistent in equity markets due to information asymmetry and it is pretty significant in emerging markets. New issue market experience underpricing phenomenon especially during an Initial Public Offerings (IPOs). IPO is a mechanism through which firms raise capital directly from the public. Prospective investors read the offer document to know information about each investor class's price band and reservations. Short-term horizon participants expect immediate listing day gain and others for capital gains over time. Thou primary market is intended for long-term capital raising and expected that the investors anticipate capital gain over time; in practice, people subscribe for IPOs shares expecting listing day gains. Increasingly, it is noticed that most of the IPOs are underpriced either deliberately or accidentally. Firms resort to underpricing to boost the demand for their shares, granting extra money for taking the risk in the company or due to the underwriter inability to find the fair value of shares grants more money on the table for investors on listing day. Apart from these, there could be different other factors that influence the listing day performance of IPOs. Empirical researches have shown some evidence of firm characteristics influencing the IPO valuation. However, still, it is a debatable issue as varied findings across the markets, and there are no consensuses on the degree of its influence.

Further, the level of information asymmetry differs significantly across developed to emerging nations. Information beyond available in the offer document has a far more significant impact on valuation. It is one of the persistent issues causing price imperfections and differential returns for different categories of investors. In recent times, as some large issue size public offerings have fared poorly on the day of listing, it has discouraged small investors as they lack the expertise to judge and leave with the losses. Only some prominent players dominate the issue right from allotment to profit booking on listing day. Underpricing is perceived to be good as it passes on wealth to the shareholder's post listing. However, there is a lack of consensus on the determinants.

Company fundamentals drive the basic valuation of stocks, but market discount for earnings potential of the firm in creating value for shareholders in the long term. Can the number of times shares subscribed determine the listing day gain? This signifies the demand for the public offering, and the higher the subscription rate, the greater the probability of listing day gain. Kamat.M.S and Phadke, M.Kedar (2018) found a positive relationship between subscription rate and listing day returns. Other macroeconomic factors like index return on the day of listing are vital determinants of the IPO performance. If the index sentiments are positive, the expected return of IPO shall be greater on listing day. Ross (1970), in their arbitrage pricing theory, asserts that macroeconomic factors influence the asset's returns. These are primarily systematic risk factors. An imperfect market provides an opportunity for unusual returns. Company fundamental and future earnings potential usually considered for built IPO pricing; sometimes misprice the public issue. However, on the day of listing, the market eventually accounts for all other macroeconomic factors. It corrects the price to bring it back to the fair price levels, and arbitrageurs expecting the price variations between primary and secondary markets would like to take advantage of any deviations from fair market value. However, there is no consistent evidence on the same. Evidence shows that even oversubscribed shares posted listing day losses, indicating the overvaluation of shares. Firm size, issue size and general market sentiments may factor in IPO pricing; however, there is no empirical evidence to prove it.

2. REVIEW OF LITERATURE

IPO underpricing is the most fascinating and time tested research area of interest for academicians and practitioners in most countries. However, the dynamics of IPO markets are ever-changing, so the factors that influence IPO performance. In this section, an attempt has been made to understand the current research findings on this topic and discussions on the gap of knowledge that can be filled up with newer studies. Iqbal Thonse Hawaldar, K.R. Naveen Kumar & T. Mallikarjunappa (2018) examined the listing day performance of IPOs and book-built IPO's and found that book-built IPOs are underpriced lesser magnitude as compared to fixed price IPO's. Lee, P., Taylor, S., & Walter, T. (1999) find their study that large investors' presence in IPOs results in higher initial returns due to the quick and the quality of information that they possess being informed investors. Kim, K. a., Kitsabunnarat, P., & Nofsinger, J. R. (2004) examined the relationship between firm ownership and IPO performance and found that managerial ownership experience and a high level of ownership have a positive influence on the IPO performance.

The signalling hypothesis asserts that a higher promoter stake in the pre IPO period signals confidence of promoters in the business, thus the expected return from the business in future. Banu Durukan, M. (2002) examined the abnormal initial returns from IPOs and confirmed that there is a winner's curse hypothesis working in the market by posting an abnormal return on a listing day in Istanbul Stock Exchange (ISE) and further states market automatically corrects itself the price imperfection of either overvaluation or under-pricing of IPOs once shareholders realize the profits on a listing day. Underpricing leaves money on the table and profit booking persists under such imperfect markets. Sinha, Nitish & TPM,. (2004) examines the role of book built IPOs in Indian markets in IPO underpricing and finds that the book built IPOs has less probability of being underpriced than the conventional fixed price issues and underpricing is more dominant in the case of smaller issue sizes. Peristiani, S., & Hong, G. (2004) verified the role of pre-IPO financial performance of firms and found that sound pre-IPO financials significantly influence the post listing IPO performance of the firm. It also asserts an increasing trend in firms with poor financial quality going for IPO, and such firms are struggling to sustain their business in the post-listing period financially. Its failure rates are increasing significantly, especially in the post tech boom period. Jaskiewicz, P., González, V. M., Menéndez, S., & Schiereck, D. (2005). Found a positive firm size effect on the IPO performance of family and non-family-owned firms IPO listed in German and Spanish markets. Zheng, S. X., & Stangeland, D. A. (2007) finds that the IPO underpricing is positively factored by sales growth rate and EBIDTA and not positively influenced by the growth in earnings. Pukthuanthong-Le, K., & Varaiya, N. (2007) find IPO underpricing related to the block selling in the post IPO period. There is a positive influence on the IPO return of the rate of difference between the intrinsic value and offer price. Information about the block selling rate influences the listing day return as it benchmarks the price levels for listing day open price. Kenourgios,

D.F., Papathanasiou, S. and Rafail Melas, E. (2007) document a significant underpricing in Greek IPOs and the underwriters' prestige and the times of oversubscription significantly affect the underpricing level of the IPOs.

Chopra,R.I.& Kiran.R, (2009) examines the short-run and long-run IPO underpricing and found a strong short-run underpricing in Indian markets. The study also confirms that the initial return of IPO returns is influenced by subscription level, Issue size, Listing Lead time and Age. Mishra, A.K. (2010) found there is significant positive underpricing in Indian IPO market and there is no difference in underpricing by method of public issue such as fixed and book built. Ghosh, S. (2011) examines the underpricing and post listing volatility of stock return and confirms the existence of negative relation between underpricing and volatility. This study confirms the existence of optimism during the pre-issue period and high volumes of subscriptions are attributed to the hot market hypothesis. Van Heerden, G., & Alagidede, P. (2012) examines the short-run IPO performance and finds a significant underpricing in the short run, specifically for the financial sector in the South African market. Chiraz, D. & Anis, J. (2013) found no evidence of IPO initial return and discretionary current accruals in French markets and confirms that the firms engaged in aggressive earnings management may post initially positive returns but fails to sustain in the short run and fails as a public company and goes for delisting. Deb, P. (2013) examines the firm specific characteristics during the IPO, signaling the firm quality and finds that underwriter reputation and patents are positively related to the post listing performance of IPO. Rani, P. (2014) found no influence of firm characteristics IPO pricing specifically with regard to the firm age, turnover, leverage of the firm and promoters stake in the firm in the pre IPO period. Banerjee, S., & Rangamani, K. T. (2015) finds that the subscription level of an IPO is influenced by the FII Inflow, Market P/E, Money supply, DE ratio and board size. Bhatia, S. (2017) finds the correlation between the long run performance and listing day returns. Similarly, it confirms the role of issue size and market conditions influence on the post listing IPO performance. Hawaldar, I. T., Naveen Kumar, K. R., & Mallikarjunappa, T. (2018) documents lesser level underpricing of book built IPOs in India as compared to the fixed price IPOs. Shenoy, S. V., & Srinivasan, K. (2018) confirms the presence of underpricing of IPOs in India and asserts that the listing day performance is well explained by the firm P/E, RoNW and NAV. Gao, S., Brockman, P., Meng, Q., & Yan, X. (2020) studied the price factor and found that IPO issue price is positively related to the quantity-weighted average bid price and the first-day closing price is positively related to the market-clearing bid price.

From the literature survey it is clear that the characteristics of IPOs are country specific and changes over time and predominantly the underpricing of IPOs are due to the information asymmetry, underwriter's reputation, firm size, type of public issue and age of the issuing firm. There are no conclusive evidences on the role of issue size and market momentum effect on listing day performance of IPOs in the context of Indian market.

3. METHODOLOGY

This study verifies the effect of issue size and market momentum on listing day performance of IPOs considering the issue-specific, firm-specific and market-specific characteristics on listing day Absolute Return (AR) and Market Adjusted Return (MAR) of IPOs. It verifies the differential issue size-specific variables such as total subscription rates, category-wise subscription rate, listing delay and firm-specific characteristics such as firm size, revenue and earnings capacity. Also, the study verifies the market momentum specific characteristics such as Market Volatility, Average Market Return and Market Sentiment.

For the study, data of 180 Book Built IPOs that went public between 2011 and 2020 has been collected from National Stock Exchange (NSE) IPOs database. Company financial information is collected from the CMIE PROWESS database, and we considered only IPOs listed on NSE and Nifty as benchmark market index. This study attempts to verify the validity of the over-optimism hypothesis on investors, money left on the table, and signalling hypothesis in the new issue market in the Indian context. The strong existence of undervaluation supports the hypothesis and factors that influence the undervaluation explains the degree of relationship between the explanatory variables and the listing day performance.

3.1 Listing Day-Absolute Return (LD-AR)

Listing day 't' stock return for the sample firm 'i' is obtained by comparing the offer price and listing the day closing price of the stock ' i'. It is computed as follows.

$$AR_{it} = \left(\frac{P_{it}}{P_{i0}} \right) - 1 \underline{\hspace{4cm}} (1)$$

AR_{it} is the listing day return of the stock 'i' on day' t'. P_{it} is the closing price of stock 'i' on the listing day and P_{i0} is the offer price of stock 'i'.

Market return is benchmarked to the Nifty Index. Nifty is India's leading broad-based market index of National Stock Exchange (NSE). Market Index return is obtained by considering the total of daily index return and the number of trading days between the IPO's offer last day and listing day. It is calculated as follows.

$$ER_t = \frac{\sum_{i,t}^{n} \left(\frac{P_{it}}{P_{i0}} \right) - 1}{N} \underline{\hspace{4cm}} (2)$$

ER_{it} is the market average listing day return on day 't'. N is the number of trading days between the IPO's offer last day and the listing day.

3.2 Listing Day-Market Adjusted Return (LD-MAR)

Further to measure the underpricing of the sample IPO stock 'i', the standard method of listing day return calculation is followed. Listing Day market-adjusted return is obtained by taking into account the listing day absolute return and market index return on a listing day 't'.

$$MAR_{it} = \left(\left[\frac{1 + ER_{it}}{1 + AR_{it}} \right] - 1 \right) \times 100$$

MAR_{it} is the market-adjusted return. ER_{it} is the listing day Nifty returns on day 't'. AR_{it} is the listing day return of the stock 'i' on day 't'. The total subscription rate is the ratio between the number of shares offered and the number of shares demanded by the applicants. Category wise subscription rate is considered as per the classification of investors as per the SEBI norms. It includes Qualified Institutional Bidders (QIBs), Non-Institutional Investors (NIIs), and Retail Investors (RIIs) (Chopra,R.I.& Kiran.R, (2009)).

Firm size is measured by taking the assets of the firm (Jaskiewicz, P., González, V. M., Menéndez, S., & Schiereck, D (2005). The average total assets are derived based on the immediate three previous year annual asset value. The average annual revenue for three immediate previous years represents the cash flows of the firm. The earnings capacity is measured through the average PAT for the last three years (Zheng, S. X., & Stangeland, D. A. (2007)). Listing delay is calculated by taking the number of days between offer close day and listing day.

3.3 Ordinary Least Squares

OLS models were used to verify the influence of issue-specific, firm-specific and market-specific factors on listing day Absolute Return (AR) and Market Adjusted Return (MAR) of IPOs based on the issue size criterion samples. Market adjusted model of measuring the underpricing phenomena is considered and initial return is computed based on the difference betwee n the offer price and the listing day closing price. Different models have been developed to analyze the impact of firm and issue-specific characteristics on underpricing. The momentum effect is verified by taking the moving average return of the market for ten previous trading sessions. Data normality has been verified using the Augmented Dickey-Fuller test and confirmed that the sample data is normally distributed.

3.4 Hypotheses:

The study attempts to verify the following test hypotheses

$H_{01:}$ Listing delay has no statistically significant impact on the listing day performance.

$H_{02:}$ Firm size has no statistically significant impact on the listing day performance.

$H_{03:}$ Cash flows of the firm have no statistically significant impact on the listing day performance.

$H_{04:}$ Earnings of the firm have no statistically significant impact on the listing day performance.

$H_{05:}$ Aggregate and Category wise investors' subscription rate has no statistically significant impact on the listing day performance.

$H_{06:}$ There is no statistically significant difference in determinants of IPOs listing day performance for different issue sizes.

$H_{07:}$ Market momentum has no statistically significant impact on the listing day return.

To test the hypothesis, the following regression models were used considering firm and issue-specific characteristics effect on IPO underpricing

Model: 1

$$AR_{i,t} = \alpha + \beta_1 LD_{it} + \beta_2 TA_{it} + \beta_3 TR_{it} + \beta_4 EAR_{it} + \beta_5 QIB_{it} + \beta_6 NII_{it} + \beta_7 RII_{it} + \varepsilon_{i,t} \dots\dots\dots(1)$$

$$AR_{i,t} = \alpha + \beta_1 LD_{it} + \beta_2 TA_{it} + \beta_3 TR_{it} + \beta_4 EAR_{it} + \beta_5 TSR_{it} + \varepsilon_{i,t} \dots\dots\dots\dots(2)$$

Model: 2

$$MAR_{i,t} = \alpha + \beta_1 LD_{it} + \beta_2 TA_{it} + \beta_3 TR_{it} + \beta_4 EAR_{it} + \beta_5 QIB_{it} + \beta_6 NII_{it} + \beta_7 RII_{it} + \varepsilon_{i,t} \ldots\ldots\ldots\ldots(3)$$

$$MAR_{i,t} = \alpha + \beta_1 LD_{it} + \beta_2 TA_{it} + \beta_3 TR_{it} + \beta_4 EAR_{it} + \beta_5 TSR_{it} + \varepsilon_{i,t} \ldots\ldots\ldots\ldots\ldots\ldots\ldots\ldots\ldots(4)$$

4. EMPIRICAL RESULTS AND DISCUSSIONS

Table 01: Estimation Results of OLS Regression

	Model 1		Model 2	
	1	**2**	**3**	**4**
Dependent Variable	AR	AR	MAR	MAR
Independent Variable	Coef.	Coef.	Coef.	Coef.
C	-.090 (.273)	-.070 (.376)	-9.130 (0.264)	-6.987 (0.376)
LD	-.002 (.172)	-.002 (.108)	-0.198 (0.169)	-0.228 (0.107)
LnTA	-.030 (.078)*	-.028 (.097)*	-3.014 (0.079)*	-2.805 (0.097)*
lnTR	.042 (.027)**	.041 (.025)**	4.196 (0.026)**	4.153 (0.025)**
EAR	0.000 (0.647)	0.000 (0.833)	0.000 (0.673)	0.000 (0.838)
QIB	.002 (.004)***	-	0.240 (0.004)***	-
NII	.000 (.409)	-	0.023 (0.409)	-
RII	.012 (.000)***	-	1.180 (0.000)***	-
TSR	-	.004 (.000)***	-	0.429 (0.000)***
R Square	0.439	0.453	0.439	0.451
F stat	19.014 (.000)	23.925 (.000)	19.018 (.000)	23.692 (.000)
Durbin-Watson	1.985	2.028	1.989	2.027
N	180	180	180	180
VIF Mean	2.55		2.737	

Note: *** $p < 0.01$, ** $p < 0.05$, * $p < 0.1$.

The above table shows the regression results of two OLS models developed to test the IPO listing day performance on an aggregate sample basis. Under Model 1, two different equations were tested using multiple regression on listing day absolute return and specific factors such as firm size, cash flows, earnings, a subscription rate of different categories of investors and the aggregate subscription rate. In model 1 equations, we document that the listing day absolute returns are significantly influenced by the firm size, revenue, subscription rate of QIBs and RIIs, confirming the findings of Kenourgios et al. (2007). Interestingly, it is found that there is a negative influence of firm size on absolute returns. It confirms that the firm-specific factors like firm size and revenue of the firm act as a determining factor for listing day performance. Firms with large asset size and strong revenue bases attract institutional and retail investors too, and their subscription rate can indicate the listing day gain. However, in OLS equation 2, the aggregate subscription rate has a significant influence on the listing day performance as measured by its absolute returns. Therefore, the null hypothesis is rejected, confirming that the firm-specific factors influence the listing day performance of Indian listed IPOs. Model 2 was framed to verify the impact of firm-specific factors on listing day underpricing as measured by the market-adjusted returns. Two different equations were tested, and we find no statistically significant evidence of listing delay and earnings of the firm influencing the underpricing. However, other explanatory variables have shown positive coefficients except for the firm size, which has a negative relationship and is statistically significant. Thus, we reject the null hypothesis and conclude that firm-specific factors can determine the underpricing of IPOs.

4.1 Issue Size Effect

The issue size is the offer volume of capital proposed to be raised by the firm through public issues. The investors' reaction varies across small size to large public offers (Van Heerden, G., & Alagidede, P. 2012). Though there are no theoretical evidence to prove the phenomenon and categorize IPOs as what is called as small and large sized public issues, considering the median issue size in Indian primary market, an issue size of less than 500 crore rupees is termed as small size and above 1000 crore is a large size IPO. In this study, an attempt has been made to verify the effect when samples are differentiated based on the issue/offer size and verify the effect of the issue size on listing day absolute return and market-adjusted return. IPOs were categorized into small-cap, mid-cap and large-cap when the issue size is below ₹500 Cr, between ₹500 and ₹1000 Cr and ₹1000 Cr, respectively. The number of sample firms and the mean subscription rate of the category are as follows.

$H_{06:}$ There is no statistically significant difference in determinants of IPOs listing day performance for different issue sizes.

$$AR_{i,t} = \alpha + \beta_1 LD_{it} + \beta_2 TA_{it} + \beta_3 TR_{it} + \beta_4 EAR_{it} + \beta_5 QIB_{it} + \beta_6 NII_{it} + \beta_7 RII_{it} + \varepsilon_{i,t} \dots\dots\dots\dots(3)$$

$$MAR_{i,t} = \alpha + \beta_1 LD_{it} + \beta_2 TA_{it} + \beta_3 TR_{it} + \beta_4 EAR_{it} + \beta_5 QIB_{it} + \beta_6 NII_{it} + \beta_7 RII_{it} + \varepsilon_{i,t} \dots\dots\dots(4)$$

Table 03: Issue size, mean AR, MAR and Category wise Subscription rate

Model	Issue Size (₹)	N	AR	MAR	Issue Size (₹)	(AR) t	(MAR) t	QIBs	NIIs	RIIs
1	<500	92	0.094	9.365	<500, 500≥1000	-.902 (.373)	-.907 (.370)	16.42	72.20	7.71
2	500≥1000	37	0.162	16.276	500≥1000, >1000	.068 (.946)	.090 (.929)	34.25	93.08	6.59
3	>1000	51	0.121	12.126	<500, >1000	-.403 (.689)	-.441 (.661)	33.22	59.82	2.52

The above table shows a higher listing day mean absolute return and underpricing for moderate issue size IPOs than small and large size IPOs. However, it is statistically insignificant when verified for mean differences among the observed groups. It means that moderate issue size IPOs signal a high probability of underpricing and leaves more money on the table.

Qualified Institutional Bidders (QIBs) are large entities reserved with a minimum of 50% of the total issue size and includes SEBI registered entities like Public Financial Institutions, Commercial Banks, Mutual Funds and Foreign Portfolio Investors. Among the sample firms, the average QIBs subscription rate is more when the issue size is greater than ₹500 crores. Non-institutional investors (NIIs) or High Net Worth (HNIs) investors are vested with a minimum of 15% reservation in total issue size. They include Resident Indian individuals, Eligible NRIs, HUFs, Companies, Corporate Bodies, Scientific Institutions, Societies and Trusts who subscribe with a minimum of ₹2 Lakhs and more shares in an IPO. Among the sample firms, the average NIIs subscription rate is more when the issue size is greater when the issue size is between ₹500 crore to ₹1000 crore. NIIs play a dominant role in terms of subscription rate and their presence in IPO is highly significant across the issue size category. Retail individual investors (RIIs) are vested with a minimum of 35% reservation in total issue size. They apply for not more than ₹2 lakhs shares in an IPO and include Resident Indian Individuals, NRIs and HUFs. Among the sample firms, it is observed that on average, RIIs subscription rate is more when the issue size is lesser than ₹500 crore.

Table 04: Estimation results of OLS regressions

Issue Size (Cr.)	<500		500≥1000		>1000	
Model	1		2		3	
Dependent Variable	AR	MAR	AR	MAR	AR	MAR
Independent Variable	Coef.	Coef.	Coef.	Coef.	Coef.	Coef.
C	-.147 (.248)	-14.761 (.248)	.090 (.516)	8.914 (.864)	-.173 (.176)	-17.242 (.332)
LD	-.002 (.211)	-.223 (.210)	.007 (.013)**	.670 (.597)	.011 (.009)***	1.081 (.246)

LnTA	-.057 (.094)*	-5.731 (.094)*	-.042 (.057)*	-4.227 (.463)	.000 (.019)**	-.058 (.976)
lnTR	.075 (.037)**	7.515 (.037)**	.024 (.034)**	2.378 (.492)	.008 (.021)**	.853 (.686)
EAR	5.283 (.835)	5.414 (.831)	2.308 (.000)***	.002 (.573)	-5.128 (.000)***	-5.023 (.858)
QIB	.000 (.895)	.025 (.893)	.004 (.003)***	.425 (.112)	.003 (.001)***	.301 (.002)***
NII	.000 (.435)	.032 (.436)	.000 (.001)*	.011 (.896)	.001 (.001)*	.080 (.231)
RII	.016 (.000)***	1.563 (.000)***	.002 (.005)***	.209 (.706)	-.014 (.019)**	-1.373 (.469)
R Square	.445	.443	.630	.628	.632	.626
F stat	8.324 (.000)	8.260 (.000)	5.743 (.000)	5.688 (.000)	8.577 (.000)	8.376 (0.00)
Durbin-Watson	2.132	2.133	1.599	1.600	1.758	1.761
N	92	92	36	36	49	49
VIF Mean	2.99	2.99	4.75	4.75	3.79	3.79

Note: *** $p < 0.01$, ** $p < 0.05$, * $p < 0.1$.

Two different OLS equations were tested under different levels of the issue size to verify the effect of issue sizes on the listing day return and underpricing. For this purpose, the IPOs were grouped based on their volume of capital raised. Three models were developed where Model 1 is for an issue size of less than ₹500 Cr, Model 2 is for an issue size of more than ₹500 cr, but less than ₹1000 Cr and finally Model 3 is for above ₹1000 cr issue size. Listing day returns were measured at its Absolute Return (AR) and the underpricing using a Market Adjusted Return (MAR). The model 1 results reveal that when IPO issue size is small, the listing day returns both at absolute terms and market-adjusted terms (Underpricing) are significantly influenced by the firm size confirming the findings of Chopra,R.I.& Kiran.R, (2009), the total revenue, and the subscription rate of RIIs. It is observed that listing returns variations are explained 44.5% by the explanatory variables with the goodness of fit. However, in Model 2 (500≥1000), the listing day absolute returns (AR) are significantly influenced by listing delay, firm size, profitability, revenue, and the subscription rate of all categories of investors with an explanatory strength of 63%. However, there was no evidence of IPO underpricing (MAR) impact by model explanatory variables.

Large IPOs attract different clusters of applicants as compared to the small issue size IPOs. It is observed that Institutional investors look for large size firms, and their subscription rate is higher than the normal compared to small-sized issues. In the case of Model 3 (1000>), the AR is influenced by listing delay, firm size, profitability, revenue, and the subscription rate of all categories of investors with an explanatory strength of 63%. However, there is a statistically significant influence on IPO underpricing (MAR) by the market momentum and the subscription rate of QIBs.

Table 05: Underpricing and Overpricing of IPOs

	All sample*		Sample Category issue size*					
	Under pricing	Over pricing	Underpricing			Overpricing		
			<500	500≥1000	>1000	<500	500≥1000	>1000
N	110	70	52	27	31	41	10	19
Mean MAR	28.16	-14.77	32.66	25.196	23.200	-20.570	-7.803	-5.942
Nifty**	.0009	-.0012	0.0001	0.0026	0.0012	0.0001	0.0025	-0.0601

*Note: Underpricing is when the Listing Day MAR is Positive and Overpricing is when the Listing Day MAR Negative. **Nifty benchmark mean return

From all sample observations, it is found that predominantly IPOs are underpriced with a mean return of 28.16%. Underpricing is associated with the positive benchmark return. The overpricing is found with the mean negative returns of 14.77% and considerably associated with the negative benchmark return. The relative strength of underpricing phenomena is greater, and it substantiates the investors over-optimism and loss aversion biases in the market. At its segment-wise sample based on the issue size, it is found that price imperfections, i.e. underpricing or overpricing and issue size, have a negative correlation, wherein, as the issue size increases, the price imperfections decreases. It means a fair price is possible when a large volume of capital is raised as the merchant bankers' active interest in such IPOs is greater than the small IPOs.

4.2 Market Momentum

H07: Market Momentum has no statistically significant impact on the listing day return.

Listing day and immediate previous week benchmark index volatility signal the listing day performance of IPOs. Irrespective of other fundamentals, volatility around the listing day can significantly affect the price movements. The participant's attention and sentiments support volatility predictions and price performance, although the magnitudes of the improvements are relatively small from an economic point of view (Audrino, F., Sigrist, F., & Ballinari, D. 2020). Market momentum shows the speed of change in stock price and indicates the strength or weakness of stock price. It affects the investors' short run sentiments and helps traders time their trade, especially for retail investors (Dorn, D. 2009). The *day of the trade sentiment hypothesis* states that the listing day benchmark volatility has a more significant influence on the IPOs performance. Market sentiments likely to change between offer close day and the listing day. We notice that when the market is gripped with persistent bear sentiments during this period, even fundamentally strong IPOs listing day expected return will get adversely affected.

In this study, the market momentum is considered an explanatory variable for determining the listing day return and underpricing. The proxies to market momentum taken is index volatility (*Vol*), index ten days moving average return (*Iavgret*), listing day index trend (*trend*) and listing day index return. Volatility is computed by taking the standard deviation of the immediate previous ten days price changes. Index trend is the dummy variable created by assigning zero for negative closing price and one for the positive closing price of Index. Listing day return is the percentage change in return as compared to the previous day (*ret*). Momentum effect on IPO listing day absolute return and underpricing is verified using Generalized Method of Moments (GMM) estimation. GMM estimation is used with two-stage least squares and standard errors and covariance computed using the estimation weighting matrix. The benchmark index average returns for ten previous trading sessions immediate to the listing day were calculated as follows.

$$Iavgret_{i,i} \frac{\sum_{i,t}^{n=10}\left(\frac{p_{it}}{p_{i0}}\right)-1}{N} \tag{3}$$

Iavgret$_{it}$ *is the simple moving average of a benchmark index. N is the previous ten trading sessions immediately before listing day 't'.* The hypothesis tested here is $H_{07:}$ Market Momentum has no statistically significant impact on the listing day return. The market momentum effect is verified in the following equation.

$$AR_{i,t} = \alpha + \beta_1 Iavgret_{it} + \beta_2 trend_{it} + \beta_3 vol_{it} + \beta_4 ret_{it} + \varepsilon_{i,t} \dots\dots\dots\dots (1)$$

$$MAR_{i,t} = \alpha + \beta_1 Iavgret_{it} + \beta_2 trend_{it} + \beta_3 vol_{it} + \beta_4 ret_{it} + \varepsilon_{i,t} \dots\dots\dots\dots (2)$$

Table: 06: Estimation results of Generalized Method of Moments

Dependent Variable	1	2
	AR	MAR
Independent Variable	Coef.	Coef.
Iavgret	17.878 (0.035)**	1717.125 (0.043)**
Trend	0.026 (0.703)	2.560 (0.703)
Vol	-11.650 (0.076)*	-1175.280 (0.073)*
Ret	-3.729 (0.247)	-382.540 (0.235)
C	0.207 (0.003)	20.772 (0.003)
R Square	0.064	0.062
Adjusted R-squared	0.043	0.041
Method: Generalized Method of Moments; Estimation weighting matrix: Two-Stage Least Squares, Standard errors & covariance computed using estimation weighting matrix, N=180;DW Stat: 2.0416; Note: *** p < 0.01, ** p < 0.05, * p < 0.1.		

The GMM estimation output shows that the index moving average return and the Index volatility influences the absolute return and the IPO underpricing. The simple moving average has a significant positive influence, whereas the Index volatility has a significant negative influence on the listing day gains and underpricing. The *day of the trade sentiment hypothesis* confirms that the day effect either on listing day or immediate previous week market trend or a sudden short-run persistent bull or bear momentum between offer close and listing day adversely affect the price movements as any sudden change in trend affects expected return and valuations of shares. Technical analysts assert that the immediate previous ten-day market trends have more probability of influencing the stock prices. This study observed that irrespective of its fundamental factors, the market momentum as measured by the moving average has a strong positive influence on determining the IPOs listing day performance. It means a poor market trend was persisting in the immediate one to two weeks before the listing day should signal that the expected returns may deviate on listing day. Also, it is observed that volatility is negatively correlated with the listing day gain and underpricing. The shift in volatility trend affects the return adversely, and an increase in average returns has a positive influence. This signals that the market momentum is a determining factor for evaluating the underpricing and listing day performance of a firm irrespective of company fundamentals. Interestingly it is observed in our study that there is no influence of listing day benchmark index performance. We used the Nifty trend to take the index's closing value as positive or negative for the day and found that it does not matter for the newly listed shares performance. Similarly, the Nifty listing day return has no significant influence.

5. CONCLUSIONS

Determining a fair price for an IPO is a challenging task as there are no previous reference prices. Therefore, price depends on the quality of information disclosed by the firm in the offer document. However, empirical evidence shows that one can draw clues about the listing day performance by understanding certain firms and Issue-specific characteristics of an IPO. It signals market its fair price and investors based on their understanding of the firm's financial condition and industry prospect or the intermediary's recommendation to respond to the IPOs. Generally, investors perceive that a firm offers shares at less than its fair value and thus expects a listing day positive returns leaving more money on the table.

This study document verifies the role of differential issue size and market momentum on IPO performance and documents that the firm size, cash flows, and subscription rate of QIBs and RIIs significantly influence the Listing day absolute return the underpricing. It verifies the signalling hypothesis confirming that offer size and market momentum signals IPO listing day performance. We find that market momentum has a significant influence on IPO performance. Predominantly, the Book Built IPOs in India are underpriced and the issue size determines the degree of listing day returns and underpricing. We also find a direct relationship between the issue size and the underpricing wherein a moderate to large issue size has more underpricing with an increased return. Offer size and listing timing are critical as the market sentiment drives the valuations and any swing in the market sentiments on a listing day adversely influences the IPO returns. The probability of dramatic change in sentiments around the listing day affects the investors as they apply for shares based on the current market sentiment. Any unusual movement in the benchmark index disrupts their expected return affecting the stock to react differently than expected on a listing day. It is observed that irrespective of company fundamentals, IPOs post an unexpected return on the day of listing due to momentum and issue size effect.

REFERENCES

1. Aruğaslan, O., Cook, D., & Kieschnick, R. (2004). Monitoring as a Motivation for IPO Underpricing. The Journal of Finance, 59(5), 2403–2420. Retrieved May 30, 2020, from www.jstor.org/stable/3694828
2. Audrino, F., Sigrist, F., & Ballinari, D. (2020). The impact of sentiment and attention measures on stock market volatility. International Journal of Forecasting, 36(2), 334–357. http://doi.org/10.1016/j.ijforecast.2019.05.010
3. Bajo, E., & Raimondo, C. (2017). Media sentiment and IPO underpricing. Journal of Corporate Finance, 46, 139–153. http://doi.org/10.1016/j.jcorpfin.2017.06.003
4. Banerjee, S., & Rangamani, K. T. (2015). Determinants of investor's subscription level of IPOs: Evidence from indian capital market in post mandatory IPO grading regime. DLSU Business and Economics Review, 24(2), 77–91.
5. Banu Durukan, M. (2002). The relationship between IPO returns and factors influencing IPO performance: Case of Istanbul Stock Exchange. Managerial Finance, 28(2), 18–38. http://doi.org/10.1108/03074350210767672
6. Bhatia, S. (2017). A Study on the Long-Run Performance of Initial Public Offerings in India. SSRN Electronic Journal, (April). http://doi.org/10.2139/ssrn.2926872
7. Binay, M., Gatchev, V., & Pirinsky, C. (2007). The Role of Underwriter-Investor Relationships in the IPO Process. The Journal of Financial and Quantitative Analysis, 42(3), 785-809. Retrieved May 30, 2020, from www.jstor.org/stable/27647320
8. Boulton, T. J., Smart, S. B., & Zutter, C. J. (2011). Earnings quality and international IPO underpricing. Accounting Review, 86(2), 483–505. http://doi.org/10.2308/accr.00000018
9. Bouzouita, N., Gajewski, J., & Gresse, C. (2015). Liquidity Benefits from IPO Underpricing: Ownership Dispersion or Information Effect. Financial Management, 44(4), 785–810. Retrieved May 30, 2020, from www.jstor.org/stable/24736541
10. Chambers, D., & Dimson, E. (2009). IPO Underpricing over the Very Long Run. The Journal of Finance, 64(3), 1407–1443. Retrieved May 30, 2020, from www.jstor.org/stable/20488005
11. Chiraz, D. (2013). Earnings management and performance of French IPO companies. Journal of Accounting and Taxation, 5(1), 1–14. http://doi.org/10.5897/jat2013.0106
12. Chopra, R. I. (2009). Price Performance of IPOs in Indian Stock Market. Social Sciences, (2009).
13. Deb, P. (2013). Signaling type and post-IPO performance. European Management Review, 10(2), 99–116. http://doi.org/10.1111/emre.12012

14. Deb, P. (2014). Cutting The 'Gordian Knot': Director Ownership, Underpricing, And Stock Liquidity In IPO Firms. Journal of Managerial Issues, 26(2), 130-156. Retrieved May 30, 2020, from www.jstor.org/stable/43488946

15. Dolvin, S., & Kirby, J. (2016). The Impact of Board Structure on IPO Underpricing. The Journal of Private Equity, 19(2), 15–21. Retrieved May 30, 2020, from www.jstor.org/stable/44396791

16. Dorn, D. (2009). Does Sentiment Drive the Retail Demand for IPOs? The Journal of Financial and Quantitative Analysis, 44(1), 85-108. Retrieved July 15, 2020, from www.jstor.org/stable/40505916.

17. Fitza, M. Lerner, D. A. (2010). IPO underpricing from the perspective of the issuing firm: Money left on the table or strategic gain? Frontiers of Entrepreneurship Research, 30(1). Retrieved from http://proquest.umi.com/pqdweb?did=2149726741&Fmt=7&clientId=5239&RQT=309&VName=PQD

18. Flagg, D., & Margetis, S. (2008). What Characteristics of Underwriters Influence Underpricing? The Journal of Private Equity, 11(2), 49-59. Retrieved May 30, 2020, from www.jstor.org/stable/43503549

19. Gagnon, L., & Karolyi, G. (2009). Information, Trading Volume, and International Stock Return Comovements: Evidence from Cross-Listed Stocks. The Journal of Financial and Quantitative Analysis, 44(4), 953–986. Retrieved July 15, 2020, from www.jstor.org/stable/40505976

20. Gao, S., Brockman, P., Meng, Q., & Yan, X. (2020). Differences of opinion, institutional bids, and IPO underpricing. *Journal of Corporate Finance*, *60*(January 2018), 1–19. http://doi.org/10.1016/j.jcorpfin.2019.101540

21. Garfinkel, J. (1993). IPO Underpricing, Insider Selling and Subsequent Equity Offerings: Is Underpricing a Signal of Quality? Financial Management, 22(1), 74–83. Retrieved May 30, 2020, from www.jstor.org/stable/3665967

22. Ghosh, S. (2011). Revisiting IPO Underpricing in India. SSRN Electronic Journal. http://doi.org/10.2139/ssrn.703501

23. Hawaldar, I. T., Naveen Kumar, K. R., & Mallikarjunappa, T. (2018). Pricing and performance of IPOs: Evidence from Indian stock market. Cogent Economics and Finance, 6(1). http://doi.org/10.1080/23322039.2017.1420350

24. Jaskiewicz, P., González, V. M., Menéndez, S., & Schiereck, D. (2005). Long-run IPO performance analysis of German and Spanish family-owned businesses. Family Business Review, 18(3), 179–202. http://doi.org/10.1111/j.1741-6248.2005.00041.x

25. Kenourgios, D.F., Papathanasiou, S. and Rafail Melas, E. (2007), "Initial performance of Greek IPOs, underwriter's reputation and oversubscription", Managerial Finance, Vol. 33 No. 5, pp. 332–343. https://doi.org/10.1108/03074350710739614

26. Kim, J., Shin, S., Lee, H. S., & Oh, K. J. (2019). A machine learning portfolio allocation system for IPOs in Korean markets using GA-rough set theory. Sustainability (Switzerland), 11(23). http://doi.org/10.3390/su11236803

27. Kim, K. a., Kitsabunnarat, P., & Nofsinger, J. R. (2004). Ownership and operating performance in an emerging market: Evidence from Thai IPO firms. Journal of Corporate Finance, 10(3), 355–381. http://doi.org/10.1016/S0929-1199(02)00019-6

28. Kimutai, G., Aluvi, P. A., Durairaj, Y. A., & Kareem, S. A. (2013). International journal of business economics & management research. Internaltional Journal of Business Economics and Management Research, 3(5), 3–6.

29. Krishnamurti, C., Thong, T. Y., & Ramanna, V. (2012). Grey Market for Indian IPOs: Investor Sentiment and After-Market Performance. SSRN Electronic Journal, (August). http://doi.org/10.2139/ssrn.1972478

30. Lee, P., Taylor, S., & Walter, T. (1999). IPO Underpricing Explanations: Implications from Investor Application and Allocation Schedules. The Journal of Financial and Quantitative Analysis, 34(4), 425–444. doi:10.2307/2676228

31. Lee, P., Taylor, S., & Walter, T. (1999). IPO Underpricing Explanations: Implications from Investor Application and Allocation Schedules. The Journal of Financial and Quantitative Analysis, 34(4), 425–444. doi:10.2307/2676228

32. Leone, A., Steve Rock, & Willenborg, M. (2007). Disclosure of Intended Use of Proceeds and Underpricing in Initial Public Offerings. Journal of Accounting Research, 45(1), 111–153. Retrieved May 30, 2020, from www.jstor.org/stable/4622024

33. Li, R., Liu, W., Liu, Y., & Tsai, S. B. (2018). IPO underpricing after the 2008 financial crisis: A study of the Chinese stock markets. Sustainability (Switzerland), 10(8), 1–13. http://doi.org/10.3390/su10082844

Whether Impact of the Acquisition is Reflected on Share Price of Acquiring Companies! - A Study Based on Few Acquisitions by Indian Corporates.

Mr. Sudipta De
Assistant Professor
Commerce and Management Department
St. Xavier's University, Kolkata
West Bengal, India
desudipta26@gmail.com

Dr. Ashoke Mondal
Assistant Professor,
Commerce and Management Department
West Bengal State University, Barasat
West Bengal, India
ashokemondal@wbsu.ac.in,
mondal_ashoke@rediffmail.com

Abstract

Merger and Acquisition become an important avenue for restructuring of business across the globe. The corporates involve in acquisition may have different motives. The ultimate motive is to increase the value of business by generating positive synergy. The synergy is mainly reflected on the overall performance of the company and ultimately on its share prices. The ultimate success of an acquisition is reflected on improvement of performance and increase in share price of the companies involved in the acquisition process. The motive of the investors is to gain by investing on the shares of the companies involved in the acquisition process. The conflict between the perceived performances of the management of companies with the general investors may be observed in many cases and in many cases the perceptions of company management and general investors are congruent. In many cases the share values of the involved companies in the acquisition process are influenced by the perception of investors. In this paper, an attempt has been taken to study the impacts of acquisition based on abnormal returns. The hypothesis is based on the assumption that there will be significant change in share price and returns of the acquiring companies due to acquisition. The research is conducted on most of the important acquisitions by Indian corporates during 2017 to 2019. The statistical evaluation is done by using MS-Excel.

Keywords: Acquisition, India, acquisition announcement, return, risk, paired sample t test. Cumulative abnormal return, Abnormal return.

INTRODUCTION

Merger and acquisition (M&A) is a path to achieve growth globally. Indian context is not different. Presently many companies are also following alternatives to traditional M&A (like partnerships, alliances, joint ventures, and other alternative investments) to achieve growth and to overcome crisis[1]. Good acquisitions lead to achieve new avenues for growth and exploit new business models. Many incidents may boost or reduce the pace of M&A deals. These events may be national or international. The number of merger and acquisition deal was declined in India during 2017, especially in the second half of 2017. The Indian economy has experienced two major economic events in the years 2016 and 2017. These are demonetization and implementation of GST respectively. M&A is not only beneficial for the expansion and improvement of performance of the company but also it is beneficial for the economy. Indian government encourages M&A activity primarily to increase the performance of the companies and smooth flow of inbound and outbound investment. The other reason is that the stock market and participants in the stock market become more efficient and knowledge of the shareholders is improved. They are now forced to take decision whether to participate or not in the acquisition process without knowing the actual outcome of the acquisition.

Many researchers and experts have focused on the performance appraisal of acquisition with respect to operating and economic synergy. Many have focused upon the abnormal return to shares of the acquirer and target companies. Impact of acquisition announcement over the share price of the acquiring company with respect to a specific sector or with respect to few cross border M&A are also tested in many literature. The impact of acquisition announcement (irrespective of a specific sector or a specific type of acquisition) by Indian acquirers on the share price, cumulative abnormal return (CAR), average abnormal return (AAR) of acquiring companies may be nurtured in this article.

The impact on share price of the acquiring company depends upon the declared synergy (depends upon the synergy, control and complexity due to acquisition process) by the acquiring firm and perceived synergy (depends upon the perception of the experts and individual shareholders etc.). Intrinsic value of the acquiring company depends upon three parameters synergy, control and complexity due to acquisition process (Prof. Aswath Damodaran). Many acquiring companies offered substantial control premium on assumption that the performance of the target company would improve under new management and/or the combine operation would fetch substantial synergy.

In this research all major acquisition initiated by Indian acquirers (listed in any recognised stock exchange in India) are considered during 2017 to 2019. The research is conducted to see the impact of acquisition announcement news upon the share price, abnormal return of the listed acquirer companies. In this paper, an attempt has been taken to study the impacts of acquisition based on abnormal returns. The hypothesis is based on the assumption that there will be significant change in share price, return of the acquiring companies due to acquisition.

---

[1] M&A Trends Survey: The future of M&A, Deal trends in a changing world, October 2020 by Deloitte US

LITERATURE REVIEW

The implication of M&A may be discussed in two ways. One is the implication from the perspective of share price (stock market based) and another is from the perspective of the performance of the company (Accounting based). Market based studies gave emphasis upon impact of acquisition over stock price, return etc. Many researchers have investigated the impact of merger and acquisition over the share price, volatility and investment outcome on the acquirers and target companies.

Anson Wong (2009) has evaluated the impact of M&A announcements on security prices with respect to acquirer firms as well as target firms in Asia. The study was conducted in the light of Asian financial crisis and Information Technology crisis. The study revealed that the impact of acquisition over the shares of acquiring company was favourable but the same for the shares of target companies was not favourable. The author examined CAR to measure the impact of M&A over the participating companies and revealed that the impact of acquisition on the share price of the target firm was not favourable whereas the impact was favourable for the acquiring firms.

David M. Barton and Roger Sherman (1984) have investigated the impact of acquisition on price and profit derived from different product lines. The resulted synergy due to acquisition was favourable and adequate with respect to analysis of two firms in this research.

Julian Franks et al have analysed post-merger performance instead of analysis of abnormal return due as announcement effects. The authors have evaluated the post-merger performance with respect to few portfolio benchmarks and identified no abnormal performance due to M&A.

Few researchers have evaluated the impact of acquisition by using event study method evaluated the impact of M&A by measuring Cumulative Abnormal Return (Sunny Oswal et al, Panayides, P. M et al, John Doukas et al, Paul Asquith et al).

Panayides, P. M et al investigated the impact of acquisition announcement over the stock market with respect few shipping companies. The authors have conducted event study method to see the impact of M&A. The authors have estimated the CAR and AR of few liner shipping companies to see whether the impact of acquisition over is significant. The study revealed that the outcome of the M&A over the synergy and shareholders wealth is significant and favourable.

E Akben-Selcuk et al have investigated the impact of acquisition over Turkish companies with respect to change in operating performance as well as with respect to stock price movement. As per their research the returns for stocks of Turkish acquirers were more than average return for the short time window. The authors have also identified decrease in operating performance of the acquirers in post-acquisition period.

John Doukas and Nickolaos (1988) had conducted a research on the US acquiring companies. It had been revealed from their research that the negative abnormal return become high when the acquiring firm enters into a new business or in a new geofigureical market.

Paul Asquith et al have identified the impact of M&A over the shares of acquiring firms. The have also revealed that the gain of acquiring company (through positive abnormal return) is not at a cost of sacrificed return of target company.

RESEARCH OBJECTIVE

Many researchers have analysed the impact of M&A through analysis of abnormal return. Many have evaluated the impact of M&A with respect to a specific industry or with respect to a specific type of acquisition. In this paper, an attempt has been taken to study the impacts of acquisition based on abnormal returns. The hypothesis is framed to check whether there is a significant impact on abnormal return during the event window due to acquisition. The research is conducted on the acquisition during the period 2017 to 2019 in India where the acquiring companies are Indian listed companies.

RESEARCH METHODOLOGY

The data is mainly collected from the secondary sources. The stock price of listed Indian acquiring companies are collected mainly in two sections from the website of Indian recognised stock exchanges like BSE and/or NSE. The two sections are i) 180 (-180 days prior to -20th days from the date of acquisition) days share prices of post-acquisition period before post 20th days from the date of announcement of acquisition and ii) before and after 20 days (+/-20 days) share price with respect to the date of announcement of acquisition. Focus is given on acquisition during 2017 to 2019 where the acquiring company is a listed Indian company irrespective of any industry or type of acquisition. The objective is to focus upon all types of acquisition. The return is calculated on the basis of daily return.

The Cumulative Abnormal Return (CAR) for individual acquiring company, Cumulative Average Abnormal Return (CAAR) for all the acquiring companies, Average Abnormal Return (AAR) for the individual companies are calculated for the +/-20 days' time horizon with respect to the date of acquisition for the analysis purpose.

The beta value is calculated based of daily percentage change in return of a security due to change in 1% daily market return. The market return is calculated based on SENSEX closing value. The expected return of a security is calculated based on Capital Asset Pricing Model. Abnormal return (AR) of a particular day (t) is calculated by subtracting expected daily return from the actual daily return of the security.

Calculation of daily Beta (β)

The value of daily β, which is the volatility of share price of a company with respect to market, has been evaluated as:

$$\dagger = \frac{\%\ \text{Change in Return of Company}}{\%\ \text{Change in Return of Sensex}} \quad \text{..........(1)}$$

Calculation of Expected Return

The values of Expected Return on daily basis are calculated by using the CAPM model as:

Expected return = Risk free return + [β*" ("Sensex return-Risk free return")].............(2)

Calculation of Abnormal Return

The values of Daily Abnormal return from the company are calculated as:

Abnormal return = Return from company - Expected return.......................(3)

Calculation of Cumulative Abnormal Return

The cumulative values of abnormal return have been calculated as:

Cumulative abnormal return on n^{th} day = Abnormal return on n^{th} day + Cumulative abnormal return till $(n-1)^{th}$ day......................(4)

Calculation of Average of Abnormal Return
The average of abnormal returns of all companies each day is calculated as:

$$\text{Average Abnormal return for } n_{th} \text{ day} = \frac{\sum \text{Abnormal return of company for } n_{th} \text{ day}}{\text{Number of companies}} ...(5)$$

Conducting t-test of hypothesis

Test for equality of two mean - t-test of hypothesis has been done to validate the existence of Abnormal return.

For doing t-test of hypothesis, first of all, the value of t is calculated as:

$$\text{Calculated value of } t = \frac{m_1 - m_2}{\sqrt{\frac{S_1^2}{N_1} - \frac{S_2^2}{N_2}}} ....(6)$$

Where,
m_1 = Mean obtained from sample space of 180 days
m_2 = Mean obtained from sample space of 40 days
S_1 = Standard deviation obtained from sample space of 180 days
S_2 = Standard deviation obtained from sample space of 40 days
N_1 = Number of elements in sample space of 180 days
N_2 = Number of elements in sample space of 40 days

Now,

- If |*Calculated value of t*| > *Critical value of t, Then, Alternate hypothesis is accepted and Null hypothesis is rejected.*

- If |*Calculated value of t*| < *Critical value of t , Then,Alternate hypothesis is rejected and Null hypothesis is accepted*

T-test of hypothesis for single sample space
For doing t-test of hypothesis for single sample space, the value of t has to be calculated as:

$$\text{Value of } t = \frac{\overline{x} - \sigma}{(\frac{s}{\sqrt{n}})} .....(7)$$

Here, $\bar{x}$ = Mean value of sample space
μ_0 = Threshold mean value
S = Standard deviation
n = Number of elements

Now, if Calculated value of t < Critical value of t, then, Null hypothesis is satisfied and Alternate hypothesis is rejected.

And if Calculated value of t > Critical value of t, then, Alternate hypothesis is satisfied and Null value is rejected.

In our consideration, Null Hypothesis: Average Abnormal Return=0

And, Alternative hypothesis: Average Abnormal Return>0

Plotting of figures

Finally, the figures of abnormal return of each of the companies are plotted for the event period.

This shows the scenario of abnormal returns during few days before and after the event of acquisition.

The hypothesis for this study are as follows:

1. H_1 = AR during acquisition period (-20 to +20) for the acquiring firm is positive.
2. H_2 = There is a significant change in average abnormal return (AAR)

To test the above hypothesis, the 180 days average of average annual return [Avg(AAR)] before the 20th day of the post-acquisition period is compared with the Avg(AAR) of the acquisition period (i.e +/-20 days w.r.t acquisition).

DATA DESCRIPTION, ANALYSIS AND RESULT

The study covers all the acquisition by Indian listed acquiring companied during the period 2017 to 2019. The objective is to analysis the impact of acquisition irrespective of type of acquisition and irrespective of any industry. Based on all the acquisition during 2017 to 2019, 8 acquisitions are selected, where the acquirer is Indian Listed Company (Table 1).

Table 1: Acquisition by Indian Listed Acquirer

Name of the Acquirer Company	Name of the Target company	Date of Acquisition announcement
Airtel	Telenor	14-May-2018
Axis Bank	Freecharge	27-July-2017
Torrent Pharmaceuticals	Unichem	14-December-2017
Havells	Lioyds	18-February-2017

IndusInd Bank	Bharat Financials(SKS Microfinance)	10-June-2019
ONGC	HPCL	20-January-2018
Tata Steel	Bhushan Steel	18-May-2018
Power Finance Corporation	Rural Electrification Corporation Limited	22-March-2019

Table 2: CAAR based on the 8 acquiring companies

Day	Airtel 40 days CAR	Axis Bank 40 days CAR	Havells 40 days CAR	IndusInd Bank 40 days CAR	ONGC 40 days CAR	Power Finance Corporation 40 days CAR	TATA Steel 40 days CAR	Torrent Pharma 40 days CAR	Average CAR
-20	-0.28%	-1.32%	-0.08%	1.40%	0.01%	0.00%	0.42%	0.00%	0.02%
-19	-0.32%	-1.33%	-0.10%	1.62%	0.02%	0.02%	1.60%	-0.03%	0.19%
-18	-0.41%	-1.36%	-0.10%	1.61%	0.00%	0.17%	1.55%	-0.48%	0.12%
-17	0.27%	-1.26%	-4.64%	1.39%	0.03%	0.11%	2.04%	-0.59%	-0.33%
-16	0.63%	-1.56%	-4.68%	1.41%	0.02%	0.20%	2.44%	-0.60%	-0.27%
-15	-0.19%	-1.55%	-4.76%	1.44%	0.05%	-0.11%	2.42%	-0.60%	-0.41%
-14	-0.01%	-0.58%	-4.75%	1.51%	2.39%	-0.08%	2.35%	-0.59%	0.03%
-13	-0.10%	-0.58%	-4.76%	0.85%	2.81%	-0.10%	2.36%	-0.60%	-0.01%
-12	-1.06%	-0.57%	-5.03%	0.84%	2.83%	0.04%	1.92%	-0.61%	-0.21%
-11	-1.10%	-0.55%	-5.26%	0.86%	2.88%	0.26%	1.61%	-0.61%	-0.24%
-10	-1.05%	-0.56%	-5.49%	0.44%	2.86%	0.13%	1.65%	-0.61%	-0.33%
-9	-1.08%	-0.60%	-5.46%	0.17%	2.86%	-0.21%	1.75%	-0.62%	-0.40%
-8	-1.13%	-0.52%	-5.64%	0.13%	2.68%	-0.12%	1.68%	-0.37%	-0.41%
-7	-1.01%	-0.49%	-5.48%	0.14%	2.68%	-0.02%	1.83%	-0.42%	-0.35%
-6	-0.80%	-0.49%	-5.99%	0.65%	2.58%	-0.03%	2.10%	-0.40%	-0.30%
-5	-0.82%	-0.25%	-5.50%	0.70%	2.55%	-0.08%	2.58%	-0.38%	-0.15%
-4	0.50%	-0.25%	-4.09%	0.51%	2.55%	-0.08%	1.41%	-0.38%	0.02%
-3	0.50%	-0.30%	4.17%	0.51%	2.55%	1.54%	9.79%	-0.39%	2.30%
-2	-0.03%	0.22%	-13.17%	0.99%	2.60%	-0.91%	9.76%	-0.38%	-0.11%
-1	-2.44%	0.31%	-13.05%	1.09%	2.57%	13.63%	9.72%	-0.37%	1.43%
0	Event Day	Event Day	Event Day	Event Day	Event Day	Event Day	Event Day	Event Day	Event Day
1	-0.88%	-6.46%	-0.04%	-0.20%	2.53%	15.51%	9.67%	-0.38%	2.47%
2	-0.99%	-6.46%	-0.31%	0.03%	2.80%	15.35%	9.72%	-0.38%	2.47%
3	-1.05%	-6.32%	0.08%	0.03%	2.82%	15.63%	9.38%	-0.38%	2.52%

4	-1.07%	-6.28%	0.72%	0.07%	2.86%	15.65%	9.37%	-0.39%	2.62%
5	-1.07%	-6.14%	0.41%	-3.56%	2.86%	13.37%	9.43%	-0.36%	1.87%
6	-1.19%	-6.12%	0.41%	-4.02%	2.86%	13.04%	9.42%	-0.36%	1.75%
7	-1.22%	-6.12%	-0.21%	-4.02%	2.80%	13.27%	9.41%	-0.45%	1.68%
8	-1.23%	-6.13%	0.44%	-3.95%	2.80%	13.67%	9.24%	-0.42%	1.80%
9	-1.23%	-6.05%	0.44%	-3.69%	2.77%	13.64%	9.14%	-0.42%	1.83%
10	-1.21%	-6.05%	0.45%	-3.55%	2.76%	14.18%	9.06%	-0.39%	1.91%
11	-1.20%	-6.14%	0.38%	-3.55%	2.77%	14.33%	9.06%	-0.38%	1.91%
12	-0.97%	-6.13%	0.49%	-3.55%	2.77%	14.37%	8.84%	-2.37%	1.68%
13	-1.08%	-6.14%	0.35%	-3.38%	2.77%	14.31%	8.85%	-2.29%	1.67%
14	-0.97%	-5.20%	0.34%	-3.48%	2.76%	12.81%	8.92%	-2.32%	1.61%
15	-0.98%	-5.22%	-0.57%	-3.44%	2.75%	12.89%	8.85%	-2.28%	1.50%
16	-0.69%	-5.19%	-0.53%	-3.39%	2.74%	12.89%	10.49%	-2.28%	1.76%
17	-0.64%	-5.08%	-3.06%	-3.42%	2.75%	13.37%	10.46%	-2.37%	1.50%
18	-0.67%	-5.08%	-2.47%	-3.52%	2.73%	13.37%	9.40%	-2.36%	1.43%
19	-0.82%	-5.01%	-11.20%	-3.57%	2.74%	13.38%	9.40%	-2.23%	0.34%
20	-3.06%	-5.02%	-11.08%	-3.56%	2.76%	12.37%	8.39%	-2.24%	-0.18%

Table 3: CAR value based on (-/+ 20 days) of the Listed Indian Acquirer

No.	Indian acquirer (Listed)	CAR (-/+20days)
1	Airtel 40 days CAR	-3.06%
2	Axis Bank 40 days CAR	-5.02%
3	Havells 40 days CAR	-11.08%
4	IndusInd Bank 40 days CAR	-3.56%
5	ONGC 40 days CAR	2.76%
6	Power Finance Corporation 40 days CAR	12.37%
7	TATA Steel 40 days CAR	8.39%
8	Torrent Pharma 40 days CAR	-2.24%

Fig. 1: *Percentage of Abnormal Return for the individual acquiring company*

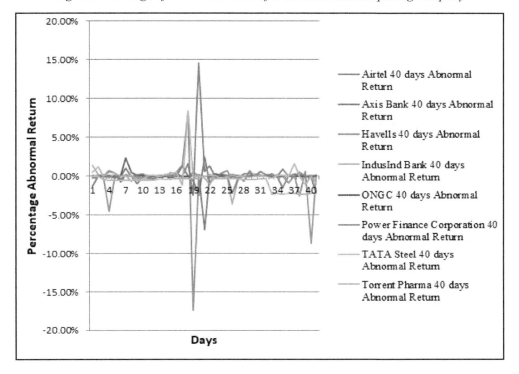

Both the figure 1 and figure 2 sows the abnormal return during (before 20days to after 20 days from the date of acquisition) event period. Therefore the day 21 signifies the date of acquisition in the figures.

The abnormal return is observed during the +/- 2 days from the date of acquisition from the figureical presentation and gradually that stabilises. This is observed for individual acquiring companies (figure 1). The average abnormal return is also very high during +/- 2 days with respect to all eight companies (figure 2).

Result of Hypothesis 1: H_1 = AR during acquisition period (-20 to +20) for the acquiring firm is positive.

The t test result shows by Considering the sample space as Average Abnormal Return, the calculated value of t is1.437, which is less than the critical value of t (i.e. 1.684). Hence, Null hypothesis (i.e Average Abnormal Return=0) is satisfied and Alternate hypothesis (i.e Average Abnormal Return > 0) is rejected. The result depicts that the abnormal return during the sample window is not positive.

Result of Hypothesis 2: H_2 = There is a significant change in average abnormal return (AAR)

The t test result shows that there is no significant change in abnormal return with respect to all eight acquiring companies during the +/-20 days with respect to acquisition. Here the average abnormal return of 180 days before the 20th day of the acquisition is compared with the average abnormal return during pre-acquisition 20 days to post acquisition 20 days. (Excluding the date of acquisition).

Fig. 2: *Average abnormal return of 8 acquiring companies:*

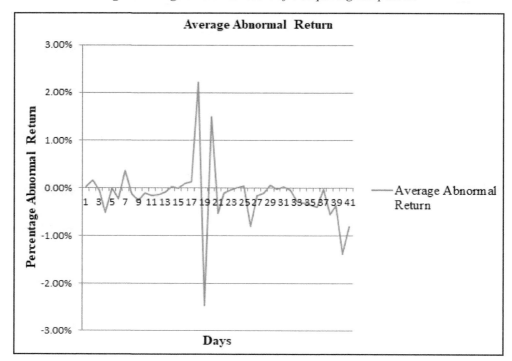

The t value is calculated by taking "Average180 days before the 20th day of the acquisition Abnormal Return" as the first Sample Space and "Average 40 days (+/- 20 days w.r.t date of acquisition) Abnormal Return" as the second Sample Space. By taking "Abnormal return does not exists" as Null Hypothesis and "Abnormal return is exists" as Alternate Hypothesis, the value of t is calculated as 1.899.

Now the calculated t value of 1.899 is less than the critical t value of 1.96752 (taking p=0.05 in Critical t value table).

This implies that in this case, the Null Hypothesis, which is "Abnormal return does not exists", is satisfied and Alternate hypothesis is rejected.

Therefore, in this scenario, for the data of before 200 days and after 20 days of Acquisition event of the companies considered, the existence of abnormal returns are not significant.

CONCLUSION

Abnormal returns from the securities of all eight acquiring companies are high during +/- 2 days with respect to the date of acquisition and gradually become stabilized. The t test result shows that the abnormal returns during the event period (i.e +/- 20 days) are not significantly different compared to normal time. The average abnormal return is not also positive during the event period (+/- 20 days). Therefore it can be concluded that there may be change in abnormal return only during +/-2 days from the date of acquisition but that is not significantly different compared to the abnormal returns earned during normal time and the acquisitions could not fetch any positive abnormal return.

Limitations and Future scope:

The study was conducted from the perspective of acquirers. The consequence of acquisition upon target companies are not evaluated. The time horizon for the study is from 2017 to 2019. The other macro-economic factors could influence the price and return of sampled companies were not considered and therefore the obtained result was not free from error.

REFERENCES

1. Akben-Selcuk, E., and A. Altiok-Yilmaz. "The impact of mergers and acquisitions on acquirer performance: Evidence from Turkey." Business and Economics Journal 22 (2011): 1–8.
2. Anson Wong, Kui Yin Cheung. "The effects of merger and acquisition announcements on the security prices of bidding firms and target firms in Asia." International journal of economics and finance, *1*(2) (2009): 274 – 283.
3. Asquith, Paul, and E. Han Kim. "The impact of merger bids on the participating firms' security holders." The Journal of Finance 37, no. 5 (1982): 1209–1228.
4. Barton, David M., and Roger Sherman. "The price and profit effects of horizontal merger: a case study." The Journal of Industrial Economics (1984): 165–177.
5. Doukas, John, and Nickolaos G. Travlos. "The effect of corporate multinationalism on shareholders' wealth: Evidence from international acquisitions." The Journal of finance 43, no. 5 (1988): 1161–1175.
6. Franks, Julian, Robert Harris, and Sheridan Titman. "The postmerger share-price performance of acquiring firms." Journal of Financial economics 29, no. 1 (1991): 81–96.
7. Liang, Chen. "The impact of merger and acquisition announcements on firms' stock performance: evidence from Hong Kong stock market." (2013).
8. Oswal, Sunny, and Kushagra Goel. "The Impact of Merger and Acquisition Announcements on Acquirer's Share Price: An Analytical Study Using Random Effects." IUP Journal of Applied Economics 19, no. 3 (2020): 8–25.
9. Panayides, Photis M., and Xihe Gong. "The stock market reaction to merger and acquisition announcements in liner shipping." International journal of maritime economics 4, no. 1 (2002): 55–80.
10. M&A Trends Survey: The future of M&A, Deal trends in a changing world, October 2020 by Deloitte US.
11. Schipper, Katherine, and Rex Thompson. "The impact of merger-related regulations on the shareholders of acquiring firms." Journal of Accounting Research (1983): 184–221.

CHAPTER 13

An Analysis of Efficiency of Foreign Exchange Reserve Among Nine Countries: An Application of DEA

Dr. Rachna Agrawal
Department of Management Studies
J.C. Bose University of Science and
Technology, YMCA
Faridabad, India
rachna.aggr@gmail.com

Ashima Verma
Department of Management Studies
J.C. Bose University of Science and
Technology, YMCA
Faridabad, India
ashimaverma421@gmail.com

Abstract

As per the guidelines of IMF 2013, it becomes imperative to maintain the appropriate level of foreign exchange reserves by countries especially developing economies. The study focuses on determining the efficiency of foreign exchange reserves among nine selected countries. It is an inter-country analysis where a comparison is made to probe countries that are most profound in dealing with foreign exchange reserves. The study employs statistical measures and data envelopment analysis (DEA) to measure the efficiency of the management of foreign exchange reserves of the countries. Here, exports and foreign direct investment inflows are taken as inputs and foreign exchange reserves as output. The findings are enthusiastic and motivate the countries for being efficient regarding forex reserve management. Four out of nine countries were found efficient. This analysis will suggest the countries make their reserves efficient so that the ultimate objective of reserves management can be achieved. With the help of this model, inefficient countries can bring about a change that is provided in absolute terms to become efficient in working of foreign exchange reserves.

Keywords: Foreign exchange reserves, Input, Efficiency, Data Envelopment Analysis, Output.

1. INTRODUCTION

The Past, present, and future of the economy of every country is always a matter of discussion among policymakers, researchers, and academicians. Foreign exchange is a distinguishable and leading economic sign to magistrate an economy. It mainly refers to foreign currencies and assets. The foreign exchange is the result of inflows and outflows where the flows can relate to trade, unilateral transactions, investments, commercial borrowings, and any other related flow of currency between or among nations. The foreign exchanges are kept in form of the reserves with mostly central banks of nations to support their trade, investments, and other obligations (Sandri, 2011). Foreign exchange reserves according to International Monetary Fund (1993) are readily available external assets that are under the control of monetary authority for improving external payment imbalances directly or indirectly through exchange markets by changing the currency rates and for distinct purposes.

Developed and developing countries travelled a long economic journey with historic ups and downs (Sharma and Singh, 2014). In this series, the economic situation and reforms play a huge role in determining policies and strategic planning and implementation of countries. The whole picture regarding trade and investments can be depicted with the BOP situation of the countries. BOP is having three significant accounts, one of which is foreign exchange reserves, after current and capital account. Foreign exchange reserves are an important indicator of the economic development of a developing economy if it is managed properly (Aizenman and Lee, 2007). The appropriate level of reserves always remains a topic of debate. Guidelines issued by International Monetary Fund in 2013 and 2015 have stopped arguments on this issue by providing models for making reserves appropriate to its member countries. But the management issues and their efficiency-related questions are still on and the answers are attempted in this research.

The literature review represents that all the studies about foreign exchange are relating to the optimum level of reserves and its management regarding the use of these huge reserves assets but no research has been found regarding the efficiency of the countries in managing foreign exchange reserves given its inputs. The significance of the management of foreign exchange reserves for the countries is obvious and acceptable by the IMF itself. Most of the countries maintain it at a higher level and strongly claim it as an important indicator of economic growth and development. In this way, it becomes important to see reserves' efficiency in comparison to other nations.

The reason for selecting this area is its eminence which is relatively less recognized. The top ten countries in terms of their reserves' holdings are not developed countries. Therefore, it is essential to analyze them in a better way. The study uses data envelopment analysis for studying the efficiency of management of foreign exchange reserves of the countries. Here, exports and foreign direct investment (FDI) inflows are taken as inputs and foreign exchange reserves (FER) as output. The number can be considered less but their importance can define the strength of international transactions of a nation and they considerably affect the foreign exchange reserves as inputs. The current study fills the research gap by focusing on comparative efficiency analysis among countries.

2. LITERATURE REVIEW OF THE STUDY

Every country in this world is aware of the significance of foreign exchange reserves and their management but it is an area that has fewer researches in almost every country (Budina, 2013; Shi and Nie, 2017). It can be firmly stated that an efficient approach of reserves can give better results in its management in the future. Most of the countries hold reserves but return and liquidity have been avoided and only the safety parameter to hold the reserves is considered. When the in-depth novel gaps among existing studies are found out, the efficiency analysis seems to come into picture.

Some scholars claim that the reserves holding is excessive as per the expected requirements and the reserves must be maintained efficiently. The literature regarding foreign exchange reserves is somewhat available on an individual country basis regarding management and maintenance issues. As per the IMF report (2005) export plays a prominent role in maintaining FER amount so it should be considered as an important component in making reserves huge.

Machlup (1996) puts forth an interesting theory towards the accumulation of FER by the central bank to his wife's passion for clothes; though her wardrobe was full, she does not feel satisfied and wants more clothes. According to him, monetary authorities are in the same position and maintain maximum reserves to ensure the smooth functioning of the monetary system. Archer and Halliday (1998) describe the reason for keeping an international trade and the study supports having a large reserve for future payment in the international market. Fischer (2001) expressed that the availability of foreign exchange gives strength for the economic and financial crisis but the reserves must be effectively managed. Edison (2003) explains that opportunity cost has an impact on the level of the reserves with any nation. Here opportunity cost has been defined as subtracting productivity from alternative investment from the yield from the reserves. The study concluded that there exists an inverse relationship between opportunity cost and reserves.

Rybinski and Sowa (2009) postulate that global reserves management by the central banks has become important news in the 21st century by developed as well as developing countries. This has become imperative during the economic shocks and consequentially gives financial stability. Cheung and Qian (2009) use international reserves' demand and concludes that reserves proliferation can be beneficial for developing firms as acts as a shield against crisis, domestic or international. Sengupta and Sengupta (2013) discuss the Indian perspective of maintaining foreign exchange reserves. They are of the view that the post-financial crisis and around 2011 efforts by RBI like a more flexible exchange rate regime and various instruments have led to the sound management of the reserves. Vermeiren (2014) claims a positive influence on the accumulation of FER. It attributes to export oriented-growth regime because of which the positives of accumulation have outgrown the negatives.

Sahu (2015) states that there are two important components of FER accumulation, one is potential risks and the other is the costs of reserves holdings. Foreign exchange reserves must be maintained to pay import, debt, and other obligations and maintain broad money (M2). The conclusion of this research doesn't justify the previous studies and states that India's reserves are not adequate with the required model of the research. If he takes individual obligations like import or debt or broad money, it seems appropriate but collectively, the reserves are not appropriate for India. Nie (2017) analyses the impact of FER on macroeconomic variables. The paper utilizes a pure-sign restriction approach which concluded that the accumulation of reserves shows a positive impact during later years in comparison to the initial years when the impact was not very vivid. Allegret and Allegret (2019) suggest that foreign exchange reserves definitely act as absorbing the financial crisis shocks in developed and developing countries but they are also of the view that this positive impact does not completely save the banks from difficulties during a crisis if this accumulation crosses a certain threshold.

Data envelopment analysis (DEA) has long been employed in various industries like the Banking industry (Karlsson, Haggqvist and Hedberg, 2020; See and He, 2015; Wang, Lu and Liu, 2014), Manufacturing industry (Azad, *et al.,* 2018; Ge and Yang,2017), the Insurance industry (Nourania, *et al.,* 2016; Cummins and Xie 2009), Education Industry (Andersson, *et al.,* 2015), railway Industry (Park, 2015) among others. It not only measure efficiency but ranks them in comparison to its peers (Lam, 2010; Mao, Li and Liu, 2014). It is considered a promising model for benchmarking performances (OECD, 2017). The use of input and output (I/O) variables provides a flexible model for analysis and is one of the most important decisions in this linear programming model (Kwoka and Pollitt, 2010; Omrani and Alizadeh Naghizadeh, 2019).

3. CONCEPTUAL FRAMEWORK OF RESEARCH

FER are a component of the economy that can be used in an efficient manner and its efficient application can give better results to the nations. The comparison studies between the two nations are common but to analyze efficiency among countries in holding reserves is quite an innovative contribution. When the reserves are observed and their sources are analyzed, the two remarkable sources – Export and FDI inflow came into the picture. The study of Chen, L.-T. & Zhang, Z.-N. (2009) also supports these two components as significant contributors to the foreign exchange reserves of a nation. The present study is about efficiency in terms of FER. In this way, the following model has been used:

Figure1: *Diagrammatic representation*

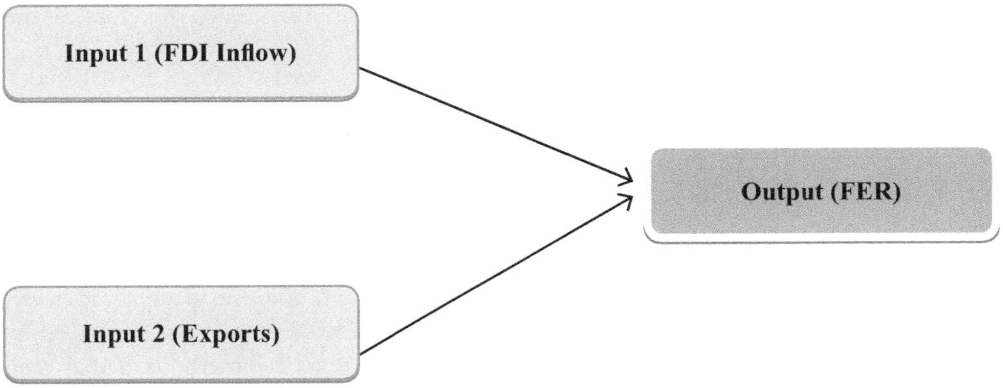

Source: Authors' compilation

Selecting I/O variables is a noteworthy step in the development of a research model based on DEA. There is no study found in the academic literature that attempts to comprehend the efficiency of management of FER. Hence, a thorough understanding of this area of research is required to select I/O variables. Focusing on such a novel idea of research brings curiosity about the results but is also necessitated the determination of I/O variables after a lot of brainstorming. The significant aim of the study is to show the I/O relationship among selected countries with peer analysis.

4. RESEARCH METHODOLOGY

The study follows the analytical research design. The research analyzes data of countries to check efficiency in context to their FER. The data for this study has been collected from secondary sources. It is always a challenge to collect data if more than one country is to be represented. Most of the data has been taken from central banks of nations, government information sources, and the International Monetary Fund. The objective of this sample is to check the efficiency of those countries that claim their reserves among the highest. Therefore, a sample of the top ten countries in terms of reserves' holdings are taken for analysis.

The researchers have taken data from nine countries among the top ten countries. Incomplete data was found for one country and when availed from other sources, it created mismatch and ambiguity. Therefore, the final data set comprised of 9 countries. For removing any obscurity in the selection of countries, the ranking of countries as per the International Monetary Fund having 189 member countries is considered (IMF, 2020). DEA is employed for checking the efficiency of countries in terms of FER. It is a non-parametric approach developed by Charnes et al., (1978) and detailed later by Banker et al., (1984). It has been used in the present study because of its many inherent advantages. First, there is no necessity to define a functional form for the mathematical programming techniques (Al-Refaie, Wu & Sawalheh, 2017; Kanwar & Sperlich, 2019; Mahajan, Nauriyal & Singh, 2018). Second, numerous inputs and outputs can be analyzed together to reveal efficiency (Aduba & Asgari, 2019; Saranga, 2007; Sales-Velasco, 2018). Third, it provides a comprehensive relative measure with the other units taken for analysis and not a statistical measure (Avkiran, 2006). The analysis is useful for countries to know their situation and make efforts for improvements. The data has been collected in April 2020. Therefore, all the countries must be on the same front.

5. DATA ANALYSIS AND DISCUSSION

Technical efficiency is an important issue describing the degree to which inputs such as exports, FDI inflows are converted into outputs, relative to benchmarks. DEA provides very accurate results and is considered a well-founded parameter for analyzing efficiency. Further, it measures inefficiency by estimating the distance between efficient groups. However, some scholars believe that it shows overestimated efficiency. DEA was first suggested by Charles, Cooper, and Rhodes in 1978 and is one of the most practiced methods of analyzing efficiency in management sciences.

Table 1: Data Presentation of Input-output

Name code	Country	Input 1	Input 2	Output
C1	China	139.04	017605.70	3399.90
C2	Japan	009.80	101354.60	1387.40
C3	Switzerland	087.20	000455.90	0850.80
C4	Russia	003.65	008008.48	0562.30

C5	Saudi Arabia	003.20	001163.93	0501.80
C6	Hong Kong	021.75	001007.49	0578.90
C7	India	003.20	001163.93	0501.80
C8	South Korea	003.20	001163.93	0501.80
C9	Brazil	047.27	000792.39	0684.93

Source: IMF, UNCTAD

Table 1 shows the data from 9 countries and the corresponding values of output (FER), Input 1 (FDI Inflows), and Input 2 (Exports). All the figures are in $ Billion. The annual value of nine countries under respective heads have been taken for analysis purposes.

Table 2: Descriptive Statistical Analysis of Inputs

Particulars	Input1	Input2	Output
Mean	53.63	109410.23	935.5
SD	47.23	241911.3	921.6
Highest Value	139.04(C1)	788279(C8)	3399.9
Lowest Value	3.2(C5)	455.9(C3)	359.4

Source: Author's compilation

Table 2 summarizes baseline measurements for the selected countries from C1 to C9. The standard deviation of input variable 1 near to its mean, same with output and input variable 2 is greater than relatively larger means. It suggests that there is a large variability in the size of the countries. Therefore, the VRS model is suitable for this particular database analysis.

Table 3: Efficiency Initial summary using a multi-stage method

Name Code	CRSTE*	VRSTE**	SCALE***
C1	0.411	1.000	0.411
C2	0.903	1.000	0.903
C3	1.000	1.000	1.000
C4	0.270	0.275	0.982
C5	1.000	1.000	1.000
C6	0.155	0.188	0.822
C7	0.072	0.076	0.943
C8	0.181	0.222	0.816
C9	0.405	0.773	0.525

Note: *Technical efficiency of CRS DEA

**Technical efficiency of VRS DEA

***Scale efficiency

Table 3 mentions the efficiency of different countries in terms of FER. The mean values are 0.488, 0.615, and 0.822 of CRSTE, VRSTE, and SCALE respectively. CRS (constant returns to scale) shows the technical efficiency and VRS (variable returns to scale) shows the technical efficiency difference between CRS and VRS. The CRS technical efficiency shows C3 and C5 are efficient in managing their reserves. On the other side, the VRS technical efficiency shows that C1, C2 and C5 as efficient countries.

Scale efficiency is obtained by dividing CRSTE and VRSTE. Scale efficiency shows if the returns show an increasing or decreasing trend. C1, C2 and C4 show decreasing returns to scale, C3 and C5 show constant returns to scale and the remaining countries show an increasing return to scale. If a change in output is less than a proportional change in input, it is called decreasing returns to scale (DRS). If this change in output is more than proportional change in input, it is called increasing returns to scale (IRS). Therefore, for input oriented the input need to make necessary changes to increase efficiency. The input-oriented VRS of C7 is 0.076 and has an IRS. This means that the input needs to increase by 92.4 % and the output is increasing with more proportion in comparison to the inputs.

Table 4: Summary of Peer Weights

Country	Peers	Countries peers' weights	CPWD	Peer Count
C1	1	1.000	0.000	0
C2	2	1.000	0.000	1
C3	3	1.000	0.000	2
C4	52	0.932	0.068	0
C5	5	1.000	0.000	5
C6	35	0.221	0.779	0
C7	5	1.000	0.000	0
C8	5	1.000	0.000	0
C9	35	0.525	0.475	0

Source: Analysed and complied by authors

The peer count indicates the number of times an efficient country acts as a reference for the inefficient countries. The inefficient country C4 can follow country C5 and C2 in that order to become efficient (this efficiency by input-oriented VRS, so change in inputs). A similar application can be applied for countries C6, C7, C8 and C9.

Table 5: Country by Country Results

Country	Variables	OV	R M	SM	PV
C1	Output	3399.900	0.000	0.000	3399.900
	Input 1	139.040	0.000	0.000	139.040
	Input 2	17605.700	0.000	0.000	17605.700
C2	Output	1387.400	0.000	0.000	1387.400
	Input 1	9.800	0.000	0.000	9.800
	Input 2	101354.600	0.000	0.000	101354.600
C3	Output	850.800	0.000	0.000	850.800
	Input 1	87.200	0.000	0.000	87.200
	Input 2	455.900	0.000	0.000	455.900
C4	Output	562.300	0.000	0.000	562.300
	Input 1	13.300	-9.649	0.000	3.651
	Input 2	31932.500	-23166.955	-757.063	8008.482
C5	Output	501.800	0.000	0.000	501.800
	Input 1	3.200	0.000	0.000	3.200
	Input 2	1163.930	0.000	0.000	1163.930
C6	Output	475.600	0.000	103.308	578.908
	Input 1	115.600	-93.841	0.000	21.759
	Input 2	5352.600	-4345.102	0.000	1007.498
C7	Output	473.300	0.000	28.500	501.800
	Input 1	42.200	-39.000	0.000	3.200
	Input 2	3752.200	-34676.915	-1681.355	1163.930
C8	Output	409.700	0.000	92.100	501.800
	Input 1	14.400	-11.200	0.000	3.200
	Input 2	788279.000	-613105.889	-174009.181	1163.930
C9	Output	359.400	0.000	325.538	684.938
	Input 1	61.200	-13.921	0.000	47.279
	Input 2	1025.700	-233.310	0.000	792.390

Note: OV= Original Value, RM= Radial Movement, SM= Slack Movement, PV= Projected Value

Since C1, C2. C3 and C5 are already efficient countries; this implies that there are 0 radical and slack movements. Looking at C4, if we have a projected value of input 1 as 3.651 and input 2 as 8008.482, then the decrease in returns to scale will be 562.3. C4 can decrease its input 1 by 9.649 and input 2 by 23166.955 to make it efficient. Similarly, the in case of C6, the projected value of Input1 is 21.759 and the corresponding figure for input2 is 1007.498, the increase in returns to scale will be 578.908. C6 can decrease the usage of input1 by 93.841 and input2 by 4345.902 to make it efficient and reach the projected value. C7 is also an inefficient country. Here, the projected value for input1 is 3.2 and for input 2 is 1163.930, and the same for output is 501.8. Again, if C7 reduces input 1 and input 2 reduces by 39 and 34676.915 respectively, it can reach its efficiency i.e. projected value. For C8, the projected values for input1 and input 2 are 3.2 and 1163.9 respectively. The radical movement values for input1 and input 2 are being 11.2 and 613105.889 respectively. Finally looking at C9, the projected values for input 1 and input 2 being 47.279 and 792.39 respectively and output is projected to reach 684.938. The change required for input 1 and input 2 is13.921 and 233.310 to reach an efficient level.

6. CONCLUSION

6.1. *Theoretical Implications*

FER are the backbone of a country. It is pivotal for reserves to be efficient. The present study evaluates the efficiency of the FER of the selected countries. The countries seem to be efficient as they lay in the top ten countries about the amount of reserve in the world. The countries which are found inefficient should take correction measures like an increase in export or/ and foreign direct investment inflow. However, it is not an easy task because economic policies should build on parameters like an increase in exports and opening up the FDI silent sectors with more liberal policies. The changes in policies may open new gateways to improve inflows and this increment may directly relate with enhancement with efficiency.

Conclusively, it is paramount to state that reserves are presented with the amount but it is pivotal to see its physical strength (Sahu, 2015). The representation concerning its efficiency for a specific country is merit for the nation. In reality, it is a challenge to convert the inputs as per the direction of research because there are global (external) factors that play more strongly than the internal strength of a single country yet the countries have to take steps regarding it and the results can be seen positive in a long run.

6.2. *Practical Implications*

The present study looks at FER from a novel lens distinct from past studies. Here, a recognised technique DEA has been used to draw a significant conclusion. The technique is never used in this area of research with the best of the knowledge of researchers. The findings are enthusiastic and motivate the countries for being efficient. There is always each country's motive to enhance export (Nie, 2017) but to what extent and how can it make the scenario change, is important to be seen and analyzed. It is an inter-country analysis where a comparison is made among countries that are most profound in dealing with foreign exchange reserves. With the help of this model, inefficient countries can bring about a change that is provided in absolute terms to come to the efficient working of foreign exchange reserves. C1, C2, C3, and C5 are efficient in terms of technical efficiency and scale efficiency. The model clearly defines the amount by which the inputs need to be increased or decreased that would impact the reserves positively. Also, the model specifies the inefficient countries that should follow the steps of efficient countries that too in a specific order. For instance, C6 should first pursue C3 followed by C5. This is of great help when the world environment is so turbulent and dynamic. Therefore, the right use of inputs to make the output efficienct is the main goal of Data Envelopment Analysis, and this paper aims and analyses the same.

7. LIMITATIONS AND SCOPE OF FUTURE RESEARCH

The study focuses on an important parameter i.e., efficiency analysis. In this study, nine countries have been taken so more numbers can be taken in future research. The study may go by taking a broader scope, for instance, increasing the number of economic indicators for analysis and supplement it with a comparative analysis. Furthermore, a deeper dive into the foreign exchange area will aid in finding numerous other inputs in future research. The inclusion of diverse variables may add value to this research. It might be interesting for comparative research between advanced and emerging nations in terms of efficient management of FER. Research into the quality of the reserves can also bring engrossing results.

8. REFERENCES

Aduba, J. & Asgari, B. (2019). Productivity and technological progress of the Japanese manufacturing industries, 2000–2014: estimation with data envelopment analysis and log-linear learning model. *Asia-Pacific Journal of Regional Science*, 4, 343–387. https://doi.org/10.1007/s41685-019-00131-w

Allegret, J.P. & Allegret, A. (2019). Did Foreign Exchange Holding influence growth performance during the global financial crises. *World Econ*omics, 42, 1–41. https://onlinelibrary.wiley.com/doi/abs/10.1111/twec.12701.

Al-Rafaie, A., Wu, C. and Sawalheh, M. (2017), "DEA window analysis for assessing efficiency of blistering process in a pharmaceutical industry", *Neural Computing and Applications*. https://doi.org/10.1007/s00521-017-3303-2

Andersson, C., Antelius, J., Månsson, J. & Sund, K. (2017). Technical efficiency and productivity for higher education institutions in Sweden. *Scandinavian Journal of Educational Research*, 61(2), 205-223. http://doi.org/10.1080/00313831.2015.1120230

Archer, D. & Halliday, J. (1998). The Rationale for holding foreign currency reserves. *Reserve's bank of New Zealand Bulletin*, 61(4), 346– 354. (Online 2016)

Avkiran, N.K. (2006). *Productivity analysis in the service sector with data envelopment analysis,* 3rd ed., University of Queensland Business School, The University of Queensland, Brisbane.

Azad, A., Munisamy, S., Talib, M & Saona, P. (2018). Productivity changes of pharmaceutical industry in Bangladesh: Does process patent matter? *Global Business Review*, 19(4), 1013–1025. http://doi.org/10.1177/0972150918772966

Aizenman, J. and Lee, J. (2007), "International Reserves: precautionary versus mercantilist views, theory and evidence", *Open Economics Review*, Vol. 18, pp. 191–214. http://doi.org/10.1007/s11079-007-9030-z

Banker, R.D., Charnes A. & Cooper, W.W. (1984). Some models for the estimation of technical and scale inefficiencies in data envelopment analysis. *Management Sciences*, 30(9), 1078–1092.

Budina, N.,Angers, P.,Wiegand, J., Crivelli, E. and Fayad, G. (2013) *Euroization, Liquidity Needs, and Foreign Currency Reserves.* IMF Country Report 13/223, 13–16. https://www.imf.org/external/pubs/ft/scr/2013/cr13223.pdf (Assessed on 7 October 2020)

Charnes, A., Cooper, W.W. & Rhodes, E. (1978). Measuring the Efficiency of decision-making units. *European Journal of Operations Research*, 2(6), 429–441.

Chen, L.-T. & Zhang, Z.-N. (2009). *FDI, export and foreign exchange reserves- Test with the time series data from 1997-2009.* Chongqing University, Chongqing, China.

Cheung, Y. & Qian, X., (2009). Hoarding of international reserves: Mrs. Machlup's Wardrobe and the Jonesses. *Review of International Economics*, 17(4), 824–843. http://doi.org/10.1111/j.1467-9396.2009.00850.x

Cummins, J.D. & Xie, X. (2009). Market values and efficiency in US insurer acquisitions and divestitures. *Managerial Finance*, 35(2), 128–155. https://doi.org/10.1108/03074350910923482

Edison, H. (2003). *Are foreign reserves in Asia too high?* World Economic Outlook, International Monetary Fund: Washington (Assessed on 15 December 2020)

Fischer, S. (2001). *IMF/World Bank International Reserves: Policy Issues Forum.* Retrieved from http://www.imf.org/external/np/speeches/2001/0 42801.htm. (Assessed on 20 November 2020)

Ge, H. & Yang, S.-Y. (2017). Study on the R&D performance of high-tech industry in China - based on data envelopment analyses. *Journal of Interdisciplinary Mathematics*, 20(3), 909-920. http://doi.org/10.1080/09720502.2017.1358890

International Monetary Fund (2003). *World Economic Outlook.* Retrieved from www.imf.org (assessed on 16 October 2020)

Kanwar, S. & Sperlich, S. (2019). Innovation, productivity and intellectual property reform in an emerging market economy: evidence from India. *Empirical Economics*, 59. 933–950. http://doi.org/ 10.1007/s00181-019-01707-3

Karlsson, L., Haggqvist, H. & Hedberg, P. (2020). Market structure and efficiency in Swedish commercial banking. *Scandinavian Economic History Review,* 1912–1938. http://doi.org/10.1080/03585522.2020.1772359

Kwoka, J. & Pollitt, M. (2010). Do mergers improve efficiency? Evidence from restructuring the US electric power sector. *International Journal of Industrial Organization*, 28, 645-656. https://doi.org/10.1016/j.ijindorg.2010.03.001

Lam, K.F. (2010). In the determination of weight sets to compute cross-efficiency ratios in DEA. *Journal of Operational Research Society*, 61, 134–143. https://doi.org/10.1057/jors.2008.138

Machlup, F. (1966). The need for monetary reserves. *PSL Quarterly Review*, 175–222.

Mahajan, V., Nauriyal, D.K. & Singh, S.P. (2018). Domestic market competitiveness of Indian drug and pharmaceutical industry. *Review of Managerial Science,* 14, 519–559. http://doi.org/10.1007/s11846-018-0299-7.

Mao, Y., Li, J. & Liu, Y. (2014). Evaluating business performance of China's pharmaceutical companies based on data envelopment analysis. *Studies on Ethno-Medicine,* 8(1), 51–60. http://doi.org/10.1080/09735070.2014.11886472

Nie, L. (2017). Macroeconomic impact on China's foreign exchange reserves accumulation: a vector auto regression analysis using pure-sign restriction approach. *Applied Economics,* 49(11), 1055-1070. http://doi.org/10.1080/00036846.2016.1210778

Nourani, M., Devadason, E., Kweh, Q. & Lu, W. (2016). Business excellence: the managerial and value-creation efficiencies of the insurance companies. *Total Quality Management & Business Excellence,* 28 (7-8), 879-896. http://doi.org/10.1080/14783 363.2015.1133244

OECD (2017). Benchmarking higher education system performance: conceptual framework and data. *Enhancing Higher Education System Performance*, Paris: OECD.

Omrani, H., Alizadeh, A. & Naghizadeh, F. (2020). Incorporating decision makers' preferences into DEA and common weight DEA models based on the best-worst method (BMW). *Soft Computing,* 24, 3989-4002. http://doi.org/10.1007/s00500-019-04168-z

Park, J. (2015), *Efficiency analysis for urban railway operating agencies based on public performance: Focusing on the DEASBM model*, PhD. Thesis, Chonnam National University, Gwangju, Korea.

Rybinski, K.I. & Sowa, U (2009). Global Reserves Management. http://dx.doi.org/10.2139/ ssrn.985071

Sahu, S (2015). *Adequacy of India's foreign exchange reserves* (Monthly Newsletter, CCIL). Retrieved from https://www.ccilindia.com/Documents/Rakshitra/2015/Mar/ Article.pdf (Assessed on 34 September 2020)

Sandri, D. (2011), "Precautionary savings and global imbalances in world general equilibrium", IMF working paper WP/11/122, International Monetary Fund. https:// www.imf.org/external/pubs/ft/wp/2011/wp11122.pdf. (Assessed on 5 September 2020)

Saranga, H. (2006). Multiple objective data envelopment analysis as applied to the Indian pharmaceutical industry. *Journal of the Operational Research Society*, 58, 1480–1493.

Sengupta, A. & Sengupta, R. (2013). *Management of capital flows in India* (Working paper no. 17) Retrieved from Asian Development Bank website. http://www.adb.org/sites/ default/files/publication/30234/management-capital-flows-india.pdf.

See, K.F. & He, Y. (2015). Determinants of technical efficiency in Chinese banking: A Double Bootstrap Data Envelopment Analysis Approach. *Global Economic Review*: *Perspectives on East Asian Economies and Industries,* 44(3), 286-307. http://doi.org/1 0.1080/1226508X.2015.1014392

Sharma, C., and Singh, S.K. (2014), "Determinants of International Reserves: Empirical evidence from Emerging Asia", *Economics Bulletin*, Vol. 34 No. 3, pp. 1696–1703.

Shi, K. and Nie, L. (2017), "Did China Effectively Manage Its Foreign Exchange Reserves? Revisiting the Currency Composition Change", *Emerging Markets Finance and Trade*, Vol. 53 No. 6, pp. 1352–1373. http://doi.org/10.1080/1540496X.2017.1300771

United Nations Conference on Trade and Development (UNCTAD) (2019). *World Investment Report, Special Economic Zones* (UNCTAD/WIR/2019) Retrieved from www.unctad.org (Assessed on 15 September 2020)

Vermeiren, M. (2014). Reserves' accumulation and the entrapment of Chinese monetary power. *Power and imbalances in the Global Monetary System*, 121–149. http://doi. org/10.1057/9781137397577_5

Wang, W., Lu, W. & Liu, P. (2014). A fuzzy multi-objective two-stage DEA model for evaluating the performance of US bank holding companies. *Expert System with Application,* 41(9), 4290-4297. https://doi.org/10.1016/j.eswa.2014.01.004

CHAPTER 14

Product Complexity Of Indian Exports: Restructuring Due to Covid-19

Dr. Purvi Pujari
Associate Professor
Bharati Vidyapeeth's Institute of
Management Studies and Research
Navi Mumbai (Mumbai University)
drpurvipujari@bvimsr.com

Abstract

The COVID-19 pandemic has brought lots of realizations to the Governments all over the globe regarding their international trade. Be it over-dependence of exports on few countries or exports centered on few low complexity products or services. This research paper has attempted to analyze how the pandemic has transformed complexity of India's exports. The product complexity of a country's exports is a wonderful tool to assess the growth potential of a country. Atlas of Economic Complexity (ACE) theory by Ricardo Hausmann, Cesar A. Hidalgo has been taken as a base for this research. The researchers have compared the data of Indian exports from the last two years. The purpose is to identify whether the product complexity of Indian exports is increasing or not. This paper also assesses the need and process of restructuring of Indian Exports. The Research Methodology is exploratory and the data collected has been through authentic government websites and e-portals. Over the years not much has been done to enhance the complexity of Indian exports. Most of the products exported by India across the globe are of low and medium complexity. Not much has changed post COVID-19 too. This pandemic has created a need for transformation of the structure of Indian exports in the global international trade. There is a need for strategic intervention to improve the growth potential of the country through more complex exports.

Keyword: India, Exports, Atlas of Economic Complexity, COVID-19, Product Complexity

1. INTRODUCTION

Growth propensity of any country has always been of lots of interest to researchers worldwide. Apart from the traditional source of Gross Domestic Product (GDP), National Income etc. the knowledge and technological sophistication of exports also present a wonderful tool to assess the growth propensity. Exports of any country are the best reflection of its economic growth potential and performance. They are the best tool to analyze the manufacturing and know-how accumulation of an economy (Hausmann, Hidalgo, S., A., & Yildirim, 2014). It also is a good parameter to understand and identify the products and services, where the country can get a better trade balance. To assess the growth potential of exports understanding its complexity is required. Economic complexity (EC), has been considered a reflection of a nation's cumulative knowledge in terms of its production level especially exports. (Hausmann, 2014). EC of exports of a country are good robust predictor of its growth. (Hidalgo, Hausmann, & Dasgupta, 2009). Hence, exports have always been a better reflection of industrial development and growth potential of any economy. Growth prospects are more in the countries which export complex products (Felipe, Kumar, Abdon, & Bacate, 2012). The COVID-19 pandemic has proved to be an inflection point for various industries across the globe. The purpose of this research is to analyze the impact of the pandemic on India's exports. It also has attempted to analyze the complexity of its Indian exports as per Atlas of Economic Complexity (ACE). The more complex the exports of a country are, higher are the chances of it having a sustainable development. Complex exports would enable the country to identify more such products which it can manufacture and exports

2. LITERATURE REVIEW

The product space and EC relation was first proposed in 2007 (Hidalgo, Klinger, Barabási, & R., 2007) Economic Complexity (EC) and income growth have been extensively studied by Hartmann et al. (Hartmann, Guevara, Jara-Figueroa, Aristarán, & Hidalgo, 2017). The research analyzed the connect between production of new goods and differences in income.

ACE was reviewed by Josiah Hickson (Hickson, 2017). This discussion paper has discussed the theory in depth. It also discusses the strengths and weaknesses of the ACE. Countries' complexity significance as per the occurrence in the high income and low-income nations and also the process of reducing the gap between the two have been discussed in the paper. (Gala, Rocha, & Magacho, 2018)

India's growth potential has also been studied. The researchers concluded that India on account of its knowledge Management practices has the best growth projection as per EC and it also concluded that Russia won't be able to achieve much of growth as it has least amount of knowledge management practices (Priscila Rubbo, 2018). One more study analyzes the significance of generating jobs vis-à-vis the complexity in the advanced sectors. (Gala, Rocha, & Magacho, 2018). A study about the impact of EC on natural rents was done. It concluded that EC has a less effect on these in general except the coal. (Nguyen, Schinckus, & Thanh, 2020). The link between Balance of payments of a nation has also been studied by few researchers (Sepehrdoust, Davarikish, & Setarehie, 2019). Many benefits of increased complexity and trade liberalization on Balance of Payments have been identified in this research.

A study by Gala et al studied and concluded that a bigger level of income distribution over the population in a country is usually reflected in manufacturing of high knowledge products and vice-versa. (Gala, Camargo, & Freitas, 2017). Majority of the studies and researches are focused on countries other than India.

The detailed literature study of the topic resulted in a literature gap where there have not been many studies which have analyzed Indian exports vis-à-vis its complexity. The researcher has found a research gap that there is a need to study India's exports as per EC of exports as well analyze the impact of COVID-19 pandemic on its products offerings.

Atlas of Economic Complexity (ACE)

ACE a 2011 economics book by Hausmann et al. A revised 2014 edition is published by the MIT Press (Hausmann, Hidalgo, S., A., & Yildirim, 2014). The Atlas explains EC a measure of preference and efficiency of total output produced by a country which is measured majorly through its exports and also, is impacted by the knowledge potential of the nation. (Hausmann, Hidalgo, S., A., & Yildirim, 2014).

This theory tries to bring out the correlation between complexity and know-how which is embedded in production sector and resulting, export basket of an economy. This concept of ACE has been taken as a base for this paper. The Atlas has created ranking of export products as per the sophistication and know-how embedded in them. It also ranks the countries on the basis of the goods produced by them and exports to other countries. This ranking reflects the individual countries potential to grow and their level among other countries in the world. The higher complexity of exports of a country reflects higher value creation and it also helps the country to identify related industries where it can grow its exports. Product Complexity Index depicts the hierarchy of products as per the technical knowledge required to produce them. The countries with export products with higher ranking will have more propensity to grow in related industries. Hence, this paper has studied complexity of exports.

3. RESEARCH METHODOLOGY

This research is aimed specifically on impact and resulting restructuring of India's exports sector. The research is having an exploratory research design and it uses descriptive method. This research is done with an analysis of secondary data taken from the Department of Commerce, Export Import Data Bank. The objectives have been decided after extensive literature review of the research papers based on the concept of ACE. To understand the impact of COVID-19 on Indian Exports, the export data from the last two years have been compared. The research methodology is based on previous literature review. Main focus of the research was on the analysis of product complexity of Indian exports. The impact of complexity of exports have been not explored much. There are very few research papers which are focused specifically on India.

Objectives:

The objectives of this paper are as follows:

4. **To understand the Product Complexity (PC) of India's Exports**
5. **To analyze the impact of COVID-19 on PC of Indian Exports**

Hypothesis:

$H1_1$: PC of India's Exports is high as per ACE
$H1_0$: PC of India's Exports is not high as per ACE

4. DATA ANALYSIS

India's exports and its product mix has always been more concentrated towards agricultural and primary products. As a new global order is emerging post COVID-19, it is the right time to analyze India's offerings to the world. This research paper has focused on analyzing the complexity of Indian exports.

This research paper analyses the data of Indian exports as taken from the Commerce Department of Indian Government statistics. Table 1 gives the comparison of top 30 Exports with a positive growth from India in the April-August period of year 2019 and 2020. Though the data is not very concrete but it shows growth in the product category of Drug Formulations, Biologicals and Bulk Drugs, Drug Intermediates of 25.2% and 17.24% respectively. These being a comparatively complex product is good for Indian exports in the long term.

The negative aspect is that maximum growth is in the product categories of Rice (Other Than Basmati)-91.34%, Sugar-69.39%, Iron Ore-65.83%, Iron and Steel -53.67%, which are from low complexity products ranking (PCI).

Table 1: Comparison of Top 30 Commodities with Positive Growth Percentage

S. No.	Commodity	Apr-Aug 2019	Apr-Aug 2020(P)	%Growth	%Share
1	Rice (Other Than Basmati)	6,046.44	11,569.56	91.34	1.57
2	Sugar	4,915.58	8,326.68	69.39	1.13
3	Iron Ore	8,314.94	13,788.93	65.83	1.87
4	Iron And Steel	25,981.38	39,925.33	53.67	5.43
5	Drug Formulations, Biologicals	45,025.16	56,373.26	25.2	7.66
6	Bulk Drugs, Drug Intermediates	11,379.43	13,341.06	17.24	1.81
77	Plastic Raw Materials	10,773.35	12,498.71	16.02	1.7
8	Aluminium, Products Of Aluminum	14,024.19	16,196.93	15.49	2.2
9	Rice -Basmati	12,621.24	13,659.82	8.23	1.86
10	Agro Chemicals	8,921.68	9,532.04	6.84	1.3
11	Spices	11,413.69	11,645.07	2.03	1.58
12	Ship, Boat And Floating Struct	19,558.80	19,047.24	-2.62	2.59
13	Residual Chemical And Allied Prod	16,928.72	16,383.54	-3.22	2.23

14	Organic Chemicals	25,417.93	24,209.63	-4.75	3.29
15	Cotton Yarn	7,538.82	7,076.71	-6.13	0.96
16	Electric Machinery And Equipment	24,518.44	22,833.81	-6.87	3.1
17	Electronics Instruments	8,368.36	7,181.38	-14.18	0.98
18	Marine Products	18,961.99	15,889.57	-16.2	2.16
19	Buffalo Meat	9,146.98	7,609.36	-16.81	1.03
20	Indl. Machinery For Dairy Etc	15,973.08	12,526.77	-21.58	1.7
21	Cotton Fabrics, Made Ups Etc.	17,504.70	13,581.95	-22.41	1.85
22	Products Of Iron And Steel	20,263.67	15,252.85	-24.73	2.07
23	Other Commodities	11,284.70	7,741.48	-31.4	1.05
24	Auto Components/Parts	15,896.59	9,743.90	-38.7	1.32
25	Manmade Yarn,Fabrics,Made Ups	13,667.70	8,162.87	-40.28	1.11
26	Rmg Cotton Incl Accessories	26,072.12	15,498.85	-40.55	2.11
27	Petroleum Products	124,167.78	63,787.06	-48.63	8.67
28	Pearl, Precs, Semiprecs Stones	64,101.36	31,147.78	-51.41	4.23
29	Motor Vehicle/Cars	23,448.65	10,791.51	-53.98	1.47
30	Gold And Other Precs Metl Jewelry	39,475.45	11,309.19	-71.35	1.54

Source: Researcher's analysis from Structure of Indian Exports:

Department of Commerce, System on Foreign Trade Performance Analysis (FTPA) Version 3.0
Values in Rs. Crores, (P) Provisional

Table 2: Top 20 Products sorted as per % growth share between 2018-19 and 2019-20

S. No.	HS Code	Commodity	2018-2019	%Share	2019-2020	%Share	%Growth
1	47	Pulp of Wood or of Other Fibrous Cellulosic Material; Waste And Scrap Of Paper Or Paperboard.	2,476.68	0.0011	6,248.46	0.0028	152.29

2	26	Ores, Slag And Ash.	1,290,944.88	0.5594	2,240,051.12	1.0091	73.52
3	75	Nickel And Articles Thereof.	46,488.33	0.0201	65,324.86	0.0294	40.52
4	92	Musical Instruments; Parts And Accessories Of Such Articles.	14,021.47	0.0061	19,552.34	0.0088	39.45
5	17	Sugars And Sugar Confectionery.	1,140,470.65	0.4942	1,558,246.55	0.702	36.63
6	99	Miscellaneous Goods.	104,265.92	0.0452	141,463.09	0.0637	35.68
7	65	Headgear And Parts Thereof.	32,047.23	0.0139	42,610.42	0.0192	32.96
8	98	Project Goods; Some Special Uses.	29,823.43	0.0129	39,504.30	0.0178	32.46
9	46	Manufactures Of Straw, Of Esparto Or Of Other Plaiting Materials; Basketware And Wickerwork.	28,130.13	0.0122	35,440.83	0.016	25.99
10	97	Works Of Art Collectors' Pieces And Antiques.	71,806.42	0.0311	88,403.00	0.0398	23.11
11	69	Ceramic Products.	1,113,632.91	0.4826	1,357,371.55	0.6115	21.89

12	85	Electrical Machinery And Equipment And Parts Thereof; Sound Recorders And Reproducers, Television Image And Sound Recorders And Reproducers And Parts.	8,919,233.08	3.8649	10,766,974.19	4.8503	20.72
13	93	Arms And Ammunition; Parts And Accessories Thereof.	77,871.63	0.0337	93,409.48	0.0421	19.95
14	67	Prepared Feathers And Down And Articles Made Of Feathers Or Of Down; Artificial Flowers; Articles Of Human Hair.	155,055.84	0.0672	184,913.49	0.0833	19.26
15	59	Impregnated, Coated, Covered Or Laminated Textile Fabrics; Textile Articles Of A Kind Suitable For Industrial Use.	180,461.84	0.0782	206,510.63	0.093	14.43
16	58	Special Woven Fabrics; Tufted Textile Fabrics; Lace; Tapestries; Trimmings; Embroidery.	263,862.70	0.1143	296,891.08	0.1337	12.52

17	16	Preparations Of Meat, Of Fish Or Of Crustaceans, Molluscs Or Other Aquatic Invertebrates	303,042.74	0.1313	340,859.36	0.1536	12.48
18	30	Pharmaceutical Products	10,323,992.70	4.4737	11,547,303.19	5.2018	11.85
19	38	Miscellaneous Chemical Products.	3,239,659.32	1.4038	3,566,292.61	1.6065	10.08
20	94	Furniture; Bedding, Mattresses, Mattress Supports, Cushions And Similar Stuffed Furnishing; Lamps And Lighting Fittings Not Elsewhere Specified Or Inc	1,196,532.91	0.5185	1,317,09526	0.5933	10.08

Source: Researcher's analysis from Structure of Indian Exports, , System on Foreign Trade Performance Analysis (FTPA) Version 3.0, Top 30 Commodities of Export Values in Rs. Crores, (P) Provisional, https://tradestat.commerce.gov.in/eidb/ecom.asp, Accessed on 05/11/20 at 15:00 pm.

After the analysis of Table 2, we can safely deduce that maximum growth in the post COVID-19 period has been in pulp of wood etc. which are low complexity products. Sugar and Ores and Slag are again low complexity export products. We see approx. 20% growth in Electrical Parts which is the 12th largest export and similarly approx. 20% growth in Arms category when we compare the data of years 2018-19 and 2019-20.

If we analyze the data from Commerce Ministry, Government of India, major commodities/ commodity groups which reflected increase figures in October 2020 as compared to October 2019 are other cereals (378.23%), Rice (113.62%), Oil meals (78.57%), Iron ore (74.14%), Oil seeds (54.21%), Carpet (37.67%), Cereal preparations & miscellaneous processed items (36.18%), Ceramic products & glassware (34.92%), Spices (21.85%), Drugs & pharmaceuticals (21.85%), Jute mfg. including floor covering (18.73%), Meat, dairy & poultry products (16.66%), Handicrafts excl. handmade carpet (11.38%), Fruits & vegetables (9.87%), Mica etc. including processed minerals (9.64%), Cotton etc. (6.68%), RMG of all textiles (6.32%), Tobacco (4.33%), Organic & inorganic chemicals (1.94%) and Tea (0.12%). Apart from Drugs and pharmaceuticals and organic and inorganic chemicals most of products are of low complexity.

Major commodities/commodity groups which reflected a decreased growth in the period of October 2020 as compared to October 2019 are Petroleum products (-52.04%), Cashew (-21.57%), Gems & jewellery (-21.27%), Leather & leather products (-16.67%), Man-made yarn/fabs./made-ups etc. (-12.8%), Electronic goods (-9.36%), Coffee (-9.23%), Marine products (-8.09%), Plastic & Linoleum (-6.86%) and Engineering goods (-3.75%). The analysis of export products which have seen a negative growth shows that few of them like Electronic goods and Engineering goods are of good complexity ranking as per PCI.

5. FINDINGS

Now, when we consider the impact of COVID-19 and recent shifts, a different picture emerges. The detailed analysis of above data brings out a very interesting scenario. Over the last year, there has been lots of changes in the composition and direction of Indian exports. Composition of Indian Exports has changed towards primary commodities where India already had a competitive advantage. Based on this data our fastest growing exports are:

1. RICE - a primary commodity. Rice has always been an important part of Indian exports. India always had a comparative advantage in this commodity. India's weather and topography has always been suitable for the crop. Over the period of time, Indian farmers have gained skilled labour and cost advantage for the same. Basmati Rice has been exported of quantity 1680813.61(MT) of approx. Rs 1134187.53 and Non-Basmati Rice of quantity 2999254.76(MT) worth Rs.890340.56 during the period 2020-21(April-July)

2. SUGAR- a primary commodity, similarly for sugar, the climate and topography has been suitable. An availability of labour for this labour intensive commodity has added advantage for Indian exports. The government subsidy has also significantly given advantage to the economy and has increase the exports.

3. IRON ORE- a primary commodity. Our neighbouring country China imports in this category have surpassed last eight year records in the first six months of the year 2020. The value of iron ore exported from India amounted to nearly 186 billion rupees in fiscal year 2020. This export value was significantly higher than the previous financial year's value of about 92 billion rupees.

4. IRON AND STEEL- a manufactured product with some transformation. Exports of Iron & Steel in India reduced to $ 2966.98 Million in 2020 from $ 6393.58 Million in 2019.

5. DRUGS AND FORMULATIONS- a manufactured product with some complexity. Drug formulations and biologicals, contributing to almost 72 per cent of exports, have shown 9.5 per cent growth in FY 2020.

Most of the medium and high complexity products have faced a decline in the recent years. For example, the products like Motor Vehicles/cars which is a product requiring technical know-how has reduced share. Auto components are one more export product which is a medium complexity product where the share has gone down. Products of Iron and Steel, this is again one category, where growth should have been there.

6. CONCLUSION

After extensive analysis of the data, we can safely conclude that our hypothesis cannot be accepted and we have to accept our null hypothesis, that is, Product Complexity of India's Exports is not high as per ACE. As over the last two years main growth has taken place in the products in low and medium complexity products. The impact of complex products is very good on Balance of Payments. Higher the complexity of the products, the money value of such products is usually higher too. A strategy should be devised to ensure a positive value enhancement in terms of Balance of payments through exports. The Government should give boost to knowledge intensive industries and give incentive to such initiatives. New policies can be enforced through Atmanirbhar Bharat and other similar Government schemes.

This drift towards low complexity must be taken in cognizance by the policy-makers. As India struggles to be a manufacturing giant with Make in India and Start-up India, a shift towards primary commodities is not a welcome sign.

7. REFERENCES

1. Buhari, D., Oana, M. D., Lorente, D. B., & Shahzad, U. (2020). The mitigating effects of economic complexity and renewable. *Sustainable Development.*, 1–12.
2. Canh, N. P., Schinckus, C., & Su Dinh Thanh. (2020). The natural resources rents: Is economic complexity a solution for resource curse?,. *Science Direct.*
3. Caria, S., Troyano, M. C., & Martí, R. D. (2017). Can the Monkeys Leave the Export Processing Zones? Exploring the Maquiladora Bias in the Economic Complexity Index in Latin America. *Journal of Economics and Development Studies, Vol. 5*(1), 20–28.
4. Estmann, C., Soerensen, B. B., Ndulu, B., & John, R. (2020). *Merchandise export diversification strategy for Tanzania - promoting inclusive growth, economic complexity and structural change.* Copenhagen: DERG working paper series 20-02, University of Copenhagen. Department of Economics. Development Economics Research Group (DERG).
5. Feix, R. D., Colussi, J., Stefani, R., & Zawislak, P. A. (2019). HOW SOPHISTICATED IS BRAZILIAN AGRIBUSINESS? AN EXPLORATORY ANALYSIS BASED ON ECONOMIC COMPLEXITY APPROACH. *Anais do IV Encontro Nacional de Economia Industrial e Inovação, 6*(1), 53–71.
6. Felipe, J., Kumar, U., Abdon, A. M., & Bacate, M. (2012). Product Complexity and Economic Development. *Structural Change and Economic Dynamics, 23*, 36–68.
7. Ferraz, D., Moralles, H., Campoli, J., Oliveira, F., & Rebelatto, D. (2018). Economic Complexity and Human Development: DEA performance measurement in Asia and Latin America. *Gestão & Produção, 25*, 839–853.
8. Gala, P., Camargo, J., & Freitas, E. (2017). The Economic Commission for Latin America and the Caribbean (ECLAC) was right: scale-free complex networks and core-periphery patterns in world trade. *Cambridge Journal of Economics*, 633–651.
9. Gala, P., Rocha, I., & Magacho, G. (2018). The structuralist revenge: economic complexity as an important dimension to evaluate growth and development. *Brazilian Journal of Political Economy,*, 38(2), 219–236.

10. Hartmann, D., Guevara, M. R., Jara-Figueroa, C., Aristarán, M., & Hidalgo, C. A. (2017). Linking Economic Complexity, Institutions, and Income Inequality,. *Science Direct*, Pages 75–93.

11. Hausmann, R., Hidalgo, B. C., S., C. M., A., & Yildirim, M. A. (2014). *The atlas of economic complexity: Mapping paths to prosperity.* Mit Press.

12. Herrera, W. D., Strauch, J. C., & Bruno, M. A. (2020). Economic complexity of Brazilian states in the period 1997–2017. *AREA DEVELOPMENT AND POLICY*.

13. Hickson, J. (2017). The Atlas of Economic Complexity: A Review. *NEWCASTLE BUSINESS SCHOOL STUDENT JOURNAL*.

14. Hidalgo, C. A., Hausmann, R., & Dasgupta, P. S. (2009). The Building Blocks of Economic Complexity. *Proceedings of the National Academy of Sciences of the United States of America, 106*(26), 10570–0575.

15. Hidalgo, C. A., Klinger, B., Barabási, A., & R. H. (2007). The Product Space Conditions the Development of Nations. *Science, 317*(5837), 482–487.

16. Morrison, G., Buldyrev, S. V., Imbruno, M., Doria Arrieta, O. A., Rungi, A., Riccaboni, M., & Pammolli, F. (2017). On Economic Complexity and the Fitness of Nations. *Scientific Reports, 7*(1), 15332–15343.

17. Nguyen, C., Schinckus, C., & Thanh, S. D. (2020). The drivers of economic complexity: International evidence from financial development and patents. . *International Economics., 164*.

18. Paulo, G., Jhean, C., Guilherme, M., & Igor, R. (2018). Sophisticated jobs matter for economic complexity: An empirical analysis based on input-output matrices and employment data,. *Science Direct*, Pages 1–8.

19. Priscila Rubbo, C. T. (2018). Knowledge management practices and economic complexity in BRIC countries from 2001 to 2014. *International Journal of Knowledge Management Studies*, 9:1, 1–17.

20. Ren, Z.-M., Zeng, A., & Zhang, Y. (2020). Bridging nestedness and economic complexity in multilayer world trade networks. *Humanities and Social Sciences Communications, 7*(1), 156.

21. Sciarra, C., Chiarotti, G., & Francesco, L. (2020). Reconciling contrasting views on economic complexity. *Nature Communications, 11*(1), 3352–3362.

22. Sepehrdoust, H., Davarikish, R., & Setarehie, M. (2019). The knowledge-based products and economic complexity in developing countries,. *Heliyon, 5*(12).

23. Sørensen, B. B., Estmann, C., Sarmento, E. F., & Rand, J. (2020). *Economic complexity and structural transformation: the case of Mozambique*.

CHAPTER 15

Nexus Between Financial Liberalization, Financial Stability Index and Crises

Dr. Anjala Kalsie
Associate Professor
Faculty of Management Studies
University of Delhi
Delhi, India
kalsieanjala@gmail.com

Dr. Jappanjoyt Kaur Kalra
Assistant Professor
Sri Guru Gobind Singh College
of Commerce, University of Delhi
Delhi, India
kalrajappanjyot.research@gmail.com

Abstract

Purpose: The study is an attempt to construct the Financial Stability Index (FSI) and evaluate the impact of Financial Stability and Financial Liberalization (FL) over the occurrence of Banking and Currency Crises for 43 nations for the period from 2003-13.

Study design/methodology: To construct the Financial Stability Index, data reduction technique of principal component analysis is applied. To analyze the impact of financial stability indices and financial liberalization on the likelihood of banking and currency crisis a panel logit approach is applied.

Findings: Panel Logit Regression results shows that in case of banking crises; Government Finance Index and Monetary, External Vulnerability and Liquidity Index plays the significant role. In the case of the currency crises all the four financial stability indexes with Dejure Financial Liberalization impacts the likelihood of Currency Crises.

Keywords: Financial Liberalization, Financial Stability Index, Banking Crises, Currency Crises, Logit Regression.

I. INTRODUCTION

"Crisis prevention rather than crises rescues must be the primary long-term objective" (Davidson, 1997) (Caruana, 2010) explains the responsibility of the financial authorities to promote financial stability and states that central banks need to follow more systemic approach, as funding illiquid and insolvent assets may hike fiscal cost and bank failures. Financial liberalization improves the efficiency of economic variables, boosting economic growth and stability, through better allocation and monitoring of capital. Financial liberalization suppress financial risk (Gou & Huang, 2018)which in turn can be used to improve human capital accumulation, socioeconomic status, and long-run economic development. One way to enhance households' access to and usage of the financial system, especially the formal banking system, is to ensure that an adequate infrastructure exists within their community. We use data from the 2013 Chinese Household Finance Survey to investigate how the infrastructure affects the usage of formal bank loans for both urban and rural households in the People's Republic of China (PRC, and gradual liberalization policies amplify both financial stability and economic growth in presence of strong market and institutional environment. But various nations also witnessed crises post liberalization, (Allegret et al., 2003) especially in banking sector.

In the integrated financial system the risk of crises in one part of the system spreads quickly to others and makes it vulnerable to speculative attack (Alves et al., 1999). (Eichengreen et al., 1995)including doing nothing. For Europe, the alternative, namely failure to complete the transition to the European monetary unit (EMUalso explains that the interest rate speculations, volatility in capital flows and fluctuations in the exchange rate are the real threat to the even working of the economy. The financial stability limits the risk, reduces chances of the occurrence of crises as well as reduces the cost and damage from these crises if they occur.

II. REVIEW OF LITERATURE

A. Literature Review on Financial Stability Index

(Nelson & Perli, 2005) analyzed selected indicators for financial stability based upon interest rates, asset prices, market liquidity, bond risks and spreads (volatility), mortgage market indicators and trade variables. (Aspachs et al., 2006) constructed a metric to measure "financial fragility", which captures probability of default "(PD)".(Fell, 2005; Houben et al., 2004)explains that financial stability should focus on monitoring and analyzing macroeconomic condition, financial markets performance, strength of financial institutions and financial infrastructure, to access the occurrence of crises. (Gray et al., 2007) proposed a framework by using contingent claim analyses for the banking system to analyze and manage the financial risk of an economy. (Morris, 2010), developed and aggregate financial stability index (AFSI), by evaluating micro and macro fundamentals and international factors related to the banking sector. (Brave & Butters, 2011) proposed a financial condition index (FCI) which is the weighted averages of financial system health indicators, to monitor financial stability of a nation. (Ülgen, 2013) stated the importance of the "cognitive bias" which helps to identify the disequilibrium in the economic system which can lead to crises and macroeconomic instability. (Čihák, 2006) takes into account the role of Central Banks to promote Financial Stability through maintenance of FSRs (Financial Stability Reports), which in turn define risk and exposures in the banking sector. (Oosterloo & de Haan, 2004) discovered a lot of heterogeneity in the way Central Banks and supervisory authorities perform their role in maintaining the financial stability. Strong institutional environment and reforms in monetary system supporting capital account openness policies helps to obtain financial stability (Botta, 2018; Jahjah, 2001).

B. Literature Review on Financial Liberalization, Financial Stability Index and Crises

(Rastovski, 2016) capital inflows decreased the probability of banking crises and with the increase in long term borrowings and equity investments, likelihood for banking crises increased. Monitoring of international capital inflows and outflows by regulators (Wei et al., 2016) and reevaluation of utility of capital account openness (Gallagher, 2015), may prevent nations from financial risk.

Current account is impacted most due to appreciation or depreciation in exchange rate lead by capital account liberalization(Kim et al., 2004). (Ayhan Kose et al., 2011) defines the thresholds for direct investment, portfolio equity are lower than the debt flows. In case of capital reversals, openness of capital account increases economic vulnerabilities, worsening the impact of banking crises (Joyce & Nabar, 2009). Level of country's development impacts the relationship between CAO and banking crises, in low-income nations CAO reduces banking crises than in high-income nations (Qin & Luo, 2014). Nations which have witnessed banking crises in past are more likely to suffer with more banking crises, but middle-income countries in presence of financial openness suffer with lesser number of banking crises (Aizenman & Noy, 2013). Lower level of capital account openness and fixed exchange rate regimes leads to disturbances in international trade and even chances for banking crises increases (Chong et al., 2016). Korea suffered from volatile capital flows in a liberalized environment which invited crises, even in the presence of floating exchange rate(Kim & Yang, 2012). (Azis, 2018) points that the capital flows channelized through the banks are riskier flows and implementation of taxes on such flows may make the situation more dangerous through contagion of crises. (Aizenman & Ito, 2014) studies the hypothesis of the trilemma and found that the high levels of international reserves can help emerging markets avoid the debt crises but at the same time chances for the currency crises increases if wider policy divergence occur.

Corruption, lack of transparency in the system and "weak democracies" inflate negative aspects of capital account openness, as emerging economies witnessed more speculative attacks and frequent crises (Alper & Öniş, 2001). The increasing interest rate have minimized effect upon currency crises if capital account is open, and monetary policy is strong as it supports exchange rate policies (Eijffinger & Goderis, 2008). Financial liberalization should be ensued only if, sound monetary and financial system is in place (Eichengreen et al., 2009). Macroeconomic stability, robust domestic financial system, sequential capital account liberalization are preconditions to achieve growth and reducing risk of crises (Daianu & Vranceanu, 2003; Obadan, 2006). In presence of weak policies and market fundamentals, international capital flows makes banking sector more fragile and puts pressure on international investments (Joyce & Nabar, 2009; Nixson & Walters, 2002). There is limited literature appraising the relationship among financial stability, financial liberalization and crises. The present study is an attempt to fill this gap.

III. OBJECTIVE AND METHODOLOGY

The objective of the paper is to construct the financial stability index, analyze, and measure the impact of Financial Stability index and Financial Liberalization on the Likelihood of Banking Crises and Currency Crises on 43 nations[1] for the period 2003-13.

Data Sources: The definition and the data for the dependent variable banking and currency crises is adopted from (Reinhart & Rogoff, 2009). For financial liberalization the dejure measure (the Kaopen) developed by (Chinn & Ito, 2007) and defacto measure as developed by (Lane & Milesi-Ferretti, 2001, 2007) for the capital assets and liabilities is used as explanatory variable. Four financial stability indices; namely; "External Payment and Debt Index (EPDI)", "Monetary, External Vulnerability and Liquidity Index (MEVLI)", "Economic Structure and Performance Index (ESPI)" and "Government Finance Index (GFI)" was constructed using data provided in Statistical Handbook (Moody's, 2013)

A. Methodology

• Principal Component analysis

$(X'X)$ are eigen values of original variables X and total variation is explained using following ratio (Brooks, 2008) equation 1

$$\varphi i = \frac{\lambda_i}{\sum_{i=1}^{k} \lambda_i} \tag{1}$$

Where; λ_i is the ordered eigenvalues of variables ($i = 1\ldots\ldots\ldots k$), explaining the variation of $(X'X)$. Highly correlated variables from the original dataset were dropped initially. Following the varimax procedure the four indices were constructed by multiplying component score (weights) with each value of the variable extracted using PCA, as given in equation 2.

$$x_j = w_j z_{it} \tag{2}$$

Where; x_j is the selected variable based on the component score, w_j is the respective weight of the obtained variable and z_{it} value of the variable for i^{th} observation at time t. After multiplying the weights with respective observation of extracted variables and summating them, the indices were constructed using the following equation:

$$k_n = \sum_{j=1}^{p} w_j x_j \tag{3}$$

---

[1] Angola, Egypt, Korea, Philippines, Uruguay, Argentina, El Salvador, Malaysia, Poland, Venezuela, Bolivia, Ghana, Mauritius, Romania, Zambia, Brazil, Guatemala, Mexico, Russia, Chile, Honduras, Morocco, South Africa, China, Hungary, Nicaragua, Sri Lanka, Colombia, Iceland, Nigeria, Taiwan, Costa Rica, India, Panama, Thailand, Dominican Republic, Indonesia, Paraguay, Tunisia, Ecuador, Kenya, Peru and Turkey.

Where; k_n is the index and p is the total number of components extracted to construct index, x_j is the selected variable based on the component score and w_j is the respective weight of the obtained variable.

- Panel Logit Model[2]

In the Logit model to measure the correct predicted values the restrictions are imposed and model transformation is done in two steps. Firstly, the probability is converted into odds, which is the ratio of occurrence of the event to the non-occurrence of the event. For the smaller probability the odds are very long and vis-s-vis and if the odds is equal to one the chances of the occurrence and the non-occurrence becomes equal.

If the probability approaches to one and odds approaches to positive infinity that implies that positive logit and the negative logit represent the equal chances of the occurrence and the non-occurrence of the events. By taking the exponentiation-estimated logit we get the odds value as below:

$$\pi_{ij} = logit^{-1}(n_{ij}) = \frac{e^{n_{ij}}}{1+e^{n_{ij}}} \tag{4}$$

After exponentiation, the logit model for the ith unit at time t with *odds* is as following:

$$\frac{\pi_{ij}}{1-\pi_{ij}} = \exp\{x'_{ij}\beta_i\} \tag{5}$$

and the probability would be :

$$\pi_{it} = \frac{\exp\{x'_{ij}\dagger_i\}}{1+\exp\{x'_{ij}\dagger_i\}} \tag{6}$$

In the Logit Regression, the model can be interpreted in log odds and the impact of covariates on the dependent variable with logistic errors can be studied. Hence, for the purpose of analyses and interpretation in the paper, we report log-odds ratio. The panel Logit equations used in the paper are listed in the Table 1.

Table 1: The Panel Logit Regression Equations

Sr.no	Crises	Equation
1/6		$BC_{i,t}/CC_{i,t} = \beta_{i,t} + \beta_{1i,t}(ESPI_{i,t}) + \beta_{2i,t}(GFI_{i,t}) + \beta_{3i,t}(EPDI_{i,t})$ $+ \beta_{4i,t}(MEVLI_{i,t}) + \xi_{i,t}$
2/7	Banking Crises/ Currency Crises	$BC_{i,t} = \beta_{i,t} + \beta_{1i,t}(ESPI_{i,t}) + \beta_{2i,t}(GFI_{i,t}) + \beta_{3i,t}(EPDI_{i,t})$ $+ \beta_{4i,t}(MEVLI_{i,t}) + \beta_{5i,t}(Kaopen_{i,t}) + \xi_{i,t}$
3/8		$BC_{i,t}/CC_{i,t} = \beta_{i,t} + \beta_{1i,t}(ESPI_{i,t}) + \beta_{2i,t}(GFI_{i,t}) + \beta_{3i,t}(EPDI_{i,t})$ $+ \beta_{4i,t}(MEVLI_{i,t}) + \beta_{6i,t}(NFA_{i,t}) + \xi_{i,t}$

[2] The Logit Model Methodology has been referred from (Cameron & Trivedi, 2009; Rodríguez, 2007)

| 4/9 | $BC_{i,t} / CC_{i,t} = \beta_{i,t} + \beta_{1i,t}(ESPI_{i,t}) + \beta_{2i,t}(GFI_{i,t}) + \beta_{3i,t}(EPDI_{i,t})$ $+ \beta_{4i,t}(MEVLI_{i,t}) + \beta_{7i,t}(TA_{i,t}) + \xi_{i,t}$ |
| 5/10 | $BC_{i,t} / CC_{i,t} = \beta_{i,t} + \beta_{1i,t}(ESPI_{i,t}) + \beta_{2i,t}(GFI_{i,t}) + \beta_{3i,t}(EPDI_{i,t})$ $+ \beta_{4i,t}(MEVLI_{i,t}) + \beta_{8i,t}(TL_{i,t}) + \xi_{i,t}$ |

Source: Author's Compilation (equation 1-5 are for banking crisis and equation 6-7 are for currency crisis)

Where; represents the Banking Crises in country i at time t, represents the Currency Crises in country i at time t represents the constant coefficient in country i at time t, represents the Coefficient for the Economic Structure and Performance index in country i at time t represents the Coefficient for the Government Finance index in country i at time t, represents the Coefficient for the External Payment and Debt index in country i at time t, represents the Coefficient for Monetary, External Vulnerability and Liquidity index in the country i at time t, represents the Coefficient for Financial Account Openness Index (Kaopen) in the country i at time t, represents the Coefficient for Net Financial Assets in the country i at time t, represents the Coefficient for Total Assets in the country i at time t, represents the Coefficient for Total Liabilities in the country i at time t andrepresents the error component in regression equation.

IV. ANALYSIS & INTERPRETATIONS

The component score and KMO value of the four FSI indices are reported in table 2.

Table 2: The Components of the Four Indexes and Their Expected Effect over the Financial Stability

S.No.	Components of the Index	Component Score	Scaling	FSI and Crises
Economic Structure and Performance Index (KMO: 0.711)				-
1	Population	0.839	+	
2	Inflation	0.759	+	
3	Openness of the Economy	0.847	+	
Government Finance Index (KMO: 0.684)				+
1	General Government Debt to General Government Revenue	0.915	+	
2	General Government Foreign-Currency and Foreign-Currency-Indexes Debt/ General Government Debt	0.965	+	

External Payment and Debt Index (KMO: 0.652)				+
1	Official Foreign Exchange Reserves	0.836	+	
2	External Debt/Current Account Receipts	0.714	+	
3	Interest Paid On External Debt	0.594	+	
4	Net Foreign Direct Investment	0.519	+	
5	Real Effective Exchange Rate	0.466	+	
Monetary, External Vulnerability and Liquidity Index (KMO: 0.645)				+
1	External Vulnerability Index	0.890	+	
2	M2 % Change	0.734	+	
3	Liquidity Ratio	0.730	+	

Source: Author's Compilation

A. Interpretations for the Logit Regression of FL and FSI on Banking Crises

Table 3 reports the result of equation 1 to 5 stated in the Table 1. The MEVLI, GFI and EPDI significantly impact the probability of occurrence of banking Crises. The positive sign indicates that as the value of said indices increases occurrence of the banking crises increases. None of the financial Liberalization parameters measured by (Chinn & Ito, 2007) and (Lane & Milesi-Ferretti, 2001, 2007) turns out to be significant.

GFI: it evaluates the sovereign risk of a nation, which is the construct of fiscal balances and government debt stocks at central, state or regional levels. Speculative foreign capital flows or short-term cross-border funds will be employed to meet the immediate deficits which increases the bank burden as the flows channelizes through bank. The amount of Government Debt proportional to Gross Domestic Product is one of the significant indicators explaining the stress on public debt. If the taxes collected are used to repay the interest and borrowing than the government revenues cannot be channelized into development projects.

EPDI: Real Effective Exchange Rate (REER) directly impacts imports and exports capacity of a nations. The large deficits mean higher external borrowing, which if done through Foreign Direct Investments Inflows or equity investments in domestic companies, which poses less risk. But if the same is financed by short-term borrowings and speculative flows, fear of imbalances may create the negative sentiments among the investors leading to capital flee, eliciting asset market declines and currency depreciation. The rapid changes in the amount of external debt impact the refinancing of foreign funds, increases the rollover risk. If the cost of debt payment is high, interest payments and principal repayment may obstruct, leading to internal as well as external bank imbalances and liquidity problems. In presence of such circumstances, fixed exchange rate and instable financial system may increase the risk of banking crises.

MEVLI: The amplification of money supply in an economy may indicate inflationary pressure in future which can destabilize the investors' confidence in domestic currency. The easing of the monetary policy feeds the economy with easy and cheaper credit to all sectors of the economy signaling future credit boom and higher financial intermediation for managing the movement of funds between lender and borrowers. But expansion of credit may also head towards higher defaults as the funds may not be utilized for the undersigned purpose, thus increases the level of Non-Performing Assets of the financial institutions. Hence, stable Fiscal Policy, Monetary Policy and Credibility of the Government are very important elements for examining the economies vulnerability to banking crises.

Table 3: Logit Regression Analyses for the Impact of FSI and FL on the Banking Crises (Odds Ratio) (Equations 1-5)

VARIABLES	odds ratio	odds ratio	odds ratio		
Dependent Variable: Banking Crises		(Chinn & Ito, 2007)	(Lane & Milesi-Ferretti, 2001, 2007)		
ESPI	-0.991	-0.984	-0.992	-0.986	-0.987
	(0.008)	(0.0117)	(0.00791)	(0.00963)	(0.00859)
GFI	1.007	1.010*	1.007	1.008	1.007*
	(0.0052)	(0.00556)	(0.00493)	(0.00505)	(0.00424)
EPDI	1.005	1.007*	1.005	1.002	1.002
	(0.0016)	(0.00421)	(0.00319)	(0.00388)	(0.00332)
MEVLI	1.003*	1.003	1.003*	1.003**	1.003**
	(0.0016)	(0.00177)	(0.00162)	(0.0017)	(0.00159)
KAOPEN		-0.467			
		(0.285)			
NFA			-1		
			(3.44E-06)		
TA				1	
				(2.11E-06)	
TL					1
					(2.05E-06)
Observations	473	473	473	473	473
Number of CountryCode	43	43	43	43	43
Standard errors in parentheses					
*** p<0.01, ** p<0.05, * p<0.1					

Source: Author's Compilation

B. Interpretations for the Logit Regression of FL and FSI on Currency Crises

Table 4 reports the result of equation 6 to 10 stated in the Table 1. The ESPI, MEVLI, GFI and EPDI significantly impact the probability of occurrence of currency Crises. The positive sign of GFI, EPDI and MEVLI indicates that as the value of said indices increases occurrence of the currency crises increases, whereas the negative sign of ESPI indicates that as the value of index increases the chances of currency crisis decreases. Among the CAO indices the Dejure CAO index by (Chinn & Ito, 2008) is significant and negative sign directs that with the increase in financial liberalization in the presence of financial stability reduces the chances of currency crises. The economies with the open financial account suffer with the surges and sudden stop of capital flows, leading to currency crisis.

Table 4 Logit Regression Analyses for the Impact of FSI and FL on the Currency Crises (Odds Ratio) (Equations 6-10)

VARIABLES	odds ratio	odds ratio	odds ratio		
Dependent Variable: Currency Crises		(Chinn & Ito, 2007)	(Lane & Milesi-Ferretti, 2001, 2007)		
ESPI	-1.002*	-1.002	-1.002*	-1.002*	-1.002*
	(0.00123)	(0.00117)	(0.00125)	(0.00128)	(0.0013)
GFI	0.991***	0.991***	0.991***	0.990***	-0.990***
	(0.00327)	(0.00309)	(0.00326)	(0.00334)	(0.00328)
EPDI	0.996*	0.996*	0.996*	0.997	-0.997
	(0.00207)	(0.00199)	(0.00206)	(0.00261)	(0.00234)
MEVLI	1.003***	1.003***	1.003***	1.003***	-1.003***
	(0.00098)	(0.000907)	(0.000993)	(0.00112)	(0.00103)
KAOPEN		-0.756*			
		(0.125)			
NFA			1		
			(1.53E-06)		
TA				-1	
				(1.48E-06)	
TL					-1
					(1.14E-06)
Observations	473	473	473	473	473
Number of CountryCode	43	43	43	43	43
Standard errors in parentheses					
*** p<0.01, ** p<0.05, * p<0.1					

Source: Author's Compilation

EPDI: The 'overvalued' Real Effective Exchange Rate (REER) is one of the vital indicator of future devaluation of money which in the presence of structural imbalances; namely high external debt and high net foreign flows, can root self-fulfilling currency crises. If external debtors or non-residents withdraw their capital either in domestic denomination or foreign denomination it can initiate currency crises. The currency depreciation accompanied with the very high interest rates can stress the borrowers, which may lead to defaults and bankruptcy due to increased credit risk and maturity mismatch.

MEVLI: The components of MEVLI index evaluate the nation's vulnerability in case of fragility in the banking sector and depreciation or devaluation of nation's currency. The nations with the weak banking sector, unstable currency and open financial account have to face larger cost of such crises. The ratio of M2 to the country's central bank's reserves points the pressure of a currency or banking crisis due to the withdrawal of domestic currency investments by money holders and investing into foreign currency assets, indicating run on liquid assets, thus causing currency crises. The external vulnerability ratio indicates the ability of the nation to repay the currently maturing external debt with the available exchange resources even if creditor's refuses to repay within a given year in case of run on the currency and loss of investors' confidence. The other important indicator is the proportion of foreign currency denominated deposits to the total deposits in the domestic banks due to currency instability and the vulnerability of market fundamentals.

ESPI: The Real GDP growth indicates the rise in the standard of living, increase in the ability to face crises but on the other side the rapid unsustainable growth indicates risk of inflationary pressure and increase in external deficits. But rapid growth in presence of monetary and financial instability can disseminate inflationary pressure impacting investments and returns as inflations impacts both demand side and supply side. The financial openness means the deregulation of the cross-border capital flows and free currency conversions, leading to surges and sudden stop of the capital flows. Trade balances are also impacted by the capital flows and exchange rate mechanism. The freedom to flee at the time of instability leads to crises.

GFI: Government financial stocks along with the external payments are significant indicators describing the sovereign risk and relative growth of the domestic economy in comparison to the foreign markets. Government debt impacts foreign exchange market, if the country has high debt and lesser revenues which can negatively impact value of the currency. Easing of monetary policy will escalate the supply of domestic currency, causing the currency to depreciate and in the absence of macroeconomic fundamentals leads to currency crisis.

V. CONCLUSION

Emerging economies in the past few decades have suffered with many banking and currency crises, which had foster the requirement of stable financial system. The paper is an attempt to construct the Financial Stability Index and evaluate the impact of Financial Stability and Financial Liberalization over the occurrence of Currency and Banking Crises. The Panel Logit Regression results points that in the case of banking crises; Government Finance Index and Monetary, External Vulnerability and Liquidity Index plays the significant role. The positive direction indicates that with the increase in value of both the indexes, chances of the incidence of banking crises increases. In the case of currency crises all the four indexes that are; "Economic Structure and Performance Index, Government Finance Index, External Payment and Debt Index and Monetary, External Vulnerability and Liquidity Index" along with Dejure Financial Liberalization impact the occurrence of Currency Crises. The negative sign of GFI, EPDI and CAL indicates that with the increase in the value of these indices the probability of the occurrence of currency crises reduces.

The rapid increase of global liquidity, financial integration and increased capital flows to the emerging nations and the frequent crises, specially the global financial crises raised the concern for financial stability of the nations. Financial stability index takes into account various aspects related to the structure and performance of economy, government expenditures and revenues, external debt and payments due and different aspects related to monetary and fiscal policies, capturing the vulnerability of an economy to banking and currency crises in the presence of different risks. The exchange rate, interest rate, trade integration, saving and investment patterns, price mechanism and monetary policy are entangled to each other, i.e. changes in one simultaneously cause's changes in others. The economic mechanisms such as; "Purchasing Power Parity (PPP)", "Interest Rate Parity", Exchange Rate and the other factors like; Political Risk, Regulation and Deregulation of Capital Flows and Trade causes currency depreciation and bank runs. In the era of globalizations markets are majorly driven by the investor's sentiments, confidence and perception about the present and future of the economy. Financial innovations, regulatory aspects for managing the fragility in the different sectors, government effectiveness and bank's ability to manage complex credit and funding liquidity problems helps in tackling the challenges of the integrated financial markets. The uncertainties of the markets, liquidity squeezes, volatile flows, balance sheet mismatch and high leverage makes it really important for the emerging economies to build a stable and safer financial system, by enhancing the surveillance and risk management practices, identifying potential risks and immediate policy responses and implementation of regulation to avoid the fragility in the banking sector and devaluation of the currency.

VI. REFERENCES

Aizenman, J., & Ito, H. (2014). The more divergent, the better? Lessons on trilemma policies and crises for Asia. *Asian Development Review*, *31*(2), 21–54.

Aizenman, J., & Noy, I. (2013). Macroeconomic adjustment and the history of crises in open economies. *Journal of International Money and Finance*, *38*, 41–58. https://doi.org/10.1016/j.jimonfin.2013.03.002

Allegret, J.-P., Courbis, B., & Dulbecco, P. (2003). Financial liberalization and stability of the financial system in emerging markets: the institutional dimension of financial crises. *Review of International Political Economy*, *10*(1),73–92. https://doi.org/10.1080/0969229032000048880

Alper, C. E., & Öniş, Z. (2001). Financial Globalization, the Democratic Deficit and Recurrent Crises in Emerging Markets: The Turkish Experience in the Aftermath of Capital Account Liberalization. *Ssrn*. https://doi.org/10.2139/ssrn.288367

Alves, A. J., Ferrari, F., & De Paula, L. F. R. (1999). The Post Keynesian critique of conventional currency crisis models and Davidson's proposal to reform the international monetary system. In *Journal of Post Keynesian Economics* (Vol. 22, Issue 2, pp. 207–225). https://doi.org/10.1080/01603477.1999.11490237

Aspachs, O., Goodhart, C., Segoviano, M., Tsomocos, D., Zicchino, L., Group, F. M., & Industry, F. (2006). Searching for a Metric for Financial Stability. *Lse Financial Markets Group Special Paper Series, 167*, 1–38.

Ayhan Kose, M., Prasad, E. S., & Taylor, A. D. (2011). Thresholds in the process of international financial integration. *Journal of International Money and Finance, 30*(1), 147–179. https://doi.org/10.1016/j.jimonfin.2010.08.005

Azis, I. (2018). Coping with the dangerous component of capital flows and Asia's ineffective cooperation. In J. Pixley & H. Flam (Eds.), *Critical Junctures in Mobile Capital* (pp. 52–67). Cambridge University Press. https://doi.org/10.1017/9781316995327.003

Botta, A. (2018). Financial and Capital Account Liberalization, Financial Development and Economic Development: A Review of Some Recent Contributions. *Forum for Social Economics, 47*(3–4), 362–377. https://doi.org/10.1080/07360932.2017.1383286

Brave, S., & Butters, R. A. (2011). Monitoring financial stability : A financial conditions index approach. *Economic Perspectives, 35(1)*, 22–43.

Brooks, C. (2008). *Introductory econometrics for finance. 2nd edition.* https://doi.org/10.1111/1468-0297.13911

Cameron, A. C., & Trivedi, P. K. (2009). Microeconometrics using Stata. In *Business and Economics* (5th ed.). Stata Press. https://doi.org/10.1016/S0304-4076(00)00050-6

Caruana, J. (2010). The great financial crisis: Lessons for financial stability and monetary policy. *An ECB Colloquium Held in Honour of Lucas Papademos, May*, 14–21.

Chinn, M. D., & Ito, H. (2007). A New Measure of Financial Openness. *Journal of Comparative Policy Analysis, 10*(3), 309–322.

Chinn, M. D., & Ito, H. (2008). A New Measure of Financial Openness. *Journal of Comparative Policy Analysis: Research and Practice, 10*(3), 309–322. https://doi.org/10.1080/13876980802231123

Chong, T. T. L., He, Q., & Chan, W. H. (2016). From Fixed to Float: A Competing Risks Analysis. *International Economic Journal, 30*(4), 488–503. https://doi.org/10.1080/10168737.2016.1204343

Čihák, M. (2006). Central Banks and Financial Stability: A Survey of Financial Stability Reports. *Seminar on Current Developments in Monetary and Financial Law Washington, D.C., October 23-27, 2006*, 1–31.

Daianu, A. D., & Vranceanu, R. (2003). Opening the Capital Account of Developing Countries : Some Policy Issues. *Acta Oeconomica, 53*(3), 245–270. https://doi.org/10.1556/AOecon.53.2003.3.2

Davidson, P. (1997). Are grains of sand in the wheels of international finance sufficient to do the job when boulders are often required? *Economic Journal, 107*(442), 671–686. https://doi.org/10.1111/j.1468-0297.1997.tb00033.x

Eichengreen, B., Gullapalli, R., Panizza, U., Del, U., Orientale, P., & Avogadro, A. (2009). *Capital account liberalization, financial development and industry growth : a synthetic view Capital Account Liberalization, Financial Development and Industry Growth : A Synthetic View. June.*

Eichengreen, B., Tobin, J., & Wypolsz, C. (1995). Two cases for sand in the wheels of international finance.pdf. *The Economic Journal, 105*(428), 162–172. https://doi.org/10.2307/2235326

Eijffinger, S. C. W., & Goderis, B. (2008). The effect of monetary policy on exchange rates during currency crises: The role of debt, institutions, and financial openness. *Review of International Economics*, *16*(3), 559–575. https://doi.org/10.1111/j.1467-9396.2008.00745.x

Fell, J. (2005). Assessing Financial Stability: Exploring the Boundaries of Analysis. *National Institute Economic Review*, *192*(192), 102–117. https://doi.org/10.1177/002795010519200110

Gallagher, K. P. (2015). Contesting the Governance of Capital Flows at the IMF. *Governance: An International Journal of Policy, Administration, and Institutions*, *28*(2), 185–198. https://doi.org/10.1111/gove.12100

Gou, Q., & Huang, Y. (2018). *Will Financial Liberalization Trigger the First Crisis in the People's Republic of China? Lessons From Cross-Country Experiences* (No. 818; ADBI Working Paper Series, Issue 818).

Gray, D., Merton, R., & Bodie, Z. (2007). New Framework for Measuring and Managing Macrofinancial Risk and Financial Stability. *NBER Working Paper Series*, *13607*(November). https://doi.org/10.3386/w13607

Houben, A., Kakes, J., & Schinasi, G. (2004). Toward a Framework for Safeguarding Financial Stability. In *IMF Working Paper* (WP/04/101).

Jahjah, S. (2001). *Financial Stability and Financial Crises in a Monetary Union* (WP/01/210; December).

Joyce, J. P., & Nabar, M. (2009). Sudden stops , banking crises and investment collapses in emerging markets. *Journal of Development Economics*, *90*(2), 314–322. https://doi.org/10.1016/j.jdeveco.2008.04.004

Kim, S., Kim, S. H., & Wang, Y. (2004). *Macroeconomic Effects of Capital Account Liberalization : the Case of Korea*. 8(4), 624–639.

Kim, S., & Yang, D. Y. (2012). Are capital controls effective? the case of the republic of korea. *Asian Development Review*, *29*(2), 96–133.

Lane, P. R., & Milesi-Ferretti, G. M. (2001). The external wealth of nations: Measures of foreign assets and liabilities for industrial and developing countries. *Journal of International Economics*, *55*(2), 263–294. https://doi.org/10.1016/S0022-1996(01)00102-7

Lane, P. R., & Milesi-Ferretti, G. M. (2007). The external wealth of nations mark II: Revised and extended estimates of foreign assets and liabilities, 1970-2004. *Journal of International Economics*, *73*(2), 223–250. https://doi.org/10.1016/j.jinteco.2007.02.003

Moody's. (2013). *Moody's Statistical Handbook Country Credit* (Issue November).

Morris, V. C. (2010). *Measuring and Forecasting Financial Stability : The Composition of an Aggregate Financial Stability Index for Jamaica*. 1–19.

Nelson, W. R., & Perli, R. (2005). *Selected Indicators of Financial Stability. June 2005*, 30.

Nixson, F., & Walters, B. (2002). Regulatory and development dilemmas in the post-crisis Asian economies. *Journal of the Asia Pacific Economy*, *7*(1), 95–112. https://doi.org/10.1080/13547860120110489

Obadan, M. I. (2006). Globalization of finance and the challenge of national financial sector development. *Journal of Asian Economics*, *17*(2), 316–332. https://doi.org/10.1016/j.asieco.2005.11.002

Oosterloo, S., & de Haan, J. (2004). Central banks and financial stability: a survey. *Journal of Financial Stability*, *1*(2), 257–273. https://doi.org/10.1016/j.jfs.2004.09.002

Qin, X., & Luo, C. (2014). Capital account openness and early warning system for banking crises in G20 countries. *Economic Modelling*, *39*, 190–194. https://doi.org/10.1016/j.econmod.2014.02.037

Rastovski, J. (2016). The Changing Relationship between Banking Crises and Capital Inflows. *Review of Development Economics*, *20*(2), 514–530. https://doi.org/10.1111/rode.12242

Reinhart, C. M., & Rogoff, K. S. (2009). *This Time Is Different: Eight Centuries of Financial Folly*. Princeton: Princeton University Press. https://doi.org/10.1017/CBO9781107415324.004

Rodríguez, G. (2007). Logit Models for Binary Data. In *Lecture Notes on Generalized Linear Models*. http://data.princeton.edu/wws509/notes/

Ülgen, F. (2013). Institutions and Liberalized Finance: Is Financial Stability of Capitalism a Pipedream? *Journal of Economic Issues*, *47*(2), 495–504. https://doi.org/10.2753/JEI0021-3624470223

Wei, Y. S., Suhaimi, R. H., & Hui, J. K. S. (2016). Analysis of international capital mobility in ASEAN-5 countries: Savings-Investment nexus. *Jurnal Ekonomi Malaysia*, *50*(2),155–166. https://doi.org/10.17576/JEM-2016-5001-13

CHAPTER 16

Relationship Between Portfolio Flows and Currency Crisis: an Empirical Analysis

Dr. Anjala Kalsie
Associate Professor
Faculty of Management Studies
University of Delhi, Delhi, India
kalsieanjala@gmail.com

Ms. Jyoti Dhamija
Senior Research Scholar
Faculty of Management Studies
University of Delhi, Delhi, India
jyoti.d_phd16@fms.edu

Abstract

Purpose: The paper aims to empirically investigate the relationship between the portfolio capital inflows and currency crisis. The analysis is conducted on BRIC nations.

Methodology: econometric methodology of Two Stage Probit Least Square (TSPLS) which uses cdsimeq command in stata software, is adopted to prove the hypothesis. The study analyses portfolio flows in its aggregate form as well as with its components namely, portfolio debt inflows and portfolio equity inflows. The data collected is for the time period spanning from 1996 till 2018.

Findings: The results reveal that the total portfolio inflows and currency crises hold a statistically significant relationship. Also, the analysis divulges that out of the two components of portfolio inflows, portfolio debt inflows have a significant relationship with currency crises.

Value: The paper makes an attempt to uncover the bidirectional relationship that exists between portfolio flows and currency crisis.

Keywords: Currency Crisis, Portfolio Flows, BRICS, TSPLS

I. INTRODUCTION

It is well known that foreign capital can increase growth and investment in the receiving country but at the same time the volatility of foreign flows makes a country prone to crises. The sequence of crises in the emerging market economies in the 1990s alongside the financial globalization has rekindled the interest amongst the academicians and the policy circles to analyse the benefits of global financial integration. The severity and frequency of the currency crises in recent years has become a major concern for not only developing but also for industrial economies. The effects of currency crises are dramatically detrimental to the economy. Literature suggests that inflow of foreign capital in the economy helps the economy to grow but undoubtedly it also sometimes hinders the growth process. To obtain the benefits of international flows a country needs to have strong fundamentals and the policies must be drafted keeping in consideration the composition of flows. Foreign Direct Investment, Portfolio Investment and Bank loans are the components that make up the international capital flows. Amongst the three components, FDI is known to be the most reliable source as it does not leave the economy in the hard times. Portfolio flows and Bank loans have qualified to be the ones to leave the country in hard time and create the situation of crises. The present study is concerned with exploring the relationship between Portfolio flows and currency crises.

Portfolio flows are known to be a volatile component of private capital flows. They are a short-term source of capital which are motivated by immediate gains and hence are very volatile. Portfolio flows are pro cyclical in nature which makes an economy vulnerable to crises. Many studies have empirically proved that these short- term flows bring about the situation of crises in the economy. They are the most unreliable sources of funds. (Frankel & Rose, 1996), (Wei, 2000), (Wei & Wu, 2002) and, (Licchetta, 2011) etc. have all talked about the composition of flows in their studies and have even proved that the composition of capital flows matters more than the size of flows in explaining the onset of the crises.

The rest of the paper is organized as follows: Section II presents the Review of Literature. Section III outlines the Data and Methodology used to analyze the relationship between Portfolio Flows and Currency Crisis. Section IV discusses the Results and Section V concludes the key findings.

II. LITERATURE REVIEW

Inefficient foreign exchange markets and weak market fundamental may lead to self-fulfilling currency crises. In the integrated financial system, the risk of crises in one part of the system spreads quickly to others and makes it vulnerable to speculative attack. The markets in general are more speculative in financially globalized and integrated system. Hence, it is very important to make the domestic financial system stable and strong, to limit the impact of financial crises. The keys macroeconomic variables that impact currency crises are Real Interest Rates and the Real Effective exchange rate to name a few.

There is a vast literature which talks about the relationship between international capital flows and currency crises. International capital flows appear to have turn out to be leading force in explaining the inception of currency crises in emerging market (Licchetta, 2011). Many researchers have theoretically as well as empirically examined the relation between the two. The events in last decade of the 20th century very well explain the contribution of international capital flows towards the outbreak of currency crises in the economies. The ERM crisis of 1992-93, Mexican Peso crisis of 1994-94, East Asian crisis of 1997-98, all these instances make it clear as to the type of relationship foreign flows and currency crises hold. Various factors that trigger currency crises are globalization and capital flows, fiscal imbalances, excessive credit creation, large current account deficit, moral hazard, pegging of currency, inflation, interest rates, bank runs and deep recession ((Aschinger, 2001);

(Dornbusch et al., 1995); (Glick et al., 2011); (Marković, 2015)). (Frankel & Rose, 1996) in the article make an empirical analysis of the currency crashes in the emerging economies and find that, crisis hit countries tend to have high proportion of short-term flows in their external capital structure. (Ghosh et al., 2016) states that the economies receiving larger share of flows in the form of debt are more likely to end with the episode of crisis. (Frost & Saiki, 2014) explains that capital flows of short-term nature like portfolio flows may increase this risk of currency crisis. gross portfolio flows increase the risk of a currency crisis for advanced economies

Studies suggest that out of the two types of portfolio flows namely, portfolio debt flows and portfolio equity flows, it is portfolio debt flows which are more of risky kind. Portfolio equity flows have a negligible effect on the incidence of crises. Portfolio debt flows are associated with larger macroeconomic imbalances and financial vulnerabilities in the economies (Qureshi & Ghosh, 2016). Portfolio debt flows spread higher levels of volatility than portfolio equity flows (Mukharaev, 2017). (Claessens et al., 1995) highlight that FDI and portfolio equity flows exhibit much less volatility over short periods than do the other short-term flows. Large inflow of debt flows increases the probability of all types of crises while equity portfolio and FDI inflows have insignificant effects. (Licchetta, 2009) divulge that the likelihood of currency crisis increases with total external gross liability and decreases with the share of gross FDI in total gross liabilities. It shows that the composition of external liability greatly influences the country's degree of susceptibility to crises than the size of liability. Also, the study puts forward that, emerging market economies are more sensitive to external balance sheet variables than advanced economies. Also, (Frost & Saiki, 2014) reveal that the risk of currency crisis increases in industrial economies, with an increase of gross portfolio flows.

Present study makes an attempt to contribute to the existing literature by trying to find out the relationship between portfolio flows and currency crisis.

III. DATA AND METHODOLOGY

To explore the relationship between portfolio flows and currency crisis, the present study uses annual data for the period from 1996 to 2018 for BRIC nations. The right-hand side variables are lagged by 1 year in order to know the precise impact of portfolio flows on currency crisis.

Table below presents the variables used in the study and their source of data.

Table I: Variables and their Sources

Sr. No.	Name of the Variable	Source of Definition
1. *Continuous Endogenous Variable*		
	a. Total Portfolio Inflows b. Portfolio Debt Inflows c. Portfolio Equity Flows	International Financial Statistics, IMF
2. *Dichotomous Endogenous Variable*		
	Currency Crisis	Reinhart & Rogoff

3. *Exogenous Variables*		
I	Real effective exchange rate (CPI-based)	World Development Indicator
II	Consumer price index (2010 = 100)	World Development Indicator
III	Current account balance as percentage of GDP	World Development Indicator
IV	Globalization Index (0-100)	theglobaleconomy.com
V	Corruption	theglobaleconomy.com
VI	Broad money (% of GDP)	World Development Indicator
VII	Monetary freedom index (0-100)	theglobaleconomy.com
VIII	Real interest rate: Bank lending rate minus inflation	World Development Indicator
IX	Debt service on external debt, total (TDS, current US$) / GDP	theglobaleconomy.com
X	Foreign exchange reserves including gold billion USD	theglobaleconomy.com
XI	Trade freedom index (0-100)	theglobaleconomy.com

A.   METHODOLOGY

In order to carry out the analysis simultaneous equation framework is used. Since one dependent variable in the study is dichotomous and the other dependent variable is continuous, the econometric model of Two Stage Probit Least Square, proposed by (Maddala, 1983), is adopted. The cdsimeq command in stata is used to prove the hypothesis.

An overview of the of the methodology formulated by Maddala is presented below:

$$y_1 = \alpha_1 y_2 + \beta_1 X_1 + \varepsilon_1 \qquad (1)$$

$$y_2 = \alpha_2 y_1 + \beta_2 X_2 + \varepsilon_2 \qquad (2)$$

Where,

y: continuous endogenous variable

y: dichotomous endogenous variable.

Matrices X and $X2$ contain the exogenous variables.

$\beta 1$ and β: parameter vectors.

α_1 and α: parameter vectors of endogenous variables

ε_1 and ε_2: error terms.

In the present study, Portfolio flows are continuous endogenous variable and currency crisis is dichotomous variable which takes value 1, if the crisis has occurred and zero otherwise. In order to study the impact of Portfolio flows on the probability of currency crisis, we take three different variants of portfolio flows, namely, total portfolio flows, portfolio debt flows and portfolio equity flows. The three type of portfolio flows are analysed to find out if the composition of flows has an impact on currency crisis. Hence, we regress three models outlined below, to explore the relationship between portfolio flows and currency crisis.

Model 1:

Y_1 = Total portfolio inflows to GDP

Y_2 = Currency Crisis

Model 2:

Y_1 = Portfolio debt inflows to GDP

Y_2 = Currency Crisis

Model 3:

Y_1 = Portfolio equity inflows to GDP

Y_2 = Currency Crisis

Matrix X includes: Broad money of GDP, Consumer price index, Monetary freedom index, Real effective exchange rate, Real interest rate, Trade freedom index, Debt service on external debt, and Foreign exchange reserves.

IV. RESULTS

To study the relationship between portfolio flows and currency crisis, we draw on panel data for BRIC nations and use the technique of simultaneous equation model. Out of the three models regressed, two models give us statically significant results, revealing positive relation between the inflow of portfolio capital and the outbreak of the crisis. The results underline the importance of the role played by the composition of flows. Table below present the results of the empirical analysis.

Model 1 of the table 2, at 5% level of significance, divulges that total portfolio inflows increase the probability of the occurrence of currency crisis, i.e., with the inflow of total portfolio flows in the recipient economy, the odds of the outbreak of currency crisis increase in the following year. Also, variables like Consumer price index, Monetary freedom index, Real effective exchange rate, and Debt service on external debt are found to have a bearing on the happening of currency crisis. On the other hand, when we have total portfolio flows as dependent variable, and currency crisis as instrumental variable, we find real effective exchange rate, consumer price index, current account balance and globalization index, all have a significant impact on total portfolio flows. Real effective exchange rate and globalization index are positively related to total portfolio flows.

Results of Model 2 in table 4, where we have Portfolio debt flows as our continuous endogenous variable, also finds a statistically significant relation between Portfolio debt flows and Currency Crisis. With the inflow of Portfolio debt, the probability of currency crisis increases. Other variables like Consumer price index, Monetary freedom index and Real effective exchange rate again have an impact on currency crisis. Furthermore, in the second equation of the same model with Portfolio debt flows as dependent variable, we find the relationship between Portfolio debt flows and real effective exchange rate, consumer price index, current account balance and globalization index, to be statistically significant.

Our third model where we try to explore the relationship between Portfolio equity inflows and the happening of currency crisis, accepts the null hypothesis that the above mentioned two variables do not hold any relationship. The corrected standard error table reveal that there is no statistically significant relationship between the two variables. The inflow of portfolio equity in an economy has no impact on currency crisis.

V. CONCLUSION

The paper argues that the inflow of portfolio capital in an emerging economy positively impacts the occurrence of currency crisis. Portfolio flows are known to be a volatile component of private capital flows. They are a short-term source of capital which are motivated by immediate gains and hence are very volatile. Portfolio flows are pro cyclical in nature which makes an economy vulnerable to crises. Studies suggest that out of the two types of portfolio flows namely, portfolio debt flows and portfolio equity flows, it is portfolio debt flows which are more of risky kind. Portfolio equity flows have a negligible effect on the incidence of crises. The results of our empirical analysis also put forward that portfolio flows increase the odds of the occurrence of currency crisis. Furthermore, when the analysis was conducted on the components of portfolio flows, portfolio debt flows were found to be significantly significant. Some general conclusions to be drawn from the study are that the emerging markets should make efforts to keep the proportion of this short term / volatile capital low in the external capital structure and try to attract more of longer-term capital in order to reap the benefits of international capital flows.

Table II: TSPLS model to study relationship between total portfolio flows and currency crisis

| Variables | Model 1 | | | | | |
| | First stage (1) | | Two-step probit with endogenous regressors (2) | | Two-step probit with endogenous regressors (Corrected Standard Error) (3) | |
	Total Portfolio Flows	Currency Crisis	Total Portfolio Flows	Currency Crisis	Total Portfolio Flows	Currency Crisis
I_Currency Crises	-	-	-2.48	-	-1.67	-
			(1.1189)**		(1.6589)*	
I_Portfolio Flows	-	-	-	2.47	-	2.3
				(0.0528)**		(0.0568)**
Real effective exchange rate (CPI-based)	-0.84	2.44	3.3	2.42	2.67	2.03
	0.1545	(0.0576)**	(0.1328)***	(0.0376)**	(0.1638)***	(0.0449)**
Consumer price index (2010 = 100)	-2.67	-2.95	-4.42	-2.16	-3.52	-1.73
	(0.0726)***	(0.0438)***	(0.1227)***	(0.0271)**	(0.1542)***	(0.0338)*

Current account balance as percentage of GDP	-3.76	-2.69	-4.55	-	-3.27	-
	(0.5495)***	(0.1991)***	(0.7707)***		(1.0707)***	
Globalization Index (0-100)	1.94	0.66	3.89	-	2.83	-
	(0.5745)**	0.1900	(0.4748)***		(0.6511)***	
Corruption	1.08	-1.69	-0.51	-	-0.38	-
	3.4811	(1.1486)*	3.2913		4.4162	
Broad money (% of GDP)	1.28	-0.98	-	-0.78	-	-0.88
	0.0756	0.0283		0.0196		0.0174
Monetary freedom index (0-100)	-1.8	2.28	-	2.53	-	2.27
	(0.1090)*	(0.0323)**		(0.0246)**		(0.0274)**
Real interest rate: Bank lending rate minus inflation	0.5	-0.69	-	-1.42	-	-1.28
	0.1883	0.0438		0.0271		0.0302
Trade freedom index (0-100)	0.22	1.44	-	1.5	-	1.33
	0.2166	0.0697		0.0501		0.0567
Debt service on external debt, total (TDS, current US$) / GDP	-2.06	0.91	-	1.75	-	1.62
	(0.0000)**	2.72E-08		(0.0000)*		3.17E-08
Foreign exchange reserves including gold billion USD	-1.16	0.46	-	0.31	-	0.35
	0.0032	0.0009		0.0009		0.0007

*The table above shows t / z statistics with robust standard errors in parenthesis. *** Indicate 1% level of significance, ** Indicate 5% level of significance and * Indicate 10% level of significance*

Table III: TSPLS model to study relationship between portfolio debt flows and currency crisis

Variables	Model 2					
	First stage (4)		Two-step probit with endogenous regressors (5)		Two-step probit with endogenous regressors (Corrected Standard Error) (6)	
	Portfolio Debt Flows	*Currency Crisis*	*Portfolio Debt Flows*	*Currency Crisis*	*Portfolio Debt Flows*	*Currency Crisis*
l_Currency Crises	-	-	-3.42	-	-1.89	-
			(0.9827)***		(1.7815)*	
l_Portfolio Flows	-	-	-	2.6	-	2.32
				(0.0658)***		(0.0738)**
Real effective exchange rate (CPI-based)	-0.13	2.44	4.16	2.16	2.94	1.83
	0.1385	(0.0576)**	(0.1166)***	(0.0380)**	(0.1648)***	(0.0448)*
Consumer price index (2010 = 100)	-2.28	-2.95	-5.38	-2.28	-3.7	-1.91
	(0.0651)**	(0.0438)***	(0.1077)***	(0.0283)**	(0.1565)***	(0.0339)**
Current account balance as percentage of GDP	-3.69	-2.69	-5.43	-	-3.26	-
	(0.4927)***	(0.1991)***	(0.6768)***		(1.127761)***	
Globalization Index (0-100)	2.09	0.66	5.07	-	3.1	-
	(0.5152)**	0.1900	(0.4170)***		(0.6828)***	
Corruption	0.53	-1.69	-1.43	-	-0.9	-
	3.1214	(1.1486)*	2.8906		4.5969	
Broad money (% of GDP)	1.45	-0.98	-	-0.89	-	-0.98
	0.0678	0.0283		0.0193773		0.0175
Monetary freedom index (0-100)	-3.29	2.28	-	2.98	-	2.74
	(0.0977)***	(0.0323)**		(0.0317)***		(0.0345)***
Real interest rate: Bank lending rate minus inflation	-0.03	-0.69	-	-0.87	-	-0.77
	0.1688	0.0438		0.0241		0.0273
Trade freedom index (0-100)	-0.14	1.44	-	1.6	-	1.46
	0.1942	0.0697		0.0521		0.0569

Debt service on external debt, total (TDS, current US$) / GDP	-0.85	0.91	-	1.38	-	1.22
	1.15E-07	2.72E-08		2.47E-08		2.78E-08
Foreign exchange reserves including gold billion USD	-1.1	0.46	-	0.28	-	0.31
	0.0028	0.0009		0.0008		0.0007

The table above shows t / z statistics with robust standard errors in parenthesis. *** Indicate 1% level of significance, ** Indicate 5% level of significance and * Indicate 10% level of significance

Table IV: Tspls Model To Study Relationship Between Portfolio Equity Flows And Currency Crisis

Model 3						
	First stage (7)		Two-step probit with endogenous regressors (8)		Two-step probit with endogenous regressors (Corrected Standard Error) (9)	
Variables	*Portfolio Equity Flows*	*Currency Crisis*	*Portfolio Equity Flows*	*Currency Crisis*	*Portfolio Equity Flows*	*Currency Crisis*
I_Currency Crises	-	-	1.05	-	1.01	-
			0.5610		0.5796	
I_Portfolio Flows	-	-	-	1.39	-	1.05
				0.2067		0.2731
Real effective exchange rate (CPI-based)	-1.5	2.44	-0.71	2.64	-0.73	1.8
	0.0740	(0.0576)**	0.0666	(0.0374)***	0.0648	(0.0548)*
Consumer price index (2010 = 100)	-1.3	-2.95	0.61	-2.05	0.62	-1.37
	0.0348	(0.0438)***	0.0615	(0.0251)**	0.0601	0.0376
Current account balance as percentage of GDP	-0.94	-2.69	0.44	-	0.44	-
	0.2631	(0.1991)***	0.3864		0.3901	

Globalization Index (0-100)	0.15	0.66	-1.13	-	-1.13	-
	0.2751	0.1900	0.2381		0.2393	
Corruption	1.25	-1.69	1.48	-	1.48	-
	1.6670	(1.1486)*	1.6503		1.6472	
Broad money (% of GDP)	-0.05	-0.98	-	-0.6	-	-0.46
	0.0362	0.0283		0.0166		0.0217
Monetary freedom index (0-100)	2.4	2.28	-	-0.02	-	-0.02
	(0.0522294)**	(0.0323441)**		0.0359937		0.0529622
Real interest rate: Bank lending rate minus inflation	1.1	-0.69	-	-1.21	-	-0.85
	0.0901888	0.0438027		0.0406907		0.0575218
Trade freedom index (0-100)	0.72	1.44	-	1.68	-	0.94
	0.1037	0.0697		(0.0334)*		0.0599
Debt service on external debt, total (TDS, current US$) / GDP	-2.7	0.91	-	1.3	-	0.94
	(0.0000)**	2.72E-08		4.31E-08		6.01E-08
Foreign exchange reserves including gold billion USD	-0.38	0.46	-	0.17	-	0.15
	0.0015	0.0009		0.0007		0.0008

The table above shows t / z statistics with robust standard errors in parenthesis. *** Indicate 1% level of significance, ** Indicate 5% level of significance and * Indicate 10% level of significance

VI. REFERENCES

Aschinger, G. (2001). Why do currency crises arise and how could they be avoided? *Intereconomics*, *36*(3), 152–159. https://doi.org/10.1007/bf02973784

Claessens, S., Dooley, M. P., & Warner, A. (1995). *I i 'S Portfolio Capital Flows : Hot or Cold ?* 153–174.

Dornbusch, R., Goldfajn, I., Valdes, R. O., Edwards, S., & Bruno, M. (1995). Currency Crises and Collapses. *Brookings Papers on Economic Activity*. https://doi.org/10.2307/2534613

Frankel, J. A., & Rose, A. K. (1996). Currency crashes in emerging markets: An empirical treatment. *Journal of International Economics*. https://doi.org/10.1016/S0022-1996(96)01441-9

Frost, J., & Saiki, A. (2014). *Early Warning for Currency Crises : What Is the Role of Financial Openness ? 22*(4), 722–743. https://doi.org/10.1111/roie.12124

Ghosh, B. A. R., Ostry, J. D., & Qureshi, M. S. (2016). *When Do Capital Inflow Surges End in Tears ? †. 106*(5), 581–585.

Glick, R., Guo, X., & Hutchison, M. M. (2011). Currency Crises, Capital Account Liberalization, and Selection Bias. *SSRN Electronic Journal.* https://doi.org/10.2139/ssrn.560142

Licchetta, M. (2009). Common determinants of currency crises: The role of external balance sheet variables. *Bank of England, Bank of England Working Papers, 16.* https://doi.org/10.2139/ssrn.1395597

Licchetta, M. (2011). Common determinants of currency crises: The role of external balance sheet variables. *International Journal of Finance and Economics.* https://doi.org/10.1002/ijfe.425

Maddala, G. S. (1983). *Limited-dependent and qualitative variables in econometrics.* Cambridge University Press. https://doi.org/10.1017/CBO9780511810176

Marković, M. (2015). Domestic and External Factors of Currency C. *FACTA UNIVERSITATIS - Economics and Organization, 12*(2), 121–128.

Mukharaev, A. (2017). *Capital flows volatility and subsequent finan- cial crises in EMEs.*

Qureshi, M. S., & Ghosh, A. R. (2016). *Capital Inflow Surges and Consequences Atish. 585.*

Wei, S.-J. (2000). Corruption, Composition of Capital Flows, and Currency Crises. *World Bank Policy Research Working Paper.*

Wei, S.-J., & Wu, Y. (2002). Negative Alchemy? Corruption, composition of capital flows, and currency crises. In *Preventing Currency Crises in Emerging Markets.*

CHAPTER 17

Impact of Corporate Governance on the Dividend Policy: Empirical Evidence from the Indian Corporate Sector

Dr. Ruchita Verma
Assistant Professor, Department of
Financial Administration
Central University of Punjab
Bhatinda
ruchitaverma@cup.edu.in

Dr. Dhanraj Sharma
(Corresponding Author)
Assistant Professor, Department
of Financial Administration
Central University of Punjab
Bhatinda
dhanrajsharma@cup.edu.in

Ms. Priyanka
Research Scholar
Department of Financial
Administration
Central University of Punjab
Bhatinda
priyanka.chughmks@gmail.com

Abstract

The study is conducted to investigate the effect of corporate governance on the dividend policy and financial performance of public companies listed on NSE (National stock exchange of India) by taking the sample of top Nifty 100 companies. This data is collected for the period of 11 years starting from 2009-10 to 2019-20. This study categorized independent variables into board characteristics (board size, board composition, CEO duality, gender diversity) and ownership structure (foreign ownership, institutional ownership, director's ownership, corporate ownership, government ownership), whereas firm size, liquidity ratio, and leverage ratio as control variables. Dividend payout ratio (proxies for dividend policy) and Return on Assets (proxies for financial performance) are taken as dependent variables. The result based on panel regression analysis shows that out of board characteristics; the board size, board composition, and gender diversity impact dividend payout ratio (DPR), but no effect on return on assets (ROA). But in the case of ownership structure, the adverse effects of foreign ownership and government ownership on dividend payout ratio (DPR) has been found in the study. The results also found the impact of foreign ownership, directors' ownership, and government ownership on return on assets.

Keywords: Corporate Governance, Board Characteristics, Ownership Structure, Panel Regression Analysis and National Stock Exchange

1. INTRODUCTION

Due to divergence in ownership and management, agency cost arises. By agency cost, the manager may choose a dividend policy that provides personal benefit, not a dividend policy that maximizes the shareholder's value (Jensen, 1986). According to Shleifer & Vishny (1997), corporate governance aims to ensure that investors supplying finance to firms receive a fair return on their investment either through a dividend or capital gain. Corporate governance can monitor firm performance and play an essential role in avoiding and managing the conflict between shareholders and management (Marendino & Meloille, 2019).

As per agency theory, dividend may mitigate the agency cost as it distributes free cash flows, which can be used for private or unprofitable projects by the management (Jensen, 1986). The dividend is the income paid to the shareholders from the company's earnings (Ahmad & Muquaddas, 2017). Various factors affect the dividend policy of the firms, such as growth rate, availability of external financing, investment opportunities, earning, firm's target capital structure.

Corporate governance and dividend policy are considered substitute tools for mitigating agency costs (Rozeff, 1982). Corporate governance is used to mitigate the agency cost as it influences its dividend policy (Shehu, 2015). The nexus between corporate governance and dividend policy to minimize the agency problem has been investigated by various researchers, but it provides inconclusive results. Some studies show the positive effect of corporate governance on dividend policy (Mitton, 2004). Some state an insignificant relationship between them (Aydin & Cavdar, 2015; Tahil, Sohai, Qayyam & Mumtaz, 2016). Most previous studies have focused on the developed countries, but there is a lack of studies that focus on developing countries like India. Thus, the study is conducted to analyze the association between corporate governance and dividend policy of NSE-listed companies. This study also focuses on the influence of corporate governance on financial performance.

Section 2 covers the reviews of relevant studies relating to the nexus between corporate governance, dividend policy, and the firm's performance. Section 3 covers the objective of the study. Section 4 covers the sample, description of variables, and methodology. Section 5 includes findings and discussion. Section 6 concludes and covers some policy implications and limitations.

2. REVIEW OF STUDIES

2.1 Board characteristics and dividend policy

Bolbol (2012) tried to observe the effect of board characteristics on dividend payout by taking a sample of Malaysian firms. They found that board size, board composition, and gender diversity have no relation with dividend payout. But contrary to the above, Sanan (2019) found the negative impact of independent directors and gender diversity on the dividend policy.

Shehu (2015) found that only independent directors have an impact on dividend payout from the board characteristics. In contrast, Mansourinia, Emangholipour, Rekabdarkolari & Hozoori (2013) found the positive effect of board size on dividend policy. Schellenger, wood & Tashokori (1989) found that board composition affects the dividend policy, whereas Abdelsalam, Masuy & Elsegini (2008) found no relation between board composition and dividend policy.

Chen, Lenug & Goergen (2017) investigate the impact of the presence of women directors on dividend payout and observe that the greater the percentage of female directors on the board, the larger the will be dividend payout. By taking a sample of 8876 companies in 22 countries; Ye, Deng, Liu & Chen (2019) tried to examine the influence of the presence of female directors on dividend policy for the period 2000 to 2013, and they found that when the female senior executive has a shareholding, then this relationship becomes more substantial.

2.2 Board Characteristics and firm performance

Stukeri & Shaari (2012) investigated the affect of board characteristics on the performance of 300 Malaysian companies and found that the firm's performance has been positively affected by the board size but negatively by the board independence. Whereas, García-Ramos & García-Olalla (2011) tried to examine the nexus between boards of directors' characteristics and performance in the presence of founders, taking a sample of European companies and found the negative affect of board size and positive impact of independent directors on the performance of founder-led businesses. They also found that when the founder leads a firm, CEO duality has no effect and board meeting has a weaker impact on the financial performance.

Masum, Khan (2019) found that board size, independent directors, and the women director on board do not affect the performance of Bangladesh listed companies. Jermias & Gani (2014) found that CEO duality and board independence negatively affect performance and that board capital reduces the adverse effect.

Conyon & Peck (1998) found that large boards may destroy corporate value and found the adverse impact of board size on performance. Dakhlallh, Roshid, Abdullah & Dakhlallh (2019) observed that the firm performance has been negatively affected by the board size, board independence & CEO duality when managerial ownership is taken as a mediating variable.

2.3 Ownership structure and dividend policy

Ramili (2010) found that companies make higher dividend payouts when the shareholding of the most significant shareholder increases. Short, Zhang & Keasey (2001) found the positive impact of institutional ownership and a adverse effect of managerial ownership on the dividend payout.

Schooley & Barney (1994) examine the relationship between dividend policy and CEO stock ownership. They observed that with the increase in CEO stock ownership, agency cost reduces a dividend yield, decreases up to CEO become entrenched but beyond that point, increase in rising in CEO stock ownership there will be increased in the dividend yield.

Kumar (2006) found that corporate ownership and director's ownership positively impact dividend payout in level. In contrast, institutional ownership has a inverse relation with the dividend payout in level and its squares. But Aydin & Cavdar (2015) found that dividend payout enlarges with the increase in the foreign ownership but become deteriorate with the increase in ownership concentration and managerial ownership.

2.4 Ownership structure and firm performance

Using the sample of 76 listed non-financial firms, Olufemi, Adebisi & Adeleye (2010) observed that performance has been positively affected by the foreign ownership. In contrast, Amin et al. (2018) establish the adverse impact of foreign ownership on performance.

Olufemi et al. (2010) observed adverse association between concentrated ownership and performance. But Saleh, Halili, Zeitun & Salim (2017), Huang & Boateng (2013) found that financial ownership has been positively affected by concentrated ownership. In contrast, Shah & Hussain (2012) found no link among focused ownership and firm performance.

The studies like Fauzi & Lock (2012), Huang & Boateng (2013), and Colombo & Croce (2014) have observed that financial performance has been positively affected by managerial ownership. But Mrad (2015) observed the negative effect of managerial ownership on the firm's performance.

3. DATA AND METHODOLOGY

3.1 Sample

We study the impact of corporate governance on the dividend policy and financial performance of Indian firms taking NSE (National stock exchange) listed companies. We select the NSE nifty 100 companies for our study as it represents 76.8% of the free-float market capitalization of the stock listed on NSE (www.nseindia.com). Due to disparity in regulatory requirements and financial reporting, the banks have been excluded from the study (Alassed, 2006). We also exclude the companies having missing data for two consecutive years. We also exclude companies that zero dividend payments in any year. Therefore, data has been collected from 54 companies out of 100 nifty companies for 11 years from 2009-10 to 2019-20. The economic data has been collected from the ProwessIQ 1.94 database of CMIE (Centre for Monitoring Indian Economy), and governance data is collected from the companies' annual reports.

3.2 Variables

a) Dependent variables
This study used two dependent variables – Dividend payout ratio (DPR) as a measure of dividend policy and Return on assets (ROA) to measure financial performance. These variables are taken from previous literature (Mitton 2004; Yilmaz & Buyuklu 2016).
b) Independent variables and control variables

This study employs corporate governance and its various mechanisms as an independent variable. Corporate governance has been divided into two parts: - Board characteristics and ownership structure. Board characteristics cover board size (BS), board composition (BC), CEO duality (duality), and gender diversity (GD) taken from previous literature (Bolbol 2012; Mansourinia et al., 2013; Masum & Khan, 2019). Ownership structure includes foreign ownership (FO), institutional ownership (IO), director's ownership (DO), corporate ownership (CO), and government ownership (GO) taken from the previous literature (Haung & Boateng 2013; Aydin & Cavdar 2015; Mrad 2015). Besides Independent variables, other factors can explain the variation in firm performance. Therefore, several control variables are used: Firm size (FS), Liquidity (LIQ), and Leverage (LEV).

3.3 Methodology

This study covers time series and cross-sectional data; therefore, the panel data method has been used in this study. Panel data regression has been significantly used by the researcher in the field of finance. This study used a static model of panel regression method. Hausman test has been used in the study for choosing between fixed and random effect models.

We categorized the data analysis into two sections. In the first sections, we analyze the effect of board characteristics on firm performance and dividend policy by estimating the following model via the panel data regression through Eviews 9.

$$ROA_{it} = \alpha + \beta_1 BS_{it} + \beta_2 BC_{it} + \beta_3 Duality_{it} + \beta_4 GD_{it} + \beta_5 LIQ_{it} + \beta_6 LEV_{it} + \beta_7 FS_{it} + e_{it}$$

$$DPR_{it} = \alpha + \beta_1 BS_{it} + \beta_2 BC_{it} + \beta_3 Duality_{it} + \beta_4 GD_{it} + \beta_5 LIQ_{it} + \beta_6 LEV_{it} + \beta_7 FS_{it} + e_{it}$$

Whereas,

ROA_{it} = Return on assets is taken as net income divided by total assets.

DPR_{it} = Dividend payout ratio is the dividend per share divided by earning per share (EPS)

BS_{it} = number of members on the board

BC_{it} = Board composition includes the proportion of independent directors on the board

$Duality_{it}$ = It is a dummy variable. 1 if the CEO is chairman as well and 0 for otherwise

LIQ_{it} = liquidity is taken as total current assets divided by total current liabilities

LEV_{it} = leverage is taken as total liabilities to total shareholder's funds

FS_{it} = Firm size is taken as the log of total assets

e_{it} = Error term

In the second section, we analyze the impact of ownership structure on firm performance by estimating the following model via the Panel regression method.

$$ROA_{it} = \alpha + \beta_1 FO_{it} + \beta_2 IO_{it} + \beta_4 CO_{it} + \beta_5 DO_{it} + \beta_6 GO_{it} + \beta_7 LIQ_{it} + \beta_8 LEV_{it} + \beta_9 FS_{it} + e_{it}$$

$$DPR_{it} = \alpha + \beta_1 FO_{it} + \beta_2 IO_{it} + \beta_4 CO_{it} + \beta_5 DO_{it} + \beta_6 GO_{it} + \beta_7 LIQ_{it} + \beta_8 LEV_{it} + \beta_9 FS_{it} + e_{it}$$

Whereas,

ROA_{it} = Return on assets is taken as net income divided by total assets.

DPR_{it} = Dividend payout ratio is the dividend per share divided by earning per share (EPS)

FO_{it} = % of shareholding by foreign investors

IO_{it} = % of shareholding by institutional investors

CO_{it} = % of shareholding by Corporate bodies

DO_{it} = % of shareholding by directors

GO_{it} = % of shareholding by government

LIQ_{it} = liquidity is taken as total current assets divided by total current liabilities

LEV_{it} = leverage is taken as total liabilities to total shareholder's funds

FS_{it} = Firm size is taken as the log of total assets

e_{it} = Error term

4. FINDING AND DISCUSSION

Table 1: Descriptive Statistics

	N	Minimum	Maximum	Mean	Std. Deviation
BS	594	6.000	22.000	11.439	2.592
BC	594	0.000	0.833	0.509	0.121

Duality	594	0.000	1.000	0.357	0.479
GD	594	0.000	5.000	1.118	0.918
FO	594	0.000	82.600	27.148	19.340
IO	594	0.000	42.410	10.962	7.992
DO	594	0.000	75.190	3.660	12.555
CO	594	0.000	66.530	11.745	17.187
GO	594	0.000	100.000	14.863	27.667
FS	594	5.607	13.784	9.888	1.438
LEV	594	0.000	8.638	1.113	1.313
LIQ	594	0.185	18.404	2.206	2.195
DPR	594	0.016	3.058	0.367	0.271
ROA	594	0.000	0.783	0.127	0.100

Source: Authors' Compilation

Table 1 presents the results of the descriptive statistics. It indicates that the average board size of an Indian company is 11, where minimum is six members and the maximum is 22 members. The average board composition (BC) is 0.509 which states that on average, 51% of the board includes independent directors. The average duality (CEO duality) is 0.357. The average gender diversity (GD) is 1.118. The average foreign shareholding (FO) is 27.148% which varies from 0% to 82.60%. The average ownership of institutional shareholders (IO) is 10.962%, ranging from 0% to 42.410. The mean value of shareholding by Directors (DO) is 3.660%. The minimum shareholding of Directors is 0%, and the maximum is 75.190%. The average ownership of the corporate bodies (CO) is 11.745%, whereas minimum and maximum are 0% and 66.53%, respectively. The average ownership by the government (GO) is 14.863% which can vary from 0% to 100%. The average Firm size (FS) is 9.888. The average Leverage Ratio (Lev) is 1.113, where the minimum is 0.005, and the maximum is 8.638. The average Liquidity ratio (LIQ) is 2.206. The average dividend payout ratio (DPR) is 0.367. The average Return on Assets (ROA) 0.127.

Table 2 shows the result of the Correlation Matrix and variance inflation matrix (VIF). It shows that the value of VIF of all variables is less than 5, which means that there is no collinearity problem. It shows that board size (BS) positively relates to CEO duality, Gender diversity, Institutional ownership, government ownership, firm size, and dividend payout ratio. But it has a negative relation with foreign ownership, director ownership, and liquidity ratio. Board composition has a positive association with foreign ownership but negative relation with duality, government ownership, firm size, leverage, and dividend payout ratio. We also find CEO duality has a connection with foreign ownership, Institutional ownership, Corporate ownership, government ownership, firm size, leverage, and dividend payout ratio. Gender diversity has a negative and significant relation with director ownership, corporate ownership, and leverage, but the positive link with dividend payout ratio and returns on assets. Foreign ownership also relates to director ownership, corporate ownership, Government ownership, liquidity ratio, firm size, leverage, and return on assets. Institutional ownership has a significant relationship with firm size, liquidity, and return on

Table 2: Correlation Matrix

	BS	BC	Duality	GD	FO	IO	DO	CO	GO	FS	LEV	LIQ	DPR	ROA	VIF
BS	1														1.260
BC	-.003	1													1.358
Duality	.097*	-.243**	1												1.827
GD	.155**	.059	-.123*	1											1.150
FO	-.132**	.155**	-.269**	.055	1										1.742
IO	.233**	-.023	.103*	.002	0.037	1									1.229
DO	-.217**	-.014	.007	-.104*	-.086*	-.042	1								1.295
CO	.008	.075	-.215**	.090*	-.244**	-.043	-.098**	1							1.285
GO	.183**	-.466**	.615**	.038	-.467**	-.027	-.156**	-.138**	1						2.985
FS	.307**	-.141**	.309**	.059	-.251**	.276**	-.341**	.013	.400**	1					1.859
LEV	.011	-.098*	.088*	-.194**	.123**	-.072	-.066	-.168**	.054	.248**	1				1.339
LIQ	-.176**	.018	-.063	-.024	-.148**	-.092*	-.048	.148**	.071	-.103*	-.174**	1			1.154
DPR	.135**	-.179**	.134**	.159**	.021	.011	-.024	-.065	.198**	-.018	-.018	-.036	1		1.131
ROA	-.051	.050	-.88*	.081*	.127**	-.092*	.077	-.045	-.024	.371**	-.311**	.120**	.339**	1	1.311

Source: Authors' Compilation

assets. Corporate ownership has a relation with government ownership, Liquidity ratio, and leverage ratio. The matrix shows the positive and significant relationship of government ownership with firm size and dividend payout ratio. The relationship between leverage ratio, liquidity ratio, firm size, and return on assets has been also observed.

Table 3: Regression Result

a) Impact of board characteristics on dividend payout and the firm's performance

Model	1	2
Dependent variable	DPR	ROA
Methodology	Random effect	Random Effect
Intercept	0.370114 (2.414657)**	.353545 (7.586300)***
BS	0.014476 (2.723805)***	0.001834 (1.383293)
BC	-0.379730 (-3.325471)***	-.023212 (-0.798478)
DUALITY	0.014846 (0.470569)	0.009381 (1.164196)
GD	0.051754 (4.110735)***	-0.002555 (-0.829339)
LIQ	-0.010644 (-2.202593)**	-0.000136 (-1.20467)
LEV	-0.008687 (-0.624471)	-0.012267 (-3.187981)***
FS	-0.000564 (-0.039100)	-0.022579 (-5.157081)***
R-Squared	0.069410	0.077919
Adjusted R-squared	0.058293	0.066904
Durbin-Watson stat	1.333289	0.734839
F-statistic	6.243978	7.074138
Prob (F-statistic)	0.000000	.000000
Hausman test	10.2892	2.8296

Source: Authors' Compilation

*Note: - *, ** and ** means significant at 10%, 5% and 1% respectively in the two-tailed.*

Table 3 represents the panel regression results of the effect of board characteristics on dividend policy and firm performance. The significant value of the Hausman test states that the fixed effect model should be preferred over the random effect model. Based on this, it is concluded that the random effect model is appropriate for models 1 and 2.

Column 2 represents the results of Model 1. It shows that dividend payout ratio (DPR) has been positively affected by board size and Gender diversity but negatively by board composition and liquidity. With the increase of independent directors on the board, a decrease in the dividend payout ratio consistent with the finding (Mansourinia et al. 2013, Bolbol & Islam, 2012). Column 3 represents the results for model 2, which shows that firm's performance is negatively affected by leverage and firm size. The result shows no impact of board characteristics on a firm's performance contrary to the finding (Stukeri, Shin & Shaari, 2012).

Table 4: Regression Results

b) Impact of ownership structure on dividend payout and the firm's performance

Model	3	4
Dependent variable	DPR	ROA
Methodology	Fixed effect	Fixed Effect
Intercept	-0.129284 (-0.604266)	0.442775 (9.334540)***
FO	-0.004779 (-2.478374)**	0.000832 (1.945859)*
IO	-0.000792 (-0.281577)	-0.000946 (-1.517609)
DO	-0.001613 (-0.438200)	-0.001663 (-2.038717)**
CO	0.001862 (0.848364)	-0.000698 (-1.434650)
GO	-0.010664 (-3.582173)***	-0.001882 (-2.851167)***
LIQ	-0.011413 (-2.249718)**	-0.000213 (-1.89779)
LEV	-0.024138 (-1.276586)	-0.007736 (-1.845473)*
FS	0.083857 (3.955170)***	-0.028115 (-5.981358)***
R-Squared	0.514263	0.823883
Adjusted R-squared	0.458568	0.803689
Durbin-Watson stat	1.506678	0.830670
F-statistic	9.233509	40.79865
Prob(F-statistic)	.0000000	.000000
Hausman test	40.9090***	16.3766**

Source: Authors' Compilation

*Note: - *, ** and ** means significant at 10%, 5% and 1% respectively in the two-tailed.*

Table 4 represents the panel regression results for the impact of ownership structure on dividend policy and firm performance. on the basis of hausman test, it is concluded that fixed effect model is appropriate for model 3 and model 4. Column 2 represents the results of Model 3. It shows that the dividend payout ratio (DPR) has been negatively affected by foreign ownership (FO) and government ownership (GO). With the rise in foreign ownership and government ownership, there will be a decline in dividend payout ratio inconsistency with the findings (Schooley & Barney 1994). The positive effect of firm size (FS) on the dividend payout ratio (DPR) has been observed which states that with the rise in the size of corporate firms, there will be an increase in the dividend payout ratio (DPR). The findings also show negative effect of liquidity (LIQ) on the dividend payout ratio (DPR). Column 3 represents the results for model 4, which shows that return on assets (ROA) is positively affected by foreign ownership (FO) whereas negatively by director ownership (DO) and government ownership (GO), consistent with the findings (Olufemi et al.,2010, and Mrad, 2015). Leverage (LEV) and firm size (FS) also has adverse impact on return on assets (ROA).

5. CONCLUSION

The study tries to assess the effect of corporate governance on dividend policy and financial performance of public companies listed on the NSE stock exchange by taking the sample for 11 years from 2009-10 to 2019-2020. In this study, we divide corporate governance into parts- board characteristics and ownership structure. Using the panel regression analysis, it is found that out of board characteristics, the board size, and gender diversity positively impact dividend policy. In contrast, board composition has an adverse effect on dividend policy. It indicates that women directors distribute a sizeable portion of the firm's earning, but independent directors retain a considerable part of the firm's earnings for investment opportunities and distribute less. The study found no impact of board characteristics on the financial performance of the Indian listed firm. The study observed the negative effect of foreign ownership and government ownership on the dividend policy, which means that there will be a decrease in the dividend payout with the increase in the proportionate share of foreign ownership and proportionate share of government ownership. The study observed that the financial performance of Indian companies has been positively affected by the foreign ownership which indicates that if there is a rise in foreign ownership, there will be a rise in the return on assets. The finding also shows the negative effect of government ownership (GO) and directors ownership (DO) on return on assets (ROA) which states that proportional increment in their shareholding leads to depletion of the financial performance of NSE listed companies.

Our study has made several contributions and implications. First, our finding is based on the corporate governance of public companies listed on the National stock exchange (NSE), thus enriching the literature of an emerging country like India. Our findings would benefit researchers, policymakers, and practitioners as they may provide a better understanding of the nature of corporate governance of Indian firms and its impact on dividend policy and financial performance. In this study, NSE Nifty 100 companies are employed. We believe that companies in this study are already using corporate governance principles, and it should not be easy to observe the difference caused by corporate governance. Therefore, further research can be extended by increasing the number of companies in these types of studies.

6. REFERENCES

Abdelsalam, O., El-Masry, A., and Elsegini, S. (2008). Board composition, ownership structure, and dividend policies in an emerging market. *Managerial Finance, 34*(12), 953–964.

Ahmad, I., & Muqaddas, M. F. (2017). Determinants of dividend payout policy: An empirical study of the banking sector of Pakistan. *Applied Studies in Agribusiness and Commerce, 10*(1033-2017-146), 106-101.

Alsaeed, K. (2006). The association between firm-specific characteristics and disclosure: The case of Saudi Arabia. *Managerial Auditing Journal, 21*(5), 476–496.

Aydin, A. D., & Cavdar, S. C. (2015). Corporate governance and dividend policy: An empirical analysis from the Borsa Istanbul corporate governance index (xkury). *Accounting and Finance Research, 4*(3), 66–76.

Bolbol, I. I. (2012). *Board characteristics and dividend payout of Malaysian companies* (Doctoral dissertation, Universiti Utara Malaysia).

Chen, J., Leung, W. S., & Goergen, M. (2017). The impact of board gender composition on dividend payouts. *Journal of Corporate finance, 43*, 86–105.

Colombo, M. G., Croce, A., & Murtinu, S. (2014). Ownership structure, horizontal agency costs, and the performance of high-tech entrepreneurial firms. *Small Business Economics, 42*(2), 265–282.

Conyon, M. J., & Peck, S. I. (1998). Board size and corporate performance: evidence from European countries. *The European Journal of Finance, 4*(3), 291–304.

Dakhlallh, M. M., Rashid, N. M. N. N. M., Abdullah, W. A. W., & Dakhlallh, A. M. (2019). The Mediating Effect of the Managerial Ownership towards the Influence of the Board of Directors on the Firm Performance among Jordanian Public Shareholders Companies. *Journal of Environmental Treatment Techniques, 7*(3), 760–767.

Fauzi, F., & Locke, S. (2012). Board structure, ownership structure, and firm performance: A study of New Zealand listed firms. *Asian Academy of Management Journal of Accounting and Finance, 8*(2), 43–67.

García-Ramos, R., & García-Olalla, M. (2011). Board characteristics and firm performance in public founder-and non-founder-led family businesses. *Journal of Family Business Strategy, 2*(4), 220–231.

Huang, W., & Boateng, A. (2013). The role of the state, ownership structure, and the performance of real estate firms in China. *Applied Financial Economics, 23*(10), 847–859.

Jensen, M. C. (1986). Agency costs of free cash flow, corporate finance, and takeovers. *The American economic review, 76*(2), 323–329.

Jermias, J., & Gani, L. (2014). The impact of board capital and board characteristics on firm performance. *The British Accounting Review, 46*(2), 135–153.

Kumar, J. (2006). Corporate governance and dividends payout in India. *Journal of Emerging Market Finance*, *5*(1), 15–58.

Mansourinia, E., Emamgholipour, M., Rekabdarkolaei, E. A., & Hozoori, M. (2013). The effect of board size, board independence, and CEO duality on dividend policy of companies: Evidence from Tehran stock exchange. *International Journal of Economy, Management and Social Sciences*, *2*(6), 237–241.

Masum, M. H., & Khan, M. M. (2019). Impacts of Board Characteristics on Corporate Performance: Evidence from Bangladeshi Listed Companies. *International Business and Accounting Research Journal*, *3*(1), 47–57.

Merendino, A., & Melville, R. (2019). The board of directors and firm performance: empirical evidence from listed companies. *Corporate Governance: The International Journal of Business in Society*, 19(3), 508–551.

Mitton, T. (2004). Corporate governance and dividend policy in emerging markets. *Emerging Markets Review*, *5*(4), 409–426.

Mrad, M. (2015). Post-privatization ownership structure and firm performance: what is the matter?. *International Journal of Monetary Economics and Finance*, *8*(1), 85–108

Obembe Olufemi, B., Adebisi, S.A., & Adeleye, O.K. (2010). Corporate governance, ownership structure, and performance of manufacturing firms in Nigeria. *Corporate Ownership and Control, 8*(1), 696–708.

Ramli, N. M. (2010). Ownership structure and dividend policy: Evidence from Malaysian companies. *International Review of Business Research Papers*, *6*(1), 170–180.

Rozeff, M., 1982, Growth, beta and agency costs as determinants of dividend payout ratios, *Journal of Financial Research, 5*, 249–59.

Sanan, N. (2019), "Impact of board characteristics on firm dividends: evidence from India", Corporate Governance: *The International Journal of Business in Society*, https://doi.org/10.1108/CG-12-2018-0383

Saleh, A. S., Halili, E., Zeitun, R., & Salim, R. (2017). The global financial crisis, ownership structure, and firm financial performance: An examination of listed firms in Australia. *Studies in Economics and Finance*, *34*(4), 447–465.

Schooley, D. K., & Barney Jr, L. D. (1994). Using dividend policy and managerial ownership to reduce agency costs. *Journal of Financial Research*, *17*(3), 363–373.

Schellenger, M. H., Wood, D. D., & Tashakori, A. (1989). Board of directors composition, shareholder wealth, and dividend policy. *Journal of Management*, *15*(3), 457–467.

Short, H., Zhang, H., & Keasey, K. (2002). The link between dividend policy and institutional ownership. *Journal of Corporate Finance*, *8*(2), 105–122.

Shah, S. Z. A., & Hussain, Z. (2012). Impact of ownership structure on firm performance evidence from non-financial listed companies at Karachi Stock Exchange. *International Research Journal of Finance and Economics*, *84*, 6–13.

Shehu, M. (2015). Board characteristics and dividend payout: Evidence from Malaysian public listed companies. *Research Journal of Finance and Accounting*, *6*(16), 35–40.

Shleifer, A., & Vishny, R. W. (1997). A survey of corporate governance. *The journal of finance*, *52*(2), 737–783.

Shukeri, S. N., Shin, O. W., & Shaari, M. S. (2012). Does the board of director's characteristics affect firm performance? Evidence from Malaysian public listed companies. *International Business Research*, *5*(9), 120.

Tahir, S. H., Sohail, S., Qayyam, I., & Mumtaz, K. (2016). Effect of corporate governance index on dividend policy: An investigation of the textile industry of Pakistan. *Journal of Economic and Social Development*, *3*(1), 139.

Ye, D., Deng, J., Liu, Y., Szewczyk, S. H., & Chen, X. (2019). Does board gender diversity increase dividend payouts? Analysis of global evidence. *Journal of Corporate Finance*, *58*, 1–26.

Yilmaz, C., & Buyuklu, A. H. (2016). Impacts of corporate governance on firm performance: Turkey case with a panel data analysis. *Eurasian Journal of Economics and Finance*, *4*(1), 56–72.

SECTION III

Contemporary Issues and Challenges in OB and HRM

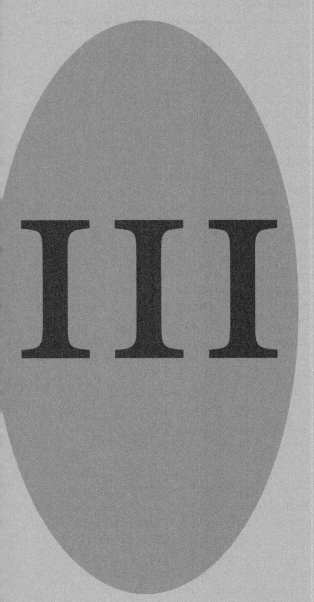

Chapter 18 *Job Performance and Its Correlates: An Empirical Study of Public Sector Employees*

Chapter 19 *Understanding Employer Branding Through Sentiment Analysis of Employee Reviews of India's Best Companies to Work for*

Chapter 20 *Work from Home During and After COVID: Need for Competence Satisfaction and Its Implications for Employee Wellbeing*

Chapter 21 *Integration of Artificial Intelligence in to Human Resources: Challenges and Scope*

Chapter 22 *Developmental Idiosyncratic Deals and Career Commitment: Mediation Effect of Organization Commitment*

Chapter 23 *Grittier and Embedded: An Analysis of Hotel Employees During Covid 19 Pandemic*

Job Performance and its Correlates: An Empirical Study of Public Sector Employees

Iqra Zaffar*[1]
Department of Management Studies
Central University of Kashmir
zaffar.iqra08@gmail.com

Abdul Gani[1]
Department of Management Studies
Central University of Kashmir
abdulgani@cukashmir.ac.in

Abstract

The present study examines the dimensions and correlates of the job performance of employees working in public sector organisations across northern India. The sample for the study comprised 400 public sector employees selected across the health, education, banking, and manufacturing sectors. The study adopted a quantitative methodology. The respondents self-reported their performance using a structured questionnaire. Statistical techniques, including mean, one-way analysis of variance (ANOVA), and independent-sample t-test were used, and the data were analysed using SPSS (Statistical Package for the Social Sciences). While most of the employees are contented with the level of their job performance, their overall level of performance is not very high. The results identify the task and contextual performance as highly-rated dimensions of employee job performance. The analysis of variance substantiates that age and years of experience significantly affect employee performance at work. The study findings will help in improving our understanding of the dynamics impacting job performance and lead to improved managerial practices that will help in contributing to employee performance.

Keywords: Job Performance, Correlates of Job Performance, Public Sector, India

INTRODUCTION

Human resources are the backbone of an organisation and the prime cause of organisational success or failure. Employees are considered to be a powerful tool that can transform an organisation and retention of a talent pool is one of the biggest strategic challenges that an organisation faces. The quality of the employees working in an organisation is pivotal in ensuring that the long-term organisational goals are met, for which the employees should be skilled, committed, and knowledgeable, which will help them perform well and make valuable contributions to the organisation. Job performance is one of the most important dependent variables and a key factor that helps organisations gain a competitive advantage. While the competitive advantage is considered more significant for the private sector, it can be extended to the public sector as well since the main objective of the public sector is to serve the common masses. Previous research has shown that improved employee job performance contributes to service delivery and customer satisfaction (Vermeeren *et al.*, 2009). An individual public sector employee's job performance reflects the performance of the government machinery at large. Hence, employees working in the public sector must be prepared to walk an extra mile and serve beyond the expectations of the public (Caron & Giauque, 2006). Realising the importance of employee job performance, public sector organisations pay more attention to formulating policies for improving employee health, safety, and the environment at work. A healthy work environment ensures that an employee remains engrossed in work; is satisfied with his job; and adds to the organisation's overall productivity. Therefore, for improving employee job performance, it is important to understand and explore the antecedents and factors contributing to employee performance at the workplace. The present study is an attempt in this direction.

LITERATURE REVIEW

Job performance has been a long-established subject of interest amongst management practitioners (Schiemann, 2009). Assessing and managing employee performance has been an indispensable part of human resource management, and as a part of the HR portfolio, it is a preferred developmental intervention (Bateman & Snell, 2007). For an organisation to succeed, its performance goals must be aligned with the organisational policies to achieve a strategic employee-centric orientation (Pradhan & Jena, 2017). An employee's performance at work is one of the most significant variables studied in the organisational setting and is considered one of the determinants of the quality of working context in organisations (Koopmans *et al.*, 2011). It is viewed as the accomplishment of the tasks by the employees after exerting the requisite efforts (Karakas, 2010).

There is no consensus among researchers about the conceptualisation of job performance, and many terms like presentism, performance, or productivity are used synonymously to describe an employee's performance at work (Koopmans *et al.*, 2011). Some researchers view job performance as a single dimension, whereas others conceptualise it as multi-dimensional (Conway, 1999). While some view it as a generic construct applicable to all jobs, others think it needs to be customised as per the job requirements (Brief & Motowidlo, 1986). Job performance is conceptualised from the behavioral perspective and the outcome perspective, though both these conceptualisations overlap (Roe, 1999). The behavioural perspective focuses on what the employees do at work (Campbell, 1990), while the outcome perspective focuses on the consequences, i.e. the result of the behaviour (Viswesvaran & Ones, 2000). The dimensions of job performance also vary from subjective (like ratings by the supervisor), to objective (like sales targets), and to a mixture of both (Moynihan *et al.*, 2012).

Early research on employee performance primarily emphasised task performance (Borman & Motowildo, 1993). Performance, comprising of explicitly stated behaviours as a part of the job description and job responsibilities, is called task performance (Pradhan &

Jena, 2017). Task performance includes task related knowledge, skill, and habits (Conway, 1999), and the bond between a supervisor and a subordinate to complete a delegated task (Sonnentag *et al.,* 2008). It includes the impact the individual's involvement will have on the organisation's overall performance and encompasses the completion of requirements that are included in the employment contract (Motowidlo, 2003). Campbell (1990) categorised job performance into eight factors amongst which five represented task performance, including job-specific and non-job-specific task proficiency; supervision; communication skill; management. The contextual performance comprises activities that are not included in the job description and indirectly supports the organisation's overall performance by assisting task performance (Sonnentag *et al.,* 2008). Contextual performance is multi-dimensional and consists of different non-uniform behaviours (Van Dyne & Le Pine, 1998), volunteering; persistence while accomplishing tasks; helping colleagues and peers; abiding by rules; guarding the organisation's mission, vision and objectives(Borman and Motowidlo,1993). Contextual performance has further been divided into interpersonal citizenship performance, organisational citizenship performance, and job-task responsibility performance (Coleman & Boreman, 2000). Ever since adaptive performance was introduced by Allworth and Hesketh (1999), several researchers have coined different terms to refer to adaptive performance. It is also referred to it as role flexibility and is considered synonymous with the ability to incorporate new learning experiences (Murphy & Jackson, 1999). Adaptive performance is multi-dimensional and includes eight dimensions ranging from crisis management to cultural adaptability (Pulakos *et al.,* 2000). While contextual and task performance focus on the employee's previous performance, adaptive performance concentrates on identifying factors that forecast the employees' future performance (Ma, 2003).

Previous research has revealed that an individual's job performance is an amalgamation of organisational policies, practices, employee engagement and knowledge management practices (Anitha, 2014). Managing employee workplace performance is a planned process comprising of positive reinforcement and continuous feedback which helps shape performance outcomes in terms of the employer's expectations (Islami *et al.,* 2018). While some researchers have linked job performance to the work environment(Smith and Bititci, 2017), and physical factors and non-physical factors (Pawirosumarto *et al.,* 2017), contemporary research has linked improvement in employee performance at work to the availability of the internet, which helps facilitate better communication and aide task knowledge (Isaac *et al.,* 2017).

While there is ample research, highlighting the contextual understanding of job performance and its dimensions, limited research has been conducted to identify the correlates of job performance. Previous research has focused on identifying the factors influencing employee performance by analysing literature and meagre empirical evidence. Since the correlates of employee job performance vary with culture and context, it is not clear which correlates and determinants of job performance, as understood from previous studies, hold a significant value for employees working in India's public sector. This study intends to fill this gap in the existing research by examining the dimensions of employee job performance and identifying the correlates and demographic variables that affect the employee's performance at work by providing supporting evidence.

Objectives

The study seeks to:

1. Determine the level of job performance of employees working in public sector organisations of northern India.
2. Identify the factors affecting the job performance of employees.
3. Explore the impact of demographic variables on employee job performance.

RESEARCH METHODOLOGY

Population and Sampling

This multi-sector, descriptive cum cross-sectional study adopted a quantitative methodology. The sample for the study comprised 400 full-time public sector employees belonging to the health, education, banking, and manufacturing sectors of northern India. The respondents were selected using stratified proportionate sampling. The study made use of self-administered questionnaires for eliciting information from the respondents and a response rate of 85.1% was recorded.

Sample Profile

As depicted in table 1 and table 5, out of the 400 respondents, the majority of the respondents were male (54.5%). More than 55 % of the respondents were within the age group of 21-30 years and 9% of the sample comprised of people above the age of 40 years. Majority of the respondents were married (56%), out of which 34 % of the respondent's spouses were employed. In all, 66% of the respondents resided in nuclear families. About 60% of the respondents had a master's degree, and 18% possess a bachelor's degree. Over 42% of the respondents had up to 3 years of work experience, followed by 26.3% of respondents having 3-7 years of experience. 35% of the respondents included in the study have an income of Rs 10,000- 30,000, followed by 26.8 % of respondents who fall in the income group of Rs 30,000- 50,000. Respondents were distributed almost equally among the banking, education, health, and manufacturing sectors.

Table 1: Descriptive Statistics and ANOVA for Job Performance

Demographic Variables	Categories	N	Percentage	Mean	F	Sig.
Age	Up to 20 years	12	3.0	3.9171	3.675	.006*
	21-30 years	223	55.8	4.0334		
	30-40 years	126	31.5	4.0635		
	40-50 years	16	4.0	4.4109		
	50 years or above	23	5.8	4.4170		

Education	Up to Higher Secondary	6	1.5	4.0913	.594	.667
	Diploma	2	0.5	4.1778		
	Bachelor's degree	72	18.0	3.9973		
	Master's degree	239	59.8	4.1113		
	Above Master's degree	81	20.3	4.0409		
Income	Less than 10,000	43	10.8	4.0068	1.778	.132
	10,000- 30,000	138	34.5	4.0260		
	30,000-50,000	107	26.8	4.0382		
	50,000-100,000	74	18.5	4.1838		
	100,000 and above	38	9.5	4.2380		
Experience	Up to 3 years	170	42.5	3.9337	4.507	.001*
	3-7 years	105	26.3	4.0140		
	7-11 years	62	15.5	4.1265		
	11-15 years	24	6.0	4.1489		
	Above 15 years	39	9.8	4.3970		
Marital Status	Unmarried	225	56.3	4.0474	1.254	.290
	Married	171	42.8	4.1030		
	Divorced	2	0.50	4.6579		
	Widowed	2	0.50	4.5103		
Sector of Employment	Bank	120	30.0	4.0881	.197	.898
	Manufacturing	80	25.0	4.1025		
	Education	100	25.0	4.0758		
	Health	100	20.0	4.0398		

*Significant at 5 per cent level of significance.

Instrument

The study follows a descriptive and cross-sectional research design. An 18-item structured questionnaire founded on a five-point Likert scale was used, ranging from 1' as 'strongly disagree' to '5' as 'strongly disagree'. The job performance scale developed by Pradhan and Jena (2017) in the Indian context was adopted. This scale comprises of the following dimensions of job performance: task performance, adaptive performance, and contextual performance. The model has also confirmed reliability for each scale, i.e. task performance (α-0.85); adaptive performance (α-0.641), and contextual performance (α-0.862), which is greater than 0.60. One item (*I lose my cool when faced with criticism from my co-workers*) was deleted from the dimension adaptive performance to improve the scale's reliability since Chronbach's alpha value of less than 0.60 indicates low internal consistency (Hair *et al.*, 2006). As Chronbach's alpha value for each dimension and the entire scale (α=0.931) is more than 0.60, it indicates that the scale has internal consistency.

Pilot Study

A pilot study was conducted to ensure the feasibility of research, identify any mistakes in the questionnaire, and improve the instrument's language to ensure adeptness, cultural and gender sensitivity. The pilot study included a sample of 40 respondents who were later excluded from the main study. The results of the pilot study led to some modifications in the language of the questionnaire and helped in improving its efficacy.

Tools of Analysis

The SPSS version 23 was used for analysing the data collected through questionnaires. Skewness and kurtosis were used for measuring the normality of the collected data. The frequency test showed that no missing responses were found. Outliers were excluded using the minimum and maximum values in item-to-item outliers. Mean and standard deviation was used for describing the characteristics of the respondents and constructs. Inferential statistical techniques including mean, ANOVA (one-way), and independent-sample t-test were used to examine the current state of job performance and the divergence in the perception of the employees working in different sectors concerning selected demographic factors. The constructs adopted in the study had a Skewness of 1.663 (SE= .122), Kurtosis of 2.348 (SE= .243) and were normally distributed. Kurtosis scores were found within the acceptable range, which established normal distribution of the data.

KMO and Bartlett's Test of Sphericity

Before performing the exploratory factor analysis for identifying problematic variables, KMO & Bartlett's tests of Sphericity were conducted. The results of KMO (0.937 > 0.6) suggests that job performance explains 93% of the variance (see Table 2 for details). The sample is adequate for conducting statistical analysis as the threshold value has been met.

Table 2: KMO and Bartlett's Test

KMO Measure of Sampling Adequacy		0.937
Bartlett's Test of Sphericity	Approx. Chi-Square	3716.630
	Df	153
	Sig.	.000

Factor Analysis

Factor analysis was conducted with the principal component method and varimax rotation for identifying the factors influencing the job performance of employees. The variables loaded a value of 0.50 or above on each factor. The results (see Table 3) show that job performance constitutes 64 per cent of the total variance. Since there were no cross-loadings, no item was deleted.

Table 3: Factor Analysis of Job Performance

Factors	No. of items (18)	Item (label) Code	Rotated Factor Loading	Eigen Value	Variance Extracted
(Factor I) Task Performance	6	I maintain a high standard of work.	.845	**8.417**	**46.763**
		I handle assignments without supervision.	.849		
		I am very passionate about my work.	.731		
		I am capable of handling multiple assignments for fulfilling organisational goals.	.705		
		I finish my assignments on time.	.651		
		My co-workers consider me a high performer in the organisation.	.524		
(Factor II) Adaptive Performance	5	I can mobilise the collective intelligence of my team for the effective fulfilment of goals.	.553	**1.283**	**7.126**
		I am capable of handling job changes, as the situation demands.	.585		
		I can lead my work team effectively in the face of change.	.638		
		Mutual understanding between colleagues can lead to a feasible solution within the organisation.	.575		
		I am at ease with job flexibility.	.842		

(Factor III) Contextual Performance	7	I handle organisational changes well.	.844	1.040	5.778
		I help my peers whenever asked or needed.	.744		
		I enjoy handling extra responsibilities.	.701		
		I am compassionate towards my colleagues when they're in trouble.	.872		
		I participate actively in meetings and discussions at work.	.740		
		I derive satisfaction by encouraging others in the organisation.	.800		
		I love sharing ideas, experiences and knowledge with my team members.	.818		
CUMULATIVE % OF VARIANCE					59.667%

ANALYSIS AND DISCUSSION

Dimensions of Job Performance

The key findings related to various dimensions of job performance, based on the data contained in Table 4, are as under:

Table 4: Descriptive Statistics

Factors	Mean	Std. Deviation
Task Performance	4.0833	.70028
Adaptive Performance	4.0495	.64892
Contextual Performance	4.0968	.64965
Total	3.3884	4.0765

Contextual performance (M=*4.0968*; SD=*.64965*) is the most important contributing factor amongst the dimensions of the job performance of employees understudy, which indicates that the organisations are making sufficient efforts to create a better workplace environment wherein the employees are engaged and willing to go beyond their specified job roles, volunteer for extra work, cooperate with others, help peers in solving problems, uphold enthusiasm at work, abide by rules and support the organisational decisions for change. This kind of culture helps the organisation in achieving individual productivity as well as overall organisational effectiveness.

The second most important contributing dimension is the task performance (M=*4.0833*; SD= *.70028*) which implies that there is job clarity and the job occupants have the requisite technical knowledge and experience to fulfill the task requirements without much supervision. The lowest mean score for adaptive performance (M=*4.0495*; SD=*.64892*) indicates that the respondents do not contend with their adaptive performance. Thus, employees should be reasonably equipped to deal with the varied requirements of their roles and to deal with any volatile situation and changed circumstances with their peers and subordinates.

Correlates of Job Performance

The main results of the study regarding the key correlates of job performance are contained in Table 5, followed by the discussion thereon:

Table 5: Descriptive Statistics and Independent Sample t-test for Job Performance

Demographics	Categories	N	Percentage	Job Performance		
				Mean	t-value	Sig.
Gender	Male	218	54.5	4.1018	.067	.796
	Female	182	45.5	4.0463		
Type of family	Nuclear	264	66.0	4.0572	.455	.500
	Joint	136	34.0	4.0865		

*At 5 percent level of significance.

Gender: There is no significant difference between the level of job performance as far as the gender of the employees is concerned, since the p>*0.05*. The job performance of the male employees (M=*4.1018*; S.D= *.59627*) is slightly better than their female counterparts (M= *4.0463*; SD= *.61005*). According to Eagly and Johannesen-Schmidt (2001), females are better decision-makers, democratic leaders, team players, problem solvers, and perform better than men. Employers usually set higher standards for females, constantly compare their performance to that of men and expect them to have fewer faults (Morrison *et al.*, 1992). This unfair comparison leads employers to believe that the tasks performed by women lack accuracy (Green *et al.*, 2009). Some researchers are of the view that all employees have the same capabilities irrespective of the gender they belong to, but since male employees are subjected to lesser discrimination, they tend to have the upper hand and perform better (Hopkins & Bilimoria, 2008).

Type of Family: The statistical results reveal no significant difference in employee job performance based on the type of their family since the p> *0.05*. However, job performance is reported to be better among employees living in joint families (M= *4.0865*). Employees having larger families perform better as they experience a better work-family balance. Since there are more people around to share responsibilities at home, the employees can focus more on their goals and accomplish more in comparison to employees living alone or in nuclear families. Moreover, a healthy and happy environment at home results in more creative and committed employees, having a sense of purpose, and improved job performance (Rose *et al.,* 2006). They are also able to contribute more to the organisation.

One-way analysis of variance (ANOVA) was performed to check whether any variation exists in the job performance of employees categorised by select demographic factors. Results of the study (see table 1 for details) in this regard are presented below.

Age: Age group of the employees has a significant impact on their job performance ($p<0.05$). With the increase in the age of the employees, their job performance improves and is maximum among employees above 50 years of age (M=*4.4170*). Organisations must tap the knowledge and abilities of the employees of this age group and involve them in mentoring and training programs so that younger employees can benefit from their experience and expertise. Senior employees in comparison to younger ones not only ensure consistency in their performance but also make sure that the tasks performed are accurate (Ghould,1979).

Educational Qualification: While the current study reveals that the educational qualification of the employees does not have any statistically significant effect on job performance (p>0.05), some earlier research suggests that employee's educational qualification significantly affects the profitability, training, and quality decisions of the organisation (Ross, 2012). Organisations that hire better-qualified employees are more likely to withstand change than organisations that do not (Collier *et al.,* 2011). A qualified workforce ensures that the next level of leadership can be proactively developed (Nyberg, 2010).

Income: Improvement in the employees' financial incentives and income has been reported to decrease turnover rates and improve job performance (Nyberg, 2010). When employees are dissatisfied with the remuneration paid to them, their commitment decreases, and they continue to look for opportunities for a job change (Agarwala, 2003). Such behaviours adversely affect the accomplishment of goals assigned to the employees, leading to a significant decrease in job performance (Kelly, 2004). The current data shows a gradual increase in the mean scores concerning job performance, which is maximum (M= *4.238*) for employees in the income group of Rs 100,000 and above. This suggests that money is an important contributing factor to employee job performance, though the difference in the mean values is not significant (p> *0.05*).

Experience: Experience-wise analysis of job performance showed a significant difference in the means (p<*0.05*). The highest mean score of job performance was reported in the case of employees with more than 15 years of experience and lowest for employees with up to 3 years of experience. While earlier research did not consider work experience as an essential predictor of job performance (Fiedler, 1970), contemporary studies have shown that experience is a crucial contributor to job performance (Chan & Schmitt, 2002). More experienced employees outperform employees who are new to the organisation because of the skills that they have amassed (Hunter & Thatcher, 2007). Since experience provides a means for learning; a long tenure can be linked to improved job performance (Sturman 2003). While there is ample evidence to support the impact of job experience on task performance, the data to support the linkage between contextual performance and job experience is comparatively weak particularly, concerning the indicators of organisational citizenship behaviour (Chan & Schmitt, 2002). Experience has a weak positive relationship with adaptive performance, especially concerning the indicators of change (Allworth & Hesketh, 1999).

Marital Status: ANOVA results indicate that there is no significant difference in the job performance of employees based on their marital status ($p>0.05$). Organisations while hiring prefer married candidates over unmarried ones in anticipation that they will perform better and achieve better work outcomes (Selmer and Lauring, 2011). Past research has shown that married employees earn more than their unmarried counterparts mainly due to the difference in their productivity (Korenman & Neumark, 1990). While some researchers have highlighted the positive impact, marriage has on workplace performance; some others have contradicted the claims made by these researchers (Chun & Lee, 2001; Cornwell & Rupert, 1997).

The sector of Employment: The current data reveals that the difference in employee job performance based on the sector of employment is not significant as $p> 0.05$. Employees working in the banking ($M=4.1217$) and manufacturing ($M=4.0850$) sectors record higher mean scores for their job performance, mainly because the jobs performed by employees in these sectors are mostly repetitive. This allows them to specialise and gain mastery over tasks that positively impacts their performance at work. Also, public sector banks conduct frequent training to improve their employees' job performance.

CONCLUSION AND RECOMMENDATIONS

Overall, the employees under study are contented with their job performance. Of the factors contributing to job performance, the least influential factor came out to be adaptive performance. Thus, organisations should ensure that employees are fairly equipped to understand and adjust to the change in the work environment by demonstrating mastery-oriented leadership aimed at helping employees attain new skills or upgrade existing knowledge, skills, and abilities which will help the employees perform better in dynamic work environments. For sustaining the contextual performance of employees, which is a vital contributing factor in the overall happiness of the employees at work, organisations should provide opportunities to cooperate. Monitoring and rewarding employees for participating in volunteer work will encourage other employees to participate and feel appreciated.

Organisations work in dynamic environments which cause frequent changes within and outside the organisations. Uncertainty and constant changes have a negative impact on an employee's job performance if he/she is not equipped to deal with the same. To improve adaptive performance, managers should create an environment where change is welcome by ensuring transparent and honest communication regarding the impending change. Organisations should conduct training in crisis management, stress management, creative problem solving, cultural adaptability, technological change, etc., to equip the employees with the requisite skills to deal with change. Managers and team leaders should also frequently meet with their teams and educate them about the developments and the impact the change will have on them. To boost task performance, organisations should proactively provide frequent feedback. Good performance should be reinforced with positive feedback, and areas of improvement should be highlighted and communicated to the employees.

The study showed mixed results about the correlates of employee job performance. Age, education, income, and years of experience were found to significantly affecting employee performance. The study revealed mixed results in respect of other demographics like gender, family type, marital status, sector of employment, etc which implies that these dimensions do not substantially impact the performance of individuals at the workplace in a similar way across sectors and contexts. To improve the overall performance of employees at work, organisations need to enhance the understanding of their employees and their work-life, provide them with a supportive environment to work, reduce negative organisational experiences and improve employee engagement and motivation by increasing workplace transparency, providing feedback proactively, clarifying goals and encouraging flexibility.

LIMITATIONS AND DIRECTIONS FOR FUTURE RESEARCH

The present study focused on full-time employees working in public sector organisations across the banking, health, education, and manufacturing sectors in northern India. Future studies could include employees working in private sector undertakings in different industries and other parts of the country. This will help in improving the generalisation and predictive value of the results and facilitate comparisons with the present research. The present study also followed a cross-sectional design while future studies can consider adopting a longitudinal design. Furthermore, the data were collected only from one source i.e. employees, which increases the chance of common method bias. Future studies could focus on collecting data from multiple sources using a different scale. It will help in identifying more causal linkages.

REFERENCES

Agarwala, T. (2003). Innovative human resource practices and organisational commitment: an empirical investigation. *International Journal of Human ResourceManagement*, 14(2), 175–197.

Allworth, E., & Hesketh, B. (1999).Construct-oriented biodata: Capturing change-related and contextually relevant future performance, *International Journal of Selection and Assessment, 7*, 97–111.

Anitha, J. (2014). Determinants of employee engagement and their impact on employee performance. *International journal of productivity and performance management*.

Bateman, T.S., & Snell, S.A. (2007). *Management: Leading & collaborating in a competitive world*. Boston: McGraw-Hill.

Borman, W. C., & Motowidlo, S. M. (1993). Expanding the criterion domain to include elements of contextual performance. In N. Schmitt and W. Borman (eds), *Personnel Selection in Organisations* (pp. 71–98). New York: Jossey-Bass.

Brief, A. P., & Motowidlo, S. J. (1986). Prosocial organisational behaviors. *Academy of Management Review*, 11(4), 710–725.

Campbell, J. P. (1990). Modeling the performance prediction problem in industrial and organisational psychology. In M. D. Dunnette and L. M. Hough (eds), *Handbook of Industrial and Organizational Psychology* (pp. 687–732). PaloAlto: Consulting Psychologists Press.

Caron, D. & Giauque, D. (2006). Civil servant identity at the crossroads: New challenges for public administration. International Journal of Public Sector Management, 19(6), 543–555.

Chan, D., & Schmitt, N. (2002). Situational judgment and job performance. *Human Performance, 15,* 233–254.

Chun, H., & Lee, I. (2001). Why Do Married Men Earn More: Productivity or Marriage Selection. *Economic Inquiry*, 39(2), 154.

Coleman, V. I., & Borman, W. C. (2000). Investigating the underlying structure of the citizenship performance domain. *Human resource management review*, 10(1), 25–44.

Collier, W., Green, F., Kim, Y., & Peirson, J. (2011). Education, training and economic performance: Evidence from establishment survival data. *Journal of Labour Research,* 32, 336–361.

Conway, J. M. (1999). Distinguishing contextual performance from task performance for managerial jobs. *Journal of Applied Psychology*, 84(1), 3.

Cornwell, C., & Rupert, P. (1997). Unobservable Individual Effects, Marriage and the Earnings of Young Men, *Economic Inquiry*, 35(2), 151.

Eagly, A.H., & Johannesen-Schmidt, M.C. (2001).The leadership styles of women and men. *Journal of Social Issues*, 57, 781–97.

Fiedler F.E. (1970). Leadership experience and leader performance: Another hypothesis shot to hell. *Organisational Behavior and Human Performance*, 5, 1–14.

Ghould, S., Age, Job Complexity, Satisfaction, and Performance (1979). *Journal of Vocational Behaviour,* 14, 209–223.

Green, C., Jegadeesh, N., & Tang, Y. (2009). Gender and Job Performance: Evidence from Wall Street. *Financial Analyst Journal*, 65(6), 65–78.

Hair, J. F., Black, W. C., Babin, B. J., Anderson, R. E., & Tatham, R. L. (2006). Multivariate data analysis (6th Ed.). New Jersey: Pearson-Prentice Hall.

Hopkins, M.M., & Bilimoria, D. (2008). Social and emotional competencies predicting success for male and female executives. *Journal of Management Development, 22,* 13–35.

Hunter, L. W., & Thatcher, S. M. B. (2007). Feeling the heat: Effects of stress, commitment, and job experience on job performance. Academy of Management Journal, 50, 953–968.

Isaac, O., Abdullah, Z., Ramayah, T., & Mutahar, A. M. (2017). Internet usage, user satisfaction, task-technology fit, and performance impact among public sector employees in Yemen. *The International Journal of Information and Learning Technology.*

Islami, X., Mulolli, E., & Mustafa, N. (2018). Using Management by Objectives as a performance appraisal tool for employee satisfaction. *Future Business Journal*, 4(1), 94–108.

Karakas, F. (2010). Spirituality and performance in organisations: A literature review. *Journal of business ethics*, 94(1), 89–106.

Kelly, S. (2004). An event history analysis of teacher attrition: salary, teacher tracking, and socially disadvantaged schools. *Journal of Experimental Education*, 72(3), 195–220.

Koopmans, L., Bernaards, C. M., Hildebrandt, V. H., Schaufeli, W. B., de Vet Henrica, C. W., & van der Beek, A. J. (2011). Conceptual frameworks of individual work performance: a systematic review. *Journal of occupational and environmental medicine*, 53(8), 856–866.

Koreman, S., & Neumark, D. (1990). Does Marriage Really Make Men More Productive?. *Journal of Human Resources*, 26(2), 283–307.

Ma, K. (2003). Adaptive performance [J]. *Business research*, *22*, 15–17.

Morrison, A.M., White, R.P., Van Velsor, E. (1992). *Breaking the Glass Ceiling: Can Women Reach the Top of America's Largest Corporations?*. Addison-Wesley: Reading, MA.

Motowidlo, J. S. (2003). Job Performance. *Handbook of Psychology, Industrial and Organisational Psychology*, 12, 39–55.

Moynihan, D. P., Pandey, S. K., & Wright, B. E. (2012). Prosocial values and performance management theory: Linking perceived social impact and performance information use. *Governance*, 25(3), 463–483.

Murphy, P. R., & Jackson, S. E. (1999). Managing Work Role Performance: Challenging the Twenty-first Century Organisations and Their Employees. In D. R. Ligen & E. D. Pulakos (eds), *The Changing Nature of Performance: Implications for Staffing, Motivations, and Development* (pp. 325–365). San Francisco: Jossey-Bass.

Nyberg, A. (2010). Retaining your high performers: Moderators of the performance-job satisfaction-voluntary turnover relationship. *Journal of Applied Psychology,* 95, 440–453.

Pawirosumarto, S., Sarjana, P. K., & Gunawan, R. (2017). The effect of work environment, leadership style, and organisational culture towards job satisfaction and its implication towards employee performance in Parador Hotels and Resorts, Indonesia. *International Journal of Law and Management*.

Pradhan, R. K., & Jena, L. K. (2017). Employee performance at workplace: Conceptual model and empirical validation. *Business Perspectives and Research*, 5(1), 69–85.

Pulakos, E. D., Arad, S., Donovan, M. A. & Plamondon, K. E. (2000). Adaptability in the workplace: Development of a taxonomy of adaptive performance, *Journal of Applied Psychology*, 85, 612–624.

Roe, R. A. (1999). Work performance: A multiple regulation perspective. *International review of industrial and organisational psychology*, 14, 231–336.

Rose, C., Beh., Uli., & Idris., (2006). Quality of Work Life and Human Resource Outcomes. *Industrial Relations*. 30(3), 469–479.

Ross, R. (2012). Managing perfectionism in the workplace. *Employment Relations Today,* 39, 1–6.

Schiemann, W.A. (2009). Aligning performance management with organisational strategy, values and goals. In J.W. Smither & M. London (Eds), *Performance management: Putting research into action*. San Francisco, CA: Jossey-Bass.

Selmer, J., & Lauring, J. (2011). Marital status and work outcomes of self-initiated expatriates, Cross-Cultural Management: An International Journal, 18(2), 198–213.

Smith, M., & Bititci, U. S. (2017). Interplay between performance measurement and management, employee engagement and performance. *International Journal of Operations & Production Management.*

Sonnentag, S., Volmer, J., & Spychala, A. (2008). Job performance. *The Sage handbook of organisational behaviour*, 1, 427–447.

Sturman, M. C. (2003). Searching for the inverted u-shaped relationship between time and performance: Meta-analyses of the experience/performance, tenure/ performance, and age/performance relationships, Journal of Management, 29, 609–640.

Van Dyne, L. and LePine, J. A. (1998).Helping and voice extra-role behaviors: Evidence of construct and predictive validity, *Academy of Management Journal*, 41, 108–119.

Vermeeren, B., Kuipers, B., & Steijn, B. (2009). A Study of HRM, Employee Attitude and Behavior and Public Service Quality of Dutch Municipalities. In *EGPA Conference.*

Viswesvaran, C., & Ones, D. S. (2000). Perspectives on models of job performance. *International Journal of Selection and Assessment*, 8(4), 216–226.

CHAPTER 19

Understanding Employer Branding Through Sentiment Analysis of Employee Reviews of India's Best Companies to Work for

Dr. Tavleen Kaur
Assistant Professor
ICFAI Business School-Gurgaon
Gurugram, Haryana
tavleenkaur@ibsindia.org

Dr. Chirag Malik
Associate Professor
BML Munjal University
Gurugram, Haryana
chiragmalik@yahoo.com

Dr. Neeraj Singhal
Assistant Professor
Management Development Institute
Murshidabad
West Bengal
neeraj.singhal@mdim.ac.in

Abstract

Purpose: To explore employer value propositions of companies rated as "India's Best Companies to Work for" by "Great Place to Work Institute".

Design/methodology/approach: 5015 employees' reviews of 20 "India's Best Companies to work for", were obtained from employee review website "Glassdoor". These 20 companies consist of top 10 companies and bottom 10 companies that scored the ranking 1-10 and 87-100 in the ranking scoreboard of India's 100 best companies to work for. Statistical software, R, was used to mine data (qualitative) from the website and natural language processing (NLP) technique was applied to analyse the data.

Findings: There are seven value propositions which are most sought after by employees namely: economic value, social value, application value, development value, interest value, management value & work life balance.

Research Limitations/Implications: The study was restricted to 5015 reviews of 20 "India's Best Companies to Work for". Understanding employer value propositions helps companies to compete better for highly qualified and skilled talent. The study also demonstrates the importance of employer value propositions for an organization to be recognised as a best place to work.

Originality/value: This paper is a first attempt at understanding employer value propositions, using NLP technique in the Indian context.

Keywords: Text Mining, NLP, Employer value propositions, Sentiment Analysis, Employee Reviews

INTRODUCTION

The term war for talent coined and highlighted by Michels, Handfield-Jones, Axelrod in 2001 referring to challenges associated in acquiring and retaining talented candidates is still a topical issue. In this war for talent the organizations have to put continuous efforts to remain attractive for the job seekers. Ambler and Barrow (1996) applied brand management techniques to the employment situations and they found that linking brand management with employment can be mutually beneficial for the organizations and prospective candidates. The popularity of employer branding has since then been increasing, there have been numerous attempts to investigate the impact of employer branding techniques on HR outcomes, particularly the impact of employer branding on job seekers (Sokro; 2012., Dabirian, Pashchen and Kietzman 2019).

Employee testimonials can be disseminated either by word of mouth or electronic word of mouth known as "word of mouse"-one that happens on web/internet (Van Hoye and Lievens (2007). The information available through word of mouse is easily accessible to job seekers and has been found to impact organizational attractiveness (Kaur & Dubey 2020; Van Hoye and Lievens; 2009; 2007). Though there have been numerous attempts to investigate the impact of employee testimonials (posted on company website) on organizational attractiveness, research is relatively silent on impact of employee testimonials available on employee reviews website like Glassdoor.

The current study uses Glassdoor: an employer review website where the current and former employees anonymously review the organization and its management. Glassdoor, having 50 million monthly visitors (www.glassdoor.com), emphasizes on employee driven reviews, comments, information about organizational culture & benefits. The current study conducted sentiment analysis of the employee reviews posted on Glassdoor for "India's Best Companies to Work For 2019-2020" rated by "Great Place to Work for Institute".

EMPLOYER BRANDING & EMPLOYEE TESTIMONIALS

Employer branding refers to application of brand management techniques in employment context. Ambler & Barrow (1996) defined employer brand "*as the package of functional, economic and psychological benefits provided by the employment and identified with the employing company*" (pg:187).

Employer branding can be conceptualized in two ways namely: internal branding and external branding (Backuas & Tikko; 2004). Internal branding refers to keeping the promises made to recruits once they are hired. External branding is about establishing an organization as a "great place to work" thereby enabling the organization to hire talented candidates who are rare to be found (Dabirian, Pashchen and Kietzman 2019)

The initial studies on employer branding highlighted three major benefits of employer branding namely functional, economic and psychological benefits (Ambler & Barrow; 1996, Backhaus & Tikko; 2004). The functional benefits are the developmental, useful activities and career advancement opportunities. The economic benefits refer to monetary rewards, the benefits and salary. The psychological benefits refer to feeling of association, belongingness with the organization (Ambler & Barrow; 1996, Dabirian, Kietzmann & Diba; 2019). In a similar attempt, Berthon, Ewing & Hah (2005) identified five dimensions of employer branding: interest value, social value, economic value, development value and application value. Interest value refers to the extent to which individuals are attracted to organizations that provide exciting work environment, novel work practices which help employees make innovative products and services. Social value refers to the extent to which an individual is attracted to an organization which offers people focused culture. Economic value refers to the extent to which individuals are attracted to organizations which offer monetary rewards, compensation, benefits etc. Development value refers to the extent to which an individual is attracted to an organization which offers career advancement opportunities, recognition, and professional development avenues. Application value refers to the extent to which an individual is attracted to an organization which offers opportunities to apply the concepts learned, teaching others. The five dimensions given by Berthon et al., (2005) can be seen as an extension and refinement of dimensions propounded by Ambler & Barrow (1996). The interest value and social value capture psychological benefits, development and application value capture functional benefits and economic dimension suggested by Berthon et al., (2005) matches with economic dimension given by Ambler & Barrow (1996). Dabirain, Kietzmann and Diba (2017) added two more dimensions to the existing dimensions of employer branding namely: management value and work life balance. Management value refers to the extent to which individuals are attracted to organizations which offer supportive management, peers and leaders with a vision and inspiration. Work life balance refers to the extent to an organization which provides arrangements to maintain an identity outside of being just an employee and maintain balance between business obligations and personal responsibilities.

Van Hoye and Lievens (2009) highlighted "word of mouse" and found that testimonials available on review website had higher association with organizational attractiveness and organizational pursuit behaviour when testimonials provided information about organization, and since then employee testimonials on review websites have been widely accepted (Dabirain, Kietzmann and Diba 2017 and Dabirian, Paschen & Kietzmann 2019)

Taking inferences from the extant literature the current study makes an attempt at conducting sentiment analysis of employee reviews available on Glassdoor for "India's Best Companies to work for, 2019-2020". "The Best Companies to Work For", survey conducted by "Great Places to Work Institute" is a survey which reveals 100 Indian best companies to work for annually. The current study has taken 20 companies from 2019-2020 list and these comprise of organizations ranked between 1-10 and those ranked between 87-100 in 100 best Indian companies to work for survey

METHODOLOGY

To understand the types of attributes employees, care about in their evaluation of an employer brand, we extracted employee reviews of organizations ranked between 1-10 (Top 10) and 87-100 (Bottom 10) in "India's Best 100 Companies to Work for" survey conducted by "Great Places to Work Institute". The organizations represent Information Technology & ITES, Manufacturing & Production, Financial Services and Insurance, Retail, Hospitality, Telecommunications, Transportation, Bio Technology & Pharmaceuticals, Construction,

Infrastructure and Real Estate, Education & Training, Hospitals and Health Care Services, Media, Industrial Services, Professional Services and Others.

The objective of the current study is to analyse the unique aspects and common attributes of top 10 and bottom 10 organizations within the "India's 100 Best Companies to Work For" list. Thus, to achieve this objective employee reviews of top10 and bottom 10 organizations were extracted from Glassdoor. Table I shows the ranking of each of the 20 companies.

Table I: List of Top 10 & Bottom 10 companies

Rank	Top 10 Name	Rank	Bottom 10 Name
1	SAP Labs India Pvt Ltd.	100	Tata Starbucks Pvt Ltd.
2	Intuit India	99	Power Grid Corporation of India Ltd.
3	DHL Express	98	VIP Industries Ltd
4	Tata Power	97	Ingersoll – Rand Technologies & Services Pvt Ltd
5	Music Broadcast	96	Ericsson India
6	Ujjivan Small Finance Bank	95	Metlife Global Operations Support Centre Pvt. Ltd
7	Adobe Inc.	94	JK Paper Ltd
8	Mahindra & Mahindra Financial Services	93	Teleperformance India
9	Indus Towers	89	Tata Communications
10	BMC Software	87	Akamai Technologies India Pvt Ltd

Four organizations namely ADP Pvt Ltd (ranked 92), Metro Cash & Carry India Pvt Ltd (ranked 91), Gabriel India (ranked 90), KLAY Prep Schools & Daycare (ranked 88) were skipped from the bottom 10 list due to non-availability of reviews on Glassdoor for the year 2019-2020.

With 50 million monthly visitors globally, 1.3 million employers and 70 million reviews and insights (www.glassdoor.com), Glassdoor is the most popular employee review website. Glassdoor has been used as a data source in related studies (Dabirian, A., Paschen, J., & Kietzmann, J; 2019, P. Tambie, Ye & Capelli; 2017), following similar approach, we utilize Glassdoor as a data source of this study.

In order to do the natural language processing and sentiment analysis, a statistical computing software R has been used. Four text files were collected from Glassdoor using web scrapping techniques (using R). Positive reviews of top 10 companies (ranked between 1-10), negative reviews of top 10 companies, positive reviews of bottom 10 companies (ranked between 87-100) and negative reviews of bottom 10 companies, in total 5015 reviews were analysed

Word clouds were formed based on the frequency of a term used in the text. Sparse terms (Terms which had a frequency of one) were removed using the package "tm". To perform the sentiment analysis, "syuzhet" package was used. Syuzet associates each text word with a sentiment attribute and assigns a score to it on the basis of 10748 built in words (Sentiment Dictionary). On the basis of the sentiment dictionary each word is given a score, higher the score, more positive are the sentiments and vice-versa. The sentiment categories are, anger, anticipation, disgust, fear, joy, sadness, surprise, trust, negative, positive.

ANALYSIS

The popular open-source statistical software, R text mining package used in the current study analyses word frequency (Maceli, 2016). Table II shows words that are frequently used among all reviews in our data set.

Table II: Word Frequency: overall positive reviews and overall negative reviews

Overall Negative Reviews		Overall Positive Reviews	
WORD	FREQ	WORD	FREQ
Work	647	Work	1583
Management	283	Good	1392
Good	274	Life	562
Company	266	Balance	536
Growth	231	Great	451
Salary	218	Company	429
Nothing	204	Culture	376
Less	198	Environment	336
Much	163	Best	287
Life	160	Employee	257
People	158	Place	248
Working	150	Benefits	231
Employees	143	Salary	207
Time	131	Learning	200
Politics	122	Friendly	198
Balance	121	Working	172
Team	113	Employees	166
Slow	109	Learn	156
Low	105	Management	154
Culture	96	Opportunities	153
Managers	96	Free	141
Get	92	People	133
Employee	89	Food	130

Now	88	Lot	112
Poor	88	Policies	110
Bad	87	Nice	107
Think	84	Team	107
Job	80	Growth	106
Level	79	Flexible	98
Career	77	Can	97
Need	73	Opportunity	96
Manager	72	Job	92
HR	70	One	92
Pressure	70	Get	90
Opportunities	66	Technologies	83
Process	64	Exposure	79
Like	63	Facilities	77
Pay	62	Amazing	75
Everything	60	Excellent	74

The word frequency analysis suggests that there are few common attributes that organizations in both the categories of employers (top 10 & bottom 10) are offering, however, the words reflect negative connotation when used while providing negative reviews and reflect positive connotation when used while giving positive reviews. For example, the word "opportunity" when reflected in negative reviews suggests the organizations does not provide enough opportunities to its employees inclusive of top 10 and bottom 10 organizations. On the other hand, the word "opportunity" when reflected in positive reviews suggests the organizations offer enough opportunities to its employees. Top 10 and bottom 10 organization both have pros and cons associated with working with them. Similarly, the word "balance" when reflected in negative reviews suggests that work life balance is poor inclusive of top 10 and bottom 10 organizations and when "balance" is reflected in positive reviews it suggests that the organization provides a work life balance to its employees inclusive of top 10 and bottom 10 organization. It can be concluded that there are pros and cons of working with any organization as reflected in overall positive and negative reviews. Organizations between 1-10 may have challenges associated with them and organizations ranked between 87-100 have unique offerings.

After getting frequencies, two separate word clouds were generated (Figure 1&2), word cloud for overall negative reviews of top 10 and bottom 10 companies and word cloud for overall positive reviews of top 10 and bottom 10 companies. The two-word clouds reveal some common categories that are frequently mentioned in overall positive and negative reviews including work, good, balance, management, great etc. The words are represented according to their frequency in the data set. As can be seen in the overall positive word cloud, work is in centre surrounded by good, balance, great, company etc. This suggests that certain positive aspects of employment like work life balance, supportive management, free food, culture, team spirit, salary, benefits etc are offered by both the category of companies: top 10 and bottom 10 organizations, however the magnitude is different as reflected in the word frequency analysis. The word cloud also suggests that even organizations ranked between 87-100 have unique offerings and a positive experience to offer to their employees. The word cloud suggests that employees look for attributes like good organizational culture, growth, work life balance, salary, benefits, nature of work etc. in exchange to their service.

Figure 1: *Word Cloud of Overall Positive Reviews*

Figure 2: *Word cloud of overall negative reviews*

As can be seen in the overall negative word cloud (Figure 2) work, management, work life balance, salary, growth are frequently used words. This suggests that even organizations ranked as 1-10 have challenges like poor work life balance, slow growth, less opportunities etc. The overall word frequency analysis and word clouds suggests that organization ranked between 87-100 have some unique offerings and organizations ranked between 1-10 have some challenges associated. To strengthen the analysis, a comparison of word frequency between four categories namely positive reviews of top 10 companies, positive reviews of bottom 10 companies, negative reviews of top 10 companies and negative reviews of bottom 10 companies was also done as reflected in Table III.

Table III: Word Frequency: Positive and Negative Review of Top & Bottom 10 Companies

Terms	Bottom 10 Negative Reviews	Bottom 10 Positive Reviews	Top10 Negative Reviews	Top 10 Positive Reviews
Balance	35	188	60	255
Company	92	167	112	204
Culture	31	125	51	191
Environment	14	155	25	125
Good	98	513	127	473
Great	16	122	28	176
Life	58	183	77	285
Management	116	60	120	61
Salary	92	96	63	73
Work	236	563	277	733

Table III emphasises upon number of times commonly used words have been used in the four categories. As it can be seen from Table III, the word "balance" is used 35 times in negative reviews of bottom 10 companies, 188 times in positive reviews of bottom 10 companies, 60 times in negative reviews of top 10 companies and 255 times in positive reviews of top 10 companies. The word "balance" has a negative connotation when it is reflected in negative reviews, and positive connotation when reflected in positive reviews. This suggests that organizations ranked between 87-100 in "India's Best Companies to Work for" are providing work life balance, however, it is less as compared to companies ranked between 1-10. The employees working in organizations ranked between 1-10 find work life balance missing, however employees of organizations ranked between 87-100 find their work life balance more compromised. To strengthen the analysis a comparison cloud between the four categories was created (Figure 3).

Figure 3 shows the comparison between positive reviews of top 10 and bottom 10 companies and negative reviews of top 10 and bottom 10 companies. The figure suggests that employees working in bottom 10 organizations feel good about being associated with their employer, the organizations are offering learning and growth opportunities etc. The top 10 organizations provide work life balance, opportunities to grow, benefits, perks, free food, positive culture etc. Words like "less", "politics", "bad", "poor", "low" are reflected in negative review of bottom 10 companies. These words suggest the overall negative experiences employees have of working with organizations ranked between 87-100. On the other hand, there are challenges associated even with organizations ranked between 1-10 as reflected in the negative reviews of top 10 companies. Word like "hierarchy", "growth" "processes" suggests challenges or negative experiences associated with employment with top 10 companies.

Figure 3: *Comparison Cloud of four categories:*

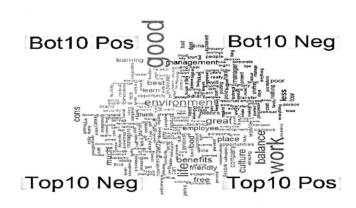

Table IV further shows most frequently used words in four categories. The table shows attributes most commonly used be employees while providing reviews about top 10 and bottom 10 organizations. The attributes mentioned closely match with the established employer brand value propositions.

Table IV: Most Frequent Words in all the four Categories of Text Files

Negative Reviews of Bottom 10 Companies					
Work	Management	Good	Company	Salary	Cons
236	116	98	92	92	79
Positive Reviews of Bottom 10 Companies					
Work	Good	Balance	Life	Company	Environment
563	513	188	183	167	155

Negative Reviews of Top 10 Companies					
Work	Management	Good	Company	Cons	Growth
277	120	127	112	118	107

Positive Reviews of Top 10 Companies					
Work	Good	Life	Balance	Company	Culture
733	473	285	255	204	191

Further, in order to understand the sentiments getting reflected in positive and negative reviews of top 10 and bottom 10 companies, a sentiment analysis was conducted. To perform the sentiment analysis, "syuzhet" package was used. Syuzet associates each text word with a sentiment attribute and assigns a score to it on the basis of 10748 built in words (Sentiment Dictionary,). On the basis of the sentiment dictionary each word is given a score, higher the score, more positive are the sentiments and vice-versa. The sentiment categories as reflected in Table V are, anger, anticipation, disgust, fear, joy, sadness, surprise, trust, negative, positive.

Table V: Overall Sentiment Score

Text	Anger	Anticipation	Disgust	Fear	Joy	Sadness	Surprise	Trust	Negative	Overall Sentiment Score
Negative Reviews of Bottom 10	79	102	49	88	83	83	42	157	196	13.55
Positive Reviews of Bottom 10	26	81	15	29	85	31	37	138	53	188.8
Negative Reviews of Top 10	79	112	63	94	90	99	49	175	226	35.65
Positive Reviews of Top 10	28	106	18	40	95	33	39	158	67	195.95

The overall sentiment score of all the four categories is positive, higher the score more positive the sentiments are. The comparison of overall sentiment score of negative reviews of bottom 10 companies and negative reviews of top 10 companies suggest that though there are challenges in working with top 10 companies as well (Overall Sentiment Score; 35.65), however, those challenges are lesser in magnitude as compared to challenges of working with bottom 10 companies (overall sentiment score; 13.55).

The sentiment score of 35.65 as compared to 13.55 reflect those negative reviews of top 10 companies are less severe as compared to negative reviews of bottom 10 companies. Similarly, the overall sentiment score of positive reviews of top 10 companies (195.85) is higher than overall sentiment score of positive reviews of bottom 10 companies (188.8).

DISCUSSION

Our results extended the previously established seven dimensions of employer brand. The results confirm the previous seven employer brand value propositions namely: economic value, development value, social value, application value, management value, interest value and lastly work life balance (Ambler and Barrow, 1996; Berthon et al., 2005, Dabirian, Kietzman and Diba; 2017).

The economic value proposition focuses on the tangible rewards & benefits an organization offers to its employees in exchange of their services. Employees primarily are concerned with compensation offered both monetary and non-monetary in exchange of their services. The word "salary" has been used frequently in all four categories positive reviews of top 10 companies, negative reviews of top 10 companies, positive reviews of bottom 10 companies and negative reviews of bottom 10 companies. Reviews and comments like "free food", "perks" "benefits", "salary" "salary is low", "no salary correction has been done" reveal the importance of rewards and benefits in an employer brand. This suggests the importance of salary as an attribute in employer brand such that its presence and absence has been highlighted by employees while providing their reviews.

"Work" is the most frequently used word inclusive of positive and negative reviews of top 10 and bottom 10 companies. This reflects the application value and interest value dimensions of employer brand. Interest value refers to the extent to which the work is interesting and challenging. On the other hand, application value refers to the extent to which the work is meaningful and invites the application of knowledge and skills. The word "work" has been used 733 times in positive reviews of top 10 companies suggesting the positive nature of work and its importance as an attribute in an employer brand. Comments like "scope of work is unlimited", "Responsibility conferred to the employee while at work is impressive and helpful in your career growth", "Social cause associated with work, "responsive HR team "brilliant exposure to how fortune 500 organizations work" "stagnation in career" etc. reflect the presence of interest value and application value in organizations ranked between 1-10 and 87-100. This attribute emerged as most frequently used word while providing positive and negative reviews.

Development value proposition refers to the extent to which an organization offers enough career advancement opportunities enabling the employee to grow. Words like "growth", "opportunities" "learning", "career" etc. reflect development value proposition.

The word "growth" has been used 106 times in overall positive reviews and 231 times in overall negative reviews, "opportunities" has been used 153 times in overall positive reviews and 66 times in overall negative reviews. This suggests that like salary, career advancement opportunity is crucial attribute for an employer brand such that the employees highlight its presence and absence in their reviews.

Social value dimension refers to the extent to which the organization offers a great organizational culture and it's a fun place to be with. It refers to the gratification employees get by working with others. The results suggest that employees value "team" "people" "culture". The word "culture" has been used 191 times in positive reviews of top 10 companies and 125 times in positive reviews of bottom 10 companies. This suggests that even for organizations which have been ranked between 87-100, culture is an important attribute that employees attach value to.

Management Value refers to the extent to which the managers respect and trust employees, they are good, honest leaders who inspire employees. Words like "management", "people" "managers", "HR" "internal politics", "leaders are selfish", "some folks in management are biased" etc. reflect the management value dimension of employer brand. The word management has been used equally in the four categories 116 times in negative reviews of bottom 10 companies reflecting the dissatisfaction of employees with respect to management of the organization. On the other hand, the word management has been used 120 times in negative reviews of top 10 companies. The presence of management value proposition in negative reviews of top 10 and bottom 10 companies reflect that even organizations ranked between 1-10 may have some challenges associated with culture/people/manager. However, it also reflects the crucial nature of management value proposition that employees highlight the presence/absence of supportive management while providing reviews.

Work life balance refers to the extent to which the working arrangements are flexible enough to achieve success on and off the job. Words like "balance", "flexible", "life", "hours", "time" reflect the work life balance proposition. The word "life" has been used 285 times in positive reviews of top 10 companies which indicates the employees of organizations ranked between 1-10 are satisfied about the life provided by their respective employers. The results also suggest that organizations ranked between 87-100, also offer as balanced work life. Similarly, the usage of word "balance" in positive reviews of top10 and bottom 10 companies reflect the important nature of this attribute and highlights that bottom companies are providing some degree of work life balance.

CONCLUSION

Our analysis of 5015 reviews of 20 best Indian companies (ranked between 1-10 and 87-100) extend the previous discussions of employer branding. The study emphasizes on positive and negative reviews of top 10 and bottom 10 Indian best companies to work for ranked by "The Great Place to Work Institute". The study reflects seven employer brand propositions highlighted by employees reviews inclusive of top 10 and bottom 10 companies. The study indicates that employer brand value propositions namely economic value, management value, application value, interest value, development value, social value and work life balance are important to the employees irrespective of bottom and top 10 organizations.

The presence of these value propositions in both the categories reconfirms the fact that all these companies are India's best companies to work, however the magnitude of brand propositions is varying in organizations ranked between 1-10 and those ranked between 87-100

IMPLICATIONS

The objective of study was to analyse the employer brand value propositions offered by top 10 and bottom 10 companies ranked in India's top 100 companies to work with list. The organizations ranked between 87-100 can compare the magnitude of brand value propositions offered by top 10 companies and rethink on how the presence of the propositions can be further strengthened and help improve the ranking in the subsequent surveys. The overall sentiment score of four categories is positive, however it is highest in case of positive reviews of top 10 organizations (195). On the other hand, the overall sentiment score of positive reviews of bottom 10 companies is 188.8, this suggests that organizations ranked between 87-100 are definitely doing something right and offering value propositions which is reflected in overall sentiment score of 188.8, however, the score can be further strengthened to improve the ranking and emerge in top 10 best companies to work for. The study also implies to the managers of top 10 and bottom 10 organizations that they need to mitigate the negative aspects where reflected. In negative reviews of organizations ranked between 87-100. "work" has been highlighted the most followed by "management". The mangers need to redesign the work in such a way that it reflects the interest value and application value proposition. Similarly, the negative reviews of top 10 organizations reflect the need to rethink about the work profile in such a way that it reflects interest value and application value proposition of employer brand. The study also implies that the managers of organizations ranked between 1-10 and 87-100 definitely have reason to celebrate and further strengthen their unique aspects. Attributes like "work", "management, "balance" should be strengthened more to hold the position in best companies to work for list. The organizations ranked between 87-100 can climb the ranking list by taking leverage of their positive attributes like nature of work, work life balance, culture and environment. Paying attention to what matters most to employees can help the organizations especially those ranked between 87-100 focus their resources and climb the great place to work list. Lastly, in an attempt to do sentiment analysis, our study demonstrates how data mining of employee reviews websites can help managers to extract meaning from reviews and understand the overall sentiment towards the organization.

LIMITATIONS AND FUTURE RESEARCH

The current study is limited to the reviews available on glassdoor.com, future research can analyse employee blogs, articles to provide more insights. The study is limited to Great Place to Work Institute's list of best Indian companies to work for, future research can attempt to analyse other rankings like Forbes' list of best companies and compare the brand value propositions. The current study is limited to 5015 reviews, future study can include more reviews and analyse the overall sentiment and value propositions offered by organizations.

REFERENCES

Ambler, T., & Barrow, S. (1996). The employer brand. *Journal of brand management, 4*(3), 185–206.

Backhaus, K., & Tikoo, S. (2004). Conceptualizing and researching employer branding. *Career development international.*

Berthon, P., Ewing, M., & Hah, L. L. (2005). Captivating company: dimensions of attractiveness in employer branding. *International journal of advertising, 24*(2), 151–172.

Dabirian, A., Kietzmann, J., & Diba, H. (2017). A great place to work!? Understanding crowdsourced employer branding. *Business horizons, 60*(2), 197–205.

Dabirian, A., Paschen, J., & Kietzmann, J. (2019). Employer branding: Understanding employer attractiveness of IT companies. *IT Professional, 21*(1), 82–89.

Dellarocas, C. (2003). The digitization of word of mouth: Promise and challenges of online feedback mechanisms. *Management science, 49*(10), 1407–1424.

Kaur, T., & Dubey, R. K. (2020). Employee Review Websites as Source of Recruitment Communication: The Role of Source Credibility, Realistic Information, and Specific Information. *Journal of Electronic Commerce in Organizations (JECO), 18*(3), 74–94.

Maagaard, C. (2014). Employee testimonials: Animating corporate messages through employees' stories. *Discourse, Context & Media, 6*, 22–32.

Maceli, M. (2016). Introduction to text mining with R for information professionals. *Code4Lib Journal*, (33).

Michaels, E., Handfield-Jones, H., & Axelrod, B. (2001). *The war for talent.* Harvard Business Press.

Sokro, E. (2012). Impact of employer branding on employee attraction and retention. *European Journal of Business and Management, 4*(18), 164–173.

Tambe, P. R. A. S. A. N. N. A., Ye, X. U. A. N. N., & CAPPELLI, P. (2016). Poaching and retention in high-tech labor markets. Working Paper, Georgia Tech. http://scheller. gatech. edu/academics/conferences/poaching-high-techtyc. pdf) (Retrieved October 2, 2016), 1–19.

Van Hoye, G., & Lievens, F. (2007). Investigating web-based recruitment sources: Employee testimonials vs word-of-mouse. *International Journal of Selection and Assessment, 15*(4), 372–382.

Van Hoye, G., & Lievens, F. (2009). Tapping the grapevine: A closer look at word-of-mouth as a recruitment source. *Journal of Applied Psychology, 94*(2), 341.

CHAPTER 20

Work From Home During and After Covid: Need for Competence Satisfaction and its Implications for Employee Wellbeing

Navya Kumar
Birla Institute of Technology and
Science
Pilani - Hyderabad Campus
p20190426@hyderabad.bits-pilani.ac.in

Dr. Swati Alok
Birla Institute of Technology
and Science
Pilani - Hyderabad Campus
swati@hyderabad.bits-pilani.
ac.in

Dr. Sudatta Banerjee
Birla Institute of Technology
and Science
Pilani - Hyderabad Campus
sudatta@hyderabad.bits-pilani.
ac.in

Abstract

Purpose: Post-COVID, work from home (WFH) would continue for numerous white-collar employees as employers anticipate same/greater productivity as work from office at lower costs. Given worker wellbeing's significance for productivity, job task and resource conditions under WFH and their implications for employees' short- and long-term wellbeing in the form of stress and career anxieties are investigated. **Approach:** Qualitative responses from a pilot study involving 23 Indian white-collar employees are examined from a perspective blending Job Demand-Resource Model and Self-Determination Theory's psychological need for competence (NFC) satisfaction. **Findings:** NFC satisfaction at job task execution, hence task characteristics and job resources of technology and conducive work environment, affect short- and long-term stress under WFH. Technology was necessary but insufficient for NFC satisfaction, while low-distraction work environment could be elusive. For long-term career anxiety related to improving and proving competence, job resources of colleague interactions, experiential learning opportunities, supervisory support, and performance appraisal were crucial for satisfying NFC. Virtual-only colleague interactions, also unchallenging, routine tasks as feasible under WFH hindered improving competence. Shared WFH experience made supervisors supportive. But appraisal processes valuing visibility to prove competence frustrated NFC in WFH. **Implications:** Paper identifies work conditions that aid/hinder employee short- and long-term wellbeing under WFH, also offers recommendations.

Keywords: Work from Home; Telework; Job Demand-Resource; Self-Determination Theory; Need for Competence

INTRODUCTION

COVID-19 triggered a swiftly executed, mass work from home (WFH) exercise globally. In India too, numerous white-collar employees (henceforth: white-collars) have operated from home since the end of March 2020, when approximately 96% of organizations operationalized WFH (Jayadevan, 2020). Given that prior to March 2020, only 19% of organizations had implemented the practice (Jayadevan, 2020), the move into WFH occurred rapidly. But, due to pandemic vagaries and expected business benefits, organizations are in no hurry to move out of WFH. Given similar/greater productivity with potential cost savings compared to work from office, many large employers across industries intend to make WFH a standard, long-term practice (e.g., Bhattacharyya & Verma, 2020).

With this fast, exuberant embrace of long-term WFH by employers, it becomes important to pause and examine the viewpoint of employees—the core affected party and instrumental to sustaining new ways of working. Employees have been provided information & communication technologies (ICT) (Livemint, 2020) to continue the same tasks as before from a place of presumable personal comfort—home. Yet, concerns have surfaced (e.g., Chakrabarti, 2020). Thus, WFH must be scrutinized not just for tools, tasks, or productivity/cost benefits, but also employee psychological consequences. However, over the years, most global and Indian research on WFH (e.g., Arora & Suri, 2020; Bathini & Kandathil, 2015; Bloom, Liang, Roberts, & Ying, 2015; Shamir & Salomon, 1985) tend largely to cover its (dis)advantages but not implications for individuals' basic psychological needs, and thereby wellbeing. Scarce works that do cover WFH explicitly/implicitly from basic psychological needs standpoint (e.g., Gajendran & Harrison, 2007; Orsini & Rodrigues, 2020) seldom explore long-term consequences, particularly when WFH may be involuntary.

Thus, there remains a need to understand short- and long-term outcomes of WFH from a psychological perspective for employees of varied industries, given for many WFH has already stretched into several months and may extend further, irrespective of personal choice.

In this context, this paper aims to present WFH implications for Indian white-collars in relation to productivity-driven preference of work location. Employers note productivity gains as a motivator for preferring home as work location. Employees too will likely prefer a work location that makes them feel competent and productive. This motivation to achieve competence is the psychological need for competence (NFC) identified under Self-Determination Theory (SDT). Through the perspective of NFC, this work seeks to answer:

- Do employees feel competent under WFH?
- What determines employees' feeling of competence under WFH?
- Given employees' feeling competent/incompetent under WFH, what is the effect on worker's short- and long-term wellbeing?
- How can WFH be made a win-win for employers and employees?

NEED FOR COMPETENCE AND WORK FROM HOME

According to the Job Demands-Resource Model (JD-R), job demands (JDs) are job aspects that require physical/mental effort and strain workers, while job resources (JRs) are aspects that help achieve work goals and lead to wellbeing, including by reducing strain (Schaufeli & Taris, 2014). However, JD-R describes which JDs-JRs may lead to certain outcomes but not the psychological mechanisms of how JDs-JRs affect outcomes such as wellbeing (Schaufeli & Taris, 2014). Knowing how helps appreciate why despite ICT and other JRs, WFH may not be rewarding. Hence, this work leverages SDT's concept of psychological need fulfilment.

SDT recognizes three basic, inborn psychological needs whose satisfaction/thwarting results in wellbeing/illbeing; viz. the need for autonomy or choice in activity, need for relatedness or interpersonal connectedness, and NFC (Ryan & Deci, 2000).

NFC is a person's need to feel effective at current tasks (task-referential competence [TRC]), improve skills over time (past-referential competence [PRC]), and prove competence versus others competitively (other-referential competence [ORC]) (Elliot, McGregor, & Thrash, 2002). NFC thus concerns present task execution also long-term career prospects. Need satisfaction drives wellbeing, such as job satisfaction (Van den Broeck, Vansteenkiste, De Witte, Soenens, & Lens, 2010). In turn, JDs-JRs affect NFC satisfaction (Van den Broeck *et al.*, 2010). Work location, e.g., home in WFH, can affect NFC satisfaction (Gerdenitsch, 2017) by affecting JDs-JRs, such as limiting access to some JRs.

Task Characteristics

Employee homes, unlike employer premises, are not necessarily primed for best possible task execution. Hence, task characteristics are critical to WFH success (Beauregard, Basile, & Canonico, 2019; Guimaraes & Dallow, 1999; Limburg, 1998). Are tasks feasible for WFH, including long term WFH? Tasks that are routine, well-defined, with little need for people-connect likely suit WFH, while those needing frequent or unscheduled in-person interactions and special facilities available only at office (Guimaraes & Dallow, 1999; Limburg, 1998) may not be performed competently from home. Hence, the proposition:

- Tasks that are predictable, clearly stated, or scarcely requiring in-people interactions can satisfy NFC in WFH. Tasks that need special facilities or frequent/spontaneous in-people interactions can frustrate NFC in WFH.

Job Resources

JRs may be "physical, social, or organizational" and include performance feedback, peer and supervisor support, also professional development opportunities (Schaufeli & Taris, 2014). JRs affect task execution, growth, and development (Schaufeli & Taris, 2014) thereby NFC satisfaction, while WFH affects JR availability/adequacy.

Technology Infrastructure: Organizations quickly deployed ICT resources (Livemint, 2020) for COVID lockdown, ICT being fundamental to enabling WFH (Arora & Suri, 2020; Beauregard *et al.*, 2019). But available may not mean adequate for NFC satisfaction. E.g., ICT's limitations in conveying non-verbal cues (Duxbury & Neufeld, 1999) may make ICT-based communication under WFH frustrating for NFC. ICT availability itself may be hampered by electricity and internet challenges in India (Arora & Suri, 2020). Hence, the proposition:

- ICT is necessary but not sufficient to satisfy NFC in WFH

Workplace Characteristics: No/low commute and fewer distractions could assuage JDs, such as time pressure and cognitive demands, respectively. WFH eliminates travel to reduce stress and boost productivity but presents more distractions due to family/household needs (Guimaraes & Dallow, 1999). Hence, the proposition:

- Commute time savings directed to task execution satisfies NFC in WFH. But distractions at home frustrates NFC in WFH

Colleague Support: Colleagues are approached spontaneously for aiding task execution (Schaufeli & Taris, 2014), even skill development. But WFH's ICT-based working limits spontaneous outreach and relationship building within teams (Bernstein, Blunden, Brodsky, Sohn, & Waber, 2020), thus frustrating NFC. Hence, the proposition:

- Virtual-only colleague interactions as possible from home frustrate NFC in WFH

Supervisor Support: Supervisor's trust, guidance, communication of expectations, and feedback help WFH succeed (Beauregard et al., 2019; Guimaraes & Dallow, 1999) and satisfy employee NFC (Legault, 2017; Orsini & Rodrigues, 2020). Shared circumstances of COVID-lockdown may have made supervisors more tolerant and enabling, even as they struggle with own tasks (Singer-Velush, Sherman, & Anderson 2020). Hence, the proposition:

- Supervisors with empathy from own WFH experience help satisfy team's NFC when WFH. But with people-centric task characteristics, supervisors find own NFC frustrated when WFH.

Learning Opportunities: Challenging tasks help learn and improve, thus satisfy NFC (Legault, 2017). Coaching and mentoring are other powerful learning mechanisms. But WFH can mean lesser access to challenging work and coaching/mentoring (Cooper & Kurland, 2002; Raghuram, London, & Larsen, 2001). Hence, the proposition:

- Limited learning opportunities frustrates NFC in WFH

Performance Appraisal: Performance appraisal combines JRs of "receiving performance feedback" and "opportunity to participate in decision-making" (Farndale, 2017). Proving competence at appraisal satisfies need for ORC, with appraisal being a situation of "interpersonal competition" (Grubb, 2007). But WFH may reduce visibility, hence chances at appraisal and advancement (Challenger, 1992), thus frustrating NFC. Hence, the proposition:

- Limited visibility or opportunities to demonstrate competence frustrates NFC when WFH

Effect of Individual Characteristics

Individual characteristics could determine who feels enabled/frustrated, hence invigorated/stressed, by which aspect of WFH and to what extent. Gender may be an especially significant characteristic. In India or where "traditional norms on gender roles are prevalent," flexi-work such as WFH would increase women's domestic burden (Chung & van der Lippe, 2020) leading to greater work interruptions for them. Hence, the proposition:

- Women more likely struggle with family intrusion into work, finding NFC frustrated in WFH

Short- and Long-Term Employee Wellbeing

Basic need satisfaction/frustration leads to wellbeing/illbeing (Ryan & Deci, 2000). This study investigates NFC satisfaction/frustration's impact on short- and long-term stress and long run career anxieties under WFH. In short-term, state of current task execution and related determinants (e.g., task characteristics) were anticipated to affect wellbeing. In long-term too, task execution would likely continue affecting NFC, thereby wellbeing. Hence, the proposition:

- In short-term and long-term, task execution enablement/challenges would satisfy/ frustrate TRC to trigger wellbeing/illbeing when WFH.

In long run, factors such as skill development and career growth and their related determinants (e.g., coaching and visibility) were also expected to affect wellbeing. Since WFH can adversely affect access to challenging assignments, learning, and visibility (Challenger, 1992; Cooper & Kurland, 2002; Raghuram *et al.*, 2001), the proposition:

- In long-term, limited learning opportunities would frustrate PRC and limited opportunities to demonstrate capabilities would frustrate ORC to trigger illbeing when WFH.

METHODOLOGY

To investigate short and long-term implications of WFH on employee wellbeing through NFC satisfaction/frustration and provide recommendations, this paper employed a small pilot study.

Sample Selection

Since white-collars under WFH during COVID-lockdown were being studied, individuals were chosen from urban Indian middle-class, the group most representative of white-collars (Sridhar, 2004). Diversity of gender, role, and industries was sought for diversity of circumstances. Married persons were selected to comprehend domestic responsibilities' effect. Researchers first approached personal contacts (convenience), then requested them for additional connections (snowballing). Total 25 persons were approached.

Data Capture

Open-ended questions were emailed from late-May (2 months into COVID-lockdown) through end-June 2020. WFH was explored as experienced before and during COVID, also as expected under potential compulsory long-term WFH post-COVID. Questions probed major job tasks; ICT support availability and satisfaction; task performance ease and satisfaction; supervisor attitude and behaviour towards respondent's WFH; experience/ expectation of impact to assignments, skill development, and career growth; and experience/ expectation of stress. Respondents also shared suggestions/views on WFH, including compulsory WFH.

Data Set

Of 25 persons emailed, 2 did not respond. Final sample of 23 consisted of 9 females and 14 males, with 6 aged 25-35 years, 14 aged 36-45 years, and 3 aged above 45 years. Five held bachelor's degree only, while 16 held master's degree and 2 doctoral. Eighteen were parents, while 5 were not. Ten were employed in IT, 5 in manufacturing, 4 in business services (BS), and 1 each in financial services (FS), government, hospitality, and utility. Fifteen were in core revenue-generating functions, while 8 were in support. By role, 4 were staff/individual contributors (S/ICs), while 2, 10, and 7 were in junior management (JM), middle management (MM), and senior management (SM), respectively. Pre-COVID, for 10 WFH was disallowed, 10 could WFH as/when needed, and 3 were under extended WFH by personal choice.

Regarding 17 respondents quoted verbatim in the paper, in terms of name code, role, function, and industry: Female1 is in MM, core function, and IT industry; Female2—MM, core, manufacturing; Female3—JM, support, BS; Female4—MM, support, IT; Female5—S/IC, support, IT; Female6—S/IC, core, IT; Female7—SM, support, IT; Female8—MM, core, IT; Male1—SM, core, IT; Male2—SM, core, FS; Male3—MM, support, manufacturing; Male4—MM, core, government; Male5—SM, core, IT; Male6—JM, support, BS; Male7—MM, core, BS; Male8—S/IC, core, IT; and Male9—MM, core, utility.

FINDINGS

Task Characteristics

Study confirmed that routine tasks with little need for people-connect were WFH-suitable. E.g., Male1: "WFH looks possibly good when the routine is fixed and the activities are defined." Also, Female1: "Individual contributor roles can be easily fulfilled in a WFH situation." But tasks reliant on people-connect and special facilities were WFH-unsuitable. E.g., Male2: "Couldn't do a major part of my job – meet people." And Male3: "Difficult to do collaborative work in WFH environment." Also, Female2: "It is impacting my annual commitments and target because labs, equipment and hardware is important for my team to develop products."

Job Resources

Technology Infrastructure: Pilot study found available employer-provided ICT resources were satisfying NFC for now. E.g., Female3: "Yes, I have all the infrastructure needed. Our organization, since March has started disbursing Rs.1000 additionally into salaries towards sustaining a good internet connection." Yet, ICT was insufficient for some tasks. For example, Male2: "Meeting on Zoom is still not as good as meeting in person." Internet issues hampering JR availability were also confirmed—Male4: "there was no internet connectivity on the day when I had to present something…"

Workplace Characteristics: Commute time savings did boost productivity under WFH for some—e.g., Male4: "it did increase my productivity as there was no travel involved." But many preferred office for ease and low distraction. E.g., Female4: "work can be little faster and easier when we work from office." Also, Female5: "office would always score better because workplace allows that focus to be there on the work. There are no major distractions."

Colleague Support: Challenges to colleague interactions under WFH's virtual-only functioning was confirmed, which frustrated NFC for task execution and learning. E.g., Male3: "miss hallway conversation and chit-chats with team and peers which many time leads to innovative solutions." And Female4: "office give you different prospect of learning and develop other social and professional skill which we learn when we personally meet our team."

Supervisor Support: Respondents affirmed supervisor empathy following COVID's shared WFH experience. E.g., Female2: "His attitude towards WFH is more open and welcoming than before. He has understood the need of the hour and is WFH himself. Very cooperative and respects everyone's personal commitments." But supervisors can struggle with own NFC under WFH, given their people-centric tasks. E.g., Male5 (a supervisor): "Actually, during WFH there were several instances where situations can be handled much better when in office. Proper coordination, tracking of subordinate work, clearing doubts/confusion, making a common consensus is a lot easier." To retain effectiveness in WFH, supervisors may overcompensate, stifling the team—Male6: "team check-ins have doubled" and Male1: "more tight co-ordination due to virtual status, which induces a feeling for tight monitoring."

Learning Opportunities: Study confirmed that along with learning via peer interactions, learning-by-doing can also get limited under WFH, thus frustrating NFC. E.g., Male7: "The guys present in office do get to work on more proposals at hand." Also, Male5: "There are more opportunities to explore/refine/excel when personally in office."

Performance Appraisal: WFH, especially long-term WFH, was confirmed to limit visibility and opportunities to demonstrate achievements, thwarting NFC. E.g., Female5: "When one is WFH most of the time, visibility in the organization could become a challenge. One's interaction with the larger audience (higher management) in the organization may get limited. This may result in someone else taking away the credit."

Effect of Individual Characteristics

Women were confirmed to be more likely to mention domestic distractions in WFH. E.g., Female1: "when you are at home, toddler expects you to spend time with him/her while you have work commitments on your mind all the time." Also, Female5: "sometimes, I am not able to focus on work if my kid is cranky or clingy."

Short- and Long-Term Employee Wellbeing

Short-Term Wellbeing: Study confirmed that mostly, stress in short-term was related to TRC. And task characteristics, ICT, and workplace environment satisfied/frustrated NFC to influence stress. E.g., **Feasible task:** Male8, an "individual contributor" with "minimal client interaction," said that "I fulfil [tasks] efficiently, and my peers/supervisor are satisfied" and "WFH during COVID has proven beneficial for my body and mind ... No stress!" **Less feasible task:** Male2 could not meet people, a major part of his job, and experienced "More stress than before. Somehow felt lesser in control even though was working longer." **Temporarily deficient ICT:** Female3 noted "Mostly, I didn't feel really stressed. Only a few times, due to network issues, things might have taken a little longer or due to network, a call might have been disrupted," when WFH. **Deficient work environment:** "WFH is stressful when one has to attend to family chores as well as work deliverables at the same time. This is especially applicable to women colleagues who have small kids," noted Female5, mother to toddler.

For short-term stress, beyond TRC, Male7 unexpectedly raised issues of ORC—virtual work hindered proving utility, driving anxiety. Male7: "constant anxiety of being available and accessible either online or on phone … constant fear among employees of proving that they are doing something useful, remaining visible and contributing to the organisation."

Long-Term Wellbeing: Stress

Study found WFH meant less stress for many. Such individuals likely felt their TRC satisfied from home, with tasks being feasible or JRs manageable. E.g., "I believe stress levels will be less," noted Female6, who mentioned, "my physical presence at work is not necessary." And "I love WFH … because I save time and energy both while WFH. Also able to take care of my family even if I am at work," stated Female4, who fulfilled tasks easily under WFH.

But those with TRC frustrated under long-term WFH would stress. E.g., "More stressed as work would suffer and household tasks would increase," felt Male2 who could not fulfil a major part of his job—meeting people, when WFH. Interestingly, some expected stress under long-term WFH because of monotony. E.g., Female7: "So far it [WFH] is not so long, so seems good, in the later period, there may be some feeling of monotonous activities may creep in."

Long-Term Wellbeing: Career Concerns

Career concerns from potential frustration of PRC and ORC due to assignment, skill development, and growth challenges were explored. Nine of 23 responders felt that long-term WFH would not impact their assignments, another 4 were unsure. Remaining 10 felt that assignments, as well as skill development and career growth would be impacted. Skilling and growth concerns surfaced even among some not expecting assignments to be affected. For instance, Male9: "long term WFH will not affect my assignments. But long-term WFH will certainly affect my skill development and career growth." Also, Male4: "It might affect the type of tasks assigned. It might also affect the learning of skills that usually happen when you sit across each other face to face." And Male3: "I guess it will impact growth as your networking abilities reduces." Additionally, Male5: "Until everyone is practicing WFH, it does make a difference to the task/assignment/opportunities one is provided with. In long term it may result in role/designation change or may be termination."

DISCUSSION AND IMPLICATIONS

WFH is likely to remain for a notable percentage of white-collars across industries in India and abroad. While employers have rapidly deployed ICT to enable WFH under lockdown, productive long-term WFH will likely need ensuring employee wellbeing. This study identified determinants of short- and long-term worker wellbeing in the context of productivity under WFH. The work combined JD-R and SDT to explore how various task characteristics and JRs affected NFC satisfaction/frustration to influence stress and long-term career anxiety.

Stress was largely influenced by TRC, hence by task characteristics and JRs of ICT and work environment. Routine, well-defined tasks with little need for in-person contact were WFH-feasible—concurring with Guimaraes and Dallow (1999) and Limburg (1998)—hence satisfied TRC to limit short- and long-term stress. For some, routine monotony may trigger long-term stress; as Legault (2017) notes, "boring or easy" thwarts development hence PRC.

Meanwhile, ICT was necessary, confirming previous works (Arora & Suri, 2020; Beauregard *et al.*, 2019). But ICT was not always sufficient for NFC satisfaction in WFH, such as for communication, similar to prior noted full-time teleworkers' communication challenges (Ramsower, 1985 as cited in Duxbury & Neufeld, 1999). ICT was also not always available due to internet hiccups, confirming Arora and Suri (2020). And domestic demands made low-distraction work environment elusive in WFH, confirming Guimaraes and Dallow (1999).

For long-term career anxiety related to improving and proving competence, JRs of colleague interactions, learning opportunities, supervisory support, and performance appraisal were important for satisfying/frustrating PRC and ORC. Virtual-only colleague interactions were suboptimal for developing select skills, aligning with Cooper and Kurland's (2002) finding that telework limited learning. WFH also restricted experiential learning via challenging assignments, consistent with prior research (Raghuram *et al.*, 2001).

Meanwhile, empathy from shared lockdown WFH experience have made supervisors tolerant and enabling, confirming Singer-Velush et al. (2020). But performance appraisal mechanisms still valuing visibility to prove competence frustrate NFC in WFH. Previous works (Bloom *et al.*, 2015; Challenger, 1992; Lamond, 2000) affirm WFH can limit visibility, thereby adversely affect career advancement prospects. Notably, lack of visibility, thus challenges in proving utility, also contributed to short-term stress according to one study respondent.

RECOMMENDATIONS

Employee wellbeing drives productivity (Ward, De Neve, & Krekel, 2019). In turn, employee wellbeing can increase with employers helping workers be productive i.e., satisfy their NFC. With several employers considering extending WFH post-COVID, it is important to identify how they can help satisfy employees' NFC at home. Rapid deployment of ICT addressed immediate needs under lockdown. But long-term WFH success requires deliberating upon task characteristics, supervisor support, learning opportunities, and appraisal mechanisms.

Task Characteristics

Well-defined tasks with little need for people-connect suit WFH, confirmed by this study and previous works (Guimaraes & Dallow, 1999; Limburg, 1998). Conversely, tasks involving ambiguity, special facilities, and frequent interpersonal connect suit the office. E.g., as Male1 shared: "unplanned tasks or future research cannot be carried out in continuous WFH" with research requiring "office premises with collaboration." Organizations may need to evaluate tasks' WFH-suitability basis current/imminent technological feasibility, as well as "social, psychological, and business needs" (Mokhtarian & Salomon,1994). But choosing some tasks hence teams for WFH, may create "primary" (office) versus "secondary" (home) groups, where "secondary" receive lesser job security, training, and advancement opportunities (Shamir & Salomon, 1985). And often, WFH tasks are female-dominated, hence women risk becoming "secondary" (Shamir & Salomon, 1985). Such equity concerns may be addressed through JRs.

Job Resources

Anxieties concerning long-term career prospects may be assuaged via learning opportunities and reimagined performance appraisal and supervisor support. Interpersonal skills built via in-person team interactions was identified multiple times in the study as important but unattainable over tele-exchanges. Such learning may be provided through periodic in-office presence. As Female8 suggests: "Restrict the number of [WFH] days for a week … This will ensure at least few team members (not all again) can rely on direct interactions than virtual."

Office visits may also address WFH's visibility concerns (Lamond, 2000), which likely affects chances at performance appraisal. However, appraisal fairness may be better achieved not through greater virtual/physical visibility, but through JR of goal clarity (Schaufeli & Taris, 2014) or clear, measurable expectations in view of WFH constraints. As Male7 suggests: "I think the stress level will go down if there are clearly define KRAs taken into considerations the WFH environment and the employee is clear what needs to be achieved."

Shifting from visibility to measurable value may require a new kind of supervisor support based on trust and avoiding bias. As previous works (Beauregard *et al.*, 2019; Guimaraes & Dallow, 1999) and study respondent Female4 suggest, "Trust your employee." Invisible workers are not necessarily shirkers. Meanwhile, biases were noted about supervisors' attitude on respondents' choosing extended WFH pre-COVID. E.g., Female3: "I feel that my career also became stagnant due to this [extended WFH] as I was not considered for career progressions, award etc. There is a subtle bias that is difficult to observe here." Similarly, Female1: "It is not easy as there is an inherent bias in the minds of supervisors and peers but with time people have adjusted." Such biases may arise from traditional notions about women leveraging flexi-work to focus on household (Chung & van der Lippe, 2020). Training interventions may help supervisors adopt egalitarian outlooks for the new normal of WFH.

Trust-based, unbiased, and objective supervision and appraisal gain more significance when extended WFH is implemented not as team directive but individual choice. In their absence, WFH may remain underutilized, with employees equating growth with office alone.

CONCLUSION, LIMITATIONS, AND FUTURE RESEARCH

Numerous Indian white-collar employees are under WFH due to COVID. Several employers intend retaining WFH as a standard practice for a significant percentage of their employee-base even post-pandemic, for potential productivity and cost benefits. Most previous studies on WFH pros and cons have not explored WFH's implications for basic psychological needs that substantially influence employee wellbeing. The scarce works that do explore WFH in the context of basic psychological needs seldom consider long-term significance.

In this context, this paper makes multiple contributions. It focuses on India, which has been relatively less researched for WFH, and captures employee voices from diverse industries and with varying degrees of previous WFH exposure. This work explores how WFH may satisfy/frustrate the basic psychological need for competence to drive employee wellbeing/illbeing in the short and long term. The study demonstrates the impact of different task characteristics and JRs on NFC satisfaction, then makes practical recommendations for a win-win WFH experience. Gendered perspectives have also been consciously included.

The paper's reliance on cross-section data, that too from a small convenience sample is its main limitation, which also presents opportunities for future works. A larger, more diverse pool of employees followed over an extended period would potentially yield better insights. Close exploration of a single industry may also offer unique perspectives and targeted recommendations. Furthermore, a quantitative study, leveraging established instruments may help statistically test the propositions. Works may also develop the concepts of short-term and long-term worker wellbeing under WFH as distinct constructs.

REFERENCES

Arora, P., & Suri, D. (2020). "Redefining, relooking, redesigning, and reincorporating HRD in the post Covid 19 context. *Human Resource Development, 23*(4), 438–451.

Bathini, D. R., & Kandathil, G. (2015). Work from Home: A Boon or a Bane? The Missing Piece of Employee Cost. *Indian Journal of Industrial Relations, 50*(4), 568–574.

Beauregard, T., Basile, K. A., & Canonico, E. (2019). Telework: Outcomes and facilitators for employees. In R. N. Landers (Ed.), *The Cambridge Handbook of Technology and Employee Behavior* (pp. 511–543). Cambridge University Press.

Bernstein, E., Blunden, H., Brodsky, A., Sohn, W., & Waber, B. (2020, July 15). The Implications of Working Without an Office. *Harvard Business Review*. Retrieved from https://hbr.org/2020/07/the-implications-of-working-without-an-office

Bhattacharyya, R., & Verma, P. (2020, April 3). *Work-from-home going to stay, even after Covid-19 scare is over. The Economic Times*. Retrieved July 6, 2020, from https://tech. economictimes.indiatimes.com/news/corporate/work-from-home-going-to-stay-even-after-covid-19-scare-is-over/74958787

Bloom, N., Liang, J., Roberts, J., & Ying, Z. J. (2015). Does Working from Home Work? Evidence from a Chinese Experiment. *Quarterly Journal of Economics, 130*(1), 165–218.

Chakrabarti, A. (2020, April 8). *Not a win-win situation — why we should not work from home after the Covid-19 lockdown. The Print*. Retrieved from https://theprint.in/opinion/pov/not-a-win-win-situation-why-we-should-not-work-from-home-after-the-covid-19-lockdown/397284/

Challenger, J. E. (1992). Telecommuters Risk Becoming Invisible Workers. *Management World, 20*(1), 8–10.

Chung, H., & van der Lippe, T. (2020). Flexible Working, Work–Life Balance, and Gender Equality: Introduction. *Social Indicators Research, 151*(2), 365–381.

Cooper, C. D., & Kurland, N. B. (2002). Telecommuting, professional isolation, and employee development in public and private organizations. *Journal of Organizational Behavior, 23*(4), 511–532.

Duxbury, L., & Neufeld, D. (1999). An empirical evaluation of the impacts of telecommuting on intra-organizational communication. *Journal of Engineering and Technology Management, 16*(1), 1–28.

Elliot, A. J., McGregor, H. A., & Thrash, T. M. (2002). The Need for Competence. In E. L. Deci, & R. M. Ryan (Eds.), *Handbook of Self-Determination Research* (pp. 361–388). The University of Rochester Press.

Farndale, E. (2017). Two-country study of engagement, supervisors and performance appraisal. *Journal of Asia Business Studies, 11*(3), 342–362.

Gajendran, R. S., & Harrison, D. A. (2007). The Good, the Bad, and the Unknown About Telecommuting: MetaAnalysis of Psychological Mediators and Individual Consequences. *Journal of Applied Psychology, 92*(6), 1524–1541.

Gerdenitsch, C. (2017). New Ways of Working and Satisfaction of Psychological Needs. In C. Korunka, & B. Kubicek (Eds.), *Job Demands in a Changing World of Work* (pp. 91–109). Springer, Cham.

Grubb, T. (2007). Performance Appraisal Reappraised: It's Not All Positive. *Journal of Human Resource Education, 1*(1), 1–22.

Guimaraes, T., & Dallow, P. (1999). Empirically testing the benefits, problems, and success factors for telecommuting programmes. *European Journal of Information Systems, 8*(1), 40–54.

Jayadevan, P. (2020, March 30). *Coronavirus lockdown leads to enterprise-wide working from home (WFH) in India. CIO India.* Retrieved July 6, 2020, from https://www.cio.com/article/3533248/coronavirus-lockdown-leads-to-an-enterprise-wide-work-from-home-wfh-in-india.html

Lamond, D. (2000). Managerial Style and Telework. In K. Daniels, D. Lamond, & P. Standen (Eds.), *Managing Telework* (1st ed., pp. 103–112). Thomson Learning.

Legault, L. (2017). The Need for Competence. In V. Zeigler-Hill, & T. K. Shackelford (Eds.), *Encyclopedia of Personality and Individual Differences.* Springer.

Limburg, D. O. (1998). Teleworking in managerial context. In R. Suomi, P. Jackson, L. Hollmen, & M. Aspnas (Ed.), *Teleworking Environments: Proceedings of the Third International Workshop of Telework. TUCS General Publication No. 8*, pp. 93–106. Turku, Finland: Turku Center for Computer Science.

Livemint. (2020, April 3). *Laptop sales surge in India as employees work from home during lockdown.* Retrieved July 8, 2020, from https://www.livemint.com/companies/news/laptop-sales-surge-in-india-as-employees-work-from-home-during-lockdown-11585902958056.html

Mokhtarian, P. L., & Salomon, I. (1994). Modeling the Choice of Telecommuting: Setting the Context. *Environment and Planning A: Economy and Space, 26*(5), 749–766.

Orsini, C., & Rodrigues, V. (2020). Supporting motivation in teams working remotely: The role of basic psychological needs. *Medical Teacher, 42*(7), 828–829.

Raghuram, S., London, M., & Larsen, H. H. (2001). Flexible employment practices in Europe: country versus culture. *International Journal of Human Resource Management, 12*(5), 738–753.

Ryan, R. M., & Deci, E. L. (2000). Self-determination theory and the facilitation of intrinsic motivation, social development, and well-being. *American Psychologist, 55*(1), 68–78.

Schaufeli, W. B., & Taris, T. W. (2014). A Critical Review of the Job Demands-Resources Model: Implications for Improving Work and Health. In G. F. Bauer, & O. Hämmig (Eds.), *Bridging occupational, organizational and public health: A transdisciplinary approach* (pp. 43–68). Springer.

Shamir, B., & Salomon, I. (1985). Work-at-Home and the Quality of Working Life. *Academy of Management Review, 10*(3), 455–464.

Singer-Velush, N., Sherman, K., & Anderson, E. (2020, July 15). Microsoft Analyzed Data on Its Newly Remote Workforce. *Harvard Business Review*. Retrieved from https://hbr.org/2020/07/microsoft-analyzed-data-on-its-newly-remote-workforce

Sridhar, E. (2004). The Growth and Sectoral Composition of India's Middle Class: Its Impact on the Politics of Economic Liberalization. *India Review, 3*(4), 405–428.

Van den Broeck, A., Vansteenkiste, M., De Witte, H., Soenens, B., & Lens, W. (2010). Capturing autonomy, competence, and relatedness at work: Construction and initial validation of the Work-related Basic Need Satisfaction scale. *Journal of Occupational and Organizational Psychology, 83*(4), 981–1002.

Ward, G., De Neve, J.-E., & Krekel, C. (2019, July 18). It's official: happy employees mean healthy firms. World Economic Forum and LSE Business Review. Retrieved July 8, 2020, from https://www.weforum.org/agenda/2019/07/happy-employees-and-their-impact-on-firm-performance/

Integration of Artificial Intelligence Into Human Resources: Challenges and Scope

Shreya Srivastava
Vibhav Khand, Gomti Nagar, Lucknow
(U.P.), India
ss4@somaiya.edu

Oamkaar Sadarangani
19th Road, Khar, Mumbai
oamkaar.s@somaiya.edu

Abstract

Technological innovations are an integral part of our lives- as individuals, or organizations. Like any new idea, the advent of Artificial Intelligence (AI) into the field of Human Resources has the world divided into: the supporters, the skeptics, and the opposers. Through this conceptual paper, the researchers address the myths surrounding the integration of AI into the HR processes, the need for reinvention, the underlying challenges, and the opportunity costs of not moving with the times. We talk about the need for a transfiguration of mindset from 'Humans v/s Machines' to 'Humans with Machines', cite relevant, real-life instances of AI in HR, and the need for a personalized AI-HR system in each organization. The paper will focus on the benefits of applying real-time analytics to key performance indicators, automation of repetitive tasks through Machine Learning, automation in talent acquisition and retention, employee engagement through AI, the use of machine intelligence to replicate and augment human understanding, et al. The researchers also address the inevitable replacement of the human workforce because of this automation, in contrast with the infinite opportunities and avenues it opens up. The resistance to change is an emotion that has no place in today's dynamic and ever-changing organizations, and we seek to prove, through this paper, that there is no reason to resist this particular change, either. Although, the real-life application of AI will point towards a structural shift in workforce and reskilling would be the need of the hour.

Keywords: Artificial Intelligence, Human Resources, Real-time Analytics, Machine Learning, Automation, Structural shift

1. INTRODUCTION

1.1 About AI

Artificial Intelligence (AI) is a school of thought, a science, a field of study; it is a process so vast and convoluted with wider interpretations, that the term hasn't accepted a unified definition of itself. At its core however, AI is merely the use of computer algorithms to calculate and qualify parameters too vast or numerous for a human to quantify without help. At the risk of undermining, AI is technology that exhibits behavior generally associated with humans such as abstract pattern matching, knowledge gathering and insight assembly. At its crux, it emphasizes on machines emulating human intelligence to achieve a task. What sets AI apart from regular analytics is that it is capable of learning on its own once a model is built, as opposed to humans feeding data and writing algorithms for every set of parameters. AI is able to apply past experience and cluster matching to current situations and with a reasonable degree of accuracy predict outcomes. The emphasis is on 'intelligence' because the machines accomplish tasks that would require humans to display and exhibit intelligence, previously known to be a human thing.

Alien as the term may sound, AI is pervasive in modern human life. From speech recognition to spam filters, from the friendly "bot" Alexa to product suggestions based on your buying history, and to Tesla's automated cars; narrow AI has taken the human world by storm and it continues to do so in fields never thought of before. Even in Human Resource Management, narrow AI is used in employee onboarding and recruitment processes by consultancy firms and other companies that value efficiency. What we refer to as AI in this paper, however, includes Machine Learning using models and pattern mapping using Neural Networks

1.2 Opportunity Costs of Not Integrating With AI

History is our witness, at the dawn of every technological revolution, there have been masses that cried out wolf, predicting to be replaced by technology. But again, history is our witness; human civilization has come out on the other side, better equipped, with advanced skills, and more opportunities to take on the world. It is to be noted that AI, like any other technology, will contribute to growth and development of the world, and create more job opportunities than it disrupts. There will be obsolescence, but not of humans, of skills, which is why, reskilling would be the need of the hour. We will be looking at a structural shift, a new wave of opportunities, and the only way to not drown would be to go with the flow.

That being said, we map the opportunities forfeited, associated with not moving with the times. When organizations choose to not apply AI processes in their organizational structure and their conduct of business operations, they lose out on the chance to streamline their processes and grow and expand into the market. AI no longer remains an option, but is proving to be an imperative that companies have to get on terms with. Not doing so has strong opportunity costs involved:

a) There will be a disequilibrium of information in the market, because the organizations who have adapted to the newer technology would have more knowledge (also known as insights gathered through relevant information), which may lead to an intellectual monopoly. Organizations as mammoth as Amul have been known to not have an allocation in the name of innovation. Setting out a large budget for AI may not seem wise in such cases but the loss of competitive edge will cost more than AI ever will.

b) A business that is late to an innovation is at the risk of losing its competitive edge in hiring as well as development of Human Resources. Integration of AI with any given process streamlines operations and gives opportunities for real-time analytics and fore vision that aid in better development of this resource.

c) The belief that the return won't be worth the investment is often a cause for hesitation while investing in AI. In reality, wide scale implementation of processes is a mundane investment, much like any other investment in Research and Development activity. And the return on investment is really only limited by the vision of the top-minds of an organization.

1.3 AI in Human Resources

As previously stated, AI is finding practical applications in all the spheres of the world. And yet, there seems to be the looming question of 'To AI or not to AI'. Resistance to change is an emotion that has no place in a dynamic organization, and it needs to be addressed whether this hesitation is warranted or not. A 2020 survey by Oracle and Future Workplace exhibited that Human Resource (HR) practitioners conceded that integration of AI into HR would simplify the processes and reduce the time and labor quotient associated with the workaday routines. However, the resistance stemmed from the fact that they had a hard time keeping up with the technological changes, which takes nothing away from the relevance of the aforementioned integration, but forces the organizations to take a long and hard look at their structural reforms. It is the willingness to readily accept changes and make implementation of newer, better technologies that sets great organizations apart.

It is evident that AI will have multifold implications and opportunities in the field of HR, and it would behoove HR professionals around the globe to familiarize themselves with the process, and begin to understand the technology as well as the need for upskilling to remain relevant in the face of an innovational revolution. The very first step of acceptance would be a change of mindset from 'Humans v/s Machines' to 'Humans with Machines'. For an HR practitioner, it would be nothing less than a blessing to automate mundane processes, so that the majority of the efforts are directed towards a higher form of Human Resource Management. The authors would like to point out that Outsourcing, which is a practice now common in every organization, was brought to life in consistency with the Core Competence theory, which propagated the view that organizations should outsource all mundane jobs outside the business, and focus on doing what the company does the best. Well, the integration of AI may be seen as an evolved and more specialized version of that theory, where every sphere in an organization can outsource its workaday job in the name of technology, and focus on analyzing, interpreting, and forecasting to propagate the growth and development needs on a macro level.

1.4 Machine Learning in Human Resource Management

"Machine learning (ML) is the study of computer algorithms that improve automatically through experience. It is seen as a subset of artificial intelligence. Machine learning algorithms build a model based on sample data, known as 'training data', in order to make predictions or decisions without being explicitly programmed to do so." Machine Learning is all around us. It is imperative to point out that while Machine Learning and Artificial Intelligence are widely used interchangeably, Machine Learning is a part of Artificial Intelligence. To quote real-life examples, ML is being used by companies by feeding them data of customer engagement and deriving analysis and interpretation as well as predictions and forecasts about their behavioral patterns. In the field of Human Resources, Machine

Learning is being used to screen and narrow down prospective applicants as well as to match job descriptions with suitable applicants. The benefit in application is feeding the machine huge amounts of data and picking patterns that would not fall under the cognitive capabilities of humans, while the human touch is reserved for relationship-building and providing personalized services.

In Human Resource processes, this model would mean screening prospective applicants' resume and crucial information and matching it against the job description. The system analyses what a certain position requires, and matches these qualities against the application of the prospect. Another use of Machine Learning is survival analysis. In this process, the time taken to fill a job position is analyzed and the probability of it being vacant way past the due date is determined. Inputs from the market are used to arrive at the desired results about factors such as job openings in the given field, and number of applicants looking to fill that position and so on. This helps in identifying the at-risk vacancies and hence, additional resources that can be committed to filling these positions. This ensures a smooth running of the machinery that is an organization. Such analyses are ground-breaking from the point of view of HR professionals, for it gives them the power to nip the problems in the bud. With such innovation solutions to problems specific to the field of Human Resource Management, Artificial Intelligence and Machine Learning are bound to end up as an indispensable tool in the tool-kit of a Human Resource manager.

2. LITERATURE REVIEW

2.1 AI in Human Resource Management

Artificial Intelligence (AI) is completely transforming the ways in which Human Resource functions are carried out. It has seeped its way into our lives to such an extent, that the transition seems to have been drastic, and yet seamless. With implications that can be categorized into basic, intermediate, and advanced, AI is now capable of predicting metrics such as vacations planning, tracking the moods of the employees as well as flight response, i.e. attrition rate. That being said, no technology has ever taken over that did not have its own set of pitfalls. AI is a system that feeds on historical data to identify patterns, and if the data is biased, compromised, or discriminatory, the repercussions would seep into the analysis and hence, the predictions. It is to be noted that AI is an aid to augment human understanding, not replace it, which is why it would be a good idea to exercise discretion that stems out of human cognitive mechanisms. The breakthroughs and groundbreaking accomplishments into the field of Human Resources continue to co-exist, and it is up to the organization to decide what works the best for its strategic requirements. Organizations will have the prerogative to either let the technology pass them by, or to introduce the changes in small, gradual steps, or to revolutionize the entire workflows altogether. (Ahmed, O, 2018)

2.2 Impact of AI in Human Resource Management

AI is taking the world by storm. The Human Resources Organization is no different. Each Human Resource practice, right from recruitment, selection, training and development to employee appraisal, retention, and engagement is being automated with the many applications of AI. Robots, chat bots, Artificial Intelligence infused assistants are taking over every aspect of Human Resource Management. Inevitably, this is inducing fears in the minds of the workforce about being replaced by machines. Considering the effects of AI so far, and its scope in the future, fears about mass employment are also in the cards, which may eventually lead to social unrest. But, it is to be considered here that in the past, every step ahead in the field of technology has only turned out to be a boon for mankind, not only creating infinite opportunities for employment, but also considerably contributing to the overall economic growth of a nation, in terms of Gross Domestic Product (GDP) as well as standard of living. Moreover, resisting change in case of an innovative technology like AI may cause the organizations to lose their competitive edge, thereby making it difficult for them to survive and usher in the new era of innovation. The real challenge would be to witness how well Human Resource Organizations adapt to this era of change, and emerge as leaders in these times, to nurture a population of change-ready workforce. (Matsa, P; Gullamajj, K; 2019)

2.3 Challenges and a Way Forward

Despite AI being all the buzz these days, there is an extent to which it is worth the hype. There are gaps in what it theoretically can be and what it is, in the present. There are certain challenges in the implementation of Artificial Intelligence into Human Resource Management such as the complexity of HR as a function, which makes it difficult to analyze variables objectively. For instance, there are no set parameters for a "job well done"; or, it may be impossible for the efforts of an individual to be extracted and quantified, from a job that largely required a team effort. Also, some tasks may not leave a digital trace, and hence, run the risk of going unnoticed, despite being a set of operations that happened in the backend. Secondly, the data sets that are fed to the machines are not large enough to have reliable sets of patterns. Machine Learning is all about feeding huge sets of data, and picking up patterns that humans cannot. So, availability of small data sets negates the entire process in the first place. Thirdly, there are ethical, moral, and legal implications of collecting and analyzing employee data for the purpose of decision-making. Privacy concerns on the part of the employees may end up creating an unfavorable work-environment, thereby reducing productivity, morale and in the longer run, employee retention. Also, concerns about taking managerial decisions on the basis of algorithms that are not foolproof in the first place may be a cause of resentment in the workforce. (Cappellii, P ; Tambe, P; Yakubovichii, V; 2019)

2.4 Future of AI in Human Resource Management

The integration of AI with HR in no way means that HR will be replaced by AI. The easily repeatable administrative tasks like job posting, creating job descriptions, screening resumes, recording expenses, timesheets, scheduling leaves and interviews will be taken care of through automation, freeing up the HR personnel to create relationships with the employees, invest in long-term strategic thinking, and use creative problem solving for the betterment of the organization. That being said, there will be initial challenges in implementation, which can easily be taken care of, by keeping a unified and futuristic mindset. For instance, provision of data that is skewed will give unreliable results. Hence, making sure that quality data is available for analysis would be a prerequisite. Secondly, organizations need to create an environment that makes their workforce feel comfortable about the usage of their data. Immaculate security and privacy provisions must be made to make sure that the data provided by the employees is used for permissible purposes only, and not handled recklessly. AI may not be foolproof yet, but it is doing a commendable job at eliminating human errors and biases, which is why several organizations are rushing to integrate AI into their HR processes. It has been widely proven that the advantages and opportunities for innovation created by the multifold features of AI will overpower its advantages. Moreover, practice makes perfect, and only by using the AI systems, can we begin to identify the challenges and learn to tackle them. (George, G; Thomas, M R; 2019)

3. AI IN HR PROCESSES AND ITS BENEFITS

Recruitment and Onboarding

Implementation of AI in recruitment streamlines the process for the organization as well as the pool of candidates. AI can be used to create Job descriptions and application forms that are optimized and more applicant-friendly, ensuring that the candidates go through filling the form as well as matching the Job description with the applicant as closely as possible. Recruitment is the stage of inviting applications to form a pool of candidates. AI can be used to better optimize the collected data to match the pooled applications with new openings in the company. With AI chat bots, the applicants or the new employees can have their queries addressed 24*7, without putting an extra pressure on the management or the administration.

Retention

Gone are the days when employees of an organization were considered to be a mere source of manpower. For decades now, Human Resources are being increasingly recognized as the living organism of the workforce. It is because of this reason that it becomes imperative to understand the importance of not only acquiring, but also, retaining workforce in the organization. With the help of AI, the entire system of recognition of employees and seeking feedback can be made objective and automated, which helps in monitoring the overall level of job satisfaction and efficiency without subjective biases. AI can identify elements such as candidates worthy of a promotion, or at risk of attrition. Such inputs can considerably lower costs by reducing turnover, and saving the costs of hiring such as onboarding and training through increased employee retention.

Automation and Engagement

Automation of workaday administrative tasks can considerably reduce the time and effort of HR professionals, leaving them more time for strategy-formulation and policy making. The former tasks, while extremely important in the bigger picture can be easily taken care of by AI integration. These would include screening resumes, designing application forms, scheduling interviews, et al. With these routine tasks taken care of, the HR professionals can contribute to the overall benefit of the workforce by engaging with them, analyzing employee reports, and taking actions for the betterment of the organization.

Training and Development

Training and Development activities of an organization will stand to receive much benefit on account of Training and Development. Instead of modules for the entire organization, AI-based modules can be made available to each employee, tailored to their gaps in skills and knowledge. This will allow the employees to address their individual needs in terms of growth and career plans, and keep them from falling in a rut of obsolescence. Feedback surveys can also be generated, with no human intervention to keep abreast of the sentiments and sensitivities of the workforce. AI chat bots are capable of query resolution about the training and development activities, 24*7, and can keep up with parallel conversations.

Information

Employees count on their HR departments for day-to-day information such as monthly statements of Income, remaining leaves, tax deductions, et al. AI assistants can automate these tasks to be carried out with no human intervention. Through this HR professionals are free from the monotony of repeatable tasks and administrative knowledge bases, and can contribute to the strategic environment of the organization once the AI has been trained in said task.

4. REAL-LIFE INSTANCES OF AI IN HR

According to a 2019 report by Oracle and Future Workplace, 64% of the respondents conceded that they would rather count on the advice of bots to their managers. Integration of AI into Human Resource processes is no more a distant dream, but something that is being accomplished every day.

Digital Resumes

As pointed before, recruitment is largely a process of inviting prospective candidates to form a pool for the current and future job openings. AI is being used to extract the relevant information and store it digitally, as opposed to reentering the same information over and over again, at multiple steps of the process. In this way, the important information is stored to be used over further steps, and gets entered automatically. Screening and matching of resumes with the best possible job descriptions is another way in which AI is making things easier for Human Resource professionals. Careful implementation of this practice ensures that the right candidates get selected for the job position, or Right person for the right job, thereby considerably reducing employee turnover, and aiding employee retention, which in turn, results in cost savings for the organization.

Referrals

AI can develop a deeper understanding of employee referrals by analyzing the success rates of previous recommendations. By doing this, results such as which employee referred the best applicants as well as referrals that stand close to the ones which proved successful in the past can be gained. This kind of automation really frees up the HR professionals from being entangled in mindless, repetitive tasks, and leaves them more time to engage with the employees and gather valuable feedback.

Data-driven Feedback

AI allows for the collection of data straight from the horse's mouth. Suggestions, solutions, and recommendations can be gathered directly from the workforce, and implementation can be personalized accordingly. This enables the management to build a cohesive environment, by providing exactly the environment the workforce asks for. This goes a long way in building morale, creating loyalties, and enhancing employee retention by reducing employee turnover. Better analysis of the data received from the employees is possible through AI, and it also aids with interpreting the feedback received from them.

Conversational AI

AI chat bots have completely changed the conversational experience, by bringing the ease of time and place. Employees can chat with their AI assistants at any time of the day to have their queries addressed, at no extra efforts from the HR professionals. These conversations are then analyzed and interpreted to gain valuable insights about grievances, sentiments, sensitivities, obstacles to productivity and so on. These inputs are real-time insights into the problems of the employees, and such information in the hands of the management can really take the field of Human Resource Management by storm. It can ease the process of appraisals, provide deeper understanding into the training and development needs, and really enhance the morale of motivation of employees by giving them the ease of being heard.

Real-time Analytics

AI can be used to analyze workforce data to predict attrition, productivity and employee involvement and create a personalized desirable work-environment for the employees, thereby improving employee retention. It is also achievable to use AI for real-time scheduling and enable leave requests. This gives the employees the ability and freedom to live a more balanced life, especially those who are supposed to be on the line of defense all the time. Moreover, automation of these tasks gives the HR professionals the ability to direct their time and effort into more productive agendas. It also enables the management to analyze the effects of leaves and absences on the overall functioning of the organization. Having such insights gives a fore vision to predict and identify problems at their roots.

Skill-based Hiring

Skill-based hiring is a new trend in the area of Human Resource acquisitions. Under this, employees are screened and evaluated purely on the basis of their skills, and not academic credentials or relevant experience in the field. This practice is increasingly being adopted by corporate giants to perpetrate the idea of inclusivity and hire relevant talent, despite certain reservations. AI can help organizations in the transition from traditional hiring to skill-based hiring, thereby making sure that the pool of prospective candidates is vast and diverse. AI assistants and bots can also be used to replace the process of testing the individuals on the basis of their skills by analyzing their aptitude, creative thinking, problem-solving and so on.

5. CHALLENGES IN THE IMPLEMENTATION OF AI

Nothing, more specifically, no technology ever comes with no drawbacks. While there are infinite upsides to integrating AI with HR, there can be some challenges in the implementation process.

The Human Touch

While human lives toil away in front of screens, there remains some level of hesitation while conversing with chat bots. Some humans prefer the human touch, and would rather have conversations with an actual person to have their queries resolved. It has been observed that the identical information coming from humans is more believable and comforting than when coming from an AI assistant. The conversational monotone of a bot also drives the users uninterested, for there has to be some gap between a human dialogue, and one with an AI-infused virtual figurine. It is not capable of gauging the wide range of human emotions, and may prove as an ineffective conversationalist.

Questionable Efficiency

Being in the preliminary stage still, AI systems can display flaws and exhibit inconsistent behavior. Firstly, the amount of data available may not be adequate for deep analysis. The data received from recruitment drives and employees is not enough to generate accurate results. Secondly, as a system that functions of steadfast rules, it may rule out the prospective candidates who do not meet the specific requirements, exactly as mentioned in the job description. It may screen according to a stringent set of pre-established standards and even the slightest divergence from those may lead to the candidate not getting shortlisted.

May Still Infuse Human Error

AI feeds on historical data. Machine Learning (ML) is the process of predicting new outcomes on the basis of past patterns, without being programmed to do so. So, if for instance, data predating 10 years is fed to the system, it may identify and pick up certain patterns on its own, despite not having been fed so. In this way, if the past 10 years exhibit a trend of, say, not recruiting people from a certain age group, the system may continue to screen candidates on the basis of this bias.

Job Performance Analysis

AI may prove inefficient in measuring job performance because with the increasingly complex nature of jobs these days, there are no predetermined standards of performing well at a job. Moreover, elements of a job may be impossible to be separated from the efforts of a job, or may not leave a digital footprint. In such cases, it becomes hard to measure performance.

Privacy Concerns

The most crucial factor against the implementation of AI is the privacy and security concern. AI can make use of sensitive data from the employees, which is why it is an imperative on part of the organization to seek permission before extracting data, and making sure that the employees are protected from any breach or invasion of privacy. Appropriate security measures must be taken.

6. CONCLUSION

With a three-step approach of Automating, Augmenting, and Amplifying, AI will continue to find varying applications in various HR processes. While automation has certainly pervaded the spaces by automating routine processes, augmenting (humans and AI coming together to enhance the collective cognitive capabilities and use them for decision-making) and Amplifying (redesigning work processes through AI) will be the next to follow. From using AI to develop insights and strategies (augmenting human understanding) to revolutionizing the processes, we are only limited by our vision to take advantage of the incredible opportunities that wait. It is to be noted that there will be no one-fits-all approach to integrating Artificial Intelligence with Human Resource Management. It will be a prerogative of the organization to work closely with its management and workforce to come up with a personalized AI-HR system, keeping in mind the needs and capabilities of the organization.

That being said, introducing an AI system in the HR organization of a company is not the all-in-one solution to every HR activity. Nevertheless, it is an important tool with various opportunities, and needs to be readily accepted as one. Ensuring that the challenges in implementation do not overpower the entire system is a job that falls on the management and Human Resource organization. Ensuring privacy and transparency, establishing Key Performance Indicators to measure job performance, maintaining databases to feed to the systems so that the patterns identified are genuine and desirable, and constant monitoring for any human biases that may have crept into the machines are some of the measures to ensure that the transition is smooth and seamless. But, it is worthy of a reiteration that abandoning an entire system of innovation because of the fear not being able to keep up is not the spirit of business. There is a need for a shift of mindset from one of hesitation and resistance to one of acceptance and readiness. With this mindset, HR leaders can instill an environment of innovation in the workforce. By accepting automation, the net result of human efforts and capabilities is also bound to rise. It is, therefore, up to us to ready ourselves for the future, the one with machines.

7. REFERENCES

Ahmed, O., December 2018, "ARTIFICIAL INTELLIGENCE IN HR", (E-ISSN 2348-1269, P-ISSN 2349-5138), Volume 5, Issue 4, www.ijrar.org

Berhil,S., Benlahmar, H., Labani, N, April 2020 , "A review paper on artificial intelligence at the service of human resources management", Indonesian Journal of Electrical Engineering and Computer Science, Vol.18, DOI:10.11591/ijeecs.v18.i1.pp32-40, https://cutt.ly/jmY9GSJ

Cappelli, P., Tambe. P, & Yakubovich.V, April 8, 2019, Artificial Intelligence in Human Resources Management: Challenges and a Path Forward, Available at SSRN: http://dx.doi.org/10.2139/ssrn.3263878

Johansson, J, Herranen, S, May 2019 ,"The application of Artificial Intelligence (AI) in Human Resource Management: Current state of AI and its impact on the traditional recruitment process", https://www.diva-portal.org/smash/get/diva2:1322478/FULLTEXT01.pdf

New Study: 60% of people trust a robot more than their manager https://www.oracle.com/corporate/pressrelease/robots-at-work-101519.html

Nicastro D, "7 Ways Artificial Intelligence is Reinventing Human Resources" at https://www.cmswire.com/digital-workplace/7-ways-artificial-intelligence-is-reinventing-human-resources/, accessed on 14 Jan. 2021

O'Connor S.W., "ARTIFICIAL INTELLIGENCE IN HUMAN RESOURCE MANAGEMENT" https://cutt.ly/rmY7Hu3, accessed on 01 Jan, 2021

Steveson, M., "AI IN HR" at https://www.hrexchangenetwork.com/hr-tech/articles/ai-in-hr, accessed on 05 Jan, 2021

Developmental Idiosyncratic Deals and Career Commitment: Mediation Effect of Organization Commitment

Biswa Prakash Jena
HR&OB,BSOM
Birla Global university
Bhubaneswar, India
bjena1990@gmail.com

Dr. Archana Choudhary
HR&OB, BSOM
Birla Global university
Bhubaneswar, India
archana.choudhary@bgu.ac.in

Dr. Manas Kumar Pal
DS & OM, BSOM
Birla Global university
Bhubaneswar, India
manas.pal@bgu.ac.in

Abstract

Purpose: This research paper designed to explore the role of Developmental Idiosyncratic deals on individual employee's career commitment. It also tries to examine the mediation effect of organization commitment between developmental idiosyncratic deals and career commitment, increasing their career commitment and leading to employee retention.

Design: This paper develops a conceptual framework by reviewing the literature available from developmental idiosyncratic deals, organization commitment, and career commitment. The model was empirically tested among executives working across various sector in India.

Findings: The study found that by using developmental idiosyncratic deals, career commitment can be maximized, which will be instrumental in employees' retention. Further, we established that Organization Commitment mediates the relation between developmental idiosyncratic deals and career commitment.

Research implications: This paper provides inference for researchers in the career management area as to how by providing developmental idiosyncratic deals and increasing organizational commitment in the context of social exchange theory, career commitment can be enhanced.

Originality: This paper gives insight into how developmental idiosyncratic deals can positively affect employees› career commitment through organizational commitment. The conceptual model created and empirically tested in one country with limited sample will create opportunities for its empirical testing in other context with larger sample also.

Keywords: Developmental idiosyncratic i-deals; Organization commitment; Career commitment

Paper type: Research Paper

INTRODUCTION

Developmental I-deals (D-Ideals) generate ample opportunities for individuals looking forward to utilizing their abilities and seeking career growth and success (Hornung, Rousseau, et al., 2016). It may actually reinforce the work relationship by enhancing noteworthy individual's commitments such as expanded execution, extra time, and higher responsibility (Hornung et al., 2008). Previous findings on developmental I-deals support organizational commitment for two reasons. To start with, people who opt for developmental I-deals might be especially amped- up for being the one and only one to get uncommon and esteemed assets. These upgraded positive feelings would straightforwardly fortify organizational commitment (Hornung et al., 2008). Second, and all the more important, the grant of developmental idiosyncratic deals may increase individual's trust in their supervisors and strengthen their bond with them (Rousseau et al, 2006). Organizational commitment is considered to be an approach identified with people's attachment to their organization (Allen and Meyer 1990). As previously indicated by scholars, the career-related components of organizational variables are often related to the degree of organizational commitment of the members, and when the employee feels that their organization has proactive career-related practices, their attachment towards the organization gets stronger (Gaertner and Nollen, 1989). Moreover, organizational commitment is the key individual variable that is linked to career commitment (London, 1983). It has also been observed that individuals who are dedicated to their organizations, are additionally dedicated to their careers also (Goulet and Singh, 2002) as organizational chances for advancement might lead to upgrading one's vocation development or get identified with one's own career (Hall, 1971).

Career commitment has been defined as a type of work responsibility that an individual has on his/her career (Morrow, 1993). Hence, it is essential to build up the capacity, as a responsibility towards a career causes one individual to develop specific abilities (cf. Perrow, 1986). People with strong career commitment will show more significant prerequisites and assumptions required by an organization with which they have developed a relationship. It likewise expresses that those profoundly dedicated to their careers are more influenced when their career projection are fulfilled by the organization (E Chang,1999). So, commitment towards an organization should be the key individual variable playing its role in career commitment (London, 1983).

SOCIAL EXCHANGE THEORY

This study is supported by Social Exchange Theory , which is be one of the distinct reasonable ideal models for understanding work environment conduct (Russell et al, 2005). Inside SET, these interactions are generally seen as related and dependent upon someone else's activities (Blau, 1964). Social exchange theory proposes that by giving individuals some specific work plans, the firm creates a reason for correspondence with its workers (Rousseau, 2005). Idiosyncratic deals reinforce the social exchange among supervisors and employees; for example, both adaptability and advancement Idiosyncratic deals relate manager's responsiveness to explicit clear-cut individual employee needs (Rousseau et al., 2009). So, it can be said that developmental Idiosyncratic deals are linked to social exchange theory. When employees opt for developmental I-deals, they know that the organization trusts them and that the employee will try their new abilities/information for the improvement of the organization (Liu et al, 2013). The chance of accomplishing better goals through developmental I-deals additionally ought to actuate the self-improvement framework (Korman, 2001). Developmental I-deals may help the employee in upgrading their skill and contributing towards the organizational performance. (Liu et al,2013). In addition to this, the social exchange way to deal with commitment makes the overall recommendation that individuals feel bound to an element to the degree that it is related to favorable encounters for them (Goode, 1960; Mowday et al., 1982). It appears that in different individual settings, work attributes, work experience, and underlying qualities of the organization can and regularly have an influence in deciding career commitment (Arnold, 1990). Commitment offers a regularly examined result of social exchange, in that individuals apparently ought to fortify their own binds alongside with their organizations via their social exchanges (Eisenberger et al., 2010). When individuals perceive positive cues from the organizational settings, they reciprocate by developing more attachment and commitment towards the company (Liu et al,2013).

THE MEDIATING ROLE OF ORGANIZATIONAL COMMITMENT

According to research, the notion of organizational commitment has been attracting a lot of interest for understanding the factors leading to the stability and the intensity of an employee's dedication to his/her organization (Mester, Visser, Roodt & Kellerman 2003). Organizational commitment is referred to as an attitude related to individuals' stable mindsets that they have for their organization (Allen & Meyer 1990). According to research, a distinction is found between affective commitment, continuance commitment, and normative commitment (Meyer & Allen, 1991). The affective, normative, and continuance components of commitments describe an employee›s intention to quit or stay in the organization or in other words, whether an employee needs to, wants to, or ought to remain in the same organization (Allen & Meyer, 1987). According to studies, the career-related aspects of organizational factors are given due importance as it influences the extent of organizational commitment of the employees, and when an employee feels that the organization gives due emphasis to career-oriented practices, their attachment towards the organization also increases (Gaertner & Nollen, 1989). Organizational opportunity for growth is assumed to consist of organizational support and work challenge, as a result, the organizational opportunity for growth is hypothecated directly to influence career commitment and indirectly through organizational commitment and career satisfaction (Samuel Aryee & Kevin Tan, 1992). According to research, organizational commitment is the key individual variable that explains career commitment (London, 1983). Employees, who are dedicated to their organizations, are also committed to their careers (Goulet & Singh, 2002). Organizational opportunities for growth may add to one's career growth or related career-roles (Hall, 1971) as there is a positive correlation between organizational commitment and career commitment (Blau, 1985; Steffy & Jones, 1988; Darden, Hampton, & Howell, 1989). So, in the present paper, we focus on the mediating part of organisation commitment in the relation between Developmental I deals and career commitment.

Fig. 1: *shows the proposed model.*

(Figure -1 - Conceptual Model)

Source: Authors' own

Based on the above proposed conceptual model, we predict the following:

Hypothesis 1: Grant of Developmental Idiosyncratic deal will lead to Career commitment

Hypothesis 2: Organization Commitment will mediate the relationship between developmental ideals and career commitment.

METHODS

We collected data from executives working across various sector within India. We approached the respondents through convenience sampling. The survey participants consisted of 299 respondents out of which 117 were female, and 181 were male. Age was asked in different ranges like 26-35, 36-45, 46-55 and over 55 years, which was coded from 1 to 4. Most respondents i.e., 230 were in the age category of 26-35 years, 68 respondents in the range of 36-45 years and only 1 in the age category of 46-55 years. Educational achievement was coded as 1 for graduate, 2 for the individuals who are post graduate, 3 for the individuals who have Ph.D. and 4 for other courses. So, from the respondents list, 150 individuals were graduates, 147 were post graduates and 2 were having doctorate. Years of total experience in an organization was asked in the range of 1 to 7 where less than 3 years was categorized as 1, 3-5 years as 2, 6- 8 years as 3, 9-11 years as 4, 12-14 years as 5, 15-17 years as 6 and over 18 years as 7. The respondents consisted of 36 people having less than 3 years of experience, 166 having 3-6 years of experience, 82 having 7-10 years of experience, 12 people having 12-14 years of experience and 3 people having 15-18 years of experience.

MEASURES

Developmental Idiosyncratic Deals: We used Rousseau et al. (2008) four-item scale to measure negotiation and grant of Developmental I-deals. Executives rated the item on five-point scale (1 for strongly agree to 5 for strongly disagree). Sample items comprise 'My employer and I have successfully negotiated a unique arrangement that allows me special opportunities for skill development'. The Cronbach alpha for this measure 0.811.

Career Commitment: We used Carson and Bedeian (1994) twelve item scale to evaluate career commitment measure. Executives rated the item on five-point scale (1 for strongly agree to 5 for strongly disagree). Sample items comprise 'The costs associated with my line of work/career field sometimes seem too great'. The Cronbach alpha for this measure is 0.764.

Organization Commitment: We used Porter, Crampon & Smith's (1976) nine item scale to measure organization commitment measure. Executives rated the item on a five-point scale (1 for strongly agree to 5 for strongly disagree). Sample items comprise 'Willing to put in unexpected effort to help organization'. The Cronbach alpha for this measure is 0.773.

ANALYSIS

To scrutinize our hypotheses, we conducted mediation analysis using Amos to check the significance between the career commitment (dependent variable), organization commitment (mediation variable) and developmental idiosyncratic deals (independent variable).

Results:

Table 1: Regression Weights of cc & did

			EST	Std.Error	Critical Ratio	P	Label
cc	<---	did	.081	.024	3.303	***	

Fig. 2: *Relation between CC & DID*

As P value is significant, so here we can interpret that developmental Ideals (DID) has significant relationship with career commitment (CC).

Table 2: Regression Weights of cc, did & oc

			EST	Std.Error	Critical Ratio	P	Label
oc	<---	did	.070	.029	2.428	.015	
cc	<---	did	.060	.023	2.596	.009	
cc	<---	oc	.294	.046	6.425	***	

Fig. 3: *Relation between CC,OC & DID*

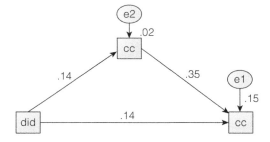

As P value is significant in all cases, so here we can interpret that OC has partial mediation role between the relationship of DID and CC.

Confirmatory Factor Analysis (CFA)

Fig. 4: *Structural equation modelling*

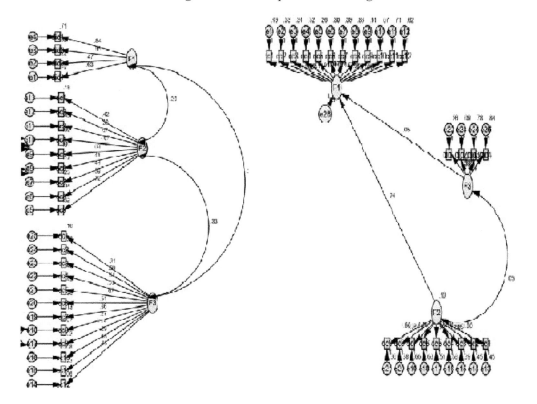

Table 3: CMIN analysis of model

Model	NPAR	CMIN	Degree of Freedom	P	CMIN/DF
Def model	57	730.686	268	.000	2.726
Sat. model	325	.000	0		
Indp model	25	2145.686	300	.000	7.152

Table-4: RMR, GFI analysis of model

Model	Root Mean square Residual	Goodness of Fit Index	Adjusted Goodness of Fit Index	P Goodness of Fit Index
Def model	.049	.936	.901	.889
Sat. model	.000	1.000		
Indp model	.132	.550	.513	.508

Table-5: Baseline Comparisons

Model	Normed Fit Index Delta1	Relative Fit Index rho1	Incremental Fit Index Delta2	Tucker Lewis Index rho2	Comparative Fit Index
Def model	.959	.919	.954	.949	.969
Sat. model	1.000		1.000		1.000
Indp model	.000	.000	.000	.000	.000

Table-6: Root mean square error of approximation

Model	RMSEA	LO 90	HI 90	PCLOSE
Def model	.046	.090	.093	.000
Indp model	.144	.138	.149	.000

From the above tables it is clear that the model is high compatible to the data. CMIN=2.72; RMSEA=0.046; Normed Fit Index =0.95, Comparative Fit Index =0.96, Tucker Lewis Index =0.94 in line with the recommendation of HU and Bentler (1999). All the path loadings from latent constructs were also noteworthy as shown in above figure.

DISCUSSION

We examined the relation among developmental idiosyncratic deals, career commitment, and organization commitment in the present study. Departing from the previous literature using social exchange theory as a supporting mechanism of developmental I deals, we proposed and empirically found that organization commitment mediated the relationships between developmental idiosyncratic deals and career commitment.

IMPLICATIONS

These results have several implications for both theory and practical implications. Social exchange theory is mostly applicable under the working environment of an organization. Previous findings done by scholars theorized that social exchange theory is the mediating factor, or social exchange theory is the catalyst between Developmental I-Deals and Organization Commitment. But in our study, we propose that due to social exchange theory, the individuals who opt for developmental i-deals, helps them to advance in their capabilities. So, basically individuals those who are committed to their organizations are also committed to their careers as developmental i-deals leads to career commitment, where organizational commitment works as a mediation between them. Social Exchange plays a massive role, as not everyone is suitable for developmental i-deals. So, our study mostly focuses on developmental i-deals and career commitment and organizational commitment as a mediating role. The individuals who got developmental I-deals from their organizations are concerned about their organizational responsibilities that they will apply all their skills for the betterment of their company by enhancing their skills which will lead to career commitment which is supported by findings of Rousseau et al., 2009 and Samuel and kevin ,1992.

CONCLUSION AND LIMITATION

This paper developed and empirically tested a relationship model among developmental idiosyncratic deals, organizational commitment, and career commitment, which draws the below conclusion. By providing developmental idiosyncratic deals to individual employees, their commitment level towards organization and career can be enhanced, leading to growth and success for both organization and individual employee. Finally the author have put forwarded that developmental I deals can be a measure to enhance the level of commitment from both organizational and career point of view. Although this research presents to the literature and the findings have important managerial implications, it is not without some limitation. The sampling strategy chosen in this is convenience sampling with limited sample size. The study results should be generalized with caution. Future research can be done with more samples across all sectors. This study is based only on a quantitative approach, so future researchers can also use qualitative inquiry and a quantitative confirmatory approach.

REFERENCE

Allen, N. J., & Meyer, J. P. (1990). Organizational socialization tactics: A longitudinal analysis of links to newcomers' commitment and role orientation. *Academy of management journal, 33*(4), 847–858.

Aryee, S., & Tan, K. (1992). Antecedents and outcomes of career commitment. *Journal of Vocational Behavior, 40*(3), 288–305.

Arnold, J. (1990). Predictors of career commitment: A test of three theoretical models. *Journal of Vocational behavior, 37*(3), 285–302.

Blau, G. (1985). The measurement and prediction of career commitment. *Journal of Occupational Psychology, 58*, 277–288.

Blau, P. M. 1964. Exchange and power in social life. New York: John Wiley

Carson, K. D., & Bedeian, A. G. (1994). Career commitment: Construction of a measure and examination of its psychometric properties. *Journal of vocational Behavior, 44*(3), 237–262.

Chang, E. (1999). Career commitment as a complex moderator of organizational commitment and turnover intention. *Human relations, 52*(10), 1257–1278.

Darden, W., Hampton, R., & Howell, R. (1989). Career versus organizational commitment: Antecedents and consequences of retail salesperson's commitment. *Journal of Retailing, 65*, 80–106.

Eisenberger, R., Karagonlar, G., Stinglhamber, F., Neves, P., Becker, T. E.,Gonzalez-Morales, M. G., & Steiger-Mueller, M. (2010). *Leader–member exchange and affective organizational commitment: The contribution of supervisor's organizational embodiment. Journal of Applied Psychology, 95*, 1085–1103. doi:10.1037/a0020858

Goode, W. J. (1960). Norm commitment and conformity to role-status obligations. *American Journal of Sociology, 66*, 246–258.

Gaertner, K. N., & Nollen, S. D. (1989). Career experiences, perceptions of employment practices, and psychological commitment to the organization. *Human relations, 42*(11), 975–991.

Goulet, L. R., & Singh, P. (2002). Career commitment: A reexamination and an extension. *Journal of vocational behavior, 61*(1), 73–91.

Hall, D. T. (1971). A theoretical model of career subidentity development in organizational settings. *Organizational Behavior and Human Performance, 6*(1), 50–76.

Hu, L. T., & Bentler, P. M. (1999). Cutoff criteria for fit indexes in covariance structure analysis: Conventional criteria versus new alternatives. *Structural equation modeling: a multidisciplinary journal, 6*(1), 1–55.

Hornung, S., Rousseau, D. M., & Glaser, J. (2008). Creating flexible work arrangements through idiosyncratic deals. *Journal of Applied Psychology, 93*(3), 655.

Korman, A. K. (2001). *Self-enhancement and self-protection: Toward a theory of work motivation. In M. Erez, U. Kleinbeck, & H. Thierry (Eds.), Work motivation in the context of a globalizing economy (pp.121–130). Mahwah, NJ: Erlbaum.*

Liu, J., Lee, C., Hui, C., Kwan, H. K., & Wu, L. Z. (2013). *Idiosyncratic deals and employee outcomes: The mediating roles of social exchange and self-enhancement and the moderating role of individualism. Journal of Applied Psychology, 98*(5), 832.

Liao, C., Wayne, S. J., & Rousseau, D. M. (2016). Idiosyncratic deals in contemporary organizations: A qualitative and meta-analytical review. *Journal of Organizational Behavior, 37*, S9–S29.

London, M. (1983). Toward a theory of career motivation. *Academy of management review, 8*(4), 620–630.

Morrow, P. C. (1993). *The theory and measurement of work commitment.* Jai Press.

Mester, C., Visser, D., Roodt, G., & Kellerman, R. (2003). Leadership style and its relation to employee attitudes and behaviour. *SA journal of industrial psychology, 29*(2), 72–82.

Meyer, J. P., & Allen, N. J. (1991). A three-component conceptualization of organizational commitment. *Human resource management review, 1*(1), 61–89.

Meyer, J. P., & Allen, N. J. (1987). A longitudinal analysis of the early development and consequences of organizational commitment. *Canadian Journal of Behavioural Science/Revue canadienne des sciences du comportement, 19*(2), 199.

Mowday, R. T., Porter, L. W., & Steers, R. M. (1982). Employee-organization linkages: The psychology of commitment, absenteeism and turnover. New York: Academic Press.

Porter, L. W., Crampon, W. J., & Smith, F. J. (1976). Organizational commitment and managerial turnover: A longitudinal study. *Organizational behavior and human performance, 15*(1), 87–98.

Perrow, C. (1986). Complex organizations (3rd ed.). New York: Random House .

Social Exchange Theory: An Interdisciplinary Review, Russell Cropanzano and Marie S. Mitchell, Journal of Management 2005; 31; 874, DOI: 10.1177/0149206305279602.

Rousseau, D. M., Ho, V. T., & Greenberg, J. (2006). I-deals: Idiosyncratic terms in employment relationships. *Academy of management review, 31*(4), 977–994.

Rousseau, D. M., Manning, J., & Denyer, D. (2008). 11 Evidence in management and organizational science: assembling the field's full weight of scientific knowledge through syntheses. *Academy of Management Annals*, *2*(1), 475–515.

Rousseau, D. M., Hornung, S., & Kim, T. G. (2009). Idiosyncratic deals: Testing propositions on timing, content, and the employment relationship. *Journal of Vocational Behavior*, *74*(3), 338–348.

Steffy, B., &L Jones, J. (1988). The impact of family and career planning variables on the organizational, career, and community commitment of professional women. *Journal of Vocational Behavior, 32*, 196–212.

CHAPTER 23

Grittier and Embedded: An Analysis of Hotel Employees During Covid 19 Pandemic

Kerwin Savio Nigli
Department of Hotel Management
CHRIST (Deemed to be University)
Bangalore, India
kerwin.nigli@christuniversity.in

Shruti Agrawal
Department of Hotel Management
CHRIST (Deemed to be University)
Bangalore, India
shruti.agrawal@bhm.christuniversity.in

Abstract

Research suggests that Grit and Job Embeddedness are essential for employees of the hospitality industry. Although prior studies have emphasised on the importance of these traits in hotel employees, little is known about whether their dimensions Perseverance of Effort, Organization Fit, Community Link, have a relationship with each other. The purpose of this paper is to research these relationships. The relationships were assessed in a sample size of 265 five-star hotel employees in Bangalore using correlation and regression. The results showed a significant positive correlation between Grit and Job Embeddedness. Perseverance of Effort has a significant positive correlation with Organization Fit and Community Link. Perseverance of Effort has a statistically significant impact on both the dimensions of Job Embeddedness. HR departments in hotels should adopt strategies that make an employee more perseverant, potentially increasing Job Embeddedness and reducing turnover.

Keywords: Grit, Perseverance of Effort, Job Embeddedness, Organization Fit, Community Link, Hotel Industry, COVID 19, Pandemic

I. INTRODUCTION

A. *Covid 19 Pandemic*

A pandemic impacting countries across the globe leads to drastic changes in the society as we know it, and such has been the impact of the novel coronavirus disease i.e., COVID 19 on us. The disease originated in China and waved through the globe, spreading over 213 countries in no time. It was declared a global pandemic by WHO. As on January 11, 2021, the number of COVID cases worldwide are 90.4 million (World Health Organization,

2021). Each day, as this number increases, the global economy continues to be pushed into recession. According to the IMF's World Economic Outlook, April 2020 report, the global economy is expected to shrink by 3% in 2020 because of the pandemic which is even worse than the 2008-09 financial crisis (International Monetary Fund, 2020). Millions of individuals have lost their jobs while others have faced a salary cut. The pandemic is the biggest economic shock the world has been a witness to in decades, with economic activity at a global level, collapsing as a result (The World Bank, 2020).

B.   *Covid 19 impact on hospitality industry*

Across the globe, the travel and tourism sector is without a doubt the biggest casualty of this pandemic. As the virus spreads and countries go into lockdown, all reservations of hotels are being postponed or cancelled. Domestic and international borders were closed as quarantine measures were introduced (The World Bank, 2020). Hotels have been hit hard, wrestling with the low demand, sharp decline in occupancy rates and revenues and all restaurants were forced to shut their dine-in operations. The present hospitality work environment is afflicted with uncertainty caused by technological changes, economic downturn, and/or political instability (Etehadi & Karatepe, 2019). In India, the travel and tourism sector generated $194 billion or 6.8% of India's GDP in 2019 (India Brand Equity Foundation, n.d.). In the Travel and Tourism Competitiveness Report 2019, India is placed 34th globally, with the largest improvement over 2017 among the top 25% of all nations assessed in the report (World Economic Forum, 2019).

In a combined report of STR and Howarth HTL, the Indian hotel industry has seen an aggregate rooms revenue loss of Rs. 4,810 crores from March to June 2020, compared to 2019 (STR & Horwath HTL, 2020). Hotels have either temporarily closed or significantly scaled down operations. The accumulated loss of revenue for 3 months from March to June is about Rs. 80 bn (Rs. 8,000 crores), said the report in its conclusion (STR & Horwath HTL, 2020). Deep fear and confusion, along with physical confinement has enforced the hospitality industry to learn how to function in ways not seen before (Djeebet, 2020). To overcome this crisis, gentle and non-aggressive communication is crucial to reach out to customers, reassuring them of the safety of traveling again. A survey conducted by Gursoy et al. (2020) showed that over 60% of individuals are not willing to dine at a restaurant immediately after lockdown restrictions are eased. Over 12% indicated that only when the vaccine becomes available, would they be comfortable in dining at a restaurant. What customers expect from restaurants and hotels is clear and evident efforts of sanitization for example hand sanitizers at the entrance, wearing of masks by all employees, implementation of social distancing, careful and continuous disinfection of high-touch surfaces in common areas and other key safety procedures (Gursoy et al., 2020).

This sector thrives on personal touch and now must contend with no-contact operations. Hotels are turning to staycation, renting out rooms and engaging in home delivery of food from restaurants to generate revenue. They are looking for new and creative ways to reach out to their guests. For example, THE Park Hotels, curated the 'Chef and Bartender at Home' service for guests, that offers customized menu for food and drinks at various price points. Well- trained teams are equipped to prepare the delicacies in the confines of their home ("THE Park Hotels introduces 'Chef and Bartender at Home' service", 2020). Taj

West End, Bangalore has been actively pushing the 'Hospitality at Home' campaign under which, through Taj's butler service, packed food orders, hampers and laundry services for regular guests were done, ensuring maintenance of hygiene standards (Ray, 2020). In June, Hilton announced CleanStay programme globally, ITC introduced the 'WeAssure initiative', Wyndham Hotels and resorts has its 'Count on Us' initiative all focusing on revised protocols of health and safety and heightened sanitization measures (Miller, 2020). Despite facing hardships and restrictions in the new normal, employees are coming together to support hotel brands in delivering unique experiences to guests. Without their effort, dedication, and willpower, this would not be possible.

C.   *Grit and Job Embeddedness*

Grit is defined as passion and perseverance for long-term goals (Duckworth et al., 2007). It involves working vigorously towards challenges, while perpetuating effort and enthusiasm over time regardless of being faced with failure and adversities (Duckworth et al., 2007). Grit has two dimensions-perseverance of effort and consistency of interest. Perseverance of effort measures the tendency of an individual to persist and perpetuate their efforts despite being faced with setbacks and hardships in life. Consistency of interest refers to a person's tendency to maintain a consistent set of interests over time.

Grit is thought to be a higher order construct by some authors, while others suggest studying its two dimensions separately. A meta-analysis on grit literature conducted by Credé et al. (2017) revealed that perseverance of effort is a better predictor of performance than consistency of interest. They based their findings on 548 effect sizes from 88 independent samples suggesting that perseverance is the most promising area of further research on grit. Perseverance of effort is more strongly influential compared to consistency of interest on students' self-efficacy and achievement orientation goals (Alhadabi & Karpinski, 2020). Datu et al. (2016) state that perseverance of effort appears to be a stronger predictor of positive outcomes. In comparison to consistency of interest, Bowman et al. (2015) argued that perseverance of effort predicted better satisfaction. Salisu et al. (2020) found that perseverance of effort had a stronger link with resilience than consistency of interest.

Previous studies on grit have found that grit increases performance of employees (Jachimowicz et al., 2018), it predicts GPAs of students (Duckworth et al., 2007; Jachimowicz et al., 2018) and is associated with well-being (Kannangara et al., 2018). For an organization to be gritty, its leaders, faculty members should promote a culture that emphasizes on the concept (Bashant, 2014; Casper et al., 2019; Caza & Posner 2019; Alhadabi & Karpinski, 2020). Grit is negatively associated with reduced turnover intention (McGinley et al., 2020; McGinley & Mattila, 2019); positively related to job satisfaction (Dugan et al., 2018) and growth mindset (Sethi & Shashwati 2019). Duckworth et. al. (2007), concluded that in all the different professional fields, grit may be as important as talent for high accomplishment. Suzuki et al. (2015) state that gritty individuals are likely to engage positively in their work.

The concept of Job Embeddedness (JE) (Mitchell et al., 2001) emerged to answer the question about why people continue to stay in one organization. Since the organizational and personal costs of turnover are high, retention is always a priority for managers. The concept of Job Embeddedness has 6 dimensions -: Link, fit and sacrifice can be applied in an individual's organizational as well as community context.

Links - Formal or informal connections between a person and institutions or other persons are referred to as links (Mitchell et al., 2001). Links connect employees to work as well as nonwork friends and groups. Higher the number of links an employee forms, the more he is attached to the job. The importance of family and other social institutions on individuals is recognized by Community Link. (Holtom et al., 2006). It can be increased by encouraging employee involvement in local schools, community-based civic organizations and sponsoring little-league teams for children. Community Link has a positive relationship with affective commitment (Agrawal & Singh, 2017).

Fit - An employee's perceived compatibility or comfort with a company and his or her environment is characterized as fit (Mitchell et al., 2001). It is important for organizations to hire employees whose personal values, career goals, and future plans, match company culture (Holtom et al., 2006). Additionally, an employee's skills and knowledge must fit the demands of the job. The better the employee fits in the organization, the more likely he is to stay in it, as it increases attachment to the organization. Organizational Fit can be increased by providing training and development opportunities that help employees meet their long-term career goals and using realistic job previews (Holtom et al., 2006). Employees that are a good fit for the job, will be willing to and successful in dealing with customers' requests demonstrating high levels of job performance (Karatepe & Ngeche, 2012). Organizational Fit and turnover intentions are negatively related (Coetzer et al., 2019). It is positively related to life satisfaction (Ampofo et al., 2017). It predicts job performance (Kapil & Rastogi, 2017) and is positively correlated to innovative work behaviour (Susomrith & Amankwaa, 2019). An employee will also consider how well he/she fits in the community or surrounding environment.

Sacrifice - The perceived cost of material or psychological rewards that may be lost by leaving a job is captured by sacrifice (Mitchell et al., 2001). Quitting a job and leaving an organization would result in personal losses like giving up friendships with colleagues, working on challenging and interesting projects and other perks of the organization. Giving up opportunities of job stability, career advancement and sabbaticals are additional sacrifices associated with quitting a job. If an employee has to relocate, he would have to leave the community in which he is living.

Job embeddedness is often associated with reduced turnover intention in hotels (Safavi & Karatepe, 2019; Arasli et al., 2017). It is positively related to life satisfaction (Ampofo et al., 2017; Ampofo et al.,2018), innovative work behaviours (Coetzer et al., 2018; Susomrith & Amankwaa, 2019), work engagement leading to better performance (Kapil & Rastogi, 2017). It reduces job stress (Rafiq & Chin, 2019).

II. PURPOSE

Perseverance of effort explains why an individual continues to persevere even in the face of difficulties and Job Embeddedness, along with its dimensions, explain why employees choose to stay in the industry despite it being so challenging. As we progress into the 10th month of the pandemic, hotels have adapted to the situation, coming up with creative ways of curating guest experiences, ensuring that all safety and hygiene measures are followed. This would not have been impossible without employee aid. This pandemic can be a learning lesson for future generations leading hotels on how to handle crises and generate revenue while ensuring employees are looked after. Analyzing how gritty and embedded employees are, even during this situation of uncertainty, can provide helpful insights to the HR department. Understanding their levels of perseverance, organization fit, and community link and the relationship between these dimensions, can help in understanding the industry and employees better. Thus, there is a need to investigate the existence of a relationship between the dimensions and suggest possible implications. After studying the literature, it can be observed that although an indirect relationship between Grit and Job Embeddedness through the framework of job satisfaction and job attitudes has been established, there is yet no study examining the direct relationship between their dimensions. This gap points out the necessity for further studies to explore the relationship between Perseverance of effort, Organizational fit and Community link in the hotel industry. To our knowledge, this is the first study to investigate such a relationship. The current crisis, although may have temporarily forced hotels to stop operations, it didn't stop their will and determination to curate new and safe experiences for their guests.

III. CONCEPTUAL FRAMEWORK

A.   *Grit in hotels*

All research is of the understanding that employees equipped with grit have a significant reason for pushing themselves to work better. The industry is heavily reliant on employees to deliver high quality services to customers because their actions directly influence the perceptions of the hotel. The quality of service is affected by frontline employees' effort, interest and skills while interacting with different customers. A part of the hospitality product, which is intangible, is offered through employee services that are essential to the customer's enjoyment of the product and experience. (Yam et al., 2018).

Amidst the task uncertainty, it is the employee's purpose for learning that increases his persistence and motivates him to work diligently. Perseverance of effort is essential in the hotel context, as it encourages employees to stay in the organization even after facing setbacks in their interactions with customers. Employees are under immense pressure as they need to constantly work towards exceeding expectations of guests. Grit may help them deal with this stress by driving them to put their best foot forward. Kim et al. (2019) through their study showed that frontline employees with high grit and job satisfaction are more customer oriented. Developing customer orientation can empower employees to take their own decisions in customer interactions and increase positive feedback, which in turn allows them to feel a stronger consistency of interest towards their work.

The hotel industry, globally, is troubled with high employee turnover. Since this is a major concern for many hotels across the world, hotel managers are left frequently dealing with new staff. Poor human resource decisions and expectations of newcomers that are left unmet, are frequently the causes of turnover in this industry (Yang, 2008). One way in which this issue could be tackled and encourage employees to stay long-term is to increase their grit levels. McGinley et al. (2020) found that gritty hospitality managers would continue in organizations despite the path being uncertain than their less gritty counterparts. McGinley and Mattila (2019) found that passion is required for success and longevity in the hospitality industry.

B.   *Job Embeddedness in hotels*

Despite the hospitality industry being a labour intensive one, it has always been plagued with high turnover levels (Robinson et al., 2014; Hinkin & Tracey, 2000). Turnover has several detrimental effects on the organization in terms of direct and indirect costs. Hinkin and Tracey (2000) found that the costs of employee turnover may be as high as 40 % of total operational expenses. This in turn leads to inconsistency delivering a service and a dissatisfied customer. According to Afsar et al. (2018), any organization's goal is to keep their best frontline personnel for as long as possible. Employees in the hotel sector should be encouraged to be actively engaged with visitors in order to offer a distinctive guest experience. Employee engagement, dedication, and task performance improve as a result of job embeddedness, making them less likely to leave the company. In order for hotels to succeed, jobs need to be made meaningful, interesting, challenging and employees must have the freedom to experiment with new ideas (Afsar et al., 2018).

Safavi and Karatepe (2019) recommend hiring the right people who fit the job well to increase Job Embeddedness. This way good work can be expected from them. In order to motivate employees to be deeply embedded in the organization, hotel managers should attempt to increase employees' links, fit and sacrifice (Yang et al., 2019). Yam et al. (2018) in their study concluded that job embeddedness may play a role in explaining why employees stay in the hospitality industry. Recruitment of operational staff can be done from local communities resulting in employees who are already highly embedded in the organization and are thus less likely to leave. This is because the authors argue that employees based in a community for a long time have strong ties and fit well in the community, making what they would have to sacrifice, a lot, if they choose to leave. A hotel's workforce, at all levels, contributes their dedication, leadership, and personal involvement to the establishment of a great service culture, going above and beyond to provide a positive guest experience (Arasli et al., 2017). By establishing a strong service culture orientation and increasing employee engagement, job embeddedness can be increased. Ensuring an organizational culture where employees freely express their opinions, feel that their contributions are valued by the organization and that their personal interests are taken care of can increase job embeddedness (Akgunduz & Sanli, 2017). While recruiting, hotels should focus on employees whose attitudes are consistent with the future plans, purposes, and values of the organization, increasing their Organizational Fit.

In recent decades, the hotel industry has grown at an unparalleled rate, and it now plays an increasingly vital role in emerging markets. (Yao et al., 2019). The success of the sector is highly dependent on service-oriented behaviors of employees. Factors such as a high sense of belonging and switching costs can help managers improve retention. Karatepe and Ngeche (2012) conclude that through job embeddedness retaining competent frontline employees is possible. They too are of the opinion that employees' values should fit the organization's values. Providing growth opportunities will increase embeddedness. Agrawal and Singh (2017) studied the role of job embeddedness in retaining employees in the hotel industry collecting data from 164 employees from 10 hotels operating in Lucknow and Varanasi. The results showed that, after controlling for job satisfaction and organizational commitment, job embeddedness predicted turnover. Community embeddedness better predicted turnover intentions. HR managers should not only focus on rewards and benefits that an employee would have to sacrifice if he leaves but also should develop an organizational climate such that the employee would not want to leave.

C. Grit and Job Embeddedness in hotels

Dugan et al. (2018) conducted a study the effects of grit on performance of salespeople and their job satisfaction in a business-to-business sales setting. They focused only on the Perseverance of Effort dimension. Salespeople are required to meet their quarterly/annual sales mark, which gritty people will attain by expending effort. A survey was conducted in a B2B firm through an online platform and 256 employees responded to it. The results showed that grit has a positive relationship with competitiveness and performance. Grit positively impacts job satisfaction which in turn leads to high job embeddedness. The study is specific to the sales industry.

McGinley et al. (2020) conducted a study to examine why some employees have higher tendencies to resign from their jobs than others in the hospitality industry and which future-oriented factors could provide an explanation for this phenomenon. The sample size of the study consisted of 1,151 US hotel employees who were currently employed. The results showed that Perseverance of Effort positively related to job attitudes and job insecurity moderated this relationship. Job attitudes positively related with Job Embeddedness and negatively with turnover intentions. Authors suggest that individual dimensions of grit should be studied separately rather than considering grit as a higher order construct.

D. Hypothesis of the study

The study hypothesizes the following - There is no significant relationship between Perseverance of Effort and Organization Fit, and Perseverance of Effort and Community Link.

Fig. 1: *Conceptual model of the study*

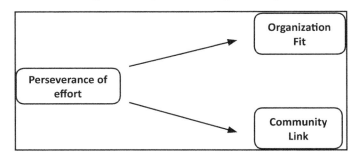

IV. METHODOLOGY

A. Sample and data collection

Data was collected from employees of 5-star hotels in Bangalore using the technique of convenience sampling. Prior to data collection, a pilot study with 50 employees was conducted. A pilot study is conducted to show that the data collected from the questionnaire is valid and reliable implying that the questionnaire is consistent and reproducible

(Williams, 2003). It can help remove any ambiguities identified, by revising questions. Once this was done, questionnaires were sent to respondents via mail. Respondents were assured that the data provided by them would be kept confidential and will be used for research purposes only. 265 responses were collected and used for data analysis.

B. Measures

Grit was measured using a 10-item questionnaire from Duckworth (2016), consisting of the 2 subscales - perseverance of effort and consistency of interest. Sample items from perseverance of effort are - 'I am a hard worker' and 'I finish whatever I begin'. Sample items from consistency of interest are - 'My interests change from year to year' and 'New ideas and projects sometimes distract me from previous ones'. The scale was rated on a 5-point scale from 'Very much like me' to 'Not like me at all'. An 18-item Job Embeddedness questionnaire was used to measure Job Embeddedness consisting of questions pertaining to its 6 dimensions. Sample items include 'My job utilizes my skills and talents well', 'I really love the place where I live' and 'I am a member of an effective work group'. A 5-point scale was used for this too, ranging from 1 (Strongly Disagree) to 5 (Strongly Agree). Reliability analysis was done for both measures by calculating Cronbach's alpha. Its value for Grit scale was 0.82 and for Job Embeddedness scale was 0.89. A score higher than 0.70 indicates that the scale will be internally consistent. In this case, thus, both scales are internally consistent and reliable.

C. Data Analysis

The analysis was done using SPSS. The researchers used Correlation and Regression as they wanted to study the relationship between the variables, their dimensions, and the prediction of Grit on Job Embeddedness. Regression analysis is done to quantify the relationship between a dependent variable and one or more independent variables, to analyze which one has a big impact, which matters the most and which ones can be ignored. An approach for assessing the relationship between two quantitative, continuous variables is correlation. Pearson's correlation coefficient denoted by 'r' represents the strength of the association between the 2 variables.

V. FINDINGS

A. Descriptive statistics

From 265 respondents, 57% were male (n=151) and 43% were female (n=114). A mixed population of respondents from human resources (19.2%), food and beverage service (16.2%), front office (15.1%), housekeeping (15.1%), sales and marketing (12.8%) and kitchen (5.3%) was found. The remaining 16.2% belonged to 'others' category. A large number of respondents were in the age bracket of 21-40 years with 45.3% in 21-30 years and 33.2% in 31-40 years age category. About 17.4% were in 41-50 years and very few respondents were of age 51-60 years (4.2%). Both married (54.0%) and unmarried (46.0%) respondents participated in the study.

B. Grit and Job Embeddedness

TABLE I: Grit and Job Embeddedness score statistics

Variables	Statistics		
	N	Mean	Std. Deviation
Grit score	265	3.989	.5825
Job Embeddedness score	265	4.023	.6275
Perseverance of Effort score	265	4.400	.4964
Organization Fit score	265	4.410	.6856
Community Link score	265	3.210	1.1579

The above table shows the mean Grit score of a hotel employee is 3.989 and the mean Job Embeddedness score of an employee is 4.0231. This shows that even during a severe pandemic, employees have high levels of Grit and Job Embeddedness. Gritty individuals are more successful and accomplish more than less gritty individuals (Duckworth et al., 2007). Grit is positively related to employee engagement (Guan, 2018; Suzuki et al., 2015) indicating that gritty employees are more likely to be engaged in their jobs. As Kim et al. (2019) found, Gritty hotel employees are more likely to be customer oriented. Gritty employees tend to display high job performance (Jachimowicz et al., 2018).

Embedded employees will be willing to and successful in dealing with customers' requests displaying high levels of job performance (Karatepe & Ngeche, 2012). Employees' proactive customer service performance can be motivated by on-the-job embeddedness (Chan et al., 2019). Retention of best talent is critical to an organization's success and retention can be increased by increasing job embeddedness (Ma et al., 2018). Kapil and Rastogi (2017) found that JE and work engagement led to better job performance in employees.

Perseverance of effort has a mean score of 4.4, indicating that employees don't give up in the face of challenges, such as this pandemic. They are resilient and are able to provide safe experiences to guests in this situation of chaos. Salisu et al. (2020) found that perseverance of effort had a stronger relationship with resilience than consistency of interest. According to Dugan et al. (2018), salespeople who were high in the perseverance element of grit performed better and had higher work satisfaction than their less gritty counterparts. Perseverance, according to Crede et al. (2017), was a superior predictor of both performance and retention. Kim et al. (2019) conclude that perseverance of effort significantly affects job satisfaction.

The mean Organization Fit score is 4.4 which indicates that employees perceive themselves to be a good fit for the organization. Their values are aligned with those of the organization and their skills are a fit for the job. Organizational Fit has a negatively relationship to turnover intentions (Coetzer et al., 2019) and positively related to life satisfaction (Ampofo et al., 2017). It predicts job performance (Kapil & Rastogi, 2017) and is positively correlated to innovative work behaviour (Susomrith & Amankwaa, 2019). The mean Community Link score is 3.2 which indicates that employees are not very well linked in their community. One reason for this could be the odd and long working hours in this industry.

C.   Correlation and Regression

TABLE II: Correlation between Grit and Job Embeddedness score

Independent Variable	Dependent Variable
	Job Embeddedness score
Grit score	.219**

**Correlation is significant at the 0.01 level (2-tailed)

The results show that there is a significant positive correlation between Grit and Job Embeddedness (Table II). Linear Regression Model explaining the relationship between the 2 variable is given as – JE score = 3.081 + (0.236) x Grit Score. 0.236 is a significant contributor to Job Embeddedness score. The findings of the study reveal that gritty employees are more embedded in their jobs. The researchers have also found that the hospitality employees are grittier and have a high level of attachment to the industry during the pandemic.

TABLE III: Correlation between Perseverance of Effort, Organization Fit and Community Link score

Independent variable	Dependent variables	
	Organization Fit score	Community Link score
Perseverance of Effort score	.277	.142

The results, as per Table III, indicate that a significant positive correlation between Perseverance of Effort and Organizational Fit score exists. Similarly, Perseverance of Effort and Community Link have a significant positive correlation. Perseverance of Effort has a statistically significant impact on both the Job Embeddedness dimensions. This indicates that employees with high Perseverance of Effort, are more engaged in the job which decreases turnover and increases their Organization Fit. Despite the long working hours, employees with high perseverance find a way to form and nurture links in the community which makes them embedded in their community. Thus, hiring employees who have high perseverance should be considered. Employees who are gritty will stay in the organization for longer duration. Human resource department should consider including questions on grit in the selection process of employees.

VI. IMPLICATIONS AND CONCLUSION

The study aimed at examining the relationship between Perseverance of Effort, Organization Fit and Community Link in the hotel industry. The findings reveal the existence of a positive relationship between the dimensions. Perseverance of effort predicted Organization Fit and Community Link in employees of the hotel industry. This is the first research that examines the direct relationship between the two variables and their dimensions. Gritty people are aware of what they care about and what they will pursue in life. This is something that they are passionate about, that will motivate them to keep working till their goals are achieved. They refuse to give up in the face of adversities and keep persevering. In a work environment, gritty individuals can motivate themselves to put in more effort and work harder. It leads individuals to continue working despite challenging tasks and even after facing disappointment (Kim et al., 2019). The key to any organization's success is its workforce. Grit can help reduce turnover leading to success and longevity in the industry (McGinley et al., 2020, McGinley & Mattila 2019).

Perseverance of Effort is a greater predictor of psychological outcomes when compared to consistency, according to Datu et al. (2016). Kim et al. (2019) found that perseverance significantly affects job satisfaction. Thus, hotel managers should consider developing perseverance of a hotel employee to increase his job satisfaction, his organization fit, community link which will increase his job embeddedness. A greater organization fit will reduce turnover intention (Coetzer et al., 2019), increase life satisfaction (Ampofo et al., 2017) and innovative work behaviour (Susomrith & Amankwaa, 2019). Community Link has a positive relationship with affective commitment (Agrawal & Singh, 2017). Limited research has examined the relationship between Perseverance of Effort, Organization Fit and Community Link in the hotel industry. The study adds on to the existing literature of Grit by identifying the impact of Perseverance of Effort on 2 dimensions of Job Embeddedness and providing a deeper understanding of the relationship. Gritty employees will be less likely to give up in the face of adversity. Training programs can be focused on making employees more perseverant. The major recommendation of the study for hospitality industry is to adopt strategies that enhance perseverance of employees which can potentially increase Job Embeddedness and reduce turnover. Employees who highly persevere to achieve their goals will have stronger embeddedness towards the industry. The study also recommends studying the dimensions of Grit separately.

VII. LIMITATIONS AND FUTURE STUDY

In the present study, due to the paucity of time, convenience sampling was used to gather data. Hence, future research can use probability sampling techniques whose results can be replicated. It should also consider widening the population to entire India or going multi-national. The current study focused on employees of 5-star hotels only. Future studies can include 1-star, 2-star, 3-star and 4-star hotels category. Further studies can test the relationship by adding moderating or mediating variables. Additionally, a distinction between managers and employees may be considered.

VIII. REFERENCES

Afsar, B., Shahjehan A., & Shah S. I. (2018). Frontline Employees' High-Performance Work Practices, Trust in Supervisor, Job-Embeddedness and Turnover Intentions in Hospitality Industry. *International Journal of Contemporary Hospitality Management* 30(3):1436–52.

Agrawal, H., Singh, A. (2017). Understanding Employee Retention through the Lens of Job Embeddedness: A Study of Indian Hospitality Industry. International Journal of Engineering Technology, Management and Applied Sciences, 5(7).

Akgunduz, Y., & Sanli, S. C. (2017). The effect of employee advocacy and perceived organizational support on job embeddedness and turnover intention in hotels. *Journal of Hospitality and Tourism Management, 31,* 118–125. https://doi.org/10.1016/j.jhtm.2016.12.002

Alhadabi, A., & Karpinski, A. C. (2020). Grit, Self-Efficacy, Achievement Orientation Goals, and Academic Performance in University Students. *International Journal of Adolescence and Youth* 25(1):519–35.

Ampofo, E. T., Coetzer, A., & Poisat, P. (2017). Relationships between job embeddedness and employees' life satisfaction. *Employee Relations, 39*(7), 951–966. https://doi.org/10.1108/er-10-2016-0199

Ampofo, E. T., Coetzer, A., & Poisat, P. (2018). Extending the Job Embeddedness-Life Satisfaction Relationship: An Exploratory Investigation. *Journal of Organizational Effectiveness: People and Performance* 5(3):236–58.

Arasli, H., Bahman Teimouri, R., Kiliç, H., & Aghaei, I. (2017). Effects of service orientation on job embeddedness in hotel industry. *The Service Industries Journal, 37*(9–10), 607–627. https://doi.org/10.1080/02642069.2017.1349756

Bashant, J. (2014). Developing Grit In Our Students: Why Grit is Such a Desirable Trait, and Practical Strategies for Teachers and Schools. *Journal for Leadership and Instruction.* Published.

Bowman, N. A., Hill, P. L., Denson, N., & Bronkema, R. (2015). Keep on Truckin' or Stay the Course? Exploring Grit Dimensions as Differential Predictors of Educational Achievement, Satisfaction, and Intentions. *Social Psychological and Personality Science, 6*(6), 639–645. https://doi.org/10.1177/1948550615574300

Casper, A. M., Eddy, S. L., & Freeman, S. (2019). True Grit: Passion and persistence make an innovative course design work. *PLOS Biology, 17*(7), e3000359. https://doi.org/10.1371/journal.pbio.3000359

Caza, A., & Posner, B. Z. (2019). How and when does grit influence leaders' behavior? *Leadership & Organization Development Journal, 40*(1), 124–134. https://doi.org/10.1108/LODJ-06-2018-0209

Chan, W. L., Ho, J. A., Sambasivan, M., & Ng, S. I. (2019). Antecedents and outcome of job embeddedness: Evidence from four and five-star hotels. *International Journal of Hospitality Management, 83,* 37–45. https://doi.org/10.1016/j.ijhm.2019.04.011

Coetzer, A., Inma, C., Poisat, P., Redmond, J., & Standing, C. (2019). Does job embeddedness predict turnover intentions in SMEs? *International Journal of Productivity and Performance Management, 68*(2), 340–361. https://doi.org/10.1108/ijppm-03-2018-0108

Coetzer, A., Inma, C., Poisat, P., Redmond, J., & Standing, C. (2018). Job embeddedness and employee enactment of innovation-related work behaviours. *International Journal of Manpower, 39*(2), 222–239. https://doi.org/10.1108/ijm-04-2016-0095

Credé, M., Tynan, M. C., & Harms, P. D. (2017). Much ado about grit: A meta-analytic synthesis of the grit literature. *Journal of Personality and Social Psychology, 113*(3), 492–511. https://doi.org/10.1037/pspp0000102

Datu, J. A. D., Valdez, J. P. M., & King, R. B. (2016). Perseverance Counts but Consistency Does Not! Validating the Short Grit Scale in a Collectivist Setting. Current Psychology, 35(1), 121–130. https://doi.org/10.1007/s12144-015-9374-2

Djeebet, H. (2020). *What is the Impact of COVID-19 on the Global Hospitality Industry? | By Hassan Djeebet – Hospitality Net*. Hospitality Net. Retrieved 15 October 2020, from https://www.hospitalitynet.org/opinion/4098062.html.

Duckworth, A. L. (2016). Grit: The Power of Passion and Perseverance. New York: Scribner.

Duckworth, A. L., C. Peterson, M. D. Matthews, and D. R. Kelly. (2007). Grit: Perseverance and Passion for Long-Term Goals. *Journal of Personality & Social Psychology* 92: 1087–1101. doi:10.1037/0022-3514.92.6.1087.

Dugan, R., Hochstein, B., Rouziou, M., & Britton, B. (2018). Gritting their teeth to close the sale: the positive effect of salesperson grit on job satisfaction and performance. Journal of Personal Selling & Sales Management, 39(1), 81–101. https://doi.org/10.1080/088 53134.2018.1489726

Guan, J. (2018). Understanding Grit and Its Relationship to Employee Engagement and Psychological Capital (PsyCap*).* (Ph.D). The Chicago School of Professional Psychology.

Gursoy, D., Chi, C. G., & Chi, O. H. (2020). COVID-19 Study 2 Report: Restaurant and Hotel Industry: Restaurant and hotel customers' sentiment analysis. Would they come back? If they would, WHEN? (Report No. 2), Carson College of Business, Washington State University. UNWTO. (2020). UNWTO world tourism barometer (Vol. 18, Issue 2, May 2020).

Hinkin, T. R., & Tracey, J. B. (2000). The Cost of Turnover: Putting a Price on the Learning Curve. *Cornell Hotel and Restaurant Administration Quarterly*, *41*(3), 14–21. https://doi.org/10.1177/001088040004100313

HOLTOM, B. C., MITCHELL, T. R., & LEE, T. W. (2006). Increasing human and social capital by applying job embeddedness theory. *Organizational Dynamics*, *35*(4), 316–331. https://doi.org/10.1016/j.orgdyn.2006.08.007

Hon, A.H.Y. & Lui, S.S. (2016). Employee creativity and innovation in organizations: Review, integration, and future directions for hospitality research. *International Journal of Contemporary Hospitality Management,* Vol. 28 No. 5, pp. 862-885. https://doi.org/10.1108/IJCHM-09-2014-0454

India Brand Equity Foundation. (n.d.). *Tourism & Hospitality Industry in India*. Department of Commerce, Ministry of Commerce and Industry, Government of India. Retrieved January 2, 2020, from https://www.ibef.org/industry/tourism-hospitality-india.aspx

International Monetary Fund. (2020, April). *World Economic Outlook, April 2020: The Great Lockdown.* United Nations. https://www.imf.org/en/Publications/WEO/Issues/2020/04/14/weo-april-2020

Jachimowicz, J. M., Wihler, A., Bailey, E. R., & Galinsky, A. D. (2018). Why grit requires perseverance and passion to positively predict performance. Proceedings of the National Academy of Sciences, 115(40), 9980–9985. https://doi.org/10.1073/pnas.1803561115

Kannangara, C. S., Allen, R. E., Waugh, G., Nahar, N., Khan, S. Z. N., Rogerson, S., & Carson, J. (2018). All That Glitters Is Not Grit: Three Studies of Grit in University Students. Frontiers in Psychology, 9. Published. https://doi.org/10.3389/fpsyg.2018.01539

Kapil, K., & Rastogi, R. (2017). JOB EMBEDDEDNESS AND WORK ENGAGEMENT AS PREDICTORS OF JOB PERFORMANCE. Journal of Strategic Human Resource Management, 6(3), 28–33.

Karatepe, O. M., & Ngeche, R. N. (2012). Does Job Embeddedness Mediate the Effect of Work Engagement on Job Outcomes? A Study of Hotel Employees in Cameroon. *Journal of Hospitality Marketing & Management*, *21*(4), 440–461. https://doi.org/10.1080/19368623.2012.626730

Kim, M., Lee, J. & Kim, J. (2019), «The Role of Grit in Enhancing Job Performance of Frontline Employees: The Moderating Role of Organizational Tenure», *Advances in Hospitality and Leisure* (*Advances in Hospitality and Leisure, Vol. 15*), Emerald Publishing Limited, Bingley, pp. 61-84. https://doi.org/10.1108/S1745-354220190000015004

Ma, Q. K., Mayfield, M., & Mayfield, J. (2018). Keep them on-board! How organizations can develop employee embeddedness to increase employee retention. *Development and Learning in Organizations: An International Journal*, *32*(4), 5–9. https://doi.org/10.1108/dlo-11-2017-0094

McGinley, S., & Mattila, A. S. (2019). Overcoming Job Insecurity: Examining Grit as a Predictor. Cornell Hospitality Quarterly, 61(2), 199–212. https://doi.org/10.1177/1938965519877805

McGinley, S., Line, N. D., Wei, W., & Peyton, T. (2020). Studying the effects of future-oriented factors and turnover when threatened. International Journal of Contemporary Hospitality Management, 32(8), 2737–2755. https://doi.org/10.1108/ijchm-12-2019-1002

McGinley, S., Mattila, A. S., & Self, T. T. (2020). Deciding To Stay: A Study in Hospitality Managerial Grit. Journal of Hospitality & Tourism Research, 44(5), 858–869. https://doi.org/10.1177/1096348020909537

Miller, D. (2020, July 24). Hotels Enhance Cleaning Protocols in Light of COVID-19. *CoStar.* https://www.costar.com/article/575929040

Mitchell, T. R., Holtom, B. C., Lee, T. W., Sablynski, C. J., & Erez, M. (2001). Why people stay: Using job embeddedness to predict voluntary turnover. *Academy of Management Journal* 44(6):1102- 1121.

Rafiq, M., & Chin, T. (2019). Three-Way Interaction Effect of Job Insecurity, Job Embeddedness and Career Stage on Life Satisfaction in A Digital Era. *International Journal of Environmental Research and Public Health* 16(9):1580.

Ray, B. (2020). This is the time for survival, before the revival: Somnath Mukherjee. *Ethospitalityworld.* Retrieved from https://hospitality.economictimes.indiatimes.com/news/hotels/this-is-the-time-for-survival-before-the-revival-somnath-mukherjee/76298699

Robinson, R. N. S., Kralj, A., Solnet, D. J., Goh, E., & Callan, V. (2014). Thinking job embeddedness not turnover: Towards a better understanding of frontline hotel worker retention. *International Journal of Hospitality Management*, *36*, 101–109. https://doi.org/10.1016/j.ijhm.2013.08.008

Safavi, H. P., & Karatepe, O. M. (2019). The effect of job insecurity on employees' job outcomes: the mediating role of job embeddedness. Journal of Management Development, 38(4), 288–297. https://doi.org/10.1108/jmd-01-2018-0004

Salisu, I., Hashim, N., Mashi, M. S., & Aliyu, H. G. (2020). Perseverance of effort and consistency of interest for entrepreneurial career success. *Journal of Entrepreneurship in Emerging Economies*, *12*(2), 279–304. https://doi.org/10.1108/jeee-02-2019-0025

Sethi, D., & Shashwati, S. (2019). Say No to Setbacks: Grit & Growth Mindset Have Got Your Back. International Journal of Innovative Studies in Sociology and Humanities, 4(3). Retrieved from https://www.academia.edu/38557375/Say_No_to_ Setbacks_Grit_and_Growth_Mindset_Have_Got_Your_Back

STR & Horwath HTL. (2020). *India Hotel Market Review – H1 2020.* https://www. hospitalitynet.org/file/152008889.pdf

Susomrith, P., & Amankwaa A. (2019). Relationship between Job Embeddedness and Innovative Work Behaviour. *Management Decision* 58(5):864–78.

Suzuki, Y., Tamesue, D., Asahi, K., & Ishikawa, Y. (2015). Grit and Work Engagement: A Cross-Sectional Study. *PLOS ONE, 10*(9), e0137501. https://doi.org/10.1371/journal. pone.0137501

THE Park Hotels introduces 'Chef and Bartender at Home' service. (2020). *Hotelier India.* Retrieved from https://www.hotelierindia.com/fb/11900-the-park-hotels-introduces-chef-and-bartender-at-home-service

The World Bank. (2020). *Global Economic Prospects.* United Nations. https://www. worldbank.org/en/publication/global-economic-prospects

Williams, A. (2003). How to … Write and analyse a questionnaire. *Journal of Orthodontics, 30*(3), 245–252. https://doi.org/10.1093/ortho/30.3.245

World Economic Forum. (2019). *The Travel & Tourism Competitiveness Report 2019 - Travel and Tourism at a Tipping Point.* http://reports.weforum.org/ttcr

World Health Organization. (2021, January 11). *WHO Coronavirus (COVID-19) Dashboard.* United Nations Economic and Social Council. https://covid19.who.int/

Yam, L., Raybould, M., & Gordon, R. (2018). Employment stability and retention in the hospitality industry: Exploring the role of job embeddedness. *Journal of Human Resources in Hospitality & Tourism, 17*(4), 445–464. https://doi.org/10.1080/153328 45.2018.1449560

Yang, J.-T. (2008). Effect of newcomer socialisation on organisational commitment, job satisfaction, and turnover intention in the hotel industry. *The Service Industries Journal, 28*(4), 429–443. https://doi.org/10.1080/02642060801917430

Yang, Q., Jin, G., Fu, J., & Li, M. (2019). Job Insecurity and Employees Taking Charge: The Role of Global Job Embeddedness. *Social Behavior and Personality: An International Journal, 47*(4), 1–12. https://doi.org/10.2224/sbp.7538

Yao, T., Qiu, Q., & Wei, Y. (2019). Retaining hotel employees as internal customers: Effect of organizational commitment on attitudinal and behavioral loyalty of employees. *International Journal of Hospitality Management, 76*, 1–8. https://doi.org/10.1016/j. ijhm.2018.03.018

SECTION IV

Contemporary Issues and Challenges in Operations and SCM/ ITM/ Business policy, Strategy and Entrepreneurship

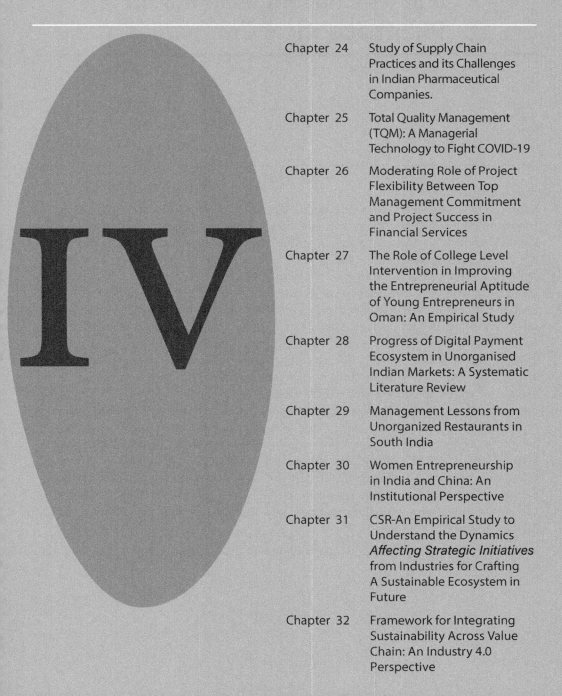

Chapter 24 Study of Supply Chain Practices and its Challenges in Indian Pharmaceutical Companies.

Chapter 25 Total Quality Management (TQM): A Managerial Technology to Fight COVID-19

Chapter 26 Moderating Role of Project Flexibility Between Top Management Commitment and Project Success in Financial Services

Chapter 27 The Role of College Level Intervention in Improving the Entrepreneurial Aptitude of Young Entrepreneurs in Oman: An Empirical Study

Chapter 28 Progress of Digital Payment Ecosystem in Unorganised Indian Markets: A Systematic Literature Review

Chapter 29 Management Lessons from Unorganized Restaurants in South India

Chapter 30 Women Entrepreneurship in India and China: An Institutional Perspective

Chapter 31 CSR-An Empirical Study to Understand the Dynamics *Affecting Strategic Initiatives* from Industries for Crafting A Sustainable Ecosystem in Future

Chapter 32 Framework for Integrating Sustainability Across Value Chain: An Industry 4.0 Perspective

CHAPTER 24

A Study of Supply Chain Practices and its Challenges in Indian Pharmaceutical Companies

Dr. Mritunjay Kumar
Army Institute of Management and
Technology
Greater Noida
mritunjay370@gmail.com

Abstract

Supply chain management in pharmaceutical industries can be helpful for the organisational transformation which makes better use of resources, enhances shareholders value, generates profits for organisation and also satisfies the customer demand. Pharmaceutical companies and its supply chain play an important role. During Covid (during coronavirus) period the supply chain, a good supply chain of medicines becomes crucial. The drug supply chain is complex in nature because of its interesting qualities of items. It's exceptionally divided with complex activities with tremendous driving requests and high development rate. In spite of the fact that industry is having colossal development potential, it is still battling with premise infrastructural issues and government intervention. The legislature of India has been attempting to invest energy to comprehend the ground real factors of such supply chains. The exploratory examination has been directed to three significant clusters of nation to comprehend the commonness of supply chain rehearses and their impact on the exhibition. The investigation involves poll based meeting reviews; gathered information has been introduced as rate examination. This study would upgrade the clearness over supply chain development point of view toward vital approach detailing. However it is tough to identify a suitable supply chain model for any particular business or industry because it is affected by infrastructure and government policy also. This study focuses on overall supply chain management of Pharma companies. The study based on theoretical aspects of supply chain management. The sample size of the study is taken100 for convenience.

Keyword: Supply Chain Management, Pharmaceutical Companies, MSME, Inventory, 3PL.

1. INTRODUCTION

Supply chain management is defined as the movement of material, finance, information from manufacturers to wholesalers to retailers to customers. In the supply chain material, moves in the forward direction while finance moves in backward direction. It means materials moves from manufacturer to customer while finance moves from customers to manufacturer. Supply chain management involves the coordination and integration within the organisation as well as among the different organisations.

For all needs of supply chain management proper forecasting and plan is required. Demand planning, capacity planning and inventory planning are part of good supply chain activities. Purchasing and procurement are the one of the important components of supply chain management. Under the purchasing and procurement agreement and contract is formed between the company and suppliers.

Supply Chain Management (SCM) is the way toward arranging, actualizing and controlling the activities of the supply affix with the reason to fulfill client prerequisites as effectively as could reasonably be expected. SCM is a cognizant and conscious control, integration, and the management of the business capacities. SCM contributes and influences that supply move through the business to improve execution, costs, adaptability and so on, which brings a definitive advantage to the end clients or customers. There are several sub area incorporated under supply chain function, for example, Planning and Forecasting, Procurement, logistics, Inventory, Operations, transportation, warehousing and so on. Logistics are exclusively handling the transportation, movements of material and goods. Purchasing activity is limited to the commercial transactions while procurement includes acquisition of material and its logistics and performance management. Operations deal the effective use of resources and/or optimum use of resources to meet the customer needs and requirement. Inventory management includes planning, controlling and coordinating of material acquisition, its handling, and possible sale of materials. It also includes component parts, replacement parts, sub-assemblies and other assets that are needed to meet customer needs and wants. Transport management involves the control over the fleet of vehicles to manage material movement and also manage the transport facilities of third party logistics providers. Warehousing includes the control of warehouse the management of warehouses hired from the third party.

India is the one of the leading pharma producers of cost-effective generic drugs and vaccines and it is supplying approximately 20 percent of the total global demand by volume. Pharmaceutical supply chain is a progression of hysterical endeavors made within a complex climate upheld by IT framework to serve a number of inner and outside clients. The productivity and adequacy of such supply chains are extremely pivotal under risk and uncertainty. The rising managerial and administrative issues, profoundly value delicate business sectors made pharmaceutical organizations to react proactively. Administrative endeavors are proposed to figure techniques to improve supply chain execution and nimbleness. The mission of such gracefully tie is to give fundamental drugs conveyed at the opportune spot at the correct time.

Pharmaceutical company supply chain includes drug research, development, manufacturing and distribution of wide range healthcare services. The Pharma and

Healthcare industry is too complex because it includes a large number of products, processes, market and intermediaries (Whewell,2009). Any risk could be a hindrance, influencing supply of medicine; a danger to a patient's life. The risk is clearly visible in all parts of significant value chains including solutions and use of medicines (Jaberidoost et al., 2015). The organizational changes, innovation in technology and uncertainty are challenges for the present-day and future drug industry (Breen, 2008). The business is confronting an immense risk in terms of steady basic change, volume estimating, request expectation, shortage of raw material, and nature of medication (Jaberidoost et al., 2013; Narayana et al., 2014).The research work done by Privett and Gonsalvez (2014),they identified the ten most important challenges for worldwide medicine or pharma supply chain such as Inventory management, Lack of coordination, , Absent demand information, Order management, Human resource dependency, Shortage avoidance, Temperature control, Expiration, Warehouse management, Shipment visibility. .

A medical care framework is described both as a circumstance and logical results after effects of economic advancement. As such, the pharma industry is described as a significant part that can add to the monetary improvement in addition it gives outstanding financial advantages to the overall population through the formation of supply chain, work creation and network advancement. it additionally assumes a significant function in mechanical advancement which can decrease the expense of assembling. Pharmaceutical companies need to oversee inconceivably complex supply chains and deal with the operational difficulties of working and communicating with a huge number of suppliers contributing fixings and segments to medicine production. Currently, they have to meet track and follow mandates and consent to new serialization guidelines that expect stock to be auditable as it travels through the supply chain. Various companies in the pharmaceutical industry incorporate branded medication producers, the generic manufacturer, firms creating bio-pharmaceutical items, non-prescribed medication producers, and firms undertaking contract research.

Pharmaceutical industries in India are highly diversified in terms of size, capacity, and research and development. In India, a large network of 3000 drug companies and about 10,500 manufacturing units of Pharma industry with growth potential 15-16% are present. Indian pharmaceutical industries are the highest growing industries of the world. Quality of medicine is a significant concern in India because of poor infrastructure; the overseeing transitory items like meds, serum plans and medications, and so forth could be debased as they move along the supply chain.

The major Pharmaceutical cluster is situated in Uttarakhand, Andhra Pradesh Maharashtra, Gujarat and Goa. It is located in Ahmedabad, Vadodara ,Mumbai, Pune, Aurangabad, Hyderabad Haridwar, Visakhapatnam .

2. LITERATURE REVIEW

It is broadly acknowledged that literature review provides the understanding and idea of issues associated to research. It is helpful to justify the research under study also helpful in finding the research gap. Numbers of articles, research papers, books, and reports on the topic of supply chain management (SCM) have been studied for the research work.

Supply chain management (SCM) is defined as a set of different activities implementing a management theory and philosophy (Mentzer,J.T et.al,2007). Seven different activities have been identified - Integrated behavior, corporation, integration of process, mutually shared information, same goal and same focus serve the customer, mutually shared risk and rewards and maintain long term relationship with the partners. For the Pharmaceutical and Healthcare industry, medical products and commodities are necessarily delivered on time to meet the customer needs and customer satisfaction by using effective supply chain management(Enyada,2009).As the pharmaceutical and healthcare marketplace facing major issues with various stakeholders which are demanding the healthcare products to be affordable, strategic planning would be of the essence (Holdford, 2005; Birdwell, 1994).

Chopra and Mendil, 2007 defined the Supply Chain as "the management of a network of retailers, distributors, transporters, storage facilities and suppliers that participate in the sale, delivery and production of a particular product".

Handfield and Nichols (1999) defined pharmaceutical supply chain as "the integration of all activities associated with the flow of and transformation of raw materials through to the end-user, as well as associated information flows, through improved supply chain relationships to achieve a sustainable competitive advantage".

Dubey and Kumar (2007) mentioned that "effective supply chain management can impact and improve upon virtually all business processes, such as data accuracy, operational complexity reduction, supplier selection, purchasing, warehousing and distribution. The benefits of SCM are included as quicker customer response and fulfillment rates, shorter lead time, greater productivity and lower costs, reduced inventory supply throughout the chain, improved forecasting precision, fewer suppliers and shorter planning cycles."

Handfield and Dhinagaravel (2005) expressed that "different functions happening consistently are forming the serious and administrative climate wherein channel individuals work their business. They brought up that controllers are requesting that wholesalers and makers uncover evaluating and are testing the expense of drug dissemination. Market channels, for example, mail request, direct delivery and site drug stores are likewise significant serious channels to consider. They saw that in spite of the fact that the way toward assembling and appropriating marked and nonexclusive medications is very comparable; the plan of the dissemination channel may be considerably extraordinary. They additionally noticed that numerous conventional organizations are investigating associations with Indian and Chinese makers to showcase their items. Given these changes, it is little wonder makers, wholesalers, drug stores, medical clinics, and different members are baffled with the variety of different serious difficulties that face them".

Chopra and Mandel explained that "the goal of the pharmaceutical supply chain emphasizes regulatory compliance and safety of product. It also includes responsiveness in the supply chain to meet the customer need. Supply chain excellence in the pharmaceutical industry plays important rules not only for the customer but also for the company. It improves demand-forecast accuracy and all financial measures of the company".

Svantesson (2009) has expressed that "drugs, being high worth products, request a protected cycle at all centers in the chain, and security estimations must be fit and thoroughly checked over the working paths with its sub-stockrooms and on/off stacking places. He further expressed that the significance of using as not many on/off stacking spots and changes of transport mode is one of the difficulties for a period compelling and secure arrangement; this at a limited cost level. As per Svantesson the market requests worldwide arrangements and customers are mentioning the capacity to arrange right amounts and lower stock levels. This circumstance carries a change to the request profile; with orders decreasing and creation evolving in like manner. This is a test to the dispersion of drugs and union prospects that can meet with the lead time interest to the end client are exceptionally significant". Svantesson noticed that a difference in routine in the Supply chain (SCM) can have effective impacts if supply chain not appropriately executed at all different levels. With clear correspondence, the expense of progress decreases significantly. Worldwide harmonization upgrades the chance of amplifying the impacts in a supply chain management.

3. OVERVIEW OF INDIAN HEALTHCARE AND PHARMACEUTICAL INDUSTRY

Pharmaceutical industry of India is the world's third largest industry by production volume. India contributes approximately 60% of Global vaccine production. Indian pharmaceutical companies also fulfill 40 to 60% WHO demand of diphtheria tetanus and pertussis (DTP). In United Kingdom, approximately 25% of medicine brands are made in India.(Press Release Government of UK, 5 October 2015).Indian pharmaceutical industries contributing Indian economic growth. As per estimate, the pharma Industry directly and indirectly provides approximately 2.7 million employments. This industry also generates approximately USD 11 billion of trade surplus every year.(IDMA Report).Indian Pharma Industry is one of the growing industries, its growth rate is 15% per annum. Indian Pharmaceutical sector accounts globally about 2.4% by value term and 10% in volume term. It is expected to grow approximately 15-16% annual growth and become US $ 55 billion by 2020.In vision 2030, it is expected that Indian pharmaceutical industry annual revenue can grow upto USD 80-90 billion by 2030.

The Indian Pharmaceutical Industries are facing major challenges. First major challenge is lack of stable pricing and government policy uncertain environment for research and innovations. Second major challenge is limited Government support in innovations. But there is a scope to get rid of this challenge by improving the collaboration between Government organisations and pharmaceutical industry on innovation focused research. Third major challenge is dependency on the external market for intermediaries and API. For Active Pharmaceutical Ingredients (API), most of the Indian companies depend on China because 80% (approximately) of API is supplied by Chinese companies.

The government can play an important role three to five to help the industry achieve self-sufficiency in API and intermediates. The government can support industry by establishing three to five dedicated clusters for API/intermediate industry. These clusters could offer some benefits like subsidised land, tax free or low tax for the industry. The facilities can help the to reduce the overall production cost of Pharma industries. It could further support the industry to improve research and development in manufacturing as well as API development.

4. RESEARCH METHODOLOGY

In this section problem definition, data collection, sample selection, design of questionnaire will be discussed. In the literature review, it is observed that operations and supply chain play major roles in the pharmaceutical industry. At present, the pharma companies of India supply more than 80 percent of the anti--viral medicines which is used in whole world to fight against AIDS (Acquired Immuno Deficiency Syndrome). During 2017-18, Indian Pharmaceutical Companies exported medicines products of worth 17.27 billion dollars. By the year 2020, the pharma industry's estimates the exports to grow by 30 per cent to reach 20 billion dollar and is achieved by the companies. The United State is the most attractive generics medicine market for India's pharmaceutical industry. It is estimated at around 60 billion US dollar and accounts for around 25 percent of India's total export. During 2017-18, India shipped about 3.21 billion dollar worth of generic medicines to the United States, despite the tough regulatory environment in the country. With branded or vital medicines going off patent during the year 2017-19, pharma research organizations estimate the export of generic medicines to the United States to rise by about 55 billion US dollars. India's other important exporting countries in which the United Kingdom (383.3 million US dollars), South Africa (367.35 million US dollars), Russia (283.33 million US dollars) and Nigeria (255.89 million US dollars) have been included. (Source-Department of Pharmaceutical –GOI)

The pharmaceutical big companies like Sun pharma , Ranbaxy, Cipla, Dr Reddy perform well in supply chain management. But small companies of pharmaceutical industry are unable to perform according to their requirement.

In this research exploratory research technique has been used. The sampling technique used for this research is convenience sampling. The data have been collected through interviews and industrial visits. The data analysis has been done by bar chart, pai chat, factor analysis and Structural equation modeling.

The Indian Pharmaceutical MSMEs become the major strength of industry and India may lead in pharmaceutical and medicines production. The quality of product and its supply chain make the industry enable to compete with the world price sensitive market.

5. SUPPLY CHAIN PRACTICES IN PHARMACEUTICAL INDUSTRY:A DISCUSSION

Excellent SCM is a competitive advantage over the competitors. It enables the firm in lowering operations cost, decrease inventory level, increase serviceability, lower the number of backorders, decrease order cycle time, and increase customer satisfaction. In this study, various factors have been identified which will be helpful in reducing the operating cost, increase profitability and improve the quality of the supply chain.

There are so many factors affecting the supply chain of the Pharmaceutical industry. For the factor identification different literature review helpful identify the various factor world class Pharmaceutical supply chain Practices. For this research paper only 15 factors have been identified for study. These Factors have been rated on a 5-point likert scale. The lowest assign value is 1 and highest assign value is 5 that is from extremely unimportant to extremely important. The most prevalent practices in pharmaceutical companies are e-procurement, 3PL, Outsourcing, JIT supply, Quality purchasing, Preventive maintenance etc found more important in the supply chain. E-procurement or electronic procurement is also known as supplier exchange. It is business to customer, business to business and business to government purchase and sales of goods services and work through the electronic or internet platform.3PL or TPL is used to describe the outsourcing of logistic management companies are turning over warehousing and distribution to companies that are specialized in these area.

From the factor analysis it is found that quality practices, inventory practices and outsourcing practices are major three factors. Quality practices include quality purchasing, preventive maintenance, benchmarking, continuous improvement grouped together with higher contribution factor. Inventory practices have also so many factors which contribute to supply chain decisions. Inventory components are e-procurement, vertical integration, warehouse safety Outsourcing practices includes 3PL, and subcontracting, lean certification .All the above major factor and sub major factors have been studied to know the Indian pharmaceutical company's supply chain. All the factors impact has been shown in the following diagram 1.

Diagram 1

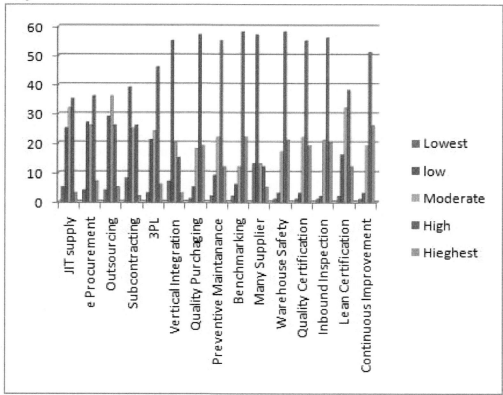

6. CONCLUSION

The study is based on major three clusters of the pharmaceutical industry. The clusters are Haridwar, Ahmedabad and Mumbai- Pune cluster. Measure of responses received from Haridwar and Mumbai Pune clusters. The Haridwar cluster faced a major challenge of infrastructure and Government support in operational policies for pharma Industry.

Most of the respondents are male and their educational qualification is at least graduate. Most of the information collected from personal interviews at the level of GM and CEO. Approximately 80% data has been collected from the higher authority i.e from GM and CEO. The age groups of respondents are more than 35 years.

MSMEs and Small scale pharmaceutical companies are doing well besides the infrastructure hurdles and lack of proper government policies. Pharmaceutical companies are also struggling with basic technology issues.

7. REFERENCES

1. Jaberidoost, M., Nikfar, S., Abdollahiasl, A., & Dinarvand, R. (2013). Pharmaceutical supply chain risks: a systematic review. Daru : Journal of Faculty of Pharmacy, Tehran University of Medical Sciences, 21(1), 69.
2. Jaberidoost, M., Olfat, L., Hosseini, A., Kebriaeezadeh, A., Abdollahi, M., Alaeddini, M., & Dinarvand, R. (2015). Pharmaceutical supply chain risk assessment in Iran using analytic hierarchy process (AHP) and simple additive weighting (SAW) methods. Journal of Pharmaceutical Policy and Practice, 8(1), 1–10.
3. Balarajan, Y., Selvaraj, S., & Subramanian, S. (2011). Health care and equity in India. The Lancet, 377(9764), 505–515.
4. Breen, L. (2008). A Preliminary Examination of Risk in the Pharmaceutical Supply Chain (PSC) in the National Health Service (NHS). Journal of Service Science and Management, 01(02), 193–199.
5. Who, W. H. O. (2012). World Health Statistics. WHO World Health Organization (Vol. 27).

CHAPTER 25

Total Quality Management (TQM): a Managerial Technology to Fight Covid-19

Ashutosh Samadhiya
Department of Management Studies
Indian Institute of Technology Roorkee
Roorkee, India
asamadhiya@bm.iitr.ac.in

Rajat Agrawal
Department of Management Studies
Indian Institute of Technology Roorkee
Roorkee, India
rajat@ms.iitr.ac.in

Abstract

COVID-19 has shaken the world financially and socially by impacting society's essential factor, i.e., human well-being. The pandemic situation, like COVID-19, has created enough chaos globally, which is easily visible at even the micro-level of any sector. These lockdowns and social distancing processes became useful in terms of controlling the virus spread, but parallelly the physical space among people has hit most of the sectors. Total Quality Management (TQM) has always been seen as a managerial philosophy that helps organizations improve their performance in various dimensions. Top Management (TM) involvement is an essential part of TQM, making all the crucial decisions related to corporate welfare. TM involvement used to shape the administrative activities with its effective management. This article represents the TM role's analogy in corporate administration and country administration during COVID-19. It compares and explains how all India's top authorities operate as a manager during the COVID-19 situation. Prime Minister, chief ministers, and all other ministers have played their role as a member of the country's top management with a clear commitment to control the spread of coronavirus and empower the local administration, doctors, safaiwala etc. Empowerment of local administration led to the continuous improvement of society by learning from each other, which reduces the speed of virus spread. This way, it finally leads to India's safety and fulfilling their essential needs. This paper presented a graphical framework to provide an analogy platform for COVID-19 management with top management's role as per the TQM understanding.

Keywords: TQM, COVID-19, Top Management, Well-being, Human life

1. INTRODUCTION

The world has suffered so much in the last few months due to the pandemic situation created by coronavirus spread. The collateral of COVID-19 was more than the death of 50 million people, which is the most frightening event in human history since 1918 influenza pandemic (**Tyagi et al., 2021**). India is the second-largest country population-wise globally and has faced the most difficult times in its history during the lockdown period. Still, a developing country like India has done a tremendous job to manage the COVID-19 situation. The first case of coronavirus was identified in late January 2020 in India's Kerala state (**Patrikar et al., 2020**). After that, few more cases came in India in late February (**Basu, 2020**). This way, the COVID-19 wave starts in India, and there were almost 1 lakh cases of coronavirus at the mid of may (**Ghosh et al., 2020**).

One report on India COVID-19 cases by (**Statista, 2021**) shows the quantified values of covid cases till now in India. This report is summarized with the help of four factors: deceased people by a coronavirus, active cases of covid-19, recovered people from coronavirus, and the confirmed cases from the covid-19. The quantitative values of these four factors show the potential of the Indian government and its members of top management such as different ministers, doctors, police officers, administrative persons, and lower chain people such as safaiwala, municipality people etc. The facts mentioned in Fig.1. shows that 1.4% of people are deceased, and 96.58% are recovered from this disease. The report developed by (**Statista, 2021**) shows the death rate was recorded at 2.14%, and the recovery rate was recorded at 71.72% globally as of January 2021. It means that India has given better performance than the rest of the world with such limited resources. This statistics shows the dedicated commitment of top management members, which helps control this crisis in a growing country like India.

Fig. 1: *Covid-19 Cases in India as of January 17, 2021*

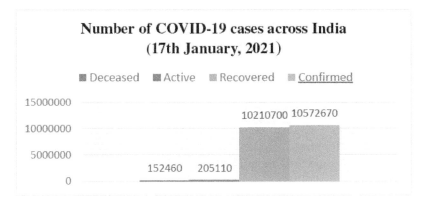

Both state and central government has worked to reduce the coronavirus cases and resolved the issues at the local and global level by involving various frontline workers such as doctors, medical nurses, police, safaiwala, and other lower chain of people (**Sharma et al., 2020; Shetti et al., 2020; Konwar and Borse, 2020; Chandra et al., 2017**). The Indian government has involved these frontline workers in handling and minimizing this pandemic's collateral damage (**Ghosh et al., 2020**). This massive crisis management led the author to think of the analogy between the TQM and all the contributors.

TQM mainly focused on continuous improvement (**Wang et al., 2012**), which projects a proven global competition survival practice. It used to improve the employee's morale and ameliorate the efficiency of the company (**Lazari & Kanellopoulos, 2007**).

TQM is such a managerial approach which focuses on different aspects of organizations such as customer satisfaction, human prioritization, continuous improvement, strategic based decision implementation, proper involvement of employees, and combined group effort (**Sureshchandar et al., 2001**). It is very popular and the most reliable and long term running philosophy for any organization (**Benavides-Velasco et al., 2014**). This is such a holistic strategy that gives a competitive advantage to any organization with the help of its different principles which finally leads to customer satisfaction, somehow the most important aspect of every business firm (**Shan et al., 2013**). W.Edward Deming has given the concept of TQM, which says the good quality advanced to higher productivity, and it minimizes the wastes. Also it reduces the cost of the item and improves the customer satisfaction, which enhances the financial value of the organization and helps to strengthen its reputation.

Various factors influence TQM. Top management ™ is an essential key factor of the TQM system, which acts as a driving element to effective TQM practices to satisfy the consumers and improve the firm performance (**Chowdhury et al., 2007**). Some past researches show that ineffective top management leads to the failure of TQM and further deprives the desirable outcomes. It is quite apparent that TM influences differ from firm to firm.

Some past research also shows that good leadership can lead organizations towards more sustainability, which creates an immense pressure on top management to lead the organization to give better outcomes of every TQM principles (**Dóci and Hofmans, 2015**). Even some previous research empirically finds the significant relationship between the TQM, effective leadership, and the ability to execute the decisions. Although we know that TQM is a long term strategy, and the pandemic situation is some crisis management. Still, it is imperative to integrate such a management system to fight this emergency. The well-established preparedness and integrated management system will help the organization/country prepare for such unexpected problems wave. It will help the organization (country) to sort this kind of problems in a shorter period with more effectiveness.

This study will elaborate by the analogy of how top management and their execution ability highlight TQM as a managerial technology to fight with COVID-19 in the country context. One graphical framework is also presented in this study to understand the parallel relationship between country and organization management.

2. GRAPHICAL FRAMEWORK AND ANALOGY

Past literature shows the TM as a useful indicator for the effective implementation of TQM in an organization to provide better survival strength, improved customer satisfaction, and improved other outcomes. This paper's previous discussion also declares that TQM not only delivers a worthwhile long-term goal but could also be used for emergency circumstances like COVID-19. This way, the author includes the TM at the centre of the framework. There are four essential aspects of this framework presented circularly in the diagram to shows the interlinking of these aspects. The circular framework also shows the interdependency and importance of all these four aspects on each other. This section of the paper will explain the graphical framework with some examples of COVID-19 management in India during the pandemic period.

2.1. Four Interlinking Factors

Fig. 2. is representing the graphical framework of the present studies, which shows top management commitment at its centre. Further, the other interlinking aspects of the frameworks are empowerment and commitment, continuous improvement and learning from each other, reducing the virus, and providing the citizen's safety with delivering the essentials. These four factors are explained further.

Fig. 2: *Graphical framework of TQM implementation in the country context*

2.1.1. Top Management

Top management involves the managers placed at top positions in organizations, making some extraordinary decisions for the firm's benefit. Here, this study considers different ministers as the top managers because they are the country's decision-makers. These decisions lead the country/ organization to succeed, or failure depends on the influence of various external factors at their conclusion. Fig. 3. presents the top 10 countries performed the maximum number of COID-19 tests till January 18, 2021 **(Statista, 2021)**.

Fig. 3. Shows that the U.S performs the maximum number of tests, but India came at the second number. As for the comparision purpose, India's resources are much lesser than the U.S. Still India shows its potential with sufficient decision-making capability, which shows the healthy mindset of top management persons.

It is easily observable that India was suffering from a massive financial, but top management of the country has decided for social welfare. With the limited resources, the top heirerchy projects their thought process towards social sustainability. It is challenging for an organization to practice social sustainability during these difficult times. Top management was taking the decisions, but their choices totally depended on the empowerment and commitment of the people involved in this process at the execution level.

Fig. 3: *Number of tests for COVID-19 in countries worldwide as of January 18, 2021.*

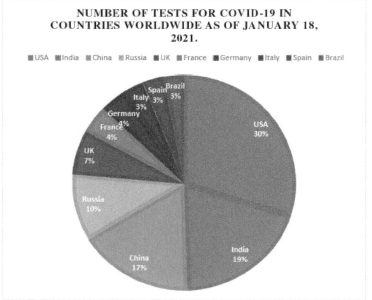

2.1.2. Empowerment and commitment

The empowerment and commitment of various people, such as doctors, nurses, police officers, and safaiwalas depend on their social welfare responsibilities. It requires a strong dedication to work for non-profit values. There is a need for extreme leadership style, which relies on the charity, voluntary participants with limited resources and less money-oriented goals in non-profit works **(Herman, 2016)**.

During COVID-19, local administration, and the other people involved in this process contributes to succeeding the fundamental achievements. As this virus spreads from the various medium, which makes it very dangerous even for people like doctors and nurses, who were taking all the precautions. In this paper, it is previously discussed that the cases of COVID-19 start at the end of January 2021 in India and further spread continuously. India has begun practising the lockdown and social distancing at the end of March 2020, but this lockdown was only for the country's public. The local administrative people, such as medical officers, police, and other medical staff were on duty even in the lockdown period. They were not getting any extra payment for this service, but the empowerment and commitment of those people avail country to fight this hectic and critical situation.

Doctors dealt with the thousands of patients related to the coronavirus and other general diseases. Still, they were willingly taking risks to handle this situation with matuarity even after various medical persons' deaths. It shows their dedication towards humanity and effective empowerment and commitment. This empowerment and responsibility are also essential aspects of the TQM practice, which reflects during the COID-19 situation by various front line warriers.

People are not used to wearing masks and maintaining social distancing in countries like India, where multiple cultures exist on the same platform. So it was an arduous task to monitor and supervise the general public to follow these protocols. Still, local administrators and police officers were sincerely doing this work by hook and crook to minimize the cases of COVID-19. Their working way reflects its potential and selfless efforts, which is a necessary factor for the respective attribute.

The pandemic situation was new for every person, so it was challenging to cope with this new lifestyle. People were scared to tell if they have some cold symptoms and fever because they thought that even simple cold could be converted into the COVID-19. Government of India starts the quarantine protocols, and different areas were marked as red, green, and yellow zones. Some people were appointed to sanitize these zones, and it was a real risk to enter in those zones and do the sanitization process. Sanitizing people and safaiwalas have done a tremendous job to recover the coronavirus affected zones during the lockdown period and after that.

In this section, the paper has explained with the examples of three different types of people that all these people show their empowering mindset with strong commitment attitudes.

2.1.3. Effects of continuous improvements and everyone learning from each other

People were not taking this pandemic seriously until the government announce the lockdown of 21 days. After the passing of this period, people start horrifying when lockdown extends. The lockdown period guidelines were not very relieving because it was for people's welfare, which makes it very strict. People start panicking because of the various unwanted factors such as non-delivering the essentials and closing the necessary medical facilities.

Fig. 4: *Stress measurement by respondents during COVID-19*

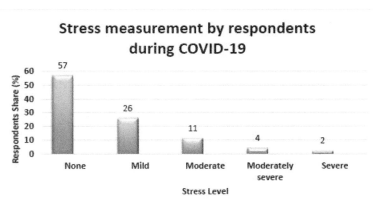

After extending the second lockdowns, people start to adopt the change in lifestyles as per the COVID-19 guidelines. Fig. 4. shows a data set generated by **(Statista, 2021)**, which is developed with the help of an online survey to predict the stress level in respondents during the COVID-19 in India. As shown in Fig. 4. that majority of respondents show the negligence of the stress during the COVID-19, and the least people felt severe stress, which leads that the people of India were not much mentally affected by this COVID-19. This kind of strong mental aptitude led to the continuous improvement phase, and the wave was very rapid because people were learning from each other. The learning phase helps people follow covid protocols such as wearing masks, maintaining social distancing, sanitization, and going outside only for the essentials. This disciplined routine plays a significant role in controlling the covid wave and minimizing the collaterals due to the virus spread. Continuous improvement is an integral part of the TQM practice. In past research, TQM outcomes can be achieved by focusing on continuous improvements. So this aspect of the graphical framework also shows the parallel paradigm of the TQM in the country context.

2.1.4. Reducing the spread of the virus, the safety of citizens, and fulfilling the essential needs

This graphical framework's previous aspect was vital, helping to achieve the awareness and sincereness towards this pandemic. This particular aspect leads India's people to follow the daily routine by reducing the virus's spread and safety and delivering the essentials.

(Statista, 2021) has done an online survey of 7847 people from April 9 to April 30, 2020 to determine people's mental status for safety from coronavirus after purchasing the items. Fig. 5. Represents the data collected from the people who had purchased items in the bulk quantity during the pandemic and after the shopping, they feel safe.

Fig. 5: *Share of respondents for the safe feeling after purchasing during COVID-19*

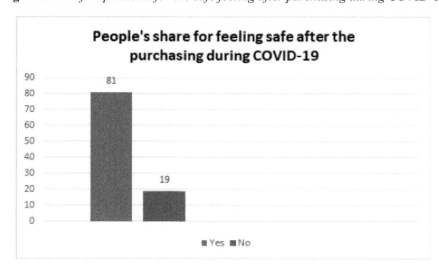

The figure's statistics show that 81 % of the people who had their purchasing were feeling safe. It reflects that most people were feeling safe after getting their essentials. So it was an influential agenda during the COVID-19 to deliver the requirements apart from the citizens' safety. Some more survey was performed and lived in **(Statista, 2021)** during the pandemic times, which shows the percentage of performed activities. This report shows the people's most involved activities during the pandemic were getting household chores with 59%. It means the delivering essentials were one of the most top priority in COVID-19 times.

The awareness among people and learning from each other lead to continuous improvements, and government also caught the pace of different activities to control the virus within this period. Top management, such as different ministers, had actively participated in solving the issues with their effective decision-making skills. The coordination of local administrative helps to reduce the effect of the virus by their dedicated working style and reflects their managerial skills as the analogous to the TQM tools.

3. ANALOGY

This pandemic situation (COVID-19) has a huge impact on every sector and part of the country and needs to be controlled. Controlling of such case depends on the various brain storming before taking any steps. Variables play an important role in handling any problem and show a way to solve it. So it is also important to understand the priority variables that needed to be controlled first, such as reducing the spread of the virus, citizens' safety, and providing the essential goods to all. There are other variables like the economy of Country, the growth of the industry, unemployment, social needs etc. but a pandemic situation like this needed to find a constraint variables so that the solution could work fast. The variables are essential to understand so that the proper decentralization of problem could be possible, which will finally ease problem-solving. The analogy of TQM for both the bodies (organization and Country) is important. A pictorial flow diagram explains the analogy of TQM in organization and Country.

Fig. 6: *Analogy of TQM in Organization and Country*

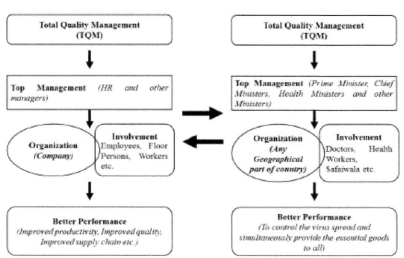

The above analogy shows the role plays by top management in both cases. Top management plays an essential part in every situation because of its decision-making capability and understanding its seriousness. Human resource managers and other managers are the top managers involved in various decision-making processes for the organization. The decisions used to improve organization performance with multiple training sessions, policy changing, etc. Similarly, Prime Minister, Health Ministers, and other government ministers participate and are involved in various country decision-making processes. These decisions involve lockdown, different policy implementation for this kind of situation etc. Employees, floor persons, and other organizational workers participate to succeed in any company's top management decisions. Similarly, Doctors, health workers, safaiwalas etc. involves fulfilling the decisions taken by top management to prevent the coronavirus and treat the infected persons with providing the essentials to all. This flow from top management to some persons' involvement leads to better organization performance. The company could get a better quality of the product, improve productivity, profit, improve supply chain, etc. For Country, it results from all the persons involved in this fight like virus prevention, people treatment etc.

As employees are essential in any organization achieving the desirable outcomes, similarly people of the country play an important part in successfully implementing the protocols, guidelines, and other important decisions to reduce coronavirus spread. This way, the paper explains the analogy between the TQM practices in organization and country at the same time.

4. CONCLUSION

This paper addresses how TQM practice helps manage its pandemic situation. Ministers of this country work as top management of the organization, local administrative, doctors, nurses, and safaiwalas were other associates succeeding in reducing and controlling the coronavirus. India is a developing country, and has minimal resources. It is also not very strong as per the economy side. Country with such geographical and cultural diversity has its demerits to handle this kind of situation. Still, they have effectively managed this situation with their strong administrative skills. Tuned coordination catalyzed the whole process to become successful and effective.

The philosophies of TQM were implemented in the country context and elaborated in this paper with the help of analogy. So it is very clear that a country can fight with this kind of pandemic problem by using a managerial technology like TQM in the context of country also. The whole process is implemented sequentially. Top management was at the centre of the framework and shows its importance for TQM in the country's context. It helped the country expose itself as a fighter for such a kind of war. TQM is a managerial philosophy implement in organization to achieve the quality outcomes by focusing on different factors. Still, it projects itself as a managerial technology to solve a problem. This way TQM is very helpful and supportive for even this kind of disasters and it can be seen as short-term management rather than only long term management.

5. REFERENCES

Basu M. (2020). How Coronavirus Spread in India — 39 of the First 50 Patients Came from Italy, Iran, China. Available at: https://theprint.in/health/how-coronavirus-spread-in-india-39-of-the-first-50-patients-came-from-italy-iran-china/379941/ accessed on 18th January, 2021.

Benavides-Velasco, C., Quintana-García, C., & Marchante-Lara, M. (2014). Total Quality Management, Corporate Social Responsibility and Performance in the Hotel Industry. International Journal of Hospitality Management, 41, 77–87. [CrossRef]

Chandra P., Nee Tan Y., Singh S.P. Spinger; 2017. Next Generation Point-of-care Biomedical Sensors Technologies for Cancer Diagnosis. [CrossRef]

Chowdhury, M., Paul, H., & Das, A. (2007). The impact of top management commitment on total quality management practice: An exploratory study in the Thai garment industry. Global Journal of Flexible Systems Management, 8(1–2), 17–29. https://doi.org/10.1007/bf03396517

Dóci, E., & Hofmans, J. (2015). Task complexity and transformational leadership: The mediating role of leaders' state core self-evaluations. The Leadership Quarterly, 26(3), 436–447. [Crossref]

Ghosh, A., Nundy, S., & Mallick, T. K. (2020). How India is dealing with COVID-19 pandemic. Sensors International, 1, 100021. https://doi.org/10.1016/j.sintl.2020.100021

Herman, R. D. (2016). Executive leadership. In D. O. Renz, et al. (Eds.), The Jossey-Bass handbook of nonprofit leadership and management (pp. 167–187). Wiley: San Francisco, CA. [Crossref]

Konwar A.N., Borse V. (2020). Current status of point-of-care diagnostic devices in the Indian healthcare system with an update on COVID-19 pandemic. Sensors Int.;1:100015. doi: 10.1016/j.sintl.2020.100015. [CrossRef]

Lazari, C.G. and Kanellopoulos, D.N. (2007) 'Total quality management in hotel restaurant: a case study in Greece', Journal of Engineering and Applied Sciences, Vol. 2, No. 3, pp. 564–571. [Crossref]

Patrikar S., Poojary D., Basannar D.R., Kunte R. (2020). Projections for novel coronavirus (COVID-19) and evaluation of epidemic response strategies for India. Med. J. Armed Forces India. 1–8. doi: 10.1016/j.mjafi.2020.05.001.

Shan, S., Zhao, S., & Hua, F. (2013). Impact of Quality Management Practices on the Knowledge Creation Process: The Chinese Aviation Firm Perspective. Comput. Ind. Eng., 64(1), 211–223. [CrossRef]

Sharma S., Basu S., Shetti N.P. (2020). Aminabhavi T.M. Current treatment protocol for COVID-19 in India. Sensors Int.;1:100013. doi: 10.1016/j.sintl.2020.100013. [CrossRef]

Shetti N.P., Srivastava R.K., Sharma S., Basu S. (2020). Aminabhavi T.M. Invasion of novel corona virus (COVID-19) in Indian territory. Sensors Int.;1:100012. doi: 10.1016/j.sintl.2020.100012. [CrossRef]

Statista. (2021, January 18). Coronavirus (COVID-19) in India. https://www.statista.com/study/71584/coronavirus-covid-19-in-india/ accessed on 18th January, 2021.

Sureshchandar, G., Rajendran, C., & Anantharaman, R. (2001). A Holistic Model for Total Quality Service. International Journal of Service Industry Management, 12, 378–412. . [CrossRef]

Tyagi, I., Mahfooz, Y., Kashif, M., & Anjum, A. (2021). COVID-19: Journey so far and deep insight using Crowdsourced data in India. MAPAN. https://doi.org/10.1007/s12647-020-00416-y

Wang, C. H., Chen, K. Y., & Chen, S. C. (2012). Total quality management, market orientation and hotel performance: The moderating effects of external environmental factors. International Journal of Hospitality Management, 31(1), 119–129. [Crossref]

CHAPTER 26

Moderating Role of Project Flexibility Between Top Management Commitment and Project Success in Financial Services

Pankaj Tiwari
PhD Research Scholar
School of Business and Management
CHRIST (Deemed to be University)
Bengaluru
pankaj.tiwari@res.christuniversity.in

Suresha B
Associate Professor
School of Business and Management
CHRIST (Deemed to be University)
Bengaluru
suresh.b@christuniversity.in

Abstract

Purpose – The aim of this paper is to study the moderation effect of project flexibility on top management commitment and project success in the Financial Services industry.

Design/methodology/approach – A survey of project managers was carried out. To find the association between the study variables, correlation was established. An ordinal regression analysis was performed to explore the direct effects of independent (top management commitment) and moderating variable (project flexibility) on dependent variable (project success).

Findings – The study variables have weak to moderate correlations. The ordinal regression analysis shows that project flexibility moderated the direct effects of top management commitment on project success in a positive direction.

Research limitations – The present study uses a cross-sectional data from Financial Services organizations, and uses the managers' perspective in achieving project success.

Managerial implications – Project managers should understand business and project vision to create business value and enable project groups to undergo continuous learning and accomplish expected outcomes. Senior managers should aim for professional development of project managers, ensure effective decision-making and promote transformational leadership style to foster business benefits.

Originality/value – The present study explored the effects of top management commitment and project flexibility on the IT project success in the Financial Services industry.

Keywords: project flexibility, top management commitment, project success, project performance, business success, project size, financial services.

I. INTRODUCTION

Established organizations are continuously engaged in technology projects execution to manage and mitigate the threat of technological disruptions (Clayton, 1997). Despite technology advancements and project management related processes, failures in projects still occur. With digitalization and globalization as the key drivers of change; established organizations have to adapt and face challenges that come with the change. Several organizations have been embracing the need for technology-led digital transformation. Along similar lines, financial services organizations have been digitizing business processes (since 1990s) and creating new financial products and services through online and offline channels. However, with the stiff competition that continuously sees improved financial products and services; financial organizations need to keep innovating and improving their offerings to stay ahead. Due to the 2008 financial crisis, it has been difficult to continue to be competitive in these dynamic conditions with new competitors and greater market instability. A few organizations have been able to execute innovative projects to offer new services and products to consumers in new markets. Based on present business dynamic, reputable financial services organizations face challenges with evolving technologies to discover new business opportunities. Such technology-intensive, projects depend on the technical skills and expertise of the involved to be successful and beneficial for the business (Nguyen et al., 2021).

The project management literature is proliferated with research conducted on key factors related with success of projects (Vrchota et al., 2021); however, very few studies address the contingency approach needed to ensure these factors influence successful implementation of the project resulting into business benefits (Ahimbisibwe et al., 2015). This research paper emphasizes top management commitment required during IT project implementation as one of the critical success factors. In this paper, contingency perspective is applied with project context, to show that commitment from senior leadership leads to success (Nunes et al, 2020; Garousi et al., 2019).

The research on senior leadership commitment is imperative because superficial support and commitment or involvement in a project does not make a project successful. Commitment means active involvement in projects, and selecting the right set of projects to achieve strategic goals (Hermano et al., 2016). Several factors results in project success and these factors can only be addressed by top management and related channels. Top management can easily manage budget and schedules related issues. The expected benefits from a project and overall scope are very important parameters to be managed because the benefits closely relate to the project's justification and funding. In case, top management is not actively engaged in projects (especially new projects with technological advancement), the project issues do not typically reach senior management following formal channels. As there can be various project stakeholders, the definition of success in a project varies. To achieve business benefits, top management should focus on successful projects crucial to the organization's future rather moving away from IT project failures (Khattak et al., 2020).

Strategies to manage risks should remain the prime consideration while managing projects to improve project performance and positively influence overall organizational efficiency and business benefits (Muller and Jugdev, 2012). Various strategies are recommended in studies to mitigate project risks and reduce delays occurring in business. The effectiveness of such recommended strategies to mitigate risks and reduce the interruptions in projects is not investigated empirically. Projects with higher complexity, innovativeness and uncertainties due to the use of advanced technologies should have thorough risk management plans and a formalized process with project controls. But conventional practices limit project managers to deal with any changes and contingencies. Consequently, operational flexibility and systemic thinking in projects add value to managerial activities by emphasizing project based performance measures and outcomes such as scope, schedule and cost. Thus, flexibility in projects relates to the preventive approaches while managing project risks in a dynamic environment (McNally et al., 2010; Salomo et al., 2007; Shenhar et al., 2001).

Given the continuous change in market settings, financial services need to remain agile with processes, stakeholder negotiations, responsiveness over inflexible planning and management of project risks, and emphasis on technology intensive projects to advance the likelihood of success. Further research is required to find the application of project flexibility in different dynamic settings with an aim to develop an effective project management approach leading to success (Curtis et al., 2019; Kapasali, 2011). Thus, the present paper will examine the impact of flexibility in financial services projects. To achieve this, general research questions are posed:

RQ1. *To what extent commitment by top management influences the success of projects?*
RQ2. *To what extent project flexibility impacts the association between commitment by top management and success of the project?*

By addressing the anticipated research questions, this study adds value to the project management literature and managerial practices. First, the paper adds to different organizational theories such as contingency theory, by considering managerial roles to achieve project success. Second, the current study offers an alternative explanation to why different managerial expertise can lead to a different project and business outcomes. Finally, this research provides insights for managers to realize project success more effectively through improved capabilities and understanding project attributes needed for a dynamic environment.

II. REVIEW OF LITERATURE

Top Management Commitment

The senior leadership in an organization is referred as top management. Commitment from top management is observed in different ways such as involvement, engagement, leadership, focus, and support of executive management in a project management environment. Support from top management is imperative because resources are controlled within an organization by the top management. Having top management commitment during project scope changes, budget overruns, delays in project schedules, and similar crises helps to obtain required resources and approvals. Specifically, for IT projects, budget allocation and extra funding for process engineering and additional training can be easily managed if they have top management commitment (Oh and Chois, 2020). Top management support encourages managers to set clear project objectives in achieving desired business outcomes and achieve customer satisfaction. As organizations want to increase the chances of accomplishing business success through projects, top management should be committed to optimizing business operations and exploring more opportunities by taking pioneering risks (Nunes et al., 2020). Technology based projects and their successful implementation depends on the intensity and sustained commitment by top management. With no involvement and support from senior management, it becomes difficult for managers, who run projects in silos, to manage when any complex issue arises. Senior management should clarify the rationale behind any projects with great enthusiasm and by applying their experience on project's activities to enrich the business outcomes. Quite a few studies recognize support from upper management as a significant aspect for executing technology-based projects and their success. However, top management commitment still need attention (Nguyen et al., 2021; Amoako et al., 2018; Young et al., 2013).

Project Success

The rate of failure or success in projects depends on how the stakeholders view it. It is important to outline success measures while defining scope in the initial stages of the project lifecycle (PMI, 2013). Both conceptual, as well as operational perspectives are important in project management. Success in projects is the combination of schedule, customer satisfaction, quality, and cost (Pinto et al., 1991). The three aspects of project success are: the way overall business, clients, and employees get influenced by the projects; how efficient the project is; and how it prepares the stage for future opportunities (Carvalho et al., 2017). Also, success in projects can be seen as the derivative of quality, time, budget, several external controls, user satisfaction, health & safety, and most importantly project's commercial value (Wu et al., 2017). In most cases, there can be different stakeholders for a single project. As a result, multiple project goals and different performance measuring parameters may exist. Thus, selecting one predominant goal to represent each project stakeholder becomes challenging. Moreover, due to the varying preferences in projects, the project goals also change. For example, extending of project duration changes all other parameters in a project. Thus, the observed performance of projects is regarded as a proxy demonstrating project outcomes. Organizations aim to improve business outcomes considering long term perspectives. For any organization, the success lies in fulfilling customer requirements by developing a service or product and showcasing the capability to offer business value. Thus, overall success incorporates the degree to which various projects realize organizational strategy and its ability to react to the dynamic environment by aiming for long term opportunities (Zhao et al., 2021).

Project Flexibility

By incorporating a flexible approach, projects can manage uncertainty, remain flexible in schedules and protect themselves from indefinite consequences. Project flexibility is generally expected in the initial stages to make sure that changes can be adapted by organizations especially in dynamic settings. Projects that showcase flexibility support long term plans of the organization, suggest strategies or evolving methodologies needed to accomplish success and utilize any overlooked opportunities by altering project capacities (Floricel et al., 2012;Olsson, 2008). Competent organizations remain flexible, sustain in dynamic settings and market competition by continued focus on potential clients or customers. Thus, any organization's success rate is based on the ability to react to dynamic scenarios (Skorstad et al., 2016). Project flexibility does not violate any project outcomes decided previously. Rather, it reduces complexities and uncertainties by risk mitigation approaches required in dynamic settings. Hence, when uncertainty is high organizations should maintain flexibility and advance effectiveness in projects (Zailani et al., 2016; Nandakumar et al., 2013).

III. HYPOTHESES DEVELOPMENT AND CONCEPTUAL FRAMEWORK

In the turbulent and rapidly changing environment, organizations should be proactive and remain innovative to gain competitive advantage. Some of the aspects such as organizational culture can be managed by senior leaders. To achieve innovativeness and offer innovative culture, top management should be committed, initiate the creative process, support creative ideas and continuously focus on technological advancements by encouraging managers to take risk. Commitment from senior leadership is important to manage project risks, project autonomy and overall project success. Top management can align individual activities by synergizing, to attain the organizational goal and is a crucial component for project success (Tzempelikos, 2015; Gemünden et al., 2005). Studies described that whenever environmental strategies are assimilated in organizational processes they enhance organizational and project performance by having top management commitment with improved the project management processes (Unger et al., 2012; Gustafson et al., 1995). Hence, proposed:

H1: *Top management commitment is significantly associated with project success.*

Typically during project initiation, project managers know how to overcome project challenges by planning ahead, establish problem-solving groups in projects to cope with uncertain events and maintain a status quo of project tasks. Flexibility in projects provides the ability to make changes with minimal variations in cost, time or performance. It describes the capacity of project to manage changes in its scope with suitable management actions, measures and defined policies. Project flexibility is a critical element to make sure that the project remains as per plan considering time, quality and cost (Atkinson, 1999). Flexibility in projects aligns the organizational short-term and long-term success as well as goals. In project based organization, risk mitigation strategies are used to overcome project related uncertain events. Customary attention in project management befits uncertainties and progressive environment. Hence, conceptual framework is depicted in Fig 1 and also proposed:

H2: *Project flexibility greatly influences success in projects.*
H3: *Project flexibility moderates the influence of top management commitment on success of the projects.*

Fig. 1: *Conceptual Framework*

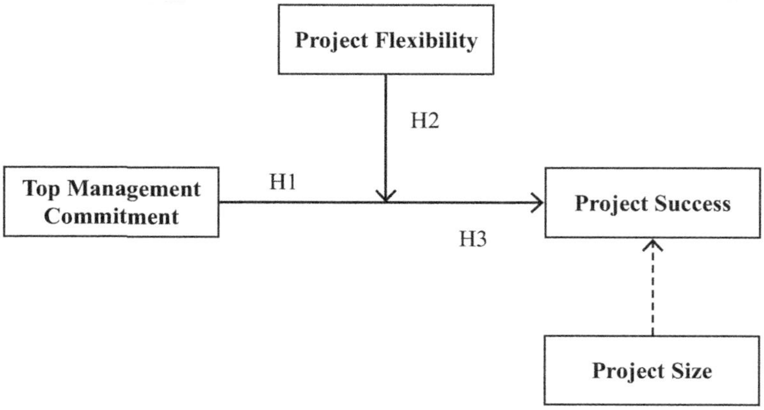

IV. RESEARCH METHODOLOGY

Sample and Data Collection

To test the hypotheses testing, 162 datasets were used as sample. Data analysis was carried on information technology projects executed and implemented between 2014 and 2020. A questionnaire in the form on web survey was shared with over 400 managers in Financial Services through email between December 2019 and June 2020. All responses received from the participants were carefully double-checked for accuracy of information. The response rate of the web-based survey questionnaire was 27.6%. There was no significant difference (alpha 5%) in the initial and later responses. A 'dual-informant' approach was applied to reduce the 'bias-risk' through common-method variance by including managers from different management responsibilities to assess study variables (Hair et al., 2010; Podsakoff et al., 2003; Armstong et al., 1977).

Sample Characteristics

About 37% of the managers who responded stated the duration of project as over three years, about 43% between one and three years, and 20% indicated project duration of less than a year.

Measures

The variables with multiple-item scales used in the present study were referred from the available project management literature. A few scales were re-worded and adapted to align with the context of this study. Five industry-specific professionals from the sample firms were consulted to evaluate all items with 7-point Likert scale and by averaging the particular items each study variable was constructed. A double blinded back-translation approach was taken into consideration to ensure meaning accuracy. A pilot test was conducted using inputs from consultants representing the Financial Services industry for the validation of all measures (Hair et al, 2010). PCFA (principal components factor analysis) was used to verify the items scale validity, along with CFA (confirmatory factor analysis). To ensure loadings from all items form a single factor, the PCFA was performed. Cronbach's alpha (α) for all scales was observed more than 0.7 as acceptable values and indicates the scale reliability (Guide et al., 2015; Ketokivi et al., 2004). The model fit was acceptable at CMIN/DF = 3.012, CFI = 0.982, RMSEA = 0.072, SRMR = 0.0260 (Hu & Bentler, 1999). **Project success** is measured based on seven items (α = 0.836) as developed by Shenhar et al. (2001). **Top management commitment** is measured using a 6-item scale (α = 0.802) developed by Ahmad (2016). The moderating variable **Project Flexibility** is measured using three items (α = 0.705) as stated by Zailani et al. (2016). **Project size** as a control variable is important for project success and is captured by calculating the natural logarithm of the project budget used, project duration, and project effort (Boehm, 1981; Barki et al., 2001).

V. RESEARCH FINDINGS AND DISCUSSION

Descriptive statistics

Correlations among study variables along with the means and standard deviation are shown in the Table 1.

Table 1: Correlations, Means and Standard deviations

Variables			0	1	2	3
Mean			5.021	5.045	4.912	3.843
Std. Dev.			1.256	1.071	1.093	1.495
Kendall's tau_b	0	Project Success	1			
	1	Top Management Commitment	.387***	1		
	2	Project Flexibility	.421***	.365***	1	
	3	Project Size	(-).156**	(-).123**	.027	1
Spearman's rho	0	Project Success	1			
	1	Top Management Commitment	.538***	1		
	2	Project Flexibility	.553***	.475***	1	
	3	Project Size	(-).211**	(-).169**	.033	1
***Sig. at 0.01 level (2-tailed).						
**Sig. at 0.05 level (2-tailed).						

Moderation analysis

To evaluate the effects of study variables with a 7-point Likert scale, regression was performed using ordinal logistic approach (Norusis, 2008). To find any assumptions that were violated or not in ordinal regression, diagnostic tests were carried out before conducting the final analysis. The data distribution was observed as normal (i.e. acceptable range for skewness and kurtosis values as -3 and + 3) with no missing values (Kline, 2005). Thus, SPSS V22 was used to perform the ordinal regression analysis. Table 2 shows the outcomes of data analysis performed based on the ordinal regression method. The results of the first regression model (i.e. model 1) without interaction term indicated that project flexibility and top management commitment significantly relate with project success ($p<0.001$). In model 1 (in Table 2), the variables indicated 48.7 percent (Cox and Snell pseudo-R^2) of the variation in project success. The model 2 (in Table 2) added interaction term to model 1 to examine the moderation effect of the project flexibility variable. Model 2 showed the variation inflation factor (VIF) as 2.34. The variables in model 2 explain 50.1 percent (Cox and Snell pseudo-R^2) of variation.

Table 2: Ordinal Regression Analysis

Study Variables	Project Success			
	Model 1		Model 2	
Control Variable				
Project Size	(-) 0.178	(-0.096)	(-) 0.165	(-0.097)
Independent variable				
Top Management Commitment	0.713***	(0.170)	0.798***	(0.175)
Moderating variable				
Project Flexibility	1.399***	(0.202)	1.481***	(0.208)
Interaction				
Top Management Commitment * Project Flexibility			0.237**	(0.109)
-2 log likelihood	1035.205		1035.205	
Likelihood ratio (Chi-Square) χ^2	110.860***		115.537***	
Cox and Snell Pseudo R²	0.487		0.501	

Unstandardized coeficients and Std. errors are shown in parenthesis. (N=162)

***Sig. at 0.01 level (2-tailed).
**Sig. at 0.05 level (2-tailed).

Discussion

This study addresses the research gaps and provides evidence to support that commitment from senior management and project flexibility has substantial effect on the success of projects. The positive direct effect of senior management on overall success has been supported by the present study. The strong influence of top management commitment helps in achieving business success and is in congruence with upper echelon behavior that focuses on the effect of top management support like advice seeking, behavioral integration, entrepreneurial drive, and risk taking on business benefits. The study outcome shows the positive impact of top management that is identified at the organization level can also be found at the project team level (Khattak et al., 2020; Zailaini, 2016).

Study outcomes indicate that commitment from senior management is essential to motivate project stakeholders to achieve project goals and project success. Thus, commitment from top management creates more chances of achieving project based goals, has greater influence on internal and external stakeholders, and eventually organizational success. The project success varies across different project based on various conditions and project approaches adopted. The effect of project flexibility as the prospective factor for project success is supported by the study findings. Managers executing projects can use flexibility in projects as a project risk mitigation strategy to protect project from any uncertain conditions, and avoid any failure in projects. The current study demonstrates that the effect of top management commitment on project success is positively moderated by project flexibility. The strength of the relationship increased for projects with greater flexibility. Hence, top management is more persuasive for greater success in projects with more flexibility in projects (Zaman, 2019; Albert et al., 2017).

Initial risk analysis and strategies to mitigate project risks along contingent factors reduce the unfavorable outcomes of unforeseen events. Innovations in projects expose them to uncertain situations due to lack of sufficient information to outline project plan to manage risks. Consequently, resource allocation should be focused towards collating appropriate project information required for planning. Improper project planning may create to the perception that the cost of project planning counterbalances its benefits. Additionally, detrimental effects of flexibility on project success should increase with high levels of flexibility in projects. This is reinforced by study findings and shows a significant moderation effect of project flexibility on success as managers handling projects may have varying capabilities, viewpoints and preferences (Patanakul, 2015).

Conclusion

As every project has different characteristics, different contingent approaches are applied since project variables fluctuate to some extent. The findings of the present paper are in line with previous researches, stating that bigger remunerations of senior leadership commitment for projects with high risks lead to project success. This research enhances the contributions that have been offered related to senior leadership's influence and project flexibility on project success. Overall, this study addresses the lack of contingency perspective as the numbers of empirically proven studies available are few.

VI. MANAGERIAL IMPLICATIONS

To attain project success along with the expected business goals, project managers should understand project vision to create business value and enable project groups to offer business benefits, like competitive advantages with new services, products, technological advancement, etc. Project managers should maintain transparency with project stakeholders, empower project groups and foster an environment that delivers value at every stage of the project. Project managers should undergo continuous learning and professional development on skills needed to work in challenging environments. Hence, organizations should ensure that project managers get trained to work on contingencies with flexible strategies and handle situations like allocation of different resources in dynamic settings, delays in project requirements reconciliation (especially in stage gate framework), deploying different approaches to plan project contingencies, etc.

Many managers acknowledge the importance of technological advancement; the study outcomes show the average involvement of senior managers in decision making, long term strategies and adoption of new technologies. Senior managers should promote an innovation-driven leadership style (for example, transformational leadership) to make use of organization's capabilities effectively, and entrepreneurial-oriented culture to promote business benefits. Furthermore, senior managers should spend more time in periodic reviews of project controls, put in more effort in promoting innovation and build dynamic capabilities at project and portfolio levels. Project or portfolio managers should seek new opportunities, learn more from market changes and improve capabilities to transform project innovativeness into better long term benefits. Therefore, managers at every level should also focus on resource development in line with strategic goals, allocate tangible and intangible assets to the entire development process, and also achieve transformational benefits such as new skills or knowledge gain, new business strategies, organizational processes, etc.

Limitation and Future Recommendations

Some of the limitations of this study can be looked at in future research - First, a cross sectional data from Financial Services organizations was used in this study. Therefore, future studies can be conducted using projects from different industries, and sectors. Second, the study uses the managers' perspective on project flexibility in achieving project success. Future studies can examine the same at organizational level flexibility to compare any differences in research outcomes. Third, although this study examines the direct effects of commitment from senior management and moderating role of flexibility in projects to achieve success, managers' decision making consists of many contingency factors. Future studies can examine other potential variables influencing the entire process.

VII. DECLARATION OF CONFLICTING INTEREST

None.

VIII. REFERENCES

Ahimbisibwe, A., Cavana, R. Y., & Daellenbach, U. (2015). A contingency fit model of critical success factors for software development projects. *Journal of Enterprise Information Management.*

Ahmed, R., & Azmi bin Mohamad, N. (2016). Exploring the relationship between multi-dimensional top management support and project success: an international study. *Engineering Management Journal, 28*(1), 54–67.

Albert, M., Balve, P., & Spang, K. (2017). Evaluation of project success: a structured literature review. *International Journal of Managing Projects in Business.*

Amoako-Gyampah, K., Meredith, J., & Loyd, K. W. (2018). Using a social capital lens to identify the mechanisms of top management commitment: a case study of a technology project. *Project Management Journal, 49*(1), 79–95.

Armstrong, J. S., & Overton, T. S. (1977). Estimating nonresponse bias in mail surveys. *Journal of Marketing Research, 14*(3), 396–402

Atkinson, R. (1999). Project management: cost, time and quality, two best guesses and a phenomenon, its time to accept other success criteria. *International Journal of Project Management, 17*(6), 337–342.

Barki, H., Rivard, S., & Talbot, J. (2001). An integrative contingency model of software project risk management. *Journal of Management Information Systems, 17*(4), 37–69.

Boehm, B.W. (1981). *Software Engineering Economics.* Prentice Hall, Englewood Cliffs, NJ.

Carvalho, M. M., & Rabechini Jr, R. (2017). Can project sustainability management impact project success? An empirical study applying a contingent approach. *International Journal of Project Management, 35*(6), 1120–1132.

Clayton Christensen M. (1997). *The Innovator's Dilemma: When New Technologies Cause Great Firms to Fail.* Boston: Harvard Business School Press.

Curtis, E., & Sweeney, B. (2019). Flexibility and control in managing collaborative and in-house NPD. *Journal of Accounting & Organizational Change.*

Floricel, S., Piperca, S. and Banik, M. (2012). Increasing project flexibility: the response capacity of complex projects. *Project Management Journal, 43*(4), 2–85.

Garousi, V., Tarhan, A., Pfahl, D., Coşkunçay, A., & Demirörs, O. (2019). Correlation of critical success factors with success of software projects: an empirical investigation. *Software Quality Journal, 27*(1), 429–493.

Gemünden, H. G., Salomo, S., & Krieger, A. (2005). The influence of project autonomy on project success. *International Journal of Project Management, 23*(5), 366–373.

Guide Jr, V. D. R., & Ketokivi, M. (2015). Notes from the Editors: Redefining some methodological criteria for the journal. *Journal of Operations Management, 37*(1), v–viii.

Gustafson, DH. & Hundt, AS. (1995). Findings of innovation research applied to quality management principles for health care. *Health Care Management Review, 20*(2), 16–33.

Hair, J., Black, W., Babin, B., Anderson, R., & Tatham, R. (2010). *Multivariate data analysis.* Pearson Prentice Hall.

Hermano, V., & Martín-Cruz, N. (2016). The role of top management involvement in firms performing projects: A dynamic capabilities approach. *Journal of Business Research, 69*(9), 3447–3458.

Hu, L. T., & Bentler, P. M. (1999). Cutoff criteria for fit indexes in covariance structure analysis: Conventional criteria versus new alternatives. *Structural Equation Modeling: a Multidisciplinary Journal, 6*(1), 1–55. doi:10.1080/10705519909540118

Kapsali, M. (2011). Systems thinking in innovation project management: A match that works. *International Journal of Project Management, 29*, 396–407.

Ketokivi, M. (2006). Elaborating the contingency theory of organizations: The case of manufacturing flexibility strategies. *Production and Operations Management, 15*(2), 215–228.

Khattak, M.S. and Shah, S. Z. A. (2020). Top Management Capabilities and Firm Efficiency: Relationship via Resources Acquisition. *Business & Economic Review, 12*(1), 87–118.

Kline, R. B. (2005). *Principles and practice of structural equation modeling.* The Guilford Press.

McNally, R. C., Cavusgil, E., & Calantone, R. J. (2010). Product innovativeness dimensions and their relationships with product advantage, product financial performance, and project protocol. *Journal of Product Innovation Management, 27*(7), 991–1006.

Müller, R., & Jugdev, K. (2012). Critical success factors in projects: Pinto, Slevin, and Prescott-the elucidation of project success. *International Journal of Managing Projects in Business, 5*(4), 757–775.

Nandakumar, M.K., Jharkharia, S. and Nair, A. (2013). Environmental uncertainty and flexibility. *Global Journal of Flexible Systems Management, 13*(2), 121–122.

Nguyen, T. S., & Mohamed, S. (2021). Mediation Effect of Stakeholder Management between Stakeholder Characteristics and Project Performance. *Journal of Engineering, Project, and Production Management, 11*(2), 102–117.

Norusis, M. (2008). *SPSS 16.0 advanced statistical procedures companion*. Prentice Hall Press.

Nunes, M., & Abreu, A. (2020). Applying social network analysis to identify project critical success factors. *Sustainability, 12*(4), 1503.

Oh, M. & Choi, S. (2020). The Competence of Project Team Members and Success Factors with Open Innovation. *Journal of Open Innovation: Technology, Market, and Complexity, 6*(3), 51.

Olsson, N.O.E. (2008). External and internal flexibility–aligning projects with the business strategy and executing projects efficiently. *International Journal of Project Organization and Management, 1*(1), 47–64.

Patanakul, P. (2015). Key attributes of effectiveness in managing project portfolio. *International Journal of Project Management, 33*(5), 1084–1097.

Pinto, M. B., & Pinto, J. K. (1991). *Determinants of cross-functional cooperation in the project implementation process.* Newtown Square, PA: Project Management Institute.

PMI Standards Committee (2013). *A Guide to the Project Management Body of Knowledge, Fifth ed..* Project Management Institute, Newtown Square, PA.

Podsakoff, P. M., MacKenzie, S. B., Lee, J. Y., & Podsakoff, N. P. (2003). Common method biases in behavioral research: a critical review of the literature and recommended remedies. *Journal of applied psychology, 88*(5), 879–903.

Salomo, S., Weise, J., & Gemünden, H. G. (2007). NPD planning activities and innovation performance: the mediating role of process management and the moderating effect of product innovativeness. *Journal of product innovation management, 24*(4), 285–302.

Shenhar, A. J., Dvir, D., Levy, O., & Maltz, A. C. (2001). Project success: a multidimensional strategic concept. *Long range planning*, 34(6), 699–725.

Skorstad, E.J. and Ramsdal, H. (2016). *Flexible Organizations and the New Working Life: A European Perspective.* Routledge Taylor & Francis Group, New York, NY.

Tzempelikos, N. (2015). Top management commitment and involvement and their link to key account management effectiveness. *Journal of Business & Industrial Marketing.*

Unger, B. N., Kock, A., Gemünden, H. G., & Jonas, D. (2012). Enforcing strategic fit of project portfolios by project termination: An empirical study on senior management involvement. *International Journal of Project Management, 30*(6), 675–685.

Vrchota, J., Řehoř, P., Maříková, M., & Pech, M. (2021). Critical Success Factors of the Project Management in Relation to Industry 4.0 for Sustainability of Projects. *Sustainability, 13*(1), 281.

Wu, G., Liu, C., Zhao, X., & Zuo, J. (2017). Investigating the relationship between communication conflict interaction and project success among construction project teams. *International Journal of Project Management, 35*(8), 1466–1482.

Young, R., & Poon, S. (2013). Top management support—almost always necessary and sometimes sufficient for success: Findings from a fuzzy set analysis. *International journal of project management, 31*(7), 943–957.

Zailani, S., Md Ariffin, H.A., Iranmanesh, M., Moeinzadeh, S. and Iranmanesh, M. (2016). The moderating effect of project risk mitigation strategies on the relationship between delay factors and construction project performance. *Journal of Science and Technology Policy Management, 7*(3), 346–368.

Zaman, U., Nawaz, S., Tariq, S., & Humayoun, A. A. (2019). Linking transformational leadership and "multi-dimensions" of project success". *International Journal of Managing Projects in Business, 13*(1).

Zhao, J., Du, B., Sun, L., Lv, W., Liu, Y., & Xiong, H. (2021). Deep multi-task learning with relational attention for business success prediction. *Pattern Recognition, 110*, 1074-69.

CHAPTER 27

The Role of College Level Intervention in Improving the Entrepreneurial Aptitude of Young Entrepreneurs in Oman: an Empirical Study

Thangarasa Tiburtrious Andrew Rohanaraj
College of Banking and Financial Studies, Boushar, Muscat, Sultanate of Oman
rohan@cbfs.edu.om, ttarohanaraj@yahoo.com

ABSTRACT

Purpose - The primary purpose of this study is to understand the role of Higher Education Institutions (HEIs) on improving the entrepreneurial aptitude of young entrepreneurs in Oman.

Methodology - The study has used exploratory factor analysis along with a linear regression model (multivariate) to identify the factors that play a useful role towards improving the entrepreneurial aptitude of young Omani entrepreneurs. The data required for this study was collected from 100 young entrepreneurs who have studied in 8 major HEIs in Oman, through a standard five-point likert scale based questionnaire.

Findings - The results found, Leadership skill, Goal orientation and Adaptability to practical situations to play a major role in improving the entrepreneurial aptitude of young entrepreneurs. This study recommends that HEIs should transform their role from being providers of knowledge to mentors, thereby facilitating development of skills and competencies among their student population.

Implications - While adding value to the existing literature and supporting the administrators in policy development, this study will help the HEIs to review their teaching model towards entrepreneurship education.

Social Applications - The findings of this study also encourage the prospective entrepreneurs to focus more on developing the required skills and competencies, as it highlights the factors that could enable them to improve their entrepreneurial aptitude and be successful entrepreneurs in future.

Future research - The findings of this study could also act as a point of reference for future researchers as well.

Originality/ Value - Unlike many other studies, this study focuses on the role of HEIs, in improving the entrepreneurial aptitude.

Key words: Entrepreneurial aptitude, Leadership skill, Goal Orientation, Adaptability, HEIs.

INTRODUCTION

Entrepreneurship plays a major role in supporting national economies of the modern world (Jami and Gokdeniz, 2020). Many governments are encouraging their population, especially younger work force, to start businesses on their own and become entrepreneurs, as it helps the administrators to manage issues related to unemployment among their younger population (Thurik et al., 2008). Higher Education Institutions (HEIs) play a useful role in imparting the knowledge on entrepreneurship through variety of programs (Pihie, 2009), by that encouraging the younger population to become prospective entrepreneurs in future. Though this action helps the students to gain knowledge related to entrepreneurship (Valerio et al., 2014) and support the governments in managing the socio-economic problems that might arise within the society due to unemployment (Thurik, 2008), the effectiveness of such programs could only be measured by the level of success achieved in improving the entrepreneurial aptitude of their students.

Entrepreneurial aptitude focuses on the entrepreneur's potential to acquire the skills required to excel in the new ventures (Ghina et al., 2017). This potential and willingness to learn will help the entrepreneurs to improve their risk perception, think out of the box, focus on effective planning, improve their ability to do multitasking and their keenness towards understanding the market dynamics (Gudluru, 2018)

Entrepreneurship, as a module, is been taught in majority of the HEIs in Oman. However, in reality, Omani entrepreneurs are experiencing higher rate of failures in their effort towards developing successful enterprises (Al-maskeri et al., 2019), even though they have learned about entrepreneurship through academic platforms. Research done by Al-maskeri et al. (2019) has found absence of entrepreneurial aptitude (potential to acquire the required skills) and lack of resilience as the major reasons for these failures. This questions the effectiveness of the knowledge provided by the HEIs and their actual role in improving the entrepreneurial aptitude of young and prospective entrepreneurs (Ibrahim et al., 2017). These failures, if left unchecked, could exert serious impact on the confidence level of the young entrepreneurs and discourage them from starting new businesses; a phenomenon already visible in Oman with around 37% drop in the number of new businesses registered in 2018, compared to 2017 (NCSI, 2018). Though studies conducted by researchers such as Jami and Gokdeniz (2020) and Pihie (2009) have shown entrepreneurship education provided at HEIs to exert significant impact on the level of desirability of the young students towards becoming an entrepreneur, its effectiveness in improving the entrepreneurial aptitude, under the current university system remains questionable (Landstrom, 2010). This requires a detailed study to understand the areas where HEIs need to focus, when providing entrepreneurship related knowledge. Hence, this study intends to understand the role of college (HEI) level intervention in improving the entrepreneurial aptitude of young entrepreneurs in Oman.

REVIEW OF LITERATURE

Entrepreneurial aptitude focuses on the entrepreneurs' potential towards learning the skills required to be successful in the market place (APA, 2009). This helps entrepreneurs to manage their organizations in such a manner that ensures success and sustainability (Cubico et al., 2010). Entrepreneurial aptitude is driven by personal traits such as creativity (Dextor, 2000; Lee et al., 2004) and passion (Cubico et al., 2010), which supports innovative mindset (Carsrud and Brannback, 2009) and drive goal-focused action (Cardon et al., 2009). These factors help the entrepreneurs to be focused in their approach towards venture creation and encourage them to be self-motivated so that they could identify and acquire the skills and competencies required to be successful in the business world. However, to what extent the entrepreneurs were able to acquire this potential becomes very much questionable in Omani context, when considering the lower rate of successes enjoyed by young entrepreneurs, who are new to the business field (Al-Shanfari, 2012). This entrepreneurial malaise, as stated by Porter (2003), could result in socio-economic issues, if left unattended. Though the Omani government is focusing on tackling the issue of unemployment through supporting entrepreneurship, fostering it at indigenous level is not an easy task, given the smaller size of the private sector (Al-Shanfari, 2012) and the limited contribution of SMEs (only around 15%) to the GDP (NCSI, 2018), along with the limited willingness among Omani students towards starting new ventures (Ibrahim et al., 2017).

Higher Education Institutions (HEIs) could play a major role in developing entrepreneurs, as they could provide the knowledge and skills required to be successful in the market (Farashah, 2013; Ibrahim et al., 2017). This can be vital for entrepreneurial success (Gibb, 2013), as HEIs could absorb the industry requirements into their teaching model (Zahra and Wright, 2011) to develop knowledgeable human capital (Gurrero et al., 2016). This intervention, and customized knowledge delivery could could be a major contributor towards developing an entrepreneurial ecosystem (Martinez and Ventura, 2020) that fosters innovation and experimentation.

Developing human capital requires the HEIs to identify the opportunities present within the market place, develop competencies required to make use of those opportunities (San & Van der sijde, 2014) and transfer them to their students to develop a focused value system and drive required to be successful in their new ventures (Morris et al., 2013), and become the catalyst of venture creation (Rizzo, 2015). Development of such competencies can greatly improve the entrepreneurial aptitude of young entrepreneurs (Bellini et al., 2019). This requires the HEIs to convert themselves to be 'entrepreneurial' in nature, so that they will be able to improve the entrepreneurial aptitude of their students by making them 'professionally' independent.

Though researchers have found number of factors to play a role in the development of entrepreneurial aptitude, researchers Messick (2008) and Favretto et al. (2003) opined that entrepreneurial aptitude could be described through the factors goal orientation, leadership skill, adaptability to situations, achievement motive, self-empowerment and fulfilment, innovative spirit, flexible approach and preference towards having their own independent space. Rauch and Frese (2007) has also found these factors to display higher correlations with both venture creation and business success. These observations were in line with the factors identified by Sartori et al., (2007) in the 'Entrepreneurial Aptitude Test' (TAI), developed to check the entrepreneurial aptitude of young entrepreneurs.

Goal orientation is determined by individual's appetite for creativity and innovation, their relentless drive towards reaching their objectives (Cubico et al. 2010) and the manner in which they handle the whole process (Favretto et al., 2003). Leadership skill and adaptability to situations help the entrepreneurs in identifying and incorporating appropriate strategies to improve the economic value, in challenging situations (Gurrero et al., 2014). This, supported by the achievement motive and strife for self-empowerment and fulfilment helps the individual to identify, choose and acquire the competencies required to manage those challenges (Chiru et al., 2012). Being innovative and the ability to reorient the strategies to suit the external situation due to their preference towards maintaining their own space could also play useful role in enhancing entrepreneurial aptitude (Sartori et al., 2007).

HEIs could play a major role in refining these competencies (Martinez & Ventura, 2020) through knowledge generation and transfer (Sam and Van der sidje, 2014). HEIs need to radically innovate and transform themselves (Ventura et al., 2019) to be truly innovation hubs, that provide guidance, knowledge and systematic support to develop truly entrepreneurial minds with enhanced entrepreneurial aptitude. The development of an integrated delivery platform that provides both entrepreneurial knowledge and training to the students (Bellini et al., 2019) along with identified competencies in a systematic manner (Chiru et al., 2012) will help the HEIs to generate human capital that are increasingly entrepreneurial in nature (Martinez & Ventura, 2020)

Oman, at present has more than 60 HEIs, providing knowledge and guidance in different fields (Al'Abri, 2019). Entrepreneurship as a subject is been taught in majority of these HEIs to support the governments initiative towards making the younger workforce to be successful entrepreneurs (Yarahmadi and Magd, 2016). Though the required infrastructure is in place (Al'Abri, 2019), the drive towards being an entrepreneur remains low among the younger generation (Ibrahim et al., 2017) who receive both knowledge and training in the HEIs. This has resulted in higher number of venture closures and reduced registration of new ventures (NCSI, 2018) as well. Research done by Al-maskeri et al. (2019) has also found the absence of entrepreneurial aptitude (potential to acquire the required skills) and lack of resilience as the major reasons for these failures. Though the studies done by researchers such as Jamie and Gokdeniz (2020), Pihie (2009) and Valerio et at., (2014) have found HEIs to play a major role in preparing the younger generation to become successful future entrepreneurs, no studies have been carried out until now to understand the direction in which such interventions should be focused in making that aspiration a reality in Oman. This makes it important to conduct a focused study to understand the role of interventions provided at the college level, by the HEIs in Oman, in improving the entrepreneurial aptitude of young entrepreneurs.

RESEARCH METHODOLOGY

This study intends to understand the direction Omani HEIs need to take, to enhance the effectiveness of their programs in improving the entrepreneurial aptitude of their students. The population for this study consisted of young entrepreneurs, who have completed their higher education in one of the eight selected HEIs in Oman, 4 public and 4 private in nature. The selection of HEIs were based on their volume of representation, among the young graduates in Oman (NCSI, 2015).

Samples were identified through stratified random sampling methodology with 65% of the samples coming from public HEIs and 35% from private HEIs. Data collection was done through a standard five point likert scale based questionnaire, from a sample of 100 entrepreneurs. A pilot test with the questionnaire, produced a Cronbach's alpha value of 0.844, showing that the survey instrument was reliable.

This study has used exploratory factor analysis (EFA) to analyse the data. The Keiser-Myer-Olkin (KMO) test (Kaiser, 1974) and Bartlett's test (Bartlett, 1954) were used to check whether factor analysis is justifiable. Principal components analysis (PCA) with varimax rotation and Kaiser normalization was used to identify the principal components. Multivariate linear regression analysis was used to identify the major factors that can improve the entrepreneurial aptitude among young entrepreneurs in Oman. As such, the improvement of entrepreneurial aptitude (Y), is modelled as,

$$Y = \alpha + \beta 1 X 1 + \beta 2 X 2 \dots + \epsilon \qquad (1)$$

where, ϵ represents the error factor and α represents the constant value while $\beta 1$, $\beta 2$ represents the influence of the independent variables. The model also considers the restrictions that $\beta 1$, $\beta 2 \dots$ to be greater than 0.

FINDINGS

The literature review helped the author to identify 22 variables and these variable were used to determine the Principal components. The Kaiser-Meyer-Olkin (KMO) measure displayed higher sampling adequacy with a value of 0.733, while Bartlett's measure of sphericity displayed significance (0.000), as displayed in Table 1. This showed that the data is suitable for factor analysis.

Table 1 – KMO and Bartlett's test result

Kaiser-Meyer-Olkin Measure of Sampling Adequacy.		.733
Bartlett's Test of Sphericity	Approx. Chi-Square	734.127
	df	231
	Sig.	.000

Exploratory Factor Analysis

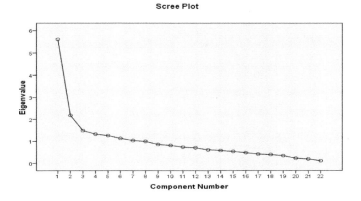

Fig. 1: *Scree Plot for the factors identified.*

Factor analysis identified seven major factors (Please refer to table 2). These factors were found to explain around 64% of the total variance. Though the percentage is reasonably higher, it indicated the presence of other factors that may also have accounted to limited portions of cumulative variance. The scree plot shown in figure 2, also supported the observation.

The first factor was dominated by variables such as, ability to take calculated risks (0.703), having a positive attitude (0.665), being able to manage different personalities (0.6), being disciplined (0.468) and being innovative in business (0.591), and was in a position to explain 25.5% of the total variance. As all these variables are related to providing strategic leadership, this factor was named as Leadership Skill.

Table 2 – Cumulative Variance

Component	Initial Eigenvalues			Extraction Sums of Squared Loadings			Rotation Sums of Squared Loadings		
	Total	% of Variance	Cumulative %	Total	% of Variance	Cumulative %	Total	% of Variance	Cumulative %
1	5.608	25.489	25.489	5.608	25.489	25.489	2.656	12.073	12.073
2	2.184	9.926	35.415	2.184	9.926	35.415	2.484	11.291	23.365
3	1.486	6.755	42.170	1.486	6.755	42.170	2.257	10.259	33.624
4	1.325	6.023	48.193	1.325	6.023	48.193	1.765	8.024	41.648
5	1.259	5.725	53.918	1.259	5.725	53.918	1.716	7.800	49.447
6	1.131	5.141	59.059	1.131	5.141	59.059	1.640	7.454	56.902
7	1.032	4.692	63.751	1.032	4.692	63.751	1.507	6.849	63.751
8	.992	4.509	68.260						
9	.854	3.880	72.140						
10	.810	3.682	75.822						

Component	Initial Eigenvalues			Extraction Sums of Squared Loadings			Rotation Sums of Squared Loadings		
	Total	% of Variance	Cumulative %	Total	% of Variance	Cumulative %	Total	% of Variance	Cumulative %
11	.732	3.326	79.148						
12	.704	3.201	82.349						
13	.607	2.758	85.107						
14	.576	2.619	87.726						
15	.535	2.430	90.156						
16	.479	2.177	92.334						
17	.416	1.892	94.226						
18	.395	1.797	96.023						
19	.343	1.559	97.582						
20	.227	1.032	98.613						
21	.195	.884	99.498						
22	.110	.502	100.000						

Extraction Method: Principal Component Analysis.

Table 3 – Rotated component matrix

	Component						
	1	2	3	4	5	6	7
Being Innovative	-.048	.018	.204	.088	.077	.094	.711
Non-Compromising Attitude	.119	.359	.660	.242	-.018	.109	.024
Developing networks that support your ideas	.189	.151	.786	-.131	-.038	.015	.138
Taking calculated risk	.703	.311	.146	.087	.064	.077	.004
Readiness to learn from success and failures	.049	.181	.190	-.085	.190	.637	.243
Being empowered	.280	.294	-.027	.180	.052	.091	.601
Positive attitude	.665	.227	.261	.138	.099	-.096	-.140
Not being disturbed by others' views	.343	-.104	.561	.147	.046	.418	.167
Managing different Personalities	.600	-.028	-.093	-.163	.032	.096	.429
Coming from a family of businessmen	-.107	-.128	.069	.178	.617	.367	.230
Being financially stable	.223	.006	-.138	.164	.761	-.210	.060
Family values towards entrepreneurship	.259	.042	.027	.324	.558	.207	-.256
Being Disciplined	.468	.077	.432	-.132	.156	.268	-.258
Supporting risk taking behaviour	.006	.236	.411	-.284	.496	.049	.195
Being innovative in business	.591	.092	.292	.212	.091	.112	.150
Accepting nothing lesser than success	.190	.893	.189	-.043	-.053	.074	.130
Being profit focused	.474	.243	.067	-.064	.053	.384	.114

	Component						
	1	**2**	**3**	**4**	**5**	**6**	**7**
Being adaptable to practical situations	.166	.212	.031	.371	-.152	.643	-.082
Passion to succeed	-.059	.062	.068	.841	.188	-.052	.128
Being a continuous learner	.128	-.108	-.028	.620	.087	.114	.062
Not giving up easily	.266	.711	.447	.089	-.073	.025	-.063
Being ethical in business	.185	.737	-.002	-.130	.154	.339	.137

Extraction Method: Principal Component Analysis.   a. Rotation converged in 10 iterations.
Rotation Method: Varimax with Kaiser Normalization.

The second factor was dominated by variables such as, accepting nothing lesser than success (0.893), being ethical in business (0.737) and not giving up easily (0.711). As all these variables are focused on achieving success, this factor was named as 'Achievement Motive'. This factor accounted for around 10% of the total variance. The third factor was dominated by variables such as, focusing on developing networks that only support their ideas (0.786), non-compromising attitude (0.66) and not being disturbed by others' views (0.561) and explained around 7% of the total variance. As all these variables are focused on non-compromising behaviour, this factor is named as 'Strategic Stubbornness'.

The fourth factor, which acconted for 6% of the total variance, was dominated by two variables, passion to succeed (0.841) and being a continuous learner (0.62). As these factors are focused on achieving the goal, the factor was named as 'Goal Orientation'. The fifth factor was dominated by the drive towards being financially stable (0.761), coming from family of businessmen (0.617), family values towards entrepreneurship (0.558) and support towards risk taking behaviour (0.496). This factor was named as 'Family Support' and was found to be in a position to explain 5.7% of the total variance.   The sixth factor was dominated by the respondents' readiness to learn from both successes and failures (0.637) along with being adaptable to practical situation (0.502). This factor accounts to around 5.1% of the total variance and is named 'Adaptability'. The seventh factor was also dominated by two variables, being innovative (0.711) and being empowered (0.601). As both these are connected to empowerment, this factor was named as 'Self-empowerment'. This factor also accounted for 5.1% of the total variances.

Model for Improving Entrepreneurial Aptitude

Once the factors were identified, researcher developed the following multivariate model to understand the relationship, using the factors identified through the exploratory factor analysis as independent variables and improvement of entrepreneurial aptitude as dependent variable. The model thus developed reads as,

$$Y = \alpha + \beta 1X1 + \beta 2X2 \quad + \beta 3X3 + \beta 24X4 + \beta 5X5 + \beta 6X6 + \beta 7X7 + \epsilon$$

along with the restriction that $\beta1$, $\beta2$, $\beta3$, $\beta4$, $\beta5$, $\beta6$, $\beta7$ should be greater than zero, where,

Y = Improvement of entrepreneurial aptitude

$X1$ = Leadership skill $X2$ = Achievement motive

$X3$ = Strategic stubbornness $X4$ = Goal orientation

$X5$ = Family support $X6$ = Adaptability

$X7$ = Self-empowerment.

Table 4 – Coefficients of Regression

Model	Unstandardized Coefficients		Standardized Coefficients	T	Sig.
	B	Std. Error	Beta		
(Constant)	3.66	0.101		36.406	0
Leadership Skill	0.23	0.101	0.215	2.273	0.025
Achievement Focus	0.132	0.101	0.124	1.309	0.194
Strategic Stubbornness	0.043	0.101	0.04	0.425	0.672
Goal Orientation	0.249	0.101	0.233	2.462	0.016
Family Support	0.053	0.101	0.05	0.524	0.601
Adaptability	0.234	0.101	0.219	2.312	0.023
Self empowerment	0.073	0.101	0.068	0.719	0.474

a. **Dependent Variable:** Improvement of Entrepreneurial aptitude

The multivariate model displayed a coefficient of determination value of 0.173, along with lower but statistically significant 'F' statistic (F = 2.751, p < 0.05), displaying model fit. The complete results of the coefficients of regression model is displayed in table 4.

The results, thus obtained showed the following.

- Leadership skill was found to display a significant positive impact towards improving the entrepreneurial aptitude (T = 2.273, P < 0.05). As such focusing on leadership skills could result in the improvement the entrepreneurial aptitude of the young Achievement focus failed to show any influence on improving the entrepreneurial aptitude of young entrepreneurs (P > 0.05).
- Strategic stubbornness also failed to display any significant influence (P > 0.05) on improving the entrepreneurial aptitude of young entrepreneurs.
- Goal orientation was found to exert positive influence towards improving the entrepreneurial aptitude of the young entrepreneurs (T = 2.462, P < 0.05).
- Family support was found to exert no influence on improving the entrepreneurial aptitude of young entrepreneurs (P > 0.05).
- Adaptability was found to have positive influence towards improving the entrepreneurial aptitude of young entrepreneurs (T = 2.312, P < 0.05).
- Self-empowerment was also found to have no influence on improving the entrepreneurial aptitude of young entrepreneurs (P > 0.05).

- The higher α value (α = 3.66) and the corresponding 'T' and 'P' values (T = 36.406, p < 0.05) denotes that the factors identified in this study will only exert limited influence towards improving the entrepreneurial aptitude of young entrepreneurs.

The results showed that the factors, Leadership skill, Goal orientation and Adaptability to situations, could play a useful role in improving the entrepreneurial aptitude of young entrepreneurs in Oman. The indicated coefficient of determination for the model (r^2 = 0.173) showed that these factors could exert around 17.3% influence towards improving the entrepreneurial aptitude on young entrepreneurs.

Leadership Skill

Table 5 – Cumulative response for variables within the factor Leadership Skill

Leadership Skill	Cumulative Response (%)					Mean	Standard Deviation
	SD	D	N	A	SA		
Taking calculated risks	0	10	17	50	23	3.86	0.89
Positive attitude	2	8	22	48	20	3.76	0.93
Managing different personalities	2	5	24	56	13	3.72	0.87
Being disciplined	5	8	19	55	14	3.66	0.99
Being Innovative in Business	4	13	32	14	37	3.67	1.12
SD - Strongly disagree, D - Disagree, N - Neutral, A - Agree, SA - Strongly Agree							

Leadership skill includes items such as taking calculated risks, managing different personalities, being disciplined and being innovative as well. Table 5 shows the results obtained for Leadership skill. The results displayed an overall mean score of 3.724, with more than 51% of respondents providing positive views for all the variables considered under this factor along with 10% -17% of respondents providing opposite views.

Goal orientation

Goal orientation is a primary factor in driving the individual to move towards the aspired goal. This includes, the passion to succeed and the ability of being a lifelong learner.

Table 6 – Cumulative response for variables within the factor Goal orientation

Goal Orientation	Cumulative Response (%)					Mean	Standard Deviation
	SD	D	N	A	SA		
Passion to succeed	10	16	26	43	5	3.15	1.13
Being a continuous learner	5	9	23	53	10	3.52	1.03
SD - Strongly disagree, D - Disagree, N - Neutral, A - Agree, SA - Strongly Agree							

The factor has also produced a mean value of 3.335. As per table 6, the passion to succeed is considered by 48% of entrepreneurs as an important variable in improving the entrepreneurial aptitude, while, 63% accepted that entrepreneurs need to be lifelong learners.

Adaptability

Table 7 – Cumulative response for variables within the factor Adaptability

Adaptability	Cumulative Response (%)					Mean	Standard Deviation
	SD	D	N	A	SA		
Readiness to learn from success and failure	2	14	19	52	13	3.59	0.99
Being adaptable to practical situations	2	3	21	53	21	3.88	0.84
SD-Strongly disagree, D-Disagree, N-Neutral, A-Agree, SA - Strongly Agree							

The factor 'Adaptability' has displayed a mean of 3.735, which is higher than the average of 3. This includes the readiness to learn from the success and failures and being adaptable to practical situations. As table 7 explains, more than 65% of the entrepreneurs agree that young entrepreneurs need to be adaptable to prevailing situations. This is opposed by lesser than 17% of the entrepreneurs, for any of the variables, considered under this factor.

DISCUSSION

This study has found 'Leadership skill' to exert positive influence towards improving the entrepreneurial aptitude of young entrepreneurs ($\beta = 0.23$, T = 2.273, p < 0.05). The factor leadership skill, is dominated by the variables ability to take calculated risks, having positive attitude towards business and being able to manage the different personalities. These variables play a major role in choosing the right strategies. This ability supported by the skills related to managing different personalities, helps the entrepreneurs to invest more on 'people' and motivate the employees. These observations are in line with the observations of Gurrero et al. (2014) along with Martinez and Ventura (2020), who found leadership skills to play a useful role in improving the potential to learn new skills. Being innovative and being disciplined also helps the entrepreneur to anticipate the market needs and learn the skills required to capitalize on those opportunities in a disciplined manner. As changing market needs brings in new opportunities to the entrepreneurs, well-groomed leadership skills can improve the potential to acquire the skills required to excel in such situations. This requires the HEIs to relook at the manner in which entrepreneurship-related knowledge is given to the students. While providing the academic knowledge, HEIs should focus more on providing opportunities that would help their students to gain practical, hands-on experience on entrepreneurship, take calculated risks and make strategic business decisions. These mentor-assisted, practical activities such as entrepreneurship competitions, opportunity to run a business within the HEIs premises, brainstorming sessions, business plan workshops, opportunities for the students to practically manage certain events happening within the HEIs, will make the students learn and improve their people management and leadership skills, through a disciplined and guided process, while being free to test their innovative ideas.

'Goal orientation' was also found to play a positive role in improving the entrepreneurial aptitude ($\beta = 0.249$, T = 2.462, p < 0.05). This observation goes in line with the observations of Cubico et al., (2010) and Sartori et al., (2007) as well. This factor is dominated by the variables 'Passion to succeed' and 'Being a lifelong learner'. The passion to succeed in business makes the entrepreneur to identify the ways and means through which success could be achieved, while lifelong learning will make the entrepreneur to be open to new ideas, thereby increasing the readiness to learn new skills. These variables motivate the young entrepreneurs to continuously seek knowledge to make their businesses successful, thereby, improving their entrepreneurial aptitude. HEIs need to make their students both focused and goal oriented. The provision of mentorship support within the HEIs, using experienced faculty members and innovative entrepreneurs on contract, could help the students with creative and innovative ideas, to develop them into business concepts, as such guidance could further boost the passion to succeed, while encouraging the participants to be lifelong learners of skills and competencies.

'Adaptability' is primarily driven by the ability to learn from both success and failure, followed by the ability to be adaptable to practical situations. The observation related to the role of 'Adaptability' goes in line with the observations of Gurrero et al., (2014) and Chiru et al., (2012), who felt that adaptability as an important skill that would help young entrepreneurs, as they support the young entrepreneurs in improving their entrepreneurial aptitude by identifying the factors that drive the success in a given situations, and look at both success and failures as opportunities, while learning new skills to fine-tune their strategies to achieve success. HEIs need to focus on setting up Innovation labs and business incubation centres within their organizations, to provide the guided platform for students to practically test their ideas and learn the skills required to convert them as a business concepts and move the 'commercially viable' ideas to the next phase through the business incubation centres.

This study has found that factors such as achievement focus, strategic stubbornness, family support for entrepreneurship and self-empowerment will not be in a position to improve the entrepreneurial aptitude of Omani entrepreneurs. This requires the HEIs to focus more on providing the right skills and support to improve the entrepreneurial aptitude of their learners. Development of an entrepreneurial eco system that encourages and supports innovation and entrepreneurship, within the HEIs, would play a major part in developing entrepreneurial mindset. While providing the academic knowledge to their students, this ecosystem provides the context for the students to test their innovative ideas within a supportive environment, learn the skills required to make their ideas 'commercially viable', thereby improving their entrepreneurial aptitude. This requires the HEIs in Oman to convert their role from that of a knowledge provider to the provider of entrepreneurial ecosystem, which encourages creativity, provides mentorship support and facilitates leadership skill development, while making the students more goal oriented and adaptable to practical situations. Such a focused intervention from HEIs in Oman could undoubtedly play a major role in improving the entrepreneurial aptitude of Omani entrepreneurs.

RESEARCH LIMITATIONS

One of the major limitations of this study was the reluctance from the part of respondents towards filling the questionnaire, which resulted in delays during data collection. The limited availability of literature on the relevant field of study was also found to be limitation for this study. Though every effort was made to identify the variables based on the available literature, there could have been more variables involved in improving the entrepreneurial aptitude of the students. Time and cost constraints also made the researcher to limit the number of respondents considered for this study. Hence, the findings need to be interpreted with due consideration to those limitations.

IMPLICATIONS

This study adds value to the available literature through focused and country specific information, identifying the factors that could improve the entrepreneurial aptitude of Omani entrepreneurs. Apart from adding value to the literature, the findings will also support the HEIs to relook at their strategy towards imparting entrepreneurship related education. The findings of this study could also contribute towards general policy development related to entrepreneurship education in HEIs in the country.

SOCIAL APPLICATION

HEIs could use the findings of this study to effectively restructure their programs and become more effective in improving the success rate of young entrepreneurs, thereby improving its social impact. These findings also provide a clear guidance to the prospective entrepreneurs, so that they could choose the HEIs based on the programs offered, to improve their knowledge and skills. These findings could also be used as a base by future researchers, who plan to conduct a focused study on improving entrepreneurial aptitude.

REFERENCES

Al'Abri, K. (2015). *Higher education policy architecture and policy-making in the Sultanate of Oman: Towards a critical understanding. Doctoral* dissertation. The University of Queensland. https://doi.org/10.1007/978-94-017-9553-1_489-1

Al-Maskari, A., Al-Maskari, M., Alqanoobi, M. & Kunjumuhammed, S. (2019). Internal and external obstacles facing medium and large enterprises in Rusayl Industrial Estates in the Sultanate of Oman. *Journal of Global Entrepreneurial Research, 9*(1)

Al-Shanfari, D.A. (2012). Entrepreneurship in Oman: A snapshot of the main challenges. *Proceedings of the United Nations conference on trade and development: Multi-year expert meeting on enterprise development policies and capacity-building in science, technology and innovation (STI)*. Switzerland.

American Psychological Association. (2009). *Concise Dictionary of Psychology.* USA

Bartlett, M. S. (1954). A note on the multiplying factors for various chi square approximation. *Journal of Royal Statistical Society, 16*(Series B), 296–298

Bellini, D., Cubico, S., Favretto, G., Noventa, S., Ardolino, P., Gianesini, G., et al. (2019). A metamodel for competence assessment: Co.S.M.O competences software management for organizations. *European Journal of Training Development, 45*(4)

Cardon, M.S., Wincent, J., Singh, J., & Drnovsek, M. (2009). The nature and experience of entrepreneurial passion. *Academy of Management Review, 34*(3), 511–532.

Carsrud, A. L., & Brännback, M. (2011). Entrepreneurial motivations: what do we still need to know? *Journal of Small Business Management, 49*(1), 9–26.

Chiru, C., Tachiciu, L., & Ciuchete, S. G. (2012). Psychological factors, behavioural variables and acquired competences in entrepreneurship education. *Procedia Social and Behavioural Sciences, 46*, 4010–4015.

Cubico, S., Bortolani, E., Favretto, G., & Sartori, R. (2010). Describing the entrepreneurial profile: the entrepreneurial aptitude test (TAI). *International Journal of Entrepreneurship and Small Business, 11*(4), 424–435.

Dexter, J. (2000). Organizational structures, entrepreneurship, and creativity: inseparably linked. *International Journal of Entrepreneurship and Small Business, 11*(4).

Farashah, A. D. (2013). The process of impact of entrepreneurship education and training on entrepreneurship perception and intention: Study of educational system of Iran. *Education and Training, 55*(8/9) 868–885.

Favretto, G., Cubico, S., & Sartori, R. (2007). *Generational transition and entrepreneurial profiles: senior in comparison with junior-A survey in a group of small sized businesses.* Paper Presented at the XIII European Congress on European Work and Organizational Psychology, Sweden.

Ghina, A., Simatupang, T. M., & Gustomo, A. (2017). *Entrepreneurship Education within Higher Education Institutions (HEIs).* https://www.intechopen.com/books/global-voices-in-higher-education/entrepreneurship-education-within-higher-education-institutions-

Gibb, A. A. (2013). *The university of the future: an entrepreneurial stakeholder learning organization?* In: Fayolle, A, Redford, D (eds) Handbook on the Entrepreneurial University. Edward Elgar, 25–64.

Gudluru, T. (2018). *The Key Skills and Ingredients Every Entrepreneur Needs to Survive.* available at: https://www.entrepreneur.com/article/316066.

Guerrero, M., Urbano, D., Cunningham, J., & Organ, D. (2014). Entrepreneurial universities in two european regions: a case study comparison. *Journal of Technology Transfer, 39*, 415–434.

Ibrahim, O. A., Devesh, S., & Ubaidullah, V. (2017). Implication of attitude of graduate students in Oman towards entrepreneurship: an empirical study. *Journal of Global Entrepreneurial Research, 7*(8).

Jami, M. Y., & Gökdeniz, I. (2020). The Role of Universities in the Development of Entrepreneurship. *Entrepreneurship Education, 6*(1), 85–94.

Kaiser, H. (1974). An index of factorial simplicity. *Psychometrika, 9*, 31–36.

Landstrom, H. (2010). *Pioneers in Entrepreneurship and Small Business Research.* Springer.

Lee, S., Florida, R., & Acs, Z. (2004). Creativity and entrepreneurship: a regional analysis of new firm formation. *Regional Studies, 38*(8), 879–891.

Martínez, S. L., & Ventura, R. (2020). Entrepreneurial Profiles at the University: A Competence Approach. *Frontiers of Psychology. 11,* 612–796. https://doi.org/10.3389/fpsyg.2020.612796

Messick, S. (2008). Test validity and the ethics of assessment. In Bersoff, D.N. (Ed.): *Ethical Conflicts in Psychology*, 273–275

Morris, M. H., Webb, J. W., Fu, J., & Singhal, S. (2013). A competency-based perspective on entrepreneurship education: conceptual and empirical insights. *Journal of Small Business Management, 51*, 352–369.

National Center for Statistics and Information. (2015). Statistical year book, 43. Oman

National Center for Statistics and Information. (2018). Statistical year book, 46. Oman

Pihie, Z. A. L. (2009). Entrepreneurship as a career choice: An analysis of entrepreneurial self-efficacy and intention of university students. *European Journal of Social Sciences, 9*(2), 338–349.

Porter, H. (2003). A Culture of Enterprise. *Business Today (Sept.)*, 51–52.

Rauch, A., & Frese, M. (2007). Born to be an entrepreneur? Revisiting the personality approach to entrepreneurship. in Baum, J. R., Frese, M. and Baron, R. (Eds.): *The Psychology of Entrepreneurship*, 41–65. Lawrence Erlbaum Associates.

Rizzo, U. (2015). Why do scientists create academic spin-offs? The influence of the Context. *Journal of Technology Transfer, 40*, 198–226.

Sam, C., & Van der Sijde, P. (2014). Understanding the concept of the entrepreneurial university from the perspective of higher education models. *Higher Education, 68*, 891–908.

Sartori, R., & Pasini, M. (2007). Quality and quantity in test validity: how can we be sure that psychological tests measure what they have to? *International Journal of Methodology, 41*(3), 359–374.

Thurik, A. R., Carree, M. A., van Stel, A., & Audretsch, D. B. (2008). Does self-employment reduce unemployment?. *Journal of Business Venturing, 23*(6), 673–686.

Valerio, A., Brent, P., & Robb, A. (2014). Entrepreneurship education and training programs around the world. The World Bank.

Ventura, R., Quero, M. J., & Díaz-Méndez, M. (2019). T*he role of institutions in achieving radical innovation.* https://doi.org/10.1108/mip01-2019-0050.

Yarahmadi, F., & Magd, H. A. E. (2016). Entrepreneurship Infrastructure and Education in Oman. *Procedia - Social and Behavioral Sciences, 219*, 792–797.

Zahra, Q., & Wright, M. (2011). Entrepreneurship's next act. *Academy of Management Perspectives, 25*(4), 67–83. http://doi.org/10.5465/amp.2010.0149.

CHAPTER 28

Progress of Digital Payment Ecosystem in Unorganised Indian Markets: A Systematic Literature Review

Aditi Mehtani
Research Scholar
IILM University
Gurgaon, Haryana
India
aditi.mehtani@gmail.com

Dr. Saima Rizvi
Professor
IILM University
Gurgaon, Haryana
India
saima.rizvi@iilm.edu.com

Abstract

The Government of India has given impetus to cashless economy by way of promoting "Digital India Initiative". Further, there has been a recent Suo Moto shift in consumer's preference due to on-going COVID pandemic to extensively use digital ecosystem viz. E-wallets like Paytm, Google Pay, PhonePe etc. to make payments. This has resulted in higher adoption of digital ecosystem not only by consumers but by small scale merchants also.

Purpose - This research paper acknowledges this shift and is an attempt to study the progress of digital payment ecosystem on the Small-Scale Merchants operating in Unorganised Indian Markets. The purpose of this paper is to find out the effect of adoption of digital payment options by the Small-Scale merchants in India, on their financial dynamics. This paper aims to answer question: How digital payment systems have made a phase wise progress in the Indian Unorganised Market sector and how this shift has influenced the small-scale merchants operating in these markets.

Findings - The result shows that penetration of digital payment systems have gained moment as an aftermath of the ongoing pandemic. To maintain social distancing norms and to match the changed preferences of consumers, small scale merchants have made this shift to sustain in the highly competitive market.

Social implication -This study has a significant social implication, particularly on the financial dynamics of small scale shop keepers who have recently shifted from cash to cashless economy and are new to M-Commerce. The results show a positive penetration of E-wallets and other digital payment systems into the unorganised markets of India.

This penetration has transformed consumer preference, which was once inclined towards purchasing from the organised market, specifically after the onset of pandemic. The unorganised sector made a quick shift to sustain in this competitive scenario and match the consumer inclination to make payments through cashless and contactless modes.

Design / Methodology / Approach - Systematic Literature review has been the base of this study relying on secondary data coll ected from RBI reports, Publications, Internet Research Engines etc. The research method used is interpretive with a descriptive approach.

Limitation - Use of primary data from the merchants operating in unorganised markets can give more realistic and in-depth results of the effects of this paradigm shift.

Originality/ Value – The paper provides insights about the technological developments and user friendly digital payment methods, which has made its way into the unorganised markets of India as well, despite of reluctance from the vendors initially. It reviews and gives insights about this shift, phase wise, from the prospective of small scale merchants.

Keywords: Digital Ecosystem, Unorganised Indian Markets, Fintech, Demonetisation, Pandemic

1. INTRODUCTION

Unorganised Retailing in Indian Markets, by business delineation, is the conventional format of low cost retailing. To name a few, the local departmental shops, general and provision stores, fruit and vegetables shops, local restaurants, single owner medical stores, hand carts and street vendors. Unorganised vendors and retailors form the core of trade and commerce in India. They also provide a great customer experience by providing prompt personalized service and sometimes monthly credits. They manage their inventory and stock quite well and run profitable businesses without much dependence on external funding.

In today's fast moving economy and lifestyle patterns there has been a shift in consumers preferred mode of payments while shopping and purchasing for their daily needs. With this dynamic change, the business transactions are constantly changing from cash based to digital modes. This shift has been well accepted by the Shop Keepers, Traders, Small Scale Merchants, Retailers as well, in order to remain in the business and not to lose their customers to the peers. These small-scale merchants or vendors who were once collecting all the receivables through cash are now accepting the transactions over digital payments. Technology has enabled the delivery of financial services innovatively, efficiently and in a cost-effective manner.With this transition in mode of collections from cash to e-cash, the present study focusses on the progress made by digitisation while penetrating in unorganised merchant groups.

The Indian markets are on a trajectory of making a paradigm shift from Cash to No-Cash. E- Wallets are gaining popularity as a preferred mode of transacting amongst the buyers and sellers even for their daily provisions. This generates research interest to study this progress of E-wallets on small scale merchants operating in Unorganised Indian markets.

This study aims to offer valuable insights about the impact of shift to Digital Ecosystem (viz. E-wallets etc.) on the business and financial dynamics of Small Scale Merchants operating in Unorganised Indian Markets (Focused group) based on secondary data.

There have been numerous studies done by various researchers over the past 2 decades on Digital Penetration and the paradigm shift this digital world has brought into Financial Economy. This study is based on these researches, with an aim to find out the progress of these digital initiatives and innovation on Unorganised Indian Markets.

2. EVOLUTION OF FINTECH PAYMENT METHODS – A SHORT OUTLINE

Unlike the Era of 1970s when all the payments and receipts were handled manually, usually in the form of cash or a cheque, much has changed today. These historical payment methods imposed delays, interruptions, manual interventions, physical presence, complex methods and moreover risks while carrying out transactions. Modern payments methods are an answer to all these negatives and gives a much better user experience in terms of customer delight and service. Also termed as the Paytech Revolution (Ref: Deloitte Research Report, SME B2B Payments), this change has revolutionized digitisation offering tailor-made and customized payment options to customers. Figure 1 gives a gist about this evolution of technology from 1970 to 2020+

Era	1970 Technology Core	1980 Technology Enablement	1990 Technology Collaboration	2000 Technology Engagement	2010 Digital	2020 Exponential
General technology	• Mainframes • Distribution terminals • Core computing	• Office computing • Mini-computers • Word processing • Spreadsheets • Home computing	• PC revolution • Network computing • Email • Relational databases • Client-servicer applications	• Internet revolution • Browser wars • Customer engagement • Intranet applications • Broadband	• Mobile • Cloud computing • Big data • Analytics • Social media • Wearables	• Artificial intelligence • Sensing • Internet of things • Digital money • Quantum computing • 3D printing
Payment technology	• First ATMs	• Credit cards • EFTPOS cards	• Telephone banking • Internet banking • Bpay • RTGS	• Card proliferation • PayPal	• Chip protection • Contactless • Digital currencies • Real-time payments	• Invisible payments • Proliferation of non-card real-time payments • Digital cross-border payments

········ Rate of change

Source: SME B2B Payments, Delloitte Research Report, 2018

Fig 1: *Broad Changes in Technology & Corresponding changes in Payment Ecosystem (1970-2020+)*

Technology has been a strategic enabler of improvements across Financial Industry and Financial Services. It has given birth to new ways of making payments and brought in changes in the financial ecosystem

Reserve Bank of India released a Booklet on Payment systems in India on 25th January 2021, which clearly indicates the movement and shift in payment choices from Manual to Digital ones over a decade. It gives a glimpse about the Journey of Payment and Settlement systems in India from 2010 to 2020, classified as a Journey in Second decade of the Millennium. This report shows some interesting facts and figures about the shift in preferred mode of payment systems in India. There has been an exponential growth in payment systems in India leading to a momentous shift in payment preference of the users.

This shift is evidenced by the fact that volume of retail payments through paper clearing declined from 60% in FY 2010-11 to 3% in FY 2019-20. Figure 2 gives a glimpse of this shift.

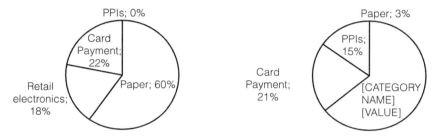

Source: RBI data (RBI Booklet released on 25th January 2021)

Fig 2: *Change in Share of Retail Payment Systems (Volume – FY 2011 to FY 2020)*

Non- bank FinTech firms issuing Prepaid Payment Instruments like cards and wallets, Bharat bill payments operating units (BBPOUs) and third-party application providers in the UPI platform has stimulated this adoption of digital payments in the country further. Reserve Bank's payment system prophecy for 2019-2021 is to enable every Indian with access to convenient, safe, fast, secure and affordable digital payment options. Aiming at Digital Bharat, these user friendly and affordable payment options are leading to an era of Fintech Revolution and Financial Inclusion.

3. Progress of DigitiSation – From Cash to E- Cash In India

The world has experienced a blizzard by the digital revolution which has emerged as a new way of transacting. No other area has witnessed such transformation as the digital ecosystem resulting in innumerable digital payments and receivables options available to a consumer and a merchant. As revealed in one of the World pay reports, digital payment options and practices are growing in the Asia Pacific countries leading to growth in CAGR of e-commerce market. It was estimated at about 12% from 2016 to 2021 in the said region, with India being one of the key enabler for the such progression. Also, within the Fintech sector, digital payment received highest investments followed by Insure tech & lending.

Global Payments Trends Report, JP Morgan 2019 shows that Indian markets which were historically cash dominating, are advancing to no cash culture to meet the rise in demand of e-commerce and online shopping ethnicity. With this transformation, payment options like cards, online transfers and digital wallets are growing in eminence.

Both non- banks and banks are offering smart pay services to the users who are using smartphones and internet as a channel to manage their financial transactions. Personal Banking platforms and fintech players are tying up with banks to create a cohesive and inclusive eco-system.

Affordable data usage prices have further triggered the adoption of digital outflows even in the rural regions. Further innovations, like scanning of QR code to make digital payments and tokenization using smartphones has emerged as new and swift techniques for making payments. These variants have solved for the social distancing requirement of the world and has done away with manual intervention while making or accepting payments. These easy and user friendly techniques have also eased the transition from cash to non-cash transactions for non-tech savvy consumers as well as merchant sector.

While the progress of digital payments can be estimated, cash transactions cannot be measured precisely. Largely, the digital payments in terms of volumes have observed a CAGR of 61% and the digital payment in terms of value have observed a CAGR of 19% around the past 5 years, representing a precipitous transference to digital ecosystem. Figure 3 depicts Digital Payment Trends in India from 2014 to 2019.

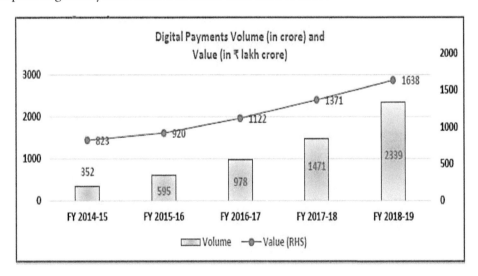

Source: RBI Data, RBI Publication dated 24th Feb 2020
https://www.rbi.org.in/Scripts/PublicationsView.aspx?id=19417

Fig 3: *Digital Payments Trends in India*

Basis RBI Publication dated 24th Feb 2020, a CAGR of 96% and 78% in terms of digital payment volume and value, respectively were noted. As per the Consumer Payments Insight Survey,2017, India is considered to be one of the top and emergent markets for digital cash adoption globally.

A widespread use of E-cash in the form of Wallets and prepaid cards, confirmed an amplified acceptance of digital payment practices. Report dated August 23, 2020 published in Financial Express mentions that Digital Payments Market in India is likely to grow 3 times to Rs 7092 trillion by 2025. E-wallets will see a steady growth in both user base and frequency thereby playing a significant role in this progression. By 2025 wallets are expected to have higher penetration amongst the users. Lower income groups would eventually to derive benefits from Fintech Platforms, the Lower income group would eventually shift their multiple small tickets transactions and day to day operations to fintech alternatives. Financial inclusion programs by Government and evolving digitisation of small scale units/ traders are the key factors supporting this growth, as per the research report. Similar revolutionary change was observed in countries like Kenya by players like M-Pesa and in Bangladesh by b-Kash."The existing 160 million mobile payment users will grow by 5 times to reach approximately 800 million by 2025." RedSeer, said in its report. The report observed COVID-19 pandemic as a stimulus to penetration of digital payments across India, like demonetisation. RedSeer Consulting founder and CEO Anil Kumar had mentioned about digital payment providers in one of their reports that "They have been quite hands-on in terms of retorting to this situation, by offering enhanced support on basics such as offering groceries, sanitisers, face masks, COVID-19 insurance, offering integration with donations to PM fund and other essential product and services,".According to a RedSeer Report, digital payments usage in grocery shopping from local stores jumped to 75 % due to the ongoing pandemic as consumers preferred and felt safe by paying through their mobile phones. Contactless payments became a new normal to uphold social distancing norms.

Not only the organised sector, the unorganised market players have also understood this consumer preference and have adopted E-Wallets as a mode of collection. This study is an attempt to highlight this progress from cash to e-cash in the contest of unorganised Indian Markets.

4.   RESEARCH METHODOLOGY

4a. Scope

- This research paper focuses on Progress of Fintech Payment methods in Unorganised Indian Markets
- Secondary data from reports and publications has been used in the study
- Paper is based on data and inputs captured through Systematic Literature Review

4b. Objective of the Research Study

- To comprehend the progress of penetration of Digital Payment Methods by Small Scale Merchants operating in Unorganised Indian Markets.

- To appraise the change, Digital Payment Ecosystem has brought in, specifically in Unorganised Indian Markets, captured through Literature review.

4c. Methodology

- Excerpts from various publications and reports have been taken to give a preview of the digital progress in India. Study is purely based on Systematic Literature Review. The data collection was Secondary and done through RBI and other reports, publications and research papers. The paper is an attempt to understand the paradigm shift brought in by the Digital and Fintech Progress, through Literature Review.

5.   LITERATURE REVIEW

Delloite Research report, 2018 and Figure 1above, give a glimpse about the digital transformation in financial sector that had started taking shape since 1970 with its First ATM installed in the said year. Looking through the phase wise development for more than two decades, technology has changed the shape of financial framework from Cash to Cashless, from E- Payments to M-Payments, from E-Commerce to M- Commerce and more. Gradually these technological advancements and payment methods, which were once the choice of big business firms and technologically advanced business houses, have now penetrated into the small shops operating in unorganised markets. Demonetisation and COVID 19 scenarios have been the driving factors behind this paradigm shift. Contactless payments have been an ask of the consumers to deal with the pandemic situations. With the increase in number of smartphone users, the M- Payment options like E- Wallets, Payment, Google Pay etc. is ruling the transaction world. Consumer is at ease to pay the seller even in odd denominations. Cash is no more a wallet requirement. A credit card or a debit card can deal with all the shopping hassles, along with the smart phone with a good network. Research Studies below show phase wise development of this sector and its successful penetration into the unorganised markets.

Mobile Commerce is defined as The Future Vehicle of E- Payment in Japan (Ogawara et al. 2002). The article mentions about the growing trend of e-shopping and providing e-services, leading to a need for secure and robust payment options which can facilitate this form of business. Innovations in Smartphone technologies have given a way to the businesses and organizations to expand using the digital space changing the traditional ways of doing business. M – business facilitates better marketing and sales activity by being an effective communication channel with the customer (Picoto et al. 2013). The study also insinuated that force from peer businesses, competition and customers are the key reasons to decide to apply M- Business practices. With digitalisation and changed shopping habits of the customers, the local traders operating through retail outlets are under an anxiety to adapt to the new technological advancements (Bollweg et al. 2016). The study had a key finding about digitalisation of Local Owners operating retail businesses. It confirmed that local competitive pressure and expectations of a customer have a positive impact on local vendors' willingness to adopt new technologies and business models. Local vendors have now realised that digitisation is here to stay and that they will have to shift their business models from cash to e-cash. The ongoing pandemic is another positive force in favour of the e-cash models. The fear of losing business to peer is another added factor which the Unorganised Market vendors have faced during the COVID times. Those enabled with e-payment options, were preferred by the customers. Contactless payments are the ask of the time and have gained moment in the unorganised markets which were once independent of these technological changes. Big business firms for expansions etc. were already exploring e-gateways etc. as a payment mode, but to sustain their businesses, these technological changes have to be adopted by the small retailers also for day to day operations.

Not only the fixed, even the small day to day expenses are being met by cashless and cheese less means. To name a few, payment for daily groceries, payment for small jobs like gardening, house maids etc., payments for vegetables and fruits, payments for utility bills, payment for hobby classes, payment for Taxis / Autos etc. have all taken an e-mode. People prefer paying through Paytm, e-wallets, google pay etc. over debit cards, credit cards and cash.

The smaller the transaction, the easier it is to pay using E- Wallets. It has even solved for the small denominations of cash and small payments being rounded off to nearest rupees. Exact payments can be done at a click of the mobile. These options are user friendly and convenient even for lower class and lower middle class users. To promote the process of financial inclusion RBI has given authorization for operation of payment banks and small finance banks. In India, e-wallets are acknowledged as a legal payment instrument. The prepaid instruments are issued under the Payment and Settlement Systems Act, 2005 as per RBI guidelines. Unlike other prepaid instruments E-wallets are only an internet based online account (Kumar N, 2016). These small payment banks are working on online transactions, promoting these even in rural areas. In the coming years, these entities are likely to play a significant role in transformation of online transactions by popularising mobile based payments (Kumar N, 2016). Enhanced use of smart phones, e-commerce and m-commerce have driven the mobile payments and expanded the use of E-wallets. As per study by Ken Research, Indian payment market comprising of Mobile banking, E-wallets, POS terminal sale etc. is estimated to reach around 8173 billion (Kumar N, 2016). In Developing economies, Mobile Applications provide a platform to focus on the set of people who do not have a bank account but possess a smart phone (Cox, 2013). Microfinance institutions earlier tried to fulfill and achieve this goal with limited success.

E-wallets are facilitating the Financial Inclusion goals as well. Evolution of payment banks along with E-wallet service providers are successful in extending the use of mobile for doing cashless transactions even to the common man, thereby enhancing the banking access to rural population as well (Kumar N., 2016). Rapid Smartphone penetration and high internet usage are the key drivers of M- Commerce. Nearly 94% of the Indian population is using mobile phones for their personal and professional use. Indian Youth are the prime drivers and are more inclined towards making payments at convenience. A study by Singh N, Srivastava S and Sinha N focusses primarily on North Indian Customers and gave good insights into the growing use of M- Wallets by North Indian Population. The study adopted a quantitative approach. Statistical techniques viz. Regression Analysis, ANOVA and T-test was applied on survey data collected from 204 North Indian Consumers. The study was based on four dimensions i.e. preference, usage rate, perception and consumer satisfaction. It revealed 81% of youth population between the age group 18 to 30 years are tech savvy and use internet based options for payment of bills, shopping expenses etc. This study indicated that women are more hands on in using plastic money than men. Choice of consumers, specifically in metro and tier -1 & tier-2 cities are changing resulting into acceptance and more penetration of mobile wallets. The volume of small transactions being done using M-Payments is quite high in Metro and tier 1 and tier 2 cities. People are preferring non-cash over cash methods for easy and secure payment options.

Consumers adopted and accepted M-Wallets for their ease and convenience. Gradually with the penetration of mobile phone into the masses, penetration of M- Payments gained momentum in the financial markets. But for Small Scale Vendors who are operating in unorganised Set up, cash was the only way of transacting until the phase of demonetization started in November 2016. A study by Tiwari & Dr. Lakshmi Shankar Iyer, 2018 is about the demonetisation of currency notes of Rs 1000 and Rs 500 and its effects on small scale vendors operating in unorganised markets. This study foresees vendor's choice to shift to digital wallets for payments as an outcome of the demonetisation phase. The study adopted an empirical approach and was based on sample data collected from 223 small vendors from two Indian Cities. Based on Decision Tree Algorithm, this study reviewed the challenges and benefits experienced by small scale vendors while implementing digital wallet as a payment method. As these vendors and common man had very high dependency on liquid cash until then, cash crunch was observed nation-wide. Consequently, people started adopting the alternative payment solutions like Cards, POS based transactions, plastic money, digital wallets and Net Banking. Plastic money replaced liquid cash. Use of digital wallets for day to day transactions had increased by over 100% (Tiwar & Iyer, 2018). The "Digital India" initiative of the Government of India is focused at creating a Cashless, Faceless and Paperless Indian Economy and for promoting this the Government is incentivizing the digital payments. A few examples of these initiative are the discounts being offered by PSUs like Indian Railways, Public Sector Insurance Companies, Central Government Petroleum units on payments made through their websites. When the customers moved from cash to cashless, there was no reason for the vendors to stay with the traditional methods of transacting. With Indian Organised Markets already making a shift from cash to cash less means, the unorganised vendors were the next to accept and adopt this shift. The current ongoing Pandemic is another key driver which has bridged this gap in making this shift from cash to cashless operations, making it convenient and secure for all.

Unorganised Markets operating in Indian Urban and Semi Urban centers, faced a major challenge to sustain their businesses during COVID. With buyers preferring contactless deliveries of daily supplies, the unorganised sector had to make this shift. From the Local Karana Shops to Vegetable vendors, Local Service Providers, Small retail electronic shops, Cloth shops, Small Repair shops etc. had to make their way to sustain in this difficult time when adopting to the new normal was the only option. Adrian Athique in his article 'A Great Leap of Faith: The Cashless Agenda in Digital India', 2019 evaluates the rationale for India's 2016 demonetisation by citing his own experiences during his visit to India during the said phase. The article had an interesting admission that India's demonetisation was closely linked to broader macro-economic considerations about the future of cash. He mentioned that cashless economies will require and subsequently endorse the development of digital infrastructure through the world.

Digital Platforms have given solutions to the many problems of the world specifically arising as a consequence of the current pandemic viz. social distancing, self- isolation, lockdown. All these measures had a wide impact on digital consumption. Technology has substantiated to be a useful tool to handle the pandemic (Galhotra & Dewan, 2020). Industry experts have characterised e-commerce as a sustenance system during this time of pandemic. Not only for the consumers but also for the retailers who need business continuity which otherwise had a major blow. Technological developments acted as a support system to keep the retail businesses running. This study gave a glimpse of digital usage phase wise during lockdown. More of the essential goods were bought as compared to the non-essential ones. With the increase in the usage of digital platform by households to purchase daily products, there was a consequent increase in this adoption by the small shops. Even the ones operating in societies had to shift to non- variables on the demand of the consumer. A study by L Puspitawati & P Gurning, 2019, used descriptive approach with interpretative qualitative methods to show that electronic payments can benefit small and medium businesses by offering discounts, cash backs, loyalty points and more such benefits. In addition to business transactions, the small vendors have started using these digital channels for payment of salaries, procurement of inventory etc., which has helped in efficient management of their businesses.

Report by McKinsey Global Institute 2019, on "Digital India: Technology to transform a connected nation", indicates that India is deemed as one of the emergent markets for digital consumers. However, acceptance of this makeover is uneven among businesses. As digital competences improve further, technology is going to change each and every sector of Indian Economy. The report had following valuable insights on digital platforms and its adoption levels in India. Looking at the figures extracted from the said report, India is among the top two countries globally on many key dimensions of digital adoption. Figure 4 gives a glimpse of global ranking of India on key dimensions of digital adoption.

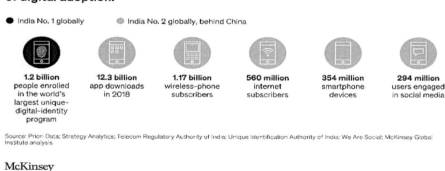

Source:https://www.mckinsey.com/business-functions/mckinsey-digital/our-insights/digital-india-technology-to-transform-a-connected-nation

Fig 4: *Digital Adoption in India*

The report specifies that Digital Technologies can also create substantial value in areas such as government services and the employment market. The report estimated that India's newly digitizing sectors have the prospective to generate substantial economic value by 2025. A few estimates as were provided in the report are from $50 billion to $65 billion in agriculture; $130 billion to $170 billion in financial services, including digital payments; $25 billion to $35 billion each in retail and e-commerce, logistics and transportation; and $10 billion in energy and healthcare (Mckinsey & Co, 2019). More than 80% of retail outlets in India function in unorganised sector mostly in the form of firms operated by sole proprietors or one man owned businesses.

They have dependence on manual store operations and their marketing practices are not effective. The prices in these unorganised stores are also more or less static. Digital solutions have actually reshaped this economic sector. It has enabled retailers to expand even without incurring capital expense on stores or own websites. Third party market sites like Amazon, Jaypore, Flipkart etc. have given an opportunity to these retail businesses to grow and expand even outside their place of business. Online market place websites have given this opportunity to the unorganised retailers to have business continuity. It has bridged the gap between the end users and actual sellers / producers of a product. With this in context, adoption of these digital platforms has become a need of an hour for these unorganised vendors operating in Indian Markets.

6.   CONCLUSION

Indian government is encouraging digital progress, from redesigning regulations to incentivizing digital payments and to improving infrastructure to support digital innovations and adoptions. To sustain and have business continuity and even expansion, small unorganised Indian Sectors should have their eyes on adoption of the digital techniques emerging in the market. Change is the only continuous thing in a world. And adapting to the change is important to survive in the new dynamics. Darwin's Survival of Fittest Theory would apply for the unorganised retail sector – Innovate, Adapt or Perish. Taking learnings from demonetisation and COVID 19 situations, Unorganised Indian retailers have well adapted to the new normal and shifted from operating in Cash to E- Cash structures. With all payments and receipts on E- Mode, these businesses have re-organized themselves. Digital adoptions have changed their way of collections and maintaining records for their business transactions. Where customer satisfaction is the key, these retailers have adjusted to the paradigm shift. They have and are successfully leveraging the digital platforms to match their business models. Giving options to the consumer to make payment, be it through Paytm, Google Pay, UPI, E-wallets etc., it's a refreshing change to the consumer to purchase from a vendor / kirana shop which is fully loaded with these digital payment options. This adaption levels should only rise in the near future, rather penetrate at rapid levels. With young entrepreneurs taking over businesses and running start –ups, this change is bound to grow with a faster pace. Matching customer preference to supply is the first driving force of a business. Our local retailers have well understood this fact and have changed their way of operations for a better and a brighter Digital Economy.

7. RESEARCH GAP AND FUTURE STUDY

This research study is based on systematic literature review. Working on primary data can give more accurate results to understand the penetration levels of E-wallets in Unorganised Markets in both urban and rural areas. Qualitative interviews can also be conducted to understand the change in financial dynamics due to adoption of digital platforms by these small-scale retailers to know the digital reality in unorganised markets from their personal experiences. Results from the primary data can be interpreted in future study to understand the consequences of this penetration.

REFERENCES

1. Adrian Athique (2019). A Great leap of Faith: The Cashless agenda in Digital India, *SAGE Journal*, Volume: 21 issue 8, pp. 1697–1713. https://doi.org/10.1177/1461444819831324
2. B. Galhotra and A. Dewan (2020). Impact of COVID-19 on digital platforms and change in E-commerce shopping trends, *Fourth International Conference on I-SMAC (IoT in Social, Mobile, Analytics and Cloud) (I-SMAC)*, Palladam, India, 861–866.
3. Bollweg, Lars; Lackes, Richard; Siepermann, Markus; Sutaj, Arbnesh; and Weber, Peter (2016). Digitalisation of Local Owner operated retail outlets: The Role of the Perception and Customer Expectations, *PACIS 2016* Proceedings. 348.
4. Delloitte Research Report (2018). SME Digital Payments, New Opportunities to Optimise, The Paytech revolution Series. Link: https://www2.deloitte.com/content/dam/Deloitte/au/Documents/financial-services/deloitte-au-fs-sme-digital-payments-270218.pdf.
5. Gary Madden, Aniruddha Banerjee, Paul N. Rappoport & Hiroaki Suenaga (2016). E-commerce transactions, the installed base of credit cards, and the potential mobile E-commerce adoption, *Applied Economics*, 49:1, 21–32, https://doi.org/10.1080/00036846.2016.1189507
6. Kalra, Neha Batra & Roopali (2016). Are Digital Wallets the New Currency? *Appeejay Journal of Management and Technology*, Vol.11, No.1.
7. Kumar N, (2016). Growth Drivers and Trends of E-wallets in India, *MANTHAN: Journal of Commerce and Management*, 3(1), 65–72. https://doi.org/10.17492/manthan.v3i1.6599
8. L Puspitawati and P Gurning, (2019). Electronic payment for Micro, Small and Medium Enterprises in Developing Countries, *IOP Conf. Ser.: Mater. Sci. Eng.662.*
9. Mckinsey & Company, (2019). Digital India: Technology to transform a connected Nation. [Report] Link-https://www.mckinsey.com/business-functions/mckinsey-digital/ourinsights/digital- india-technology-to-transform-a-connected-nation
10. Nidhi Singh, Shalini Srivastava, Neena Sinha, (2017). Consumer preference and satisfaction of M-Wallets: A study on North Indian consumers, *International Journal of Bank Marketing*, Vol. 35 No.6, pp. 944–965. https://doi.org/10.1108/IJBM-06-2016-0086

11. Phillip McGowan, (2021). Sales failure: a review and future research directions, *International Journal of Logistics Research and Applications*, 24:1, 23–50. https://doi.org/10.1080/13675567.2020.1726306

12. RBI Publication, (2020, February 24). Assessment of the progress of digitisation from cash to electronic. [Publication] Link:https://www.rbi.org.in/Scripts/PublicationsView.aspx?id=19417

13. RBI Booklet, (2021). Payment Systems in India, Booklet.
Link: https://rbidocs.rbi.org.in/rdocs/Publications/PDFs/PSSBOOKLET93D3AEFDEAF14044BC1BB36662C41A8C.PDF

14. R.Aggarwal, S. Tuteja, (2018). Paytm's wallet business: on a growth trajectory or suicide mission? *The CASE Journal*, 14. 112–138, https://doi.org/10.1108/TCJ-07-2017-0063

15. Sachiko Ogawara, Jason C. H. Chen PhD & P. Pete Chong PhD. (2002). Mobile Commerce, Journal of Internet Commerce, 1:3, 2941. https://doi.org/10.1300/J179v01n03_04.

16. Srinivasan Swaminathan, Rolph Anderson & Lei Song (2018). Building loyalty in e-commerce: Impact of business and customer characteristics, *Journal of Marketing Channels*, 25:12, 22–35. https://doi.org /10.1080/1046669X.2019.1646184

17. Trisha Tiwari & Dr. Lakshmi Shankar Iyer (2018). Adoption of Digital Wallets by Petty Vendors Post Demonetisation in India: A Prediction Approach, *Asian Journal of Research in Social Sciences and Humanities,* Vol.8, No. 6, pp. 117–130. https://doi.org/10.5958/2249-7315.2018.00095.3

18. Winnie Ng Picoto, France Bélanger & António Palma-dos-Reis (2013). M-BusinessOrganizational Benefits and Value, A Qualitative Study. *Journal of Organizational Computing and Electronic Commerce*, 23:4, 287324. https://doi.org/10.1080/10919392.2013.837789.

CHAPTER 29

Management Lessons from Unorganized Restaurants in South India

Sandeep H
Student of MBA (LOS), School of Business and
Management
CHRIST (Deemed to be University)
Bengaluru, India
sandeep.h@mba.christuniversity.in

Georgy Kurien*
Associate Professor, School of Business and
Management
CHRIST (Deemed to be University)
Bengaluru, India
georgy.kurien@christuniversity.in

*Corresponding Author

Abstract

The research aims to do a comparative study of various metrics of organized and unorganized restaurants. It also proposes a possible collaboration between organized and unorganized restaurants by deriving management lessons from the unorganized sector and their possible application in organized sector. An Exploratory Qualitative Research Methodology is used in this study. Data collection is mainly done through field visits and by means of interview using a preset questionnaire where extra questions are asked based on the type of business and other considerations. The study revealed many interesting results. Some of the unique dishes are existing only in the traditional unorganized restaurant in its purest form. Enhancement of taste using traditional methods such as usage of banana leaves, conventional cooking utensils, effectiveness of firewood as fuel, low serving times achieved through certain premixes, assurance of cleanliness and hygiene through minimum resources, experimentation of recipes and get instant feedbacks from customers etc. were some of learnings from the unorganized restaurants. The paper also recommends lessons for the unorganized sector. The research is limited to the states of Kerala and Karnataka and the sample size is only 25.

Keywords: India Uninc., Unorganized Sector, Marginal Businesses, Informal Supply Chains, small scale restaurants

INTRODUCTION

In India, the terms 'unorganized sector' and 'informal sector' are used interchangeably in popular culture. The term 'unorganized sector' is used commonly in all official records and analysis. The literature regarding this sector is so vast and so there is a multitude of conceptualizations and definitions relating to this concept. Keith Hart is the first person to introduce the term 'Informal sector' and distinguished formal and informal income opportunities on the basis of whether the activity entailed wage or self-employment (Hart, 1973). Unorganized sector is also called Informal Sector, Marginalized Sector or India Uninc. The term Uninc. was popularized by Prof. R. Vaidyanathan through his book "India Uninc." (Vaidyanathan, 2014).

Sales per square feet revenue and Return on Investment (RoI) are often better for India Uninc compared to India Inc. Distribution of money across the Supply Chain is far more equitable in India Uninc when compared to India Inc. The agility, with which street vendors change their inventory, supply chain linkages, target segmentation, pitch, product innovations is praiseworthy. The methods by which they market is remarkable considering minimum infrastructure and without the aid of much technology (Adams, 2002). The India Uninc is considered as equal opportunity provider in which skills are given more importance than experience. The India Uninc is the largest Contributor to national income (GDP) in India (NSSO, 2018). The unorganized workers are subject to exploitation significantly by the rest of the society (Raju, 1989; Datt, 2008).

This area of study is found to be relatively unexplored (Dutta, 2020). Around 25 restaurants were observed which belong to different categories: Unorganized restaurants (11), Organized Restaurants (3) and Five Star Hotels (5). The ranking is done based on the selected 19 parameters. The aim is to evaluate various unorganized restaurants and compare it with organized and 5-Star Restaurants.

IMPORTANCE OF UNORGANIZED SECTOR

India's aim to be a $5 trillion economy hinges a lot on catalyzing the unorganized sector, particularly in retail and wholesale. The self-employed form a sizeable chunk of this sector. Over 90 per cent of the $700 billion retail market in India is unorganized (Datt, 2008, Mishra, 2017, Raju, 1989).

Various businesses involved in the Unorganized Sector

The sectors that account for a dominant share of informal employment are: 1. Manufacturing; 2. Construction; and 3. Trade (wholesale and retail). They accounted for 76 per cent and 72 per cent respectively of all workers in the non-agriculture informal sector, in the rural and urban areas, as compared with 69 per cent and 59 per cent respectively of all workers in the non-agriculture sector (Gurtook 2009; Naik, 2009). However, Kolli (2007) chose to define the informal sector as consisting of all enterprises outside the public and private corporate sectors which employed five or less workers. In light of its significance, we have a motivation for research on the informal sector from a management and organization scholarship perspective.

Need of the Study

Around 50% of India's GDP is contributed by unorganized sector and they employ 90% of the workforce of our country (around 450 million people) (Gupta, 2009; Mcgahan, 2012). Yet management researchers are often ignoring this unorganized sector in several business metrics. Therefore, corporate sector and researchers are missing some useful information that can be applied for their operations (Bruton, Ireland, & Ketchen, 2012). There is a need to study and analyze the strategy used by the unorganized sector. Then we can apply it in organized sector (Darbi, Hall, & Knott, 2016). This can be done by analyzing the different processes and supply chain strategies of unorganized restaurants.

Details of the research conducted

Data collection is mainly done through field visits. Interviews were conducted using a pre-set questionnaire (self-filled questionnaire) where additional questions were asked based on the type of business and other considerations. The data collection covered various aspects of the business technology, such as supply chain strategies, marketing, turnaround management, human resources management, sustainability features of the business, innovations/distinct features of the business, pricing strategies etc. Various news articles and websites in the context of 'management lessons from unorganized sector' were also referred while doing this research (Biggs, Hall, & Stoeckl, 2012; Dimara, & Skuras, 2005; Godfrey, 2011).

A Convenient sampling technique is used to select respondents to the study. For convenience, locations that we focused were parts of Kerala and Bangalore. A sample size of 25 was chosen based on this convenience and also considering the time-bound nature of conducting study.

Criterion for Evaluation

As mentioned, 25 restaurants were studied for different criterion of performance and management practices related to the business area. Based on literature and expert opinion, a list of criterion (measures) are identified. This list of criterion were validated through a pilot study with experts in the field. Following measures and criterions are used to study and compare the restaurants (refer Table 1):

Table 1. List of Criterion Selected to Evaluate the Restaurants

Criterion	Abbreviation	Description
Hotel Amenities	H	The Infrastructure of the restaurant, Seating Arrangement etc.
Arrival & Car Parking	P	The arrival experience and the car parking Space

Criterion	Abbreviation	Description
Location	L	Consider location advantages like approachability, nearness to communication hubs etc.
Hygiene	C	The cleanliness of the table, the plates, kitchen, freshness of the raw materials, people etc.
Ambience & View	A	The overall character and atmosphere of a place.
Privacy	S	Ability of customers to seclude themselves, not observed or disturbed by other people.
Buffet Spread	B	It refers to the number of dishes or variety of dishes offered by the restaurant
Salads	S	The quality and taste of the salads
Starters	S_t	The quality and taste of the Starters
Continental Food	Co	The quality and taste of the Continental Food
North Indian Food	N	The quality and taste of the North Indian Food
South Indian Food	So	The quality and taste of the North Indian Food
Counters	L	The Customer satisfaction obtained from the live counters
Desserts	D	The quality and taste of the Desserts
Service	Se	The Customer satisfaction obtained from the services offered from the restaurant
Overall Quality of the Food	Q	The overall Freshness, taste of the food felt as a customer
Price	P	Average price spends by the customer for one visit. Lower the price, the higher the rating
Sustainability	S	It refers to how much the restaurant is ecofriendly (Mainly the usage of plastic, waste management etc)

COMPARATIVE EVALUATION AND ASSESSMENT

All the 25 selected restaurants were visited and studied. An exploratory qualitative research methodology is used in this study. Data collection is mainly done through field visits and by means of interview using a preset questionnaire and additional questions are asked based on the type of business and other considerations. The criterion mentioned in Table 1 are used to evaluate the restaurants in a scale of 1 to 5. The summary of evaluation is presented at Table 2. The ranking of restaurants is also presented at Table 2.

Table 2: Summary of Evaluation of the Restaurants

R	Name	Type	H	P	L	C	A	S	B	Ar	S	St	Co	N	So	L	D	Se	Q	P	S	F
1	Taj	Five Star	5	5	4	5	5	4	2	5	5	3	2	5	5	4	5	3	5	2	4	78
2	Crowne Plaza	Five Star	5	5	5	5	4	4	3	4	4	3	2	3	4	4	3	3	5	2	4	72
3	Grand Hyatt	Five Star	5	3	4	5	4	2	5	3	3	5	5	4	3	4	1	5	5	1	4	71
4	Le Meridien	Five Star	5	5	4	5	4	5	3	5	3	2	4	2	5	3	0	3	5	2	4	69
5	Marriott	Five Star	3	2	5	5	4	4	4	4	3	1	5	1	2	1	3	4	4	1	4	60
6	Othenans Hotel	Organized	4	4	4	4	3	3	-	-	-	-	-	-	5	-	-	4	5	4	3	43
7	Vazhiyorakkada	Organized	3	3	3	4	3	3	-	-	-	-	-	-	5	-	-	4	5	4	3	37
8	Rajapuram Toddy Shop	Unorganized	3	3	2	3	4	3	-	-	-	-	-	-	4	-	-	3	4	4	3	36
9	Thalassery National	Organized	3	4	3	4	3	2	-	-	-	-	-	-	4	-	-	4	4	4	3	38
10	Amma Mess	Unorganized	3	4	2	4	3	2	-	-	-	-	-	-	4	-	-	2	5	4	2	35
23	Mapranam	Unorganized	3	3	3	3	3	3	-	1	-	-	-	-	4	-	-	2	4	4	3	35
11	Ikayees	Unorganized	2	2	5	3	4	1	-	-	-	-	-	-	3	-	-	3	3	5	3	34
12	40 Rupees Chicken Curry Meals	Unorganized	2	2	2	4	3	2	-	-	-	-	-	-	4	-	-	3	4	5	3	34
13	Ezhuthanikada	Unorganized	3	1	2	3	2	1	1	1	-	-	-	-	4	-	2	2	3	5	3	33
14	R K Dosa Camp	Unorganized	2	2	4	2	2	2	-	-	-	-	-	-	4	-	-	3	4	5	3	33
15	Mullapanthal Toddy Shop	Unorganized	3	2	1	3	3	2	-	-	-	-	-	-	4	-	-	3	4	4	3	32
16	Kanhangad Vanitha Hotel	Unorganized	3	2	1	4	2	2	-	-	-	-	-	-	4	-	-	2	4	5	3	32

TOP RANKED RESTAURANTS IN THE UNORGANIZED SECTOR

This section gives details of the top five restaurants in the unorganized sector. A brief description with photos is presented.

Rank 1 – Rajapuram Shop (Overall Rank - 8)

Rajapuram Shop is situated in Kavalam region of Alappuzha District in Kerala. They have been doing this business for the past 65 years. It is located in the midst of a backwater and a paddy field. We can reach the restaurant only via a boat. It possesses 24 traditional food varieties which includes different fish and meat varieties which is made using their own secret recipes. Quality and Freshness of food is found to be very high.

Fig. 1: *Entrance of Rajapuram Restaurant*   **Fig. 2:** *Kozhuva (Crunchy fish dish)*

Rank 2 – Amma Mess (Overall Rank – 10)

Fig. 3: *Entrance of Amma Restaurant*   **Fig. 4:** *Service Area – Amma Restaurant*

Amma Mess is one of the most famous restaurants in Calicut which provides traditional south Indian food. They have been doing this business for the past 26 years. They have specialized meals with lot of fish varieties. They provide high quality food but with comparatively less price. Moreover, freshness of the food and hygiene atmosphere of the restaurant is commendable. They have their own secret recipe and they serve the food in banana leaves. A small hut with thatched roof is still providing a good ambience for the customers. They don't use any kind of plastic material inside the restaurant which is a good sustainable initiative. They are operated between 11:00 AM to 4 PM.

Rank 3 – Ikayees (Overall Rank – 11)

Ikayees is a moving restaurant which runs on a small converted matador tempo in Calicut. They serve delicious Malabar dishes around the city premises of Calicut. As they don't have any location constraint, they will travel to most crowded destinations within the city with enough food items in their truck. This was started by six students (Shameem, Arfath, Ulais, Naseem, Shaz, Shyma, Shameer) of Institute of Palliative Medicine, Calicut as a venture which can help unemployed women who is passionate about cooking with a capital investment of Rs. 8 lakhs.

Fig. 5: *Ikayees Restaurant serving food*   **Fig. 6:** *Graphics done on the Truck as a Promotional Technique*

Rank 4 – 40 Rupees Chicken Curry Meals (Overall Rank – 12)

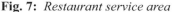

Fig. 7: *Restaurant service area*   **Fig. 8:** *Lunch served on banana leaf*

It is a small home which provides a 40 Rs. Chicken curry meals which also includes all kinds of traditional curries which is run by 65-year-old woman called Ammini. For fishes, separate charges are applied. Quality and Freshness of the food is quite commendable.

A. Rank 5 – Ezhuthanikkada (Overall Rank – 13)

Ezhithanikkada is a local restaurant in Kollam, Kerala which is famous for its mutton curry and porotta. They have been doing this business for the past 65 years. It is widely known to be the inventor of famous vettu cake and Kollam special mutton curry. Even though it has low varieties, it provides fresh and quality food. (Cooked food will not be stored for the next day). They are doing somewhat accurate demand forecasting without any aid of technology based on historical data. There were only four benches and table. Three fans are also present. It has traditional cooking utensils and Equipment only. It will provide a true village ambience to the customers even though the Kollam town is nearby (3 km).

Fig. 9: *Vettu Cake*

Fig. 10: *Dosa with Mutton Curry*

FINDINGS AND RECOMMENDATIONS

Five star hotels are in the top five as expected. But one unorganized restaurant scored above one organized restaurant (Rajapuram Restaurant). It is because of the exquisite ambience of the Rajapuram Restaurant in which customers can experience the beauty of the backwaters while having the food. If we compare the price and Quality ratio, the unorganized sector is found to better than organized and five star restaurants

	Five Star	Organized	Unorganized
■ Avg Quality Rating	4.8	4.66	3.82
■ Avg Price Rating	1.6	4	4.64

Fig. 11: *Comparison between price and Quality Ratings*

MANAGEMENT LESSONS THAT CAN BE LEARNED FROM UNORGANIZED RESTAURANTS

Collaboration

South Indian food of selected unorganized restaurants can be on par with five star and organized restaurant in terms of taste and quality but lacks presentation. In fact, some unique dishes are existing only in the traditional unorganized restaurant in its purest form. So, five-star restaurants can add those unique dishes to their south Indian buffet and live kitchen segments in which a specific percentage of profit margin can be given to the corresponding unorganized player and the dish can be named with the concerned unorganized shop's name also. The collaboration will be definitely a win-win situation for both the parties. This can be considered as a CSR activity also.

Direct interaction of chef with customers

Customization is very easy in an unorganized restaurant in which the customer can directly interact with the cook regarding his recipe requirements and he can watch the cooking process live. (The concept of live kitchen is adopted in many five-star restaurants, but it is not present in many of the organized restaurants.). This will increase the level of customer satisfaction.

Branded food trucks

Some of the unorganized restaurants do not have any location constraints (Eg: Ikayees is a moving restaurant which runs on a food truck). Therefore, branded restaurant chains can build some food trucks with their brand name attached and thus they can explore more customers and create more visibility in places where their presence is limited.

Usage of firewood as fuel for cooking

It is observed that usage of firewood would enhance the taste of south Indian food and five-star hotels like Le Meridien has adopted the fire food as fuel for specific dishes. More organized restaurants can explore this possibility.

Usage of banana leaves for serving and storing

Usage of Banana leaves will give another flavor to the dishes as hot food items will dry up the banana leaves. So organized restaurants can consider serving specific dishes in banana leaves.

Involve customers with the experimentation of different recipes and get instant feedback

In unorganized restaurants, it is easy to experiment recipes and get instant feedbacks. This should be made possible in unorganized restaurants with live kitchen facility Food with core traditional values are more often obtained in unorganized restaurants which has a legacy of several decades.

LESSONS UNORGANIZED RESTAURANTS CAN LEARN FROM ORGANIZED RESTAURANTS

Improve cleanliness

In order to improve cleanliness and hygiene, they can use gloves, hair cap and mask (some of the unorganized restaurants are found to be lacking in the cleanliness of the table, the plates, kitchen, freshness of the raw materials, people etc.)

Use marketing models

Lot of unorganized restaurants do not have any marketing plan in place. So, they should have appropriate marketing tools for better visibility and communication to the customers

Adaptation to digital payment modes

Digital payment modes are now commonly available and most people own a smart phone. Unorganized sector can use multiple mobile phone based online facility for payment (Eg-Google Pay).

Improve inventory management

Inventory should not be left over as it is a severe problem for the unorganized restaurants. For that, efficient and any kind of simplified way of demand estimation should be done based on the historical data.

CONCLUSIONS

The unorganized sector play an important role in shaping the Indian economy; is labor intensive and provides employment to a sizable section of the Indian population (Kulshreshtha, 2011; Porter & Kramer 2018). Various management lessons are learned by the study which can be applied by both the unorganized and organized restaurants in their daily operations. India uninc has lot to offer in terms of practical wisdom and local resourcefulness. The unorganized sector can also be benefitted by established management practices. The limitation of the study is that the sample size is limited to 25 and restricted to the states of Kerala and Karnataka.

REFERENCES

Adams, R. J. (2002). Retail profitability and sweatshops: a global dilemma. *Journal of Retailing and Consumer Services*, *9*(3), 147–153.

Biggs, D., Hall, C. M., & Stoeckl, N. (2012). The resilience of formal and informal tourism enterprises to disasters: reef tourism in Phuket, Thailand. *Journal of Sustainable Tourism*, *20*(5), 645–665.

Bruton, G. D., Ireland, R. D., & Ketchen, D. J. (2012). Toward a Research Agenda on the Informal Economy. *Academy of Management Perspectives*, *26*(3), 1–11.

Darbi, W. P. K., Hall, C. M., & Knott, P. (2016). The Informal Sector: A Review and Agenda for Management Research. *International Journal of Management Reviews*, *20*(2), 301–324.

Datt, R. (2008). *Growth, poverty, and equity: story of India's economic development*. New Delhi: Deep & Deep Publications.

Dutta, S., & Das, A. (2020). Street vending in the urban informal sector: A study in Silchar town in Northeast India. In Understanding Urbanisation in Northeast India (pp. 138–152). Routledge India.

Dimara, E., & Skuras, D. (2005). Consumer demand for informative labeling of quality food and drink products: a European Union case study. *Journal of Consumer Marketing*, *22*(2), 90–100.

Godfrey, P. C. (2011). Toward a Theory of the Informal Economy. *Academy of Management Annals*, *5*(1), 231–277.

Gupta, K. R. (2009). *Economics of development and planning: history, principles, problems and policies*. New Delhi: Atlantic Publishers & Distributors.

Gurtoo, A., & Williams, C. C. (2009). Entrepreneurship and the informal sector: some lessons from India. The International Journal of Entrepreneurship and Innovation, 10(1), 55–62.

Hart, K. (1973). Informal Income Opportunities and Urban Employment in Ghana. *The Journal of Modern African Studies*, *11*(1), 61–89.

Kolli, R. (2007, September). The Informal Sector in the National Accounts of India. In International Conference on Experiences and Challenges in Measuring National Income and Wealth in Transition Economies organized by the International Association for Research in Income and Wealth (IARIW) and the National Bureau of Statistics (NBS) of China (pp. 18–21).

Kulshreshtha, A. C. (2011). Measuring the unorganized sector in India. Review of Income and Wealth, 57, S123–S134.

Mcgahan, A. M. (2012). Challenges of the Informal Economy for the Field of Management. *Academy of Management Perspectives*, *26*(3), 12–21.

Mishra, S. (2017). Social Security for Unorganised Workers in India. *Journal of Social Sciences*, *53*(2), 73–80.

Naik, A. K. (2009). Informal sector and informal workers in India. In Special IARIW-SAIM Conference on 'Measuring the Informal Economy in Developing Countries' September (pp. 23–26).

NSSO (National Sample Survey Office) Annual Report (2018), Government of India Ministry of Statistics and Programme Implementation, https://www.mospi.gov.in/

Porter, M. E., & Kramer, M. R. (2018). Creating Shared Value. *Managing Sustainable Business*, 323–346.

Raju, R. S. (1989). *Urban unorganised sector in India*. Delhi, India: Mittal Publications.

Academic Foundation. (2008). *Report on conditions of work and promotion of livelihoods in the unorganised sector*. New Delhi.

Vaidyanathan, R. (2014). India Uninc. Westland.

CHAPTER 30

Women Entrepreneurship in India and China: An Institutional Perspective

Dr. Meghna Chhabra
Associate Professor
Faculty of Management Studies
Manav Rachna International
Institute of Research and Studies
Faridabad, Haryana, India
meghnachhabra28@gmail.com

Dr. Rajat Gera
Professor
Jain Deemed-To-Be-University
Bangalore, Karnataka, India
geraim43@gmail.com

Ms. Anita Sharma
Assistant Professor
K. R. Mangalam University
Gurugram, Haryana, India
anita.shandilya57@gmail.com

Abstract

This study empirically evaluates the effects of individual and normative determinants of opportunity and necessity-based entrepreneurial activity of women pertaining to nascent entrepreneurs (opportunity and necessity based) in India and China. For China, the effects of the individual factors of 'Alertness to Opportunities' and 'Self-Efficacy' on nascent entrepreneurship activity were found to be significant irrespective of gender and motivation type; whereas the mitigating impact of 'Fear of Failure' was significant for opportunity driven entrepreneurial activity only. The effects of informal normative factors of 'Social Capital of Entrepreneur', 'Desirable Social Image of Entrepreneurs' and 'Intensity of Media Exposure' were found to be moderated by gender, and type of motivation. Effect of 'Higher Household Income' and 'Education' on 'Total Early Stage Entrepreneurship' (TEA) was specific to gender and motivation type. For India, the effects of individual and informal normative factors on TEA were moderated by gender and motivation type. Social Status and Respect' in society did not have significant impact on TEA for both China and India.

Keywords: *Opportunity Entrepreneurship; Necessity entrepreneurship; Institutional Theory; China; India; Gender; Global Entrepreneurship Monitor*

1. INTRODUCTION

In developing economies, about 50% of the human capital comprises women entrepreneurs (World Bank, 2009). However, in these countries, the ratio of female to male entrepreneurs is low and it is accompanied by a lower survival rate, with the probable reasons being exclusion of women as well as inequality between men and women (Pines et al., 2010). Multi-country studies on GEM data have shown that variations in early-stage women entrepreneurship are influenced by lower perceptions of self-confidence (Koellinger et al., 2013; Langowitz and Minniti, 2007; higher fear of failure (Koellinger et al., 2013; Wagner and Sternberg, 2004), favorable opportunity perceptions and type of social network (Koellinge et al., 2013). Verhaul et al., (2006) established that individual factors differentially impact female entrepreneurship. However, entrepreneurial norms and the societal attitudes determined by cultural values and religious beliefs discourage female entrepreneurship in some countries (Baughn et al., 2006). Hence, an integrative theoretical model, which deals with the manner in which institutional contextual attributes and individual factors (Karmarkar et al., 2014) are moderated by country level socio-psychological perceptions at the individual level to motivate innovative entrepreneurial activity by women is still lacking. There are very few studies that integrate individual and institutional factors on individual entrepreneurial motivations (e.g. Estrin et al., 2016; Pathak and Muralidharan, 2016). This study aims at addressing this gap.

The antecedent factors of the two entrepreneurial GEM based classification of motivational factors i.e., opportunity based to take advantage of an opportunity and necessity based because there is no other employment option, have been found to differ by country (Crecente-Romero et al., 2016; Chhabra, 2016) and gender of the business owner (Minniti and Naudé, 2010, Chhabra and Karmarkar, 2016). This study assumes the perspective that, "Necessity and opportunity entrepreneurship is shaped by national environmental and institutional contexts regardless of level of economic development at country level", (Dencker et al., 2019) as evidenced by significant levels of necessity entrepreneurship in both OECD (21.1%) and non-OECD (41.6%) countries. The determinants of necessity-based and opportunity-based entrepreneurship are different (Verheul et al., 2010) and the results of empirical studies on the effects of individual and normative factors on necessity/opportunity types of entrepreneurships have been inconclusive (Arai, 1997).

According to Warnecke (2013) female entrepreneurship appears to be influenced by formal institutions (economic and political domains, regulations, and laws) as well as informal institutions (social norms and attitudes). The antecedents of female entrepreneurial activity in middle-income transition economies have not been adequately investigated (Chhabra et al., 2020). This study makes an attempt at filling in the gaps in literature as well as extending this stream of research that would soon branch out into two transition economies, with divergent rates of female entrepreneurial activity.

By conducting a cross-country analysis of India and China that exhibit high economic growth rates, we are attempting to answer the following research questions:

1. Whether the influence of individual and informal normative factors on female entrepreneurship is moderated by the type of motivation?
2. Whether the influence of individual and informal normative factors on female entrepreneurship is moderated by the socio-cultural context of the country?

The hypotheses were formulated based on the proposed list of determinants by the relevant theoretical studies. The findings are discussed and presented followed by the conclusions, implications, and limitations of the study.

2. THE RESEARCH CONTEXT

India and China are the world's most populous countries, with 1.31 and 1.38 billion people respectively. These two are among the fastest growing and largest economies in terms of GDP in the world. China's GDP is attributed to its manufacturing sector, whereas India's GDP is majorly driven by its service sector (Sreekumar et al., 2018). The female to male ratio of Total Early Stage Entrepreneurial Activity (TEA) is 0.58 for India whereas it is 1.34 for China (GEM, 2015). Chinese growth with regard to female entrepreneurship has been associated with structural changes that arose as a result of economic changes (Hernandez et al., 2012); on the contrary, Indian entrepreneurship appears to be stagnated as small businesses receive hardly any incentives in terms of government policies (such as taxation and regulation) that would foster their growth, and novice entrepreneurs have suffered due to a lack of support (Bhidé, 2004; Chhabra and Karmarkar, 2016).

3. LITERATURE REVIEW AND HYPOTHESIS DEVELOPMENT

Female entrepreneurs with higher levels of education were 9% more likely to be in entrepreneurship compared with those who had received a certain kind of education post-secondary level (Terjesen and Lloyd, 2015). Hence, it is proposed that:

H1: Higher levels of education of women will lead to higher female entrepreneurship levels

Some researchers have found that there is a positive association between female higher educational levels and women being involved in start-ups (Minniti, 2006). The study also proposes that:

H2: Higher household income levels will result in higher female entrepreneurship levels

Opportunity is recognized based on either potential entrepreneurial opportunities or individual subjective alertness to unexploited opportunities. This factor has been proven to be one of the key components of entrepreneurial behavior and it impacts the intentions of the actors (Arenius and Minniti, 2005). Hence, it is proposed that:

H3: Higher alertness exhibited by female entrepreneurs to economic opportunities is significantly linked to higher levels of female entrepreneurship

The self-confidence and self-efficacy have a positive relationship with higher levels of one's entrepreneurial activity (Arenius and Minniti, 2005). It is, therefore, proposed that:

H4: Entrepreneurial self-efficacy would be significantly associated with higher levels of female entrepreneurship

Fear acts as an inhibitor of entrepreneurial activity (Arenius and Minniti, 2005) for all types of entrepreneurial actions, and the risk appetite of women impacts their entrepreneurial intentions (Dawson and Henley, 2015). Hence, it is proposed that:

H5: Higher fear of failure is significantly associated with lower levels of female entrepreneurship

Social capital or 'Knowing other Entrepreneurs' has been found to be highly correlated with women's involvement with starting a new business (Minnitti, 2009; Edelman et al., 2010; Langowitz et al., 2006) found that the influence of formal as well as informal networks (Baker et al., 1997; Aldrich and Martinez, 2001) and the impact of role models (Wagner and Sternberg, 2004; Kourilsky and Walstad, 1998) is very significant when it comes to women taking entrepreneurial decisions. It is propositioned that:

H6: The ability of female entrepreneurs to know another entrepreneur is significantly linked to higher levels of female entrepreneurship

Women's involvement in entrepreneurial pursuits has been attributed to contextual factors, such as the need for self-recognition and social status (Ratten et al., 2017; Sharif, 2015). Thus the hypothesis:

H7: Female entrepreneurship activity levels would have a stronger association with status and respect

The ways in which media depicts female entrepreneurs shape perceptions of potential female entrepreneurs and the society about the features of a typical female entrepreneur and her business acumen (Achtenhagen and Welter, 2007; Anderson and Smith, 2007; Bruni et al., 2004; Langowitz and Morgan, 2003). It is proposed that:

H8: Positive representation of female entrepreneurs by the media is significantly linked to a greater level of female entrepreneurship

Any entrepreneurial tradition may be reinforced by redefining and improvising the social status enjoyed by entrepreneurs, and the extent of people's beliefs that entrepreneurship is an attractive activity (Micozzi, 2016). Hence, it is proposed that:

H9: Entrepreneurship as a socially desirable career choice is associated with higher levels of female entrepreneurship

4. THEORETICAL FRAMEWORK

The institutional theory perspective is adopted for this study, as gender gaps in entrepreneurship cannot be fully explained by either the micro-economic or macroeconomic factors (Chhabra, 2018). Recent studies have fallen within the normative context of the entrepreneurial activity (Brush et al., 2009; Baughn et al., 2006). We are dealing with level two institutions pertaining to Williamson's (2000) four-level hierarchy and three-pillar framework propounded by Scott (1995, 2005); in addition, we are also determining the range according to which those with alike socio-cognitive features—fear of failure, alertness toward perceived opportunities related to business, and entrepreneurial self-efficiency— are likely to be involved in entrepreneurial action that is determined by the institutional environment of their nation. This study crisply focuses on the evaluation of the relationship of individual and informal institutional factors with early-stage entrepreneurial activity and the moderating effects of:

A. The socio cultural and economic context of the countries

B. Type of motivation–opportunity and necessity

C. Gender

The three-pillar framework propounded by Scott (1995, 2005) serves as the basis for the institutional factors that have been selected for this study. This framework comprises informal institutions that could be divided into two categories: cognitive (which portrays cultural practices and ideologies) and normative (institutions that emphasize social obligations and expectations involved with acceptable and appropriate actions based on important and prevailing norms or ideologies in a given culture). The female perspective adopted is one of either post-social feminism or modern feminism. This philosophy holds that women and men are not fundamentally similar, and it is one that focuses on the unique values, competencies, needs, and experiences of women. Fig 1 depicts the theoretical framework of the study.

5. EMPIRICAL DESIGN

The GEM is considered a reliable, rich, and valid survey by the scholars (Reynolds et al., 2005). In each country, the survey was conducted through face-to-face or telephonic interviews with a representative weighted sample size of minimum 2000 adults in the age range 18 to 64 years. The data provide an in-depth insight into the antecedents leading to entrepreneurship of both current and aspiring entrepreneurs.

From the dataset of GEM 2015, seven binary logistic regression analyses were run of the selected nonparametric variables by evaluating the effect of 'education', 'income', individual cognitive', and institutional factors of TEA (overall, male, female), TEA Necessity (male/ female), and TEA Opportunity (male/female) for the two countries separately by using the "select case" option in SPSS version 20. The sample size was 3,413 for both India and China. The logistic regression technique is employed with the aim of assessing the data that are found appropriate according to Sánchez-Escobedo, et al. (2016), during their GEM's gender studies bibliometric review.

Total Early-Stage Entrepreneurial Activity (TEA) has been defined as the "Percentage of the adult population (18–64 years) that is either actively involved in starting a new venture or is the owner/manager of a business that is less than 42 months old" (Reynolds, et al., 2002). Respondents are directly asked whether they had started their business venture because they had no other better opportunity or because they perceived a good business opportunity.

6. DATA ANALYSIS AND EMPIRICAL RESULTS

Binomial logistic regression was conducted for the seven dependent variables from the GEM 2015 database. The dependent variables selected for the study were Total Entrepreneurial activity (TEA) overall, TEA Male, TEA Female, TEA Opportunity male, TEA Opportunity Female, TEA Necessity male and TEA Necessity Female. The data of the independent categorical variables selected for the study were tested for assumptions, that is, for

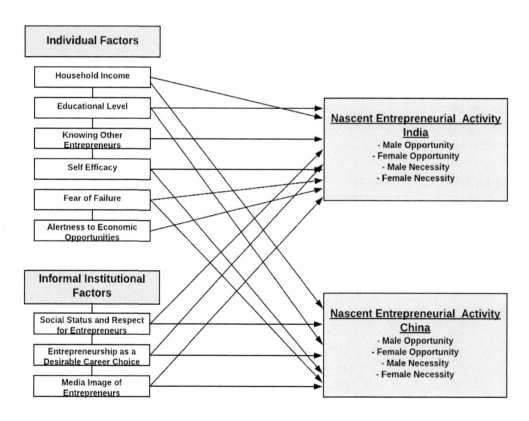

Fig. 1: *Theoretical Framework of the study*

multicollinearity among the predictors and no outliers were detected. The data were separately analyzed for the two countries selected for the study, that is, India and China using SPSS version22. The model is accepted or rejected based on the significance level of chi square values and model is accepted if significance level is less than .10 (90% confidence level) in this study. The Cox &Snell R Square and Nagelkerke R Square values indicate the percentage variance explained by the independent variables in the model tested (for example , R square value of 0.18 means that 18% variance is explained by the model). The classification index gives the correctly predicted percentage for dependent variable. The statistical significance of the independent variables are measured by Walds test and accepted if statistical significance is less than 0.1, Exp (B) is the odds ratio which indicates the odds of the event occurring (for example odds ratio of 1.56 for means the probability of TEA for age group 1 is 1.56 times higher than age group 0 or default age group. The results of binomial logistic regression for the dependent variables selected for the study are presented in Tables I and II for India and China.

Table I: Binary Logistic Regression India

Factors and Categories	TEAyy	TEAyyMAL	TEAyyFEM	TEAyyMOP	TEAyyFOP	TEAyyMNE	TEAyyFNE
Overall Model							
-2 Log likelihood	1525.43	990.0	583.4	771.54	778.77	335.5	175.32
Sig level	0.000	0.000	0.000	0.000	0.000	0.000	0.000
Cox & Snell R Square	.109	.104	.104	.089	.103	.019	.076
Nagelkerke R Square	.222	.181	0.2	.174	.283	.071	.192
Classification Index(%)	86.2	86.4	87.9	88.5	91.6	96.4	93.2
Individual variables							
HHINC1	**0.000**	**0.000**	**.000**	NS	**.000**	NS	**.001**
HHINC2	NS	NS	NS	NS	**.000**	NS	**.000**
HHINC3	NS	NS	NS	NS	.059	NS	**.028**
GEMEDUC1	**0.000**	**0.000**	**.000**	NS	.517	NS	1.000
GEMEDUC2	NS	NS	**.000**	NS	**.001**	NS	.999
GEMEDUC3	NS	NS	**.015**	NS	.084	NS	.999
GEMEDUC 4	NS	934	**.008**	581	**.002**	.522	.999
knowent	**.000**	**.000**	**.000**	NS	NS	NS	**.025**
opport	**.000**	**.000**	**.000**	NS	NS	NS	**.018**
suskill	**.000**	**.000**	**.000**	NS	NS	NS	**.001**
fearfail	**.000**	**.000**	**.000**	NS	NS	.361	.307
nbgoodc	>0.1	**.098**	**.000**	.844	NS	**.000**	.831
nbstatus	**0.000**	.450	.491	.123	NS	.307	.460
nbmedia	>0.006	**.009**	.240	**.087**	NS	**.063**	.497

Note: *Data in bold depict the probability levels that are significant at 90% confidence levels.

Table II: Binary Logistic Regression China

Factors and Categories	TEAyy	TEAyyMAL	TEAyyFEM	TEAyyMOP	TEAyyFOP	TEAyyMNE	TEAyyFNE
Overall Model							
-2 Log likelihood	1149.9	560.49	579.5	642.5	587.6	629.2	49.3
Sig level	.000	.000	.000	.000	.000	.000	.000
Cox & Snell R Square	.155	.165	.153	.142	.139	**.043**	**.038**
Nagelkerke R Square	.289	.291	.310	.323	.346	.116	.149
Classification Index(%)	87.8	86.1	89.6	91.9	93.5	93.7	96.9
Individual variables							
HHINC1	.000	.007	.000	.111	.000	.069	NS
HHINC2	.000	.002	.011	.003	.001	NS	NS
HHINC3	NS	NS	NS	NS	NS	NS	NS
GEMEDUC1	NS	NS	.089	NS	NS	NS	.079
GEMEDUC2	NS	NS	NS	NS	NS	NS	.059
GEMEDUC3	NS	NS	NS	NS	NS	NS	.045
GEMEDUC 4	NS	NS	.077	NS	NS	NS	.005
knowent	.000	.000	.000	.000	.000	.009	NS
opport	.000	.000	.003	.001	.010	.053	.092
suskill	.000	.000	.000	.000	.000	.001	.000
fearfail	.025	. NS	.048	.003	.018	NS	NS
nbgoodc	NS	NS	.062	.160	.084	NS	NS
nbstatus	NS	NS	NS	NS	NS	NS	NS
nbmedia	.002	.005	NS	.005	.088	NS	NS

Note: *Data in bold depict the probability levels that are significant at 90% confidence levels.

6.1 Summary of the results

Only 3 of the 9 hypotheses i.e., H1, H2 and H9 were partially accepted while the remaining 6 hypotheses were rejected. The summarized results are presented in Table V.

Table III: Summary results of the hypotheses tested

Objective: This study aims at evaluating the influence of informal institutional and individual factors on the activity levels of female entrepreneurship; it also aims at checking whether the effects vary with the type of motivation and the country context		Status
H_1	*Higher levels of education of women will be associated with higher female entrepreneurship levels in India and China.*	*Partially Accepted*
H_2	*Increased household income levels will result in increased female entrepreneurship levels.*	*Partially Accepted*
H_3	*Higher alertness exhibited by female entrepreneurs to economic opportunities is significantly linked to higher levels of female entrepreneurship in India as compared with China.*	*Rejected*
H_4	*Entrepreneurial self-efficacy is significantly associated with higher levels of female entrepreneurship in India and China.*	*Rejected*
H_5	*Higher fear of failure is significantly associated with lower levels of female entrepreneurship in India as compared with China.*	*Rejected*
H_6	*The ability of female entrepreneurs to know another entrepreneur is significantly linked to higher levels of female entrepreneurship in China as compared with India.*	*Rejected*
H_7	*Female entrepreneurship activity levels have a stronger association with status and respect in China as compared with India.*	*Rejected*
H_8	*Positive representation of female entrepreneurs by the media is significantly linked to a greater level of female entrepreneurship in India as compared with China.*	*Rejected*
H_9	*As a socially sought-after career option, entrepreneurship is linked with increased female entrepreneurship levels in China when compared with India.*	*Partially Accepted*

7. DISCUSSIONS OF FINDINGS

Thus, effects of individual and informal institutional factors on, probability of higher levels of nascent entrepreneurship are validated though the impact of the factors is specific to gender or motivation type only in selective instances. We can hence infer that the effects of Individual and informal institutional factors are moderated by country level economic and socio-cultural environment. Necessity-driven female entrepreneurial activity in China is associated with 'Higher Education' levels and 'Entrepreneurship as a Desirable Career

Choice' has a positive impact on female opportunity motivated entrepreneurship in China. This could be because of the transitional status of the economy as more women consider entrepreneurship as a choice-based career in China as opposed to wage employment. Higher 'Household Income' levels, self-confidence in one's entrepreneurial abilities, alertness to opportunities, and knowing another entrepreneur in India are positively associated with female necessity-motivated entrepreneurship, which could be because of the acute resource deficit being faced by potential female entrepreneurs who are motivated by push factors.

The mitigating effects of higher "fear of failure" is specific to opportunity or pull entrepreneurship in China, which could be because of the increasing uncertainty in their economic environment in the recent past. Studies (Van Trang et al., 2019) show that individuals' educational level moderates the negative impact of fear of failure on nascent entrepreneurship. Fear of failure is moderated by the institutional and cultural context (Acemoglu and Johnson, 2005; Williamson, 2000) of a country. Higher social status and respect for entrepreneurs in society was not associated with higher levels of TEA in China or India which could be because of the transitional economies of these countries or because of entrepreneurial activity in India is mostly informal (India) or small in scale (China and India).

7.3 Practical Contributions and Theoretical Implications

This study provides evidence for a culture, situation-specific approach to be adopted towards the promotion of nascent female entrepreneurship by government or developmental agencies. Broad-based, generic programs without specific entrepreneurial outcomes are unlikely to be successful in attaining their goals. A one-hat fits all approach may not be successful (Nikiforou et al., 2019). Government of India can promote nascent female entrepreneurial activity by enhancing the education levels (Chhabra et al., 2021) and household incomes (Chhabra and Goyal, 2019). Female necessity driven entrepreneurship can be promoted through capacity building actions which improve their self-efficacy, risk taking abilities, opportunity identification skills and professional network and by creating positive image of entrepreneurship as a career in society. Female opportunity motivated entrepreneurship in India is positively impacted by household income levels and education and not dependent on individual and informal institutional factors.

In China, male and female TEA motivated by opportunity and necessity factors can be promoted by enhancing the self-efficacy and opportunity identification skills of potential entrepreneurs. Opportunity driven entrepreneurial activity can be supported by improving the risk taking ability of nascent entrepreneurs and their visibility in the media. Professional networking would contribute to growth of nascent entrepreneurship except for female necessity driven TEA. Female necessity driven entrepreneurship can be developed through education and Female opportunity TEA through higher 'Household Income's'. Thus, 'Individual' and 'Informal Institutional Factors' impact on nascent female entrepreneurship is moderated by the economic and socio-cultural macro environment of transition economies of India and China. The institutional theory related to the perspective of entrepreneurship is partially supported in this study, as the effect of informal institutional factors selected for the study were not universal and were found to vary with the country's macro environment and socio-cultural context, type of entrepreneurial motivation and gender. 'Gender equality' signifies the focus of the current studies in the area of women's studies (Hassan et al., 2021). This study also lends support to the post-modern feminist theory, that is, the social role theory wherein female entrepreneurship is defined and structured by the cultural and social traditions of society.

7.4 Limitations of the Study and the Pathway for Researchers

This study is restricted to nascent entrepreneurial activity and the selective factors captured by the GEM database only hence, its results may not be extended to new ventures at different stages and types of ventures and entrepreneurial endeavors, for example social, corporate, and international entrepreneurship. Certain economic and institutional factors have not been included in the study, which makes the results specific to the context of the study. The interaction effects of individual and normative factors and the moderating effects of various country-level factors may be studied to further understand the complex dynamics of female entrepreneurship. This study may be extended to different stages of entrepreneurship, different business sectors, countries, individual characteristics as well as normative attributes and theoretical approaches.

Acknowledgements

This study was supported by Indian Council of Social Science and Research (ICSSR), research grant (No. IMPRESS/P1083 /489/18-19/ICSSR).

REFERENCES

Acemoglu, D., Johnson, S. and Robinson, J.A., 2005. Institutions as a fundamental cause of long-run growth. *Handbook of economic growth*, *1*, pp. 385–472.

Achtenhagen, L. and Welter, F., 2007. Media discourse in entrepreneurship research. *Handbook of qualitative methods in entrepreneurship research*, pp. 193–215.

Aldrich, H. and Martinez, M., 2001. Many are called, but few are chosen: An evolutionary perspective for the study of entrepreneurship (Discussion Paper). *Chapel Hill, NC: University of North Carolina*.

Anderson, A.R. and Smith, R., 2007. The moral space in entrepreneurship: an exploration of ethical imperatives and the moral legitimacy of being enterprising. *Entrepreneurship and Regional Development*, *19*(6), pp. 479–497.

Arai, A.B., 1997. The road not taken: The transition from unemployment to self-employment in Canada, 1961-1994. *Canadian Journal of Sociology/Cahiers canadiens de sociologie*, pp. 365–382.

Arenius, P. and Minniti, M., 2005.Perceptual variables and nascent entrepreneurship. *Small business economics*, *24*(3), pp. 233–247.

Baker, T., E. aldrich, H. and Nina, L., 1997. Invisible entrepreneurs: The neglect of women business owners by mass media and scholarly journals in the USA. *Entrepreneurship & Regional Development*, *9* (3), pp. 221–238.

Baughn, C.C., Chua, B.L. and Neupert, K.E., 2006. The normative context for women's participation in entrepreneurship: A multicountry study. *Entrepreneurship Theory and Practice*, *30*(5), pp. 687–708.

Bhidé, A., 2004. What role for entrepreneurship in India. *New York. A Paper presented at Columbia University.*

Bosma, N. and Harding, R., 2006. *Global entrepreneurship monitor: GEM 2006 summary results.* Babson College London Business School.

Bruni, A., Gherardi, S. and Poggio, B., 2004. Entrepreneur-mentality, gender and the study of women entrepreneurs. *Journal of organizational change management.*

Brush, C.G., De Bruin, A. and Welter, F., 2009. A gender-aware framework for women's entrepreneurship. *International Journal of Gender and entrepreneurship.*

Chhabra, M. (2016). A study of gender gap in small and micro enterprises in India. Devi Ahilya Vishwavidyalaya, Indore. http://hdl.handle.net/10603/238542

Chhabra, M., 2018. Gender Gap in 'Success Factors' among Entrepreneurs: A Study of Micro and Small Enterprises. *SEDME (Small Enterprises Development, Management & Extension Journal)*, *45*(2), 1–17.

Chhabra, M., Dana, L. P., Malik, S., & Chaudhary, N. S. (2021). Entrepreneurship education and training in Indian higher education institutions: a suggested framework. *Education+ Training.* Vol. ahead-of-print No. ahead-of-print.

Chhabra, M., Gera, R., Hassan, R., & Hasan, S., 2020. An exploratory study of cognitive, social and normative dimensions of female entrepreneurship within transition economies: Evidence from India and Vietnam. *Pakistan Journal of Commerce and Social Sciences (PJCSS)*, *14*(4), 1012–1042.

Chhabra, M., & Goyal, A. P., 2019. Education & entrepreneurial experience w.r.t female entrepreneurs. *Int. J. Res. Hum. Arts Literat*, *7*, 95–110.

Chhabra, M., & Karmarkar, Y., 2016. Effect of gender on inception stage of entrepreneurs: Evidence from small and micro enterprises in Indore. *SEDME (Small Enterprises Development, Management & Extension Journal)*, *43*(3), 1–16.

Chhabra, M., & Karmarkar, Y. (2016). Gender Gap in Entrepreneurship-A Study of Small and Micro Enterprises. *ZENITH International Journal of Multidisciplinary Research*, *6*(8), 82–99.

Crecente-Romero, F., Giménez-Baldazo, M. and Rivera-Galicia, L.F., 2016. Subjective perception of entrepreneurship.Differences among countries. *Journal of Business Research*, *69*(11), pp. 5158–5162.

Dawson, C. and Henley, A., 2015. Gender, risk, and venture creation intentions. *Journal of Small Business Management*, *53*(2), pp. 501–515.

De Clercq, D. and Arenius, P. (2006), "The role of knowledge in business start-up activity",*International Small Business Journal 24* (4), 339–358

Dencker, J., Bacq, S.C., Gruber, M. and Haas, M., 2019. Reconceptualizing necessity entrepreneurship: a contextualized framework of entrepreneurial processes under the condition of basic needs. *Academy of Management Review*, (ja).

Edelman, L.F., Brush, C.G., Manolova, T.S. and Greene, P.G., 2010. Start-up motivations and growth intentions of minority nascent entrepreneurs. *Journal of Small Business Management*, *48*(2), pp. 174–196.

Estrin, S., Mickiewicz, T. and Stephan, U., 2016. Human capital in social and commercial entrepreneurship. *Journal of Business Venturing*, *31*(4), pp. 449–467.

Global Entrepreneurship Monitor, 2015. GEM 2015 Global Report. Published online, http://www.gemconsortium.org

Hassan, R., Chhabra, M., Shahzad, A., Fox, D., & Hassan, S., 2021. A Bibliometric Analysis of Journal of International Women's Studies for Period of 2002-2019: Current Status, Development, and Future Research Directions. *Journal of International Women's Studies*, *22*(1), 1–37.

Hernandez, L., Nunn, N. and Warnecke, T., 2012. Female entrepreneurship in China: opportunity-or necessity-based? *International Journal of Entrepreneurship and Small Business*, *15*(4), pp. 411–434.

Karmarkar, Y., Chabra, M., & Deshpande, A., 2014. Entrepreneurial leadership style (s): a taxonomic review. *Annual Research Journal of Symbiosis Centre for Management Studies*, *2*(1), 156–189.

Koellinger, P., Minniti, M. and Schade, C., 2013. Gender differences in entrepreneurial propensity.*Oxford bulletin of economics and statistics*, *75*(2), pp. 213–234.

Kourilsky, M.L. and Walstad, W.B., 1998. Entrepreneurship and female youth: Knowledge, attitudes, gender differences, and educational practices. *Journal of Business venturing*, *13*(1), pp. 77–88.

Langowitz, N., Sharpe, N. and Godwyn, M., 2006. Women's business centers in the United States: Effective entrepreneurship training and policy implementation. *Journal of Small Business & Entrepreneurship*, *19*(2), pp. 167–182.

Langowitz, N.S. and Morgan, C., 2003.Women entrepreneurs. *New Perspectives on Women Entrepreneurs, Information Age Publishing Inc., America*, pp. 101–119.

Micozzi, A. and Lucarelli, C., 2016. Heterogeneity in entrepreneurial intent: the role of gender across countries. *International Journal of Gender and Entrepreneurship*.

Minniti, M. and Naudé, W., 2010. What do we know about the patterns and determinants of female entrepreneurship across countries?

Minniti, M., 2006.*Global entrepreneurship monitor: 2005 executive report*. Babson College.

Nikiforou, A., Dencker, J.C. and Gruber, M. (2019), "Necessity entrepreneurship and industry choice in new firm creation", *Strategic Management Journal*, *40*(13), pp. 2165–2190.

Pathak, S. and Muralidharan, E., 2016. Informal institutions and their comparative influences on social and commercial entrepreneurship: The role of in-group collectivism and interpersonal trust. *Journal of Small Business Management*, *54*(sup1), pp. 168–188.

Pines, A.M., Lerner, M. and Schwartz, D., 2010. Gender differences in entrepreneurship. *Equality, diversity and inclusion: An International journal*, *29*(2), pp. 186–198.

Ratten, V. and Ferreira, J.J. eds., 2017. *Sport entrepreneurship and innovation*. New York, NY: Routledge.

Reynolds, P., Bosma, N., Autio, E., Hunt, S., De Bono, N., Servais, I., Lopez-Garcia, P. and Chin, N., 2005. Global entrepreneurship monitor: Data collection design and implementation 1998–2003. *Small business economics*, *24*(3), pp. 205–231.

Reynolds, P., Bygrave, W., Autio, E. and Hay, M., 2004.GEM 2004 Summary Report.

Reynolds, P.D., Bygrave, W.D., Autio, E. and Cox, L.W., 2002. M. Hay, 2002. *Global Entrepreneurship Monitor, 2002 Executive Report.*

Sánchez-Escobedo, M.C., Fernández-Portillo, A., Díaz-Casero, J.C. and Hernández-Mogollón, R., 2016.Research in entrepreneurship using GEM data. Approach to the state of affairs in gender studies. *European journal of management and business economics*, *25*(3), pp. 150–160.

Sánchez-Escobedo, M.C., Fernández-Portillo, A., Díaz-Casero, J.C. and Hernández-Mogollón, R., 2016.Research in entrepreneurship using GEM data. Approach to the state of affairs in gender studies. *European journal of management and business economics*, *25*(3), pp. 150–160.

Scott, W.R. and Christensen, S., 1995.*The institutional construction of organizations: International and longitudinal studies.* Sage Publications, Inc.

Scott, W.R., 2005. Institutional theory: Contributing to a theoretical research program. *Great minds in management: The process of theory development*, *37*(2005), pp. 460–484.

Sharif, M.Y., 2015.Glass ceiling, the prime driver of women entrepreneurship in Malaysia: a phenomenological study of women lawyers. *Procedia-Social and Behavioral Sciences*, *169*, pp. 329–336.

Sreekumar, M. D., Chhabra, M., & Yadav, Ruchika., 2018. Productivity in Manufacturing Industries. *International Journal of Innovative Science and Research Technology (IJISRT)*, *3*(10), pp. 634–639.

Terjesen, S.A. and Lloyd, A., 2015.The 2015 female entrepreneurship index. *Kelley School of Business Research Paper*, (15-51).

Van Trang, T., Do, Q.H. and Luong, M.H. (2019), "Entrepreneurial human capital, role models, and fear of failure and start-up perception of feasibility among adults in Vietnam", *International Journal of Engineering Business Management*, *11*.

Verheul, I. and Van Stel, A., 2010. Entrepreneurial diversity and economic growth. *The entrepreneurial society*, pp. 17–36.

Verheul, I., Stel, A.V. and Thurik, R., 2006. Explaining female and male entrepreneurship at the country level. *Entrepreneurship and regional development*, *18*(2), pp. 151–183.

Wagner, J. and Sternberg, R., 2004. Start-up activities, individual characteristics, and the regional milieu: Lessons for entrepreneurship support policies from German micro data. *the annals of regional science*, *38*(2), pp. 219–240.

Warnecke, T., 2013. Targeting the 'Invisible': Improving Entrepreneurship Opportunities for Informal Sector Women. *Research to Practice Policy Brief*, *32*.

Williamson, O.E., 2000. The new institutional economics: taking stock, looking ahead. *Journal of economic literature*, *38*(3), pp. 595–613.

Wilson, F., Kickul, J. and Marlino, D., 2007. Gender, entrepreneurial self-efficacy, and entrepreneurial career intentions: Implications for entrepreneurship education. *Entrepreneurship theory and practice*, *31*(3), pp. 387–406.

World Bank. (2009). Enterprises surveys. Washington DC: World Bank.

CHAPTER 31

CSR-An Empirical Study to Understand the Dynamics Affecting Strategic Initiatives from Industries for Crafting a Sustainable Ecosystem in Future

Dr. Vaishali Rahate
Associate professor
Datta Meghe Institute of
Management Studies, Nagpur, India
vaishali1412@gmail.com

Dr. Parvin Shaikh
Asst. professor
JDCOEM, Nagpur, India
arvinshaikh05@gmail.com

Abstract

Purpose of the Study: CSR is not new to Indian corporate, but the amendments in the 'Companies Act 2013' has made it mandatory for the companies coming under the mentioned criteria.

Maharashtra is one of the states with growing industrial sector and a major hub for CSR activities. Though the companies conduct various CSR activities, still there is a need for a professional outlook which will lead to sustainable results. This can be possible with appropriate employee awareness and involvement in CSR activities.

Methodology: In the light of the changes, this research explores the awareness of CSR, involvement of employees, Assessment criteria, and CSR budget allocation among the selected 100 PSE and private sector companies. The research also highlights the key areas of concerns. These concerns if rightly addressed will be certainly helpful to policy makers to design activities suitable for overcoming the gaps in SDGs.

The research instrument comprising of 48 items was tested for reliability and validity. Various statistical tools were used in the research and analysis was done in SPSS.

Findings: The employee awareness and involvement in CSR activities was found to be less in Public sector companies compared to Private companies. Most of the companies concentrate their CSR activities in Education, Health but very less focus is in the technical incubation area. Moreover, majority of the companies lack the focus on base line survey & impact assessment.

Social implications: The research provides insights for the policy makers in CSR regulatory bodies. The companies can analyze their projects and design the activities which best suits to increase social accountability by implementing meaningful CSR activities.

Limitations: The study is restricted with a sample of companies from Maharashtra State.

Keywords: CSR, Awareness, Employee involvement, Public sector companies(PSE/PSU)

INTRODUCTION

Positive growth in economy is possible only when there is balance between the industries, environment and society. Industries need input from the environment and society in terms of natural resources and human resources respectively. Also, industries need to satisfy the needs of the society without harming the environment. CSR is all about making proper utilization of the resources as it has a direct impact on the society as a whole. Organizations have to keep a watch on their activities and work so as to create a positive Impact on the surrounding.

LITERATURE REVIEW

H. Bansal, V. Parida and Pankaj Kumar (2012) conducted a research titled "Emerging trends of CSR in India". The authors concluded from their study that the organisations are changing their views towards social responsibility and are thinking beyond Profits.

Mr. Neelmani Jaysawal, Mrs. Sudeshna Saha (2015) in their study on, "Corporate Social Responsibility (CSR) in India: A Review" gave a detailed overview about the CSR initiatives of large scale companies. Authors in their study encountered some major challenges in CSR activities like Lack of available expertise in conducting CSR activities, lack of accountability of the staff, absence of assessment framework. Dr. M. R. Kumar (2013) in his research on CSR concluded that there is a need of CSR awareness amongst employees & stakeholders as well. N. Sharma, R. Chaudhary, H. Purohit (2013 – 14) in their study on, "A Comparative Study of Corporate Social Responsibility Initiatives Taken by Select Public and Private Sector Banks" concluded that though private and public sectors bank are contributing towards CSR, still Public sector banks need to showcase their work.

RESEARCH METHODOLOGY

Population of the study-

Public(PSU/PSE) and Private Companies in Maharashtra.

Sample size-

A sample of 100 Public and Private Companies (Large Scale) in Maharashtra were selected. The sample includes both manufacturing and services providers. Manufacturing includes electronics, auto ancillary, engineering, cotton, pharmaceuticals, automobile component, cement, chemical, food item, heavy engineering, metal, and others. Service providing firms under study are software, telecommunication and IT Enabled Services.

Employee related questionnaires were filled by 671 employees.

Data collection-

Data Collection-Primary & Secondary sources

The secondary data was collected from company websites, Journals, Books and information from the internet which was used as the foundation for the theoretical framework. Primary data was collected from randomly selected companies in Maharashtra with questionnaire and telephonic interview method.

Data Analysis and Interpretation-

Data analysis was done using MS Excel and SPSS software. Various tools like mean, percentage, standard deviation, correlation, regression, ANOVA etc, are used for descriptive and inferential statistics.

OBJECTIVES

1. To analyze and compare the CSR activities under taken by selected companies in Maharashtra
2. To analyze and compare the CSR impact assessment criteria adopted by the selected Large Scale companies in Maharashtra
3. To assess the awareness of CSR concept amongst the employees of companies in Maharashtra.
4. To investigate the comparison of employees' involvement in CSR activities between selected companies in Maharashtra.

HYPOTHESIS

1. There is lack of employee awareness with respect to CSR in selected Large Scale Public and Private Companies in Maharashtra.
2. There is no significant difference in 'employee awareness' with respect to CSR amongst selected Large Scale Public and Private Companies in Maharashtra.
3. There is no significant difference between 'employee's involvement' in CSR activities in selected Large Scale Public and Private Companies in Maharashtra.

FINDINGS

-To analyze and compare the CSR activities under taken by selected companies in Maharashtra

Implementing CSR:

It has been observed that 38 percent of the organizations within the surveyed sample partnered with the implementing agencies, where approximately 62 percent organizations have conducted their CSR activities directly. 12% of Organizations chose conducting their CSR Activities through Trust in which 5 companies PSE and 7 are Private.

CSR Budget

Major companies have shown a higher budget outlay against the prescribed amount.

A majority 51 per cent of companies considered in the study reported an increase in their CSR Budget throughout the years 2015-16 & 2016-17, 2017-18 While 49 per cent companies reported a decline in their CSR budget.

As per sectorial analysis, there was an increase in CSR Budget in case of 22 per cent PSU companies as compared to 29 percent Private companies considered in the study.

Prominent Reasons for decrease in CSR budget:

- Lack of proper resources for CSR department in terms of specialized manpower having relevant CSR knowledge.

- Inability to select right projects and identifying thrust areas

- Lack of information about implementing agencies

- Lack of appropriate training wrt Conducting Base line surveys or impact analysis.

- Longer time duration for creating sustainable impact

CSR spending

Education, rural development and health & sanitation were the top three areas where the companies have collectively spent 73 percent of the money in the year 2015-16.

Rs 627 crore was spent for construction of classrooms in rural schools, installation of computers and providing computer training to the students, providing school uniforms, construction of toilets in schools, providing resources for teachers etc . Rs 511 crore was spent for healthcare and sanitation which included Construction of toilets, providing safe drinking water, installing hand pumps in rural areas, construction of small dispensaries and hospitals in backward areas, conducting health camps segregated for infants, adolescents and old age people. 15% of the CSR fund was utilized for environment protection activities such as cleaning of rivers, recycling the waste, providing substitutes for Plastic, conducting awareness camps for curbing pollution and conservation of natural resources. Rs 63.74 crore funds were contributed to the PM Relief Fund.

In FY17, health and sanitation activities contribution was almost 20% of the total CSR spends. The FY17 witnessed an incremental spending of CSR funds in Preservation of Environment and Rural development.26 % of the companies contributed in Developmental activities (at least 1 activity) whereas 12% of the companies contributed in more than 5 developmental activities. Almost 63% of the CSR funds was utilized in Education & Healthcare in FY 2017. 100 companies collectively spent Rs. 11,788 Crore for CSR activities. The companies have spent Rs 2,978.469 crore in the year 2015-16; Rs. 4,220 crores in 2016-17 & Rs. 4,589.7 crores in 2017-18. 27 % of the companies under this survey could not manage to spend 2% of their net profit as was prescribed.

Review of CSR activities

69% organizations conduct review of CSR activities while 31% of organizations do not have any monitoring procedure of their CSR activities.

Frequency of Review of CSR Activities

Half of the total organizations considered in the study prefer Midterm review. The preference is followed by yearly and Half Yearly reviews with 19% and 12%. Reviews after every 4 and 3 months count for 7% and 3%. Only 3% of organizations prefer reviewing their CSR activities after completion. Reviews after a month or 2 are rarely adopted by the organizations.

Assessment of CSR activities

65% or 65 of 100 companies in this study conduct Assessment of CSR activities on the target group. Out of which 23 PSEs assessed their CSR activities while 42 Non PSEs undertook assessment of their CSR activities

Reporting Frameworks/ Certifications

Of the 100 companies included in this study, 17 preferred UN Global Compact reporting while,9 organizations preferred reporting 'in accordance' with the GRI's Sustainability Reporting Guidelines. The international standard ISO 14001 is being practiced by 8 organizations. There is only one organization which is SA8000 certified. Out of total 39 reporting organizations, 4 are following other methods of reporting.

CSR work audited by third party

Out of 65% of the companies who conduct assessment of the CSR work, 61% of the companies conduct the audit through Third party such as Midstream Marketing research pvt. ltd, IPE, Hyderabad, IIM Lucknow, NABCONS, ISS, Madras School of Social Work, GRI, Tata Institute of Social Sciences, NIRD,ERM, ABF etc.

Information from audit used for future decision making

51 companies out of the 61 companies, who conduct Impact analysis audit, use the data for future decision making.

Availability of CSR Board/ Committee Composition on organization website

Though it is a mandate to make available all the information related to CSR on the respective websites of the company, 10% of the companies under study do not have/disclose CSR committee composition on the website.

Availability of Number of CSR Meetings on organization website

Only 42% of the companies under study have the details of the CSR meetings conducted displayed on the website. (12 Public companies and 30 Private companies).

Reasons for Organization to engage in CSR

The major reason responsible for Public sector organizations to engage in CSR are

- Legal obligation (42%)
- Community Pressure (40%)
- Stakeholder requirements (35%)

While the major reasons responsible for Private sector organizations to engage in CSR are

- Customer Loyalty (54%)
- Attracting potential Investors/ Customers (50%)
- Retaining & attracting employees (45%)

Support of NGOs, Environmental concerns are some non-influential factors considered by both the sectors which received relatively low results in the survey.

Driving forces behind Organization's CSR efforts (Employees Perspective)

It was observed that according to the perspective of employees, Regulatory compliance, Employee Interests and Community Environmental concern were the three driving forces behind Organization's CSR efforts.

1. To analyze and compare the CSR impact assessment criteria adopted by the selected Large Scale Public and Private Sector companies in Maharashtra

65% or 65 of 100 companies undertaken in this study are trying to maintain transparency by improved quality of disclosures beyond legislative requirements.

Sector wise distribution of organizations assessing impact of CSR activities

Table 1: Distribution of organizations assessing impact of CSR activities

Public		Sector		Total
		Private		
Impact Assessment of CSR activities	No	21	14	35
	Yes	23	42	65
Total		44	56	100

Organizations using Reporting Frameworks/ Certifications

Table 2: Organizations using Reporting Frameworks/ Certifications

Reporting Framework/ Certifications	Number of Organizations
AA1000	0
Global Compact	17

Reporting Framework/ Certifications	Number of Organizations
GRI	9
SA8000	1
ISO14001	8
EMAS	0
Others	4

Of the 100 companies included in this study, 17 preferred UN Global Compact reporting while,9 organizations preferred reporting 'in accordance' with the GRI's Sustainability Reporting Guidelines. The international standard ISO 14001 is being practiced by 8 organizations. There is only one organization which is SA8000 certified. Out of total 39 reporting organizations, 4 are following other methods of reporting as shown in Table 2 .

Impact of CSR activities audited by third party

Out of the 100 organizations undertaken for study the impact of CSR activities of 61% organizations is audited by third party. The organizations have partnered with various groups with the objective of enhanced value creation. Some of them are given below

- Midstream Marketing research Pvt ltd , IPE, Hyderabad, IIM Lucknow

- NABCONS, ISS, Madras School of Social Work

- GRI, Tata Institute of Social Sciences, Soul Ace Consultants

- NIRD, ERM' ABF

Sector wise distribution of organizations getting CSR activities audited by third party

Table 3: Sector wise distribution of organizations getting CSR activities audited by third party

Public		Sector		Total
		Private		
CSR activities audited by third party	No	23	16	39
	Yes	21	40	61
Total		44	56	100

Sector wise analysis shows that only 50% or half of Public Sector Organizations have audited their CSR activities by third party while in Private sector, majorly 70% of private sector organizations audited CSR activities by third party.

2. To assess the level of CSR awareness amongst the employees of selected Large Scale Public and Private Sector companies in Maharashtra.

Reliability Statistics for Employee Awareness

Reliability-Employee awareness		
Cronbach's Alpha	Cronbach's Alpha Based on Standardized Items	Number of Items
.763	.807	7

According to Table above the internal scale reliability of the Employee Awareness questionnaire was examined and the scale was found to have good internal consistency (Alpha = 0.763).

Employee awareness with respect to CSR

One-Sample Statistics for Employee Awareness						
	N	Mean	Std. Deviation	Std. Error Mean		
EA_Average	671	3.9521	.90272	.03485		
One-Sample t Test for Employee Awareness						
	Test Value = 3					
	t	df	Sig. (2-tailed) Lower	Mean Difference Upper	95% Confidence Interval of the Difference	
EA_Average	27.320	670	.000	.95210	.8837	1.0205

T value obtained was 27.320 at 0.00 Significance level with degree of freedom 670
Null hypothesis has been rejected and alternate hypothesis has been validated.

Descriptive for One way ANOVA for Employee awareness								
EA_Average								
	N	Mean	Std. Deviation	Std. Error	95% Confidence Interval for Mean		Minimum	Maximum
					Lower Bound	Upper Bound		
Public	344	3.3468	.72319	.03899	3.2701	3.4235	2.29	11.57
Private	327	4.5889	.57542	.03182	4.5263	4.6515	1.29	11.57
Total	671	3.9521	.90272	.03485	3.8837	4.0205	1.29	11.57

As shown in table above, The Employee Awareness of Corporate Social Responsibility result of mean comparison of the organizations shows that the mean in the Private Sector organizations with 4.5889 is a higher than 3.3468 in the Public Sector organizations.

A one-way ANOVA between-group was conducted to explore the Employee Awareness of Corporate Social Responsibility in PSE & Private Organizations, as measured by the Employee Awareness questionnaire.

One way ANOVA for Employee awareness					
EA_Average					
	Sum of Squares	Df	Mean Square	F	Sig.
Between Groups	258.658	1	258.658	602.238	.000
Within Groups	287.332	669	.429		
Total	545.991	670			

Results of the analysis showed no statistical significance between employee awareness of CSR in the Organization scores [F (1, 669) =602.238. p=.000] as seen in the above table.

Group Statistics for Independent sample t test for Employee awareness					
	Sector	N	Mean	Std. Deviation	Std. Error Mean
EA_Average	Public	344	3.3468	.72319	.03899
	Private	327	4.5889	.57542	.03182

An independent-samples t-test was conducted to compare the Employee Awareness in Public and Private Sector Organizations which concluded that some employees are still un aware of the CSR activities in their organization.

3. To investigate the comparison between employees' involvement in CSR activities among PSE& Private companies.

Employee Involvement

Reliability Statistics for Employee Involvement		
Cronbach's Alpha	Cronbach's Alpha Based on Standardized Items	N of Items
.815	.880	8

One-Sample Statistics for Employee Involvement				
	N	Mean	Std. Deviation	Std. Error Mean
EI_Avg	671	3.6403	.77197	.02980

One-Sample t Test for Employee Involvement						
	Test Value = 3					
	t	df	Sig. (2-tailed) Lower	Mean Difference Upper	95% Confidence Interval of the Difference	
EI_Avg	21.485	670	.000	.64028	.5818	.6988

Group Statistics for Independent sample t test for Employee Involvement					
	Sector	N	Mean	Std. Deviation	Std. Error Mean
EI_Avg	Public	344	3.2940	.72361	.03901
	Private	327	4.0046	.64357	.03559

An independent-samples t-test was conducted to compare the Employees' Involvement in Public and Private sector Organizations.

Independent Samples Test for Employee Involvement										
	F	Levene's Test for Equality of Variances		t-test for Equality of Means						
		Sig.	t	df	Sig. (2-tailed)	Mean Difference	Std. Error Difference	95% Confidence Interval of the Difference		
								Lower	Upper	
EI_Avg	Equal variances assumed	9.265	.002	-13.417	669	.000	-.71062	.05297	-.81462	-.60662
	Equal variances not assumed			-13.456	666.078	.000	-.71062	.05281	-.81431	-.60693

Descriptives for One way ANOVA for Employee Involvement								
EI_Avg								
	N	Mean	Std. Deviation	Std. Error	95% Confidence Interval for Mean		Minimum	Maximum
					Lower Bound	Upper Bound		
Public	344	3.2940	.72361	.03901	3.2172	3.3707	.00	5.00
Private	327	4.0046	.64357	.03559	3.9346	4.0746	.00	10.88
Total	671	3.6403	.77197	.02980	3.5818	3.6988	.00	10.88

As shown in table above, The Employee Involvement result of mean comparison of the organizations shows that the mean in the Private Sector organizations with 4.0046 is higher than 3.2940 in the Public Sector organizations.

ANOVA for Employee Involvement					
EI_Avg					
	Sum of Squares	df	Mean Square	F	Sig.
Between Groups	84.656	1	84.656	180.007	.000
Within Groups	314.625	669	.470		
Total	399.281	670			

A one-way between-groups analysis of variance was conducted to explore the Employee Involvement in Public and Private Sector Organizations, as measured by the Employee Awareness questionnaire. Results of the analysis showed no statistical significance between employee involvement in public and private sector Organizations scores [F (1, 669) =180.007, p=.000] as seen in the above table.

AREAS OF CONCERN

Review of CSR activities

69% organizations conduct review of CSR activities while 31% of organizations do not have any monitoring procedure of their CSR work. It is necessary for all the organisations to conduct the review of the CSR activities so that they can get a clear picture of the lacunas which can be improvised in the future activities.

Frequency of Review of CSR Activities

Half of the total organizations considered in the study prefer Midterm review. The preference is followed by yearly and Half Yearly reviews with 19% and 12%. Reviews after every 4 and 3 months count for 7% and 3%. Only 3% of organizations prefer reviewing their CSR activities after completion. Reviews after a month or 2 are rarely adopted by the organizations.

Assessment of Impact of CSR activities on the target group

65% or 65 of 100 companies in this study conduct Assessment of Impact of CSR activities on the target group. Out of which 23 PSEs assessed their CSR activities while 42 Non PSEs undertook impact assessment of their CSR activities

Sustainability:

Information from audit used for future decision making
51 companies out of the 61 companies, who conduct Impact analysis audit, use the data for future decision making.

Transparency

Availability of CSR Board/ Committee Composition on organization website

Though it is a mandate to make available all the information related to CSR on the respective websites of the company, 10% of the companies under study do not have/disclose CSR committee composition on the website.

Availability of Number of CSR Meetings on organization website

Only 42% of the companies under study have the details of the CSR meetings conducted displayed on the website. (12 Public companies and 30 Private companies)

Employee involvement

Involving employees in CSR activities is an important part of CSR. Involvement of the employees in CSR provides individual accountability. This can be initiated by cultivating Organisational Citizenship through various activities of the organization. The Public sector organizations need to change their corporate mindset moving towards being more customer centric.

CONCLUSION:

The research provides some insights for the companies and to the Ministry of Corporate affairs to take into consideration the facts which have come forward during this survey. The findings of the research will be useful for crafting the future strategies especially in the post Covid arena.

REFERENCES:

1. Anil Dhaneshwar, Pooja Pandey (December 31, 2015) "Status of Corporate Social Responsibility among PSUs in India".

2. BhaveshSarna, (2016)," Voluntary CSR vs. Mandatory CSR – The Sound Of Employees". Jyväskylä University School of Business and Economics

3. Chaitra R. Beerannavar (October 20, 2010), "Corporate Social Responsibility in India: The need of the hour." India.

4. Dr Ashok kumarRath (October-2016), "A Critical Study on Corporate Social Responsibility Activities of Public Sector Undertakings in India and its financial implications". IOSR Journal of Business and Management (IOSR-JBM). Volume 18, Issue 10. Ver. I, PP 31-37, Issue 10, e-ISSN: 2278-487X, p-ISSN: 2319-7668, India.

5. Hatem Radwan Ibrahim Radwan (Nov 2015), "The Impact of Corporate Social Responsibility on Employees in the Hotel Sector". International Journal of Tourism & Hospitality Review (IJTHR). Vol. 2 (1), ISSN: 2395-7654 (Online), Egypt.

6. LaxmiRajak and Dr. Kushendra Mishra (December- 2014), "A Study of Corporate Social Responsibility in Indian Organizations". Indian Journal of Applied Research. Volume: 4, Issue: 12, ISSN - 2249-555X, India.

7. ManabhanjanSahu and Dr. D. Panigrahy (January- 2016) "Corporate Social Responsibility" Public Sector Vs Private Sector – Is a Myth or Reality. XVII Annual International Seminar Proceedings. ISBN no. 978-81-923211-8-9, India.

8. Pankaj Dodh, Sarbjeet Singh and Ravita (2013), "Corporate Social Responsibility and Sustainable Development in India." Global Journal of Management and Business Studies, © Research India Publications. Volume 3, Number 6, pp. 681-688, ISSN 2248-9878, India.

9. Priscila Alfaro-Barrantes (2012) "Examining the Relationship between Employees' Perceptions of and Attitudes toward Corporate Social Responsibility and Organizational Identification". Florida State University Libraries.

10. Raja Mukherjee, Indranath Ghosh (February-2014), "Going Green: The New Strategy for Environmental Sustainability and CSR in India". The International Journal of Business & Management. Volume 2, Issue 2, (ISSN 2321 – 8916), India.

11. Rakesh H M (June 2014)," A Study on Indian perspective of Corporate Social Responsibility". IRACST – International Journal of Commerce, Business and Management (IJCBM). ISSN: 2319–2828. Vol. 3, No. 3, India.

12. Rahate, V., & Shaikh, P. (2017). A Pragmatic Approach to CSR Evaluation: A Comprehensive Framework. *IRA-International Journal of Management & Social Sciences (ISSN 2455-2267), 7*(2), 123–130.

13. Satinder Singh (April-15), "Corporate social responsibility practices in India: Analysis of Public companies". International Journal of Business Quantitative Economics and Applied Management Research. Volume 1, Issue 11, ISSN: 2349-5677, India.

14. Shah, S. &Bhaskar, S. (2010). Corporate Social Responsibility in an Indian Public Sector Organisation: A case study of Bharat Petroleum Corporation Ltd. Journal of human values.

15. Shravya Saxena (2016) "A comparative study of corporate social responsibility (CSR) of private and public sector banks". World Wide Journal of Multidisciplinary Research and Development. Volume 2, Issue 1, e-ISSN: 2454-6615, India.

16. SoheliGhose (December 2012),"A look into Corporate Social Responsibility in Indian and emerging economies." International Journal of Business and Management Invention. Volume 1, Issue 1, PP. 22–29, ISSN (Online): 2319 – 8028, ISSN (Print): 2319 – 801X, India.

17. Vani Malli Bhat (September-2015), "Employee Awareness on the CSR Activities in the Public and Private Sector Organizations: Environment Related CSR Activities". Abhinav Publication, Volume 4, Issue 9, Online ISSN-2320-0073, India.
http://aequitaslegal.co.in/?p=194
http://www.un-documents.net/poa-wssd.htm
https://www.india-briefing.com/news/corporate-social-responsibility-india-5511.html/
https://www.ncbi.nlm.nih.gov/books/NBK53982/

CHAPTER 32

Framework for Integrating Sustainability Across Value Chain: An Industry 4.0 Perspective

Dr. Neeraj Singhal
Assistant Professor (Strategy)
Management Development Institute, Murshidabad, India
neeraj.singhal@mdim.ac.in

Abstract

Present era is the digitalization time, when companies integrating information and communication technologies; to identify customer needs and wants, manufacturing systems, service facilities (Coetteleer et al., 2014). The business scenario is reshaping due to the changes in customer focus, shorter business cycles and accordingly companies adapting customization and batch size reduction (Prinz et al., 2016). The fourth industrial revolution term coined from Germany in the year 2011, as a roadmap towards manufacturing challenges. Fourth industrial revolution includes, Internet of things (IoT), Internet of services (IoS), big data, data analytics, cyber physical systems (CPS), cloud based manufacturing, augmented reality, robotics (Kagermann et al., 2013). Time and cost are the two important driving forces for the mass customization and to address the same companies are integrating Industry 4.0 in both the supply chain and value chain. The present paper is an effort to suggest the theoretical framework for integrating sustainability across value chain through industry 4.0 lenses.

Keywords: Value Chain, Industry 4.0, Sustainability

INDUSTRY 4.0 CONCEPT & DEFINITION

Authors and researchers across the globe describe the Industry 4.0 in their own perspective, but the focal theme is the integration of Industry 4.0 technologies across the supply chain and value chain activities. The table 1 describes the contribution of authors and important perspective highlighted in the definitions.

Table 1: Industry 4.0 perspective highlighted in the definitions

Author (Year)	Industry 4.0 perspective highlighted in the definition.
Koch et al., (2014)	Value chain for product life cycle, focus on individual customer requirements.
MacDougall, (2014)	Embedded systems to cyber physical systems (CPS), transforming value chain and business models.
Mckinsey and Company, (2015)	Digitalization of manufacturing systems, CPS, data analysis.
Deloitte, (2015)	Organization and management of value chain.
Hermann et al., (2015)	Decentralized decision making, machine to human interface, application of IoT, CPS.
Pfohl et al., (2015)	Digitalization trend, automation, transparency, mobility, modularization, network collaboration, and socializing of products and processes.
Geissbauer et al., (2016)	End to end digitalization of value chain.

Source: Adapted **and modif**ied, Singhal, N., (2020)

Value chain concept describes; how much amount buyer would like to pay for the company product or services. The nine components of the value chain activities; inbound logistics, outbound logistics, operations, marketing and sales, services, procurement, human resource development, technological development, infrastructure (Porter, M.E., 1985). Most of the authors highlighted industry 4.0 integration with one or more component of the value chain perspective.

INDUSTRY 4.0 APPLICATIONS & IMPORTANCE

The first stage, second stage and third stage of the industrial revolution respectively based on mechanization, electrification and information. The fourth and the present state focused on integration of the three with internet based modern technologies such as IoT, IoS, CPS, cloud based manufacturing, robotics, data analytics. Schneider, P., (2018) describes industry 4.0 perspective in the context of innovative economy, manufacturing challenges, customer centric production, human centric production. This study also focused on smart decision making processes based on adaptive business models, customization and human-machine interface. The table 2 highlights the Industry 4.0 applications across different sectors and its importance.

Table 2: Industry 4.0 Applications and Importance

Authors (Year)	Application in (Sector)	Importance	Context
Zhang (2016)	Manufacturing	Implementation of Industry 4.0	China
Baldassarre (2017)	Manufacturing	Manufacturing performance	Italy
Lin (2017)	Automobile	Government policies, production technologies	China
Szozda (2017)	Automobile	Supply chain from production, procurement and distribution perspective	United States, Germany, Japan
Yi & Xie (2017)	Logistics	Third party logistics	China
Mládková, (2018)	Aviation	Human and technology interface	China, Malaysia
Vaidya et al., (2018)	Generalized	Industry 4.0 overview	India
Balwant & Awasthi (2019)	Generalized	Industry 4.0 future perspective	India
Rajput & Singh (2019)	Generalized	Circular economy, Artificial intelligence, service and policy framework	India
Ramingwon et al., (2019)	Automotive, electronics, plastic, rubber, food	Industry 4.0 and human skills	Thailand
Yasar & Ulusoy (2019)	Automotive, electronics, food, transportation, information technology	Lowering production cost, increasing production quality, innovation	Turkey
Singhal (2020)	Information technology, Automobile, Shipping, Financial Services, Pharma	Industry 4.0 application, challenges	India

Source: Adapted and modified, Singhal, N., (2020)

INDUSTRY 4.0 BENEFITS AND CHALLENGES

The Industry 4.0 applications derives several benefits and challenges, varies from company to company, industry to industry. Yasar & Ulusoy (2019) conducted a study in Turkey and identified several benefits and challenges of industry 4.0 implementation, Singhal (2020) also conducted a study in Indian context across different company representing different sectors. The table 3A compiled the benefits and Table 3B compiled challenges identified by various authors.

Table 3A: Industry 4.0 Benefits

Author (Year)	Benefits
Koch et al., (2014)	• Productivity enhancement • Cost reduction • Operational efficiency • Revenue growth • Logistics automation
BCG (2015)	• Productivity enhancement • Employment opportunities
McKinsey (2015)	• Operational efficiency • Revenue growth • Logistics automation • Employment opportunities
Uglovskaya (2017)	• Planning and controlling • Demand response • Stock level response • Resource efficiency • Energy efficiency • Quality improvement • Flexible production • Productivity enhancement • Market changes response • Customization • Customer satisfaction • Competitive advantage • Cost reduction • Waste reduction • Safety • Enhanced revenue • Brand image • Wok life balance
Karre et al., (2017)	• Work efficiency • Human machine interface • Efficient problem solving • Reduction in physical working • Efficient information retrieval • Error reduction

Author (Year)	Benefits
Pereira et al., (2017)	• Digital production • Decentralization • Mass customization • Modular products • Innovative models • Value chain responsiveness • Competitiveness • Productivity enhancement • Job transformation • Skills upgradation
Yasanur (2018)	• Logistics cost savings • Delivering time reduction • Transport delay reduced • Inventory reduction • Loss/damage reduction • Efficient service • Accurate forecasting • Reliability improvement • Flexible systems • Digitalized logistics • Transport volume rationalization
Singhal (2020)	• Higher productivity • Decrease in labour cost • Lower production cost • Enhanced customer satisfaction • More competition • Higher revenue

Source: Adapted & modified, Mohamed, M. (2018), Singhal, N. (2020)

Table 3B: Industry 4.0 Challenges

Author (Year)	Challenges
Nilsen & Nyberg (2016)	• Integration • Product end to end interface • Human-machine interface
Stock & Seliger (2016)	• Manufacturing automation • Flexibility • Employability challenges • Workforce reduction • Organization complexity • Decentralized controlling • Additive manufacturing

Author (Year)	Challenges
Wang et al. (2016)	• Intelligent decision making • Autonomy • Strong network protocol • Modelling and analysis • Flexible physical artefacts • Dynamic production configuration
Dennis et al. (2017)	• Financial benefits uncertainty • Inter-organizational coordination • Skills gap • Motivational issues • Cyber security
Saurabh et al.(2018)	• Cyber security • Big data interpretation • Financial investment • Sustaining innovation • Increased Customization • Flexible production • Organization hierarchy • Sustainability
Singhal (2020)	• Trained employees • Uncertainty about investment recovery • Reluctance for innovation • Data security • Low prioritization • Higher investment

Source: Adapted & modified, Mohamed, M. (2018), Singhal, N. (2020)

SUSTAINABILITY

Elkington (1998), coined the term triple bottom line in the context of social, environmental and financial context, since than the term create curiosity among policy makers, corporate and researchers. Lynes and Dredge (2006), describe the sustainability from the stakeholder's perspective and also explored the regulatory, competitive advantage and ethical dimensions. Frederick (2006), highlighted the issues of corporate resources and its philanthropic interface. Carroll and Shabana (2010) suggested the strategic perspective of triple bottom line concept in the corporate settings.

FRAMEWORK FOR INTEGRATING SUSTAINABILITY ACROSS VALUE CHAIN THROUGH INDUSTRY 4.0

Ding, B (2018), conducted an extensive literature review covering the integration of sustainability across different pharmaceutical supply chain (PSC) components through Industry 4.0 lenses. The paper focuses on potential sustainability barriers of PSC, and investigate how industry 4.0 can be applied in sustainable PSC. The study explored the different components of supply chain starting from the role of regulatory bodies, end customer awareness, initiatives by competitors or peers. The other important component of the study includes sustainable pharmaceutical product life cycle, addressing the future operations and production challenges, integrating technology and innovation across production lifecycle, highlighting the integration challenges across the different supply chain stages, the challenges of human resources expertise and training, the cost component is the most important from financial perspective. The sustainability impact is discussed in the study from financial viability and cost perspectives, the social aspect addressed in the perspective of social wellbeing and environmental concern addressed how to mitigate waste and pollution at different stages of PSC.

The figure 1 depict the proposed framework for integrating sustainability across value chain from an Industry 4.0 perspective, based on the literature review and content analysis conducted for this study. The whole value chain is represented through input, process and output, the central theme is the integration of industry 4.0 across the three stages and also address the sustainability concern. The input stage comprises different driving forces such as initiatives on the part of the regulatory bodies due to the change in the global business practices in the preview of social, environmental and economic concern. The organizations are also facing challenges due to the peer initiatives or due to the change in the consumer behaviour. The organizations are minimizing the challenges through integration of different component of industry 4.o such as as IoT, IoS, CPS, cloud based manufacturing, robotics, data analytics.

Fig. 1: *Framework for Integrating Sustainability across Value Chain through Industry 4.0*

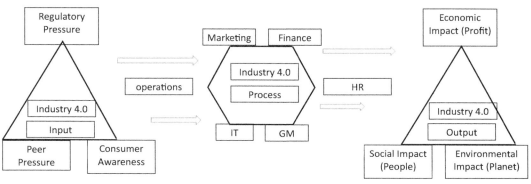

Source: Author Compilation

The process stage incudes the different management functional areas of an organization such as marketing, operations including production, information technology (IT), general management (GM) covering issues such as corporate social responsibility, general administration etc., human resources (HR), finance. The companies are putting their best efforts to integrating industry 4.0 components across the all functional areas and analysing the impact in terms of efficiency enhancement; customer satisfaction, customer relationship, product and brand improvement, sales increase, market share as far as marketing function concerned. The operation and production outcome measurement is in terms of increase in production capacity, reduction in defect levels, optimization of machines, automation of production lines etc. The information technology is the backbone of the organizations in the present scenario, how fast the information can transit between the different department and verticals of the organization, spread across the globe, is addressed through integration of industry 4.o components.

The organizations have lots of responsibilities towards society in the present time including concern for survival, growth and profitability but keeping in view the social, economic and environmental agenda as the central theme. The adaption of technological changes is very fast in the organizations due to disruptive technologies, the industry 4.0 adaptation opening the new windows of challenges related to human resource training and employability skills. The financial perspective is the most important dimension of any technological shift, the organizations have concern for financial viability with integration of industry 4.0 and sustainability perspective across the value chain.

The output is the most important dimension of the proposed framework and issue of concern for most of the stakeholder, as it requires the equal attention for social (people), economic (profit) and environmental (planet) concerns. Today the companies are adopting the practices in such a way so that they can address the all stakeholder concerns.

CONCLUSION

The study proposed the theoretical model based on the literature review and content analysis for integration of sustainability perspective across the value chain of an organization. The industry 4.0 is used as the central theme for developing a conceptual interface for 3 stages of value chain such as input, process and outcome. The input stage further discussed from the regulatory, peer and customer perspective. The process stage is the integration of marketing, operations including production, information technology (IT), general management (GM), human resource (HR) and finance. The output stage is addressing the stakeholder concern related to social (people), economic (profit) and environmental perspective. The challenges are at every stage of the integration from both sustainability and industry 4.0 perspective. The training, awareness is required at the level of all stakeholders for addressing regulatory perspective, peer perspective and consumer concerns at input stage. A more proactive action is required at process stage on the part of organizations for the skill set training of employees, awareness among suppliers, buyers and other important stakeholders of the value chain. The output challenges are always in terms of measurement yard stick, the appropriate yard stick is required for the measurement of social, economic and environmental concerns with respect to appropriate parameters.

LIMITATION

The proposed framework is based on the literature review and content analysis; the important limitation of the study is testing the framework in the corporate situations. The other future course of action for this study is collecting the opinion of experts from industry and academia, those playing an important role in value chain of any organization.

REFERENCE

Baldassarre, F., Ricciardi, F., and Campo, R. (2017). The Advent of Industry 4.0 in the manufacturing industry: Literature review and growth opportunities. Dubrovnik: University of Dubrovnik. Retrieved from https://search.proquest.com/docview/2068860672?accountid=33465

Balwant, S. M., and Awasthi, I. C. (2019). Industry 4.0 and the future of work in India. FIIB Business Review, 8(1), 9–16.

Carroll, A. B. and Shabana, K.M. (2010). "The business case for corporate social responsibility: a review of concepts, research and practices", International Journal of Management Reviews, Vol. 12, No. 1, pp. 85–105.

Coetteleer, M., J. Holdowsky, and M. Mahto, Additive Manufacturing paths to performance, innovation, and growth. Deloitte Review, 2014. 1(19): p. 32.

Deloitte. (2015). Industry 4.0. Challenges and solutions for the digital transformation and use of exponential technologies. 45774A Deloitte Zurich Switzerland 2015.

Dennis K., Nicolina P., and Yves-Simon G. (2017). Textile Learning Factory 4.0 – Preparing Germany's Textile Industry for the Digital Future. 7th Conference on Learning Factories, CLF 2017 Procedia Manufacturing, Vol. 9, pp 214–221

Ding, Baoyang (2018), Pharma Industry 4.0: literature review and research opportunities in sustainable pharmaceutical supply chains.Process Safety and Environment Protection, Vol 119, pp 115-130. https://doi.org/10.1016/j.psep.2018.06.031

Elkington, J. (1998), "Partnerships from Cannibals with Forks: The Triple Bottom Line of 21st-Century Business. *Environmental Quality Management,* Vol. 8 No1, pp. 37–51.

Frederick,W.C. (2006),"Corporation, Be Good! The Story of Corporate Social Responsibility", Dogear Publishing, Indianapolis, IN

Geissbauer, R., Vedso, J., & Schrauf, S. (2016). Industry 4.0: Building the digital enterprise. https://www.pwc.com/gx/en/industries/industries4.0/landing-page/industry-4.0-building-your-digital-enterprise-april-2016. pdf.

Hermann, M., Pentek, T., and Otto, B. (2015). Design principles for Industrie 4.0 scenarios: A literature review. HICSS '16 Proceedings of the 2016 49th Hawaii International Conference on System Sciences, 49, 3928–3937.

Kagermann, H., W. Wahlster, and J. Helbig, Recommendations for implementing the strategic initiative industrie 4.0. Acatech national academy of science and engineering, 2013(6).

Karre, H., M. Hammer, M. Kleindienst, and C. Ramsauer. (2017). "Transition towards an Industry 4.0 State of the LeanLab at Graz University of Technology." Procedia Manufacturing 9: 206– 213.10.1016/j.promfg.2017.04.006

Koch, V., Kuge, S., Geissbauer, R. and Schrauf, S. (2014). Industry 4.0: Opportunities and challenges of the industrial internet. Tech. Rep. TR 2014-2, PWC Strategy GmbH, United States, New York City, New York (NY).

Lin, D., Lee, C., Lau, H., and Yang, Y. (2018). Strategic response to industry 4.0: An empirical investigation on the Chinese automotive industry. Industrial Management & Data Systems, 118(3), 589–605. doi:http://dx.doi.org/10.1108/IMDS-09-2017-0403

Lynes, J. K and Dredge, D. (2006), "Going Green: motivations for environmental commitment in the airline industry. A case study of Scandinavian airlines", Journal of Sustainable Tourism, Vol. 14 No.2, pp. 116–38.

MacDougall, W. (2014). Industry 4.0: Smart Manufacturing for the Future, Germany Trade, and Invest, Berlin, available at www.gtai.de/GTAI/Content/EN/Invest/_SharedDocs/Downloads/GTAI/Brochures/Industries/industrie4.0-smart-manufacturing-for-the-future-en.pdf

McKinsey and Company. (2015). Industry 4.0: How to navigate digitization of the manufacturing sector. Tech. rep., McKinsey and Company, New York City, New York (NY).

Mládková, L. (2018). Industry 4.0: Human-technology interaction: Experience learned from the aviation industry. Kidmore End: Academic Conferences International Limited. Retrieved from https://search.proquest.com/docview/2116815603?accountid=33465

Mohamed, M. (2018). Challenges and benefits of industry 4.0: An overview, International Journal of Supply and Operations Management, 5(3), 256–265. Retrieved from https://search.proquest.com/docview/2137847267?accountid=33465

Nilsen, S., Nyberg, E (2016).: The Adoption of Industry 4.0 - Technologies in Manufacturing: A Multiple Case Study, http://www.diva-portal.org/smash/record.jsf?pid=diva2%3A952337& dswid=9006.

Pereira A.C., Romero F., (2017). A review of the meanings and the implications of the Industry 4.0 concept, Procedia Manufacturing, Vol.13, pp. 1206–1214.

Pfohl H.C., Yahsi B., Kurnaz T. (2015). The impact of Industry 4.0 on the supply chain, Proceedings of the Hamburg International Conference of Logistics (HICL) 2015, 29–58.

Porter, M.E., The Competitive Advantage: Creating and Sustaining Superior Performance, ed. N.F. Press. Vol. 1. 1985, NY, U. S. A: The Free Press.

Prinz, C., et al., Learning Factory Modules for Smart Factories in Industrie 4.0. Procedia CIRP, 2016. 54: p. 113–118.

Rajput., S., Singh., S., P. (2019) "Industry 4.0 – challenges to implement circular economy", Benchmarking: An International Journal, Vol. 49, 98–113.

Ramingwong, S., Manopiniwes, W., and Jangkrajarng, V. (2019). HUMAN FACTORS OF THAILAND TOWARD INDUSTRY 4.0. Management Research and Practice, 11(1), 15–25. Retrieved from https://search.proquest.com/docview/2197775920?accountid=33465

Saurabh V., Prashant A., and Santosh B. (2018). Industry 4.0 – A Glimpse. 2nd International Conference on Materials Manufacturing and Design Engineering/ Procedia Manufacturing, Vol. 20, pp. 233–238.

Schneider, P., Managerial challenges of Industry 4.0: an empirically backed research agenda for a nascent field. Review of Managerial Science, 2018.

Singhal N. (2020), An Empirical Investigation of Industry 4.0 Preparedness in India. Vision. October 2020. doi:10.1177/0972262920950066

Stock T., and Seliger G. (2016). Decoupling Growth from Resource Use Opportunities of Sustainable Manufacturing in Industry 4.0. 13th Global Conference on Sustainable Manufacturing CIRP, Vol. 40, pp. 536–541.

Szozda, N. (2017). Industry 4.0 and its impact on the functioning of supply chains. LogForum, 13(4), 401-414. DOI: 10.17270/J.LOG.2017.4.2

The Boston Consulting Group (2015). The Future of Productivity and Growth in Manufacturing Industries. http://www.zvw.de/media.media.72e472fb-1698-4a15-8858-344351c8902f.original.pdf

Uglovskaya, E. (2017), The New Industrial Era: Industry 4.0 & Bobst company case study, http://urn.fi/URN:NBN:fi:amk-201703012801

Vaidya, S., Ambad, P., & Bhosle, S. (2018). Industry 4.0—Glimpse. Procedia Manufacturing, 20, 233–238.

Wang S., Wan J., Li D., Zhang C., (2016). Implementing Smart Factory of Industrie 4.0: An Outlook. International Journal of Distributed Sensor Networks, Vol. 2016, pp 1–10.

Yasanur K. (2018). Sustainability impact of digitizationin logistics. 15th Global Conference on Sustainable Manufacturing Procedia Manufacturing. Vol. 21(2018), pp. 782–789.

Yasar, E., and Ulusoy, T. (2019). INDUSTRY 4.0 and TURKEY / ENDÜSTRİ 4.0 ve TÜRKİYE. Business & Management Studies: An International Journal, 7(1), 24–41. doi:http://dx.doi.org/10.15295/bmij.v7i1.1038

Yi, S., and Xie, J. (2017). A study on the dynamic comparison of logistics industry's correlation effects in china. China Finance and Economic Review, 5(1), 1–26. doi:http://dx.doi.org/10.1186/s40589-017-0059.

Zhang, X., Peek, W. A., Pikas, B., and Lee, T. (2016). The transformation and upgrading of the chinese manufacturing industry: Based on "German Industry 4.0". The Journal of Applied Business and Economics, 18(5), 97–105. Retrieved from https://search.proquest.com/docview/1855298156?accountid=33465

For Product Safety Concerns and Information please contact our EU
representative GPSR@taylorandfrancis.com Taylor & Francis Verlag GmbH,
Kaufingerstraße 24, 80331 München, Germany

Printed and bound by CPI Group (UK) Ltd, Croydon, CR0 4YY
01/05/2025
01858423-0001